INFANT SOCIAL COGNITION:
Empirical and Theoretical Considerations

List of Contributors

Marjorie Beeghly-Smith, *University of Colorado*

Inge Bretherton, *University of Colorado*

Joseph J. Campos, *University of Denver*

Dante Cicchetti, *Harvard University*

Alexandra Cortelyou, *University of Pennsylvania*

M. Ann Easterbrooks, *University of Michigan*

Douglas Frye, *Yale University*

Michael E. Lamb, *University of Utah*

Michael Lewis, *Educational Testing Service*

Sandra McNew, *University of Colorado*

Gary M. Olson, *University of Michigan*

Harriet Oster, *University of Pennsylvania*

Petra Pogge-Hesse, *Harvard University*

Lonnie R. Sherrod, *Social Science Research Council*

Elizabeth S. Spelke, *University of Pennsylvania*

Craig R. Stenberg, *University of Denver*

Marguerite B. Stevenson, *University of Wisconsin–Madison*

Stephen J. Suomi, *University of Wisconsin–Madison*

INFANT SOCIAL COGNITION:
Empirical and Theoretical Considerations

Edited by
MICHAEL E. LAMB
Departments of Psychology and Pediatrics
University of Utah

LONNIE R. SHERROD
Social Science Research Council

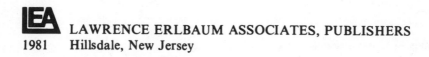
LAWRENCE ERLBAUM ASSOCIATES, PUBLISHERS
1981   Hillsdale, New Jersey

Lawrence Erlbaum Associates, Inc., Publishers
365 Broadway
Hillsdale, New Jersey 07642

Library of Congress Cataloging in Publication Data

Main entry under title:

Infant social cognition.

   Includes bibliographical references and index.
   1. Infant psychology. 2. Social perception in
children.   I. Lamb, Michael E., 1953-   II. Sherrod, Lonnie R.
B720.S63I53   155.4'13   80-21137
ISBN 0-89859-058-2

Printed in the United States of America

Contents

Preface

In this volume, we have brought together all the evidence currently available concerning the development of social cognition in infancy. The task of each author has been to synthesize research and theory concerning the central issues in this area. The result, we feel, is a set of remarkably prescient and heuristic chapters. Each of the chapters deals in detail with one aspect of the process whereby babies come to understand the social environment and their role in it. Much of the relevant research has been concerned with the development of the capacity to identify, remember, and recognize social objects—people—as distinct from inanimate objects in the environment, and these issues are discussed by several contributors. Another important area of investigation concerns development of the capacity to make inferences about the behavioral propensities, motivations, and emotions of other people. Related to these topics is the infant's ability to attribute meaning to its social experiences. Here it is generally believed that the infant's understanding is limited by the immature nature of its cognitve capacities. These limitations also define the extent to which the baby can be aware of its social experiences and open to influence by them. Finally, underlying many of the chapters is a common theme: What concept of itself does an infant develop, and what are the mechanisms subsuming the development of this concept of self?

In our opinion, the topic of infant social cognition—as defined by the above issues—must rank as one of the most important areas in developmental psychology today. It is a topic that stands at the intersection of a number of areas—perceptual, cognitive, social, emotional, and personality development. Consequently, more than any other topic, this area demands that theorists and researchers recognize the mutual influences and interrelationships among developments in many diverse areas. Despite its manifest importance, however, infant social cognition has not been accorded the integrative, coherent, and critical attention it deserves. The empirical and theoretical advances of the last decade make this effort both possible and necessary. The present volume is designed to fulfill this need.

This volume is of greatest use to professionals interested in infancy, socioemotional development, and general developmental psychology. The contributions may well be invaluable to those whose research interests embrace a concern with any aspect of infancy, for the authors draw upon all the areas (social, perceptual, cognitive, psychophysiological development) that are commonly distinct in analytic discourse. The chapters have all been written especially for this volume, and so they represent up-to-date syntheses of theory and research as well as novel perspectives on this emergent field. Our hope is that the volume provides direction and impetus to research in this area.

Michael E. Lamb
Lonnie R. Sherrod

INFANT SOCIAL COGNITION:
Empirical and Theoretical Considerations

1 Infant Social Cognition: An Introduction

Lonnie R. Sherrod
Social Science Research Council

Michael E. Lamb
University of Utah

By definition, social cognition refers to the way individuals perceive and understand other people. In this volume, we restrict our focus rather narrowly to the manner in which knowledge about people and their behavior is acquired during the first 2 years of life. Our topic, therefore, lies squarely at the interface of the developmental, social, and cognitive areas within psychology.

In the first section of this chapter, we identify major concerns in the study of developmental social cognition and trace these foci back to three areas from which the field developed. We do so not simply to highlight the history of the area, but because an acquaintance with the field's origins may help readers understand why certain phenomena are of interest, and why particular approaches have predominated. In the second section, we describe three ways in which the study of developmental social cognition can be approached most fruitfully. These approaches represent alternative ways of achieving conceptual organization, and all are represented and exemplified in this volume. In the third and final section, we summarize the contributions to this book, indicating how each advances our understanding of infant social cognition.

THE ORIGINS OF THE FIELD

In a nutshell, students of developmental social cognition have acquired from cognitive psychologists a concern with perceptual processes, reasoning, and concept formation; from social psychologists a concern with the way we

1

monitor people and social behavior; and from developmental psychologists an interest in the way these processes and capacities develop. These concerns have combined to yield a focus on person perception, the categorization of people, and the formation of expectations about the motives, feelings, and behavior of others. Despite this fusion of social psychological and cognitive interests, students of social cognition have not been able simply to borrow concepts and methodologies from either social or cognitive psychology. They have had to develop new perspectives and strategies of their own.

The area of social cognition attained importance in its own right with the adoption of a *developmental* perspective. Prior to the emergence of developmental social cognition as a separate area, research had, for the most part, been approached from the viewpoint of social psychology (see, for example, Kelley, 1972), and the cognitive social psychologists had not attempted to relate their findings to those of cognitive scientists (perhaps because the latter did not disguise their disinterest). As a result, developmental social cognition originally focused on topics that had been central to social psychology—for example, person perception, role taking, the perception of psychological causality, and moral judgment (see Shantz, 1975, for a review). Interests have since broadened to encompass research on conceptions of peer relations, friendships, the self, and social institutions. When and how, researchers now ask, do children develop the capacities to identify, remember, and recognize people as distinct from inanimate objects; make inferences about the behavioral propensities, motivations, and emotions of other people; attribute meaning to their own social experiences; remain aware of and open to influences by the social environment; and identify themselves as similar to, yet distinct from, others? These questions are still closer to the concerns of social psychologists, but developmental psychologists have made serious attempts to integrate their findings with those of cognitive psychologists. Clearly, by broadening the scope of the field, developmental psychologists have made social cognition more interesting, but several other factors also account for the popularity and importance of developmental social cognition.

Converging trends in research on socialization and cognitive development were probably most influential (Damon, 1978). Under Piaget's influence, cognitive developmentalists have long emphasized the child's active role in conceptually structuring and mastering her/his environment. Students of socialization, by contrast, traditionally emphasized the role of the environment and focused their attention on social *inputs*. Since Bell's (1968) classic reformulation, however, students of socialization have also begun to talk about the active and interactive child, thus bringing their perspective closer to that of the cognitive developmentalists. Social cognition of necessity attributes an active, constructive role to the child. It begins with the assumption that the child does not simply receive social input, but is a thinking and reasoning actor in the social world. Therefore, social cognition was, and remains, an area in which knowledge of social and cognitive behavior can be productively integrated.

Research in social cognition was also enhanced by advances in our knowledge of early cognitive development. Substantive contributions were derived from the investigation of "subjective" cognitive processes such as imagery, daydreaming, and imaginative play; from the emergence of cognitive science as an interdisciplinary area drawing upon psychology, computer science, the neurosciences, linguistics,and so forth; and, indirectly, from the technological advances making it possible to study—even in very young children—eye movements, information processing strategies, memory, and other cognitive processes.

In addition, it had long been recognized that early social experiences determine the course of development, yet little was known about the processes by which these effects were achieved. Further progress depended on understanding not simply what was done to the child, but how the child perceived what happened to it. Thus the study of social cognition was demanded, and this demand accelerated research into the processes whereby children come to understand the social environment and their role in it.

Social Cognition and Developmental Psychology

As an area, developmental social cognition promises to contribute substantially both to our understanding of social and cognitive development and to developmental psychology in general. There are a number of reasons why we expect so much from the area.

First, the study of social cognition stands at the intersection of a number of areas. Consequently, it demands that theorists appreciate the mutual influences and interrelationships among developments in perception, cognition, social relations, and personality. This yields a perspective beneficial for the field as a whole.

Second, because it attempts to integrate diverse areas of developmental psychology, the study of social cognition also facilitates consideration of broader issues that are easy to lose sight of when one's focus is too narrow. Here we are thinking particularly of the biological bases of development, cross-cultural variability, and the sociopolitical context or ecology within which development takes place.

The location of social cognitive researchers at the intersection of multiple areas within developmental psychology prevents them from embracing either a univariate approach or a linear view of development. Rather, researchers in the area must adopt a multivariate, transactional perspective (as proposed by e.g., Sameroff, 1975), which stresses complex interrelationships among variables changing at several levels over time.

Like others who have adopted a transactional perspective, scholars who study social cognition have found their attention drawn to issues concerning the continuity and stability (or discontinuity and instability) of development because the phenomena of interest to them are relevant to infants, as well as children, adolescents, and adults. Social cognition is a topic that lends itself to a life-span perspective. Inasmuch as people are always part of the social environment, persons of all ages have to monitor, interpret, and respond to the behavior of other people.

Finally, social cognition lends itself to a focus on the quality, quantity, etiology, and development of individual variability because it emphasizes the child's role as an active and independent thinker.

APPROACHES TO THE STUDY OF SOCIAL COGNITION

Because social cognition involves the study of both cognition and social behavior, it is a broad area. When one acknowledges that cognitive capacity and salient aspects of the social world vary developmentally, the area becomes even broader and more diverse. There are, however, several ways of organizing the area conceptually in order to control, and even to capitalize on, this breadth. Three such approaches seem especially promising: (1) focusing on a limited developmental period; (2) examining the importance of critical aspects of the social environment; (3) investigating cognitive processes that may have major implications for conceptualization of the social world. Although we describe these approaches independently in the paragraphs that follow, they are not mutually exclusive. Indeed, if we are to attain a comprehensive understanding of social cognition, the three approaches should complement one another.

Infancy

Within developmental psychology, there are many precedents for focusing on a particular chronological period or developmental stage. In the present volume, we concentrate on the infancy period. We do this partly out of respect for and commitment to the importance of beginnings, partly because infant social cognition has received less attention than other developmental phases, and partly because exploration of the infant's social understanding holds the key to further theoretical advances in the study of infant social development.

Even on the basis of superficial criteria, a focus on "beginnings" seems more logical and less arbitrary than a slice through the middle of the developmental spectrum. It seems reasonable to believe that a successful beginning makes a second successful step more likely, without at the same time implying that a "critical" period exists or that the subsequent course of development involves an irreversible linear process. Infants are encountering people for the first time and so must begin to develop an understanding of social behavior. This means that researchers obtain a better sense of the developmental starting point than they do when studying older individuals who have a history of unique experiences and idiosyncratic perspectives. And because individuals develop more rapidly in infancy than at any other point in their lives, the interrelationships among social, cognitive, emotional, and perceptual development are most clearly evident at this stage.

Over the last 3 decades, students of social development have come to recognize the manner in which the child shapes its own socialization. For the most part, however, theorists still conceive of infants' characteristics and propensities as determinants of the adults' behavior; they fail to consider the infants' motives and the role these play in affecting the socialization process. Further progress in the conceptualization of development requires that we cease seeing the infant as an organism that simply acts and start exploring the reasons why it behaves as it does. Infant social cognition promises to achieve some balance.

Yet there are problems in attempting to enter this field. Because they are preverbal organisms with limited cognitive capacities, infants require quite different research strategies than do older children. This may explain why students of social cognition have, in the main, failed to develop issues of special relevance to infancy. It is true, of course, that recent advances in our knowledge of perceptual, cognitive, conceptual/linguistic, and social competence in infancy have removed earlier barriers to progress in this area. Nevertheless, one cannot lose sight of the infant's severe cognitive limitations because the limitations themselves are constantly changing with age—thereby complicating matters still further.

Actually, cognitive limitations and developments have largely shaped the research agenda for theorists of infant social cognition. This has certainly been true of those investigators who have attempted to describe the social environment from the perspective of the young infant. These researchers assume that various aspects will become more (or less) salient to the infant as it develops, and so they have attempted to determine how the social environment is perceived at different stages of development.

Despite the importance of these issues, we know little about the way infants attend to and use the different types of information that people provide, and just as little about the manner in which use of this information varies as cognitive capacities develop. One wonders, for example, whether infants of various ages attend to and make sense of different types of information; whether different types of information are used to construct concepts of people rather than to recognize individual persons, and whether differentiations are based on the characteristics of the stimulus or on the reactions evoked in the infant. These are the basic issues that must be addressed. As such, they resurface repeatedly throughout this volume.

The Social Environment

The social environment is, of course, composed of people, and there are at least two major ways in which encounters with people affect the child's development. First, persons can be studied as physical stimuli along dimensions such as contour, contrast, movement, color, and so forth. Although there has been considerable research of this nature (for example, on recognition of facial form), this work has not been related either to research on perceptual development in a manner permitting analysis of "the person as a physical stimulus," or to other research on cognitive, perceptual, or social development. This seems likely to change with the recognition that person perception may well have formative developmental significance. For example, people are complex stimuli. Consequently, encounters with people may facilitate the infant's attempts to integrate its world across sensory modalities and thereby form multimodal concepts.

Second, one can emphasize social processes, because people substantially affect socioemotional development. People are social partners who interact with infants, inside and outside of caretaking routines, pacing the infant's behavior, and modeling the reciprocal patterns that characterize social interaction. Adults—particularly parents—also satisfy basic biological needs in response to the infant's signals, and by doing so they foster feelings of personal effectiveness in the infant. A sense of efficacy is of crucial significance to the development of a concept of "self," which is also aided by the fact that people are more "like-self" than any other objects the infant encounters. And in addition to providing stimulation of various forms directly, people mediate environmental stimulation—modifying the quality and quantity of nonsocial stimulation. Finally, whatever specific stimuli they provide, social partners serve to arouse infants, thereby facilitating the occurrence, differentiation, and expression of emotion.

Cognitive Processes

As noted earlier, an alternative means of approaching social cognition involves analyzing the cognitive and perceptual processes involved in social behavior or attainments and considering the infant's cognitive capacities at different phases of development. This approach requires that the focus of analysis shift from the environment (or stimulus) to the infant as we examine the cognitive processes that have major implications for social cognition. Visual attention is one such topic, for it is important to determine how the infant's attention is attracted to specific aspects of the social world and how this changes with age. Identification of the cognitive prerequisites for the recognition of specific others is another central topic. Concept formation, too, can be examined from the perspective of social cognition. Are social concepts and concepts of the physical world formed in the same way? Is the same type of information relied upon? What concepts of the social world are developed first? Do they emerge at about the same time as similar concepts of the physical world? Must the infant have developed schemas and the ability to integrate information across modalities before it can form social concepts and recognize specific individuals? When are infants able to learn, and how does this ability influence social development? These are examples of the types of questions that might be posed regarding the cognitive processes involved in social cognition.

Other Issues

Several of the contributors to this volume exemplify yet another approach to the study of social cognition—one focusing on issues that truly stand at the interface of social and cognitive development and can only be studied from the viewpoint of social cognition. Two examples are development of the self-concept and emotional (or affective) development. What concept of itself does an infant have, and what mechanisms underlie the development of this concept? What emotions does the infant experience, and when do these come to color the infant's perception of people and events? How do infants learn to recognize and attribute meaning to the emotional expressions of others?

THE PRESENT VOLUME

The task set for the present volume is formidable. Our goals are: (1) to impart some conceptual structure to a relatively new area of endeavor; (2) to address a myriad complex questions like those outlined in the preceding paragraphs; (3) to suggest a research agenda that will insure the systematic development of the field. Each chapter reflects an appreciation of the complex, transactional nature of development and the potential importance of examining individual variability, although the contributors have adopted different approaches and perspectives, as outlined in the preceding section.

People as Stimuli

Several authors emphasize the unique stimulus properties of social objects and explore the implications of this for the development of infant social cognition. In Chapter 2, for instance, Sherrod considers the human face as a physical stimulus of special interest and importance to young infants. His focus is limited to visual attention in the first few months of life on the grounds that visual attention is a peculiarly important mode of interaction with the environment during this period. Sherrod asks whether physical properties of the face shape early responses to people and affect later patterns of interaction. For example, are those physical properties that are peculiar to people (such as facial configuration) more salient than those properties people share with other stimuli (such as contour density)?

Noting that people provide multimodal sensory information, Spelke and Cortelyou (Chapter 4) examine the integration of information across modalities and the development of multimodal (e.g., audio-visual) concepts of people in general and specific persons (e.g., mother or father) in particular. Olson, too, goes beyond characterizing social stimuli to ask about the prerequisites for the recognition of specific persons (Chapter 3). What cognitive capacities are needed to recognize mothers or fathers, he asks, and at what age do infants exhibit these capacities? Do babies learn to recognize physical objects at the same time that they start recognizing specific persons? Are people especially easy or difficult stimuli to remember and to recognize?

People as Social Partners

The remaining chapters focus on the *behavior* of other people rather than on their physical characteristics. In Chapter 7, Lamb speculates that the emergent capacity to associate and remember events (i.e., to learn) affects the ability to recognize the contingent relationship between the infant's own behavior and that of others. Lamb concentrates on the development of expectations regarding the way others behave because these expectations permit the infant to develop faith in the predictability of others as well as a belief in its own efficacy as a member of the social world. By definition, expectations about the predictability of others' behavior develop differently depending on the consistency of the adults involved. Thus there is every reason to explore the factors accounting for individual differences in the predictability and sensitivity of parental behavior, and this topic occupies the attention of Lamb and Easterbrooks in Chapter 6. Suomi (Chapter 8), too, explores the mechanisms whereby infants develop a sense of personal efficacy, and his account is supplemented by the results of experimental investigations involving rhesus monkeys raised in contingently responsive and noncontingent social environments.

Emotional Development

Three chapters deal with aspects of emotional development. Oster's treatment (Chapter 5) is focused on the infant's ability to recognize emotions in others. She also discussed her earlier work on the expression of emotions; however, her primary concern is with the capacity to perceive and attribute meaning to subtle social signals emitted by the infant's partners. By contrast, both Cicchetti and Pogge-Hesse (Chapter 9) and Campos and Stenberg (Chapter 10) deal less with the *recognition* of emotions than with the developing capacity to *experience* emotions and associate them with persons and events. Both selections propose a close relationship between cognitive and affective development, although they portray this relationship rather differently.

Cognitive Development and Social Understanding

In general, the authors of the first 10 chapters portray cognitive capacities as limitations on the rate and nature of social or affective development. This position is articulated and defended more systematically by Frye in Chapter 11. Frye's hypothesis is that the stages of cognitive development described by Piaget have implications for the understanding of social objects and relationships. In Chapter 13, however, Stevenson and Lamb focus on the extent to which social experiences affect the development of cognitive competence. Between them, the authors of these two chapters illustrate the complex and bidirectional relationship between aspects of cognitive and social development.

Finally, Chapters 12 and 14 consider more general aspects of social cognition. Bretherton, McNew, and Beeghly-Smith (Chapter 12) examine children's knowledge of people as revealed in the everyday language and communicative skills of 1- to 3-year olds. They argue that young children have a fairly sophisticated model of others and of themselves as psychological beings, even though they make errors of attribution and have difficulty manipulating several aspects of their person knowledge. Among the questions raised is whether such knowledge facilitates social interaction as well as leading to the acquisition of further knowledge. Lewis (Chapter 14) discusses the interaction of gender identity (a category of self) and sex role. He suggests that gender identity (differentiating identity and constancy) is one category that the child acquires between 1 and 2 years of age as it develops a notion of self. He elaborates this idea as he describes the mediation of sex-role development by gender identity.

CONCLUSION

Overall, the contributors to this volume discuss a variety of basic issues in infant social cognition. In many cases, the data presented were not originally intended to address issues in this area, so that the authors have had to attempt careful, evaluative reviews supplemented by their own interpretations. Their syntheses represent novel, if necessarily speculative, perspectives on an exciting, emergent field and these different perspectives may not, in all cases, be perfectly compatible. Our hope is that these aspects of this volume highlight the need for fresh and innovative research and encourage others to enter an area that, more than any other, promises to advance our understanding of development in infancy.

REFERENCES

Bell, R. Q. A reinterpretation of the direction of effects in studies of socialization. *Psychological Review,* 1968, *75,* 81–95.

Damon, W. (Ed.). Editor's notes. *Social Cognition* (No. 1). San Francisco: Jossey-Bass, 1978.

Kelley, H. H. Attribution in social interaction. In E. E. Jones, D. E. Kanouse, H. H. Kelley, R. E. Nisbett, S. Valins, & B. Weiner, (Eds.), *Attribution: Perceiving the causes of behavior.* Morristown, N. J.: General Learning Press, 1972.

Sameroff, A. Transactional models in early social relations. *Human Development,* 1975, *18,* 65–79.

Shantz, C. U. The development of social cognition. In E. M. Hetherington (Ed.), *Review of child development research* (Vol. 5). Chicago: University of Chicago Press, 1975.

2 Issues in Cognitive-Perceptual Development: The Special Case of Social Stimuli

Lonnie R. Sherrod
Social Science Research Council

In this chapter, infants' perception and cognition of some physical-stimulus properties of people are examined. In addition to being social behavers, caregivers, and attachment figures, people are also physical stimuli composed of parameters such as contour density and color. Except for facial form (or configuration), the physical properties of people have not been systematically and thoroughly studied, perhaps because the socioemotional qualities of people seem more powerful. The role of people's physical characteristics in infants' early responses to the social world requires some specification. Such specification is provided in this chapter by examining two relatively straightforward questions: (1) which physical properties of people are most salient to young infants? and (2) how significant for early development are perception and cognition of these physical parameters of people? The major thesis presented in answer to these questions is that infants' attention to certain physical-stimulus properties of people represents an early and basic form of social cognition that has implications for both social and cognitive development. That is, the physical characteristics of people call out the attentional strategies that the infant brings to his or her initial contacts with the environment and facilitate the development of these strategies into more mature and adaptive modes of interaction with the world, social *and* nonsocial.

This general thesis, in fact, represents a theme that appears throughout this volume. A number of contributors argue that certain early forms of social cognition have broad developmental consequences. For example, Lamb describes the role of social interaction in the development of generalized notions of personal effectiveness, and Spelke and Cortelyou discuss the cross-modal integration of social stimuli and its implications for schema development. The focus on infants' attention to the physical parameters of the person is, however, unique to this chapter and, to a lesser extent, the next, in which Olson considers infants' ability to recognize specific persons.

The focus of this chapter is limited to visual attention—not because vision is more important to the infant's early interaction with his or her environment than the other sensory modalities such as olfaction—but because a vast amount of literature exists on the infant's visual system, its functional status at birth, its early maturation, and its role in early environmental interaction. An emphasis on visual attention can, therefore, serve to highlight the paucity of, and consequently the need for, empirical knowledge on the other sensory systems and their role in early development. Additionally, visual attention is both an index and a mediator of information acquisition. Other behaviors, such as smiling, may *indicate* that the infant is extracting and processing information from the environment, but unlike looking, smiling is not a response by which these processes occur. The chapter also limits its attention, for the most part, to the human face, although other characteristics of the person (such as behavior) and other parts of the body (such as the hands) are obviously important. This focus, as with that on visual attention, represents an attempt to impart some structure from the perspective of social cognition to an enormous literature. Finally, the transactional and constructivistic nature of development is emphasized.

The organization of the chapter can be simply described. It first considers "what there is for the infant to respond to," attempting an analysis of the physical-stimulus characteristics of the person[1]—a task that is far more ecological than psychological. Thereafter, it examines "what the infant can respond to." Knowledge of the infant's cognitive capacities and limitations, especially as they intersect with infant visual attention, is a well-developed area of infant psychology, and several excellent reviews are available (Cohen & Salapatek, 1975; Haith, 1979; Kessen, Haith, & Salapatek, 1970). Thus, the chapter simply outlines the scope of our information. Third, it considers the infant's visual preferences, "what the infant does, in fact, respond to." Finally, the chapter offers a series of speculations on the role of social cognition in the development of general strategies of attention.

THE PERSON AS A PHYSICAL STIMULUS

A preliminary consideration in any study of cognition involves definition of the stimulus set used in the investigation of a particular cognitive behavior. Studies of infant social cognition, particularly research on attention to the

---

[1]Throughout the chapter, I use the terms "person" and "social stimulus" interchangeably; this usage is entirely from the adult's viewpoint and does not imply that the infant differentiates social and nonsocial or recognizes specific persons.

human face, have been neglectful in this regard. This section outlines some of the problems that can result from such neglect and suggests some guidelines for future research.

In Chapter 1, Lamb and I argue that people present several different levels or forms of information such as physical stimulus properties, social reinforcement, interactive behaviors, and emotional qualities. Each of these broad categories of information can be further subdivided into a number of different characteristics; for example, the person presents an array of physical properties—contrast, contour, curvature, movement, color, and brightness. The infant's selective extraction and use of this physical-stimulus information is especially interesting because the person offers such a diverse array of information. Although the selectivity of attention to these various characteristics of people may operate at any of several levels of organization—such as sensory function, cognitive capacity, or behavioral response—the level of organization at which selectivity occurs is less central to the theme of this chapter than is the diversity of information potentially available to the infant.

Attention to, and processing of, the diverse physical properties of people may be an important aspect of infants' early responses to people, yet there has been very little theoretical treatment of those issues. For example, physical properties may be especially important before a differentiation of "social" and "nonsocial" has been well-established. Although the infant does, of course, eventually come to differentiate people and nonsocial stimuli, to develop expectations of people's behaviors, to make inferences about people's motives, and to develop theories of people's behaviors and attitudes,[2] he or she comes into the world with very little or no knowledge of people. Thus, initial responses are as likely to involve the physical parameters of people as their social behaviors. The earliest transaction of interpersonal interaction and person perception may involve some physical properties of the person, particularly of the human face.

An extensive literature exists on infants' recognition of, and response to, the human face. With the exception of research on infants' response to facial form, however, these studies are based on infants' preferences for stimuli and do not adequately analyze the stimulus structure that mediates the preferences.

An ecological analysis of the physical stimulus structure of the person is called for. For example, certain qualities of people, such as facial configuration, are unique to social stimuli; other characteristics such as contour density, are shared by social and nonsocial stimuli. Yet, we know very little about either the qualitative or quantitative variation between social

---

[2]Such developments are, indeed, central issues for developmental social cognition, and the beginnings of these developments occur during the infancy period (and are explored in certain chapters of this volume).

and nonsocial stimuli or between different social stimuli. Thus, on the whole, faces may possess more contour density than other stimuli; if so, this quantitative difference in contour density might be used by infants to qualitatively differentiate social and nonsocial stimuli. Likewise, how much quantitative variation in contour density exists between different faces? Could contour density provide the basis for recognition of specific individuals or for the differentiation of categories of social stimuli, such as males versus females? There are few studies that systematically examine infants' responses to people as a function of quantitative (or qualitative) variation in physical properties of the face.

Some researchers have attempted to reduce variation in one property of facial stimuli in order to examine infants' responses to another characteristic. Thus, certain investigators of infants' attention to facial configuration have attempted to control for characteristics like symmetry, complexity, and contour density (for example, Caron, Caron, Caldwell, & Weiss, 1973; Goren, 1975; Haaf & Bell, 1967; Haaf & Brown, 1975; Thomas, 1973). Perhaps one of the best examples is a series of studies by Haaf and Brown (1975) in which they examined the relative influences of facial resemblance and degree of complexity on infants' attention to achromatic facial representations. The stimuli, which varied across the dimensions of "faceness" and "complexity," were presented to infants of various ages. Resemblance to the face ("faceness") was defined by the number of appropriately placed facial features, and complexity by the number of details or elements. The two dimensions were either orthogonal to one another or positively correlated in the set of stimuli. From the results of these studies, Haaf and Brown concluded that infants under 10 weeks respond to the complexity of the stimuli, but that between 10 and 15 weeks of age, infants begin to respond to the facial quality of the stimuli as well as to complexity. Although the particular operational definitions of "facial resemblance" and "complexity" (and hence the conclusions) are questionable, the design and goals of the study are noteworthy. These investigators did attempt to define operationally and control the structure of their stimuli. The creation of two dimensions, which varied in either a correlated or orthogonal manner, represents a reasonable and useful strategy. A more typical strategy is to present infants with a diverse collection of objects such as a face, panda bear, checkerboard, and bottle (Kagan & Lewis, 1965) or to present various photographs of faces that vary across orientation or pose (Cornell, 1974; Fagan, 1977b). In these more typically employed strategies, the investigator cannot determine the particular aspect of the stimulus to which the infant responds or even whether the subject is responding to qualitative or quantitative variation in the stimulus set.

Garner (1978) has presented one of the most powerful statements of the necessity for the researcher to command precise, operational control over the structure of the stimulus set. Although Garner's argument is oriented to adult cognitive psychologists, several points are relevant to the considerations in this chapter; particularly relevant is his taxonomy of stimulus structure.

Garner differentiates component and wholistic properties of stimuli. Component properties can be either featural or dimensional in nature. Dimensions vary across mutually exclusive levels. Features exist at a single level; the feature is present or not, but does not vary across a variety of levels. Zero can also denote nonexistence of a dimension (for one of a qualitative nature), or it can function as one of the positive levels on a quantitative dimension. Regarding social stimuli, dimensions include color and contour density. (A number of investigators have also evaluated the possible existence of a "faceness" dimension—see later section, "Faceness.") Features could include properties such as the presence or absence of ornamentation (hats, jewelry, and makeup) as well as facial characteristics (eyes, nose, and mouth).

Wholistic properties are of three types: simple wholes that equal the sum of the parts; templates that are prototypal forms or schema; and configurations in which the whole is greater than the sum of its parts. Configuration is of special interest because it is an emergent property of the component properties. That is, it is not simply equivalent to the whole set of elemental properties but emerges from them. It is this emergent characteristic of configuration that is perhaps responsible for researchers' interest in infants' response to facial configuration; the particular elements or features can be varied (for example, dots substituted for eyes) without eliminating the essential properties of the arrangement.

Garner stresses the importance of the investigator's definition of the stimulus set by documenting the relationship between stimulus structure and the organism's processing of the stimulus set. Featural processing involves search for the presence of each of the single features with a question and separate search for each. For example, does the face have a nose? Yes. Does it have a finger? No. This continues through a list of features. Dimensional processing involves search for levels on the dimension. For example, is the face pink or blue or yellow? There is one question with one answer: pink. Often, adult human subjects may treat dimensionally structured stimuli with a feature-type interrogation; that is, with a question and search for each level as if each were a feature. For example, is the face blue? No. Is it pink, then? Yes. If both component and configurational properties are available, organisms may respond only to the wholistic properties, regardless of whether the components are featural or dimensional. Thus, infants might respond to contour density as a dimension differentiating specific social stimuli and/or as a feature differentiating social and nonsocial stimuli. On the other hand, the arrangement of eyes, nose, and mouth (facial configuration or form) may be the primary differentiator of social and nonsocial, irrespective of component qualities like contour density.

In summary, the researcher must have operational command of the stimulus set in order to determine "how" the subject responds, and the infant researcher must have such control also to determine "to what" the subject responds. Garner's taxonomy of stimulus structure provides one means of considering the physical-stimulus nature of the person. Very little attention has been given to the definition and measurement of the physical parameters of social stimuli. The literature on the neonate's responses to social stimuli can be reviewed in terms of these considerations, but having considered the physical nature of the stimulus and before addressing infants' responses to stimuli, we must examine the organism's structure. What cognitive-perceptual capabilities and what attentional strategies does the neonate bring to his or her earliest interactions with the social and nonsocial worlds?

THE NEONATE'S COGNITIVE-PERCEPTUAL CAPABILITIES AND ATTENTIONAL STRATEGIES

The infant is by no means born a tabula rasa nor is the infant born blind or deaf as was believed less than a century ago. Our knowledge of infant capacity has increased significantly during the past decade or so (Haith, 1979; Kessen & Nelson, 1974; Salapatek, 1975; Sameroff, 1978). Piaget (1952) has argued that the first mode of interaction that the infant brings to the environment is the reflex scheme with the accompanying strategies of assimilation and accommodation. But the infant brings much more structure to its initial environmental interaction than is implied by Piaget's descriptions. For example, at birth or shortly thereafter, the infant can divide parts of the world categorically. Perhaps most notable, especially for the theme of this chapter, is the infant's tendency to organize the visual spectrum in the same color categories as adults (Bornstein, 1975), but this tendency to categorize the world also extends to taste (Nowliss, 1974) and sound (Eimas, Siqueland, Jusczyk, & Vigorito, 1971).

In particular, the looking scheme is adequately functional at birth. Although the neonate's visual cortex is immature, and aspects of visual performance are poor compared to adult standards, visual interactions with the world do not seem to be severely handicapped (Deacon & Konner, 1978). For example, although ability to visually accommodate to different focal lengths is immature during the first few months, infants exhibit a similar degree of visual acuity across several distances (Salapatek, Bechtold, & Bushnell, 1976). Although infants tend to err in the direction of undershoot, soon after birth, they become capable of moving their eyes to the side of a visual field if a peripheral target is introduced (Salapatek, 1975).

Additionally, the infant brings to early environmental interaction a number of what Kessen and Nelson (1974) call "middle-range strategies," which are more limited than the strategies of accommodation and assimilation described by Piaget (1952), but more general than specific reflex activity. These "middle-range strategies" include a tendency to seek out and respond to movement (Haith, 1966; Wickelgren, 1969) and to contour density (Karmel, Hoffman, & Fegy, 1974; Kessen et al., 1970; Salapatek, 1975). With age, infants develop preferences for curvature (Salapatek, 1975), complexity (Fantz, 1965; Kessen et al., 1970), novelty (Jeffrey & Cohen, 1971), and aperiodicity of stimulation (Vietz, Friedman, & Foster, 1974). In addition to responding preferentially to certain dimensions and features of stimuli, infants also prefer certain levels on the dimensions. Typically, medium levels of stimulation are preferred, and the preferences are expressed as an inverted U function of visual attention and dimensional measurement (Kessen et al., 1970).

The development of visual attention over the first few months has been carefully described. First, there is an overall increase in visual attention to the environment during the first 6 months of life (Haith, 1979; Salapatek, 1975; Sherrod, 1979). Second, before 2 months, visual attention seems to be "captured" by limited featural aspects of the stimulus. The number of contour elements per unit area (contour density) and the size of contour elements control the infant's gaze behavior prior to 2 months. That is, before 2 months of age, and perhaps even beyond 2 months, visual perception of stimuli is part, not whole, oriented (Salapatek, 1975).

Fantz, Fagan, and Miranda (1975), from an extensive series of studies on visual selectvity and discrimination in infancy, report a similar developmental pattern. Potency of pattern definition, characterized by high contrast, sharp contours, and large elements, is succeeded by potency of pattern quantity or complexity (number of elements, contour length, density of contour), which is succeeded by pattern quality or configuration (shape, regularity, concentricity, orientation). These authors argue that this pattern can be related to the maturation of the visual system.

This development from response on the basis of pattern definition, to response on the basis of pattern quantity, and finally to response on the basis of pattern quality corresponds with the transition from Stage I to II of Piaget's (1952) description of infancy—a transition also occurring around the age of 2 months. That is, initially the infant responds to objects on the basis of his or her reflex schemes; stimuli exhibit characteristics such as contour and movement, which elicit activity of the looking scheme. Stage II is heralded by the initial differentiation of assimilation and accommodation; infants no longer simply exercise their reflex schemes such as looking (assimilating the world to them), they begin to accommodate to the world. Their exercise of the looking scheme is changed to allow them to experience objects more exhaustively; they scan more globally allowing for the pickup of information on wholistic properties and the construction of stimulus characteristics such as form. Once this construction of form occurs, the stimulus' configuration itself may determine the infants' scanning style by leading their gaze to specific foci of interest.

Thus, the infant brings to his or her initial social contacts a fairly well-developed visual system, a tendency to categorize the world in certain ways, and a number of visual preferences or attentional strategies. Development consists primarily of a move from attention directed to limited featural, contour aspects of the world to a more global scan and attention to configurational properties. In the following section, infants' early social cognition is examined in terms of the physical properties of the face and the development of visual attention.

INFANTS' VISUAL PREFERENCES FOR SOCIAL STIMULI

Much research has focused on infants' attention to, and recognition of, social stimuli (primarily facial stimuli). The unifying theme across these studies is the infant's differentiation of the social world. The literature is extensive, and a summary review is presented in Table 2.1. The types of differentiations examined, some sample references, and some general age trends are offered in this table.

This is a difficult body of literature with which to come to grips. Summarization and comparison across studies is problematic due to the diversity of approaches involved. Such difficulties include the following:

1. A number of different response indices are employed to measure infants' attention to, or preferences for, social stimuli. These responses include visual fixation, smiling, head turning, cardiac rate, tongue protrusion, and general body movement. Because so little is known about the processes indexed by these various responses or the interrelationships of these different responses, it is risky to compare results of studies based on different infant responses. The problem is compounded further by the fact that different measures may be taken of the same behavioral response. Thus, visual fixation can be measured as total amount of fixation on a stimulus, length of first fixation, longest consecutive fixation, number of discrete fixations, and/or latency to first fixation. These different measures of infant visual behavior may also index different aspects or processes of attention. This diversity of response and measurement, compounded by a lack of understanding about the processes indexed by particular responses, indicates the need for multiple measures of several infant responses *within* infant studies (Kagan, 1971).

TABLE 2.1

Infants' Differentiations of the Social World:
A Summary Review of the Literature

Differentiation	Age Trends in Visual Preferences[a]	Examples of References
Social vs. nonsocial	Social are preferred at all ages	Fantz & Nevis, 1967; Fitzgerald, 1968; Kagan & Lewis, 1965; Sherrod, 1979; Spitz & Wolf, 1946.
Faces vs. representations of faces	Faces are preferred by 1 to 2 months	Ahrens, 1954; Dirks & Gibson, 1977; Lewis, 1969; McCall & Kagan, 1967; Polak et al., 1964; Wilcox, 1969.
Animate (sound, moving) vs. inanimate (silent, nonmoving) faces	Animate preferred by 1 to 3 months	Carpenter, 1974b; Field, 1979; Haith et al., 1977b; Piaget, 1952; Sherrod, 1979.
Regularly arranged vs. scrambled or altered faces	Regular preferred until 5 to 6 months	Caron et al., 1973; Goren, 1975; Haaf & Brown, 1975; Kagan et al., 1966
Correctly oriented vs. disoriented faces (or changes in pose)	Can recognize invariance across variance by 5 to 6 months	Cornell, 1974; Fagan, 1976; Watson, 1966.
Familiar vs. unfamiliar faces	Familiar preferred by 5 months	Bigelow, 1977; Carpenter, 1974a; Maurer & Salapatek, 1976; Sherrod, 1979.

[a]Most typical finding across several studies.

2. The method of presenting stimuli to infant subjects also varies across studies. The stimuli may be presented singularly and serially or in paired comparisons. They may be presented from within closed or open boxes or in a more naturalistic, interactive context. The infant may be seated in an infant chair, seated on a person's lap, held on someone's shoulder, or lain on his or her back in a crib. Such factors may influence infants' performance; for example, recent research has shown that the mode of presentation of the stimuli (singular or paired) can influence the infant's relative responses to the set of stimuli (Greenberg & Blue, 1977).

3. Studies of infants' responses to social stimuli also vary considerably in design and in age group sampled. One month, 3 months, and 5 to 6 months are heavily sampled age groups because they index fairly rapid and noticeable transitions within the infancy period. This diversity is, in many ways, the easiest with which to deal.

4. The diversity of response measurement is paralleled by an equally great variety of "social" stimuli employed in studies of infant social cognition. The large variety of stimuli is due, at least in part, to inadequate attention to the structural properties of the stimuli. Thus, photographs of faces, moving pictures of faces, facial line drawings, paper-mâché masks, heads of mannequins, live faces (familiar, novel, adult, child, midget, black and white), dolls, and teddy bears have all been used in studies of infants' attention to, and preferences for, facial stimuli. These stimuli may share a few characteristics (for example, facial configuration), but they also vary across many others such as contour density, brightness, color, complexity, and movement properties. Even within a category of stimuli such as "face drawings" there exists considerable variation between studies; some "face drawings" represent simple geometric stimuli composed of dots and straight lines whereas others may include detailed drawings of facial features. Few studies, exceptions being Thomas (1973) and Sherrod (1979), utilize face drawings from previous research and thus fail to allow direct comparisons of results.

5. Perhaps even more problematic than the diversity of stimuli is the fact that most studies use only one example of each stimulus. Thus, a comparison of infants' responses to a live face versus a photo of a face may use only one live face and one photo. We know that, especially in the first months, the infant's gaze is easily captured by a limited featural aspect of a stimuli. Thus, comparisons of infants' responses to stimuli using only one exemplar may reflect a response pattern based entirely on the peculiarity of a particular example, not the characteristics of a category such as live face versus photo of face. This problem also reflects the fact that few studies of infant social cognition pay careful attention to the physical stimulus properties other than the one or two being explicitly examined, and few place their findings within the context of what is known about the infant's cognitive-perceptual development.

Given these criticisms of this literature on infant social cognition, it is a testimony to the power of social stimuli in eliciting and holding attention that we are able to extract any conclusions with confidence. Wholistic properties, such as configuration (arrangement of facial features—eyes, nose, and mouth) and animated movement, both of which are specific to facial stimuli, emerge as most conclusive and interesting. Although such wholistic properties are represented in the literature tabulated in Table 2.1, component properties of facial stimuli are hardly represented at all. Using Garner's (1978) taxonomy, we delineate at least the following component properties of the face: contrast, color, contour, curvature, and brightness, and it is exactly these component properties that figure prominently in the research on young infants' cognitive-perceptual development. With the exception of facial configuration and animation, not one of the differentiations listed in Table 2.1 involve only one property of the stimuli or sets of stimuli being compared. It is possible, for example, that many of the differentiations in Table 2.1 are based on response to contour density, up to and including the differentiation of specific faces.

The following section considers in detail the research on two wholistic properties, configuration and animation, for the following reasons:

1. Most research attention has been given to infants' interest in facial configuration and in the movement properties of the face.
2. These two lines of research, in many ways, represent the best work in the area.
3. They have implications for infants' social cognition of other stimulus characterstics.

Facial Configuration

Although physical properties such as contour and movement (or complexity and animation) may be necessary, they are not sufficient criteria for definition of the human face. That is, one might construct some nonsocial stimulus, a mobile for example, which would possess many of the same physical properties as the face. One characteristic of the face, however, that cannot be removed without altering the "faceness" of the stimulus is configuration, or arrangement of the features, eyes, nose, and lips. Facial configuration is, in fact, more specific to the face than is animation; the arrangment of facial features may, therefore, be of paramount importance to the infant's early cognition of the person.

Many researchers (the most notable group being the ethologists) have, in fact, argued that human infants are very attentive to configuration. The argument is that infants are born able to recognize and respond to the form of the face, or that they very rapidly develop this tendency. The configuration of the face is seen to be similar to a releaser stimulus for animal imprinting. The alternative view—that of the cognitive-developmentalists—is that infants learn to recognize the form of the face in the same way that they learn to recognize the form of any other stimulus, that there is nothing inherently attractive about the arrangement of the human facial features. Infants' recognition of, and response to, the configuration of the face has inspired much research, and two general approaches have been used.

One method is to alter facial form by adding, omitting, or scrambling facial features. The infant's ability to discriminate the regular and altered facial stimuli or the preference for one or the other stimulus is then assessed. Responses such as smiling (Ahrens, 1954; Fantz, 1965; Futterman, 1963; Takahashi, 1973) and visual fixation (Fantz, 1965, 1966; Haaf, 1977; Haaf & Bell, 1967; Kagan, 1967; Kagan, Henler, Hen-Tov, Levine, & Lewis, 1966; Lewis, 1969) are usually employed to measure the infant's recognition of the alterations in facial form. Such studies usually examine only one age group or are cross-sectional in design.

As mentioned earlier, it is difficult to compare results across studies because they make use of different age groups, different response measures, and different types of facial stimuli (line drawings, photographs, mannequins, and so forth), yet, on the average, two trends can be extracted from these studies: (1) There is a developmental progression in the saliency of specific elements of the facial configuration. Thus, infants first attend to the contour of the head, then the eyes become attractive, and finally the nose-mouth area is noticed at around 5 months (Caron et al., 1973; Futterman, 1963; E. Gibson, 1969; Kagan, 1966); (2) Under 6 months, infants prefer to look at regularly arranged rather than scrambled or altered faces (Fantz, 1965, 1966; Fantz & Nevis, 1967; Haaf & Bell, 1967; Kagan 1966, 1967; Kagan & Lewis, 1965; Kagan et al., 1966; Lewis, 1969; McCall & Kagan, 1967). These results are usually interpreted to mean that only when infants are attending to all elements of the face are they able to appreciate facial configuration and thereby assimilate and deal with an altered face. That is, the face schema is developing during the first 6 months (Kagan, 1966, 1967). These are the general findings that can be extracted from many of these studies. However, there are contradictory specific results. For example, Hershenson (1967) with newborns, Koopman and Ames (1968) with 2½-month olds, and Wilcox (1969) with even older infants report no difference in visual fixation between regular and scrambled faces. Wilcox also found no differences in smiling responses to the distorted and regular faces. On the other hand, Goren (1975) reports that newborns preferentially track a regularly arranged face over scrambled faces! The contradictions in results cannot be attributed to the use of different response measures because studies using the same responses

(Fantz, 1965, 1966 and Wilcox, 1969, for example) report contradictory results.

The second method used to study infants' recognition of facial configuration assesses the infant's ability to recognize the invariance of a stimulus (facial configuration, in this case) across variance in the stimulus (for example, changes in orientation, position, and poses of the face).

By 5 to 6 months, infants can recognize live faces, photos, and line drawings of faces across rotations through 360°. However, no changes with age have been found in visual fixation or smiling to different (nonupright) rotations of the face (Fagan, 1972; Watson, 1966). Furthermore, Fagan (1977b) reported that the recognition memory of similarly aged infants for photos of faces was interfered with by intervening presentations of upright photos of similar faces but not by rotated photos of the familiarized face.

Studies of the second type often use the habituation paradigm; for example, infants are habituated to one view of a face (using photos) and then presented with two different views of the same face or with a different face in a similar pose. Dishabituation to the new facial stimulus is assessed. Cornell (1974) reports that in 23-week-old infants, looking decreased to repeated presentations of the same face; there was less decrement to different poses of the same face, and no decrement over trials to different faces of the same pose. Dirks and Gibson (1977) habituated infants to repeated presentations of a live face and measured dishabituation to a photo of the same face or of a novel face. Dishabituation occurred in response to the photo of the novel face but not to the photo of the previously exposed live face. Although live faces and photos of faces differ in regard to information relating to three-dimensionality and other such characteristics, they possess the same distinctive features of faces. Dirks and Gibson argue, therefore, that their infants must have been responding to these distinctive features.

Fagan (1976), using the habituation paradigm, presented a preference test on the dishabituation trials. Thus, if on the preference test the infant looked at the more novel stimulus, then one could conclude that the infant recognized the old stimulus and discriminated the two stimuli. Using this paradigm in a series of five studies, Fagan (1976) found that 7-month-old infants could discriminate different faces of the same sex, as well as different poses of the same face. Fagan (1976, 1979) generally concludes, in agreement with Cornell (1974), that 7-month-old infants recognized unique aspects of a particular face as well as general characteristics such as configuration. These habituation studies reinforce one finding of the majority of the studies that scramble or alter faces—that perception of facial form continues to develop throughout the first 6 months.

Sherrod (1979) investigated infants' attention to facial configuration as one facial characteristic along with complexity, animation, and familiarity. Several examples of each stimulus were used in order to insure that infants' responses were based on response to the stimulus category, not to specific examples. It was found that even very young infants (1-month-old exhibited visual preferences for facial configuration; the preference was not statistically significant, but the trend was consistent. Compared to other characteristics such as animation and complexity, facial configuration was not especially important in determining response to the face.

Thus, review of the research on infants' attention to facial configuration implicates a view of the importance of facial configuration somewhere between that of the ethologists and the cognitive-developmentalists. Facial configuration is attractive to very young infants, yet infants also continue to learn about facial configuration during the first 6 months. And facial configuration alone, independent of other characteristics of the face such as complexity, is not responsible for the interest infants display in facial stimuli.

Investigations of infants' visual scanning of faces generally support the above summary of the research on infants' attention to facial configuration. Although the developmental pattern of visual scanning (limited contour/potency of pattern definition to configurational/potency of pattern quality) has been found in regard both to live faces (stationary and unresponsive) and to representations of faces (Hainline, 1978; Haith, Bergman, & Moore, 1977b; Maurer & Salapatek, 1976; Salapatek, 1975), some qualifications are in order. That is, under 2 months of age, infants predominantly scan the limited contour (edges) aspects of faces—the hairline and chinline of the face. By 2 months, they have shifted their gaze to internal features of the face—scanning eyes, for example. Nonetheless, in regard to faces, infants never exhibit the extreme limited contour scanning displayed to geometric stimuli such as triangles—implying some special regard for faces very early (Donnee, 1973). Second, addition of an auditory component to the face, which need not be a voice, facilitates internal scanning, especially of the eyes (Haith, Bergman, & Mann, 1977a).

On the whole, infants tend to scan faces in the same way they scan other objects—implying that under 2 months, information on configuration would not be picked up by the infant. However, certain characteristics of the face—including properties like audition, movement (see next section), and perhaps the nature of configuration—tend to pull the infant's scan away from this limited featural style, thereby facilitating a more global style and allowing pickup of information on wholistic properties.

Movement Properties of the Face

Aside from configuration, the other characteristic that is rather unique to faces is animation. Indeed, it is difficult to define animation in terms other than those relating to a live organism, but a definition must include motion or movement, a stimulus characteristic to which infants are preferentially responsive.

Gibson, Owsley, and Johnston (1978) investigated infants' capacity to recognize motion as an invariant property of objects. They habituated 5-month-old infants to three types of rigid motion and then measured dishabituation (with visual fixation as the dependent measure) to a different, rigid movement or to a deforming, elastic motion. Dishabituation was greater to the deforming than to the different rigid motion. The infants exhibited the capacity to detect the rigidity of the object as an invariant property; deforming motion was recognized as a different property than rigidity (see also Gibson, Johnston, & Owsley, 1977). Thus, infants as young as 5 months recognize and attend to at least two categories of stimulus motion—rigid, side-to-side, rotating motion and deforming, continuous, undulating, elastic motion. As Gibson et al. (1978) note, these findings raise important questions about the role of motion as an object-defining property, and this issue is especially important regarding infants' perceptions of faces. Faces exhibit both kinds of motion—rigid (nodding, for example) and deforming (facial expressions, for example). Deforming motion is, therefore, at least one way of characterizing animation. At any rate, rigid movement and more fluid, animated motion of the face represent two different types of stimulus movement, and they should be separately studied in regard to infants' visual preferences.

Rigid movement is important to infants' attention both to social and nonsocial stimuli. Newborns have been found to shift their gaze in the direction of moving lights (Wickelgren, 1969) and to suppress sucking in response to moving visual stimuli (Haith, 1966). Further, 2- and 7-week-old infants prefer to look at moving rather than stationary heads (Carpenter, 1974b). Piaget (1952) observed that moving heads elicited the attention of 1-month-old Laurent, and movement has been found to elicit head fixation in 3 to 5-week-old infants (Haith et al., 1977a).

The role of deforming motion or animation is, however, less clear. Field (1979) argued that animate faces attract lower levels of attention than inanimate faces and suggested that animation such as changing facial expressions place greater demands on the infants' information-processing abilities. Field examined responses of 3-month-old, term and preterm, infants to animate and inanimate faces. She used a spontaneous mother-infant session as animate mother, a mother imitating infant session as inanimate mother, a raggedy-Ann doll as inanimate nonmother, and a nodding, talking raggedy-Ann doll as animate nonmother. She found a pattern of looking response ranking the stimuli (low to high preference): animate mother, inanimate mother, animate doll, inanimate doll. Mother was looked at less than the doll, and the animated doll was looked at less than the inanimate doll. The Field study exemplifies the inadequate assessment of the physical properties of stimuli in studies of social cognition. First, the doll–mother comparison is confounded across a range of characteristics including animation as well as complexity, color, contrast, brightness, contour density, and so forth. The animate–inanimate doll comparison indexes rigid movement, not animated deforming motion. It is also not clear how an imitative-of-infant mother is less animated than a spontaneously responsive mother; this comparison, in fact, would seem to index expectations of the infant regarding mother's behavior—expectations that are well-developed by 3-month-old infants (see Chapter 7). It is not surprising that the infants looked less at a strangely responding mother—who represents a novel, even bizarre, stimulus—than at a normally responding mother. The failure to replicate the finding of increased looking to a rigidly moving as opposed to a nonmoving stimulus is, however, surprising. It may also represent a response based on violation of expectation because the infants were familiar with the doll; in this case, however, the violation of expectation works in the opposite direction to that with mother. The fact that addition of sound to the doll resulted in decreased looking also contradicts past research indicating that addition of an auditory component increases looking at the stimulus (Culp, 1973).

Field cites several other studies supporting her results of lesser attention to animated stimuli (Brazelton, Koslowski, & Main, 1974, comparing mother and a toy monkey; Carpenter, 1974b, Carpenter, Tecce, Stechler, & Friedman, 1970, comparing mother and a mannequin; Field, 1978, comparing a raggedy-Ann doll and mother). However, with the exception of the Carpenter studies, similar criticisms can be applied to the findings. Mother versus a toy monkey or a raggedy-Ann doll are not appropriate comparisons for indexing the infant's response to the animation of the stimuli; these comparisons index a host of characteristics other than animation. Carpenter compared infants' responses at 1 month of age to the stationary, unresponsive faces of mother and a department-store-type mannequin. This comparison would index rigid and deforming motion as well as familiarity of the specific faces of mother and the dummy; a more appropriate comparison might be stranger–mannequin. Although other component properties may modestly differ across the comparison, a live-face-mannequin comparison is as close as we can come to a comparison that indexes response to animation—rigid and/or deforming motion—of the face.

Sherrod (1979) compared infant responses to the stationary, nonresponsive, faces of mother, a female stranger, and a mannequin (among other stimuli) in 1-, 3-, and 5-month-old infants. There were five examples of each stimulus so that infants' responses to the stimulus category could be examined across a number of exemplars of the category, allowing for intercategory variation in properties such as contour density. It was found that, at all ages, infants preferred the animated faces and, in factor analyses of looking behavior, animation emerged as one dimension critical to infants' responses to the entire set of stimuli. The contradiction between Sherrod's and Carpenter's studies can only be resolved through replication of the studies. It is possible, however, that some peculiarity of the mannequin used by Carpenter is responsible for that response because she did not use multiple exemplars. Also, subtle auditory-stimulus characteristics may have influenced infants' responses in the Carpenter study; although her stimuli were silent, they were not presented from behind sound-proof windows, as in the Sherrod study. Finally, Carpenter's study used single-stimulus presentations, not paired comparisons as in the Sherrod study, so that Sherrod's results may be more reliable for judging relative response to the stimuli.

Thus, movement properties of the face, including rigid motion like nodding and the more animated quality of motion found in facial expressions, are especially important to infants' attention to the face. Motion of the face may, in fact, represent one characteristic by which infants initially differentiate the social world. More research is needed, such as that of Gibson et al. (1978) and Sherrod (1979), to delineate the significant characteristics of motion that are of interest to young babies and that might serve to identify people.

"Faceness"

The importance of examining the physical properties of the person and of carefully assessing the stimulus structure in studies of social cognition is documented by the preceding review of the research on animation and facial configuration. On the one hand, the power of facial configuration in eliciting infant attention has been overemphasized, due to the fact that this characteristic is peculiar to social stimuli and the fact that its importance was not examined in the context of other characteristics like complexity and animation. On the other hand, the power of motion, especially animated motion, has been underrepresented in studies of infants' attention to the face—partly because research was being devoted to characteristics like configuration and partly because motion per se has not been adequately defined in regard to social stimuli.

There can be little question that a variety of factors operate in attracting infants' attention to the face. In order to fully understand the infant's social cognition of the human face, it is necessary to consider as many facial characteristics as is possible. A line of research that attempts to do this is the one investigating the existence of a "faceness" dimension.

The concept of faceness rests on the idea that a complete, unaltered face is more facelike than a scrambled face or one without eyes, nose, or mouth. This research questions whether infants construct a concept or dimension of faceness, and whether such a construction influences their response to facial stimuli.

Thomas (1973) argued that babies' looking behavior belongs to a theory of preferential choice behavior. Infants' responses, according to Thomas, are at best ordinal structures, and infants can, therefore, be considered replications of one another only if, as individuals, their responses produce the same ordinal preferences. Using data from the Koopman and Ames (1968), Fantz (1961), and Haaf and Bell (1967) studies, and employing the undimensional scaling technique (Coombs, 1964) to uncover the scale or dimension underlying infants' looking preferences (in paired-comparison stimulus presentations), he found that the most probable scale determining the infants' looking responses was that of symmetry; infant responses could not be ordered according to the faceness scale, which Haaf and Bell had established. Jones-Molfese (1975) came to a similar conclusion. Yet, these authors concluded that 2- and 3- month-old infants did not randomly rank face-like stimuli. Infants seem to respond to some dimensional aspect of faces, but no one has yet been successful in uncovering the content of the dimension.

In paired-comparison trials, Sherrod (1979) presented 1-, 3-, and 5-month-old infants with all comparisons of five stimuli: mother, a female stranger, a female department-store-window mannequin, a three-dimensional schematic face, and a three-dimensional geometric stimulus composed of the same elements as the schematic face. A Coombsian–unfolding-technique analysis of looking behavior did not reveal an underlying dimension of faceness or personness at any age, although infants did tend to order the five stimuli transitively, especially at 5 months. The total complex of characteristics that the face possesses seem to be responsible for infants' interest in the face, and global factors of animation and complexity seemed to be the most specific factors that could be described as underlying the response pattern.

It can be concluded, therefore, that infants do not construct a dimension of faceness although they do rank facial stimuli. The ranking appears to be based on the total complex of characteristics offered by the human face, emphasizing the necessity of examining many different properties of the face and indicating the importance of physical properties to infants' responses to facial stimuli.

SUMMARY AND CONCLUSION

This chapter has reviewed research analyzing the properties of the face, the neonate's attentional strategies, and infant social cognition of the human face. It has argued in favor of examining infant social cognition of physical properties of the face; it has supported such analysis as necessary for an understanding of infants' attention to the face. The chapter now offers some speculations on the possible developmental consequences of this early form of social cognition.

Attention to Social Stimuli:
Alternative Strategies

Review of the literature on early cognitive-perceptual development as well as that on attention to faces indicates that before 2 months, infants generally scan limited-feature contour aspects of objects including faces. However, exceptions regarding attention to the human face indicate that faces "push" the infant beyond this primary strategy. To review the exceptions: (1) scanning of the face is never quite as limited featurally as is the scanning of geometric forms (Donnee, 1973); (2) auditory characteristics of the face facilitate more global, internal scanning of the face (Haith et al., 1977b); (3) infants exhibit a tendency to look preferentially at facial configurations; (4) infants appreciate global properties of faces such as animation and complexity (Sherrod, 1979) indicating attention to other than limited features.

Infants come into the world with the "middle-range" strategy of scanning contour, a strategy based on the maturational level of the visual system and the infants' information-processing capacities. With age, infants develop a tendency to escape the capture of their gaze by contour and to scan more globally, especially the inside of objects (that is, the eyes, rather the chinline or hairline). Social stimuli, with their frequency, meaningfulness, the saliency of facial configuration, and their animation, "push" infants toward the more global scanning style. (This argument does not imply that for a single incident, infants would necessarily scan a face more "globally" than a nonface. Rather, over several incidents and longer time periods, one would expect the scanning of faces and nonfaces to differ.) After more global and/or internal scanning is facilitated, the face may serve to hold attention there. For example, the configuration of the face may serve to hold attention to the eyes (Arnheim, 1969), a very animated part of the face, thus setting the stage for mutual visual regard, a developmental milestone for later social relations (Robson, 1967).

The limited-feature contour scanning style involves attention to component properties of the stimulus whereas the more global, internal style is more focused on wholistic properties like configuration (though not exclusively so). To connect these strategies with the conceptual structure proposed by Garner (1978) also implies a characterization of the strategies in terms of analysis and synthesis (J. Gibson, 1950, 1966; Hebb, 1949; Neisser, 1967). When attention is focused on elements, appreciation of more global aspects of the stimulus requires a synthesis or organization of those elements and details into a whole; attention to wholes implies that analysis of wholistic properties must be used to determine the elemental components.

Therefore, it is possible to describe two general styles of interaction with the world; one global scanning style, involving attention to wholistic properties, and analysis of these properties; and the other involving limited-featural scanning, attention to component properties, and synthesis. The infant is born predisposed to the latter strategy given its biological-structural characteristics; gradually the child develops the more global style and interactions with social stimuli facilitate the development.[3] The argument for a developmental shift does not necessarily mean that the two strategies cannot coexist. The frequency of use of the two strategies varies across development, and we argue, also between social and nonsocial stimuli. This difference in strategy of attention may also vary between individuals, thereby contributing to individual variability in responsiveness to social stimuli.

Researchers have noticed different styles of infant interaction with social and nonsocial stimuli, and these differences can be interpreted to correspond to the two types of scanning strategy described above. Brazelton et al. (1974) report sustained, captured attention (quiet "stares") to nonsocial stimuli; response to nonresponsive and responsive social stimuli is much more dynamic, involving looking away, vocalizing, moving, and so forth. Likewise, Carpenter casually mentions that during the interstimulus intervals, infants displayed sustained, "captured" attention to dimly blinking lights on the door of the stimulus presentation box; response to the "social" stimuli did not exhibit this sustained character (Carpenter, 1974b; Carpenter et al., 1970). Sustained attention to nonsocial stimuli could be interpreted to indicate exhaustive search, feature by feature, whereas dynamic response to social stimuli could be interpreted as brief attention to more global qualities with frequent looks away to moderate the informational input.[4] Thus, by developing strategies for interacting with persons, the stage may be set for the development of more general styles of environmental interaction. This chapter has considered this issue only from the perspective of early attention to the physical properties of the human face. The person, as a stimulus, however, has both physical and social properties, and the "social" properties may also "push" cognitive development throughout the sensory-motor period. This point can be briefly reviewed before summarizing the overall argument.

The "Development-Stimulating" Nature of Social Stimuli

During the sensory-motor period, as developmental milestones such as crawling, babbling, walking, and talking are reached, more and more of the

---

[3]I do not intend to imply in this speculative scheme, or in any other section of this chapter, that knowledge of the physical properties of the face is exhausted during early infancy. Carey and Diamond (1975) as well as Mann, Diamond, and Carey (1979), for example, present results of children's developing knowledge of physical properties of the face.

[4]Recently proposed models of infant attention (for example, Fagan, 1977a; Jeffrey, 1976) do not address the possibility of differential strategies of interaction with social and nonsocial objects.

world is opened up to the infant. Infants are, however, much less dependent on sensory-motor acquisitions for interaction with social stimuli than they are for exploration of the physical world. Infants need not come to mother because she comes to them. They do not need to manipulate mother, turn her round and round in order to see all her sides—mother turns herself round and round. All infants need to do is look, to pay attention to mother as she naturally behaves in the environment. Infants can lie in their crib and follow mother through appearances and disappearances of her person and her behavior; all they need do is look and listen. Infants can search with their eyes; they need not search with their hands. They must, however, handle, and manipulate physical objects in order to explore their properties and aspects.

Piaget (1952, 1954) argues that the infant cannot "know" an object without acting on it. Because of the physical-stimulus properties (and behavior, of course) of persons, it is less necessary to act on the social environment than on physical objects. The "experience" of the person is a sufficient form of "acting-on" social objects. As a result, a positive décalage may occur in the emergence of knowledge of the social environment and of the physical world. This chapter has proposed such a décalage regarding attentional structure and strategies of environmental interaction.

Furthermore, cognitive achievements reached through interaction with people facilitate the acquisition of these achievements in relation to other aspects of the environment. Through generalizing assimilation, such developments can be extended to other aspects of the environment—when the infant acquires the sensory-motor capacity for dealing with these environmental events. Thus, as Casler (1961) argued, retardation, as a result of maternal deprivation during the first 6 months may be due to perceptual deprivation—from failure to experience the boost to cognitive development that social cognition provides. Interaction with social stimuli—with *both* their physical and social properties—may provide the conditions that facilitate infants' organization until they are autonomous separate systems capable of self-organization (Korner, 1973).

In Review

This chapter has argued for: (1) more careful control and description of stimulus structure in studies of infant social cognition; (2) more attention to the person as a physical stimulus; and (3) more attention to the complex and multiproperty nature of the person-stimulus. It has emphasized the possible importance of people's physical properties in facilitating the development of alternative strategies of infant attention and suggested that this represents one specific example of the general developmental significance of infant social cognition.

By focusing on physical properties, this chapter does not intend to deny the critical importance of "social," emotional, and interactive qualities of people (as pointed out in the preceding section). One must realize that such a focus on physical properties, along with careful attention to and experimental control of stimulus structure, is both difficult and risky—possibly resulting in "throwing out the baby with the bath"—or perhaps more appropriately, "throwing out the personness with the social qualities."[5] I do not think, however, that the research attention given to the physical properties of people allows an accurate assessment of either the nature of these properties or their importance. At a minimum, the person as a stimulus can be used as a powerful tool for studying early infant cognition.

Future work in this area will demand innovative new research strategies. In one notable example, Souther and Banks (1979) attempted to construct the social world as seen through the eyes of a young infant, and then asked what information was available to an adult viewer of the world. The spatial-frequency content and contrast of facial photographs were reduced to that commensurate with the acuity-contrast sensitivity of 1-, 2-, and 3-month-old infants. Reduction to the 1-month level produced faces with fainter internal features and more distinct contours than reduction to the 3-month level. Different, specific persons could generally be discriminated by adults at both levels, though with difficulty at the 1-month level; facial expressions, however, could not be recognized at the 1-month level. In themselves, these results are not earthshaking because they simply reflect what we had already learned from studies of infants' visual scanning of objects, but the study does present a fresh perspective on methodology. Progress in studies of infant social cognition will result from creative and innovative approaches to research.

ACKNOWLEDGMENTS

I wish to thank Barbara Cornblatt, William Kessen, Michael Lamb, Gary Olson, and Elizabeth Spelke for critical readings of the manuscript.

REFERENCES

Ahrens, R. Beitrage zur entwickiung des physiognomie-und mimikicennes. *Zeitschrift fur experimentelle und angewandte psychologie,* 1954, *2,* 412–454.

Arnheim, R. *Visual thinking.* Los Angeles: University of California Press, 1969.

Bigelow, A. *Infants' recognition of mother.* Paper presented at the meeting of the Society for Research in Child Development, New Orleans, March 1977.

Bornstein, M. Qualities of color vision in infancy. *Journal of Experimental Child Psychology,* 1975, *19,* 401–419.

---

[5] I acknowledge Elizabeth Spelke for emphasizing the importance of this point.

Brazelton, T. B., Koslowski, B., & Main, M. The origins of reciprocity: the early mother-infant interaction. In M. Lewis & L. Rosenblum (Eds.), *The effect of the infant on its caregiver.* New York: Wiley, 1974.

Carey, S., & Diamond, R. From piecemeal to configurational representation in faces. *Science,* 1977, *195,* 312–315.

Caron, A., Caron, R., Caldwell, R., & Weiss, S. J. Infant perception of structural properties of the face. *Developmental Psychology,* 1973, *9,* 385–399.

Carpenter, G. Mother's face and the newborn. *New Scientist,* March, 1974, 742–744. (a)

Carpenter, G. Visual regard of moving and stationary faces in early infancy. *Merrill-Palmer Quarterly,* 1974,*20,* 181–194. (b)

Carpenter, G., Tecce, J., Stechler, G., & Friedman, S. Differential visual behavior to human and humanoid faces in early infancy. *Merrill-Palmer Quarterly,* 1970, *16,* 91–108.

Casler, L. Maternal deprivation: A critical review of the literature. *Monographs of the Society for Research in Child Development,* 1961, *26(#2).*

Cohen, L., & Salapatek, P. (Eds.). *Infant perception: From sensation to cognition.* New York: Academic Press, 1975.

Coombs, C. *A theory of data.* New York: Wiley, 1964.

Cornell, E. Infants' discrimination of photos of faces following redundant presentations. *Journal of Experimental Child Psychology,* 1974, *18,* 98–106.

Culp, R. Effect of mother's voice on infant looking behavior. *Proceedings of the 81st APA Convention,* 1973, *8,* 55.

Deacon, T. W., & Konner, M. J. *Biological and behavioral development of the human infant: A selective summary in graphs and tables.* Paper prepared for a meeting of the Social Science Research Council's Committee on Biosocial Science, New York, December, 1978.

Dirks, J., & Gibson, E. Infants' perception of similarity between live people and their photos. *Child Development,* 1977, *48,* 124–130.

Donnee, L. H. *Infants' development scanning patterns of face and non-face stimuli under various auditory conditions.* Paper presented at the meeting of the Society for Research in Child Development, Philadelphia, March 1973.

Eimas, P., Siqueland, E., Jusczyk, P., & Vigorito, J. Speech perception in infants. *Science,* 1971, *171,* 303–305.

Fagan, J. Infants' recognition memory for faces. *Journal of Experimental Child Psychology,* 1972, *14,* 453–476.

Fagan, J. Infants' recognition of invariant features of faces. *Child Development,* 1976, *47,* 627–638.

Fagan, J. An attention model of infant recognition. *Child Development,* 1977, *48,* 345–359. (a)

Fagan, J. Infant recognition memory: Studies in forgetting. *Child Development,* 1977, *48,* 68–78. (b)

Fagan, J. The origins of facial pattern recognition. In M. H. Bornstein & W. Kessen (Eds.), *Psychological development from infancy: Image to intention.* Hillsdale, N.J.: Lawrence Erlbaum Associates, 1979.

Fantz, R. The origin of form perception. *Scientific American,* 1961, *194,* 66–72.

Fantz, R. Visual perception from birth as shown by pattern selectivity. *Annals New York Academy of Science,* 1965, *118,* 793–814.

Fantz, R. Pattern discrimination and selective attention as determinants of perceptual development from birth. In A. Kidd & J. Rivone (Eds.), *Perceptual development in children.* New York: International Universities Press, 1966.

Fantz, R., Fagan, J., & Miranda, S. Early visual selectivity. In L. Cohen & P. Salapatek (Eds.), *Infant perception: From sensation to cognition* (Vol. 1). New York: Academic Press, 1975.

Fantz, R., & Nevis, S. The predictive value of changes in visual preferences in early infancy. In J. Hellmuth (Ed.), *Exceptional infant.* Seattle: Special Child Publications, 1967.

Field, T. M. Interaction patterns of preterm and term infants. In T. Field, A. Sostek, S. Goldberg, & H. H. Shuman, (Eds.), *Infants born at risk.* New York: Spectrum, 1978.

Field, T. M. Visual and cardiac responses to animate and inanimate faces by young and preterm infants. *Child Development,* 1979, *50,* 188–194.

Fitzgerald, H. Autonomic pupillary reflex activity during early infancy and its relation to social and non-social visual stimulation. *Journal of Experimental Child Psychology,* 1968, *6,* 470–482.

Futterman, S. *A study of smiling in the human infant.* Unpublished doctoral dissertation, Yale University, 1963.

Garner, W. Aspects of a stimulus: Features, dimensions, and configuration. In E. Rosch (Ed.), *Cognition and categorization.* Hillsdale, N.J.: Lawrence Erlbaum Associates, 1978.

Gibson, E. *Principles of perceptual learning and development.* New York: Appleton-Century-Crofts, 1969.

Gibson, E., Johnston, J., & Owsley, C. *Perception of invariance in five month old infants.* Paper presented at the meeting of the Society for Research in Child Development, New Orleans, March 1977.

Gibson, E. J., Owsley, C. J., & Johnston, J. Perception of invariants by five-month-old infants: Differentiation of two types of motion. *Developmental Psychology,* 1978, *14,* 407–415.

Gibson, J. J. *The perception of the visual world.* Boston: Houghton Mifflin, 1950.

Gibson, J. J. *The senses considered as perceptual systems.* Boston: Houghton Mifflin, 1966.

Goren, C. *Form perception, innate form preferences, and visually mediated head-turning in human newborns.* Paper presented at the meeting of the Society for Research in Child Development, Denver, April 1975.

Greenberg, D. & Blue, S. The visual preference technique in infancy: Effect of number of stimuli presented upon experimental outcome. *Child Development,* 1977, *48,* 131–137.

Haaf, R. Visual response to complex facelike patterns by fifteen and twenty week old infants. *Developmental Psychology,* 1977, *13,* 77–78.

Haaf, R., & Bell, R. A facial dimension in visual discrimination by human infants. *Child Development,* 1967, *38,* 893–899.

Haaf, R., & Brown, C. *Developmental changes in infants' response to complex facelike patterns.* Paper presented at the meeting of the Society for Research in Child Development, Denver, April 1975.

Hainline, L. Developmental changes in visual scanning of face and non-face patterns by infants. *Journal of Experimental Child Psychology,* 1978, *25,* 90–115.

Haith, M. M. Response of the human newborn to visual movement. *Journal of Experimental Child Psychology,* 1966, *3,* 235–243.

Haith, M. M. Visual cognition in early infancy. In R. B. Kearsley & I. E. Sigel (Eds.), *Infants at risk: Assessment of cognitive functioning.* Hillsdale, N.J.: Lawrence Erlbaum Associates, 1979.

Haith, M., Bergman, T., & Mann, L. *Eye contact and face scanning in early infancy.* Paper presented at meeting of Society for Research in Child Development. New Orleans, March 1977 (a).

Haith, M. M., Bergman, T., & Moore, M. J. Eye contact and face scanning in early infancy. *Science,* 1977, *198,* 853–855. (b)

Hebb, D. O. *The organization of behavior.* New York: Wiley, 1949.

Hershenson, M. Development of the perception of form. *Psychological Bulletin,* 1967, *67,* 326–336.

Jeffrey, W. Habituation as a mechanism for perceptual development. In T. J. Tighe and R. N. Leaton (Eds.), *Habituation: Perspectives from child development, animal behavior, and neurophysiology.* Hillsdale, N.J.: Lawrence Erlbaum Associates, 1976.

Jeffrey, W., & Cohen, L. Habituation in the human infant. In H. Reese (Ed.), *Advances in child development and behavior.* (Vol. 6). New York: Academic Press, 1971.

Jones-Molfese, V. Preferences of infants for regular and distorted facial stimuli. *Child Development,* 1975, *46,* 1005–1009.

Kagan, J. Infants' differential reactions to familiar and distorted faces. *Child Development,*1966, *37,* 519–532.

Kagan, J. Growth of the face schema: Theoretical significance and methodology issues. In J. Hellmuth (Ed.), *Exceptional infant.* Seattle: Special Child Publications, 1967.

Kagan, J. *Change and continuity in infancy.* New York: Wiley, 1971.

Kagan, J., Henler, B., Hen-Tov, A., Levine, J., & Lewis, M. Infants' differential reactions to familiar and distorted faces. *Child Development,* 1966, *37,* 519–532.

Kagan, J., & Lewis, M. Studies of attention in the human infant. *Merrill-Palmer Quarterly,* 1965, *11,* 95–127.

Karmel, B., Hoffman, R., & Fegy, M. Processing of contour information by human infants evidenced by pattern dependent evoked potentials. *Child Development,* 1974, *45,* 39–48.

Kessen, W., Haith, M., & Salapatek, P. Human infancy: A bibliography and guide. In P. Mussen (Ed.), *Carmichael's manual of child psychology.* New York: Wiley, 1970.

Kessen, W., & Nelson, K. *What the child brings to language.* Paper presented at the Fourth Annual Symposium of the Jean Piaget Society, Philadelphia, May 1974.

Koopman, P., & Ames, E. Infants' preferences for facial arrangements: A failure to replicate. *Child Devleopment,* 1968, *39,* 481–487.

Korner, A. Early stimulation and maternal care as related to infant capabilities and individual differences. *Early Child Development and Care,* 1973, *2,* 307–327.

Lewis, M. Infants' responses to facial stimuli during the first years of life. *Developmental Psychology,* 1969, *1,* 75–86.

Mann, V. A., Diamond R., & Carey, S. Development of voice recognition: Parallels with face recognition. *Journal of Experimental Child Psychology,* 1979, *27,* 153–165.

Maurer, D., & Salapatek, P. Developmental changes in the scanning of faces by young infants. *Child Development,* 1976, *47,* 523–527.

McCall, R., & Kagan, J. Attention in infancy: Effects of complexity, contour, perimeter, and familiarity. *Child Development,* 1967, *38,* 939–952.

Neisser, U. *Cognitive psychology.* New York: Appleton-Century-Crofts, 1967.

Nowliss, G. H. Taste-elicited tongue movements in human newborn infants: An approach to palatability. Cited by W. Kessen & K. Nelson, *What the child brings to language.* Paper presented at the Fourth Annual Symposium of the Jean Piaget Society, Philadelphia, May 1974.

Piaget, J. *The origins of intelligence in children.* New York: Norton, 1952.

Piaget, J. *The construction of reality in the child.* New York: Basic Books, 1954.

Polak, P., Emde, R., & Spitz, R. The smiling response to the human face: I. Methodology, quantification, and natural history; II. Visual discrimination and onset of depth perception. *Journal of Nervous and Mental Disorders,* 1964, *139,* 103–109, 407–415.

Robson, K. The role of eye to eye contact in maternal-infant attachment. *Journal of Child Psychology and Psychiatry,* 1967, *8,* 13–25.

Salapatek, P. Pattern perception in early infancy. In L. Cohen & P. Salapatek (Eds.), *Infant perception: From sensation to cognition* (Vol. 1). New York: Academic Press, 1975.

Salapatek, P., Bechtold, A. G., & Bushnell, G. W. Infant visual acuity as a function of viewing distance. *Child Development,*1976, *47,* 860–863.

Sameroff, A. J. (Ed.). Organization and stability of newborn behavior: A commentary on the Brazelton neonatal behavior assessment scale. *Monographs of the Society for Research in Child Development,* 1978, *43,* (Serial No. 177).

Sherrod, L. Social cognition in infants: Attention to the human face. *Infant Behavior and Development,* 1979, *2,* 279–294.

Souther, A. F., & Banks, M. S. *The human face: A view from the infant's eye.* Paper presented at the meeting of the Society for Research in Child Development, San Francisco, March 1979.

Spitz, R., & Wolf, K. The smiling response: A contribution to the ontogenesis of social relations. *Genetic Psychological Monographs,* 1946, *34,* 57–125.

Takahashi, M. Cross-sectional study of infants' smiling, attention, reaching, and crying responses to facial models. *Japanese Journal of Psychology,* 1973, *44,* 124–134.

Thomas, H. Unfolding the baby's mind: the infant's selection of visual stimuli. *Psychological Review,* 1973, *80,* 468–488.

Vietze, P., Friedman, S., & Foster, M. Non-contingent stimulation effects of stimulus movement on infants' visual and motor behavior. *Perceptual and Motor Skills,* 1974, *38,* 331.

Watson, J. Perception of object orientation in infants. *Merrill–Palmer Quarterly,* 1966, *12,* 73–94.

Wickelgren, L. Ocular response of human newborns to intermittent visual movement. *Journal of Experimental Child Psychology,* 1969, *8,* 469–482.

Wilcox, B. Visual preferences of human infants for representations of human faces. *Journal of Experimental Child Psychology,* 1969, *7,* 10–20.

3 The Recognition of Specific Persons

Gary M. Olson
University of Michigan

During the first year of life, the infant makes major strides in the acquisition of knowledge about the social world. Behaviors such as the fear of strangers, the formation of specific attachments, and the onset of communicative skills are all reflections of this. Central to these developments are the infant's emerging concepts of person and of specific individuals. During the first year, the infant differentiates persons from other classes of experiences, acquiring knowledge about their common properties. Further, the infant learns the characteristics of specific individuals such as mother and father, and comes to view them and others as individual members of the class of persons. These cognitive achievements are prerequisites for the major landmarks of social development, and many of the chapters in this volume deal with the components of these achievements.

In this chapter the development of the ability to recognize specific individuals is analyzed. The chapter begins with an analysis of the process of recognition in order to clarify exactly what issues are being addressed. Two types of recognition are distinguished, and this distinction provides a framework for the subsequent review of studies of recognition. This review examines the first year of life, focusing on the recognition of the mother, the discrimination of mother and stranger, and the development of the concept of a person. A developmental progression is offered, starting with the perceptual recognition of the recurrence of the mother and progressing toward the individuation of members of a mature concept of person. Finally, possible factors in the acquisition of these skills are discussed.

AN ANALYSIS OF RECOGNITION

A conceptual framework is helpful in the subsequent discussions. A schematic representation of the major components of the infant's information-processing system appears in Figure 3.1. For purposes of simplification, I limit the discussion to the processing of visual information. However, information from several modalities plays an important role in the areas to be reviewed in this chapter. The major components of the information-processing system are: (1) the *knowledge base*, the store of everything that is known; (2) the *active memory*, the currently active set of knowledge from both perception and the knowledge base; (3) the *perceptual system*, which encodes stimuli received from the external world; (4) the *response system*, which initiates and controls actions, including the *orienting system*, a special subset of the response system that controls the orientation of the perceptual analyzers; (5) the *monitor*, the set of routines responsible for the control of information processing and the regulation of system goals. These are not descriptions of different places in the nervous system, but rather they characterize the major types of internal events and states involved in responding to the environment.

Let us look a little more closely at these processes. The control of perceptual analysis by the orienting system plays an important selective role. Though information that is not attended to can influence processing (e.g., by causing attention to shift), that which is attended to dominates current activity. This is one reason why the eye movements of an alert organism are so useful in studies of cognitive processing. Perceptual analysis consists of both innate and acquired processes, and it is likely that it undergoes major development during early infancy. Information that is encoded by perceptual analysis exists in an activated state, in which a number of important things can happen. First, activated information is matched against stored memory representations, and a measure of the degree of match can influence subsequent processing (such as orienting behaviors). Second, the matching of perceptual knowledge in the knowledge base can lead to the activation of other knowledge associated with the matched trace. This activated information often affects subsequent information processing and responding. Third, information that is activated can be stored in the knowledge base, mediated by the control of the system monitor. The monitor is the control system. It is responsible for maintaining and updating the system's goals and for allocating the use of cognitive resources. Interactions between active memory, the knowledge base, and the response systems are under the control of the monitor. It uses information from perceptual analysis and from the knowledge base for decision-making and control, regulating the storage of new information, and activating the response systems. All work on the control of motor activity, from Lashley (1951) on, has recognized that the

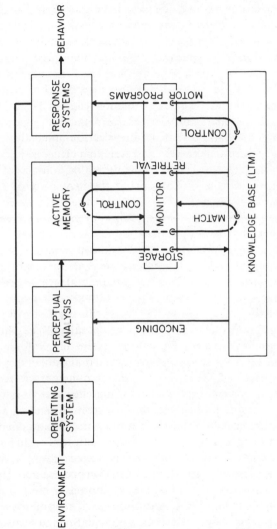

FIG. 3.1. Schematic representation of the information-processing system.

39

response systems are quite complex. Even the most casual observer is aware of the fact that there is enormous change in this domain during infancy.

What is meant by recognition in this scheme? There are two types that can be distinguished. The central process of both is the making of contact between an active perceptual trace and a stored memory trace. They differ by emphasizing somewhat different aspects of such matches. The first type, *recognition of recurrence,* is recognition that something has been experienced before. In infants, the major observable consequence of such recognition is on orienting behavior: Infants typically give greater attention to novel experiences. These shifts in behavior have been systematically investigated in studies of habituation and memory (Cohen & Gelber, 1975; Olson, 1976; Olson & Sherman, in preparation). In terms of Figure 3.1, such behaviors are produced by monitor routines that use information about the extent of the match between perceptual traces and memory traces. Recognition of recurrence must also play a role in learning generalizations about experience. This type of recognition is one important element of what is meant by recognition of specific persons.

A second type of recognition is *recognition of class membership.* This is when an organism recognizes that an experience is an example of a category or class. Such recognition has been variously referred to as pattern recognition, classification, categorization, or concept identification. Like recognition of recurrence, it is based on the matching of perceptual traces with memory traces. It differs in that the match process selectively ignores certain characteristics of the perceptual trace. The goodness of the match is evaluated with respect to selected features of the trace. Recognition of class membership is quite different from a mistaken case of recognition of recurrence. The features that are irrelevant to class membership are ignored rather than misperceived. Totally novel experiences can be recognized as members of a class. A more advanced form of knowledge is required for recognition of this type: knowledge about what to attend to and what to ignore. Further, one usually focuses on more specific consequences of such recognition than the overall reactions in recognition of recurrence.

The basis of both types of recognition is perceptual information: They differ at this level in how it is used. Now, it is necessary to consider in more detail the consequences of both types of recognition. One general consequence of the matching of a perceptual trace and a memory trace is the activation of other associated traces in memory. Such activation probably occurs as an automatic consequence of the match, though its extent and character are only now being investigated (e.g., Anderson, 1976; Posner, 1979). The result of activation is to make information from the knowledge base available to the monitor and active memory. For instance, the infant, in recognizing a recurrence of its mother, might activate the memory of an earlier pleasant experience. As the knowledge base becomes richer, the occurrence of a recognizable environmental event will activate knowledge about the dispositional characteristics of these events, leading the infant to specific expectations about what might occur next. To return to the example, the infant will learn that the appearance of the mother is associated with the occurrence of pleasurable social interaction or feeding. Such expectations could be quite complex, and which expectations are activated could depend on the infant's level of cognitive development. But, in essence, the process is straightforward. A set of eliciting conditions, based on perceptual representations of the environment, make contact with perceptual knowledge in memory, leading to the activation of associated knowledge. This associated knowledge influences subsequent activities, including observable behavior.

The importance of the activation of associated knowledge cannot be minimized, for it is an integral part of the recognition process. Learning has its primary impact through the activation of knowledge associated with perceived experiences. Such knowledge can play an important role in the process of recognition itself. For instance, an infant inspecting a face might activate the expectation that the person will smile as a result of the infant's attention. If the person does smile, the expectation has been confirmed. This contributes to the sense of recognition and in turn leads to the generation of additional expectations. One the other hand, if the person does not smile, the sense of recognition might be diminished, with corresponding effects on orienting or other behaviors. Thus, although the perceptual characteristics of persons usually define the precipitating conditions for recognition, the confirmation or disconfirmation of expectations can provide a further basis for recognition that could determine to a significant degree the infant's final response to the experience.

To sum up, two types of distinctions are important in this chapter. The first is between recognition of recurrence and recognition of class membership. Both involve comparing a current percept with a memory trace, but differ in the extent to which perceived characteristics are ignored in making the comparison. Piaget and Inhelder (1973) made a very similar distinction in their contrast between mnemonic recognition and recognitory assimilation. It is an important difference. The second distinction is between the perceptual knowledge that is the basis for the memory match and the dispositional knowledge that is activated when such a match occurs. A regular consequence of a successful match is the activation of additional information in memory. This information can have a number of influences on subsequent processing and responding. These distinctions are important for our analysis of the recognition of specific persons.

There has been far too little analysis in this literature of exactly what is being studied. This has led to confusing claims about when the recognition of specific individuals occurs. The analysis just presented should help clarify this. In essence, it is necessary to consider both the basis of the recognition and the consequences of it. The recognition of the recurrence of the mother in the absence of any general knowledge about persons is quite different from the individuation of the mother as a member of a category for which the infant has rich dispositional knowledge. It seems likely that the infant at a very young age might be capable of recognizing the recurrence of the mother as a perceptual event, given the large amount of intimate experience most infants have. Initially, little additional knowledge would be activated. Further, the very young infant may have limited abilities to notice differences among individuals. The acquisition of a rich network of knowledge about the mother will certainly alter the consequences of recognition. However, as long as there is little knowledge about other persons, the knowledge about mother will have no social context. The acquisition of an abstract concept of person, including knowledge of the individuating characteristics of specific persons, should lead to major changes in the nature and consequences of recognition. These are the developments that must be examined.

PERSONS AS SOURCES OF KNOWLEDGE

As a prelude to a more detailed examination of the literature on person recognition, we need to examine the types of information conveyed by persons that could be noticed by the infant and become either a basis for, or a consequence of, recognition. As is evident from the prior discussion, there are two classes of such information: perceptual and dispositional.

Perceptual Characteristics.   Considerable research has been devoted to the perceptual characteristics of persons. Much of this work has focused on the visual properties of the face. Sherrod (Chapter 2) reviews much of this literature as it bears upon infant attention, so there is little we need add here. Vision and hearing are the dominant senses for recognition at a distance, but during the earliest months, when many of the infant's encounters with persons are quite intimate, information from touch, smell, and even taste could provide significant components of the infant's perceptual experiences with persons. Very little is known about this kind of information. Further, there are important limitations even in the well-researched domain of faces. A good deal is known about the steady-state properties of pictorial representations of faces, but relatively little about faces as they occur in the world—with motion, three-dimensions, and concordant auditory stimulation. From what is known about infant attention, the qualities of real faces in motion are likely to be important elements of the infant's knowledge. It is important to take into account our restricted understanding of persons as stimuli when examining the research literature.

Dispositional Characteristics.   Persons are a rich source of dispositional information. They are complex, multimodal stimuli, with complex temporal patterns of behavior. Given the infant's intimate and rich interactions with persons from the very beginning of its life, it is likely that the dispositional properties of persons form an important part of what the infant learns. Examples are not difficult to generate. The sound of a person's voice might produce expectations about the types of tactile, olfactory, or visual experiences that might follow. The sight of a face might lead to expectations about particular experiences that might follow. Particularly interesting from a developmental point of view are expectations arising from the effect one's own behavior has on persons. An infant's cry is typically followed with certain responses by adults. A smile from the infant often elicits smiling from nearby persons. Additionally, individuals have particular qualities to their responses, making it possible for the infant to discriminate persons on the basis of their reactions as well as their appearances.

There is very little research on the topic of the dispositional characteristics of persons. A few studies of infant responses to persons can be discussed on these terms (see later parts of the chapter), but on the whole there is very little of substance that can be said. However, the remainder of the chapter should further substantiate the importance of carrying out research on these characteristics.

RECOGNITION OF RECURRENCE OF THE MOTHER

The dominant specific person in the normal infant's experience is the primary caregiver, usually the mother. Therefore, the earliest person recognition ought to involve the mother, and given our earlier conceptual analysis what should be recognized is that the mother has recurred. Because of both perceptual and cognitive immaturity, other individuals are likely to be mistakenly recognized as the mother, but this would still constitute recognition of recurrence in the sense we intend. Little additional knowledge is likely to be activated initially as a consequence of such recognition.

The infant apparently has the capacity to perform such recognition. Though much of the research on neonatal recognition memory has been plagued by methodological difficulties (Cohen & Gelber, 1975), there do exist several successful demonstrations of neonatal recognition memory (cf. Friedman, 1975). Because the mother is experienced more than any other entity in the infant's environment, it would be startling if she were not among the very first things in the infant's world whose recurrence is recognized.

Early recognition of the mother is likely to be based on a rudimentary set of characteristics. For instance, MacFarlane (1977) reported that 6-day-old infants can reliably discriminate the scent of their mother's breast pad from that of another woman. This report contains few methodological details, so the finding cannot be fully evaluated. But it does show what might be possible: The very young infant could recognize certain selective aspects of the mother. One would scarcely want to claim that this would constitute evidence of recognition of the mother. Rather, it represents recognition of a perceptual aspect of the mother. These are the building blocks from which a more complex representation of the mother will evolve, and even during these early periods they may have some social significance. But, the most reasonable interpretation is that the young infant has recognized that an aspect of its experience has recurred, nothing more.

Though there are virtually no carefully controlled studies of the recognition of recurrence of the mother in very young infants, there is ample observational evidence to indicate that it occurs fairly early (e.g., Piaget, 1952; Stern, 1977). However, as indicated in the previous paragraph, such recognition is likely to be based on only certain elements of the stimulus complex defining the mother. Further, it is likely that many other persons will be confused with the mother—that the infant has no differentiated concept of person. Finally, the consequences of such recognition are likely to be minimal. Little additional knowledge will be activated as a result of recognition. Thus, although recognition of recurrence of the mother may occur during the very first few months of life, it is at best a precursor of socially significant forms of recognition that will occur later. In particular, different persons are probably not individuated, and there is no concept of person or of individuals that is activated as a result of recognition.

DISCRIMINATION OF MOTHER AND STRANGER

Most of the research on infant recognition of specific persons has examined the discrimination of the mother and a stranger. Two types of studies have been done: observational studies in relatively naturalistic settings and experimental studies. The former seldom have mother–stranger discriminations as their sole focus, and because of the absence of careful controls, inferences about infant capacities and skills are difficult. Experimental studies potentially offer a firmer basis for unambiguous inferences, but, unfortunately, many of the existing studies have serious flaws. Further, most experimental studies have examined mother–stranger discriminations based on the perceptual characteristics of static, often two-dimensional stimuli. Given that the infant's experience is with dynamic, multimodal, three-dimensional stimuli, the possibility for underestimation of the infant's skills and knowledge is great.

Prior to examining the literature, it is necessary to consider some general issues that affect the interpretation of research. Studies of discrimination must employ proper controls so that the basis of the discrimination can be clearly inferred. Unfortunately, these have not always been employed, leaving many studies in this area ambiguous. The logic of a discrimination experiment is to present two (or more) stimuli and contrast the reactions given to them. The stimuli can be presented simultaneously or successively, with obvious controls for position and order. As noted by Olson (1976), infant discriminative reactions are affected by many factors. In order to examine the factors of interest, irrelevant ones must be controlled. To concretize the discussion, let us consider the visual discrimination of faces, the situation investigated in most studies. Faces have many dimensions of physical variation in space and time that affect infant attention (see Sherrod, Chapter 2). Similarly, persons who can view or interact with the infant can vary their expressions in reactions to the infant's behavior. If differences in these factors are allowed to covary with the mother–stranger difference, inferences about the basis of discrimination will be inconclusive. Unfortunately, in many studies of mother–stranger discrimination, the mother–stranger comparison has been confounded. The ideal design would be to have each mother serve as the stranger for another infant, so that the role of mother and stranger would be counterbalanced across specific persons. Many studies have used a single person (and not always a female!) as the stranger. Similarly, if live faces are used (and they should be), every effort should be made to eliminate the possibility of feedback or reinforcement from the mother influencing the infant's reactions. This is difficult to do if naturalistic behaviors on the part of the model are desired, but it is technically feasible to make the mother blind as to the identity of the specific infant viewing her. Such controls are essential if it is the infant's reaction to the face that is to be studied and not the contingent interactions between infant and mother or stranger. Most studies using live faces have tried to contol this by having mother and stranger follow a set script or display a static, expressionless faces, but these methods are less than optimal.

Conclusions about the infant's abilities must take into account the eliciting conditions used in the study and how closely these match the conditions under which the infant acquired its knowlege. Many of the studies have been observational ones, and thus have maximal similarity to the conditions of acquisition, but minimal control of the factors affecting the discrimination. Many experimental studies have used photographs or other two-dimensional representations, thus introducing a step of abstraction between the infant's knowledge and the stimuli. Although older infants are capable of generalizing between representational modes (e.g., Dirks & Gibson, 1977), younger infants are certainly going to be influenced by how the stimuli are presented. The ideal stimulus for assessing the infant's knowledge is a live model, though of course the capacity to generalize to other formats is itself an informative behavior.

Let us now turn to the research. There are a variety of observational and experimental studies examining the mother–stranger discrimination, and their findings are not consistent. However, by attending to the nature of the stimuli and the control of confounding factors, it is possible to construct a somewhat more orderly picture. The basic conclusion is that under the conditions that have been examined so far there is little evidence of mother–stranger discrimination prior to 3 months. However, there are many demonstrations of such discriminations during the second quarter of the first year.

Discrimination Prior to 3 Months. The most controversial evidence pertains to discriminations made prior to 12 weeks of age. In a nutshell, my conclusion is that there are no convincing demonstrations of discrimination. There is no evidence of discrimination during the neonatal period. The earliest reported discrimination is that described by MacFarlane (1977). A series of studies by Carpenter (Carpenter, 1973, 1974; Carpenter, Tecce, Stechler, & Friedman, 1970) suggested that infants as young as 2 weeks of age discriminated the mother's face from other faces. However, these studies have not controlled for confounding differences. For instance, several of the studies compared the live faces of the mother with that of a mannequin (Carpenter, 1974; Carpenter et al., 1970), which clearly confounds a number of differences. Further, neither these studies nor those that used live faces of strangers (e.g., Carpenter, 1973) used more than one exemplar of a stranger, thus confounding the role of stranger with a specific person. Thus, Carpenter's data cannot be taken as clear evidence of a discrimination between mother and stranger on the basis of familiarity.

Maurer and Salapatek (1976) measured the detailed eye fixations of 1- and 2-month-old infants and found that the younger ones looked less at the live image of the mother in a mirror than at the images of female and male strangers. There were no mother–stranger differences for the 2-month olds. Infants at both ages tended to fixate the perimeters of the faces rather than their central regions. Interestingly, 57% of the 1-month old's fixations were off the face entirely. It is not clear what significance to draw from these results, both because the evidence of discrimination was found at 1 month but not at 2, and because Haith, Bergman, and Moore (1977) found no mother–stranger differences in fixations for infants between 3 and 11 weeks in a very similar study. Maurer and Salapatek did use six different strangers, so the discrimination is less likely to be based on stranger effects than in the studies by Carpenter. However, the fact that the young infants spent so little time fixating the face at all, and even then most of the fixations were on the perimeter of the face, suggests that the infants were not discriminating exemplars of a facial category having a very elaborated representation.

Two studies have found that young infants seem to be able to discriminate mothers and strangers on the basis of voice. Wolff (1963), in an intensive observational study of smiling, found that the mother's voice was more effective than other voices in eliciting smiling by infants 5 weeks of age. This selective smiling on the basis of voice occurred much earlier than comparable selective smiling on the basis of visual cues. Bigelow (1977) reported that 5-week-old infants looked longer at a stranger than at the mother when their voices accompanied their face, but there was no difference in looking to the silent faces. By 13 weeks, infants discriminated the mother and stranger on the basis of visual information alone. These two studies, neither of which used careful counterbalancing of mother–stranger roles, give some support to the notion that discrimination of mother from the stranger on the basis of voice may precede discrimination based on visual information. Furthermore, several studies have shown that visual attention is affected by auditory information (Horowitz, 1975; Mendelson & Haith, 1976; see Spelke & Cortelyou, Chapter 4). These intermodal aspects of recognition clearly need further research.

There are several reports of no discrimination at ages younger than 3 months. Of course, as in any discrimination study, the lack of a difference must be interpreted with great caution because, strictly speaking, one cannot infer from the lack of discrimination the absence of discriminative capacity. Nonetheless, these negative results are worth noting because of the consistency with which positive results emerge with older infants. We have already noted the Wolff (1963), Haith, Bergman, and Moore (1977), Maurer and Salapatek (1976), and Bigelow (1977) negative results for purely visual discriminations at young ages. Other negative results include Fitzgerald's (1968) using pupil dilation and black-and-white photographs at 1 and 2 months, and Sherrod's (1979) using live models at 1 and 3 months. Though they did not explicitly compare strangers and mothers, Spitz and Wolf (1946), Ambrose (1961), and Gewirtz (1965) stressed that selective social smiling to the mother did not occur until nearly 5 months of age.

In sum, the evidence for mother–stranger discriminations prior to 3 months is very spotty. Even where positive discriminations have been found, the design of most studies has left the basis of the discrimination ambiguous. A highly restricted range of stimulus conditions has been examined with these younger infants. Thus, although there is little evidence of mother–stranger discrimination prior to 3 months, this conclusion must be qualified by the poor stimulus control in extant studies and the narrow range of conditions that have been examined.

Discrimination in 3- to 8-Month-Old Infants.   In marked contrast to the weak results at ages below 3 months, studies of mother–stranger discrimination in slightly older infants generally yield positive outcomes. The early studies of smiling, although not directly comparing mothers and strangers as stimuli, all report a decline in smiling to strangers at about 4 or 5 months, with the implication that strangers were being discriminated from mothers (Ambrose, 1961; Gewirtz, 1965; Spitz & Wolf, 1946; Wolff, 1973). Although these studies used live models, they offered no control over eliciting factors. For instance, male strangers were used in several of them. A number of experimental investigations report that infants are capable of visual discrimination between mother and stranger during the period from 3 to 5 months (Bernard & Ramey, 1977; Bigelow, 1977; Cohen, 1974; Fitzgerald, 1968; Sherrod, 1979). The studies by Cohen (1974) and Sherrod (1979) are the most careful in this set, primarily because they both used a pool of strangers to minimize the confound between the stranger role and the specific characteristics of the persons portraying that role. Sherrod also used live models who were visible to the infant behind a one-way mirror so as to eliminate nonvisual cues, something not done in other studies using live models. It is also interesting to note that Sherrod's study gives the latest evidence of a positive discrimination: 5 months, but not at 1 or 3 months (Cohen, 1974, did not test any ages below 5 months).

Not many studies have examined discriminations based on information in other modalities. An important exception is the report by Spelke and Owsley (1979). The details are presented by Spelke and Cortelyou (Chapter 4). This is also the only study that contrasts the infant's knowledge of the father and the mother. In essence, they found that by roughly 4 months (they did not test younger ages) the infant would turn to look at the face of whichever parent spoke, both for actual and tape-recorded speech. The clearest results emerged for the mother–father discriminations, where the infant looked toward the face associated with the voice. Data collected for a mother–stranger discrimination (with the role of stranger not counterbalanced) were more puzzling because the infants tended to look *away* from whomever was speaking. These studies suggest that the infant may have learned the voice–face associations for both parents by around 4 months, though much remains to be learned about this.

Thus, somewhere between 12 and 20 weeks, the ablity to differentiate the mother from other persons on the basis of perceptual information clearly appears. The detailed differences among the studies are difficult to reconcile because of differences in response measures, specific stimuli, and the precise ages tested. However, even at 3 months the results are somewhat mixed (positive: Bigelow, 1977; negative: Contole & Over, 1979; Haith et al., 1977; Sherrod, 1979), but by 5 months the results are uniformly positive, in the best designed studies. Thus, again with the cautionary note on the limited range of conditions that have been examined, the ability to discriminate the mother and a stranger on the basis of visual cues appears between 12 and 20 weeks. Discrimination on the basis of auditory cues may occur earlier, though the available research is not definitive. Very little is known about the bases of these discriminations because up to now there has been no analytic inquiry into the precise stimulus differences to which the infants are responding.

There are no studies that examine the infant's knowledge of dispositional characteristics of persons. An interesting study by Wahler (1967) suggests a way in which it might be done, but his experiment is unfortunately flawed in several ways. He examined the ability of the mother and a stranger to condition infant smiling instrumentally, and claimed to have found that the mothers were better at this than the strangers. However, as noted by Sameroff and Cavanagh (1979), the study did not include the controls needed to distinguish between the elicitation properties of the two adults and their differential effectiveness in conditioning. Furthermore, the strangers, who were undergraduates in a child psychology class, were not as experienced with infants in general as were the mothers. Thus, any differences in conditioning that might have emerged in a proper conditioning design could not be attributed to the mother's specific style and the infant's sensitivity to it. An ideal design would be one that employed the proper conditioning controls and counterbalanced the mothers so that net experience with infants between the roles of mother and stranger would be equivalent. Indeed, if one wanted to focus on the extent to which the infants are sensitive to the specific dispositional characteristics of the mother, a study in which identical twin mothers who differed in their specific experience with this particular infant would be interesting. The general point, though, is that studies of this type might allow for an assessment of the infant's knowledge of the unique dispositional characteristics of its own mother. Such research would supplement the studies focusing exclusively on perceptual characteristics.

THE DEVELOPMENT OF THE
CONCEPT OF A PERSON

Discerning when an infant first has a concept of person is complex. First, it is difficult to specify exactly what one means by a concept of person. Minimally, there are a range of such concepts, and development represents some sort of progression through them. But defining the possibilities is difficult. Second, even if one has a set of possibilities, it is difficult to interrogate the infant about the current status of its person concept. This is a classic dilemma in infant research. As the knowledge one seeks to assess becomes increasingly abstract, errors of over- or underestimation become increasingly easy to make. The controversial status of many claims concerning infant cognitive development underscores this problem.

However, it is possible to adopt a pragmatic approach. Rather than try to assess the precise character of the infant's person concept, one can seek evidence for any of a variety of indicators that, in combination, lead to the suspicion that such a concept exists. In other words, in such matters single indicators are often subject to multiple interpretations, but if there is evidence of several possible indicators of a person concept, one can tentatively infer that some such concept exists. In the present case, what we are really looking for is some indication that persons as a class are treated in some systematically different way than other experiences. The most convincing demonstration of this would be through a response that, although initially given indiscriminately, came to be given uniquely to persons. Many of the responses studied in social development, such as smiling, crying, approach, and withdrawal, approximate this criterion.

Persons have many characteristics that can serve as a basis for differentiating them from other experiences. As Sherrod (Chapter 2) has elegantly pointed out, no other source of stimulation in the infant's environment has as potent a combination of attention-getting characteristics. People cannot help but be noticed. Furthermore, no other source of stimulation so regularly reacts to the infant's behavior in a contingent fashion. Indeed, because adults seek and foster interaction with the infant, the adult's behavior is often exaggerated and emphasized in an effort to get a clear reaction from the baby (Stern, 1977). Thus, up to the limits of its attentional and perceptual skills, the normal infant is saturated with experiences of persons, and as its capacities to perceive, abstract, and differentiate develop, it can scarcely avoid learning about the perceptual and dispositional characteristics of persons.

The fact that most early experiences with persons occur in interactive situations means that the infant's knowledge of persons is likely to be associated with the dominant dimensions of its own goals and actions. Both because of motoric and perceptual immaturity, the infant's initial experiences with persons are in intimate proximal situations, with the infant's own actions constituting a significant component of the experience. Eventually, following motoric, perceptual, and cognitive development, distal, noninteractive experiences will come under the same conceptual umbrella. Persons outside the infant's immediate sphere of influence will be recognized as persons, and their actions will constitute a new type of input for the elaboration of the concept. Another major development in the concept of person will come with the recognition that oneself is of this class. This recognition will comprise the most basic and influential piece of knowledge for social cognition because it will allow for the attribution of causes for other's behavior based on analogies with one's own experience. These last two aspects of the person concept—the extensions to distal experiences and to oneself—represent elaborations that most likely occur outside the period this chapter has been focusing on, namely, the first 8 months. The extension to distal others may begin toward the end of this period, but throughout the first 8 months the infant's experiences of persons are dominated by proximal interaction. The extension to self most likely occurs outside this period (Lewis & Brooks, 1975).

In sum, the types of person concepts the infant might form during the early months will be based on perceptual and dispositional properties of persons noticed during close interactions. The face and the voice will provide major perceptual experiences, but because of the close interactions, the other senses should also make important contributions. Similarly, the contingent reactions of persons should provide the basis for dispositional knowledge (see Chapter 7). Not surprisingly, infant behaviors such as smiling, crying, babbling, and the components of feeding will constitute the major domains for dispositional knowledge. All of this suggests that the emergence of distinctive reactions to faces, and voices, and the selective use of the behaviors of interaction will constitute the first evidence of a rudimentary concept of person.

In order to demonstrate that a concept of a person has been formed, it is not sufficient to show merely that persons as stimuli are responded to differently than nonpersons. Discrimination is a necessary but not a sufficient condition. The infant's behavior must at some level be distinctive or appropriate. This can be indexed by the appearance of specific patterns of behavior based on prior learning. For example, the increase in the frequency of smiling and its primary application to persons (or person-like stimuli) would be an example of such evidence. Smiling is implicated in the early social interactions of the infant. The primary rewards for smiling come from social interactions with persons. Thus, its selective shaping by experience with persons implies not merely that persons are discriminated from nonpersons, but that they have come to be treated as a distinctive category with functional significance.

The empirical evidence on the emergence of a person concept is not very strong, but several conclusions can be reached. There is very little evidence of a person concept during the first 2 or 3 months. Faces and voices elicit much attention during this period, but the reactions they elicit appear to be due to the fact that persons have numerous properties that are intrinsically attractive to the infant (Cohen, DeLoache, & Strauss, 1979). There is little evidence that infants respond to faces as configurations, attending instead to local features such as hairline or eyes (Caron, Caron, Caldwell, & Weiss, 1973; Gibson,

1969; Maurer & Salapatek, 1976). The sense of smell, touch, and body position have not been investigated very extensively, and thus their possible contribution to a primitive concept of person is not known.

It is not long, however, before behaviors appear that suggest a rudimentary person concept. Smiling comes to be selectively elicited by human voices during the first month and by faces by 3 months, showing a great increase to social stimuli in general around 4 months (Ambrose, 1961; Gewirtz, 1965; Rheingold, 1961; Wolff, 1963). During this period, social stimuli come to control the elicitation of babbling and the termination of crying (see Bowlby, 1969). Most of these data have been collected in naturalistic settings, where it is difficult to separate elicitation and shaping of infant behaviors. However, in a number of ways the infant has begun to show special reactions to persons suggesting that its interactions with them have produced certain expectations about their behavior that distinguishes persons from other experiences.

The infant's perceptual knowledge of persons is also developing. Sherrod (this volume) has reviewed persons, in particular faces, as physical stimuli, and has summzarized the evidence on the infant's emerging appreciation of the distinctive qualities of persons as physical events. As his review suggests, virtually all of the research has focused on the static qualities of faces. These studies show that infants appear to manifest knowledge of the properties of faces by at least 6 months. For instance, Caron et al. (1973) found that by 5 months infants appreciated the configural properties of the face. Similarly, Fagan (1972) found that 5-month-old infants were able to remember right-side-up faces but not upside-down ones, suggesting they had knowledge of faces that helped them encode the properly oriented ones. Given that this work has focused primarily on static pictorial faces, it is likely to be an upper bound on the appreciation of facial form, because the infant's experience with faces is predominantly with moving, real ones. Extending the knowledge of faces to static representations is likely to be a more advanced achievement. Contrary to Field's (1979) speculations, it is likely that moving real faces constitute *less* of an information load for the infant than static ones, because information must be defined in terms of how stimuli are coded, and the real faces more closely approximate the infant's experiences than static ones. However, there is no research that bears clearly on this issue.

In sum, the infant's knowledge of persons undergoes major development during the first 6 months. Persons have many properties that attract the infant's attention, and interactions with them constitute a significant portion of the infant's experience. Most of the available evidence suggests that the great attention paid to persons during the first few months does not imply the existence of a person concept, though virtually all research has focused on reactions to visual and auditory stimuli. However, during the second quarter of the first year, the infant's behavior increasingly suggests that a rudimentary concept is present and developing.

SUMMARY: RECOGNITION OF
SPECIFIC PERSONS

During the first 6 to 8 months, the infant undergoes major development in its ability to recognize specific individuals. The analysis of recognition led us to highlight two components of this development: (1) an increased ability to recognize and discriminate among persons on the basis of their perceptual characteristics; (2) an increased knowledge about persons and individuals, which gets activated as a consequence of recognition. Both need to be taken into account in order to evaluate the infant's development in this area. Although the very young infant may respond discriminatively to an aspect of its mother and a stranger, the recognition is probaly based upon an impoverished representation of the individuals involved and activates a limited range of associated knowledge. Though such early recognition is probably a developmental precursor of socially significant person recognition, it would be inappropriate to confuse the two forms.

Unfortunately, the existing research literature provides limited information about this early development. The infant shows great attention to persons and faces during the first few months, yet there is little evidence of specific recognition prior to 3 months or of associated knowledge of either individuals or persons. The infant is not born with innate knowledge of persons or faces, though it is important that persons have many perceptual characteristics that attract infant attention. The best documented evidence of person recognition exists for the second quarter of the first year. However, because the stimulus conditions typically investigated in these studies have usually not approximated those found in natural settings, it is possible that evidence of person recognition could be found at younger ages.

MECHANISMS OF ACQUISITION

The infant does not appear to have innate knowledge about persons. Instead, the infant's knowledge about persons in general and individuals in particular is learned from experience. The behavior of caretakers appears to be optimal for learning. The caretaker is the source of satisfaction for many of the infant's most basic needs. Thus, the experience with caretakers will often be associated with pleasurable events or with the termination of noxious ones. Caretakers typically interact with the infant during periods of maximal attentiveness. Indeed, such attentiveness is often either the basis for the initiation of interactions or the result of basic caretaking activities (e.g., feeding). Further, much of the specific behavior of caretakers is elicited by the infant, meaning that the stimulation provided to the infant is contingent on the infant's behavior. Caretakers often try to shape or modify the infant's behavior, and thus are sensitive to the infant's reactions to stimulation. Further, caretakers are typically aware of the fact that they are interacting with a developing organism, and are thus eager to provide a range of experiences that are attractive to the infant and pleasurable for both participants. Caretakers are eager for the infant to learn about people and about themselves (i.e., the caretaker), so that true social interactions can occur.

How does person knowledge, both general and individuated, develop? Several factors contribute to the acquisition of this knowledge.

1. Maturation of Perceptual and Attentional Skills. The general development of the infant's perceptual and cognitive abilities places limits on what the infant will be capable of at any given age. Although it is not clear that William James' characterization of the newborn's world as a "buzzing booming confusion" is quite accurate, the newborn's sensory, peceptual, and mnemonic capacities are limited compared to what they will be even a few months later. The newborn can perceive aspects of the world around it, yet its sensory and perceptual skills are not very finely tuned. Much has been made of the fact that the newborn's limited perceptual skills seem well-adapted to perceiving the face of a caregiver while being held by her or him. However, there is no evidence of perceptual discrimination of faces at this age, and certainly the newborn is unable to perceive persons at a distance. Similarly, the newborn possesses rudimentary learning and memory skills, but these skills are quite limited relative to what will emerge over the next few months (Olson & Sherman, in preparation).

By 3 or 4 months of age, the infant's basic skills have improved dramatically (see reviews by Appelton, Clifton, & Goldberg, 1975; Cohen, DeLoache & Strauss, 1979; Sherrod, Chapter 2; Olson & Sherman, in preparation). There is little doubt that by this age the infant has the capacity to discriminate among individuals and to attend to and store a variety of different types of information about them. In approaching the question of the infant's development of the ability to individuate persons, then, one can assume that the newborn probably does not have the capacity to notice differences, and to learn and remember information about persons, but that these skills emerge by 4 or 5 months.

2. Development of Skills of Abstraction and Differentiation. Noticing of stimulation is but the first step toward knowledge. In order to have an impact, experiences must be remembered, and the common and distinguishing qualities of various experiences must be noted and encoded into memory. The investigation of the infant's ability to classify, to abstract, and to differentiate its experiences is just beginning. Recent experimental studies have demonstrated the presence of such skills in infants older than about 3 or 4 months and have identified a few of their characteristics (Cohen & Strauss, 1979; Cornell, 1974; Fagan, 1976; Ruff, 1978). The core of what the infant will be learning about people consists of general knowledge about their peceptual and dispositional properties, both of people in general and of specific individuals.

3. Broad Experience with People in Interaction. The specific experiential component of the acquisition of person knowledge is interaction with people. The important element of these interactions is the contingency that exists between the infant's behavior and the interactor's behavior. It is scarcely controversial to argue that the experience of contingencies during interactions is an important component of social development (e.g., Lamb, Chapter 7). However, the importance of these contingencies for the acquisition of knowledge about persons has not been systematically explored. The goal of person knowledge is understanding, which means the reduction in uncertainty about experiences.

Gibson's (1969) influential account of perceptual learning provides a useful framework for examining the acquisition of knowledge about persons. Though her focus was on the abstraction and differentiation of perceptual experiences, the means by which such processes occur is closely related to what we have called dispositional knowledge. The core assumption of the theory is that perceptual learning consists of modifying how one attends to the perceptual world. Information sufficient for differentiating experiences into a number of useful categories exists in the perceptual array, and the process of learning is one of coming to pay attention to those attributes that are distinctive in relation to these categories. Further, categorization is utilitarian. The partitioning of experience into categories is based on the epistemic goals of the organism. The goal of categorization is a practical one: the reduction of uncertainty. The perceptual array is overwhelming in information. The task of the learner is to distinguish those aspects of the array that are informative from those that are not. Informativeness can only be described in relation to the organism's state of knowledge and epistemic goals. It is adaptive for the organism to pay attention to those aspects of experience that are correlated with outcomes that matter.

Thus, the acquisition of perceptual and dispositional knowledge about real-world categories proceeds hand in hand. The perceptual aspects of experiences that are noticed and encoded are those that are associated with outcomes that are of significance to the organism. Faces are learned as a meaningful category both as a particular kind of perceptual array and as a class of experiences that tend to be associated with certain kinds of events or outcomes.

A number of purely perceptual factors operate as well, and their importance should not be overlooked. To take vision as an example, color, brightness, shape, and patterns of motion can all bias the organism to form certain partitions of experience. For instance, Rosch (1978) has argued that many natural categories have a basic level of organization that seems to be based on shape. Similarly, intermodal concordance can be a powerful device for calling attention to sets of experiences (see Spelke & Cortelyou, this volume). The infant's innate attentional and perceptual tendencies will naturally draw its interest toward particular elements of experience. But, these biases are not innate kowledge of these categoreis. Rather, they are the foundational skills for the acquisition of knowledge. There is undoubtedly considerable adaptive significance to having perceptual and attentional skills that lead one to notice and attend to functionally significant perceptual experiences. But, the categorization of these experiences must be learned by associating certain configurations of perceptual characteristics with significant dispositional properties.

It is not difficult to see why interactive experiences are so important to the acquisition of such knowledge. However, what we do not yet possess is a body of research that shows us exactly how the development of such knowledge depends on interaction. What is needed are studies of the development of person knowledge and person individuation that relate epistemic achievements to the nature and extent of early interactions. In principle, there ought to be important differences in this knowledge as a function of the identity and number of primary caretakers, the sensitivity of these caretakers, their particular interactive styles, and the range and quality of infant experiences with people in general. Although studies of social development have examined these types of factors, they have not been systematically related to the development of person knowledge and the individuation of specific persons. The absence of such information makes it difficult to provide more than a general sketch of the nature of this knowledge and its development.

CONCLUSIONS

It is surprising that a topic as important as the recognition of specific persons has generated such a small amount of careful and definitive research, because it has major importance for students of both cognitive and social development. In my view, progress on this topic has been hindered by the absence of a clear conceptualization of the issues. This chapter has tried to provide a cognitive framework in which questions of person recognition can be cast. Other chapters in this volume establish a social framework for the same issues. It is imperative that investigators formulate their studies in the context of a clearly defined conceptual framework—both cognitive and social—if we are to achieve an understanding of the development of person recognition.

ACKNOWLEDGMENTS

Preparation of this chapter was facilitated by a Research Career Development Award (HD 00169) and a research grant (HD 10486) from NICHD to the author. Lindsay Chase-Lansdale, Michael Lamb, Margaret Owen, Tracy Sherman, Lonnie Sherrod, and Barbara Zimmerman provided helpful feedback on an early version.

REFERENCES

Ambrose, J. A. The development of the smiling response in early infancy. In B. M. Foss, (Ed.), *Determinants of infant behavior* (Vol. 1). London: Methuen, 1961.

Anderson, J. R. *Language, memory and thought*. Hillsdale, N.J.: Lawrence Erlbaum Associates, 1976.

Appelton, T., Clifton, R., & Goldberg, S. The development of behavioral competence in infancy. In F. D. Horowitz (Ed.), *Review of child development research* (Vol. 4). Chicago: University of Chicago Press, 1975.

Bernard, J. A., & Ramey, C. T. Visual regard of familiar and unfamiliar persons in the first six months of infancy. *Merrill-Palmer Quarterly*, 1977, *23*, 121-127.

Bigelow, A. *Infants' recognition of their mothers*. Paper presented at the biennial meeting of the Society for Research in Child Development, New Orleans, March 1977.

Bowlby, J. *Attachment*. New York: Basic Books, 1969.

Caron, A. J., Caron, R. F., Caldwell, R. C., & Weiss, S. J. Infant perception of the structural properties of the face. *Developmental Psychology*, 1973, *9*, 385-399.

Carpenter, G. C. *Mother-stranger discrimination in the early weeks of life*. Paper presented at the biennial meeting of the Society for Research in Child Development, Philadelphia, March 1973.

Carpenter, G. C. Visual regard of moving and stationary faces in early infancy. *Merrill-Palmer Quarterly*, 1974, *20*, 181-194.

Carpenter, G. C., Tecce, J. J., Stechler, G., & Friedman, S. Differential visual behavior to human and humanoid faces in early infancy. *Merrill-Palmer Quarterly*, 1970, *16*, 91-108.

Cohen, L. B., DeLoache, J. S., & Strauss, M. S. Infant visual perception. In J. D. Osofsky (Ed.), *Handbook of infant development*. New York: Wiley, 1979.

Cohen, L. B., & Gelber, E. R. Infant visual memory. In L. B. Cohen & P. Salapatek (Eds.), *Infant perception* (Vol. 1). New York: Academic Press, 1975.

Cohen, L. B., & Strauss, M. S. Concept acquisition in the human infant. *Child Development*, 1979, *50*, 419-424.

Cohen, S. E. Developmental differences in infants' attentional responses to face-voice incongruity of mother and stranger. *Child Development*, 1974, *45*, 1155-1158.

Contole, J., & Over, R. Signal detection analysis of infant social behavior. *Infant Behavior and Development*, 1979, *2*, 189-200.

Cornell, E. H. Infants' discrimination of photographs of faces following redundant presentations. *Journal of Experimental Child Psychology*, 1974, *18*, 98-106.

Dirks, J., & Gibson, E. Infants' perception of similarity between live people and their photographs, *Child Development*, 1977, *48*, 124-130.

Fagan, J. F. Infants' recognition memory for faces. *Journal of Experimental Child Psychology*, 1972, *14*, 453-476.

Fagan, J. F. Infants' recognition of invariant features of faces. *Child Development*, 1976, *47*, 627-638.

Field, T. M. Visual and cardiac responses to animate and inanimate faces by young term and preterm infants. *Child Development*, 1979, *50*, 188–194.

Fitzgerald, H. D. Autonomic pupillary reflex activity during early infancy and its relation to social and nonsocial visual stimuli. *Journal of Experimental Child Psychology*, 1968, *6*, 470–482.

Friedman, S. Infant habituation: Process, problems and possibilities. In N. Ellis (Ed.), *Aberrant development in infancy*. Potomac, Md.: Lawrence Erlbaum Associates, 1975.

Gewirtz, J. L. The course of infant smiling in four childrearing environments in Israel. In B. M. Foss (Ed.), *Determinants of infant behavior* (Vol. 3). London: Methuen, 1965.

Gibson, E. J. *Principles of perceptual learning and development*. New York: Appleton-Century-Crofts, 1969.

Haith, M. M., Bergman, T., & Moore, M. J. Eye contact and face scanning in early infancy. *Science*, 1977, *198*, 853–855.

Horowitz, F. D. (Ed.). Visual attention, auditory stimulation, and language discrimination in young infants. *Monographs of the Society for Research in Child Development*, 1975, *39*, Serial 158.

Lashley, K. S. The problem of serial order in behavior. In L. A. Jeffress (Ed.), *Cerebral mechanisms in behavior*. New York: Wiley, 1951.

Lewis, M., & Brooks, J. Infants' social perception: A constructivist view. In L. B. Cohen & P. Salapatek (Eds.), *Infant perception: From sensation to cognition* (Vol. 2). New York: Academic Press, 1975.

MacFarlane, A. *The psychology of childbirth*. Cambridge, Mass.: Harvard University Press, 1977.

Maurer, D., & Salapatek, P. Developmental changes in the scanning of faces by infants. *Child Development*, 1976, *47*, 523–527.

Mendelson, M. J., & Haith, M. M. The relation between audition and vision in the human newborn. *Monographs of the Society for Research in Child Development*, 1976, *41*, Serial No. 167.

Olson, G. M. An information processing analysis of visual memory and habituation in infants. In T. Tighe & R. Leaton (Eds.), *Habituation*. Hillsdale, N.J.: Lawrence Erlbaum Associates, 1976.

Olson, G. M., & Sherman, T. Attention, learning, and memory. In M. M. Haith & J. J. Campos (Eds.), *Carmichael's manual of child psychology: Infancy and the biology of development*. New York: Wiley, in preparation.

Piaget, J. *The origins of intelligence in children*. New York: Norton, 1952.

Piaget, J., & Inhelder, B. *Memory and intelligence*. New York: Basic Books, 1973.

Posner, M. I. *Chronometric explorations of the mind*. Hillsdale, N.J.: Lawrence Erlbaum Associates, 1979.

Rheingold, H. L. The effect of environmental stimulation upon social and exploratory behavior in the human infant. In B. M. Foss (Ed.), *Determinants of infant behavior* (Vol. 1). London: Methuen, 1961.

Rosch, E. Principles of categorization. In E. Rosch & B. B. Lloyd (Eds.), *Cognition and categorization*. Hillsdale, N.J.: Lawrence Erlbaum Associates, 1978.

Ruff, H. A. Infant recognition of the invariant form of objects. *Child Development*, 1978, *49*, 293–306.

Sameroff, A. J., & Cavanagh, P. J. Learning in infancy: A developmental perspective. In J. D. Osofsky (Ed.), *Handbook of infant development*. New York: Wiley, 1979.

Sherrod, L. R. Social cognition in infants: Attention to the human face. *Infant Behavior and Development*, 1979, *2*, 279–294.

Spelke, E. S., & Owsley, C. J. Intermodal exploration and knowledge in infancy. *Infant Behavior and Development*, 1979, *2*, 13–27.

Spitz, R. A., & Wolf, K. The smiling response: A contribution to the ontogenesis of social relations. *Genetic Psychology Monographs,* 1946, *34,* 57–125.

Stern, D. *The first relationship: Infant and mother.* Cambridge, Mass.: Harvard University Press, 1977.

Wahler, R. G. Infant social attachments: A reinforcement theory interpretation and investigation. *Child Development,* 1967, *28,* 1079–1088.

Wolff, P. Observations on the early development of smiling. In B. M. Foss (Ed.), *Determinants of infant behaviour* (Vol. 2). London: Methuen, 1963.

4 Perceptual Aspects of Social Knowing: Looking and Listening in Infancy

Elizabeth S. Spelke
Alexandra Cortelyou
University of Pennsylvania

An infant encounters human beings through rich and complex patterns of sensory information. He or she comes to recognize individual persons, and to perceive their actions and expressions, by looking, by listening, and perhaps even by touching, tasting, and smelling. More importantly, the infant comes to relate these sources of information to each other. He or she eventually perceives each audible, visible, and tangible person as a unitary object. There comes a time when a child knows, for example, that a certain voice belongs to a certain person. This chapter focuses on the development of auditory-visual perception of people. The discussion centers on three capacities: (1) the ability to attend to a person by looking and listening at the same time; (2) the ability to perceive that the person one sees is (or is not) the source of a concurrent pattern of speech; (3) the ability to learn that certain patterns of light and patterns of sound specify the same individual.

In this discussion, two themes are highlighted. The first theme is substantive. Infants appear to possess innately, or to develop quickly, remarkable abilities to perceive the actions and expressions of other persons. These abilities may facilitate infants' learning about people and social encounters. The second theme is methodological. The study of infants' capacities to perceive and learn about people has only begun. This enterprise might benefit greatly from a closer collaboration between students of perception and students of social interaction. A collaborative venture could enrich both fields. Perceptual psychologists might better appreciate the earliest human capacities if they observe infants in contexts that are social. When infants confront other people, they may reveal perceptual abilities that rarely come to light in nonsocial settings. In addition, social psychologists might come to understand more about the growth of social and communicative competence if they attempt to characterize the stimulus information that is available to an infant in a communicative setting, the infant's sensitivity to that information, and the infant's consequent perception of people, actions, a nd relationships. This collaboration, difficult though it will be to achieve, might permit psychologists to turn with new force toward questions such as those we raise.

PRELIMINARIES:
PERCEIVING FACES AND VOICES

Before considering the infant's ability to relate visual and auditory information about a person, we first ask about the developing ability to perceive a face or a voice that is presented by itself. Although the evidence is somewhat contradictory (see Sherrod, this volume), it appears that infants attend to human faces and voices, detect some of their properties, and learn about them. In this section, we consider studies of attention, discrimination, and learning.

Infants attend to voices and faces from the beginning of life. Voices and voice-like sounds are among the most effective audible events for attracting the interest of newborn infants (Church, 1970; Eisenberg, 1976; Hutt, Lenard, & Prechtl, 1969; Turnure, 1971; Wolff, 1963). Similarly, a drawing of a face attracts the eye of a newborn infant in preference to a variety of other visual patterns (Fantz, 1963; Goren, 1975), whereas a real, animated face elicits strong interest and apparent attempts at communication in the first 2 months (e.g., Trevarthen, 1977; Wolff, 1963). Further evidence for the infant's interest in faces comes from studies of conditioning. Both faces and voices provide effective reinforcers for young infants. Infants of 2 months will learn to suck or turn their heads in order to see a person (e.g., Bower, 1966; Koch, 1967), whereas infants of various ages will learn to suck or press a lever in order to hear speech (e.g., Eimas, Siqueland, Jusczyk, & Vigorito, 1971; Friedlander, 1968).

Infants are able to discriminate a number of the properties of a person's face or voice. Studies of speech perception reveal that infants of 4 months or less are sensitive to some of the distinctive sound patterns of human languages (cf. Eimas, 1975) and of inanimate sounds with certain characteristics of speech (Jusczyk, Rosner, Cutting, Foard, & Smith, 1977; Jusczyk, Walley, & Pisoni, 1979). Furthermore, infants of 3 to 6 months are sensitive to the pitch of a speech sequence (Kessen, Levine, & Wendrich, 1979), 1-month olds respond to its intonation (Mehler, Bertoncini, Barriere, & Jassik-Gerschenfeld, 1978), infants of 9 months, and perhaps younger, perceive its affective tone (Lieberman, 1967), and 2-month olds appear to detect its time-spanning structure of rhythm or rhyme (Horowitz, 1974).

Studies of face-to-face interaction suggest that infants are also sensitive to some actions and expressions of the human face. For example, infants as young as 2 months evidently anticipate that a visible person will communicate with them, for they are disturbed by an immobile face (Tronick, Adamson, Wise, Als, & Brazelton, 1975; see also Bloom, 1977; Field, 1979), or by a person who suddenly becomes unresponsive (Brazelton, Koslowski, & Main, 1975; Fogel, Diamond, Langhorst, & Demos, 1979). Even when the mother is actively communicating, the infant seems to be sensitive to a lack of contingency in the exchange. Signs of distress have been observed in 2-month olds whose mothers switched their attention to another adult while continuing to face the infant (Trevarthen, 1977). Infants may also discriminate and imitate certain specific actions of the lips, tongue, and mouth (Church, 1970; Meltzoff & Moore, 1977), although the existence of early imitation has been questioned (Hamm, Russell, & Koepke, 1979; Hayes & Watson, 1979). Finally, studies of infants' responsiveness to an active adult or to a still photograph suggest an early appreciation of some of the affective expressions of another person (Barrera, 1979; Kreutzer & Charlesworth, 1973; LaBarbera, Izard, Vietze, & Parisi, 1976; Young-Browne, Rosenfeld, & Horowitz, 1977).

These investigations suggest that infants are sensitive to some of the temporal and spatial information that characterizes human utterances and expressions. Infants also have a further ability assuring that their capacity for social perception will grow: They are able to learn rapidly about human faces and voices. Infants are capable of at least two kinds of perceptual learning. First, they learn about some of the distinctive characteristics of human speech and human physiognomy. Infants learn quickly about some of the sound patterns of their own language (Eilers, Gavin, & Wilson, 1979; Streeter, 1976). They may also learn about some of the characteristics and actions of people (e.g., Caron, Caron, Caldwell, & Weiss, 1973; Gibson, 1969), although this ability is in need of further study with more natural displays. Second, infants come to recognize certain individuals by their voices and by their faces. One-month-old infants can recognize the voice of a parent (Mehler et al., 1978; see also Turnure, 1971), and they quickly learn to recognize the voice of an unfamiliar person (Horowitz, 1974). Recognition of tape-recorded voices can, nevertheless, cause some difficulty well into the school years (Mann, Diamond, & Carey, 1979). Infants also recognize the face of a parent by 1 month of age according to some criteria (Maurer & Salapatek, 1976), and by 2 to 4 months according to other criteria (Fitzgerald, 1968; Fogel, 1979). Infants learn rapidly to recognize the face of an unfamiliar person by 4 months of age, if the person moves expressively (Spelke, 1975). Until 5 or 6 months, however, they appear not to discriminate and recognize static photographs of people they do not know, even two people of opposite sex (Cornell, 1974; Fagan, 1972). Again, recognizing faces in photographs can cause some difficulties throughout childhood (Carey & Diamond, 1977).

In summary, infants explore, perceive, and learn to distinguish complex patterns of auditory and visual information about other human beings and their actions. Young infants appear especially sensitive to people whose actions and expressions change over time. They may extract visual and auditory information about a person who is communicating with them more easily than they can analyze the static, configural information in a photograph or a schematic drawing. The ability to perceive actions has, at least, been easier to document at young ages. Infants may also be more sensitive to the actions and the emotional expressions of a person than they are to a person's static features. For example, infants appear to discriminate between photographs of a face displaying different emotional expressions (e.g., Barrera, 1979) before they can discriminate between photographs of two unfamiliar faces with neutral expressions (e.g., Fagan, 1972).

The sensitivity of young infants to some human actions and expressions raises an important possibility. Many aspects of a communicative act can be perceived either by looking or by listening. The same pattern of timing may characterize both a visual and a vocal expression of surprise; the same interactional contingencies may underlie both a visual and a vocal social exchange. Infants might be able to detect such invariances and perceive a relationship between the speech and the visible appearance of a person. We return to this possibility.

With this background, the chapter now focuses on the early development of coordinated looking and listening to people. Infants' exploration, perception, and knowledge of the people whom they see and hear are considered in turn.

EXPLORING PEOPLE BY LISTENING AND LOOKING

It is commonly observed that babies tend to look at a person when he or she speaks to them. And it is also widely believed, if less often tested by parents, that babies will lose interest in a person who looks at them without speaking. These observations suggest that infants attempt to explore people by looking and listening at the same time.

What exploratory patterns underlie the infant's looking and listening to a person? Some of these patterns may be quite general. Infants are known to look attentively at times and in places in which the sounds of inanimate objects are played. When young infants are presented with a sound, they often open their eyes (Haith, 1973), increase their attention to a concurrent visual display (Horowitz, 1974), and turn in the sound's direction (e.g., Muir & Field, 1979; Wertheimer, 1961). If looking is similarly affected by animate sounds, then these exploratory patterns will tend to increase the infant's looking to a person who speaks. But a further, more interesting exploratory pattern may also underlie the infant's visual attention to a speaking person. When an infant detects a voice, he or she may tend to look specifically for a face, in preference to other displays that are visible at the same time and place.

This exploratory pattern would depend on an ability to relate auditory and visual information about a person in a special way. An infant who looked specifically for a face when hearing a voice would seem implicitly to know that voices are the kinds of sounds produced by people. We now consider evidence that an infant who hears a voice looks for: (1) an object occurring at the same time as the voice; (2) an object occurring in the same spatial direction as the voice; and/or (3) an object that looks like a face.

Do infants tend to look attentively to a face at the time that a voice is presented? A recent experiment indicates that they do. Haith, Bergman, and Moore (1977) presented infants from 3 to 11 weeks of age with a mirror reflection of the face of an adult—the mother or a stranger—under three conditions: still, moving from side to side, and moving while talking. The infant's point of fixation was calculated every half second, and scanning patterns were assessed. Infants of 7 weeks and older tended to look on or near the person's eyes. In the presence of a voice, infants slightly increased their looking at the eyes, and their scanning of the face became distinctly more concentrated. The locations of different eye fixations varied less when the adult spoke than when she was silent. These observations suggest that the presence of the voice increased visual attention to a face.

There is some doubt about whether infants tend to look at a face in the spatial direction of a voice. In an experiment by Field, DiFranco, Dodwell, and Muir (1979), infants' looking to a peripherally presented face was unaffected by the spatial direction of a voice accompaniment. While 2 ½-month-old infants looked straight ahead, a still photograph of a person was presented to one side. At the same time, a voice was heard on the same or on the opposite side. Infants looked to the face in both conditions. They looked to the face equally quickly, regardless of whether the voice was played in the appropriate direction or on the opposite side. In contrast, looking at a face was affected by the direction of a voice in a different experiment (Spelke, 1978). Four-month old infants were presented with two films, projected side by side. One film depicted a person speaking, whereas the other depicted moving, inanimate objects. A voice sound track, synchronized with the speaking person, was played either through a speaker centered between the films (at a 20° separation from the face), or through a speaker next to the film of the inanimate objects (at an 80° separation from the face). Infants looked at the person more when the spatial separation of voice and face was small than when it was large. The discrepancy between the findings of these two experiments could derive from a number of factors. For example, Spelke's infants were older, they viewed a moving, voice-synchronized face rather than a photograph, the moving face was continuously present, and the duration of infant's looking, rather than its latency, was the critical response measure.

In brief, young infants tend to look attentively at a face at the time that a voice is played. By 4 months, they also appear to look more at a face presented in the spatial direction of a voice. Do infants also tend to look specifically for a face when they hear a voice? Two kinds of comparison are needed to answer this question. Experiments must compare looking at a face in the presence of a voice with looking at a face in the presence of some other auditory pattern. Similarly, experiments must compare the effect of a voice on looking at a face with its effect on looking at other visual displays. Several such studies have been conducted. None provides evidence for a specific effect of voices on looking at faces.

Hainline (1978) studied 1- to 3-month-old infants' scanning of a photograph of a face that was accompanied by a voice, by a tone varying in frequency, or by no auditory presentation. Unlike Haith et al. (1977), she found no effect of the voice on the amount of fixation on the eye region of the face. Hainline did report that eye fixations were more concentrated in the presence of a voice, but this effect was not specific to the voice. Scanning was even more concentrated in the presence of the tone. Inanimate sounds thus may influence infants' scanning of faces in much the way that voices do. Similarly, voices may affect infants' scanning of inanimate displays much as they affect scanning of faces. Mendelson and Haith (1976) observed that newborn infants scanned simple inanimate displays with more concentrated fixations when a display was accompanied by a voice than when it was presented silently. Furthermore, the infants tended to look at the central region of the display when the voice was presented from behind, as it had been in Haith et al.'s (1977) study. This central region would seem to correspond to the location of the eyes of the person in Haith et al.'s experiment.

Although young infants tend to look at a person when he or she speaks, these studies suggest that they do not do this because of any specific effect voices have on looking at faces. The presence of any interesting sound may lead to more concentrated looking at any interesting visual display. It might be argued, however, that these experiments do not provide a sensitive test of the effect of voices on looking at faces. In each study, only one visual display and one sound were presented to the infant at any given time. Although sounds may not affect visual attention differentially under these conditions, they may have more specific effects under other conditions. For example, if the infant were given a choice between two visual displays, one of them a face, he or she might attend to that display preferentially during times in which a voice was played. The same preference might not be observed during times in which the displays were accompanied by an inanimate sound.

At first glance, an experiment by one of us would seem to provide just such evidence (Spelke, 1976). Four-month-old infants were shown a film of a person speaking, side by side with a film of inanimate objects mving into contact. Different sounds, played through a central speaker, accompanied these events. When the films were accompanied by a voice synchronized with the speaking person, infants exhibited a reliable visual preference for that person. When the films were accompanied by percussive sounds synchronized with the impacts of the inanimate objects, infants no longer preferred the film of the speaking person. In fact, they tended to look more to the film of the inanimate objects.

Although this experiment would seem to show that voices have specific effects on looking at faces, there is an alternative explanation for the infants' looking patterns. The voice sound track was temporally synchronized with the movements of the speaking person, and the percussion sound track was synchronized with the movements of the inanimate objects. Thus, the infants might have looked at the face when they heard the voice because they detected this temporal synchrony, not because they related faces to voices in general. Infants of this age are known to detect the synchrony of an inanimate sound with simple, translatory movements of an object (Spelke, 1979). In order to investigate whether they tend in general to look at a face when they hear a voice, one must present infants with a face and voice that are not temporally synchronized. We have attempted to do this in a preliminary experiment.

Experiment 1: The Effects of a Voice on Looking at a Face.   The study used a preferential looking technique. Infants were presented with a film of a face, side by side with a film of inanimate objects. In this study, as in the study just described, the face film depicted the head and shoulders of a young adult woman playing "peekaboo." The other film depicted a hand holding a baton that struck two different toy percussion instruments in an irregular rhythm. Each event was filmed with a synchronized sound track, but the films and sounds were not presented at the same time. Infants first watched the two films with no sound. Then they heard the first sound track, unaccompanied by any film. The sound track was followed again by the two silent films, which were followed by the second sound track. The session closed with a final viewing of the two films. Because the sound tracks were not concurrent with the two films, sounds and visible movements were of course not temporally synchronized, although they may have been related in more subtle ways.[1] If infants tend specifically to look at a face when they hear a voice, then we

---

[1]An ideal test of the general effect of a voice on looking at a face would present a face and voice that were not temporally related in any way. This goal is not fully achieved by presenting a voice and a moving face that are shown out of synchrony. A person tends to speak in a characteristic rhythm, and a baby might detect this rhythm by looking and listening even if the person's voice and face were not synchronized. Thus, our study can provide no conclusive test of infants' knowledge about the specific relationship between a face and voice. We hoped nevertheless that its results would be suggestive.

expected them to look at the film of the person after the voice was played. We expected this preference to be diminished after the percussive sounds were played.[2]

Sixteen healthy, full-term infants, aged 3 months, 22 days to 4 months, 19 days (mean, 4 months, 3 days), participated in the experiment. They took part in five episodes. During the first, third, and fifth episode, they were presented with the peekaboo and percussion films, side by side, projected silently for 30 seconds per session. During the second and fourth sessions, infants were presented with the two sound tracks—one per session—for 50 seconds each. The films were projected on the left and right halves of a divided screen. For each infant, the lateral positions of the films remained constant throughout the experiment. The sound tracks were played through a speaker centered between the films. The left–right positions of the films and the order of the sound tracks were counterbalanced across infants. Looking was recorded throughout the session by two observers who were unaware of the position of each sound-related film. Reliabilities averaged 87%. The proportion of looking to each side of the screen was recorded for the three preference episodes.

The experiment provided only equivocal evidence that babies look at faces when they hear voices and not when they hear inanimate sounds. Infants tended to look longer to the person playing peekaboo after presentation of the voice than after presentation of the percussion sound, but this tendency was not significant. Preference for the peekaboo film averaged .58 following the voice presentation and .51 following the percussion sound, $t(15) = .88$. These results are complicated by what can only be a spurious effect. During the initial preference test, infants looked more to whichever film did not go with the sound that was about to be played. As Table 4.1(a) indicates, infants looked about equally to the two screens during the subsequent preference episodes, but these comparisons do not take account of the initial preferences. Table 4.1(b) accordingly presents the change in the proportion of looking to each film, from the first preference episode to the subsequent episodes. It is evident from Table 4.1(b) that the presence of the sounds affected looking during the preference test that followed the first sound track, but not during the test following the second sound track. Infants reliably increased their

---

[2]This prediction requires some elaboration. In different experiments, the presence of auditory or tactile information about an object has been found to influence subsequent preferential looking to that object in two mutually exclusive ways. First, infants have sometimes looked more to an object that they had just heard (Bahrick, 1979) or felt (Meltzoff & Borton, 1979). Second, infants have sometimes exhibited a "novelty preference," looking more to an object that they had *not* heard (Spelke, in press) or touched (Gottfried, Rose, & Bridger, 1977). The latter pattern is more often observed after prolonged familiarization with an object, and it is more commonly exhibited by older infants. Because we were presenting young infants with brief, interesting displays, we expected infants to prefer the more familiar object.

TABLE 4.1
The Effects of Sounds on Subsequent Visual Preferences

	Looking to first sound film	Looking to second sound film	Preference	t (15)
(a)				
Pretest	9.1	15.5	.36	2.33[a]
Post-Test 1	13.7	10.5	.56	1.00
Post-Test 2	12.4	11.8	.49	0.13
	Change in Preference for Sound Film		t (15)	
(b)				
Post-Test 1	.18		4.32[b]	
Post-Test 2	−.12		−1.62	

[a]$p < .05$, two-tailed
[b]$p < .01$, two-tailed

looking to the film whose sound was the first to be played. This tendency was unaffected by the particular sound track presented.

Infants in the first study thus tended to look at a face after hearing a voice and to look at inanimate objects after hearing their sounds, but these tendencies were reliable in only one of several comparisons. Experiment 1 provides suggestive, but not conclusive, evidence for an ability to appreciate that faces belong with voices and that inanimate sounds belong with inanimate objects.

In summary, infants do appear to look at a person when they hear that person's voice, but this tendency seems to reflect primarily the tendency to look at an object when and where a sound occurs. There is no firm evidence that infants tend to look specifically at faces when they hear voices. It may be that infants do not appreciate that voices are the kind of sounds that are produced by objects with human faces. Alternatively, infants may implicitly know that faces and voices belong together, but they may fail to use this knowledge to direct their exploration in the situations that have been studied. New experimental procedures may uncover this knowledge. To date, however, knowledge in infancy of the general relation between faces and voices has not been conclusively demonstrated.

The tendency to look at a person when he or she speaks, whatever its perceptual or conceptual basis, is likely to aid the infant in learning about people and social exchanges. Under normal circumstances, young infants are likely to be faced directly by the persons who are talking to them, usually at close range. Infants will naturally look while listening, and they will thereby have the opportunity to learn about those persons through the interaction. But do infants realize that the person they see is the source of the sounds they hear? Do they perceive that a speaking face and its synchronized voice are aspects of a single, unitary object? This is the question to which we now turn our attention.

PERCEIVING PEOPLE AS
AUDIBLE AND VISIBLE OBJECTS

Adults usually perceive with little difficulty whether or not a person that they see is the source of a voice that they hear. This ability reflects a knowledge, perhaps a tacit knowledge, of certain auditory-visual relationships. There are at least three components to our stock of knowledge. First, we know that people with certain visible characteristics have voices with certain audible characteritics. Some of these characteristics are transient. Cheerful voices usually go with alert, smiling faces; sobbing voices usually accompany mournful faces. Other characteristics are persistent. Women have higher speech registers than men, and the old have less clear voices than the young. Thus, we more readily attribute a raspy, low-pitched, angry voice to a frowning elderly man than to the 4-year-old girl who smiles beside him. Second, we know that audible speech and visible speaking movements tend to be synchronized in certain regular ways. Visual and auditory information for speech is to some extent redundant. Because of this redundancy, adults find it easier to understand speech in a noisy environment if they can look at the speaker (Dodd, 1977; Sumby & Pollack, 1954) and some deaf people are able to understand speech by lip-reading. Our normal reliance on this redundancy may also explain the occasional discomfort caused by dubbed or poorly synchronized motion pictures. As adults, we may determine which of several people is speaking by detecting the synchrony of speech and speaking movements. Third, a speaking person is seen and heard in the same position in space. We may sometimes determine which visible person is speaking by localizing the voice. As every ventriloquist knows, however, adults can be fooled about a voice's location.

The sensitivity of infants to these auditory-visual relationships has received very little study. We know of no research asking whether infants can discover that a voice specifies a particular visible person by detecting the common spatial direction of the face and voice.[3] We also know of only one investigation of infants' ability to perceive a face-voice relationship by detecting a characteristic of a person by looking and listening: Walker (1980) has investigated infants' visual and auditory perception of a person's expressions of emotion. Finally, at the same time we began this chapter, we knew of no studies of infants' ability to determine whether a voice comes from

---

[3]The demonstration that infants will look at a face in the spatial direction of a voice does not, in itself, indicate whether they perceive the face they encounter to be related to that voice. Infants may simply localize a sound and turn to look at anything in its direction.

a particular speaking person by detecting the temporal synchrony of speech and speaking movements. One such study has since appeared (Dodd, 1979). We have, accordingly, conducted a second experiment. This section first descibes our investigation of infants' sensitivity to the synchrony of audible speech and visible expressive movements, and it briefly relates our own work to that of Dodd (1979). Next, it describes Walker's (1980) studies of infants' sensitivity to the common affective tone of a voice and a visually expressive face. All these investigations indicate that infants can sometimes determine which of two visibly speaking people is the source of an accompanying voice.

Experiment 2: Detecting the Synchrony of Speech and Expressive Movement. We confess that we approached this experiment with some trepidation. Detecting the synchrony of speech and expressive movements would seem to be a formidable task for a young infant. The temporal relationships between speech sounds and speaking movements are subtle and complex. Most articulatory movements are fully or partly invisible. Many of the movements that are visible could correspond to any of a class of speech sounds (see, for example, MacDonald & McGurk, 1978). Furthermore, only some movements of the face may correspond predictably to a stream of speech. A raising of the eyebrows, for example, may accompany any number of different sounds. In order to detect the synchrony of speech and facial movements, an infant would seem to need to attend selectively to certain facial movements and to certain aspects of the speech stream. The infant would also need to grasp the relationship between the relevant movements and sounds. Young perceivers would seem to be ill-equipped to accomplish these tasks. Their discrimination of speech sounds and facial movements is unlikely to be as good as the discrimination by adults. And infants, like adults, have been reported to look at the eyes of a speaker, not at the mouth (Haith et al., 1977). Thus, they would seem likely to miss any voice-synchronized movements that a speaking face exhibits.

Two considerations reduced our pessimism. First, the synchrony between speech and expressive movements would seem to be especially compelling in the speech of adults to infants. When a person talks to a baby, he or she tends to exaggerate facial expressions, to extend them in time and space, and to create especially full and redundant expressive displays (see Stern, Beebe, Jaffe, & Bennett, 1977). Many movements besides those of the articulators are probably synchronized with such a person's voice. Second, as our initial review indicated, the tendency to look at the eyes of a person evidently does not prevent an infant from detecting information about the person's actions and expressions. And it is just such actions that are likely to be detectable both by eye and by ear. The second experiment therefore tested infants' sensitivity to the synchrony of a person's speech and facial movements.

Four-month-old infants were presented with films of the faces of two young adult women. The women were not known to the infants. Each spoke spontaneously, while facing the camera, as if she were addressing a baby. She greeted the baby, asked about his or her daily routines, attempted to elicit a smile, and so forth. Both women exhibited the temporally extended, exaggerated expressions characteristic of speech to infants. Each spoke in a bright, cheerful manner.

Throughout the experiment, the films of the two speaking people were presented side by side. One sound track was played at a time, through a centrally placed speaker. This display arrangement insured that only the temporal synchrony of speech and facial movements could tie each voice to one person. The voices and faces were not spatially related, each voice was played concurrently with both faces, and the particular face-voice pairings were not previously known to the infants.

The experiment made use of a procedure that one of us has used before, with inanimate objects (Spelke, 1979). It consisted of two episodes within a single session. During the "preference episode," infants were presented with the films of both women projected side by side. They heard the synchronized voice of each woman in turn. Each voice has heard for one 100-second session through the central speaker. During the subsequent "search episode," the two films were projected silently while a light was flashed between them to attract the infant's attention. One voice, synchronized with the appropriate face and coming through the central speaker, was then played for 5 seconds. Eight such trials were given with each voice, the voices occurring in a random order. Throughout the experiment, each film was continuously projected on one side of the screen. The lateral position of the films and the order of the sound tracks were counterbalanced across infants.

Looking time to each film was continuously record by two observers, blind to the sound-object relationships. Their reliabilities averaged 89%. For each preference session, we calculated the proportion of total looking time that was devoted to the voice-synchronized face. For the search episode, a trial was scored if the infant was not looking at either film at the time that the voice began. Seven scorable trials, on average, were given to each infant. We calculated four measures of the tendency to look to the person whose voice was played: the number of trials that the infant looked first to the appropriate and to the inappropriate person (*first look*), the number of trials on which he or she looked at all—first or second—to each person within the 5-second trial duration (*eventual look*), and the mean *latency* and *duration* of looking to each person. Trials in which an infant did not look to a given person received a latency score of 5 seconds and a duration score of 0 seconds. Further information about these procedures is given in Spelke (1979b).

Twenty infants from the Philadelphia area participated in the experiment. The infants ranged in age from 3 months, 21 days to 4 months, 21 days, and averaged 4 months, 8 days. They were healthy and full-term.

TABLE 4.2
Looking to Voice-Synchronized Faces

	Synchronized Face	Nonsynchronized Face	Preference	t (19)
(a) Preference episode				
Session 1	49.94	37.71	.57	1.49
Session 2	44.40	32.56	.58	1.76[a]
Total	94.34	70.27	.58	3.90[b]
	Synchronized Face	Nonsynchronized Face		t (19)
(b) Search episode				
First Look	4.15	2.75		2.19[a]
Eventual Look	5.30	4.35		2.76[b]
Latency	2.09	2.45		1.74[a]
Duration	1.96	1.66		1.30

[a] $p < .05$, one-tailed
[b] $p < .01$, one-tailed

The results of this experiment appear in Table 4.2. Infants looked primarily to whichever woman they heard. They tended to prefer the "speaking" woman during each preference session. This tendency was reliable for the second session and for both sessions combined. During the search test, infants looked first, and looked eventually, more often toward the woman whose voice they heard. They also looked at her more quickly. They did not look at her for a significantly longer duration.

These results agree well with those of studies with inanimate objects (Spelke, 1979b). When infants are presented with two moving inanimate objects, accompanied by synchronized sounds during a preference episode and a search episode, they respond with looking patterns that are very similar to those observed in the present experiment. In particular, they tend to look for a sounding object on every measure of the search test except the duration measure.

The results of this experiment suggest that 4-month-old infants are sensitive to the synchrony of speech with some of the visible movements of the face. Infants can perceive a temporal relationship between the sight of a speaking person and the sound of his or her voice, even when the spatial location of the voice cannot guide their discovery of the face-voice relationship. By detecting the synchrony of speech and facial movement, infants can determine whether a particular voice belongs to a particular visible person.

The findings of this experiment have been corroborated in an experiment by Dodd (1979) and in ongoing research by Walker (1980). Dodd presented an unfamiliar, speaking person to infants who ranged in age from 10 to 16 weeks. Each infant viewed the person reciting nursery rhymes for four or more 60-second periods. During half of these periods, the person's voice was presented in synchrony with the speaking movements of the face. During the remaining periods, the voice lagged behind the facial movements by 400 milliseconds. In both conditions, the voice was played through a loudspeaker presented behind the face. Visual attention to the face was scored in each of these conditions. As in our experiment, the presence or absence of synchrony had a pronounced effect on visual attention. Infants looked at the face more when it moved in synchrony with the voice.

Walker (1980) investigated the infant's sensitivity to the affective tenor of a communication, using a method very similar to ours. Her research focused on the ability to detect the common emotional tone of a voice and a visually expressive face. In two experiments, 7-month-old infants viewed films of a person engaging in a "happy" monologue and a person engaged in a "sad" monologue. The films were projected side by side and were accompanied by a centrally located, happy or sad voice. In one experiment, each voice was synchronized with the movements of the appropriate face. In a second experiment, the voice sound tracks were delayed by 1 second, such that the faces and voices were not temporally synchronized. Infants viewed both films at once while they heard each voice in turn through a central speaker. Infants in the first experiment looked longer to the face that corresponded to each voice during both voice episodes. Infants in the second experiment—in which the faces and voices were nonsynchronized—showed no preferences during the first voice episode, and then exhibited the appropriate preference during the second voice episode. Walker concluded that infants were sensitive both to the synchrony and to the emotional tenor of a voice and a face. When faces and voices are presented out of synchrony, infants may initially be confused by this discordance and, therefore, show no preferences during the first testing period. During the second period, they may become accustomed to the lack of synchrony and so begin to exhibit the preference for the face with the same emotional tone as the voice.

The findings of these experiments raise a question that bears special emphasis. What perceptual information does an infant use in detecting a relationship between speech and expressive movements? This question is not easily answered, for the speech and expressions of a person are richly redundant. In Walker's second experiment, for example, infants might have responded to expressions of emotion per se, or they might have responded to the common tempo of sound and movement when a person is happy or sad. In our second experiment and in Dodd's research, infants could have responded to temporal relationships of many kinds. For example, infants might have detected the synchrony of particular speech sounds and articulatory movements. Alternatively, they might have responded to the pattern of speech and pauses that characterizes any natural communication. Infants might have detected the simultaneous occurrence of speaking and moving, and of pausing and resting, in the people whom they saw and heard. As a third possibility, infants in both experiments might have responded to changes with time in the affective quality of a face and voice. Although the overall emotional tones of the speakers in our experiment were not noticeably different in our judgment, every person's speech is characterized by moment-to-moment changes in affective quality. These changes may be both audible and visible, and they may create a further temporal relationship between speech and facial movement. Infants might detect both auditory and visual information for a sudden expression of surprise or glee, and they may perceive the expression they see as related to the expression they hear. It will be difficult to distinguish experimentally between these possibilities. Psychologists have neither descriptive tools with which to characterize most of these relationships, nor adequate procedures for manipulating them. We think, however, that these problems must, and ultimately can, be faced. Gross descriptions of "face-voice synchrony" or "emotional expression" can yield to more specific descriptions of the auditory-visual relationships to which an infant responds.

Despite their limitations, the above studies have uncovered a remarkable perceptual ability. When two people are seen to speak, and a voice is centered between them, infants can discover which of the people is the source of that voice. However they do this, it is clear that they are sensitive to subtle and complex relationships in stimulation to the eye and ear. Infants have revealed a striking ability to perceive auditory-visual relationships in animate events.

LEARNING ABOUT SPECIFIC
FACE VALUE RELATIONSHIPS

Thus far, we have considered the infant's exploration of a person while looking and listening at the same time, and the infant's perception of a relationship between a person's face and voice. Young babies appear both to explore people intermodally and to perceive face-voice relationships. They are therefore in a position to learn something new. They should be able to learn about further correspondences between the visible and audible characteristics of a person.

This last section focuses on one aspect of infants' learning. To an adult, the sight and sound of a familiar person are in some sense equivalent: They specify the same individual. Thus, one may determine that a certain acquaintance has entered a house by watching her cross the room, listening to her call, or even by identifying her distinctive pattern of footsteps. One has obviously had to learn that these diverse visual and auditory patterns specify a single individual. How early in life does such learning begin? We discuss infants' learning about the audible and visible characteristics of the best-known people in their lives: their parents. We ask if babies appreciate that the sound of a parent's voice goes with the sight of that parent's face.

A number of investigations have focused on the infant's knowledge of the relationship between the mother's face and her voice. Most of these use a "conflict" procedure. While the mother speaks to the infant, auditory and visual information are rearranged so that the mother's face and voice are spatially separated, or so that the mother's face is paired with a different person's voice. The infant's response to these rearrangements is observed. If infants are surprised or distressed, it is inferred that they know that the mother's face and voice normally go together. The findings of conflict studies have not always agreed, but evidence is now accumulating that young infants do expect the mother's voice to emanate from her face.

Infants studied by Aronson and Rosenbloom (1971) looked at the mother while listening to her synchronized voice first in her direction (straight ahead) and then 90° to one side. The 6-week-old infants were reported to be upset—in particular, to show marked "tonguing"—when the sound was spatially displaced. Two careful studies failed to replicate this effect (Condry, Haltom, & Neisser, 1977; McGurk & Lewis, 1974). McGurk and Lewis did, however, report one intriguing finding: Infants tended to look away from the mother's face more often in the spatial displacement condition than in the nondisplacement condition. Although this looking pattern could have reflected a simple tendency to look in the direction of the sound, a follow-up study suggested a more interesting interpretation. Lewis and Hurowitz (1977) presented 1- and 4-month-old infants with the faces and voices of the mother and of a female stranger. Infants saw one face and heard one voice at a time; the face and voice either came from the same person or from different people. In these conditions, the voice was always played from the direction of the face. Infants nevertheless looked around the room and away from a face more often if the face and voice were mismatched. Looking away may reflect a conflict reaction to the inappropriate face-voice pairing.

In the aforementioned studies, the faces and voices were synchronized when they were paired appropriately. In Lewis and Hurowitz's (1977) study, faces and voices were not synchronized when they were paired inappropriately. If infants in the latter study detected the incongruous arrangements, their detection could depend either on knowledge that the mother's face and voice go together or on the perception of face-voice synchrony. Three further experiments eliminated the possibility of a response to auditory-visual synchrony alone. Carpenter (cited in Bower, 1979) presented 2-week-old infants with the face and voice of the mother or a stranger. Faces and voices were paired appropriately or inappropriately. In all cases, the face moved in synchrony with its paired (tape-recorded) voice. Infants looked away from a face least when the mother spoke with her own voice. They were reported to avoid looking at either person's face when it was presented with the wrong person's voice. This gaze avoidance was taken to reflect a conflict reaction to a perceived discrepancy. The presence of confict would suggest that infants know about the normal relationship of the mother's voice and face.

Cohen (1974) presented 5- and 8-month-old infants with the mother and a stranger seated facing the infant, several feet apart. The tape-recorded voice of one of these adults was played through a loudspeaker. The loudspeaker was placed next to one of the people, who moved her lips in synchrony with the voice. These face-voice pairings could be either appropriate or inappropriate. Cohen recorded the latency and duration of the infant's looking to the person in the direction of the sound. She found such looking to be reduced, at 8 months of age, if either person appeared in the direction of, and moved in synchrony with, the other person's voice. There was no effect of matching or mismatching faces and voices at 5 months. Although Cohen discussed the infant's looking away from the location of the voice as evidence for conflict or discrepancy, she noted that infants may have looked toward the voice less in the mismatched conditions because they were looking toward the person to whom the voice really belonged.

A final study focused more directly on the exploratory activity of looking to a person whose voice is heard. Spelke and Owsley (1979) investigated infants' knowledge of the faces and voices of the mother and father. Infants from 3½ to 7½ months were presented with the two parents sitting side by side. While the parents remained motionless, their tape-recorded voices were heard in turn through a central speaker. Despite the absence of any face-voice synchrony, infants at all ages tended to look to the person whose voice was played. It was concluded that the infants had already come to appreciate which parent's voice belonged with each face. Spelke and Owsley repeated this procedure with 4-month-old infants in two conditions, the first with the mother and father and the second with the mother and an unfamiliar, adult woman. The results of the mother-father condition were as before, but the results of the condition with the two women were not. Contrary to expectations, infants did not look for the woman whose voice was played. In fact, they showed the opposite tendency, looking to the mother when the stranger's voice was played, and vice versa.

Sifting through these studies, it appears that babies do possess some knowledge about the relationship between a parent's face and voice. This knowledge seems to be best reflected in infants' patterns of looking. Except in one condition of Spelke and Owsley's study, infants have tended to look at the mother longer if they heard her voice than if they heard the voice of another person. They also appear to look longer at the father or at an unfamiliar woman if they hear that person's voice. These patterns may reflect an interesting exploratory activity. Just as babies look in the direction of a sound, and just as they look at an object that is synchronized with a sound, they may look for an object that they know to be the source of a sound.

There is some dispute concerning the age at which infants acquire this knowledge. Carpenter found responses to the mismatched faces and voices of the mother and stranger at 2 weeks, but Cohen observed no such responses until 8 months. The findings of Lewis and Hurowitz and of Spelke and Owsley are more consistent with those of Carpenter, because they yield evidence for knowledge at the youngest ages tested (1 and 4 months). Despite these differences, it is clear that infants are learning about the audible and visible characteristics of familiar people quite early in life. Further studies might profitably focus on the nature of the learning capacities that underlie this accomplishment.

CONCLUDING REMARKS

Human infants can perceive the communicative actions of others by looking and listening in a coordinated manner. We discussed three aspects of this coordination. First, young infants are usually able to look at a person when they hear the person's voice. They do this because of a very general tendency to look attentively at the time and in the direction in which a sound is heard. Infants may also tend to look specifically for a face when hearing a voice, but this possibility has received no clear experimental support. Because infants will tend to explore a person by looking and listening at the same time under normal viewing conditions, they are in a position to detect specific temporal relationships between the person's speech and facial movements. They are also in a position to learn about the relationship between the face and voice of a specific person. The rest of the chapter focused on these abilities.

We turned next to the ability to perceive a relationship between a face and its accompanying voice. Four-month-old infants are able to determine whether a visibly speaking person is the source of a voice by detecting some temporal relationship between the voice and face. Infants appear to be sensitive to the synchrony of certain characteristics of speech with certain visible movements of the speaker. They also appear to be receptive to the common emotional tenor of a visual and vocal communication. We do not yet know which of the many specific relationships between speech and expressive movements are detectable by infants.

Finally, we considered the infant's ability to learn about particular face-voice relationships. Such learning begins early in life. By 2 to 4 months of age, infants appear to expect the mother's face—and not the face of another person—to accompany the mother's voice. They may reveal this expectation through their exploration: When they hear the mother's voice they look toward the mother's face and away from the face of some other person, even if the mother's voice is played from some inappropriate direction.

In summary, infants explore a person by looking and listening; they can detect the synchrony of the person's face and voice; and they can learn that the person's face and voice are specifically related. These findings are the fruits of rather recent research. Thus it is clear that psychologists have learned, and are learning, about the infant's perception of people, their communications, and their actions. But it is evident that there is a great deal more to learn. Psychologists have only begun to understand how infants coordinate auditory and visual information when they perceive animate events.

The understanding that has been achieved comes primarily from a heterogeneous collection of investigations, rather than a program of systematic research. We believe that further understanding of the infant's perception of others can come only from a serious and close collaboration between those who study infants as perceivers and those who study infants as social partners. We end by presenting some questions to challenge future investigations and by suggesting how those questions could be approached through such a collaboration.

The first question concerns the nature of the temporal relationships between speech and facial movements that infants are able to detect. What is the "synchrony" to which they are sensitive? To address this question, we need a workable description of the auditory and visual information available to infants in a communicative setting and a description of the manifold correspondences between these arrays of information. Then we may attempt to manipulate systematically the information available to infants in order to reveal what relationships they detect and, ultimately, how they detect them. Both tasks may be undertaken by a collaboration between the student of social communication—who seeks to describe and analyze patterns of activity in a social exchange—and the student of perception—who could attempt, through systematic experiments, to analyze the infant's sensitivity to those patterns.

The second question concerns the development of perception of auditory-visual relationships. What kinds of correspondences between auditory and visual information do infants detect, and which are detected earliest in development? Are infants first sensitive to the common spatial location of a face and voice, to the temporal synchrony of speech and movement, to certain specific correspondences between faces and voices, or simply to the repeated cooccurrence of a voice and a particular visible face? This question has theoretical importance. According to traditional theories of learning by association, the cooccurrence or "temporal contiguity" of faces and voices should be the first relationship to which an infant responds. According to a theory that bases intermodal perception on the capacity to detect a common stimulus relationship in light and sound (Gibson, 1969), infants should first be sensitive to either spatial or temporal relationships between a voice and a speaking face. An association theory might have difficulty accounting for the ease and speed with which 4-month-old infants come to appreciate intermodal relationships of complex kinds, such as the synchrony of speech and expressive movements. But, it is difficult to decide among these theories until we understand the newborn infant's sensitivity to all the available intermodal relationships. Here, again, is a topic on which students of perception and students of social interaction might work together. Careful and systematic observations of infants' social contacts with another person might provide the best suggestions about their abilities, and inabilities, to coordinate auditory and visual information about animate events. The newborn infant's social encounters need to be described and then manipulated to control the information that is available. Such manipulations may elucidate the auditory-visual relationships available to humans at birth, and our inborn capacities to detect these relationships.

The third question concerns the development of perception of people and animate events. This chapter is sprinkled with suggestions about the infant's ability to perceive the attributes, actions, and mental states of a person. But what do infants first perceive in other people, and how does the perception of people develop? On no other question, we believe, does a wedding of studies of social interaction with studies of infant perception hold greater promise. And on no other question has work in the two traditions been more at odds. Within an experimental tradition, most studies of the infant's perception of other people present young babies with photographs or schematic drawings of faces. An implicit or explicit assumption of this research is that infants first become sensitive to static features of faces, then to configurational properties, and later to actions, expressions, communications, and the mental states that give rise to them (see Caron et al., 1973; Fagan, 1972). The simplest displays for a psychologist to describe, it is apparently assumed, are likely to be the simplest displays for a young child to perceive. In contrast, students of social interaction observe infants in natural communicative interactions with active, expressive people. The infant's ability to respond to a person's actions, and even a person's intentions, is sometimes taken as a foundation for other basic perceptual, cognitive, and linguistic developments (see Bruner, 1977; Stern et al., 1977; Trevarthen, 1977). These traditions differ not only in their assumptions and their methods, but also in their findings. Studies of perception of face photographs or drawings suggest a slow development of sensitivity to other people (cf. Carey & Diamond, 1977). Studies of social interaction suggest a rather remarkable competence to perceive others and to participate in social exchanges early in life.

Which view may we trust? Are students of face perception missing the infant's greatest capacities by focusing on impoverished stimulus displays? Or are students of social interaction inflating their estimates of the infant's abilities by focusing on situations in which the infant has an enormous prop: An adult partner who can regulate the social exchange? Does perception of people develop from detecting features to perceiving configurations, acts, and expressions, or is the developmental progression more nearly the reverse? These questions can only be answered by an approach that incorporates the best aspects of the observational and experimental traditions. Studies of the origins of perception of people should endeavor to examine infants in richly informative, social situations, but these studies must attempt to describe each situation and specify the potential sensory information available in it. Only thus can we analyze infants' sensitivity to that information and their ability to make sense of the social encounter.

These questions carry us far beyond the investigations that we have discussed. They point, however, to what we believe is an exciting direction for the study of infant social cognition. Studies of the infant as a perceiver and as a social agent might both benefit from investigations of the infant's perception of the actions, intentions, feelings, and social encounters of human beings. For the student of perceptual development, such research may yield glimpses of the infant's most advanced perceptual capacities, including capacities for coordinating sensory information from different modalities. For the student of social development, such research could shed light on some of the foundations of human social understanding.

ACKNOWLEDGMENTS

We thank Richard Evans, Rochel Gelman, and Philip Kellman for their comments. Preparation of this manuscript was supported by Grant NICHD-13248 to E.S.S.

REFERENCES

Aronson, E., & Rosenbloom, S. Space perception in early infancy: Perception within a common auditory-visual space. *Science,* 1971, *172,* 1161–1163.

Bahrick, L. *Infants' perception of properties of objects as specified by amodal information in auditory-visual events.* Unpublished doctoral dissertation, Cornell University, 1979.

Barrera, M. E. The perception of facial expressions by three-month-old infants. Paper presented at the meeting of the Society for Research in Child Development, San Francisco, March 1979.

Bloom, K. Operant baseline procedures suppress infant social behavior. *Journal of Experimental Child Psychology,* 1977, *23,* 128–132.

Bower, T. G. R. The visual world of infants. *Scientific American,* 1966, *215,* 80–92.

Bower, T. G. R. *Human development.* San Francisco: Freeman, 1979.

Brazelton, T. B., Koslowski, B., & Main, M. The origins of reciprocity: The early mother-infant interaction. In M. Lewis & L. Rosenblum (Eds.), *The effect of the infant on its caregiver.* New York: Wiley, 1975.

Bruner, J. S. Early social interaction and language acquisition. In H. R. Schaffer (Ed.), *Studies in mother-infant interaction.* New York: Academic Press, 1977.

Carey, S., & Diamond, R. From piecemeal to configurational representation of faces. *Science,* 1977, *195,* 312–315.

Caron, A. T., Caron, R. F., Caldwell, R. C., & Weiss, S. T. Infant perception of the structural properties of the face. *Developmental Psychology*, 1973, *9*, 385–399.

Church, J. Techniques for the differential study of cognition in early childhood. In J. Hellmuth (Ed.), *Cognitive studies I*. New York: Brunner Mazel, Inc., 1970.

Cohen, S. E. Developmental differences in infants' attentional responses to face-voice incongruity of mother and stranger. *Child Development*, 1974, *45*, 1155–1158.

Condry, S. M., Haltom, M. Jr., & Neisser, U. Infant sensitivity to audio-visual discrepancy: A failure to replicate. *Bulletin of the Psychonomic Society*, 1977,*9*, 431–432.

Cornell, E. H. Infants' discrimination of photographs of faces following redundant presentations. *Journal of Experimental Child Psychology*, 1974, *18*, 98–106.

Dodd, B. The role of vision in the perception of speech. *Perception*, 1977, *6*, 31–40.

Dodd, B. Lipreading in infants: Attention to speech presented in- and out-of-synchrony. *Cognitive Psychology*, 1979, *11*, 478–484.

Eilers, R. E., Gavin, W., & Wilson, W. R. Linguistic experience and phonemic perception in infancy: A cross-linguistic study. *Child Development*, 1979, *50*, 14–18.

Eimas, P. Speech perception in early infancy. In L. B. Cohen & P. Salapatek (Eds.), *Infant perception II*. New York: Academic Press, 1975.

Eimas, P., Siqueland, E., Jusczyk, P., & Vigorito, J. Speech perception in infants. *Science*, 1971, *171*, 303–305.

Eisenberg, R. B. *Auditory competence in early life*. Baltimore: University Park Press, 1976.

Fagan, J. F. III Infants' recognition memory for faces. *Journal of Experimental Child Psychology*, 1972, *14*, 453–476.

Fantz, R. Pattern vision in newborn infants. *Science*, 1963, *140*, 296–297.

Field, J., DiFranco, D., Dodwell, P., & Muir, D. Auditory-visual coordination in 2 ½-month-old infants. *Infant Behavior and Development*, 1979, *2*, 113–122.

Field, T. M. Visual and cardiac responses to animate and inanimate faces by young term and preterm infants. *Child Development*, 1979, *50*, 188–194.

Fitzgerald, H. Autonomic pupillary reflex activity during early infancy and its relation to social and non-social visual stimuli. *Journal of Experimental Child Psychology*, 1968, *6*, 470–482.

Fogel, A. *Response to maternal leave taking in one- to three-month old infants*. Paper presented at the meeting of the Society for Research in Child Development, San Francisco, March 1979.

Fogel, A., Diamond, G. R., Langhurst, B. H., & Demos, V. *Alteration of infant behavior as a result of "still-face" pertubation of maternal behavior*. Paper presented at the meeting of the Society for Research in Child Development, San Francisco, March 1979.

Friedlander, B. The effect of speaker identity, voice inflection, vocabulary, and message redundancy on infants' selection of vocal reinforcement. *Journal of Experimental Child Psychology*, 1968, *6*, 443–459.

Gibson, E. J. *Principles of perceptual learning and development*. New York: Appleton-Century-Crofts, 1969.

Goren, C. *Form perception, innate form preferences, and visually mediated head-turning in human newborns*. Paper presented at the meeting of the Society for Research in Child Development, Denver, April 1975.

Gottfried, A. W., Rose, S. A., & Bridger, W. H. Cross-modal transfer in human infants. *Child Development*, 1977, *48*, 118–124.

Hainline, L. Developmental changes in visual scanning of face and non-face patterns by infants. *Journal of Experimental Child Psychology*, 1978, *25*, 90–115.

Haith, M. M. Visual scanning in infants. In L. J. Stone, H. T. Smith, & J. B. Murphy (Eds.), *The competent infant*. New York: Basic Books, 1973.

Haith, M. M., Bergman, T., & Moore, M. J. Eye contact and face scanning in early infancy. *Science*, 1977, *198*, 853–855.

Hamm, M., Russell, M., & Koepke, J. *Neonatal imitation?* Paper presented at the meeting of the Society for Research in Child Development, San Francisco, March 1979.

Hayes, L. A., & Watson, J. S. *Neonatal imitation: Fact or artifact?* Paper presented at the meeting of the Society for Research in Child Development, San Francisco, March 1979.

Horowitz, F. D. Visual attention, auditory stimulation, and language discrimination in young infants. *Monographs of the Society for Research in Child Development,* 1974, *39,* (5-6, Serial No. 158).

Hutt, S. J., Lenard, H. G., & Prechtl, H. F. R. Psychophysiological studies in newborn infants. In L. P. Lipsitt & H. W. Reese (Eds.), *Advances in child development and behavior IV.* New York: Academic Press, 1969.

Jusczyk, P. W., Rosner, B. S., Cutting, J. E., Foard, C. F., & Smith, L. B. Categorical perception of non-speech sounds by two-month-old infants. *Perception and Psychophysics,* 1977, *21,* 50–54.

Juscyzk, P. W., Walley, A., & Pisoni, D. B. *Infants' discrimination of tone onset time differences: Some implications for voicing perception.* Paper presented at the meeting of the Society for Research in Child Development, San Francisco, March 1979.

Kessen, W., Levine, J., & Wendrich, A. The imitation of pitch in infants. *Infant Behavior and Devleopment,* 1979, *2,* 93–100.

Koch, J. Conditioned orienting reactions in two-month-old infants. *British Journal of Psychology,* 1967, *58,* 105–110.

Kreutzer, M. A., & Charlesworth, W. R. *Infants' reactions to different expressions of emotions.* Paper presented at the meeting of the Society for Research in Child Development, Philadelphia, March 1973.

LaBarbera, J. D., Izard, C. E., Vietze, P., & Parisi, S. A. Four and six month old infants' visual responses to joy, anger, and neutral expressions. *Child Development,* 1976, *47,* 535–538.

Lewis, M., & Hurowitz, L. *Intermodal person schema in infancy: Perception within a common auditory-visual space.* Paper presented at the meeting of the Eastern Psychological Assocation, Boston, April 1977.

Lieberman, P. *Intonation, perception and language.* Cambridge, Mass.: MIT Press, 1967.

MacDonald, J., & McGurk, H. Visual influences on speech perception processes. *Perception and Psychophysics,* 1978, *24,* 253–257.

Mann, V. A., Diamond, R., & Carey, S. Development of voice recognition: Parallels with face recognition. *Journal of Experimental Child Psychology,* 1979, *27,* 153–165.

Maurer, D., & Salapatek, P. Developmental changes in the scanning of faces by young infants. *Child Development,* 1976, *47,* 523–527.

McGurk, H., & Lewis, M. Space perception in early infancy: Perception within a common auditory-visual space? *Science,* 1974, *186,* 649–650.

Mehler, J., Bertoncini, J., Barriere, M., & Jassik-Gerschenfeld, D. Infant recognition of the mother's voice. *Perception,* 1978, *7,* 491–497.

Meltzoff, A., & Borton, R. Intermodal matching by human neonates. *Nature,* 1979, *282,* 403–404.

Meltzoff, A. N., & Moore, M. K. Imitation of facial and manual gestures by human neonates. *Science,* 1977, *198,* 75–78.

Mendelson, M. J., & Haith, M. M. The relation between audition and vision in the human newborn. *Monographs of the Society for Research in Child Development,* 1976, 41 (4, Serial No. 167).

Muir, D., & Field, J. Newborn infants orient to sounds. *Child Development,* 1979, *50,* 431–436.

Spelke, E. *Recognition of facial identity over varying activities in infancy.* Paper presented at the meeting of the American Psychological Association, Chicago, August 1975.

Spelke, E. Infants' intermodal perception of events. *Cognitive Psychology,* 1976, *8,* 53–60.

Spelke, E. *Intermodal exploration by four-month-old infants: Perception and knowledge of auditory-visual events.* Unpublished doctoral dissertation, Cornell University, January 1978.

Spelke, E. S. The infant's acquisition of knolwedge about bimodally specified events. *Journal of Experimental Psychology,* in press.

Spelke, E. S., & Owsley, C. J. Intermodal exploration and knowledge in infancy. *Infant Behavior and Development,* 1979, *2,* 13–24.

Stern, D. N., Beebe, B., Jaffe, J., & Bennett, S. L. The infant's stimulus world during social interaction: A study of caregiver behaviors with particular reference to repetition and timing. In H. R. Schaffer (Ed.), *Studies in mother-infant interaction.* New York: Academic Press, 1977.

Streeter, L. A. Language perception of 2 month old infants shows effects of both innate mechanisms and experience. *Nature,* 1976, *259,* 39–41.

Sumby, W. H., & Pollack, J. Visual contribution to speech intelligibility in noise. *Journal of the Acoustic Society of America,* 1954, *26,* 212–215.

Trevarthen, C. Descriptive analyses of infant communicative behavior. In H. R. Schaffer (Ed.), *Studies in mother-infant interaction.* New York: Academic press, 1977.

Tronick, E., Adamson, L., Wise, S., Als, H., & Brazelton, T. B. *The infant's entrapment between contradictory messages in face to face interaction.* Paper presented at the meeting of the Society for Research in Child Development, Denver, April 1975.

Turnure, C. Response to voice of mothers and strangers by babies in the first year. *Developmental Psychology,* 1971, *4,* 182–190.

Walker, A. *Perception of expressive behavior by infants.* Unpublished doctoral dissertation, Cornell University, 1980.

Wertheimer, H. Psychomotor coordination of auditory-visual space at birth. *Science,* 1961, *134,* 1692.

Wolff, P. H. Observations on the early development of smiling. In B. M. Foss (Ed.), *Determinants of infant behavior* (Vol. 2). New York: Wiley, 1963.

Young-Browne, G., Rosenfeld, H. M., & Horowitz, F. D. Infant discrimination of facial expressions. *Child Development,* 1977, *48,* 555–562.

5 "Recognition" of Emotional Expression in Infancy?

Harriet Oster
University of Pennsylvania

> *Children long before they can speak, or understand the language of their parents, may be frightened by an angry countenance, or soothed by smiles and blandishments.*
> Erasmus Darwin, 1794 [p. 146]

As the questioning tone of the title suggests, this chapter does not provide conclusive statements about the infant's responsiveness to human expressions of emotion. Studies spanning 50 years have failed to answer the most obvious questions, in part because of serious methodological deficiencies. A deeper problem, however, is the fact that some of the most important—but less obvious—questions have either been ignored or have been addressed only in speculative terms.

Experimental studies have focused almost exclusively on the infant's *discrimination* of emotional expressions.[1] If subjects of a given age respond differentially to stimuli representing different facial, vocal, or gestural expressions, we know that they detected some difference between the stimuli. However, different emotional expressions also differ in their purely physical

---

[1]The term "emotional expression" is used fairly loosely in this chapter to cover distinctive human patterns of facial, vocal, or gestural expression—however these have been defined in the various studies reported. The term includes, but is not limited to, the universally recognizable expressions of emotion such as joy, anger, sadness, fear, surprise, and disgust (cf. Ekman, 1973; Ekman & Oster, 1979; Izard, 1971; Tomkins, 1962). In addition, the term can cover expressions defined in terms of more general dimensions of affective meaning (cf. Scherer, 1979); expressions that may be only vaguely defined in terms of their physical characteristics or meaning (e.g., "frown"); and expressions defined primarily in terms of their signal function (e.g., "threat"). Thus the term as used here is not limited to behavior conveying information about emotion.

stimulus characteristics (intensity, contrast, spatial frequency, temporal patterning, etc.). Therefore, without adequate stimulus controls we do not know if infants' responses were based on differences that are relevant for adults' judgments of emotion. In fact, we cannot even be certain that very young infants perceive the stimuli as human faces or voices. Most investigators have simply ignored this problem. Even with adequate stimulus controls, however, the standard paradigms for testing infants' discriminatory abilities can tell us very little about the nature of an infant's responses to emotional expressions. By itself, a difference in responding cannot tell us what "meaning"—if any—a smiling or angry face, a friendly or scolding voice might have for a 3- or 6-month-old, as compared with a 3- or 20-year-old.

In this chapter, I examine some of these neglected issues and attempt to place them within a broader evolutionary and developmental framework. That is, I ask not only what kinds of distinctions infants can make among emotional expressions, but what adaptive function the ability or inability to make such distinctions might serve, and what role differential responding to emotional expressions might play in early social, emotional and cognitive development. (Do parents' facial and vocal expressions serve as positive and negative reinforcers for infants, as learning theorists assume? Are infants sensitive to subtle signs of ambivalence or hostility in their mother's behavior, as psychoanalytic theorists suggest?)

I begin by examining the preliminary question of whether human expressions of emotion can provide any reliable information about another person's emotional state or behavioral tendencies, and I review the evidence on the recognition of emotion by adults and young chldren. To provide a framework for research on the infant's responses to emotional expressions, I consider what kinds of processes might underlie different facets of the ability to "recognize" emotions at different ages. I then examine the possible biological bases of human responses to emotional expressions, and I ask what kinds of maturational constraints might govern the infant's ability to "recognize" expressions of emotion. Following these discussions, I focus on methodological problems in existing studies and suggest possible solutions to some of these problems. Finally, I suggest new directions for future research and describe some work in progress in my own laboratory.

RECOGNIZING EMOTIONS

The question of whether infants recognize emotional expressions is interesting only if we have reason to believe that the expressions themselves can provide reliable information about emotions, i.e., if there is some consistent relationship between emotional expressions and emotional states.

Opinion on this question—along with interest in infants' discrimination of emotional expression—has recently undergone a major shift.

In the 40 years from 1928 to 1968, there were only four noteworthy studies of infants' responses to emotional expressions (see Table 5.1), and two of these studies were German. During those same 4 decades, most American psychologists were convinced that *adults* could not recognize emotions from facial or vocal expressions. The consensus of opinion, based on the disappointing results of early recognition studies (cf. Landis, 1924; review by Tagiuri, 1969), was that emotional expressions did not provide any consistent information upon which judgments of emotion could be based. The only reliable source of information, it was believed, was knowledge of the stimulus situation.

In an insightful paper, Hebb (1946) rejected the prevailing view: "Human emotions are identified socially without perception of the cause. A wife knows that her husband is annoyed but does not see what he is annoyed about [p. 99]." Hebb (1946) argued instead that the "intuitive process" of recognizing emotions depends on our extensive knowledge of the individual, including his or her past as well as present behavior in circumstances similar to those observed at the moment. Most psychologists and ethologists today would agree that complex processes are called into play when we encounter expressions of emotion in another individual. Expectancies based on our knowledge of another's habitual behavior may well help us to interpret his or her expressions of emotion more accurately. (Such expectancies may likewise play a crucial role in infants' reactions to emotional displays in their caregivers.) It is also true, as Hebb (1946) saw, that in real life we are rarely presented with an isolated, momentary face or voice and asked to label the emotion it expresses.

All of the above notwithstanding, Hebb (1946) was wrong in believing that the momentary patterns of emotional expression themselves provide no consistent information about emotional states. As Ekman, Friesen, and Ellsworth (1972) point out in a critical review, the apparent variability in facial expression reported in these early studies could be largely attributed to variability in the emotional state aroused by a particular stimulus and to variability in the "display rules" governing the overt expression of emotion. Similarly, inconsistencies in observers' judgments of emotion could be largely attributed to the use of stimulus materials that did not adequately represent the intended emotion. If these extrinsic sources of variability are controlled, a close relationship between emotional expressions and emotions can be demonstrated.

There is now convincing evidence that distinctive patterns of facial and vocal expression can be reliably identified even in the absence of other cues (cf. reviews by Ekman, Friesen, & Ellsworth, 1972; Ekman & Oster, 1979;

Scherer, 1979). Cross-cultural studies, including the studies conducted by Ekman and his colleagues in isolated, preliterate cultures (reviewed in Ekman, 1973; Ekman & Oster, 1979), provide very strong evidence that certain "primary" human emotions have universally recognizable facial expressions. Although extensive cross-cultural research on the recognition of vocal expressions of emotion has not been conducted, studies within Western cultures (reviewed by Scherer, 1979) have shown that adults can identify emotional portrayals from vocal cues alone. There is also growing evidence (reviewed by Ekman & Oster, 1979) that observers' judgments of emotion can be accurate as well as reliable, i.e., that they correspond to the feelings actually reported by the observed person.

Although most experimental studies have focused on the subject's ability to label the emotions portrayed by facial or vocal expressions, this is not a necessary or even a frequent way of responding to emotional expressions in real-life situations. As Frijda (1970) noted, "recognition of emotion" often takes the form of anticipating what actions the observed person is likely to take in a given situation. Working independently within a very different theoretical framework, ethologists have confirmed specialized signals, which they call displays, do provide important information about the signaler's behavioral tendencies (cf. Hinde, 1970; Smith, 1977). The findings of ethological studies and recognition experiments are complementary, rather than contradictory. Taken together, they strengthen the conclusion that distinctive expressive patterns can provide reliable and accurate information about the performer.

Recognition of Emotion by Children

We do not know the earliest age at which children can use the information provided by emotional expressions to make accurate inferences about another person's emotional states or behavioral tendencies. On the one hand, data on the discrimination of emotional expressions by young infants are difficult to interpret; on the other hand, there have been practically no studies involving 1- to 2-year olds (cf. reviews by Charlesworth & Kreutzer, 1973; Ekman & Oster, 1979). We do know, however, that by 3 to 5 years of age children can perform a variety of tasks demonstrating a knowledge of the distinctive patterns of facial expression found to be universally recognizable by adults (e.g., happiness, sadness, anger, fear, surprise, disgust).

Preschool children can match photographs of facial expressions to standard photographs of the same expressions posed by different individuals, and they can imitate the expressions shown in these photographs (Hamilton, 1973; Odum & Lemond, 1972). They can correctly identify the facial expressions that correspond to particular emotion terms or to stories depicting emotion-eliciting situations (Borke, 1971; Izard, 1971; Odom & Lemond, 1972; Zuckerman & Przewuzman, 1979), and they can voluntarily produce recognizable facial expressions corresponding to these same emotions. (In all of these studies, certain expressions are found to be more difficult than others, and production tasks are almost always more difficult than matching or identification tasks.) The ability to recognize discrete emotional states from vocal expression appears to develop more slowly (cf. McCluskey, Albas, Niemi, Cuevas, & Ferrer, 1975).

Preschool children's understanding of emotional expressions is also demonstrated by evidence of empathic emotional responses to stories or films depicting emotion-eliciting situations (cf. Feshbach & Roe, 1968; Leiman, 1978; review by Hoffman, 1977). Main, Weston, and Wakeling (1979) have recently presented evidence of "concerned attention" to an adult's distress in 1-year olds, a finding consistent with anecdotal evidence of spontaneous empathic responding in toddlers (cf. Zahn-Waxler, Radke-Yarrow, & King, 1979; review by Hoffman, 1977).

Ethological studies of children's spontaneous social interactions in natural or experimental settings indicate that preschool children have some understanding of the social implications of emotional expressions. According to Ainsworth, Bell, and Stayton (1974), infants begin to show compliance with urgently spoken adult commands ("No!" "Don't touch!") as soon as they are able to venture away from their parents and into potential danger. The authors note that responsiveness to the tones of voice, facial expressions, and gestures accompanying such commands would have clear survival value for the infant [p. 114]. In a notable study of preschool children's social interactions in a laboratory "conflict" situation, Camras (1977) has demonstrated that a child's use of certain facial expressions that had been described in earlier ethological studies as "aggressive" predicted the child's own subsequent behavior and that of his or her partner.

The young child's skills in "recognizing emotions" are by no means fully developed by 3 to 5 years. The ability to interpret and weigh information from a variety of different sources (situational cues, facial, vocal, and gestural expressions, speech, etc.)—some of which may provide conflicting cues— develops more slowly (cf. Bugental, Kaswan, & Love, 1970; Greenspan, Barenboim, & Chandler, 1976; Watson, 1975). Children's understanding of "display rules" also develops more slowly (Saarni, 1979). Nevertheless, these findings show that preschool children possess an impressive array of skills. Although it is unlikely that these skills suddenly emerge full-blown at 2 to 3 years of age, almost nothing is known about their early precursors or developmental history.

THE DIFFERENT FACETS OF RECOGNITION

There is no reason to believe that the various "recognition" skills demonstrated by adults and preschool children reflect a single, unitary process. Different skills, governed by different kinds of mechanisms, may be called into play at different ages and in different circumstances. These various skills all involve the ability to obtain from affect expressions information that is relevant to another individual's emotional state and behavioral tendencies. It is a matter for empirical study to determine what kinds of information infants of a given age are *actually* capable of deriving from affect expressions and what kinds of mechanisms govern their responses at different ages. I attempt here to elucidate the kinds of questions that need to be systematically investigated.

Expressions as Stimulus Configurations

Our first question about infants' responses to emotional expressions is whether young infants can discriminate among different expressions on the basis of the specific configurational cues that are relevant to adults' judgments of emotion, such as raised versus lowered lip corners or rising versus falling voice intonation. The trick is to find out whether infants can perceive the relevant configurational cues independent of potentially confounding cues such as gross differences in contrast, complexity, intensity, or other stimulus dimensions that are not specifically related to human expressions of emotion. To illustrate: A smiling face with flashing teeth would have greater visual contrast than a sad face with closed mouth and downturned lip corners. Young infants might respond differentially to the smiling face solely because of the heightened contrast, without perceiving the crucial differences in the configuration of the facial features.

Even if we could be confident that infants perceived the stimuli just described as faces, they might find the "toothy grin" more attractive simply because bared teeth make the mouth a more salient feature. Unless we can show differential responses to toothy smiles versus *other* facial expressions with bared teeth (e.g., expressions of fear, anger, pain, etc.), we cannot be certain that infants perceived the distinguishing characteristic of a smile, namely the raising of the lip corners and cheeks produced by the action of the *zygomaticus major* muscle. As we shall see later, none of the studies reported to date have even tried to deal with this issue.

If infants can perceive the relevant cues for differentiating emotional expressions, the next question is whether they can also perceive the similarity between two instances of the *same* emotional expression. That is, do they perceive a smile as a smile, regardless of differences in the age, sex, or facial morphology of the person smiling? As noted by Cohen, DeLoache, and

Strauss (1979), this ability to abstract the invariant information from facial expressions is an important part of what we mean by "recognizing" emotional expressions. In adults, this ability extends to the recognition of different versions of a given expression, e.g., smiling with the lips parted or closed. It even extends to the recognition of smiling when this action is blended with other facial expressions. To my knowledge, the development of these abilities in infants has never been studied explicitly.

The preceding set of questions asked whether infants can extract the relevant configurational cues from facial or vocal expressions and whether they can use these cues as a basis for perceiving similarities or differences in expression. In raising these questions, I make no assumptions about the levels of neural information processing that might underlie such abilities. This is a separate and more difficult issue. It is possible, at least in principle, that young infants are equipped with a specific innate mechanism for detecting certain signals such as smiling or crying. Alternatively, all affect expressions might be recognized through the same general kinds of perceptual and cognitive mechanisms that are involved in perceiving ordinary, i.e., nonsocial, stimuli (cf. Banks & Salapatek, in press; Cohen et al., 1979).

Expressions as Signs of Emotion

Evidence that infants of a given age perceive emotional expressions as distinctive patterns of facial, vocal, or gestural activity would not, by itself, tell us whether these patterns conveyed any information about emotion or about particular emotional states to the infants. The ability to obtain information about emotion might take a variety of forms, not all of which would involve complex, higher level cognitive processes. The "recognition of emotion" by young infants might be based on more primitive mechanisms, such as the triggering of an emotional response by specific affect expressions. Such responses might be reactions to the emotion expressed (e.g., a fearful or defensive reaction to an angry face or tone of voice), or they might be "empathic" responses (e.g., signs of distress triggered by the sound of crying). Primitive modes of recognition such as these could be demonstrated by studying the infant's own emotional expressions in response to the stimuli presented. However, as I point out in discussing existing studies, we would need to show sufficient specificity in the relationship between particular stimulus expressions and particular emotional responses in the infant for such evidence to be convincing.

Emotional responses to affect displays in young infants might be based on an "innate releasing mechanism" of some sort (cf. Hinde, 1970), but they might also be based on classical conditioning as Hoffman (1977) points out in discussing reflexive crying in newborns. These alternatives—which are not mutually exclusive—would be exceedingly difficult to tease apart empirically, but in principle it should be possible. Whatever mechanism or mechanisms govern such responses in young infants, relatively automatic, involuntary emotional reactions to intense expressions of emotion in others do not seem to be limited to infancy.

In older infants and toddlers, the "recognition of emotion" begins to involve more complex cognitive processes, including inferences about what another individual—perceived as being distinct from the self—might be experiencing in a given situation. Hoffman's (1977) treatment of developmental stages in empathic responding can serve as a more general guide for conceptualizing the interplay of affect and cognition in infants' "recognition" of emotion in others.

As early as the second year, children begin to understand and use verbal labels for salient affect displays (e.g., crying and laughter) and for the emotions they express (cf. Main, Weston, & Wakeling, 1979; Zahn-Waxler et al., 1979). More systematic research is needed to specify the kinds of situations in which parents and children label their own or one another's feelings and affect expressions. Detailed study is also needed to specify the relationship between the infant's own nonverbal expressiveness and the ability to recognize emotions in others. Previous studies of preschool children (e.g., Buck, 1976; Odom & Lemond, 1972; Zuckerman & Przewuzman, 1979) have examined this question globally, by looking at the correlation between children's overall scores on "encoding" and "decoding" tasks. Far more interesting would be data on children's effectiveness in communicating particular emotions in natural situations and their ability to recognize these same emotions in others.

Expressions as Social Signals

The ability to use another person's nonverbal expressions as a "practical guide to behavior" (cf. Hebb, 1946) may also have roots in early infancy. A hallmark of the developing infant-mother attachment relationship is what Ainsworth, Bell, and Stayton (1974) call a "reciprocal responsiveness to signals." Ainsworth (1973), like Bowlby (1969), believes that this mutual responsiveness is based in large part on strong biological predispositions—an issue that is discussed in the following section. It is also based in large part on individual experience. Through experience, both infant and caregiver begin to develop expectancies about the kinds of responses likely to occur in a range of familiar circumstances.

Rudimentary expectations about social interaction may be present even in early infancy. This is suggested by the finding that 3- to 4-month olds engaging in social interaction with their mother show signs of distress if she suddenly becomes silent and expressionless or turns her attention from the infant (Trevarthen, 1977; Tronick, Adamson, Wise, Als, & Brazelton, 1975).

In other words, the infants behave as though some expectations about their mother's social behaviors or about the "rules" of social interaction had been violated. Beginning in the latter part of the first year, infants become increasingly mobile and increasingly active in pursuing their mothers. They also become increasingly able to anticipate her behavior and to make appropriate adjustments in their own behavior and strategies (Bowlby, 1969).

In natural social interactions, many different sources of information are available to guide the infant, including the social setting, time of day, specific stimulus events, and all aspects of the caregiver's behavior, including nonverbal signals. What is not clear from existing studies is how much the nonverbal signals themselves, as opposed to other sources of information, contribute to the infant's ability to interpret and anticipate the caregiver's behavior in a given situation. That is, can 3- or 6-month-old infants tell from their mother's facial expressions, gaze, tone of voice, and gestures, how likely she is to engage in play or to pick them up? When 1-year olds comply with their mother's commands (cf. Ainsworth, 1973; Main, Londerville, & Townsend, 1980), are they responding specifically to the urgency in her voice, to a particular facial expression or gesture, or to some other aspect of her behavior (e.g., anticipatory movements toward the infant)? How specific is the information that infants obtain from nonverbal signals? (Does the mother's command tell an infant to look at her, to stop what he or she is doing, or that what he or she is doing is dangerous?)

The implicit or explicit assumption that infants at some early age become sensitive to specific positive and negative affect signals has been central not only to modern attachment theory but also to traditional theories of development. Unfortunately, these theories have been vague with respect to all of the pertinent details. Learning theorists assume that the parents' scheduling of positive and negative reinforcers is a crucial factor in shaping their infant's behavior and personality. According to the social-learning model (cf. Gewirtz, 1969), aspects of the mother's appearance and behavior— including her nonverbal affect expressions—acquire reinforcing value by being consistently associated with "primary," functional reinforcers such as food, warmth, relief from physical pain and discomfort, etc. Thus, the mother's face and behaviors such as smiling, vocalizing, and picking up the infant become strong positive reinforcers by association with positive caretaking activities. Gewirtz (1969) notes: "Similarly, aversive social stimulus complexes, such as verbal disapproval, and component responses like frowns, acquire generalized aversive properties by being paired with various functional noxious reinforcers for the individual [p. 69]."

Let us leave aside for the moment the issue of whether certain kinds of social stimuli may actually be primary reinforcers (cf. Gewirtz, 1969). A more urgent question for social-learning theorists is whether emotional expressions, by themselves, have *any* specific reinforcing properties for infants within the first half-year or even year of life. Astonishingly, the relevant data do not seem to exist. Recent reviews of the literature on social conditioning (Millar, 1976; Sameroff & Cavanaugh, 1979) point out the difficulty of disentangling the reinforcing effects of social stimuli from their eliciting effects. This remains a serious methodological problem, but my own reservations stem primarily from another source: namely, that studies using social reinforcers have all confounded the possible reinforcing effects of specific facial or vocal *expressions* with the reinforcing effects of the human face or voice generally.

Most studies of conditioned smiling or vocalizing in 3- to 6-month-olds have used composite social reinforcers, in which a previously impassive experimenter simultaneously smiles, vocalizes, touches the infant, and in some studies picks the infant up. When presented separately, the visual, vocal, and tactile/kinesthetic components of this complex pattern of stimulation are each effective reinforcers, i.e., each increases infant smiling or vocalizing above baseline levels (see Millar, 1976, for a review of these studies). These findings show that an animated facial expression, vocalizing, and other social *behaviors* are important components of social reinforcers. In fact, the continuing presence of an expressionless, unresponsive adult—the "base-line" condition in such studies—may inhibit social responding or may actually be an aversive stimulus (cf. the studies by Trevarthen, 1977, and Tronick et al., 1975, mentioned previously). However, it has not been demonstrated that an animated and responsive but *nonsmiling* face would be any less effective as a reinforcer than a smiling face. Nor has it been shown that a frowning, angry face or an angry tone of voice would be *negatively* reinforcing.

The notion that infants are somehow sensitive to nonverbal signals has also played a key role in psychoanalytic theories of early development. For example, the concept of the "double bind" (cf. Bateson, Jackson, Haley, & Weakland, 1956) presupposes an ability to pick up the often subtle negative messages embedded in the parents' words or overt behavior. Unfortunately, data on how responsive infants actually are to such signals are largely lacking, particularly for infants less than 1 year of age.

In a recent experimental study, Volkmar and Siegel (1979) showed that children as young as 1 to 3 years of age can perceive the negative components of "mixed messages" in which friendly signals in one channel (visual or auditory) are contradicted by negative signals in the other channel. The children in this study were wary and hesitant in approaching a male stranger whose friendly smile and beckoning gesture were accompanied by a coldly spoken command to "stay away." The authors attribute the children's wariness to the discrepancy between channels and not just to the presence of a strongly negative signal. This interpretation is not justified, however, because the study did not include a condition in which the negative visual or auditory component was presented by itself.

Bugental, Kaswan, and Love (1970) studied 5- to 12-year-old children's and adults' judgments of videotaped messages containing various combinations of conflicting cues. (The verbal content, voice tone, or facial expression could be either friendly or unfriendly.) It was found that messages in which the speaker smiled while making negative statements were rated more negatively by children than by adults, who interpreted such statements as "joking." This negative bias was particularly marked if the speaker was a woman. In fact, children tended to discount a woman's positive signals and to rate the total message as negative, or at best neutral, if even one of the three components was negative. The authors conclude: "children, when confronted with a conflicting message, resolve the ambiguity by assuming the worst [p. 655]." In a study of spontaneous parent-child communication in a clinic setting, Bugental, Love, and Gianeto (1971) found that mothers (but not fathers) were as likely to smile while criticizing their children as when praising them. Thus, children may have good reason to discount a woman's smiles.

These findings are suggestive, but the picture is still far from complete. We do not know whether mothers' smiles are equally unreliable signals in more natural settings without a camera present, and we do not know how toddlers and children actually respond to "mixed messages" produced by their own mothers in natural communication situations. Nor do we know whether younger infants are aware of, and give priority to, negative signals that cooccur with positive signals such as smiling.

Psychoanalytic theorists have long viewed the first months of life as crucial for early psychosocial and emotional development. During this period, they hold, emotional conflict in the mother—produced by depression or inadmissible feelings of anger toward her infant—can lead to serious emotional disturbance in the infant. In the light of the findings that have been discussed, it is pertinent to ask how such feelings might be transmitted to the infant.

Spitz and Wolf (1946) described several case studies of infants who failed to smile at the experimenter's smiling face in the second trimester of life—when smiling at human faces is normally at its peak. In each case, according to the authors, the infant had a disturbed relationship with its mother. Furthermore, the authors note: "hostility on the side of the mother towards her child is always present, well repressed behind a surface of syrupy sweetness [p. 111]." How might 3-month-old infants detect this repressed hostility? The authors (1946) suggest that a mother's hostility and anxiety can be transmitted to her infant during the first 3 months of life by tactile/kinesthetic cues, i.e., by rough or awkward handling of the infant: The mother's movements, "perhaps by producing the sensation of lack of security, transmit the emotional attitude of the mother to the infant, via the sense of vibration and deep sensibility [p. 111]." The authors further note that the mother's face is seen by the infant "in innumerable emotionally charged situations, both during feeding as well as in every other situation of child care . . . . [p. 111]." Therefore, by the second trimester, a "visual Gestalt" of the mother's face becomes linked with the infant's total experiences of security or insecurity, of pleasurable or unpleasurable stimulation received from the mother. In cases where this total experience is negative, the human face in general, or the mother's face in particular, fails to become a stimulus for smiling or may even become an aversive stimulus for the infant.

Spitz and Wolf (1946) do not consider the possibility that infants at some age may begin to form associations between specific facial expressions produced by the mother and maternal stimulation experienced as pleasurable or unpleasurable. On the basis of their own experimental study, they believed that infants respond indiscriminately to facial expressions throughout the first half-year of life. Bühler and Hetzer's (1928) earlier study and later studies by Ahrens (1954) and by Kreutzer and Charlesworth (1973) also suggest a lack of differential affective responses to facial, vocal, or gestural signals before 4 to 5 months of age. However, as we see later when discussing these and other experimental studies, this issue is far from being resolved. We need to find out whether infants can detect subtle negative signals, and we also need to find out what infants of different ages can do when such signals are produced by their own mother or by another important person in their life. Data are also needed on the extent to which mothers may "leak" negative feelings through facial, vocal, or gestural signals.

In this section, I have considered three facets of what is commonly called the "recognition of emotion." In dissecting the phenomenon in this way, I hoped to specify more precisely what we need to learn about the infant's developing abilities to obtain information from nonverbal expressions— information about their stimulus characteristics, emotional correlates, and signal value. In each case, I suggested the possibility that young infants might initially respond to such information through fairly "primitive" mechanisms, e.g., classical conditioning or some sort of innate mechanism. In the following section, I consider what kinds of biological biases might govern the development of the ability to "recognize" emotions in others, and I speculate about the possible evolutionary significance of such constraints.

THE BIOLOGICAL BASES OF RECOGNITION

Theoretical Considerations

There is considerable evidence for the universality of the most distinctive human facial expressions (cf. review by Ekman & Oster, 1979). The vocalizations associated with crying, screaming, and laughter are clearly universal, and other aspects of human affective vocalization may also be universal (Scherer, 1979). This does not mean that distinctive human facial and vocal expressions are "innate," in the strong—and outmoded—sense that individual experience is completely unnecessary for their development (cf. Lehrman, 1970). Many questions about the specific roles of genetic factors and experience in the development of emotional expression remain unanswered (cf. Ekman & Oster, 1979; Oster & Ekman, 1978). Nevertheless, evidence from a variety of independent sources (e.g., observation of facial expressions in congenitally blind children and in identical twins, comparison of human and nonhuman primate expressions) suggests that these expressions have a strong biological basis. That is, they are evolutionarily adapted, "environmentally stable" characteristics of the human species and not arbitrarily variable cultural inventions.

Darwin recognized that evidence for the innateness of certain expressive movements does not, by itself, tell us whether the ability to recognize them is innate. Darwin (1872) reasoned, nevertheless, that "there seems to be some degree of *a priori* probability that their recognition would likewise have become instinctive [p. 357]." Modern ethologists point out that the evolution of a specialized communicative signal such as smiling would be accompanied by selection pressure to improve the efficiency of responding to that signal (cf. Hinde, 1974). However, this does not necessarily imply either "innate recognition" of the expression or "innate triggering" of a particular kind of response. Selection pressures for efficient communication may have worked in a variety of ways: The expressions themselves might have become more distinctive and discriminable (a process called ritualization); the sensory and perceptual apparatus might have become more finely "tuned" to particular kinds of stimulus patterns; mechanisms for learning about the emotional correlates or behavioral consequences of particular expressions might have become more efficient; mechanisms for arousing emotion in the receiver might have become more closely linked with the perception of specific expressive patterns in others. Such adaptations could be general purpose or relatively specific to the recognition of emotional expression or to specific expressive patterns.

The question of whether information relevant to specific affect expressions has become genetically "programmed" into the human nervous system cannot be answered on purely theoretical grounds. On the one hand, our responses to nonverbal signals must be flexible enough to be appropriate to the specific circumstances. The ability to integrate many different sources of information in making inferences about another person's emotional state or likely behavior requires a considerable amount of learning and experience. Because the human infant's prolonged period of dependency ensures repeated opportunities for learning, it might be argued that innate mechanisms are altogether unnecessary. On the other hand, the ability to respond appropriately to certain kinds of signals (a smiling or angry facial expression, an urgent tone of voice) might be crucial in early infancy, even before there is a chance for much learning to occur. In addition, as Bugental's data suggest, caregivers' signals may frequently provide contradictory or misleading information that could impede learning. Hence, it is not obvious that "ordinary" perceptual and learning mechanisms would suffice for infants to learn the meaning of signals that are crucial for effective social communication. The question, as Darwin (1872) recognized, is an empirical one: "Do our children acquire their knowledge of expression *solely* by experience through the power of association and reason? [p. 357, emphasis added]"

Empirical Evidence

In light of the foregoing, it would make little biological sense to ask whether the recognition of human affect expressions is based *solely* on innate mechanisms. It makes far more sense to take Darwin's question—quoted in the preceding paragraph—as our null hypothesis and to ask whether human facial, vocal, or gestural expressions have any "special status" as stimulus configurations or as elicitors or reinforcers of human behavior.

In fact, it would be extremely difficult to demonstrate that human beings have any specific "innate recognition mechanism"—above and beyond any innate mechanisms governing the expression of emotion. Opportunities for learning about affect expressions are present from the beginning, and recent studies have shown that human newborns are capable of certain kinds of learning. In studying the development of emotional *expression,* we can take advantage of "natural experiments" such as congenital blindness and deafness to tease apart the specific contributions of genetic programming and experience. This strategy will not work in the case of recognition. "Unnatural" experiments designed to eliminate opportunities for learning (i.e., isolation studies) would be unthinkable with human infants, but such experiments have been conducted with nonhuman primates. Although the findings of these experiments are not directly applicable to human beings, they may give some idea about the range of possible outcomes that we might expect with human subjects.

The best evidence that recognition of certain expressive displays may have an innate basis in nonhuman primates comes from a study by Sackett (1966). Rhesus monkeys were raised in total social isolation for the first 9 months of life. Twice a week, beginning at 2 weeks, the infants were shown slides of monkeys engaged in various activities, and their responses were observed. At 2½ months, the frequency of vocalizations and of "disturbed" behaviors (e.g., rocking, huddling, withdrawal) increased sharply in response to slides of threatening monkeys. From 2½ to 4 months, vocalizations and disturbed behaviors remained significantly more frequent in response to the threat pictures than to any other category of slides. During this same period, when the infants were given the chance to control the slide presentations by pressing a lever, their rate of lever pressing was significantly lower for the slides of threatening monkeys than for other categories. Fearful responses to the slides began to wane after 4 months. Interestingly, throughout the period when fearful responses were at their peak, visual and manual exploration of the threat pictures and even playing with these pictures were also at high levels. (Pictures of infant monkeys also produced higher levels of exploration and play than did other slide categories.) Sackett (1966) interprets the fairly abrupt onset of fearful responses to the threat pictures as evidence for the maturation of an innate recognition mechanism. He points out, however, that in a normal environment the *maintenance* of fearful responses probably depends on learning. Although the infants showed fearful emotional responses to the threat pictures—in the absence of any opportunity for learning their "message"—the fact that they also explored and played with the pictures suggests that the "innate program" for recognizing threat displays allows for a great deal of flexibility in the animal's overt behavioral responses.

Most research on the effects of long-term social isolation in nonhuman primates has been concerned with demonstrating the importance of experience for normal social and emotional development. Because total social isolation creates severe emotional disturbance, it is not surprising to find that monkeys raised under such conditions for the first 6 to 12 months of life are grossly deficient in social skills, including the ability to respond appropriately to species-specific signals (cf. review by Redican, 1975). After 12 months of isolation, these effects cannot be reversed by subsequent social experience. Miller, Caul, and Mirsky (1967) showed that adult monkeys raised in total isolation for the first year performed significantly worse than feral monkeys in a "cooperative-avoidance" testing paradigm. The isolates were ineffective both as "senders" and "receivers" of facial cues signaling the anticipation of shock, even when they were paired with feral monkeys. As "receivers," the isolates showed no reaction at all to the "sender's" televised facial expressions, suggesting that the isolates were not able to use another monkey's expressive behavior as a source of information relevant to their own behavior. Because the disruptive effects of total social isolation are so gross, experiments such as this cannot tell us what kind of knowledge about social signals and their appropriate use infants acquire through normal social experience.

Observations of natural social interactions in a wide variety of nonhuman primates suggest that the ability to use and respond appropriately to social signals is gradually acquired during the first year of life (cf. Redican, 1975). However, there is virtually no systematic data on infants' responses to specific signals such as threats and fear grimaces during the first 3 to 4 months—data that could corroborate Sackett's findings.

Infant monkeys of some species are closely protected by their mothers, and usually they are treated with considerable indulgence by adult males. Thus, they are not often the direct objects of threats. Kaufmann (1966), however, observed nine instances in which mature males in a free-ranging band of rhesus monkeys on Cayo Santiago threatened or even hit approaching infants. In all of these cases, according to Kaufmann, the infants completely ignored the threats and continued to approach, even after being hit or pinned to the ground. These observations suggest that infant monkeys may learn the meaning of threat signals literally "in the school of hard knocks." On the other hand, the infants' apparent obliviousness to the adult's threatening gestures, and their persistence in the face of overtly punishing behavior, suggest the possibility of biological constraints on the infants' ability to recognize or respond appropriately to aggressive displays.[2]

Kaufmann (1966) does not describe these incidents in detail, nor does he mention how old the infants were in each case. He does say that infants in this group first began to approach adult males on their own at around 8 weeks of age. And the one incident he does describe involved a 58-day-old infant, who gave a slight "fear grin" only after being hit for the second time. If the other incidents involved infants of about the same age, Kaufmann's observations would be consistent with Sackett's hypothesis that the ability to recognize threats is maturationally controlled. The fact that the infants in this free-ranging band first began to approach adult males at 2 months and seemed strongly attracted to them also fits nicely with Sackett's finding that infants' exploration of the threat pictures peaked at 2 months, 1 month before their fearful responses peaked.

Evolutionary Biases

In the absence of more systematic data, we can only speculate about the existence and possible adaptive functions of biological mechanisms governing the recognition of affect expressions in nonhuman primates and in human infants.[3] It is possible that there are no special "constraints" on the ability to learn the meaning of nonverbal expressions (cf. Hinde & Stevenson-Hinde, 1973; Seligman, 1970). The failure of young infants to respond

---

[2]It is possible that infants learn to disregard threat displays during the first 2 months of life. This might occur if the mother is occasionally threatened while she is carrying her infant. As no direct harm would come to the infant, the negative implications of this signal would not be learned. This explanation seems unlikely for two reasons. First, mothers carrying infants are infrequently threatened or attacked. Second, the mother's emotional reaction to being threatened could indirectly disturb her infant. In fact, any exposure to threat displays (such as seeing juveniles threatened and then attacked) could teach the infant about the negative consequences of these displays.

[3]In the following discussion, I go back and forth between nonhuman primates and human infants. This is because some of the issues are the same, and not because I believe that the answers will be the same. In fact, it is unlikely that the answers will be the same, given the different rates at which the nervous system matures in monkeys and in human beings.

appropriately to such signals may simply reflect general sensory or cognitive limitations that have nothing to do with the social nature of the stimuli. This seems unlikely in the case of the infant monkeys described by Kaufmann (1966). By 1 to 2 months of age, rhesus infants can undoubtedly resolve the details of an adult male's "direct, open-mouth stares and head-bobbing [p. 22]." They should also be capable of learning to avoid or escape punishment (cf. Hinde, 1974), although I have not found any studies that specifically demonstrate this ability. In the case of human infants, we must carefully consider whether the infants' performance with stimuli representing affect expressions is any better or any worse than it is with other kinds of social or nonsocial stimuli. For example, it is (logically) possible that young infants are relatively insensitive to differences in facial *expression* during the period when they are learning to recognize their mother's face and the faces of other familiar individuals.

Redican (1975) suggests that very young monkey infants have "no real need for appeasement or especially threat gestures [p. 170]" (and presumably no need to recognize such gestures), because the infants are protected from agonistic interactions by their mothers and by the indulgence of other adults. Although plausible, arguments based on a lack of "need" are not wholly satisfactory. A more intriguing possibility is that the ability to produce and to respond "appropriately" to threats and other negative affect signals in early infancy might actually be maladaptive, because such responses would interfere with the infant's development of secure attachment relationships with the mother and with other significant adults in its life. Because of their extreme dependency in the first months of life, human infants—to an even greater extent than rhesus infants—have no place to turn but their caretaker (e.g., mother), sourpuss or not.[4] (The fact that the father, grandmother, or some other person may be a more appealing surrogate does not help in the first months of life because the infant cannot select which person will care for it.)

Given their "captive" status, what can very young infants do with the information that their mother is angry or depressed? If the infant responds "appropriately" (for a 1- or 2-month old) by becoming distressed and crying, this could have the unwanted effect of increasing the mother's anger or depression. In fact, an infant's best "strategy" might be to "assume the best" and smile beguilingly. The case of "Ned S." described by Sander (1969) illustrates how such a strategy might work. According to Sander, when Ned was 2½ months old his smiling response blossomed. "The charm of his smile

---

[4]Commenting on the finding that rhesus infants returned repeatedly to "evil artificial mothers" (mechanical devices designed to repel clinging infants), Harlow, Harlow & Suomi (1971) note: "In retrospect, it should have been obvious—to what else can a frightened, contact-seeking infant cling?"

and his readiness to respond delightfully to a social interaction even by 12 weeks was outstanding [p. 207]." As a result, Ned's mother—a "vigorous, aggressive, garrulous" woman who had been suffering from anxiety and depression and who had avoided contact with her infant—"gradually succumbed to this irresistable influence [p. 207]." Bowlby (1969), Spitz and Wolf (1946), and Wolff (1963) similarly recognized the infant's *active* use of the smile to attract and "win over" the mother. A certain amount of indifference to the mother's initial emotional state may be necessary for this strategy to work.

The ability to discriminate fine nuances of expression and to recognize negative cues embedded in the mother's smiles and "syrupy" tone of voice may become adaptive only toward the end of the first year, when the infant is better equipped (in terms of cognitive and motor skills) to develop more flexible strategies for coping with this information. I am thinking here of Main's recently proposed theory that the syndrome of avoidance of the caregiver in 1-year olds reflects an evolutionarily adapted "alternative strategy" that is available to infants for coping with rejecting or ambivalent mothers (Main, in press). Unlike the limited strategies available to 1- to 2-month-olds, such a strategy would depend on the development of keen sensitivity to the mother's facial, vocal, and gestural expressions.

This line of reasoning suggests that the infant's developing abilities to "recognize" affect expressions may be governed by specific biological predispositions and constraints, which would serve initially to facilitate the development of secure attachment relationships with the mother and other caregivers. Specifically, in the first 3 to 4 months of life, an "optimistic" view of the caregiver's affect expressions might help to initiate and sustain the kinds of social interactions that create mutual satisfaction and delight (cf. Stern, 1977). This hypothesis is purely speculative at present, but it fits with what is known about the young infant's perception of affect expressions, that is: (1) a responsiveness to the animated quality of facial, vocal, and gestural expressions and to expressions that are responsive to (i.e., contingent on) the infant's behavior; (2) a readiness to perceive and reciprocate smiles; (3) an insensitivity to the negative emotional correlates or signal value of negative affect expressions.

The difficult task will be to find out whether these "optimistic" characteristics of the infant's responses to affect expressions are the product of specific biological biases, and not just incidental side effects of an immature nervous system. To demonstrate the former, we would have to show that the infant's pattern of responding to specific affect expressions is peculiarly advanced or retarded in comparison with responses to nonsocial stimuli or even with other aspects of social stimuli (such as visual or auditory features that are relevant to individual recognition). Because the kinds of constraints previously hypothesized might operate differently on different facets of the "recognition" process, we might expect to find inconsistencies in the infant's performance. For example, young infants might show differential visual fixations to positive versus negative affect expressions (indicating discrimination of the stimulus configurations), but smile as readily at the latter as the former. As we see in the next section, such inconsistencies have been found *between* studies. To test this and alternative hypotheses about the development of responsiveness to affect expressions, it will be necessary to design studies that consider more than one facet of "recognition" at a time.

EXPERIMENTAL FINDINGS

Table 5.1 summarizes experimental studies on infants' discrimination of emotional expressions conducted in the last 50 years—or at least those studies that have survived in the literature. In discussing these studies, I focus primarily on methodological problems that are relevant to the issues raised in the preceding sections.

A quick glance at Table 5.1 should reveal a number of major differences between the three "classical" studies conducted before 1960 and the more recent studies. In the three older studies, infants were shown live portrayals of facial expressions, and the experimenter made live, real-time judgments of their emotional responses. Most recent studies have used still photographs or filmed portrayals of facial expressions as stimuli and visual fixation as the response measure. The authors of the recent studies point out the advantages of their procedures over those used in older studies: better experimental control and more "sensitive" response measures. However, it is also likely that these response measures tap different kinds of discrimination processes than those tapped by earlier studies. The fact that recent studies have found evidence of differential responding to smiling versus nonsmiling faces at an earlier age than older studies does not necessarily mean that infants "recognize" smiles (as expressions of emotion or as social signals) earlier than had previously been thought. The question of what various response measures actually measure is dealt with in the final part of this section. But, first I consider some problems associated with the presentation of stimuli.

Stimulus Expressions

The experiments summarized in Table 5.1 used a wide variety of stimulus materials: live portrayals of emotion, drawings presented on paddles, photographs, slides, films, and audiotapes of infant cries. In evaluating these studies, we need to be concerned with two kinds of issues: (1) Did the stimuli adequately represent the target expressions? (2) How can we be sure that

TABLE 5.1
Studies of Infants' Differential Responses to Emotional Expressions

Study	Stimuli & Method of Presentation	Expressions	Dependent Measures	Subjects N, Ages	Findings
Bühler & Hetzer, 1928	Familiar person, live 30-sec. portrayals (each expression presented by itself)	Smiling vs. angry face; friendly vs. scolding voice; coaxing vs. threatening arm gesture	Emotional reactions: neutral, positive, or negative	90 Ss (10/month) 3 mos.:	*Emotional responses to Negative face and voice* 90% positive
				4 mos.:	50–60% negative
				5–7 mos.:	100% negative for face
				6–9 mos.:	100% negative for voice
				10–11 mos.:	Negative responses decline to 25% (face) and 34% (voice), neutral responses increase
					Responses to gestures
				6–7 mos.:	15–35% "show understanding"
				8–11 mos.:	65–100% "show understanding"
Spitz & Wolf, 1946	Live portrayals of facial expressions	Smile vs. a "savage" expression ("rictus")	Smiling	140 Ss, 2–6 mos.:	Indiscriminate smiling

Ahrens, 1954	Paddles with life-size drawing of boy's face; live portrayals of static or dynamic facial expressions and isolated facial movements	Smiling, attention, negative emotional reactions, avoidance	Neutral, smiling, laughing, and crying faces; isolated mouth and brow movements	76 Ss (16/month)	
				2–3 mos.:	a) Smiling at drawings of laughing (L) and neutral (N) vs. crying (C) faces Indiscriminate smiling
				4 mos.:	Differential smiling, 6/16 Ss Negative reaction to C, 3/16 Ss
				5 mos.:	Differential smiling, 11/16 Ss (no negative reactions to C) b) Static, posed expressions
				5–7 mos.:	More smiling to laughing (but not smiling) vs. neutral expression c) Dynamic facial movements
				3–4 mos.:	Smiling to any forehead or mouth movements
				5–7 mos.:	Transient negative responses to horizontal or vertical forehead wrinkles; more smiling to lateral stretching of mouth than to mouth puckering or opening and closing
				8–9 mos.:	Strong negative reaction to horizontal and vertical forehead wrinkles
				9–26 mos.:	More smiling to laughing expression than to lateral stretching of mouth
				10–24 mos.:	Stronger negative reaction to vertical than to horizontal forehead wrinkles

(continued)

Study	Stimuli & Method of Presentation	Expressions	Dependent Measures	Subjects N, Ages	Findings
Wilcox & Clayton, 1968	Films of an actress portraying static and moving versions of 3 facial expressions	Neutral, smiling, and "frowning" faces	Total looking time per presentation	Exp't. 1 (28-sec. exposures) 10 Ss, 5 mos.:	For static expressions only: longer fixation on smile vs. frown and neutral
				Exp't. 2 (60-sec. exposures) 10 Ss, 5 mos.:	No differential responses
Simner, 1971	Recordings of newborn cry, 5½-mo-old cry, computer-synthesized cry	Crying	Crying and physiological measures	235 Ss, 3-days (4 expt's)	More crying to newborn cry sounds than to 5½-mo.-old cry or synthesized cry
Sagi & Hoffman, 1976 (replication of Simner, 1971)	Newborn cry vs. computer-synthesized cry	Crying	Crying	58 Ss, mean age 34 hours	More crying to newborn cry sounds than to synthesized cry
Kreutzer & Charlesworth, 1973	Live presentations of composite expressions including face, voice, and body movement	Neutral, happy, sad, and angry expressions	Ratings of infant attention, activity, and emotional responses (positive, negative, or neutral)	40 Ss, 10 @ each age 4 mos.:	Indiscriminate responses
				6, 8, & 10 mos.:	Sad expression fixated longer than happy, angry, neutral (H = A = N); appropriate emotional response sometimes shown

Study	Stimuli	Conditions	Measure	Subjects	Results
LaBarbera, Izard, Vietze, & Parisi, 1976	Black and white slides of a male actor portraying 3 facial expression	Neutral, joy, and anger faces	Length of first fixation for each presentation	24 Ss, 12 each at 4 & 6 mos.:	Joy fixated longer than both anger & neutral; anger not discriminated from neutral
Young-Browne, Rosenfeld, & Horowitz, 1977	Colored and achromatic slides of a male actor portraying 3 facial expressions. Habituation-recovery paradigm	Happy, sad, & surprised faces	Recovery of looking time to novel expression (vs. decrement in control group)	24 Ss, 3 mos.:	Happy and surprised faces discriminated Recovery to surprise following sad but not vice versa No discrimination of happy vs. sad
Barrera & Maurer, 1979	Color slides of infant's mother's face (Exp't. 1) or of strange woman's face (Exp't. 2). Habituation-recovery paradigm	Smile vs. "frown"	Recovery of looking time to novel expression	Exp't. 1 24 Ss, 3 mos.: Exp't. 2 28 Ss, 3 mos.:	Recovery to mother's smile following frown and vice versa Recovery to stranger's smile following frown and vice versa
Oster & Ewy, 1980	Achromatic slides of a man and a woman portraying 3 expressions. Each infant shown 2 expressions by both models	Groups: 1: "Toothy smile" vs. sad face 2: Closed-mouth smile vs. sad face 3: same as (1), upside down	Total looking time per 30-sec. presentation	24 Ss, 4 mos.: (8 per group)	Group 1: toothy smile fixated longer than sad face Group 2 & 3: no differential responses based on expression

infants were responding to stimulus dimensions that are relevant for adults' judgments of emotion?

In principle, live portrayals of emotion should be the most realistic and therefore the most adequate form of stimulus presentation. This is usually not the case, however. Spitz and Wolf (1946) describe the expression that was supposed to elicit negative responses in infants as "a species of *rictus* or *risus sardonicus*... best described as that of a savage animal baring its fangs [p. 77]" and as "a terrifying expression of savage rage [p. 79]." However, if the photograph used to illustrate this expression (cf. Fig. 5.1) is representative, it is not surprising that 141 of 142 infants smiled at it. At the very least, there is reason to be skeptical about the authors' often-cited conclusion that "the *emotion* expressed in the human face has no significance for the smiling reaction of the child between its third and sixth month [p. 79]."

Even if the negative affect expressions presented are potentially more convincing (cf. the angry face described by Bühler & Hetzer, 1928), they would be difficult to perform in a natural and uniform manner, especially when the audience is an infant on the verge of smiling. The inadequacy of live performances may account in part for the failure of Bühler & Hetzer (1928), Spitz and Wolf (1946), and more recently Kreutzer and Charlesworth (1973) to find consistent differences in infants' emotional responses to positive versus negative affect expressions before the age of 5 or 6 months. However, Ahrens (1954) obtained similar results with drawings that were exaggerated, but fairly realistic, representations of the facial expressions of crying and laughter. Thus, additional factors, apart from the adequacy of stimulus

FIG. 5.1. Illustration of the "savage" expression presented by Spitz and Wolf (1946, p. 78). Copyright 1946 by Spitz and Wolf. Reprinted with permission.

expressions, may account for the consistently observed lack of differential emotional responses in young infants. The high potential for experimenter and observer bias must be considered a serious factor in studies involving live portrayals of expressions and/or live, on-the-spot judgments of the infants' emotional responses.

More recent studies have generally sacrificed the realism of live performances for the greater control of film or slide presentations. However, this does not automatically guarantee adequate stimulus expressions. Wilcox and Clayton (1968) and Barrera and Maurer (1979) do not describe the "frowning" expressions they presented to infants. These expressions probably had some of the components of either sad or angry faces, but they may not have been good full-faced representations of either. Nor are dynamic presentations of facial expressions necessarily better than static poses or still photographs, as shown by Wilcox and Clayton's (1968) findings. In this case, the attractiveness of an animated human face may have created a "ceiling effect" that obscured any discrimination among facial expressions.

Several studies have used "standardized" facial expressions, i.e., configurations shown by cross-cultural research to be universally recognized as expressions of particular "primary" emotions. LaBarbera, Izard, Vietze, and Parisi (1976) used slides from Izard's (1971) series, and two studies (Young-Browne, Rosenfeld, & Degen Horowitz, 1977; Oster & Ewy, 1980) used slides from sets developed by Ekman and Friesen. The dependent variable in these studies and in the Barrera and Maurer (1979) study, which also used slides as stimuli, was some measure of visual fixation. These investigators all found evidence of differential visual fixation to a smiling face versus some nonsmiling expression by 3 to 4 months of life. However, as seen in Table 5.1, the results of these studies are not entirely consistent. It is impossible to make sense of the discrepancies, however, because the experiments differed in so many details.

A more serious problem is that the crucial issue of stimulus control (discussed on p. 90) has been virtually ignored in research on infants' discrimination of facial expressions. As a result, we cannot be certain whether young infants' responses to facial expressions are based on relevant affect cues or solely on confounding stimulus variables such as the heightened contrast produced by bared teeth or widely opened eyes. Ahrens (1954) was the only early investigator who tried to test the specificity of infants' responses to expressive movements such as "smiling" or "frowning." He did this by comparing infants' responses to isolated facial movements that may produce differences in expression without producing gross physical differences (e.g., vertical versus horizontal forehead wrinkles) or vice versa (e.g., smile with lips closed versus a laughing expression). His results, summarized in Table 5.1, suggest that infants' responses are based largely on gross physical cues until late in the first year. (However, the many problems associated with live performances must be considered in evaluating these results.)

Stimulus Control Strategies

The Oster and Ewy (1980) experiment summarized in Table 5.1 is part of a continuing study designed to find out whether young infants are able to perceive the distinctive configurational cues on which adults' judgments of emotion are based. We are following two strategies for dealing with confounding stimulus variables: (1) systematically manipulating both relevant facial cues (e.g., raised versus lowered lip corners) and potentially confounding cues (e.g., bared teeth); (2) presenting facial expressions upside down. Inverted faces contain all of the physical pattern information (except orientation) present in upright faces, but inversion makes it more difficult to process the specifically human configurational information (cf. Diamond & Carey, 1977; Fagan, 1972; Watson, 1966).

Another question addressed by this study is whether young infants treat two instances of the same facial expression as equivalent, even when the expression is posed by two individuals who differ markedly in facial appearance. This issue has been ignored in previous studies, as none of these studies has presented individual infants with stimulus expressions posed by more than one person. By presenting two exemplars of different expressions to each infant, we can be more confident that differential responses are due to differences in relevant facial cues and not to some peculiarity of a particular person's facial features.

The details of the Oster and Ewy study will be reported more fully elsewhere. I here describe the important features of the experimental design and present the pertinent findings from three groups for which complete data are available. The experiment used a single-presentation paradigm to test spontaneous visual preferences. The subjects, 24 4-month-olds (12 male and 12 female), were divided equally into the three groups summarized in Table 5.1. Subjects in each group were shown two expressions posed by both a man and a woman: a sad face and either an open-mouth ("toothy") smile (group 1) or a closed-mouth smile (group 2). Subjects in group 3 were shown the sad faces and the "toothy" smiles upside-down. The three expressions are shown in Figure 5.2.[5]

---

[5]The six stimulus expressions used in the study were selected from a set of 110 achromatic slides published by Ekman and Friesen (1976). In addition to the four slides reproduced in Fig. 5.2, we used two slides showing a closed-mouth smile (PF1-6) and a sad face (PF2-16) posed by the female model in Fig. 5.2. Ekman requested that these two slides not be reproduced here, in order to protect the model's privacy and to discourage researchers from using photographic reproductions, which lack the high technical quality of the original slides.

The emotions portrayed in the six slides used in the study were correctly identified by 93–100% of the adult observers tested by Ekman and Friesen (1976). The "toothy" smiles posed by each model are sightly more intense (in terms of *zygomaticus major* contraction) than the closed-mouth smiles, although both are of moderate intensity. The female model's sad face has clearly downturned mouth corners, whereas the male model's sad face has only a hint of this muscle action (*triangularis*).

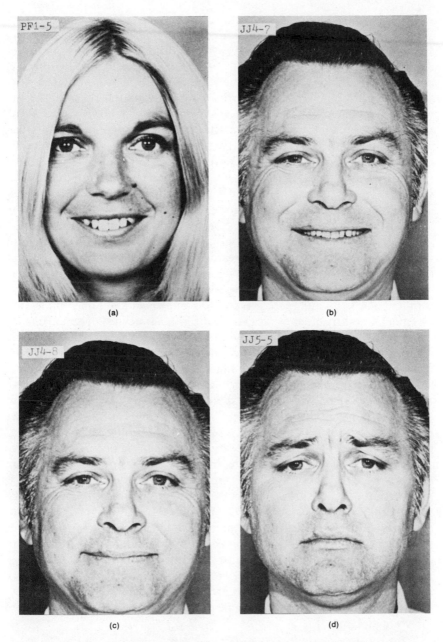

FIG. 5.2. Four of the six stimuli presented by Oster and Ewy (1980): (a & b) open-mouth smile; (c) closed-mouth smile; (d) sad face. Copyright 1976 by Ekman and Friesen. Reprinted by permission.

The four slides shown to each subject were repeated in two trial blocks. Within trial blocks, the two expressions posed by one model were followed by the same two expressions posed by the other model, with order of presentation (happy versus sad face, male versus female model) counterbalanced. Each trial lasted 30 seconds, timed from onset of first fixation. The response measure, scored from videotapes of the infant's face, was total looking time per 30-second trial per subject. The coder did not know the subjects' experimental groups or the expressions presented on a given trial. Half the subjects were scored on a separate occasion by a second coder. Interobserver reliability (Pearson r) averaged .97.

Separate ANOVAs were computed for each group of subjects in a 2 (sex of subject) × 2 (model) × 2 (expression) × 2 (trial blocks) design. These analyses revealed a significant main effect for expression only in group 1: Subjects looked significantly longer at the "toothy" smiles than at the sad faces [$F = 11.71$, $p < .025$]. Subjects in group 2, on the other hand, showed no significant preference based on expression but did look significantly longer at the male than at the female faces [$F = 6.11$, $p < .05$]. By contrast, the subjects in group 3—who saw upside down presentations of the sad faces and "toothy" smiles—showed no differential responding on the basis of either expression or model. The only other significant finding was a decline in visual fixations from the first to the second trial block in all three groups [all $p < .05$].

One strong conclusion and several tentative conclusions can be drawn from these findings. First, the fact that infants looked significantly longer at the "toothy" smiles than at the sad faces in group 1 but not group 3 (upside-down faces) strongly indicates that the subjects in group 1 were responding to differences in *facial configuration,* and not just to purely *physical* differences in contrast, contour, brightness, etc., because the stimulus patterns shown to both groups were identical in these latter respects. A number of studies have previously shown that by 4 months of age infants' responses to faces are affected by orientation, i.e., that the configuration of facial features is important for the infants' perception of *faceness* (cf. Watson, 1966) and also for recognition of individual faces (cf. Fagan, 1972; Hayes & Watson, 1979; review by Cohen et al., 1979). The present study provides the first evidence that the discrimination of facial *expression* by 4-month-olds is also based on configurational cues whose perception depends on the proper orientation of the faces. The fact that the visual responses of subjects in group 1 were governed more by differences in expression than by differences in identity further suggests that expression can be a salient dimension of the human face for young infants.

Unfortunately, it is not yet clear whether 4-month-olds can perceive the *specific* configurational cues that are crucial for distinguishing between sad and happy facial expressions (e.g., cues that may be visible in the lip corners, cheeks, and eyelids, in the brows and forehead, and in the position of the eyes and head). As the subjects in group 2 did not show differential responses to the closed-mouth smiles versus the sad faces, it is possible that infants this age do not "recognize" raised lip corners as a smile without an accompanying flash of teeth. It is even possible that young infants do not perceive the distinctively bowed curvature of the lips produced by *zygomaticus major,* and that they would respond to any lateral stretching of the lips or baring of the teeth—including a fear grimace—as a smile. This was the conclusion reached by Spitz and Wolf (1946) and Ahrens (1954), and it must remain our tentative conclusion until disproved by further evidence.[6]

We are presently testing infants' differential responses to smiling faces versus nonsmiling expressions such as fear faces that have horizontally stretched lips and/or bared teeth. We also expect to test additional groups of subjects to find out when infants are able to perceive the fairly subtle physical cues that distinguish the sad expressions used in this study from neutral faces and from other negative affect expressions (e.g., angry faces with lips pressed).[7] In addition to measuring the infants' visual fixations, we are looking for subtle signs of differential responding in the infants' own facial responses to the various expressions presented.

Of course, the need for adequate stimulus controls applies to vocal as well as visual expressions. The positive and negative tones of voice presented by Bühler and Hetzer (1928) and Kreutzer and Charlesworth (1973) were portrayed live and were therefore subject to the same kinds of problems as live portrayals of facial expressions. In an early study of "reflexive crying" in

---

[6]Although LaBarbera et al. (1976) did not try to compare the effectiveness of closed- versus open-mouth smiles, both the "joy" and neutral expressions that they used as stimuli had closed lips. Using length of first fixation as their response measure, these investigators found a significant preference for the smile versus both the neutral face and an anger expression that had bared teeth (cf. footnote 7). This finding is at odds with the results of other studies (e.g., Ahrens, 1954; Oster & Ewy, 1980) and should therefore be viewed with caution. Before concluding that 3- to 4-month old infants can perceive the distinctive cues to smiling independent of confounding cues, we would need to find similar results with expressions posed by several different models, with another measure of visual preference, and with adequate controls for experimenter and observer bias. (No such controls were reported by LaBarbera et al., 1976).

[7]Wilcox and Clayton (1968, Experiment I) and LaBarbera et al. (1976) did not find differential responses to neutral versus negative facial expressions, though these expressions were discriminated from smiling. No other investigator has reported data on infants' responses to negative versus neutral expressions. Most of the sad, angry, or "frowning" expressions presented to infants in discrimination studies have involved features such as knit and lowered brows, depressed mouth corners, and tightly pressed lips. In terms of their gross physical-stimulus properties, such expressions might differ much less from neutral faces than from a smile with bared teeth. The stimulus expressions presented by LaBarbera et al. (cf. footnote 6) were unusual in that the smiling and neutral faces both had closed lips, whereas the angry face had fully bared upper and lower teeth and glaring eyes—the expression illustrated in Izard (1971, p. 330) (LaBarbera, personal communication). In terms of its striking physical characteristics, we would have expected a significant difference between this expression and the neutral face.

newborns, Bühler and Hetzer (1928) actually presented a crying infant as the stimulus. Simner (1971) has recently provided a more carefully controlled demonstration of this phenomenon. In an attempt to find out which parameters of an infant's cries were effective in eliciting crying in newborns, Simner (1971) compared the relative effectiveness of various tape-recorded stimuli: the spontaneous crying of a newborn and a 5½-month-old, white noise, and a computer-synthesized cry that shared some of the nonvocal stimulus properties of infant crying (e.g., intensity, suddenness of onset, burst–pause patterning, etc.). The spontaneous newborn cry produced significantly more crying in 2-day-olds than the other stimuli. Sagi and Hoffman (1976), using Simner's newborn cry and synthetic cry stimuli, replicated this finding with even younger (1-day-old) infants.

Simner concluded that the infants in his study were responding to vocal properties specific to a human newborn's cry and not just to intensity or other nonvocalic properties. However, a number of nonvocal parameters of crying in newborns (e.g., variability) were not precisely controlled for in the single synthetic cry tape used in these studies. Additional study, involving a greater variety of spontaneous and synthetic cry sounds, is needed to specify which properties of spontaneous infant cries produce crying in newborns. Further research on infants' responses to different noncry affective vocalizations is also needed.

Response Measures

The trend in recent studies has been to use the most "sensitive" response measures available in order to demonstrate differential responding at the earliest possible age. Visual fixation is thought to be a more sensitive measure than smiling or other emotional responses. (Though it may just be that it is easier to measure the different parameters of visual fixation precisely and objectively.) Recovery of fixation following habituation is a more sensitive index than spontaneous visual preferences, and the two studies using this paradigm (Barrera & Maurer, 1979; Young-Browne et al., 1977) have found evidence of differential responding earlier (at 3 months) than other studies.

What most investigators have failed to appreciate fully is that the *need* to use highly sensitive response measures is a sign that the ability to recognize or discriminate among emotional expressions in early infancy may be limited or may be demonstrable only under certain kinds of circumstances or only with particular kinds of stimulus materials or emotional expressions. That this may be the case is indicated by a number of inconsistencies in the findings summarized in Table 5.1: e.g., the fact that infants discriminate smiles from certain nonsmiling expressions but not others; Wilcox and Clayton's (1968) finding that infants showed differential responses with brief, static poses but not with longer or more dynamic presentations; and the fact that infants showed differential responses to a smiling versus a sad or "frowning" face in one habituation study (Barrera & Maurer, 1979) that used the infant's own mother or a female stranger as the model but not in another habituation study (Young-Browne et al., 1977) that used a male model. Unfortunately, few comparisons can be made within studies because most investigators have reported findings based on only one procedure. We do not generally learn about procedures that were abandoned. For example, pilot work for the Oster and Ewy study indicated that it would be difficult to get differential responses with simultaneous presentations of facial expressions. (All of the reported studies have in fact used sequential presentations of the stimulus expressions.)

I do not mean to suggest that young infants are really unable to discriminate among emotional expressions or that differential fixation is not a valid or reliable measure of infants' discriminative abilities. My point in questioning the robustness of the experimental findings is that it is not enough to demonstrate—by whatever procedure and response measure will work— that young infants can respond differentially to emotional expressions. In addition, if we want to test alternative hypotheses about the kinds of biological "constraints" that govern infants' responses to nonverbal signals, we need to explain why some response measures work while others do not. And we need to ask what kinds of recognition abilities are tapped by the response measures that do work.

Visual fixation measures provide useful information about the infant's perception of the stimulus patterns presented. The basic principle is the same regardless of the specific testing paradigm or parameter of visual fixation used: If infants show significant differential responses to the stimuli, we know that they can discriminate between them. Spontaneous visual preferences for one class of stimuli versus another (e.g., smiling versus nonsmiling faces) can provide the additional information that some feature or features of the preferred stimuli have greater power to attract or hold the infant's attention. If confounding cues (such as differences in contrast) have been eliminated, consistent visual preferences may also indicate that the relevant stimulus dimension (e.g., lip corners raised versus lowered) has some special "meaning" for infants. On the other hand, an absence of spontaneous visual preferences—or of other differential responses—is always ambiguous, indicating that either: (1) infants cannot detect any difference between the stimuli; (2) they perceive some difference, but this difference does not make one stimulus more attractive than the other; or (3) some artifact of the experimental procedures or response measure used may conceal whatever preference the infant may have.

Typically, in habituation-recovery or familiarization paradigms, one of two stimuli is presented repeatedly for a fixed number of trials or until some habituation criterion is reached. The other stimulus is then introduced, and recovery of fixations to this more novel stimulus is assessed. Because this technique can induce differential responding to equally "attractive" stimuli, it may provide a more sensitive measure of the infant's discriminative abilities than spontaneous fixation. The greatest value of this technique for the questions raised here is that evidence of recovery to the novel stimulus effectively rules out simple sensory limitations as an explanation for lack of spontaneous preferences.[8] Unfortunately, no study has used both spontaneous response measures and habituation techniques with the same set of stimulus expressions.

Because the differential responses obtained in habituation studies are based on "artificial preferences" (Cohen et al., 1979), they cannot tell us whether differences in facial expression would "make any difference" to infants in real life. Even spontaneous visual fixations provide only limited information about the "meaning" particular emotional expressions might have for infants. Infants may show—or fail to show—differential visual responses for different reasons. As Sackett's (1966) data on infant monkeys show, fear-inducing stimuli may nevertheless have high attentional value. Conversely, infants may spend equally *little* time looking at a stimulus that is merely "boring" as one that is "upsetting."

Measures of infants' spontaneous emotional responses may be better able to tell us whether expressive movements and vocalizations convey any information to young infants about emotion or whether they otherwise serve as meaningful social signals. But infants' emotional responses can also provide ambiguous data. For example, Barrera and Maurer (1979) reported more crying by infants habituated to a "frowning" face than by infants habituated to a smiling face. They interpret this finding as evidence that some 3-month-old infants perceive "some of the social meaning" conveyed by the expressions. However, as the investigators did not present any neutral faces, we do not know whether more infants cried at the frowning faces because they perceived some negative message in them or merely because they found them less interesting as visual stimuli.

Indiscriminate smiling, on the other hand, does not necessarily mean that infants are unable to perceive the negative message conveyed by negative affect expressions. Smiling at sad or angry facial or vocal expressions—

---

[8]In cases where the physical differences between two expressions seem fairly gross (e.g., the anger versus neutral face used by LaBarbera et al., 1976; or the toothy smile versus sad face used by Young-Browne et al., 1977 and by Oster & Ewy, 1980), we would guess that 3-to-4-month-olds are probably able to detect the differences. More precise predictions about what kinds of differences infants of a given age *should* be able to detect can come from estimates of the infants' visual acuity and contrast sensitivity functions and from precise measurement of the visual pattern information in the stimuli (cf. Banks & Salapatek, in press; Dobson & Teller, 1978). However, such predictions must always be tested by direct behavioral measurement.

especially when these are presented live—may instead reflect an overriding tendency for young infants to respond positively to *any* potential social interaction. Unlike the previous example, this ambiguity cannot be resolved simply by using better stimulus controls.

It is possible that the relatively crude response measures used in most previous studies—e.g., the mere presence or absence of smiling and crying—failed to pick up more subtle signs of "recognition" in young infants. The use of unreliable and potentially biased live judgments of infants' emotional reactions in some studies might also have produced "false negative" results.[9] To find out whether this is the case, we will have to look much more closely at the infants' own emotional expressions. In the final section, I mention how this might be done, and I propose some new strategies for obtaining information about the responsiveness of young infants to expressions of emotion.

NEW DIRECTIONS

The Measurement of Infants' Emotional Responses

Precise and objective techniques are available for measuring infants' facial expressions and vocalizations. The most comprehensive and flexible system for describing facial movements is Ekman and Friesen's Facial Action Coding System, or FACS (Ekman, in press; Ekman & Friesen, 1976, 1978). Oster has adapted this system for measurement of infants' facial movements (Oster, 1978b, in press; Oster & Ekman, 1978). Using FACS, it is possible to detect fleeting negative expressions interspersed with smiles. It is possible to distinguish between affectively negative expressions that may precede crying and subtle expressions such as the "knit-brow face," which often precedes smiling and which appears to reflect intense interest or "puzzlement," i.e., an active effort to assimilate a stimulus (Oster, 1978b). It is also possible to obtain quantitative measures of various qualitative aspects of facial movements, such as their duration, intensity, variability, and complexity. These measures differentiate social smiles from rapid-eye-movement (REM) sleep smiles (Oster, 1978a), and they might also reveal subtle differences in

---

[9]The conclusion usually drawn from the findings of Bühler and Hetzer (1928) and Ahrens (1954)—in fact the conclusion drawn by these authors—is that infants show indiscriminate emotional responses until 5 months of age. However, as shown in Table 5.1, roughly half of the 4-month-olds in both studies either failed to smile or showed negative responses to the negative expressions. Compared with the consistently indiscriminate responses of the 2- to 3-month-olds, this suggests that a considerable proportion of infants may begin to show differential responses by 4 months of age.

young infants' reactions to positive versus negative affect expressions. Significant differences might also be found in the timing and sequencing of facial expressions (cf. Oster, 1978b) and in their coordination with gaze direction, vocalizations, or body movements. (Detailed analyses of the facial expressions produced by infants in the Oster and Ewy study described earlier are now under way, but it is too early to report any findings.)

Scherer (in press) reviews recent studies of affective vocalizations in infants and describes modern acoustic- and auditory-analysis techniques that can be used to describe these vocalizations. Such techniques could reveal differences in the quality of infants' vocal responses to different facial and vocal affect expressions. Similarly, there might be subtle differences in the quality of infants' body movements. The most powerful approach is likely to be one that looks at the patterning of two or more responses or that combines behavioral and psychophysiological responses.

The kinds of analyses that have been suggested are laborious and time consuming. Moreover, it is possible that they would yield no more clear-cut evidence of differential emotional responses in young infants than the cruder measures used in earlier studies. This would bring us closer to the conclusion that differences in affect expression—whether detected or not—really do not matter to very young infants.

Between 4 and 6 months of age, infants do begin to show differential emotional responses to affect expressions (Ahrens, 1954; Bühler & Hetzer, 1928; Kreutzer & Charlesworth, 1973; Spitz & Wolf, 1946). The detailed measurement techniques previously discussed should make it possible to determine the specificity and "appropriateness" of their emotional reactions to specific negative expressions such as anger, sadness, or fear. Such data would help to fill in the 18-month gap in the empirical data mentioned earlier.

The use of sophisticated measurement techniques probably extends traditional discrimination paradigms about as far as they can be stretched. At best, these paradigms can provide only indirect evidence concerning some of the theoretical issues raised in earlier sections. Even if we could find evidence of differential visual fixation and emotional responding in young infants, this would not tell us what role responsiveness to emotional expressions might actually play in important aspects of the infant's life such as: early learning, the development of attachment relationships, and the acquisition of social interaction skills. These issues should be investigated more directly and systematically. I here mention two promising research strategies that could be applied.

Conditioning Techniques

As noted by Cohen et al. (1979), conditioning paradigms have been used—like habituation—as a means of testing infants' discriminative abilities by artificially inducing differential responses. In addition, conditioning studies should be able to provide information relevant to two theoretically important questions:

1. Do nonverbal expressions have differential reinforcement value for young infants? That is, will infants "work" as hard for reinforcement when the "reward" is a negative affect expression as they will when it is a positive expression?
2. Are there any special constraints on the infant's ability to learn about the potential behavioral consequences of positive versus negative affect expressions in another persons? That is, how easily can infants learn to use specific positive and negative affect expressions as discriminative stimuli in different kinds of learning situations?

I have recently begun to investigate these questions in my own laboratory.

Microanalysis of Social Interactions

Data on the discriminative abilities of infants in experimental situations cannot tell us whether or not the infants would be responsive to differences in spontaneous expressions in naturally occurring social interactions. Stern's microanalytic studies of mother-infant interaction have documented features of the mother's expressive behavior that seem ideally suited to attract and hold the attention of young infants and to lead them through the basic "steps" of dyadic interaction (cf. Stern, 1977; Stern, Beebe, Jaffe, & Bennett, 1977). Stern's work further suggests that a crucial aspect of the mother's performance is its exquisite timing and sensitivity to feedback from the infant's facial expressions and vocalizations (cf. Stern & Wasserman, 1979). As mentioned earlier, infants show signs of distress if the mother suddenly becomes expressionless and unresponsive in the middle of an ongoing interaction (Trevarthen, 1977; Tronick et al., 1975). It is not known, however, whether infants or even toddlers are responsive to changes in facial or vocal expression per se, or whether they respond differentially to specific expressions.

I have begun to look for evidence of differential responding in unstructured face-to-face interactions between mothers and their 2- to 4-month-old infants. Although my analyses are still too preliminary to provide answers to the questions raised, one problem—for statistical analysis and presumably for the infants—has become clear: Some mothers have a nearly constant smile on their lips while playing with their infants. In three separate 6-minute episodes (when her infant was 10-, 12-, and 14-weeks-old), one mother smiled from 40 to 50% of the time. This makes smiling (as defined by the presence of *zygomaticus major* action) part of the background facial activity. However, big "toothy" smiles did seem to have the quality of discrete events in this mother and seemed to elicit or intensify her infant's smiles. This example should make it clear that defining the mothers' expressions and the infants' responses is not a straightforward task. Finding out whether the infants' expressions are nonrandomly related to the mothers' expressions will be even more difficult.

SUMMARY AND CONCLUSIONS

I have suggested throughout this chapter that different facets of what is loosely referred to as the "recognition of emotion" are likely to have different behavioral correlates, different biological bases, and different developmental histories. To complicate matters still further, different "solutions" to the problem of how infants acquire the abilities to recognize and respond appropriately to another person's nonverbal signals may be found for different emotions, different modes of expression (face, voice, body movement), and different kinds of natural or experimental situations.

The empirical evidence concerning the actual discriminative abilities of young infants is fragmentary and often methodologically flawed. Therefore, we cannot yet specify the effective cues for young infants' responses to distinctive expressions such as a smiling face or the sound of a newborn's cry. Because the period from 6 months to 2 years has been largely ignored in recent studies, we do not know when infants are able to perceive and finely discriminate the specific patterns of facial and vocal cues that are relevant for adults' judgments of emotion. Even less is known about the infant's responsiveness to nonverbal expressions *as* signs of emotion and *as* social signals.

In attempting to review what is known about the "recognition of emotion" in infancy and to define the kinds of questions that remain to be investigated, it is useful to view the phenomenon within a broader evolutionary and developmental perspective. I have therefore drawn on theories and findings from a wide variety of sources: the work of modern ethologists, nonhuman primate research, research on "social conditioning" in human infants, the literature on the infant-mother attachment relationship, recent "micro-analytic" studies of infant-caregiver social interaction, and experimental studies of infants' discrimination of emotional expressions.

Though incomplete, the available data from all of these sources suggest three alternative hypotheses: (1) Infants in the first 3 to 6 months of life may be unable—because of the immaturity of their sensory systems—to discrimate among facial or vocal expressions that differ in physically subtle ways. (2) They may be *peculiarly* insensitive to differences in emotional expression or *peculiarly* slow to learn the negative message conveyed by affectively negative expressions. (3) They may be able to discriminate between positive and negative expressions and may even be "sensitive" to their meaning at some level, but they may have an overriding tendency to respond positively (i.e., by smiling) to a human face or voice. I have suggested that such a tendency might in fact be adaptive, because "appropriate" (i.e., negative) responses to negative signals could interfere with the development of secure attachment relationships. Although speculative, these are eminently testable hypotheses.

The theoretical and empirical questions raised in this chapter are too complex to be resolved by any single testing paradigm or response measure. Unfortunately, existing studies have not compared several different infant responses to the same set of stimuli, e. g., visual fixations and spontaneous emotional responses. Nor have they specifically examined how difficult or easy it is to obtain differential responses at different ages—a question that is relevant to the issue of possible biological constraints. Moreover, traditional discrimination paradigms may be intrinsically limited in their ability to answer important questions about the infant's *use* of the information conveyed by emotional expressions. I have, therefore, proposed several new approaches that may be able to provide more direct answers to the questions raised. Although this chapter has raised far more questions than it has answered, I hope that by spelling out the questions and putting them within a broader framework it provides new impetus to research in this neglected area.

ACKNOWLEDGMENTS

I am indebted to W. John Smith and Mary Main for their thoughtful comments on an earlier draft of this manuscript.

REFERENCES

Ahrens, R. Beitrag zur Entwicklung des Physiognomie- und Mimikerkennens. *Zeitschrift für experimentelle und angewandte Psychologie,* 1954, *2,* 412–454.

Ainsworth, M. D. S. The development of infant-mother attachment. In B. M. Caldwell & H. N. Ricciuti (Eds.), *Review of Child Development Research,* (Vol. 3). Chicago: University of Chicago Press, 1973.

Ainsworth, M. D. S., Bell, S. M., & Stayton, D. J. Infant-mother attachment and social development: 'Socialization' as a product of reciprocal responsiveness to signals. In M. P. M. Richards (Ed.), *The integration of a child into a social world.* Cambridge, England: Cambridge University Press, 1974.

Banks, M. S., & Salapatek, P. Infant pattern vision: A new approach based on the contrast sensitivity function. *Journal of Experimental Child Psychology,* in press.

Barrera, M. E., & Maurer, D. *The perception of facial expressions by the three-month-old.* Paper presented at the Biennial Meeting of the Society for Research in Child Development, San Francisco, March 1979.

Bateson, G., Jackson, D., Haley, J., & Weakland, J. Toward a theory of schizophrenia. *Behavioral Science,* 1956, *1,* (4), 251–264.

Borke, H. Interpersonal perception of young children: Egocentrism or empathy? *Developmental Psychology,* 1971, *5,* 263–269.

Bowlby, J. *Attachment and loss* (Vol. 1). New York: Basic Books, 1969.

Buck, R. *Human motivation and emotion.* New York: Wiley, 1976.

Bugental, D., Kaswan, J. W., & Love, L. R. Perception of contradictory meanings conveyed by verbal and nonverbal channels. *Journal of Personality and Social Psychology,* 1970, *16,* 647–655.

Bugental, D., Love, L. R., & Gianetto, R. Perfidious feminine faces. *Journal of Personality and Social Psychology,* 1971, *17,* 314–318.

Bühler, C. & Hetzer, H. Das erste Verständnis für Ausdruck im ersten Lebensjahr. *Zeitschrift für Psychologie,* 1928, *107,* 50–61.

Camras, L. A. Facial expressions used by children in a conflict situation. *Child Development,* 1977, *48,* 1431–1435.

Charlesworth, W. R., & Kreutzer, M. A. Facial expressions of infants and children. In P. Ekman (Ed.), *Darwin and facial expression.* New York: Academic Press, 1973.

Cohen, L., DeLoache, J., & Strauss, M. Infant visual perception. In J. Osofsky (Ed.), *Handbook of infant development.* New York: Wiley, 1979.

Darwin, C. *The expression of the emotions in man and animals.* Chicago: University of Chicago Press, 1965. (Originally published in 1872.)

Darwin, E. *Zoonomia* (Vol. 1). New York: AMS Press, Inc., 1974. (Originally published, 1794).

Diamond, R., & Carey, S. Developmental changes in the representation of faces. *Journal of Experimental Child Psychology,* 1977, *23,* 1–22.

Dobson, V., & Teller, D. Y. Visual acuity in human infants: A review and comparison of behavioral and electro-physiological studies. *Vision Research,* 1978, *18,* 1469–1483.

Ekman, P. Cross-cultural studies of facial expression. In P. Ekman (Ed.), *Darwin and facial expression: A century of research in review.* New York: Academic Press, 1973.

Ekman, P. Methods for measuring facial action. In K. Scherer & P. Ekman (Eds.), *Handbook on methods in research on nonverbal communication.* New York: Cambridge University Press, in press.

Ekman, P., & Friesen, W. *Pictures of facial affect.* (Brochure and slides). Palo Alto, Cal.: Consulting Psychologists Press, 1976.

Ekman, P., & Friesen, W. *Facial action coding system.* Palo Alto, Cal.: Consulting Psychologists Press, 1978.

Ekman, P., Friesen, W., & Ellsworth, P. *Emotion in the human face.* New York: Pergamon, 1972.

Ekman, P., & Oster, H. Facial expressions of emotion. *Annual Review of Psychology,* 1979, *30,* 527–554.

Fagan, J. F. Infants' recognition memory for faces. *Journal of Experimental Child Psychology,* 1972, *14,* 453–476.

Feshbach, N. D., & Roe, K. Empathy in six- and seven-year-olds. *Child Development,* 1968, *39,* 133–145.

Frijda, N. H. Emotion and recognition of emotion. In M. B. Arnold (Ed.), *Feelings and Emotions: The Loyola Symposium.* New York: Academic Press, 1970.

Gewirtz, J. Mechanisms of social learning: Some roles of stimulation and behavior in early human development. In D. A. Goslin (Ed.), *Handbook of socialization theory and research.* Chicago: Rand McNally, 1969.

Greenspan, S., Barenboim, C., & Chandler, M. J. Empathy and pseudo-empathy: The affective judgments of first- and third-graders. *The Journal of Genetic Psychology,* 1976, *129,* 77–88.

Hamilton, M. L. Imitative behavior and expressive ability in facial expression of emotion. *Developmental Psychology,* 1973, *8*(1), 138.

Harlow, H. F., Harlow, M. K., & Suomi, S. J. From thought to therapy: Lessons from a primate laboratory. *American Scientist,* 1971, *59,* 538–549.

Hayes, L. A., & Watson, J. S. *Facial orientation of parents and elicited smiling by infants.* Unpublished manuscript, University of California, Berkeley, 1979.

Hebb, D. O. Emotion in man and animal: An analysis of the intuitive processes of recognition. *Psychological Review,* 1946, *53,* 88–106.

Hinde, R. A. *Animal behaviour: A synthesis of ethology and comparative psychology* (2nd ed.). New York: McGraw-Hill, 1970.

Hinde, R. A. *Biological bases of human social behaviour.* New York: McGraw-Hill, 1974.

Hinde, R. A., & Stevenson-Hinde, J. (Eds.). *Constraints on learning: Limitations and predispositions.* New York: Academic Press, 1973.

Hoffman, M. L. Empathy, its development and prosocial implications. In C. E. Keasey (Ed.), *Nebraska Symposium on Motivation* (Vol. 25). Lincoln: University of Nebraska Press, 1977.

Izard, C. E. *The face of emotion.* New York: Appleton-Century-Crofts, 1971.

Kaufmann, J. H. Behavior of infant rhesus monkeys and their mothers in a free-ranging band. *Zoologica,* 1966, *51,* (No. 1–12), 17–27.

Kreutzer, M. A., & Charlesworth, W. R. *Infants' reactions to different expressions of emotions.* Paper presented at the biennial meeting of the Society for Research in Child Development, Philadelphia, March 1973.

LaBarbera, J. D., Izard, C. E., Vietze, P., & Parisi, S. A. Four- and six-month-old infants' visual responses to joy, anger, and neutral expressions. *Child Development,* 1976, *47,* 535–538.

Landis, C. Studies of emotional reactions: II. General behavior and facial expression. *Journal of Comparative Psychology,* 1924, *4,* 447–501.

Lehrman, D. S. Semantic and conceptual issues in the nature–nurture problem. In L. R. Aronson, E. Tobach, D. S. Lehrman, & J. S. Rosenblatt (Eds.), *Development and evolution of behavior. Essays in memory of T. C. Schneirla.* San Francisco: Freeman, 1970.

Leiman, B. *Affective empathy and subsequent altrusim in kindergarten and first-grade children.* Paper presented at the annual meeting of the American Psychological Association, Toronto, August 1978.

Main, M. Avoidance in the service of proximity. In K. Immelmann, G. Barlow, M. Main, & L. Petrinovitch (Eds.), *Behavioral Development: The Bielefeld Interdisciplinary Project.* New York: Cambridge University Press, in press.

Main, M., Londerville, S., & Townsend, L. *Compliance and aggression in toddlers.* Unpublished manuscript, University of California, Berkeley, 1980.

Main, M., Weston, D., & Wakeling, S. *"Concerned attention" to the crying of an adult actor in infancy.* Paper presented at the meeting of the Society for Research in Child Development, San Francisco, March 1979.

McCluskey, K. W., Albas, D. C., Niemi, R. R., Cuevas, C., & Ferrer, C. A. Cross-cultural differences in the perception of the emotional content of speech: A study of the development of sensitivity in Canadian and Mexican children. *Developmental Psychology,* 1975, *11,* 551–555.

Millar, W. S. Operant acquisition of social behaviors in infancy: Basic problems and constraints. In H. W. Reese (Ed.), *Advances in child development and behavior* (Vol. 11). New York: Academic Press, 1976.

Miller, R. E., Caul, W. F., & Mirsky, I. A. Communication of affects between feral and socially isolated monkeys. *Journal of Personality and Social Psychology,* 1967, *7,* 231–239.

Odom, R. D., & Lemond, C. M. Developmental differences in the perception and production of facial expressions. *Child Development,* 1972, *43,* 359–369.

Oster, H. *Early social smiling: Reflex-like response or expression of affect?* Paper presented at the annual meeting of the American Psychological Association, Toronto, August 1978. (a)

Oster, H. Facial expression and affect development. In M. Lewis & L. A. Rosenblum (Eds.), *The Development of affect.* New York: Plenum, 1978. (b)

Oster, H. Measuring facial movement in infants. In P. Ekman & W. Friesen (Eds.), *Analyzing facial action.* New York: Plenum, in press.

Oster, H., & Ekman, P. Facial behavior in child development. In A. Collins (Ed.), *Minnesota Symposia on Child Psychology* (Vol. 11). Hillsdale, N.J.: Lawrence Erlbaum Associates, 1978.

Oster, H., & Ewy, R. *Discrimination of sad vs. happy faces by 4-month-olds: When is a smile seen as a smile?* Unpublished manuscript, University of Pennsylvania, 1980.

Redican, W. K. Facial expressions in nonhuman primates. In L. A. Rosenblum (Ed.), *Primate behavior: Developments in field and laboratory research* (Vol. 4). New York: Academic Press, 1975.

Saarni, C. Children's understanding of display rules for expressive behavior. *Developmental Psychology*, 1979, *15* 424–429.

Sackett, G. P. Monkeys reared in isolation with pictures as visual input: Evidence for an innate releasing mechanism. *Science*, 1966, *154*, 1468–1472.

Sagi, A., & Hoffman, M. L. Empathic distress in the newborn. *Developmental Psychology*, 1976, *12*, 175–176.

Sameroff, A. J., & Cavanaugh, P. J. Learning in infancy: A developmental perspective. In J. Osofsky (Ed.), *Handbook of infant development*. New York: Wiley, 1979.

Sander, L. W. The longitudinal course of early mother-child interaction: Cross-case comparison in a sample of mother-child pairs. In B. M. Foss (Ed.), *Determinants of infant behavior* (Vol. 4). New York: Wiley, 1969.

Scherer, K. Nonlinguistic vocal indicators of emotion and psychopathology. In C. E. Izard (Ed.), *Emotions in personality and psychopathology*. New York: Plenum, 1979.

Scherer, K. Assessment of vocal expression. In P. B. Read & C. Izard (Eds.), *Measuring emotions in infants and children, New York: Cambridge University Press, in press.*

Seligman, M. E. P. On the generality of the laws of learning. *Psychological Review*, 1970, *77*, 406–418.

Simner, M. L. Newborn's response to the cry of another infant. *Developmental Psychology*, 1971, *5*, 136–150.

Smith, W. J. *The behavior of communicating: An ethological approach*. New York: Cambridge University Press, 1977.

Spitz, R. A., & Wolf, K. M. The smiling response: A contribution to the ontogenesis of social relations. *Genetic Psychology Monographs*, 1946, *34*, 57–125.

Stern, D. N. *The first relationship: Infant and mother*. Cambridge, Mass.: Harvard University Press, 1977.

Stern, D. N., Beebe, B., Jaffe, J., & Bennett, S. L. The infant's stimulus world during social interaction: A study of caregiver behaviours with particular reference to repetition and timing. In H. R. Schaffer (Ed.), *Studies in mother-infant interaction*. New York: Academic Press, 1977.

Stern, D. N., & Wasserman, G. A. *Intonation contours as units of information in maternal speech to pre-linguistic infants*. Paper presented at the meeting of the Society for Research in Child Development, San Francisco, March 1979.

Tagiuri, R. Person perception. In G. Lindzey & E. Aronson (Eds.), *The handbook of social psychology*, 2nd ed. (Vol. 3). Reading Mass.: Addison-Wesley, 1969.

Tomkins, S. S. *Affect, imagery, consciousness* (Vol. 1). *The positive affects*. New York: Springer, 1962.

Trevarthen, C. Descriptive analyses of infant communicative behavior. In H. R. Schaffer (Ed.), *Studies in mother-infant interaction*. New York: Academic Press, 1977.

Tronick, E., Adamson, L., Wise, S., Als, H., & Brazelton, T. B. *The infant's response to entrapment between contradictory messages in face-to-face interaction*. Paper presented at the meeting of the Society for Research in Child Development, Denver, March 1975.

Volkmar, F., & Siegel, A. Young children's responses to discrepant social communications. *Journal of Child Psychology and Psychiatry*, 1979, *20*, 139–149.

Watson, J. S. Perception of object orientation in infants. *Merrill–Palmer Quarterly*, 1966, *12*, 73–94.

Watson, M. S. *A developmental study of empathy: Egocentrism to sociocentrism or simple to complex reasoning?* Paper presented at the meeting of the Society for Research in Child Development, March 1975.

Wilcox, B. M., & Clayton, F. L. Infant visual fixation on motion pictures of the human face. *Journal of Experimental Child Psychology*, 1968, *6*, 22–32.

Wolff, P. H. Observations on the early development of smiling. In B. M. Foss (Ed.), *Determinants of infant behavior* (Vol. 2). New York: Wiley, 1963.

Young-Browne, G., Rosenfeld, H. M., & F. D. Horowitz, F. Infant discrimination of facial expressions. *Child Development*, 1977, *48*, 555–562.

Zahn-Waxler, C., Radke-Yarrow, M., & King, R. Child rearing and children's prosocial initiations toward victims of distress. *Child Development*, 1979, *50*, 319–330.

Zuckerman, M., & Przewuzman, S. Decoding and encoding facial expressions in preschool-age children. *Environmental Psychology and Nonverbal Behavior*, 1979, *3*, 147–163.

Note: The following study (which used facial expressions posed by two actors) came to my attention after final revision of the manuscript: Nelson, C. A., Morse, P. A., & Leavitt, L. A. Recognition of facial expressions by seven-month-old infants. *Child Development*, 1979, *50*, 1239-1242.

6 Individual Differences in Parental Sensitivity: Origins, Components, and Consequences

Michael E. Lamb
University of Utah

M. Ann Easterbrooks
University of Michigan

Because "parental sensitivity" refers to a characteristic of adult behavior, a chapter on this topic may appear misplaced in a volume concerned with infant social cognition. Obviously, we think otherwise. Several of the chapters in this volume portray parental sensitivity as a determinant of individual differences in infant social cognition; we see it as perhaps *the* most important determinant of these individual differences. Unfortunately, neither parental sensitivity nor the mechanisms whereby its postulated effects are mediated have ever been discussed in any detailed fashion. The present chapter represents a synthesis of our evolving notions regarding parental sensitivity as well as a selective review of the literature on this topic.

Parental sensitivity may be defined as an adult's tendency to provide contingent, appropriate, and consistent responses to an infant's signals or needs. All three of these defining characteristics are important. The temporal relationship between the adult's and the infant's behavior (*contingency*) is important because this permits the infant to associate its behavior and the behavior of its interactive partner. In order for any association to be learned, however, members of the same two classes of behavior have to be associated repeatedly, hence the importance of behavioral *consistency*. But regardless of the consistency of cooccurrence, all behaviors cannot be associated with equivalent ease. Some stimuli and responses seem to complement one another in ways that facilitate the formation of associations, whereas other stimulus–response pairings are difficult to establish. Furthermore, some responses are aversive to infants, whereas others elicit pleasure: The nature of the infant's emotional reaction to the adult affects the salience on the adult's behavior. Consequently, the *appropriateness* of the adult's response is also important.

It is difficult to identify precisely which infant behaviors may serve as the stimuli that elicit adult responses. The "signals" referred to in our definition of sensitivity are diverse. Some may be as explicit as cries or as imprecise as gross motor activity. The "needs" may be as interpretable and unambiguous as the need for food or as diffuse as the need for the type of cognitive stimulation appropriate for a given age and condition.

As far as the adult's behavior is concerned, we need to consider four stages in the response process. The adult has to *perceive* the infant's signal or need, *interpret* it correctly, *select* an appropriate response from her/his repertoire, and *implement* it effectively. A deficiency in any of these stages of the reception-response sequence could result in behavior that would be labeled insensitive. There are, in sum, many ways of behaving insensitively and many reasons for behaving insensitively. We believe that the effects on the infant's development will differ accordingly.

Before pursuing this issue, we need to address a more fundamental question about the manner in which parental sensitivity affects infant social cognition. In order to understand this, it is helpful to consider the intellectual status of newborn infants. Neonates have limited perceptual and cognitive capacities: They have no knowledge of the independent existence of objects and thus no expectations regarding the behavior of persons and things. The first step in the development of social cognition may involve distinguishing between social and nonsocial stimuli. One difference between people and inanimate objects, Watson (1966) argues, is that people are more likely than objects to respond contingently and consistently. In fact, he continues, contingent responsiveness probably serves as the cue whereby social and nonsocial objects are distinguished.

Lamb argues in the next chapter that the contingent responsiveness of people has another major consequence for infants. From the repeated occurrence of sequences in which the infant's behavior serves as the stimulus eliciting a predictable adult response, the baby learns that its behavior can elicit environmental consequences. Lamb proposes that a simple stimulus (infant behavior)–response (adult behavior) association is established first. It is clear that associations can be formed without the organism's awareness, however, and we propose that awareness of the S–R association follows the realization that the adult's response is predictable. What occurs next is the most important development—the infant recognizes that it is effective, that it can elicit responses, and thus that it partially determines its own experiences.

To the extent that the adult's behavioral responses are consistent and predictable, therefore, the baby develops specific expectations of other people as well as the realization that it is an effective social agent. The development of a sense of personal effectance and the development of expectations regarding others' behavior are the major aspects of infant social cognition affected by parental sensitivity. Individual differences in the nature of the parent's behavior obviously affect both of these developments. Variations in the consistency, promptness, and quality (the nature of the response and the valence of the affect elicited) of the adult's behavior undoubtedly influence his or her representation in the infant's mind (see also Lamb, this volume).

In this chapter, we focus primarily on the origins and nature of individual differences in parental behavior. (A more extensive discussion of the ways in which parental behavior affects the course of infant development is provided by Lamb in the next chapter). Four perspectives on the nature and importance of parental sensitivity are discussed in the first section. Instead of attempting to review the literature comprehensively, however, we present only those propositions and notions that contribute most to our present understanding of parental sensitivity. Our perspective draws upon all four of the approaches reviewed, for we believe that their notions (at least those we discuss) should be viewed as complementary rather than incompatible with one another. We have indicated where we perceive incompatibilities or proposals with which we disagree.

Thereafter, we turn our attention to the origins of individual differences among parents. Here we argue that the variations one observes are the product of interrelations among several influences—notably the parents' personality traits, their infants' characteristics, and the values and attitudes characteristic of their social environment. Finally, we present a brief summary of the evidence concerning the manner in which parental sensitivity affects infant social development. Although the amount of research conducted thus far has been limited, the results are sufficiently impressive to encourage further research on the origins, components, and consequences of individual differences in parental sensitivity.

PERSPECTIVES ON SENSITIVITY

We are certainly not the first theorists to speculate about the importance of parental sensitivity, and our notions have been influenced by many others. In this section, we review four theoretical perspectives (the ethological, psychoanalytic, social learning, and "organismic") on the definition and role of parental sensitivity in infant development. These theories represent very different approaches to developmental psychology, yet they all emphasize the formative significance of sensitivity. On the other hand, they conceive of and operationally define sensitivity in different ways and they pay varying degrees of attention to issues concerning individual differences among parents. Our position is a synthesis, which draws somewhat on all of these perspectives.

The first theorists to discuss the concept were the psychoanalysts. Not surprisingly, given their emphasis on the significance of the mother-infant relationship, they focused exclusively on maternal sensitivity. Theorists like

Brody and Axelrad (1978) operationally defined sensitivity by reference to quality of affect and empathic response, pacing and tempo, and tactile stimulation. Sensitivity, in their view, involved the ability to monitor infant signals attentively, to perceive them accurately, and to respond both appropriately and contingently. Psychoanalysts perceive sensitivity as a personality trait, and consequently they discuss these characteristics as if they tend to covary. Unfortunately, their data do not permit one to assess the assumption that individuals are equivalently sensitive in all aspects of the response selection and implementation sequence. We think it more likely that the abilities to monitor signals, interpret them, select responses, and respond smoothly and appropriately vary independently and are probably influenced by different personality characteristics and attitudes (as discussed later). In any event, when psychoanalysts discuss the effects of variations in maternal sensitivity, they do not accord equal importance to these abilities; rather, they focus on the response implementation and imply that the temporal contingency and the affective quality of the mother's behavior have the greatest impact on the development of the infant's expectations regarding her accessibility and trustworthiness (Erikson, 1950).

Since Freud (1905) proposed that oral experiences were particularly important during the first 18 months of life, it is not surprising that psychoanalysts have especially emphasized maternal behavior and responsiveness in the feeding situation. Psychoanalysts generally believe, however, that personality traits are consistent over time and across situations. Even though they emphasize the formative significance of maternal sensitivity during feeding, therefore, they believe that the sensitivity evidenced in the feeding situation will be accompanied by comparable sensitivity in other situations. For similar reasons, they believe that the behavior and personality patterns established during the infant's first months of life directly predict personality traits that will still be evident during the latency period (6–12 years) and even at the onset of puberty (Brody & Axelrad, 1978). Furthermore, the effects of early parental behavior are deemed irreversible; even if a mother behaves sensitively in later developmental periods, she cannot compensate for the negative consequences of earlier insensitivity during a formative developmental phase. Thus, continuity in child behavior and personality is ensured by a broad psychological base established through early infant-mother interaction.

Psychoanalysts can certainly claim credit for stimulating interest in parental sensitivity, and it is clear that their position has had a major effect on many of the other theorists that we discuss. In the case of the ethological-attachment theorists (Ainsworth, 1969, 1972; Bowlby, 1969), an initial training in psychoanalysis undoubtedly contributed to the emphasis they place on maternal sensitivity. Like the psychoanalysts, Ainsworth views sensitivity as a stable maternal personality trait whose origins have not been explored in detail. On the other hand, the psychoanalysts have only been concerned with *whether* or not maternal insensitivity affects infant personality development. Neither their researches nor their theories have attempted to explain *how* maternal sensitivity affects infant behavior. The ethologists—particularly Ainsworth—attempt to remedy this deficiency by introducing the concept of genetically predisposed behavior propensities. Bowlby and Ainsworth propose that infants are born with the capacity to promote proximity to, and contact with, adults via signaling behaviors ("precursor attachment behaviors"), and that biological predispositions motivate adults to respond to infant signals. These signals may vary in their degree of clarity or readability, but the effectiveness of the infant's signals is wholly dependent upon the propensity of adults to respond to them. The contingency and appropriateness of maternal responses are believed to pace the development of the infant-mother attachment relationship. In a recent paper, Ainsworth (1977) wrote:

> [Securely attached infants] experienced a contingent feedback from their actions in a fairly consistent way. Such feedback makes it relatively easy for a baby to build up a set of expectancies about what his mother will do in each of a variety of sets of commonly-occurring circumstances. He gradually builds up a working model of his mother, in representational terms, as someone in whom he can have confidence as being accessible and responsive when he wants or needs her. Therein lies his feeling of security in his relations with her [p. 6]

In the course of interaction with its mother, thus, the baby develops expectations regarding the predictability of her responses to its behaviors and cues. By way of an associative learning mechanism, the infant comes to associate its own signals (e.g., crying) with a predictable adult response (e.g., being picked up). It also comes to associate the person involved (mother) with the response itself, and to associate mother with contingent responsiveness. The repeated occurrence of the signal-response sequence permits the infant to recognize the relationship between its behavior and its mother's behavior. When mother is sensitively responsive, the infant develops an expectation that she is accessible and can be relied upon to respond in a prompt and appropriate manner. This trust in the reliability of the mother lays the foundation for a secure attachment relationship. In addition, the infant learns that its own actions elicit predictable responses, and so comes to develop a sense of personal effectance. Quite clearly, Ainsworth's description of the manner in which sensitivity affects development is very similar to the one we outlined in the opening paragraphs, and that which Lamb presents in the next chapter.

Infants also develop expectations, of course, when their mothers are consistently inaccessible and either noncontingently or inappropriately responsive. When mothers are consistently insensitive, however, infants learn that their mothers cannot be relied upon to meet their needs, and insecure attachment relationships result. When mothers are inconsistently sensitive (that is, when they sometimes response contingently and appropriately, and sometimes do not) infants may fail to develop clear expectations regarding their predictability. Again insecure attachment is the result. These types of insecure relationships have very different consequences, however, as we shall show later.

Like the psychoanalysts and the ethological-attachment theorists, the "organismic" theorists—Brazelton (e.g., Brazelton, Koslowski, & Main, 1974), Sander (1975, 1977; Sander, Stechler, Burns, & Lee, 1979), and Stern (1974a, 1974b)—seem to view sensitivity as a personality trait. They differ from both the analysts and the ethologists, however, in emphasizing very early interactions (those in the first months of life). Furthermore, they believe that the crucial component of parental sensitivity is an aptitude for monitoring and interpreting infant signals. These theorists imply that any adult can emit an appropriate response provided that she or he can interpret the signal and thus determine what would be appropriate. Another major difference between these theorists and the others we have discussed lies in the portrayal of the neonate's cognitive capacity. We believe that infants develop expectations as a consequence of extensive interaction, whereas many of these theorists believe that infants are born with innate expectations regarding the structure or pattern of social interactions. Brazelton (e.g., Brazelton, Yogman, Als, & Tronick, 1979, and personal communications) implies that sensitive parents do not *create* expectations, but *fulfill* the infant's expectations by meshing their behavior with the infant's in order to achieve behavioral synchrony or reciprocity. In addition, sensitive adults should be able to read the innate cycles of attention–withdrawal in the baby's behavior and pattern their interactive behavior accordingly.

To Brazelton and Stern, sensitivity refers to the parent's ability to attend to cues regarding the infant's state, and to appreciate the baby's need for withdrawal (from stimulation and attention) following bouts of intense interaction. The sensitive parent recognizes the baby's attempts to elicit interaction and respects the baby's occasional need to be without stimulation. The parent can bring the baby to, and hold it in, the alert state that is optimal for reciprocal exchange and adjust his or her own rhythm and behavior to that of the baby in order to insure behavioral synchrony. The timing, quality, and content of the sensitive parent's response varies depending on the baby's activity level and affective mood.

From reciprocal exchanges with a sensitive and responsive adult, the infant learns what effects its behavior has on others. It thus develops a notion of its own effectance and acquires the ability to act intentionally. From interacting with a specific partner, furthermore, the baby develops expectancies about the partner's behavior and, if the interaction is mutually satisfying, the infant will seek further interaction with that person preferentially. Organismic theorists do not discuss the ontogenetic relationship between the innate expectations of people in general and these expectancies of specific people. Presumably, the latter develop in accordance with the substantiation or violation of the baby's initial "hypotheses." In any event, interaction (whose smoothness partly depends on the adult's sensitivity) affects communicative competence, cognitive mastery, the development of early coping strategies, and the understanding of social interaction. Notice that the organismic theorists emphasize both cognitive and social outcomes, whereas the psychoanalysts focus on the establishment of personality traits, and the ethological-attachment theorists stress the development of affective bonds.

Both Brazelton and Stern have been influenced by Louis Sander (1964), who has described a series of developmental stages in which the infant's social needs differ. Throughout these stages, Sander proposed, the sensitive mother is aware of the infant's capacity to perceive and process stimulus input and is able to intermesh her behavior and the infant's cyclic needs. Both Brazelton and Sander (e.g., 1977) emphasize the infant's need for physiological and psychological homeostasis in the first months and see the cycling of attention and nonattention as a manifestation of the baby's innate homeostatic mechanism.

A final and rather diverse group of theorists (Gewirtz, Watson, Lewis) now merit scrutiny. All three stress the temporal contingency of infant signals and parental responses, and pay less attention to the sources of individual differences among parents. Opinions differ concerning the importance of qualitative aspects of parental behavior, infant effects on parental sensitivity, and the role of biogenetic factors in determining whether contingency per se will be reinforcing and whether it will affect the development of perceived effectance.

As noted earlier, Watson (1966, 1979) proposes that contingency is the cue permitting the infant to distinguish between social and nonsocial objects: People respond contingently, objects do not. Watson proposes that the occurrence of contingent parental responses affects the development of infant social responsiveness, but he fails to detail the mechanisms by which contingency affects development. He treats contingency itself as a stimulus and suggests that because parents are the most consistent providers of contingent reinforcement, the baby pays special attention to people and to the context of contingent stimulation. Through repeated experiences with contingently responsive adults, infants learn the efficacy of operating on the environment. A baby reared in a social environment that is not contingently responsive will fail to develop a sense of perceived effectance; having developed perceptions regarding its own ineffectiveness in controlling its environment, it will manifest "learned helplessness" instead (Seligman, 1975), and this will have a negative effect on conditionability.

Gewirtz (1977) has also written about the importance of contingent parental responsiveness; unlike Watson, he proposes that infant temperament affects parental responsiveness. Even a parent predisposed to respond promptly and frequently, he argues, will become less responsive if the infant cries inexplicably and extensively, because such an infant will become an aversive stimulus. This claim differs from that of ethological-attachment theorists like Bell and Ainsworth (1972) who believe that maternal responsiveness affects the amount of infant crying not the reverse.

According to Gewirtz, an attachment forms when the characteristics of a social object acquire the ability to regulate the child's behavior. Consequently, the contingency of parental response provides the reinforcement necessary for an attachment to form. Attachments form despite variations in the quality of interaction, provided the adult's behavior is contingent and positively valenced. (Attachment, in Gewirtz' terms (1972), involes "positive stimulus control.") Gewirtz does not attempt to explain why "attachments" are formed to objects that do not respond contingently (e.g., blankets), or why infants only become attached to some, not all, sources of contingent reinforcement (Rajecki, Lamb, & Obmascher, 1978).

A somewhat different approach is suggested by Lewis and Goldberg (1969). They propose that from a variety of contingent experiences with the parent, the baby learns that its behavior can produce events in the environment. Strict operant-learning models (like Gewirtz's) do not account for changes in the occurrence of behaviors other than those that are specifically reinforced. Lewis and Goldberg, by contrast, believe that parental responses not only reinforce particular behaviors; they also show that acting upon the environment is worthwhile. In other words, parental responses are reinforcing and yield expectations on the part of the infant. These expectations, in turn, motivate the infant to repeat the particular action and to develop new skills that were not specifically reinforced in the past. The positive interactional behaviors of both adult and infant complement and reinforce each other, thus creating feelings of efficacy in parent and infant alike. Thus, perceptual, cognitive, and social motivation and development are all fostered.

Overview

We have certainly not provided a comprehensive review in the foregoing paragraphs, but we have attempted to represent the stated position of each theory or theorist concerning the role of parental sensitivity. Clearly, there is remarkable agreement that parental sensitivity is an extremely important influence on early infant development. Furthermore, there is near unanimity regarding the assertion that it is through interaction with sensitive adults that infants develop a notion of their own effectance. Another consequence of parental sensitivity—infant trust in specific others—is not discussed explicitly by the social learning theorists, although its development is certainly not inconsistent with their analysis of sensitivity and the development of effectance. Indeed, as the concepts are defined here, it is hard to conceive of an infant developing a perception of its own efficacy in relation to both the social and nonsocial environments without developing some form of trust. For the most part, the theorists concur that parental sensitivity assures the occurrence of contingent behavioral associations and that the perception of these is crucial to the development of social expectations. Brazelton perhaps deviates furthest in proposing that there are innate expectations regarding social interaction, but he does not explain how parental sensitivity, in interaction with these, facilitates the development of perceived effectance and trust. Unfortunately, Brazelton cites no empirical evidence to bolster the plausibility of his proposal, which appears to be at variance with other evidence concerning neonatal capacities (see Lamb, this volume). It is more parsimonious to believe that social expectations do not antedate but develop out of social experiences.

In a later section of this chapter, we discuss the consequenes of parental sensitivity more thoroughly, taking up at that point the development of individual differences among infants. Before doing so, however, we wish to discuss the origins of individual differences in the behavioral sensitivity of adults because it is to these that we attribute major differences among infants. We have alluded to differences among parents in the present section, but it is necessary to deal with the issues more thoroughly. Those theorists who have discussed these issues have attributed individual differences in sensitivity to different sources. We propose, however, that the disagreement is not a major one, for all of the sources of influence discussed—personality traits, situational and attitudinal factors, infant characteristics—are likely to affect sensitivity, and there is no reason why they could not operate synergistically. Indeed, it seems most reasonable to presume that they do operate in this fashion. In the next section, we discuss each of the influences on parental sensitivity in turn, while attempting to demonstrate the interrelatedness of their effects and modes of influence.

INFLUENCES ON PARENTAL SENSITIVITY

The effects of parental sensitivity on infant development have been discussed by theorists of many persuasions. It is clear to all that there are marked individual differences in the degree to which parents are sensitively responsive to their infants. It is widely believed, furthermore, that these individual differences largely determine variability in infant sociability and social cognition. The pervasive influence of variations in parental sensitivity makes it imperative that we identify the factors that determine and affect individual differences among parents.

The determinants of individual differences among parents have elicited some discussion in the past, although some factors have been discussed more extensively than others. No one, however, has yet attempted to synthesize the diverse views on this topic, possibly because the views tend to be associated with particular theoretical perspectives. In this section, we present our own views as well as those of the theorists from whom we have drawn.

Before discussing determinants of individual differences in parental responsiveness, however, we should address a broader question: Why do parents respond to infant signals at all? Ethologically-oriented theorists propose that adults—especially parents—are biologically predisposed to respond to infant signals. Lorenz (1935) suggests that the features of the infant's face elicit nurturant behavior, and several studies have shown that the smiles and cries of infants elicit autonomic responses (changes in blood pressure, skin conductance, and heart rate) that are the physiological precursors of the types of behavioral responses that the signals appropriately elicit (e.g., Frodi, Lamb, Leavitt, & Donovan, 1978; Murray, 1979). Other theorists, particularly social-learning theorists, are not persuaded by arguments regarding biological predispositions. Instead, they argue that infant signals, like any other stimuli, gain meaning by virtue of their association with certain contexts and experiences. Adults respond to infant signals, they propose, because they have learned that they are expected to do so, and/or because reinforcement has followed most prior interventions (e.g., the baby terminated its aversive cry). Individual differences among parents are viewed by social-learning theorists as consequences of different rearing conditions (i.e., the insensitivity of some parents results from inadequate opportunities to learn societal expectations about parenting). Social-learning theorists thus expect large individual differences in sensitivity. The ethological orientation, meanwhile, implies that there will be less variability among parents because responding to infant signals is biologically determined—at least in part. All theorists would likely agree that previous parenting experiences enhance parental sensitivity.

The origins of individual differences in parental sensitivity are complex indeed. Many factors in combination determine whether an adult will respond to an infant signal, the response latency, and the quality of the response itself. We believe that three types of factors influence parental sensitivity: enduring personality characteristics, situational influences on psychological state, and characteristics of the infant itself. Individual differences among parents may be influenced by the interaction among these variables, which means that the relative importance of the influences on parental sensitivity varies quite substantially.

Personality-Trait Approaches

Most early discussions of parental sensitivity implied that it reflected enduring personality traits or predispositions. This is not surprising because psychoanalytic theorists—proponents of a trait view of personality—were the first to address this issue. Acceptance of the idea that parental sensitivity is in some way influenced by enduring personality traits is expressed in most discussions of sensitivity and ours is no exception.

It seems likely that certain personality characteristics affect whether or not adults respond to particular infants signals, as well as the contingency and quality of the responses. Thus the phases of the perception-interpretation-selection-response sequence may be differentially affected by various personality characteristics. Several characteristics appear to be especially relevant—notably self-centeredness and adaptability. Self-centeredness affects the extent to which the parent monitors the infant's state and signals, as well as the evaluation/interpretation of the signal/need, the care with which an appropriate response is selected, and finally, the latency of the response (if any). Self-centeredness may lead to insensitivity when adults fail to put the infant's needs before their own desires.

The characteristic ways in which people approach and adapt to new situations also influence the quality of their parenting. Adaptability may be reflected in the adult's ability to tolerate ambiguity; parents who are able to tolerate some ambiguity are likely to be more sensitive. This may be especially important in the first few months during which behavior is less organized, the infant's cues are less distinct and differentiated, and the infant is less "readable."

Parental rigidity or flexibility also affects the assessment and accurate evaluation of new situations. The potential for accurately evaluating novel or ambiguous situations may also be limited by the tendency to react reflectively or impulsively. Related to this is each individual's "response-elicitation threshold"—a person will be more sensitive if subtle or low-intensity infant cues are perceived and responded to than if the intensity of the signal must escalate before a response is elicited. Persistence will affect how long parents attempt to soothe distressed infants, how patient they are in attempts to elicit and maintain the infant's alert state, and how likely they are to try alternative strategies for achieving desired goals when initial strategies are ineffective. Mood and irritability undoubtedly influence all the aforementioned characteristics.

Many of the notions discussed in the preceding paragraphs have been discussed by psychoanalysts, who believe that enduring personality characteristics are the primary (if not exclusive) determinants of individual differences in parental sensitivity. The psychoanalysts who have written about maternal sensitivity most extensively typically relate personality characteristics to sensitivity rather loosely (Brody, 1956; Brody & Axelrad, 1978). They define sensitivity by emphatic and consistent responsiveness to the infant in physical caretaking routines (primarily feeding). Mothers who were deemed to be sensitive later appeared to be more intelligent, friendly, thoughtful, and self-assured than less sensitive mothers. They also demonstrated more empathy, positive affect, and pride regarding their infants, and they were more supportive of their infants in testing situations. Mothers who were less sensitive provided more superficial accounts of their infant's home behavior, lacked the candor and self-assuredness of the sensitive mothers, and seemed cold, detached, and narcissistic during the interviews. Less sensitive mothers exhibited more anxiety and less positive affect when interacting with their infants; during the infant testing sessions, they seemed remote, negative, and/or intrusive. Intellectual or emotional problems appeared to cause inadequate maternal behavior, especially when the emotional difficulties stemmed from unresolved conflicts concerning the developmental phase that the infant was approaching or negotiating.

It is clearly necessary to specify *which* personality traits affect the ability to monitor, interpret, and respond appropriately to infant signals or behaviors and *why* they have this effect on maternal behavior. In her discussion of maternal neglect, Brody identified five traits that could yield insensitive behavior. *Ignorance,* in her view, produced a failure to monitor and interpret infant's signals, to recognize distress readily, and to adjust to the child's age-appropriate needs. *Intolerance* caused a failure to allow enough time to attribute correct motivation to the child's behavior; intolerant mothers also had expectations incongruent with their infant's capabilities. *Disinterest* brought a reluctance to be responsive to the child's needs, *excessive indulgence* a failure to exert the necessary control over the child's desires and demands, and *carelessness* a failure to monitor the infant's environment so as to insure the optimal amount and type of stimulation.

Further research regarding the effects of personality traits on maternal sensitivity has been conducted by representatives of the ethological-attachment theory. Our own perspective has been influenced by the work of Ainsworth and her colleagues (Ainsworth, Bell, & Stayton, 1971; Ainsworth, Blehar, Waters, & Wall, 1978) who identified several maternal characteristics that predict qualitative differences in later infant-mother attachment. The key dimension along which mothers were differentiated assessed the degree of *sensitivity* evident in the accurate perception of infant signals and the execution of prompt, appropriate responses. In addition to the *sensitivity-insensitivity* dimension, mothers differed with respect to: (1) their *acceptance (rejection)* of infant needs and desires; (2) the degree to which they *cooperated (interfered)* with the baby's wishes; and (3) the degree to which they were *accessible to (ignored)* their infant's signals. Using these four scales, Ainsworth et al. identified three types of mothers. One group consisted of mothers who were unempathic and emotionally unexpressive, became irritated when their infants' demands interfered with their own wishes, were relatively rigid (obsessive-compulsive) in their behavior, and showed an observable aversion to physical contact with their infants. This aversion was attributed to the mothers' anger with, and rejection of, their babies. These mothers were insensitive to infant signals and inaccessible to their infants. They took longer to respond to infant cries than did more sensitive mothers, failed to cooperate with their infants' desires, and expressed anger about, and rejection of, their infants. Another group displayed their insensitivity to infant signals differently. These women, too, frequently delayed responding to infant distress signals, or else ignored the infant cues altogether. Although they were not averse to physical contact with their babies, these mothers did not evince the tender mode of holding characteristic of the more sensitive mothers. Instead, they typically held their infants only in the course of physical caretaking routines. Finally, the sensitive mothers (group 3) were characterized by warm, empathic interaction, contingent responsiveness to infant distress cues, acceptance of the many needs and demands of young infants, and a tender, careful way of holding their babies. In Ainsworth's view, the mothers' personalities greatly affected the way in which they interacted with their infants.

Situational and Attitudinal Determinants of Parental Sensitivity

Personality characteristics certainly affect parental sensitivity, but we are convinced that they are not the sole determinants of variation in sensitivity. Elsewhere, Lamb has discussed the impact of situational and attitudinal factors, particularly the attitudes and values involved in decisions concerning maternal employment (Lamb, Chase-Lansdale, & Owen, 1979; Lamb, Owen, & Chase-Lansdale, 1980). In these discussions, as well as in the present chapter, the central concept is the adult's perception of his/her efficacy as a parent (Goldberg, 1977). Parents who believe that they are effective see themselves as competent caretakers and believe that the interactions between themselves and their infants are enjoyable for the infants. Parental skill, of course, is not the only relevant factor here. The infant's temperament, readability, predictability, and responsiveness influence the effectiveness of any adult intervention. The same behavioral intervention may rapidly soothe one infant yet seem totally ineffective when another infant is involved, leading the parents of these two infants to reach very different conclusions about their competence as parents. Through the quality and contingency of their responses, infants have a major impact on their parents' perceived effectiveness.

Perceived effectance is likely to affect parental sensitivity because the parent who feels effective is reinforced and thus motivated to engage in further interaction. The greater the amount of interaction, the greater the opportunities to learn how to read the infant's signals, interpret them correctly, and respond appropriately. Furthermore, the more rewarding the interaction, the more motivated is the parent to seek "quality" interaction again.

The quality of infant-parent interaction is not the sole determinant of perceived effectance, however. How parents define their paternal or maternal role affects the manner in which they evaluate their interactions and appraise their effectance. Consider, for example, two parents who repeatedly fail in their efforts to elicit pleasurable responses in play with their infant. If a father defines his role as that of socializer and playmate, his perceived effectance may be affected quite seriously. If a mother defines her role as one involving physical caretaking and nurturance, however, her perceived effectance may be less affected by the same experience than his is.

The assessment of one's effectiveness as a parent may have a major impact on self-esteem: Parents who consider themselves highly effective as parents may have their self-esteem enhanced. The link between perceived effectance and self-esteem is not a necessary one, however, because being an effective parent may be less important to some individuals than to others. When parenthood is valued highly, perceived effectance will have a major impact on self-esteem. On the other hand, individuals who value parenthood less may suffer little decline in self-esteem if they are ineffective parents.

The amount of time that parents have available to care for and interact with infants, and the quality of the interactions themselves, affect both perceived effectance and sensitivity because the greater the amount of interaction, the more experience the parent has reading and interpreting infant signals and implementing responses. Particularly in nontraditional families in which both parents work, however, time may be at a premium. The amount of time actually available for interaction with the infant may vary depending on the availability of support systems. Practical assistance (e.g., housekeeping) from their husbands enables working mothers to spend more time with their babies than would otherwise be possible. Other types of support—such as access to practical information about child development and child rearing—may also be comforting. Even more important is the emotional and attitudinal support available to women who are, or wish to be, employed outside the home. The husbands', relatives', and peer groups' attitudes toward maternal employment crucially affect guilt about working (if the women do work), resentment of the infant (when they wish to work but do not), self-esteem, role satisfaction and—via these mediating variables—perceived effectance and sensitivity.

Variables such as self-esteem and perceived effectance probably affect sensitivity in both mothers and fathers. It is likely, however, that some determinants of parental sensitivity are different in men and women. We now explain why we believe this to be the case.

Differential Determinants of Paternal and Maternal Sensitivity

Father-infant interaction had not been studied at all until recently (Lamb, 1976, 1978a). Even when fathers were considered, as in Brody and Axelrad's (1978) study, they were considered only as "husbands of mothers." From interviews, Brody and Axelrad determined that the men and their wives held similar attitudes and that fathers were more involved with sons than with daughters. Father-child interactions were not systematically considered in their own right, however.

Although most men do not assume primary caretaking roles, fathers can be quite sensitive to newborns; they are capable of responding as contingently and as effectively as mothers do (Lamb & Goldberg, 1981; Parke & Sawin, 1977). This suggests that maternal hormones are not necessary for the emergence of competent caretaking (Lamb & Goldberg, 1981). Although they may respond *as promptly,* however, men and women tend to respond *differently.* Parke and Sawin (1977), for example, found that fathers vocalized in response to infant vocalizations, whereas mothers provided contingent tactile stimulation. Brazelton and his colleagues (1979), meanwhile, argued that there were differences between mothers and fathers in the sequence and temporal structuring of infant-parent interaction. Father-infant interactions were playful and involved affective peaks, whereas mother-infant interactions were more smoothly modulated and contained. Following maternal vocalizations, infants vocalized more promptly than after paternal vocalizations (Brazelton et al., 1979). Lamb (1978a) and Clarke-Stewart (1978) both showed that fathers saw themselves and socializers and playmates—especially for sons.

Although much of what we have written about sensitivity applies to both mothers and fathers, several factors may influence maternal and paternal sensitivity differently. In our society, the maternal role is defined quite narrowly, and there is little disagreement about what constitutes "good mothering." Typically, the mother is primary caretaker even when the father is more actively involved in child care than is typical. As a result, value of parenthood may affect responsiveness in women more directly than in men. Women are expected to care for and interact with their infants and thus women are evaluated (by others and by themselves) on the basis of their relative success as mothers. If a woman values the maternal role highly, perceived effectance as a parent is probably a crucial influence on her self-esteem: Perceiving herself as an ineffective mother would engender guilt and a decline in self-esteem. When parenthood is not highly valued, however, perceived effectance or ineffectance will have a reduced impact on self-esteem and sensitivity because such a woman does not really care whether or not she is a "good mother."

For fathers, the link between value of parenthood and behavioral sensitivity may be more complex. Unlike the maternal role, which is quite clearly prescribed, the paternal role is defined in a variety of ways, and this determines how value of parenthood affects parent-child interaction. Inasmuch as there are few general expectations about what fathers should do with their children, value of parenthood alone may not predict paternal behavior. Measures of behavioral responsiveness may inaccurately represent parental sensitivity, especially when they assess performance in activities that men do not define as legitimate areas in which to be involved. What a father does depends very much on how he defines the paternal role. Two men may value fatherhood highly and be similarly committed to their infants as well as to the paternal role, yet their actual interactions and their responsiveness may be very different.

For traditional fathers, experience with infants is limited because much of the interaction with infants takes place during the caretaking routines that these fathers seek to avoid. Traditional fathers may appear less sensitive, for example, than fathers who participate in caretaking and thus regularly respond to distress signals and other perceived needs because over time the lack of behavioral involvement will affect sensitivity. Participative fathers have more direct involvement in caretaking and have more experience monitoring infant signals; they also receive important infant feedback contingent upon parental behavior. This experience should translate into enhanced sensitivity. Interaction facilitates the growth of parental sensitivity by providing practice differentiating among, interpreting, and responding to infant signals. Fathers who have more interaction with young infants may be better prepared for sensitive responding later than are fathers who regard themselves primarily as socializers of toddlers and have little to do with their young infants.

For both mothers and fathers, the way parental roles are defined affects whether they perceive themselves as effective. When a traditional father engages in caretaking and performs poorly (on any objective criteria), his self-esteem is unlikely to suffer because caretaking skills are not salient elements in his role definition. Other infant characteristics, such as the infant's physical appearance and its perceived similarity to one of the parents, may affect his self-esteem more.

Commitment to the infant, like value of parenthood, probably affects maternal and parental sensitivity differently. Highly committed mothers may express their commitment in behavioral terms, which doubtless enhances their sensitivity. For fathers, by contrast, the way the role is defined is crucial.

A man committed to insuring "a good life" for his offspring may demonstrate his commitment, not by interacting with his infant, but by supporting his wife emotionally and his family financially.

Infant Effects

The parents' personality and attitudes, as well as the situation in which they find themselves, undoubtedly affect parental sensitivity, but the physical and behavioral characteristics of the infant are also important. Most theorists acknowledge that infant characteristics affect parental behavior, but there is disagreement about the relative importance of parental and infant contributions to interaction and development.

Very young infants cannot construct internal representations of their parents' behavior because their behavior is too disorganized and their cognitive capacities are too limited. Consequently, they cannot alter their behavior in order to mesh their behavior and emotions with those of their interactive partners. Parents, by contrast, can generate internal models of infant behavior and alter their behavioral strategies in order to elicit specific responses and to mesh with their infant's behavior and needs. With age and experience, babies begin to interpret others' behavior. Thereafter, specific parental behaviors may be evaluated differently by different infants or by the same infant in different circumstances. Interpretation of parental behavior is affected by the infant's age, mood, and emotional reactions (Sroufe, 1979b). Our belief that propensities develop with experience differs from Brazelton's (personal communication) contention that newborns have the neurological and cognitive capacities necessary to structure infant-parent interaction, as well as the ability to discriminate among partners (e.g., mothers vs. fathers) and to expect certain types of interaction from them. Even neonates, Brazelton claims, shape parental behavior by patterning their cycles of attention–inattention and their affective responses to stimulation.

Although there is disagreement on this score, we agree with Sander (1962) that one aspect of sensitivity is the ability to perceive what developmental tasks an infant is negotiating and to modify one's behavior accordingly. An infant may be deemed responsible for initiating interaction (intentionally or unintentionally), but the success of the interaction depends on the parents' ability to respond to their infant's initiations and its need for patterned (cyclic) interaction.

Sander's emphasis on infant effects differs from that of most theorists who view maternal personality as the major determinant of sensitivity. Many do not even consider infant effects, whereas others imply that "a good fit" between the infant's temperament and its mother's personality is not significant. Coleman, Kris, and Provence (1953) explicitly reject the notion that parental adequacy depends on the ability to shift from one to another "identification with the child" when the child enters a new developmental phase. Brody and Axelrad (1978) acknowledge that infant characteristics may influence the emotionality and attitudes (and hence the responsiveness) of mothers, although they contend that the age of the infant is irrelevant. They support this contention by arguing that mothers interact similarly with infants and older children. Ainsworth, too, believes that the direction of influence is mainly from mother to infant because early infant behavior did not predict later maternal behavior, whereas early maternal behavior did predict later infant behavior. On the other hand, Ainsworth (1977) argues that the extent to which mothers accept their infants' idiosyncracies influences the extent to which maternal behavior is affected. Infants at risk because of constitutional aberrations may exert a greater influence on maternal behavior.

Most learning theorists say little about the effects of infant characteristics on parental behavior. Gewirtz (1977), however, states that the "quality of infant temperament" influences the propensity of adults to respond to infant distress signals. A difficult crying infant may become a conditioned aversive stimulus for its caretakers who will come to delay responding to its distress cues—perhaps ignoring some cues altogether. We contend, though, that the extent to which this occurs will depend on the adult's personality. Not all infants who cry excessively reduce their parents' responsiveness in this manner. Indeed, some parents of infants who cry a great deal may be motivated to monitor subtle cues so that they can intervene before incipient distress develops into a full bout of crying. Parental attitudes and traits, as well as the situation, affect the salience, interpretation of, and the propensity to respond to infant signals. Clearly, it is exceedingly difficult to talk about "paternal effects" or "infant effects" in isolation.

Our view of the manner in which infants contribute to parental sensitivity, and thus their own development, is similar to that of Goldberg (1977). Infants have innate behavioral propensities that permit them to provide contingent feedback to their parents, and this in turn creates feelings of efficacy in the parents. Behavior such as the readiness to respond to social stimulation, mutual eye contact, and soothing when held indicate to parents that their behavior is effective and is enjoyed by the infant. Furthermore, under ordinary conditions, specific infant behaviors predictably elicit from parents caretaking or social responses that allow infants to develop notions of effectance as well. Successful dyadic interaction thus helps both parents and infants to perceive themselves as effective.

Goldberg lists a number of infant characteristics that affect parental effectance, including responsiveness, readability, and predictability. *Responsiveness* refers to the extent and quality of infant responses to stimulation and readability to the definitiveness of infant behavioral signals. An "easily read" infant is one who produces unambiguous cues that allow caretakers to recognize infant states quickly, interpret infant signals promptly, and thus respond contingently. Parents are more likely to respond appropriately to "easily readable" infants. Lastly, *predictability* refers to the degree to which the infant behavior can be anticipated reliably from contextual events and/or the preceding behavior. These three infant characteristics affect the contingency and quality of parental behavior which in turn influences the infant's responses, and thereby enhances or depresses feelings of parental efficacy. As the infant develops socially, motorically, and cognitively, it becomes more readable, predictable, and responsive to stimuli. Continued interaction further promotes parental sensitivity.

Several infant characteristics other than those identified by Goldberg seem likely to influence parental behavior and sensitivity. Perceived parental effectance is surely influenced by temperamental characteristics such as: *sociability* (the readiness to respond to social stimuli), *soothability* (the readiness with which the baby can be calmed once it is distressed), *rhythmicity* (the modifiability of sleep–wake cycles), *adaptability* (the extent to which the baby can adjust to new situations, experiences, and foods), *emotional lability* (the baby's characteristic mood and irritability), and *threshold* (the amount of stimulation required for a stimulus to become salient to the infant). In addition, parents' motivation to interact with their infants may also be influenced by gender, perceived attractiveness, physical characteristics, and the rate of motor maturation. The adults' values, attitudes, and expectations regarding infants will influence the salience of infant characteristics and their effects on parental behavior.

Summary

In sum, we propose that individual differences in parental sensitivity are influenced by parental personality characteristics, situational and attitudinal factors, and infant characteristics. The factors interact in a complex manner to determine the tendency to monitor, perceive, and interpret infant signals and to select and execute responses. Considerably more research must be conducted if we are to understand the interrelated patterns of influence involved. It is clear that the factors that have been discussed combine to affect sensitivity in a multiplicative rather than additive fashion.

CONSEQUENCES OF VARIATIONS
IN SENSITIVITY

Theorists would not have paid so much attention to parental sensitivity had it not been of major formative significance. It is no coincidence that many of the writers previously discussed develop their notions in the context of empirical research on the determinants of social development. In this section, we wish to review evidence indicating that variations in parental sensitivity are causally related to individual differences among infants. We do not detail the research of either Brazelton or Watson, although the notions of these two theorists received considerable attention earlier. Brazelton has yet to demonstrate that parental sensitivity, as assessed in his paradigm, has systematic effects on infant development although, if we presume that all the theorists discussed in this chapter are dealing with a common construct—parental sensitivity—we should expect sensitivity (as assessed by Brazelton) to have effects similar to those described by others. Watson (1966, 1979; Watson & Ramey, 1972) has argued that experiences with contingently responsive objects facilitate the development of a sense of efficacy and that this permits more rapid learning in other contexts; his hypotheses have been supported empirically (e.g., Finkelstein & Ramey, 1977). Unfortunately, Watson has not studied contingently responsive social objects (i.e., people) so the relevance of his research to our present concerns is unclear. As a result, we focus primarily on three research projects—those of Sander, Brody, and Ainsworth—which have provided sufficient evidence about systematically assessed outcomes. Unfortunately, each of these researchers has chosen not only to assess sensitivity differently, but also to focus on different outcomes, so there have been few direct replications of findings. Nevertheless, the findings reported are generally complementary and consistent, so we presume that the outcomes mentioned by the different researchers can be deemed probable and coexistent effects.

Sander's (Sander et al., 1979) major contribution comes from a study of pediatric nurses, not parents. When sensitivity was assessed by the adequacy and duration of response to infant distress, Sander found that neonates cared for by the more sensitive nurse came to cry less, show more regular rhythms, and have longer periods of sleep. In Sander's view, sensitive caretakers help infants to attain homeostatic control over the state fluctuations characteristic of early infancy. Sander has also written about the effects of sensitive parenting on older infants, but his data have yet to be published.

Brody's (Brody & Axelrad, 1978) project was much larger and comprehensive than Sander's in that it involved multiple assessments of parental sensitivity and filial personality from infancy through early childhood in 120 famillies. Sensitivity was repeatedly assessed by observation as well as by interview throughout the project period and was indeed related to the children's later personality. Specifically, Brody and Axelrad (1978) reported that maternal sensitivity toward infants was related to indices of their current functioning as well as their later status:

> From the maternal reports at ages three to seven, the conclusion can be drawn that group A children [children of mothers who were sensitive from early in the project] were more satisfied, more resourceful, and more able to be occupied when alone, had better relationships with people, and were more capable of age adequate behavior [p. 243].

Whereas Brody followed her subject families for several years, Ainsworth (1979; Ainsworth, Bell, & Stayton, 1971; Ainsworth et al., 1972; Ainsworth, Bell, & Stayton, 1974) followed her's for only 1 year, during which repeated observations of mother-infant interactions were conducted. The most important outcome measure was of the infants' behavior in the "strange situation"—a standardized laboratory assessment performed when the infants were 1 year of age (Ainsworth & Wittig, 1969). Behavior in this situation was systematically related to behavior observed at home (Ainsworth et al., 1972). The situation was originally developed in a study of *mother*-infant interaction, but has since proved useful in research involving *fathers* as well (Feldman & Ingham, 1975; Lamb, 1978b). As described later, behavior in the strange situation is systematically related to behavior at home as well as to later behavior in a variety of other settings.

The focus in the strange situation is upon the organization of attachment behavior around an attachment figure in increasingly stressful circumstances (Ainsworth et al., 1978). Stress is produced by exposing the child to an unfamiliar environment and an unfamiliar adult, as well as by two brief separations from the parent. In Ainsworth's study, babies whose mothers had been sensitive (i.e., contingently and appropriately responsive) were able to use their mothers as "secure bases" from which to explore the novel surrounds, and although they did not all respond to separation with intense distress, they greeted their parents upon reunion with displays of proximity- and contact-seeking behavior or active distance interaction (this has been called the *B* pattern.) By contrast, infants whose mothers had been insensitive behaved in one of two ways. One group (the *A* infants) behaved independently in the preseparation episodes, but failed to greet their mothers: Instead, they avoided interaction and/or contact by averting their gaze, ignoring the parents' solicitations, turning their backs, or moving away. Another group of infants (the *C* infants) were unable to use their mothers as secure bases from which to explore assertively. Upon reunion, they behaved ambivalently, both seeking and rejecting contact and interaction. The *A* infants were distinguished primarily by avoidance, the *C* infants by resistance (Ainsworth et al., 1978; Connell, 1976). Although the mothers of both *A* and *C* infants had been insensitive in earlier interactions, the *C* mothers were inconsistently responsive and engaged in perfunctory contact without the same clear indices of aversion (Ainsworth, 1979). Barring marked changes in maternal behavior, there is good stability across time in the behavior patterns characteristic of individual infants (Connell, 1976; Vaughn, Egeland, Sroufe, & Waters, 1979; Waters, 1978).

As we have intimated repeatedly, we believe that the patterns of behavior observed in the strange situation reflect the expectations the babies have developed regarding their mothers' behavior. The infants' expectations mediate the relationship between maternal sensitivity and infant behavior. Consider, for example, the *B* infants who have been deemed "securely attached." These babies, through interaction with a sensitively responsive caretaker, have become confident in the reliability, predictability, and trustworthiness of their mothers, and so are able to use their mothers as secure bases and as sources of comfort when distressed. The *A* infants, by contrast, have been rebuffed frequently in the past so cannot count on their mothers to be emotionally accessible or sources of comfort. As a result, they refrain from seeking comfort from their mothers. Indeed, they ignore and avoid interaction with her in the strange situation. The *C* infants, confused by the inconsistency and unpredictability of their mothers, behave in an ambivalent fashion—seeking comfort and being angered by its uncertainty. Uncertainty about maternal predictability also accounts for the peculiar inability of these babies to gain sufficient security from the presence of, proximity to, or contact with, their mothers to enable them to explore the surroundings.

As indicated earlier, other researchers have shown that the patterns of behavior assessed in the strange situation predict infant behavior in other contexts. Main (1973) reported that securely attached (*B*) infants were later more cooperative and playful with unfamiliar adults, whereas infants who avoided their mothers later avoided strangers. Matas, Arend, and Sroufe (1978) showed that securely attached infants were more "effective" (i.e., more enthusiastic, persistent, and compliant with maternal suggestions) in a problem-solving situation, and this finding was subsequently confirmed by Gove, Egeland, and Sroufe (in preparation). The securely attached 18- to 24-month olds studied by Matas et al. (1978) later (as kindergarteners) demonstrated high ego resiliency and moderate ego control; the *A* infants were later noted for excessively high ego control, whereas the former *C* infants were deficient in ego control as kindergarteners (Arend, Gove, & Sroufe, 1979). Securely attached infants later (at 3½ years) demonstrated greater interpersonal competence in interaction with peers (Waters, Wippman, & Sroufe, 1979). Summarizing the results of these studies, Sroufe (1978, 1979a) has argued that there is continuity across time in "individual adaptation." Infants who behave adaptively in the strange situation (those who exemplify the *B* pattern of behavior), later adapt well when the developmentally appropriate task becomes either independent problem solving (in the second year) or social integration into extrafamilial networks (in the preschool years). His argument is predicated upon the assumption that sensitive mothers comprise the social environment for which infants are evolutionarily adapted and that being reared in such an environment facilitates the development of autonomous individual adaptation.

There is certainly a growing amount of evidence that behavior in the strange situation predicts performance in other contexts, and we are likely to witness an increasing number of attempts to use this procedure as a means of classifying infant-mother attachment. More poorly documented is the relationship between strange-situation behavior and antecedent patterns of mother-infant interaction. Only Ainsworth has investigated this, and in her intensive and detailed study it was possible to follow longitudinally only 23 infants. When one considers that the three patterns described *(A, B, C)* actually represent eight subgroups—each representing a different pattern of infant behavior systematically related to a specific pattern of maternal behavior—the need for further investigation into the origins of strange-situation behavior becomes obvious. At least one study has shown that infants from the different subgroups within the (securely attached) *B* group behave differently in interaction with peers (Easterbrooks & Lamb, 1979). Clearly, there is reason enough to see parental sensitivity as a formatively important dimension; further investigation will facilitate our understanding of the concept and of the manner in which infant development is affected.

In the present context, finally, it is important to note that parental sensitivity appears to affect infant development through an influence on the baby's understanding of the parent's behavior. As previously described, the patterns of behavior observed in the strange situation seem to reflect the infant's degree of certainty about the adult's behavior and its expectations about what type of responses will occur. Thus, the *B* baby perceives its parent as dependable and trustworthy and so gains security from the parent's presence as well as comfort from proximity or contact when in need of emotional refueling. The *A* infant expects rejection and unsatisfying contact and so avoids interaction with the parent. The *C* infant is uncertain what to expect because the parent has behaved unpredictably in the past. Herein lies the relevance of this chapter to the theme of this volume. Only by close focus on parental sensitivity, we venture, will we advance understanding of the origins of individual differences in infant social cognition—differences that have long-term implications for social style and personality development. Refining our understanding of the nature of parental sensitivity, as well as of the origins of individual differences therein, will advance comprehension of the relationship between sensitivity and the development of infant social cognition.

SUMMARY

In this chapter, we have advocated that considerable attention must be paid to the determinants and components of parental sensitivity if we are to understand how individual differences among parents help determine differences among infants. We began the chapter with a selective review of theory concerning parental sensitivity, noting that the concept has long been of interest to developmental psychologists. Parental sensitivity has been discussed by representatives of four "schools," but the perspectives of each can be viewed as complementary, rather than as alternatives to one another. In our review, we attempted to accentuate those aspects of each perspective that contribute most to our understanding of parental sensitivity and its effects.

Relatively few attempts have been made to consider the determinants of individual differences among parents. This may be attributable to the enormous complexity of this issue. As we pointed out in the second section, the way any parent behaves in relation to her or his infant is determined by a number of interacting and interrelated factors. The most important of these are the parent's personality, the attitudes and values held by the parent and others in his or her social network, and the characteristics of the infant itself. The complexity of the causal networks insures that the task faced by future investigators is imposing. We hope that we have adequately illustrated the enormous importance of research in this area by briefly summarizing the effects of individual differences among parents upon infant development.

ACKNOWLEDGMENTS

We are grateful to several people for suggestions and comments on this topic. Mary D. Salter Ainsworth, Lonnie Sherrod and L. Alan Sroufe provided critical comments as our ideas developed and as drafts were written. Although differences of opinion may remain, we benefited greatly from their efforts. Our thoughts about the determinants of parental sensitivity were also influenced by discussions within an informal seminar attended by Susan Bronson, Lindsay Chase-Lansdale, Ann Frodi, Wendy Goldberg, and Margaret Owen in addition to the authors.

REFERENCES

Ainsworth, M. D. S. Object relations, dependency, and attachment: A theoretical review of the infant-mother relationship. *Child Development,* 1969, *40,* 969–1025.

Ainsworth, M. D. S. Attachment and dependency: A comparison. In J. L. Gewirtz (Ed.), *Attachment and dependency.* Washington: Winston, 1972.

Ainsworth, M. D. S. *Affective aspects of the attachment of infant to mother: Individual differences and their correlates in maternal behavior.* Paper presented to the American Association for the Advancement of Science, Washington, February 1977.

Ainsworth, M. D. S. Attachment as related to mother-infant interaction. In J. S. Rosenblatt, R. A. Hinde, C. Beer, & M. Busnel (Eds.), *Advances in the study of behavior* (vol. 9). New York: Academic Press, 1979.

Ainsworth, M. D. S., Bell, S. M., & Stayton, D. J. Individual differences in strange situation behavior of one-year-olds. In H. R. Schaffer (Ed.), *The origins of human social relations.* New York: Academic Press, 1971.

Ainsworth, M. D. S., Bell, S. M., & Stayton, D. J. Individual differences in the development of some attachment behaviors. *Merrill–Palmer Quarterly,* 1972, *18,* 123–143.

Ainsworth, M. D. S., Bell, S. M., & Stayton, D. J. Infant-mother attachment and social development: 'socialisation' as a product of reciprocal responsiveness to signals. In M. P. M. Richards (Ed.), *The integration of a child into a social world.* Cambridge, England: Cambridge University Press, 1974.

Ainsworth, M. D. S., Blehar, M. C., Waters, E., & Wall, S. *Patterns of attachment.* Hillsdale, N.J.: Lawrence Erlbaum Associates, 1978.

Ainsworth, M. D. S., & Wittig, B. A. Attachment and exploratory behavior of one-year-olds in a strange situation. In B. M. Foss (Ed.), *Determinants of infant behavior IV.* London: Methuen, 1969.

Arend, R., Gove, F., & Sroufe, L. A. Continuity of individual adaptation from infancy to kindergarten: A predictive study of ego-resiliency and curiosity in preschoolers. *Child Development,* 1979, *50,* 950-959.

Bell, S. M., & Ainsworth, M. D. Infant crying and maternal responsiveness. *Child Development,* 1972, *43,* 1171-1190.

Bowlby, J. *Attachment and loss* (Vol. 1). *Attachment.* New York: Basic Books, 1969.

Brazelton, T. B., Koslowski, B., & Main, M. The origins of reciprocity: The early mother-infant interaction. In M. Lewis & L. A. Rosenblum (Eds.), *The effect of the infant on its caregiver.* New York: Wiley, 1974.

Brazelton, T. B., Yogman, M., Als, H., & Tronick, E. The infant as a focus for family reciprocity. In M. Lewis & L. A. Rosenblum (Eds.), *The child and its family.* New York: Plenum, 1979.

Brody, S. *Patterns of mothering.* New York: International Universities Press, 1956.

Brody, S., & Axelrad, S. *Mothers, fathers, and children.* New York: International Universities Press, 1978.

Clarke-Stewart, K. A. And daddy makes three: The father's impact on mother and young child. *Child Development,* 1978, *49,* 466-478.

Coleman, R. W., Kris, E., & Provence, S. The study of variations of early parental attitudes: A preliminary report. *Psychoanalytic Study of the Child,*1953, *8,* 20-47.

Connell, D. B. *Individual differences in attachment: An investigation into stability, implications, and relationships to structure of early language development.* Unpublished doctoral dissertation, Syracuse University, 1976.

Easterbrooks, M. A. & Lamb, M. E. The relationship between quality of infant mother attachment and infant competence in initial encounters with peers. *Child Development,* 1979, *50,* 380-387.

Erikson, E. *Childhood and society.* New York: Norton, 1950.

Feldman, S. S., & Ingham, M. E. Attachment behavior: A validation study in two age groups. *Child Development,* 1975, *46,* 319-330.

Finkelstein, N. W., & Ramey, C. T. Learning to control the environment in infancy. *Child Development,* 1977, *48,* 806-819.

Freud, S. *Three essays on the theory of sexuality* (1905). New York: Avon, 1962.

Frodi, A. M., Lamb, M. E., Leavitt, L. A., & Donovan, W. L. Fathers' and mothers' responses to infant smiles and cries. *Infant Behavior and Development,* 1978, *1,* 187-198.

Gewirtz, J. L. On the selection and use of attachment and dependence indices. In J. L. Gewirtz (Ed.), *Attachment and dependency.* Washington: Winston, 1972.

Gewirtz, J. L. Maternal responding and the conditioning of infant crying: Directions of influence within the attachment acquisition process. In B. C. Etzel, J. M. LeBlanc, & D. M. Baer (Eds.), *New developments in behavioral research: Theory, method, and application.* Hillsdale, N.J.: Lawrence Erlbaum Associates, 1977.

Goldberg, S. Social competence in infancy: A model of parent-infant interaction. *Merrill-Palmer Quarterly,* 1977, *23,* 163-177.

Gove, F., Egeland, B., & Sroufe, L. A. Attachment and autonomy: A replication and extension. Manuscript in preparation, 1979.

Lamb, M. E. (Ed.). *The role of the father in child development.* New York: Wiley, 1976.

Lamb, M. E. The father's role in the infant's social world. In J. H. Stevens & M. Mathews (Eds.), *Mother/child, father/child relationships.* Washington: National Association for the Education of Young Children, 1978. (a)

Lamb, M. E. Qualitative aspects of mother- and father-infant attachments. *Infant Behavior and Development,* 1978, *1,* 265-275. (b)

Lamb, M. E., Chase-Lansdale, L., & Owen, M. T. The changing American family and its implications for infant social development: The sample case of maternal employment. In M. Lewis & L. A. Rosenblum (Eds.), *The child and its family.* New York: Plenum, 1979.

Lamb, M. E., & Goldberg, W. A. The father-child relationship: A synthesis of biological, evolutionary and social perspectives. In R. Gandelman & L. W. Hoffman (Eds.), *Perspectives on parental behavior.* Hillsdale, N.J.: Lawrence Erlbaum Associates, 1981.

Lamb, M. E., Owen, M. T., & Chase-Lansdale, L. The working mother in the intact family: a process model. In R. R. Abidin (Ed.), *Parent education and intervention handbook.* Springfield, Ill.: Charles C. Thomas, 1980.

Lewis, M., & Goldberg, S. Perceptual-cognitive development in infancy: a generalized expectancy model as a function of the mother-infant interaction. *Merrill-Palmer Quarterly,* 1969, *15,* 81-100.

Lorenz, K. Companions as factors in the bird's environment (1935). In K. Lorenz (Ed.), *Studies in animal and human behavior* (Vol. 1). Cambridge, Mass.: Harvard University Press, 1970.

Main, M. *Exploration, play and cognitive functioning as related to child-mother attachment.* Unpublished doctoral dissertation, Johns Hopkins University, 1973.

Matas, L., Arend, R., & Sroufe, L. A. Continuity of adaptation in the second year of life. *Child Development,* 1978, *49,* 547-556.

Murray, A. D. Infant crying as an elicitor of parental behavior: An examination of two models. *Psychological Bulletin,* 1979, *86,* 191-215.

Parke, R. D., & Sawin, D. B. *The family in early infancy: Social interactional and attitudinal analyses.* Paper presented to the Society for Research in Child Development, New Orleans, March 1977.

Rajecki, D. W., Lamb, M. E., & Obmascher, P. Toward a general theory of infantile attachment: A comparative review of aspects of the social bond. *Behavioral and Brain Sciences,* 1978, *1,* 417-436.

Sander, L. W. Issues in early mother-child interaction. *Journal of the American Academy of Child Psychiatry,* 1962, *1,* 141-167.

Sander, L. W. Adaptive relationships in early mother-child interaction. *Journal of the American Academy of Child Psychiatry,* 1964, *3,* 231-264.

Sander, L. W. Infant and caretaking environment: Investigation and conceptualization of adaptive behavior in a system of increasing complexity. In E. J. Anthony (Ed.), *Explorations in child psychiatry.* New York: Plenum, 1975.

Sander, L. W. The regulation of exchange in the infant-caretaker system and some aspects of the context-content relationship. In M. Lewis & L. A. Rosenblum (Eds.), *Interaction, conversation, and the development of language.* New York: Wiley, 1977.

Sander, L. W., Stechler, G., Burns, P., & Lee, A. Change in infant and caregiver variables over the first two months of life: Integration of action in early development. In E. B. Thoman (Ed.), *Origins of the infant's social responsiveness.* Hillsdale, N.J.: Lawrence Erlbaum Associates, 1979.

Seligman, M. P. M. *Helplessness.* San Francisco: Freeman, 1975.

Sroufe, L. A. Attachment and the roots of competence. *Human Nature,* 1978, *2*(10), 50-57.

Sroufe, L. A. *The problem of continuity in development.* Paper presented to the Society for Research in Child Development, San Francisco, March 1979. (a)

Sroufe, L. A. Socioemotional development. In J. D. Osofsky (Ed.), *Handbook of infant development.* New York: Wiley, 1979. (b)

Stern, D. N. The goal and structure of mother-infant play. *Journal of the American Academy of Child Psychiatry,* 1974, *13,* 402–421. (a)

Stern, D. N. Mother and infant at play: The dyadic interaction involving facial, vocal, and gaze behaviors. In M. Lewis & L. A. Rosenblum (Eds.), *The effect of the infant on its caregiver.* New York: Wiley, 1974. (b)

Vaughn, B., Egeland, B., Sroufe, L. A. & Waters, E. Individual differences in infant-mother attachment at twelve and eighteen months: Stability and change in families under stress. *Child Development,*1979, *50,* 971–975.

Waters, E. The reliability and stability of individual differences in infant-mother attachment. *Child Development,* 1978, *49,* 489–494.

Waters, E., Wippman, J., & Sroufe, L. A. Attachment, positive affect and competence in the peer group: Two studies in construct validation. *Child Development,* 1979, *50,* 821–829.

Watson, J. S. The development and generalization of "contingency awareness" in early infancy: Some hypotheses. *Merrill–Palmer Quarterly,* 1966, *12,* 123–135.

Watson, J. S. Perception of contingency as a determinant of social responsiveness. In E. B. Thoman (Ed.), *Origins of the infant's social responsiveness.* Hillsdale, N.J.: Lawrence Erlbaum Associates, 1979.

Watson, J. S., & Ramey, C. T. Reactions to response-contingent stimulation in early infancy. *Merrill–Palmer Quarterly,* 1972, *18,* 219–227.

7 The Development of Social Expectations in the First Year of Life

Michael E. Lamb
University of Utah

My goal in the present chapter is to describe the development of social understanding during the first year of life. The focus thus differs from that of the preceding chapters, in which Sherrod, Olson, and Oster examined infants' responses to, perception of, and recognition of, social stimuli (as distinct from nonsocial stimuli), Spelke and Cortelyou discussed the processes by which multimodal knowledge about people is integrated into complex perceptuo-cognitive concepts, and Lamb and Easterbrooks considered the determinants and nature of individual differences in critical parental behaviors. In this chapter a related, though different, theme becomes central—a concern with the development of concepts and expectations about the behavioral propensities of specific individuals and with the manner in which these concepts and expectations come to shape the infant's social style.

I have chosen to develop my argument following a chronological organization and address three interrelated topics in turn. To begin, I discuss the interactions between caretakers and very young infants—that is, infants under 3 months of age. The major developmental issue during the first 3 months involves the modulation of psychophysiological states of arousal and there is evidence that caretakers play crucial mediatory roles in this regard. In the course of these early interactions, I propose, infants have the opportunity to learn about social stimuli in particularly propitious circumstances. Unfortunately, no good evidence exists concerning the development of social expectations during these months, so the argument in this section is heavily speculative.

During the second 3 months of life, these expectations start to become evident, although they surely reflect the infant's experience with people during the previous as well as in the current quarter. Early in the first quarter, however, the infant cannot distinguish among individuals, and so the earliest expectations probably operate as generalized expectations of people, even though they may develop out of interaction with a single caretaker. During the second quarter-year of life, the infant becomes able to differentiate among individuals more systematically. The evidence supporting this claim was reviewed by Olson and is only briefly cited in the second section of this chapter, where the focus is upon the implications of this important developmental advance. The most salient individual in the infant's life—that is, the person with whom the most stimulating and frequent interactions take place—is the primary caretaker. Consequently, this second section is concerned with the development of conceptions about the caretaker's predictability and reliability. I assume that the processes whereby expectations regarding this person develop are similar to the processes whereby expectations of others are developed during this phase of the infant's life. In the third section, I discuss the cognitive capacities necessary for expectations (and later, intentions) to develop and review evidence concerning the ontogeny of the various component capacities.

As discussed here, conceptions of predictability pertain primarily to expectations concerning the structure of interaction—that is, to the likelihood that responses of a given type will occur consistently following certain infant behaviors. Provided that the same response recurs consistently, the nature of the response appears to be unimportant in the early development of expectations. Two parents, for example, may respond to the infant's smiles with equivalent consistency except that one adult vocalizes and smiles, whereas the other smiles at and touches the infant. The behavior of the two is equally predictable. Even when individuals are equally likely to respond to the baby, however, their responses may differ in some consistent fashion (as in the example just cited). In these circumstances, the infant would be equivalently certain of the individuals' predictability, and so in one sense the expectations of the two adults would be very similar. On the other hand, the infant would also develop different expectations regarding the types of interaction that each represented. These social expectations too play an important role in social development, and their ontogeny is discussed in the fourth section. For ease of reference, I refer to the expectations discussed in the second and third sections as expectations concerning the *patterning* or *structure* of the interaction, whereas those in the fourth section are referred to as expectations regarding the *content* of interaction because they relate to the characteristic activities in which specific individuals engage the infant. Although the two types of expectations develop in tandem, with a substantial amount of overlap, I discuss the two separately in order to facilitate analysis and discussion.

Throughout the chapter there runs a theme that deserves to be made explicit at this point. Prior to the development of linguistic competence (a competence dependent upon the capacity to represent events and objects symbolically), children develop relatively sophisticated and complicated notions about the nature of social interaction in general and about the behavioral propensities of particular individuals and certain classes of persons. It is my contention that this understanding develops as a consequence of each infant's experiential history, and that is why we see variability among infants in regard to social style and expectations of other people. My goal is to describe the processes whereby these expectations or concepts are developed. Let me add one preparatory caveat, however. This is a descriptive essay in which no attempt is made to review the literature comprehensively. References are cited only as illustrations of the argument. To the best of my knowledge, however, my notions are consistent with currently available evidence about infant development.

BECOMING SOCIAL THROUGH STATE MODULATION

In this first section, my discussion is focused on the interactions between caretakers and infants during the first 2 months of life. The focus here is not simply on the development of specific expectations; it is also upon the manner in which the behavioral propensities of adults and infants complement one another in ways insuring that infants learn a great deal about their caretakers' physical characteristics and behavioral predictability.

During the first 2 months of life, human infants have some difficulty organizing states of arousal and behavior (Berg & Berg, 1979). State changes are unpredictable; neonates appear to shift with remarkable facility from the heightened arousal manifest in the distress state to the low arousal of sleep. Only around 8 to 10 weeks do the various neural components of specific states become intercoordinated. Simultaneously, state transitions become more predictable and less labile and, from this point on, longer periods of continuous time are spent in discrete states (Berg & Berg, 1979; Emde & Robinson, 1979). To the delight of parents, unambiguous, extended, and somewhat regular periods of sleep, drowsiness, and alertness become more common in the third month.

The distress state and its sequelae are of greatest interest to us, because the vocal component of distress—the infant cry—has uniquely potent and predictable effects upon adults (Murray, 1979). Upon hearing it, adults experience physiological and emotional arousal (see, for example, Frodi, Lamb, Leavitt, & Donovan, 1978; Frodi, Lamb, Leavitt, Donovan, Neff, &

Sherry, 1978), and they usually translate this arousal into an attempt to relieve the infant's distress. The most common intervention attempted by adults is to pick up and hold the crying infant, and there is evidence that the vestibular and tactile stimulations involved in being held comprise the most effective way of terminating the infant's distress (Bell & Ainsworth, 1972; Korner & Thoman, 1970, 1972).

Picking up the infant not only terminates its cry; it also puts the infant in a state of quiet alertness (Korner & Thoman, 1970, 1972). The infant opens its eyes and visually inspects its surroundings. An observer would say that it was concentrating, for the baby's other movements are stilled and the visual regard is searching. States of alert wakefulness, as noted earlier, are otherwise rare and fleeting in early infancy, so the potency of the adult's intervention is noteworthy. The relationship between holding and alertness insures that when the baby is in a state of alertness—the state in which it is most capable of inspecting and learning about its environment—it is most likely to encounter and learn about social stimuli, because it is the caretaker who is most likely to be sensed, perceived, and inspected during the periods of quiet alertness produced by interventions. The multimodal stimulation that characterizes the caretaker recurs repeatedly in a predictable constellation: The baby visually regards the caretaker while simultaneously hearing his or her voice, experiencing his or her soothing touch, and smelling his or her unique odor. These repeated co-occurrences should permit the infant to construct—or to begin constructing—a multimodal, nonverbal concept of the caretaker. As this concept depends only on the association of multiple stimuli (i.e., it involves S-S learning, as described by Bolles in 1972), the necessary learning probably begins early in infancy because this type of learning demands minimal capacity on the part of the organism. Unfortunately, the development of S-S learning capacity has not been studied much in infancy. There is, however, a provocative report by Thoman, Korner, and Beason-Williams (1977) indicating that when the sound of a woman's voice repeatedly occurred at the same time that distressed neonates were picked up for soothing, the voice alone gained some capacity to relieve neonatal distress. This finding comprises one of the earliest demonstrations of associative learning and suggests that a multimodal concept of the caretaker *as a person* can start to develop very early. Perhaps other researchers have been less successful in demonstrating early learning because the associations to be learned were not as appropriate as the vestibular and vocal stimuli Thoman et al. paired, or because the stimuli were repeatedly paired by Thoman et al. during the optimal infant states (distress, quiet alertness) and so were rendered more salient. The importance of infant state was also illustrated by Little (1970, 1973) who showed both conditioning and long-term (10-day) memory in infants as young as 20 days of age tested in an experiment on eye-blink conditioning.

Distress–relief sequences are worthy of attention, then, because of the opportunities they provide for important episodes of social learning. There is another reason why these sequences are especially worthy of examination. The infant and adult behaviors occur here in a sequence that is probably more predictable than any other (adults usually respond to crying by picking up the baby), and the events themselves are highly salient. Distress involves high arousal and unpleasant affect, and the multimodal intervention that follows usually facilitates a transition to a state of more controlled arousal and receptiveness. The salience of the events (distress, caretaker intervention, relief, and alertness) enhances the likelihood that the associations will indeed be learned rather quickly. The distress–relief sequence thus contains all the components necessary for the infant to: (1) learn that distress predictably elicits an intervention that brings relief; (2) recognize the person responsible for facilitating the transition from displeasure to pleasure; (3) develop an integrated, multimodal concept of the caretaker; (4) associate the person's features with the pleasurable outcome he or she produces.

Thus, these early and simple interactions, centered around relief of the infant's distress, appear destined to advance the developing sociability and personality of the infant in four ways. First, the circumstances are more likely than any other to permit—indeed, to promote—the dawning awareness that the caretaker is a complex multisensory, but unitary, social object. Second, the conditions facilitate the development of an affectively positive relationship and indeed may represent the origins of affective attachment bonds. Further, the distress–relief sequence is sufficiently predictable that the infant may develop expectations concerning the probability of the caretaker's responses. This is important both because it adds a behavioral component to the emerging concept of the caretaker (a point elaborated in the next section) and also because it permits the infant to develop a sense of its own efficacy. As several writers have noted (e.g., Lewis & Goldberg, 1969; Watson, 1979), perceived effectance develops when an infant recognizes that it is able to elicit certain responses predictably from the environment.[1]

The issues surrounding the development of multimodal concepts are explored in depth by Spelke and Cortelyou (Chapter 4), so I refrain from

---

[1]This notion is by no means new. Theorists have speculated for years that a sense of effectance develops from caretakers' responsiveness to cries. To my knowledge, Jean-Jacques Rousseau (1762) was the first to suggest this. Rousseau's own discussion is too lengthy to quote, and a recent summary of his position must suffice (in Bloom, 1978): "Tears are a baby's language and naturally express physical discomfort and are pleas for help. The parent or nurse responds by satisfying a real need, either feeding the baby or removing the source of pain. But at some point the child is likely to recognize that his tears have the effect of making things serve him through the intermediary of adults. The world responds to his wishes. His will can make things move to satisfy his desires. . . . His tears become commands and frequently no longer are related to his real needs but only to testing his power [p. 141–142]."

providing a necessarily abbreviated and superficial account here. Instead of pursuing this issue, I discuss the perception of contingency or predictability in the next section. In Chapter 8, Suomi analyses the concept of contingency and its operationalization; I concern myself more narrowly with the ability to perceive contingency, and the implications of this developmental milestone.

THE PERCEPTION OF PREDICTABILITY

Learning that the behavior of others is sometimes contingent upon one's behavior is the basis for two crucial developmental attainments. One of these—learning that certain others can be relied upon—is portrayed by students of infant social development as perhaps the most elementary and important social concept (e.g., Ainsworth, 1973; Erikson, 1950). The other— recognizing that one is a competent, effective individual in partial control of one's experiences—is a centrally important early self-concept. The significance of these two attainments justifies a detailed exploration of the likelihood that infants are cognitively capable of the relevant operations as early in their lives as I have suggested.

The key question has to do with sheer capacity: When does the young infant possess the cognitive skills that are necessary if it is to appreciate and expect the contingencies between its behavior and that of others? Multiple skills are involved. In order to recognize that another person's behavior is predictable and controllable, the infant must be capable of learning the association between its behavior and the adult's response; it must be aware of both the contingency and the identity of the respondent: it must remember the repeated occurrences of the contingency so that when it reflects upon the history of interactions with the caretaker it perceives the characteristic themes that permit it to develop a conception of the adult as predictable and itself as efficacious. Let us consider each of these component prerequisites.

There is considerable controversy about whether or not newborn infants can be conditioned (see, for example, Fitzgerald & Brackbill, 1976; Sameroff, 1971, 1972), but it is widely believed that classical conditioning is impossible in the first 2 months of life, and that, although operant conditioning is possible, the behavioral modifications are usually short-lived. Typically, there is not even transfer to the next training session (e.g., Papousek, 1961; Sameroff & Cavanaugh, 1979). One recent study, however, reported impressively different results. In this study, Thoman et al. (1977) conditioned 1- to 3-day-old babies to soothe to the sound of a voice that was previously paired with soothing vestibular/tactile stimulation. This finding is sufficiently provocative that it demands replication. Conceivably, Thoman et al. succeeded where others had failed because they carefully sought to associate stimuli that "naturally" went together in a meaningful way, whereas other researchers have paired events more casually. Furthermore, newborn infants may easily be distracted by extraneous stimuli that interfere with the learning process (Rovee-Collier & Lipsitt, 1981). In their recent review, Rovee-Collier and Lipsitt (1981) conclude that learning is possible during the first month of life provided that the context and task are carefully selected.

There has been extensive discussion in the 1970s about the stimuli and responses that *can* be associated. Seligman (1970) and Hinde and Stevenson-Hinde (1973) have proposed that there are "constraints on learning." As a result, certain stimuli and responses go together naturally, and so it is relatively easy to establish conditioned associations between them in both infants and adults. Other pairings, by contrast, may be resistant to association. Sameroff and Cavanaugh (1979) point out that many studies of infant learning abilities were conducted during an era in which all stimuli and responses were considered equivalently associable. This may account for the early experimental failures. The notion of preparedness also has other implications for the study of learning in infancy. Sameroff and Cavanaugh suggested in their review that associations were established in only one trial by Lipsitt, Bosack, and Kaye (1966) because the stimulus and response concerned (sucking for a liquid food reward) naturally go together. This led Sameroff and Cavanaugh to doubt whether Lipsitt et al.'s study should be considered an example of neonatal learning. Rovee-Collier and Lipsitt (1981) rejected this claim, pointing to many other instances of neonatal learning in which the stimulus and response do not obviously "go together."

Rovee-Collier and Gekoski (1979) then went further, suggesting that Sameroff's discussion of preparedness did not help us to understand the circumstances under which neonatal learning is possible. One must recognize, they argued, that infants have to compare the costs and benefits of learning associations or performing certain responses. Their perspective also implies that there may sometimes be a performance (rather than a competence) problem, which makes it difficult for infants to demonstrate their ability in some conditioning tasks. Some studies, claim Rovee-Collier and Gekoski, demand that infants perform a response that is too costly (in terms of effort and energy) relative to the size of the reward. When the response is less taxing, associations can be conditioned in infants of all ages. This notion warrants further investigation because there is little evidence currently available to support it unequivocally. The notion of response cost is not inherently incompatible with the preparedness hypothesis advanced by Sameroff, however. Both preparedness and response cost probably limit the types of learning that can be demonstrated in research laboratories, and both notions hold that newborns can be conditioned given the appropriate circumstances. Thoman et al.'s (1977) success in a classical conditioning paradigm, in which a stimulus was associated with a compatible and undemanding response, suggests that the notions of preparedness and response cost have relevance to classical as well as operant paradigms.

In the present context, I am primarily concerned with operant conditioning and the age at which infants remember operant associations from one training session to the next. For my purposes, the most convincing and extensive studies of the ontogeny of conditionability were conducted by Papoušek (1961; Papoušek & Bernstein, 1969) in The Institute for Mother and Child Care in Prague, Czechoslovakia. In the course of a longitudinal study involving healthy infants who were residents of the Institute, Papoušek showed that the behavioral modifications occurring in the first few days of life were extremely unstable and short-lived. Long-term memory of the contingency (i.e., remembering the reinforced response from one training session to the next) was common during the second month of life, after which it was possible to teach the infant new responses. For example, once they had learned to turn their heads in one direction in order to obtain reinforcement, the infants easily learned to turn their heads in the other direction. Of special importance, Papoušek observed, was the age at which training began, rather than simply the number of training sessions the infant experienced. Observations such as these suggest that a certain degree of neural maturation is necessary if stable learning is to take place. As far as our analysis of predictability is concerned, Papoušek's data suggest that social expectations are unlikely to develop before the end of the second month. This estimate may be conservative, however. Papoušek made abundantly clear that he was interested in developmental changes in the process of conditioning, not in establishing early conditioned responses. As a result, the number of training trials conducted each day was small (10).

The results of several studies conducted by Rovee-Collier and her colleagues indicate that, by 3 months of age, infants can remember associations between their behavior and interesting environmental consequences for as long as 2 weeks in a cued-recall paradigm (Rovee-Collier, 1979). Three-month-olds can remember associations for 1 and 6 days without any cueing (Fagen, Rovee, & Kaplan, 1976; Rovee & Fagen, 1976; Sullivan, Rovee-Collier, & Tynes, 1979), and Rovee-Collier (personal communication) reports that some individual infants show long-term retention as young as 20 days of age.

When considering the implications of these findings for "natural" learning in a social context, it is important to recall that the retention reported by Rovee-Collier and her colleagues is demonstrated without repeated opportunities for the consolidation of learning, whereas learning in the distress–relief sequence is repeated several times daily. It seems extremely likely, therefore, that infants are learning about and remembering their caretakers' propensities sooner than experimental studies indicate—perhaps from as early as the second month of life. If we conclude that operant learning is possible as early as this, furthermore, there is no need to pursue the controversy about how early infants start to remember learned associations. Clearly, *from the time that babies are able to recognize specific individuals,* they are able to remember associations between their own and the others' behavior. It is generally believed that infants *begin* to recognize (and behave differentially toward) specific individuals sometime during or after the second month of life (see Ainsworth, 1973 and Bowlby, 1969 for reviews).

Watson and his colleagues have addressed a somewhat different question, focusing not on conditionability but on the motivational consequences of being conditioned (Watson, 1967, 1972, 1979; Watson & Ramey, 1972). In his research, Watson has studied 4-month-old infants, who are readily able to learn simple operant responses. He has been impressed not by the fact that the infants could learn but by the fact that the infants seemed to enjoy controlling environmental stimulation; they smiled more when they controlled the movement of mobiles over their cribs than they did when the mobiles' movements were not under their control. According to Watson, this indicated that the infants enjoyed exerting control. It is, of course, difficult to demonstrate that the infants perceived contingency in this situation or that the infants actually attributed potency to themselves. Nevertheless, Watson's findings are certainly suggestive.

Drawing upon Watson's findings and interpretations, Finkelstein and Ramey (1977) showed that 6- to 10-month-old infants who had experience with response-contingent (i.e., controllable) stimulation learned new and different operant responses more easily than infants without this prior experience. According to Finkelstein and Ramey (1977), experience with response-contingent stimulation led infants to focus their attention in a balanced fashion upon both stimulus and response aspects of the task, whereas experience with noncontingent stimulation led to an attentional strategy involving major focus on the stimulus aspects. However, this explanation avoids concepts like perceived effectiveness and cannot readily explain social learning experiences.

In a later study involving 3-month-old infants, Ramey and Finkelstein (1978) found that prior experience with controllable stimulation facilitated learning in a different setting. Unexpectedly, however, Ramey and Finkelstein found that experience with noncontingent stimulation also facilitated infants' learning, suggesting that controllable stimulation does not have a special meaning for infants as young as 3 months of age. Watson (1979), too, has found that results are not reliable with infants under 4 months of age. Papoušek (1961) also found that operant learning appeared to become robust in the third month of life. Between the third and fourth months, there occurs a turning point not simply in conditionability but in the infant's understanding of the conditioning experience.

The studies by Watson, Ramey, and Papoušek are of interest here to the extent that they help define when infants are able to recognize contingent stimulation and when the "motivation" to control stimulation emerges. Unfortunately, these researchers have studied the effects of experience with contingent stimulation only in experimental contexts bearing no resemblance to the interactions from which I have suggested that infants develop confidence in their caretakers' behavior. The stimuli (i.e., the adults' behaviors) and the responses (i.e., the infants' behaviors) are much more salient in social than in nonsocial contexts—particularly if one considers the distress–response sequence as the most important type of social interaction (see previous section). In addition, social learning usually involves repeated opportunities for consolidation. On the other hand, the stimulus–response pairings are seldom as reliable in natural contexts as they are in experimental contexts. Perhaps the most regular, predictable, and salient association is that implicit in the distress–relief sequence. Herein resides another reason why this sequence may be the source of the earliest social expectations. Thoman et al.'s (1977) findings are especially noteworthy, for they suggest that the distress–relief association is learned several weeks or months before long-term learning in other contexts becomes possible.

Distress–relief contingencies and their consequences have been studied in only one longitudinal study (Bell & Ainsworth, 1972) and this study has been criticized severely by Gewirtz (1977; Gewirtz & Boyd, 1977). Bell and Ainsworth's findings clearly buttress my emphasis upon the distress–relief sequence. The more contingently (i.e., promptly) that mothers respond to their infants' cries in the first 3 months of life, the less those infants cried later in the year. Infants who had contingently responsive mothers shifted instead to more mature means of communication (e.g., nondistress vocalizations). These infants, as we note presently, also appeared to have the greatest confidence in their mothers accessibility, but as these mothers were sensitive in a variety of contexts (not only in response to cries), we do not know how crucial the responsiveness to cries per se was.

An unpublished study by Gekoski (1974) is also pertinent. Gekoski showed that some 2-month-olds ceased crying at the sound of their mothers' approaching footsteps, and the number of babies behaving in this fashion increased between 2 and 6 months of age. In Gekoski's view, the infants had developed expectations that their mothers would approach, pick them up, and soothe them.

It is not at all clear how much infants learn about the predictability of behavioral responses to their behavior from social interactions other than those dominated by distress–relief sequences. In fact, there is some controversy about whether these interactions are marked by reciprocal turn taking or by simultaneous behavior. Many studies, like those by Strain and Vietze (1975), Stern, Jaffe, Beebe, and Bennett (1975), and Vietze, Strain, and

Falsey (1975) report that simultaneous behavior, rather than reciprocal turn taking, is the norm in early social interactions. Even when turn taking occurs, there is much less predictability in positive social interactions than there is in the distress-relief sequence because positive social behaviors tend to be used rather interchangeably (i.e., a positive response may involve a smile and/or a vocalization and/or a touch. It might be interesting to determine how often these behaviors occur together, because multimodal social responses would surely be more salient than unimodal responses.). Furthermore, it is clear that cries are more likely than vocalizations and smiles to elicit responses from adults (unpublished observations). Evidently, we will not be able to say whether and when infants' experiences in positive social interactions begin to affect the development of social expectations until much more research has been conducted.

As is the case of distress–relief sequences, however, it seems that infants are capable of learning and remembering that their positive social behaviors have predictable consequences from the second quarter-year of life. When they are engaged in social interaction, for example, they expect their partners to behave and respond socially, and they appear surprised when their partners behave unpredictably and unexpectedly (e.g., Tronick, Als, Adamson, Wise, & Brazelton, 1978). They have somewhat similar expectations about their control over nonsocial objects (Piaget, 1952). Paradoxically, however, infants of this age do not act *in order to* elicit consequences or responses identified in advance. According to Piaget (1952), they are not yet capable of distinguishing between an action and its environmental consequence. The consequence or response is seen as part of the behavior of the individual infant. At this age, therefore, infants may have expectations but not intentions.

A major change takes place at around 6–8 months of age. Piaget (1952) has defined this at the point at which means and ends are differentiated in the infant's mind, making intentional behavior possible. McCall and his colleagues (1979a, 1979b; McCall, Eichorn, & Hogarty, 1977) have also identified a discontinuity at this point—a discontinuity that they attribute to the emergent ability to separate means from ends.

There is reason to believe that this transition has implications for social cognition as well. The ability to distinguish between means and ends makes it possible for infants to direct social behaviors to parents because they want the adults to perform particular behaviors in response. The infant's behaviors are thus simply *means* employed in service of other ends. Escalona (1968) has commented upon a shift in infants' sociability at this point—a shift marked by the emergence of persistent efforts to elicit social responses. Active and apparently intentional initiations of interaction now occur (Sander, 1962). Only at this age do infants laugh in the course of social play *in anticipation of* the adults' playful behavior (Sroufe & Wunsch, 1972).

The evidence regarding the elicitation of negative affect is also pertinent. Sroufe (1979) argues that in the first 6 months of life, infants may exhibit rage due to disappointment when a well-established action sequence is not continued. Sroufe (1979) writes that later (in the third quarter-year), specific anger toward people emerges because the "infant now perceives in a new sense the *cause* of an interruption [p. 487]." One likely cause of such anger is disruption of an intended action.

In sum, it is hard to determine exactly when experiences begin to influence the infants' social expectations. The most conservative estimate would be that expectations develop from later in the second or third month of life, although some would argue that they are evident far earlier. Indeed, there is an alternative perspective on the origins of social responsiveness of which I should take note. This is the notion, proposed by both Brazelton (e.g., Brazelton, Yogman, Tronick, & Als, 1979) and Condon and Sander (1974), among others, that infants are born with *innate* expectations about the reciprocal nature of social interaction. Brazelton (personal communication) has argued that even preterm newborns become distressed when adults offer an unresponsive "still face" in reaction to the infants' solicitations: The distress occurs, he claims, because the adults are violating the infants' expectations regarding turn taking and reciprocity in social interaction (Tronick et al., 1978). Brazelton has never explicitly discussed the ontogeny of social responsiveness and social expectations, so it is not clear what types of developmental changes he envisages. He clearly believes, however, that newborns behave intentionally. Individual differences in later infant social development are attributed to the failure of certain caretakers to mesh their behavior with the infants' so as to fulfill the infants' innate expectations. As yet, no data unambiguously support this interpretation, which seems implausible in the light of other evidence concerning neonatal capacities. Further research would facilitate resolution of the conflict.

SECURITY OF ATTACHMENT

Before discussing how individual differences in parental sensitivity are translated into individual differences in infant–adult attachments, I wish to discuss another cognitive competency that develops over the first 6–8 months of life. This is the development of the concept of object or person permanence. The comprehension of person permanence refers to the recognition that other people have an enduring existence, which continues regardless of whether they are currently visible and audible and independent of the infant's actions with respect to them. Piaget (1954) has written extensively about the development of the concept of object permanence, suggesting in passing that comprehension of the existence of people proceeds more rapidly than recognition of object permanence. This prediction was later tested and confirmed (Bell, 1970), although recent research indicates that the apparently more rapid development of person permanence occurs because of differences in the way object and person permanence are tested; the décalage does not seem attributable to intrinsic characteristics of social objects (Jackson, Campos, & Fischer, 1978). This finding nevertheless indicates that the conception of person permanence probably develops more rapidly than Piaget implied when he was discussing the development of object permanence and that an immature but adequate understanding of person permanence (perhaps at the Stage IV level) is achieved early in the third quarter-year of life.

Achieving some comprehension of person permanence has important implications for socioemotional development. Not only does the child recognize and distinguish among the individual adults; she or he now appreciates that the person continues to exist even when not currently visible to, or in interaction with, the child. For the first time, it becomes possible to conceive of specific attachment bonds developing, for such relationships assume this degree of cognitive sophistication. Furthermore, fully intentional social behavior (which I discussed in the previous section) cannot occur prior to this development. Before we can say that an infant is crying (for example) *in order to* summon its caretaker, it must have some understanding of means–ends relationships, and it must have some comprehension of the caretaker's continued existence despite his or her current absence. Cognitive development, therefore, permits the shift to a different role for the infant in its social interactions and relationships—a shift to being a far more active and intentionally directive participant. The relationships themselves become more mature by virtue of the infant's new ability to form discriminating and enduring bonds. We can now speak of the infant as attached and turn in the next paragraphs to individual differences in those attachment relationships.

Surprisingly few studies have explored the origins of individual differences in parent-child relationships, but the major study in this area—the longitudinal project undertaken by Ainsworth and her colleagues (Ainsworth, Bell, & Stayton, 1974)—indicated that the contingency and predictability of the adults' behavior was a major determinant of the type of relationship established between infants and mothers. Although the sample was small, Ainsworth's data indicate fairly well how infants' expectations regarding their mothers' behavior translate into different ways of interacting with them. Let us review these findings briefly.

All the infants were seen in the "strange situation," a procedure designed to permit observation of the way in which 1-year-olds organize their behavior around attachment figures when distressed (Ainsworth, Blehar, Waters, & Wall, 1978). In Ainsworth's longitudinal study, three major patterns of behavior were identified; each pattern had several variants. One group of infants behaved in a normative, adaptive fashion (the B pattern): The infants explored in their mothers' presence, sometimes sought security and proximity to their mothers when a stranger entered, were disturbed by brief separation from their mothers, and sought contact with them when they returned. Another group was characterized by avoidant behavior upon reunion (the A pattern): Instead of seeking contact, the A infants actively avoided their mothers by moving away, turning their backs, averting their gaze, and ignoring solicitations. A third group of infants behaved ambivalently (the C pattern): They strongly sought contact upon reunion, but when this was achieved, some rejected it angrily and all failed to cuddle or derive much comfort. When they were put down, they requested contact again, though they were rejecting when it was attained again.

For our present purposes, it is especially important to note that these remarkably stable patterns of infant-mother interaction (Waters, 1978) were related to earlier patterns of maternal behavior (Ainsworth, Bell, & Stayton, 1972; Ainsworth et al., 1978). Earlier in the infants' lives, the mothers of the securely attached (B) infants responded sensitively (i.e., promptly and appropriately) to their infants' signals. In the strange situation, the infants behaved as if they had faith in the predictability of their mothers' behavior—they were able to count on their mothers to provide security and comfort. In other words, when their mothers' behavior had been predictable and contingently responsive, infants later behaved in a trusting fashion.

The avoidant (A) infants, by contrast, had mothers who were not sensitively responsive and who had a deep aversion to physical contact with their infants (Ainsworth, 1979). The fact that these infants avoided seeking comfort from, or interaction with, their mothers presumably reflected either their inability to predict how their mother would behave, or their expectation that any contact would be unrewarding and unsatisfying. The mothers of C babies, finally, were also insensitive and unlikely to provide satisfying comfort. The behavior of the C infants indicates either that the infants were uncertain about how their mothers would behave, or that they were angry about the predictably unsatisfactory behavior and affect of their mothers.

Detailed analyses of these data have recently been published (Ainsworth et al., 1974, 1978), so I refrain from describing these behavioral patterns and their relation to antecedent maternal behavior in greater detail. It is worth restating however, that infants develop expectations regarding the probability of maternal responsiveness and the appropriateness of maternal responses from interactions in which mothers reveal their characteristic behavioral styles. Different expectations yield different modes of relation to mothers. Also of relevance is a study in which infants were seen twice in the strange situation, once with their mothers and once with their fathers (Lamb, 1978c). A significant proportion of the infants I studied had different types of relationships with their mothers and fathers, indicating that by 1 year of age the infants had developed expectations regarding the behavior of specific individuals, not simply of people in general. Thus, during their early interactions, infants are constructing individually discriminating expectations regarding the way their attachment figures will behave.

EXPECTATIONS OF BEHAVIORAL CONTENT

The types of expectations described in the preceding section are essentially related to the *structure* of interaction; that is, they largely reflect the infants' expectations of the probability of contingent responses from specific adults. The affective component and appropriateness of the adults' behavior is also important (as indicated by the behavior of *A* and *C* infants), but the actual *content* of the interaction (i.e., the type of behavior involved) appears less crucial. It seems likely, however, that there exist other types of expectations than those which the strange-situation procedure was designed to investigate.

Perhaps in recognition of this fact, Lewis and his colleagues (Lewis & Feiring, 1978, 1979) and Suomi (1979), have written about expectations of interactional content. Lewis has proposed that infants organize their knowledge of the social world by classifying people in a three-dimensional space, and that they expect people at different points in this space to behave differently in interaction with them. According to Lewis and Feiring (1978), the three key dimensions are familiarity, age/size, and gender. Unfortunately, Lewis and his colleagues have not systematically explored the developing ability to categorize along these dimensions, nor have they indicated whether some of the axes become salient sooner than others. By the beginning of the second year, we know that infants are able to categorize people using each of the dimensions separately but we do not know when they are able to integrate this information fully in order to perform three-dimensional classifications.

Although we do not know when infants develop expectations of members of classes (e.g., males and females), there are some data suggesting that infants may learn from their interactions within the family that different persons (mother, father, sibling) behave differently. It seems unlikely that they would see their mothers and fathers as exemplars of broader gender categories until they have had experience with other adult males and females, but these generalized expectations may grow out of individualized ones.

From the start, mothers and fathers treat infant offspring differently. Even in nontraditional families (Eiduson, Zimmerman, & Bernstein, 1977), mothers assume primary responsibility for child care, and they are likely to perform caretaking chores even when fathers are present and are capable of performing the tasks themselves (e.g., Parke & Sawin, 1977). By later in the first year, mothers are still primarily responsible for child care, and this influences the types of interactions they are likely to engage in. For example, when mothers pick up their infants, they are most likely to do so in order to initiate some caretaking routine (Belsky, 1979; Lamb, 1976, 1977). It is likely that infants come to *expect* interactions with their mothers to be characterized by caretaking. Even though mother-infant interaction does not always involve caretaking, caretaking is a highly salient characteristic that typifies mother-infant interactions and most readily permits distinctions between mother-infant and other-infant interactions.

By contrast, father-infant interaction is characterized by play— particularly vigorous, physically stimulating play (Lamb, 1976, 1977; Yogman, Dixon, Tronick, Als, Adamson, Lester & Brazelton, 1977). As a result, infants come to see their fathers primarily as playmates—not because fathers play more than mothers do (indeed, if all interactions with the two parents are considered, it becomes clear that infants play much more with their mothers than with their fathers) but because the most salient or characteristic aspect of father-infant interaction is play. Infants respond more positively to play with their fathers than with their mothers from 7 months onward (Lamb, 1976, 1977). In the second and third year of life, children are more cooperative and enthusiastic about play with their fathers than with their mothers, and they are more likely to choose their fathers rather than their mothers as playmates (Clarke-Stewart, 1978; Lynn & Cross, 1974). Thus, infants develop clear expectations regarding the types of experiences their parents each represent. Unfortunately, we will not know until further research has been conducted when these expectations first develop; I suspect that they are formed as early as the first half-year of life.

Despite the discernible differences between maternal and paternal interactional styles, it seems likely that infants perceive similarities between these styles, inasmuch as both parents are adults and both are (at least occasionally) caretakers. Siblings represent a very different type of interaction. Their social competence is only marginally greater than the infant's own, and so although there are asymmetrical roles in sibling-infant interaction, the asymmetry is not as great as it is in adult-infant interaction. When I observed 12 and 18-month olds interacting with their preschool-aged siblings, I found that the older children tended to assume a dominant role: They were more likely than the infants to take things from, give things to, and assert themselves over, their siblings (Lamb, 1978a, 1978b). The older children paid scant attention to the infants (unlike the parents, who focused their attention on the infants), whereas the babies were inordinately interested in what their sisters/brothers were doing. They were responsible for keeping close to their siblings, monitoring their actions before attempting to imitate or explore objects just abandoned by the older children. Analyses of second order effects in these studies suggested that the sibling/peer and parent interactional systems were distinct by the time infants reached their first birthdays (Lamb, 1979). If generalizable, this implies that infants have different expectations regarding the behavioral styles of siblings/peers and parents by at least 1 year of age. Other studies have also indicated that peer interactions have a unique flavor, although differentiated expectations have not been investigated systematically (see Mueller & Vandell, 1979, for a review).

Although his subjects were rhesus macaques, Suomi's (1979) findings are pertinent here. From the time that infant monkeys started to move away from their mothers, their interactions with others differed depending on the class represented by the partner. Different patterns and behaviors characterized interactions between infants and their mothers, fathers, and other females, other males, juveniles, and other infants. Differences were evident not only in the behaviors that others directed toward the infants, but also in the manner in which the infants initiated interactions with others. This implies that the infants expected others to respond in characteristically different ways, and so they selected partners depending on the type of interaction they desired (or else they proposed interactions they could expect the available partner to engage in). Human infants should be capable of forming comparable behavioral expectations at least as early as infant monkeys do. By this reasoning, we would expect human infants to develop clear expectations of the way others tend to behave during the first half-year of life. Suomi's research suggests a number of questions regarding the development of human infants that need to be addressed.

CONCLUSION

In all, then, it seems likely that by the end of the first year of life, infants have developed fairly sophisticated expectations regarding the behavioral propensities of people around them. We have discussed two types of expectations in this chapter—structural and content expectations. Structural expectations have to do with the predictability of the others' responses and seem to underlie notions of faith or trust in others. The conceptions or expectations are individualized, in that infants develop qualitatively differentiated relationships with their mothers and their fathers. Nevertheless, there is considerable generalization to encounters with novel people. When they encounter unfamiliar individuals whose behavioral propensities are unknown, infants tend to adopt the social style that characterizes their interactions with their primary attachment figures (e.g., Main, 1973). We do not know how they would behave if they had different expectations regarding the behavior of two major attachment figures: Perhaps they would behave toward males depending on the quality of the father-infant relationship and toward females depending on the quality of the mother-infant bond. It is clear nevertheless that the types of expectations infants have of their parents' predictability have important implications for the infants' later sociability.

We do not know about the formative significance of expectations of behavioral content, although these expectations are obviously major components of the infants' concepts of specific persons in their social world. These expectations seem to develop during the first year of life, and thereafter they shape the way in which infants initiate and respond to bids from specific others. They undoubtedly facilitate interaction in two ways. First, they insure that infants are ready for the types of interaction specific types of people initiate. Second, they make it possible for infants to initiate interactions selectively in a manner that maximizes the likelihood of reciprocation. These expectations, therefore, may represent essential elements of emergent social competence, and they deserve greater consideration than they have been accorded in the past.

ACKNOWLEDGMENT

I am especially grateful to Carolyn Rovee-Collier of Rutgers University for her extensive assistance and advice.

REFERENCES

Ainsworth, M. D. S. The development of infant-mother attachment. In B. M. Caldwell & H. N. Ricciuti (Eds.), *Review of child development research III*. Chicago: University of Chicago Press, 1973.

Ainsworth, M. D. S. Attachment as related to mother-infant interaction. In J. S. Rosenblatt, R. A. Hinde, C. Beer, & M. Busnel (Eds.), *Advances in the study of behavior* (vol. 9). New York: Academic Press, 1979.

Ainsworth, M. D. S., Bell, S. M., & Stayton, D. J. Individual differences in the development of some attachment behaviors. *Merrill-Palmer Quarterly*, 1972, *18*, 123-143.

Ainsworth, M. D. S., Bell, S. M., & Stayton, D. J. Infant-mother attachment and social development: 'Socialisation' as a product of reciprocal responsiveness to signals. In M. P. M. Richards (Ed.), *The integration of a child into a social world*. Cambridge, England: Cambridge University Press, 1974.

Ainsworth, M. D. S.., Blehar, M., Waters, E., & Wall, S. *Patterns of attachment*. Hillsdale, N.J.: Lawrence Erlbaum Associates, 1978.

Bell, S. M. The development of the concept of object as related to infant-mother attachment. *Child Development*, 1970, *41*, 291-311.

Bell, S. M., & Ainsworth, M. D. S. Infant crying and maternal responsiveness. *Child Development*, 1972, *43*, 1171-1190.

Belsky, J. S. Mother-father-infant interaction: A naturalistic observational study. *Developmental Psychology*, 1979, *15*, 601-607.

Berg, W. K., & Berg, K. M. Psychophysiological development in infancy: State, sensory function and attention. In J. D. Osofsky (Ed.), *Handbook of infant development*. New York: Wiley, 1979.

Bloom, A. The education of democratic man: *Emile. Daedalus,* 1978, *107,* 135-154.

Bolles, R. C. Reinforcement, expectancy, and learning. *Psychological Review,* 1972, *79,* 394-409.

Bowlby, J. *Attachment and loss* (Vol. 1). *Attachment.* New York: Basic Books, 1969.

Brazelton, T. B., Yogman, M., Als, H., & Tronick, E. The infant as a focus for family reciprocity. In M. Lewis & L. A. Rosenblum (Eds.), *The child and its family.* New York: Plenum, 1979.

Clarke-Stewart, K. A. And daddy makes three: The father's impact on mother and young child. *Child Development,* 1978, *49,* 466-475.

Condon, W. S., & Sander, L. W. Speech: Interactional participation and language acquisition. *Science,* 1974, *183,* 99-101.

Eiduson, B. T., Zimmerman, I. L., & Bernstein, M. *Single versus multiple parenting— Implications for infancy.* Paper presented to the American Psychological Association, San Francisco, August 1977.

Emde, R. M., & Robinson, J. The first two months: Recent research in developmental psychobiology and the changing view of the newborn. In J. Noshpitz & J. Call (Eds.), *Basic handbook of child psychiatry.* New York: Basic Books, 1979.

Erikson, E. *Childhood and society.* New York: Norton, 1950.

Escalona, S. K. *The roots of individuality: Normal patterns of development in infancy.* Chicago: Aldine, 1968.

Fagen, J. W., Rovee, C. K., & Kaplan, M. G. Psychophysical scaling of stimulus similarity in 3-month-old infants and adults. *Journal of Experimental Child Psychology,* 1976, *22,* 272-281.

Finkelstein, N. W., & Ramey, C. T. Learning to control the environment in infancy. *Child Development,* 1977, *48,* 806-819.

Fitzgerald, H. E., & Brackbill, Y. Classical conditioning in infancy: Development and constraints. *Psychological Bulletin,* 1976, *83,* 353-376.

Frodi, A. M., Lamb, M. E., Leavitt, L. A., & Donovan, W. L. Fathers' and mothers' responses to infant smiles and cries. *Infant Behavior and Development,* 1978, *1,* 187-198.

Frodi, A. M., Lamb, M. E., Leavitt, L. A., Donovan, W. L., Neff, C., & Sherry, D. Fathers' and mothers' responses to the faces and cries of normal and premature infants. *Developmental Psychology,* 1978, *14,* 490-498.

Gekoski, M. *Changes in infant quieting to mother or stranger over the first six months.* Unpublished masters thesis, Rutgers University, 1974.

Gewirtz, J. L. Maternal responding and the conditioning of infant crying: Directions of influence within the attachment-acquisition process. In B. C. Etzel, J. M. LeBlanc, & D. M. Baer (Eds.), *New developments in behavioral research: Theory, method, and application.* Hillsdale, N.J.: Lawrence Erlbaum Associates, 1977.

Gewirtz, J. L., & Boyd, E. F. Does maternal responding imply reduced infant crying? A critique of the 1972 Bell and Ainsworth report. *Child Development,* 1977, *48,* 1200-1207.

Hinde, R. A., & Stevenson-Hinde, J. *Constraints on learning: Limitations and predispositions.* New York: Academic Press, 1973.

Jackson, E., Campos, J. J., & Fischer, K. W. The question of décalage between object permanence and person permanence. *Developmental Psychology,* 1978, *14,* 1-10.

Korner, A. F., & Thoman, E. B. Visual alertness in neonates as evoked by maternal care. *Journal of Experimental Child Psychology,* 1970, *10,* 67-78.

Korner, A. F., & Thoman, E. B. The relative efficacy of contact and vestibular-proprioceptive stimulation in soothing neonates. *Child Development,* 1972, *43,* 443-453.

Lamb, M. E. Interactions between eight-month-old children and their fathers and mothers. In M. E. Lamb (Ed.), *The role of the father in child development.* New York: Wiley, 1976.

Lamb, M. E. Father-infant and mother-infant interaction in the first year of life. *Child Development,* 1977, *48,* 167-181.

Lamb, M. E. The development of sibling relationships in infancy: A short-term longitudinal study. *Child Development,* 1978, *49,* 1189-1196. (a)

Lamb, M. E. Interactions between 18-month-olds and their preschool-aged siblings. *Child Development,* 1978, *49,* 51–59. (b)

Lamb, M. E. Qualitative aspects of mother- and father-infant attachments. *Infant Behavior and Development,* 1978, *1,* 265–276. (c)

Lamb, M. E. The effects of the social context on dyadic social interaction. In M. E. Lamb, S. J. Suomi, & G. R. Stephenson (Eds.), *Social interaction analysis: Methodological issues.* Madison: University of Wisconsin Press, 1979.

Lewis, M., & Feiring, C. The child's social world. In R. M. Lerner & G. B. Spanier (Eds.), *Child influences on marital and family interaction: A lifespan perspective.* New York: Academic Press, 1978.

Lewis, M., & Feiring, C. The child's social network: Social object, social functions and their relationship. In M. Lewis & L. A. Rosenblum (Eds.), *The child and its family.* New York: Plenum, 1979.

Lewis, M., & Goldberg, S. Perceptual cognitive development in infancy: A generalized expectancy model as a function of the mother-infant interaction. *Merrill-Palmer Quarterly,* 1969, *15,* 81–100.

Lipsitt, L. P., Kaye, H., & Bosack, T. N. Enhancement of neonatal sucking through reinforcement. *Journal of Experimental Child Psychology,* 1966, *4,* 163–168.

Little, A. H. *Eyelid conditioning in the infant as a function of the inter-stimulus interval.* Unpublished masters thesis, Brown University, 1970.

Little, A. H. *A comparative study of trace and delay conditioning in the human infant.* Unpublished doctoral dissertation, Brown University, 1973.

Lynn, D. B., & Cross, A. R. Parent preference of preschool children. *Journal of Marriage and the Family,* 1974, *36,* 555–559.

Main, M. *Exploration, play and cognitive functioning as related to child mother attachment.* Unpublished doctoral dissertation, Johns Hopkins University, 1973.

McCall, R. B. The development of intellectual functioning in infancy and the prediction of later IQ. In J. D. Osofsky (Ed.), *Handbook of infant development.* New York: Wiley, 1979. (a)

McCall, R. B. Qualitative transitions in behavioral development in the first three years of life. In M. H. Bornstein & W. Kessen (Eds.), *Psychological development from infancy.* Hillsdale, N.J.: Lawrence Erlbaum Associates, 1979. (b)

McCall, R. B., Eichorn, D. H., & Hogarty, P. S. Transitions in early mental development. *Monographs of the Society for Research in Child Development,* 1977, *42,* Number 171.

Mueller, E., & Vandell, D. B. Infant-infant interaction. In J. D. Osofsky (Ed.), *Handbook of infant development.* New York: Wiley, 1979.

Murray, A. D. Infant crying as an elicitor of parental behavior: An examination of two models. *Psychological Bulletin,* 1979, *86,* 191–215.

Papoušek, H. Conditioned head rotation reflexes in infants in the first months of life. *Acta Paediatrica,* 1961, *50,* 565–576.

Papoušek, H., & Bernstein, P. The functions of conditioning stimulation in human neonates and infants. In A. Ambrose (Ed.), *Stimulation in early infancy.* New York: Academic Press, 1969.

Parke, R. D., & Sawin, D. B. *The family in early infancy: Social interactional and attitudinal analyses.* Paper presented to the Society for Research in Child Development, New Orleans, March 1977.

Piaget, J. *The origins of intelligence in children* (1936). New York: International Universities Press, 1952.

Piaget, J. *The construction of reality in the child* (1937). New York: Basic Books, 1954.

Ramey, C. T., & Finkelstein, N. W. Contingent stimulation and infant competence. *Journal of Pediatric Psychology,* 1978, *3,* 89–96.

Rousseau, J. -J. *Emile* (1762). London: Dent, 1911.

Rovee, C. K., & Fagen, J. W. Extended conditioning and 24-hour retention in infants. *Journal of Experimental Child Psychology,* 1976, *21,* 1–11.

Rovee-Collier, C. K. *Reactivation of infant memory.* Paper presented to the Society for Research in Child Development, San Francisco, March 1979.

Rovee-Collier, C. K., & Gekoski, M. J. The economics of infancy: A review of conjugate reinforcement. In H. W. Reese & L. P. Lipsitt (Eds.), *Advances in child development and behavior* (Vol. 13). New York: Academic Press, 1979.

Rovee-Collier, C. K., & Lipsitt, L. P. Learning, adaptation, and memory. In P. M. Stratton (Ed.), *Psychobiology of the human newborn.* New York: Wiley, 1981.

Sameroff, A. J. Can conditioned responses be established in the newborn infant? *Developmental Psychology,* 1971, *5,* 1–12.

Sameroff, A. J. Learning and adaptation in infancy: A comparison of models. In H. W. Reese (Ed.), *Advances in child development and behavior* (Vol. 7). New York: Academic Press 1972.

Sameroff, A. J., & Cavanaugh, P. J. Learning in infancy: A developmental perspective. In J. D. Osofsky (Ed.), *Handbook of infant development.* New York: Wiley, 1979.

Sander, L. Issues in early mother-child interaction. *Journal of the American Academy of Child Psychiatry,* 1962, *1,* 141–166.

Seligman, M. E. P. On the generality of the laws of learning. *Psychological Review,* 1970, *77,* 406–418.

Sroufe, L. A. Socioemotional development. In J. D. Osofsky (Ed.), *Handbook of infant development.* New York: Wiley, 1979.

Sroufe, L. A., & Wunsch, J. P. The development of laughter in the first year of life. *Child Development,* 1972, *43,* 1326–1344.

Stern, D. N., Jaffe, J., Beebe, B., & Bennett, S. L. *Vocalizing in unison and in alternation: Two modes of communication within the mother-infant dyad.* Paper presented to a Conference on Developmental Psycholinguistics and Communicative Disorders, 1975.

Strain, B. A., & Vietze, P. M. *Early dialogues: The structure of reciprocal infant-mother vocalization.* Paper presented to the Society for Research in Child Development, Denver, March 1975.

Sullivan, M. W., Rovee-Collier, C. K., & Tynes, D. M. A conditioning analysis of infant long-term memory. *Child Development,* 1979, *50,* 152–162.

Suomi, S. J. Differential development of various social relationships by rhesus monkey infants. In M. Lewis & L. A. Rosenblum (Eds.), *The child and its family.* New York: Plenum, 1979.

Thoman, E. B., Korner, A. F., & Beason-Williams, L. Modification of responsiveness to maternal vocalization in the neonate. *Child Development,* 1977, *48,* 563–569.

Tronick, E., Als, H., Adamson, L., Wise, S., & Brazelton, T. B. The infant's response to entrapment between contradictory messages in face-to-face interaction. *Journal of the American Academy of Child Psychiatry,* 1978, *17,* 1–13.

Vietze, P. M., Strain, B., & Falsey, S. *Contingent responsiveness between mother and infant: Who's reinforcing whom?* Paper presented to the Society for Research in Child Development, Denver, March 1975.

Waters, E. The stability of individual differences in infant-mother attachment. *Child Development,* 1978, *49,* 483–494.

Watson, J. S. Memory and "contingency analysis" in infant learning. *Merrill-Palmer Quarterly,* 1967, *13,* 55–76.

Watson, J. S. Smiling, cooing, and 'the game.' *Merrill-Palmer Quarterly,* 1972, *18,* 323–339.

Watson, J. S. Perception of contingency as a determinant of social responsiveness. In E. B. Thoman (Ed.), *The origins of the infant's social responsiveness.* Hillsdale, N.J.: Lawrence Erlbaum Associates, 1979.

Watson, J. S., & Ramey, C. J. Reactions to response-contingent stimulation in early infancy. *Merrill-Palmer Quarterly,* 1972, *18,* 219–227.

Yogman, M. W., Dixon, S., Tronick, E., Als, H., Adamson, L., Lester, B., & Brazelton, T. B. *The goals and structure of face-to-face interaction between infants and fathers.* Paper presented to the Society on Research in Child Development, New Orleans, March 1977.

8 The Perception of Contingency and Social Development

Stephen J. Suomi
University of Wisconsin-Madison

INTRODUCTION

The concept of contingency has long presented problems for psychologists. On the one hand, consideration of contingency, in one form or another, has concerned many of the major theories of behavior over the past half-century, including several prominent ones of the last decade. Countless empirical studies involving experimental manipulation of contingency between a subject's behavior and some outcome have been performed in carefully controlled laboratory settings, and certain robust principles have become well-established empirically. Yet, in one of the areas for which the concept of contingency has perhaps its greatest heuristic appeal, interactive social behavior and its development, our current ability to apply laboratory-based knowledge of contingency to real-life social phenomena appears to be quite inadequate.

In this chapter, I first examine some of the ways in which the concept of contingency has been viewed in the past and then turn to consider some of the problems one encounters in attempting to operationalize contingencies in social settings. Additional complexities that result when one takes a developmental perspective are then detailed. Finally, some data representative of current empirical work in the study of social contingencies are examined, and some possible strategies for future research are discussed.

DEFINITIONS OF CONTINGENCY
AND RELATED TERMS

Webster's Third New International Dictionary (1963) defines "contingency" in the following manner:

> *1*: The quality or state of being contingent: as *a* (1):the condition that something may or may not occur; the condition of being subject to chance (2): the happening of anything by chance: fortuitousness *b* (1): close connection or relationship especially of a causal nature ... *2a*: an event or condition occuring by chance and without intent, viewed as possible or eventually probable, or depending on uncertain occurrences or coincidences *b*: a possible future event or condition or unforeseen occurrence that may necessitate special measures; *c*: something liable to occur as a chance feature or accompaniment of something else ... [p. 493].

Contingency has traditionally been afforded a narrower definition in the psychological literature. To most psychologists, contingency involves the occurrence of behavior as a direct result of consequence of some event(s) or action(s) perceived by the individual displaying the behavior. Such a view of contingency carries with it two tacit assumptions. First, a degree of causality is inferred: The event(s) or action(s) perceived by the subject is (are) seen as a precipitating agent for the behavior termed "contingent." Second, some element of chance (or something most likely beyond the subject's immediate control) appears to exist: If the precipitating event or action were *not* to occur, the behavior in question probably would not occur either, at least not at that particular time and place. Put another way, contingency refers to a behavioral "strategy" by a subject that involves a particular response or pattern of responses in the event that some external event or action should occur. The response is a direct result of a judgment by the subject that the relevant event or action has transpired. That strategy could be conscious or unconscious, genetically determined and/or a product of experience, depending on the situation, the behavior, the subject, and the species under study, as well as on the theoretical bias of the investigator.

For most psychologists, the assertion that two events (and/or actions or behaviors) are contingent carries with it implications beyond those of mere proximity in time and space. The term "correlation" is usually employed to denote such time-place proximity, and this term does not share the implication of causality that contingency carries. Indeed, how many times in our scientific training have we been explicitly reminded that "correlation does not imply causality"? Yet, mistakes in attribution of causality or control to certain events (actions, behavior) on the basis of a strong correlation between their appearance and a perceived subsequent outcome are not that uncommon among scientists. One wonders how often correlated events are "wrongly" seen as reflecting contingency by untrained and/or inexperienced individuals, e.g., by human infants.

The task of distinguishing between events that are merely correlated and events that represent a truly contingent relationship would seem to grow progressively more difficult as the two events become closer in time and space, to a point (but see Garcia, Ervin, & Koelling, 1966, for a classic exception). Perhaps the single case of correlated appearance most compelling for an attribution of contingency is that where one event (action, behavior) immediately precedes the other and is contiguous in space with it (for a good example in nonhuman primate subjects, see Meyer, Treichler, & Meyer, 1965). Frequently, in cases where such temporal sequencing and special contiguity exist, it takes almost the equivalent of a scientific experiment to demonstrate convincingly that true contingency does *not* exist. In such cases, one might expect most individuals to perceive contingency, whether or not it really exists in the purely scientific sense.

To summarize, most psychologists would consider one event to be contingent upon another if the former occurred as a direct result of the appearance of the latter and if it would likely not have occurred had the latter not appeared. One event is said to cause or control the other. Mere coincidence in time and space does not necessarily insure that a contingent relationship exists, although there may be a persistent tendency on the part of some individuals to so conclude.

THEORETICAL VIEWS
REGARDING CONTINGENCY

Why has consideration of the presence (or lack thereof) of a contingency between two events (actions, behaviors) been prominent in psychological thinking in the areas of learning, perception, social behavior, psychopathology, and development? In this section some ways in which contingency has been involved in psychological theory and experimentation are reviewed.

1. Contingency in Conditioning Studies

An enormous amount of research time and effort has been devoted to studies of conditioning throughout all but the earliest of psychology's history. Concepts of contingency are involved in most past and present interpretations of both Pavlovian conditioning (e.g., Gormezano, 1977; Pavlov, 1927) and operant conditioning (e.g., Ferster & Skinner, 1957; Skinner, 1938), and both paradigms provide textbook examples of experimentally defined and controlled contingencies between events in a subject's immediate environment and the subject's behavior (and vice versa).

In Pavlovian (classical) conditioning, the display of a particular behavior pattern (UR) is initially contingent on the occurrence of some particular stimulus (US)—the behavior is a reflexive, automatic response triggered by the subject's perception of a US but not usually displayed in the absence of the US. However, through the conditioning process, other previously "neutral" stimuli reliably associated with the US can come to cause the display of that behavior pattern to occur. The pattern can then be said to be contingent on the appearance of these new stimuli, termed CS's. A great deal of research has been devoted to study of factors that influence the relative strength of the acquired contingent relationship between a given CR and its preceding CS. This research has demonstrated that numerous parameters that describe the CR are dependent upon the spacial-temporal-modality proximity or contiguity between the relevant CS and the original US (cf. Rescorla & Wagner, 1972).

In typical operant conditioning paradigms, on the other hand, there exists some contingency between the subject's operant responses and experimentally determined reinforcers. Operant conditioning theorists have concentrated on the nature of that contingent relationship, indicated by their emphasis on "schedule of reinforcement," as perhaps the most important parameter in the learning model. Thus, the "laws of learning" are said to be robust across species and behaviors selected for operant control, whereas operant control is viewed as most efficiently exercised via direct manipulation of the contingency between the subject's behavior and the reinforcement that it receives for displaying the behavior. This view has carried over to empirical studies: much of the classic operant conditioning experimental literature has focused on study of schedule manipulation (e.g., Ferster & Skinner, 1957).

2. Cognitive Interpretations of Contingency

In traditional explanations of conditioning phenomena, comparatively little emphasis was placed on possible mediational involvement by the subject in its display of experimentally modified behavior. Indeed, some proponents of rigorous behaviorism explicitly argued that consideration of mediational processes is not necessary to predict and control behavior and in fact can only serve to sidetrack progress in achieving a true science of behavior (e.g., Skinner, 1938). Such viewpoints have come under increasing attack over the past 15 years by cognitively oriented psychologists. Rather than dismissing the importance (or even the existence) of mediational activity on the part of the subject, the cognitive psychologists have made the study of mediational processes the primary focus of their research and theory.

The change in emphasis embodied by cognitive psychology has important consequences for consideration of contingency. Whereas traditional learning theorists argued that effects of contingency manipulations were automatically expressed in behavior by the subject via the laws of learning (and thus not requiring any "higher" mental activity by the subject), cognitive psychologists have explicitly implicated mediational processes by the subject in accounting for its behavior given some experimentally determined contingency. In other words, the subject is hypothesized to perceive and interpret the contingency at hand, and then to behave accordingly.

For example, in Pavlovian conditioning paradigms, a subject typically learns to exhibit a particular behavior in the presence of a previously neutral stimulus. In cognitive terms, the subject comes to perceive a contingency between the appearance of the CS and the occurrence of the US (which elicits the behavior); as a result, it comes to anticipate the occurrence of the US when it perceives the CS and consequently exhibits the appropriate behavior (the CR). Behavior in a typical operant paradigm can likewise be analyzed from a cognitive perspective. For example, a subject pressing a lever in a Skinner box for food reward can be said to have learned that acquisition of food pellets is contingent on the lever being pressed, i.e., lever pressing results in delivery of food. Once the subject perceives that this contingency exists, it need only produce the "causal" behavior (lever pressing) when it desires the contingent outcome (food pellets). Thus the cognitive approach assumes that subjects are capable of perceiving, interpreting, and evaluating contingencies in their respective environments, and that they routinely adjust their behavior accordingly.

3. Noncontingency: Learned Helplessness Theory

The cognitive approach to contingency has had perhaps its most widespread impact on contemporary psychological thinking through its application to cases of clear-cut *non*contingency between events (actions, behaviors). During the past decade extensive study of situations in which such noncontingency exists has been carried out under the banner of learned helplessness theory (Seligman, 1975). This theory argues that subjects readily perceive and make judgments about the existence (or lack thereof) and the relative strength of various contingencies between their behavior and environmental events. Perception of noncontingency between behavior and events (especially aversive events) is theorized to have three important consequences for the subject: (1) it will be more likely to perceive noncontingency in future situations, even if "real" contingency does exist, i.e., it will be impaired in its perception of future contingencies; (2) its motivation to initiate behaviors in situations for which it perceives noncontingency will be reduced; (3) it will experience a loss of affect in such situations. Such cognitive, motivational, and affective deficits are said to be a direct consequence of the perception of "helplessness," i.e., the perception that crucial events in the environment are *not* contingent on any of the subject's behavior.

Learned helplessness theory had its origins in animal studies concerned with the consequences of exposure to noncontingent aversive stimulation in carefully controlled experimental settings. Nevertheless, the theory has been used to interpret a wide range of "real-life" human phenomena. Such phenomena typically occur in naturalistic settings rather than in psychological laboratories, and they often involve naturally occurring complex social stimuli rather than experimentally controlled and calibrated nonsocial stimulation. Two applications of learned helplessness theory have been particularly emphasized by Seligman and other contemporary authors: (1) the use of learned helplessness as a model for human reactive depression; and (2) consideration of the developmental consequences of being reared in a "noncontingent" environment, i.e., one in which the subject has little or no control over salient stimulation.

In the case of learned helplessness as a model for reactive depression, it has been necessary to reformulate the original version of the theory in light of the findings indicating that not all humans who perceive themselves as being in a helpless state become depressed (c.f. Seligman et al., 1978). The Pennsylvania reformulation of learned helplessness theory (e.g., Abramson, Seligman, & Teasdale, 1978) acknowledges that although perception of lack of control over important life events may represent a necessary condition for "helplessness" (reactive) depression, such a perception is clearly not sufficient in and of itself to produce depression in all subjects; other conditions must be satisfied (see also Alloy & Seligman, 1979; Miller & Norman, 1979). Nevertheless, it has been demonstrated that: (1) experience with noncontingency between one's behavior and certain events occurring in laboratory settings produces subsequent cognitive, motivational, and affective deficits in some human subjects; and (2) these deficits in cognitive, motivational, and affective functioning are highly similar to those demonstrated by psychiatric patients diagnosed as clinically depressed. Such data are seen to be consistent with the learned helplessness theory of depression (e.g., Alloy & Seligman, 1979).

Virtually all the data designed to demonstrate the relationship between perception of noncontingency and depression have come from laboratory studies in which the relevants noncontingency is manipulated directly by the experimenter. Each subject (in human studies) is later questioned to document that his or her perception of the relative contingency (or lack thereof) between behavior and outcomes is consistent with the experimenter's manipulation. To the best of my knowledge, however, there exist no data that document *within a natural setting* a clear-cut, causal relationship between an individual's perception of lack of contingency and a subsequent depressive reaction. Although such an etiology has been hypothesized to occur (e.g., Seligman, 1975), actual contingencies (and subjects' perceptions of them) have not been operationally defined and measured in real-life settings in a manner that allows the proposed etiology to be demonstrated in scientifically convincing fashion. Until such operational definitions and associated measurement techniques have been developed, direct tests of the helplessness theory of depression in natural settings are not possible.

4. Developmental Implications of Noncontingency

The second major application of learned helplessness theory, and the one most relevant for the present essay, has occurred in the area of social and cognitive development. According to Seligman (1975), frequent and/or prolonged exposure to noncontingent stimulation during infancy and childhood should have potentially serious developmental consequences. Individuals reared in environments where they lack control over important stimuli may develop cognitive, motivational, and affective deficits that parallel the deficits found in laboratory animals and undergraduate volunteers participating in learned helplessness experiments. Seligman argues that children reared in such "noncontingent" environments may be impaired in their subsequent ability to recognize actual contingencies between their own behavior and environmental events later in life. They also will be less motivated to initiate behavior in subsequent settings and thus less likely to engage in activities that might lead to the discovery of new contingencies. Furthermore, their affect should be lower than normal, hindering the establishment of social bonds and the discovery of various social contingencies.

It is important to note that these hypothesized deficits are *not* thought to result from a lack of environmental stimulation per se. Of course, there is no question the environmental deprivation itself can have devastating developmental consequences. Such deprivation during rearing has been shown to result in profound deficits in cognitive, motivational, and affective development in a variety of species, including advanced nonhuman primates and man. Clearly, a subject will be naïve with respect to recognition of contingency between its behavior and environmental changes if it has been reared in a totally sterile environment. Rather, Seligman argues that similar deficits can emerge even among subjects reared in stimulus-rich environments. The crucial matter is whether any contingency exists between a subject's behavior and stimulus change—or more correctly, whether the subject is *perceiving* a contingency between its behavior and stimulus change.

Seligman's hypotheses concerning the developmental consequences of perceived noncontingency are intuitively appealing, and they have received the endorsement of many contemporary developmental psychologists and psychiatrists. There does exist some strong but indirect evidence from the animal literature that generally supports a learned helplessness interpretation; suggestive evidence also comes from some laboratory studies of human infants. Some of these data are examined later in this chapter. However, I am not aware of the existence of any direct evidence taken from natural settings that provides unequivocal support for Seligman's hypotheses concerning developmental consequences of not learning contingencies between behavior and events in one's environment. To provide such unequivocal support, one must first be able to identify and calibrate in a natural setting any contingency that exists between a subject's behavior and alterations in the environment. Additionally, one must be able to assess the subject's *perception* of what (or how great) each contingency might be. This is no easy matter, as is evident from the sections that follow.

PERCEPTION OF CONTINGENCY

Given the theoretical importance ascribed by helplessness theory to a subject's perception of any contingency between its behavior and subsequent events, it would seem highly important for an investigator to be able to evaluate the relative strength of the contingency, as well as the subject's ability to perceive the contingency. In a recent paper, John Watson (1978) has developed a formal representation—based on Bayesian probability theory— of factors influencing a subject's perception of contingency between its behavior and events in its environment. Two types of contingency are considered by Watson. The first is embodied in the conditional probability that a particular stimulus event will occur within a predetermined time after the subject has emitted a given behavior, symbolized by Watson as $P/R \rightarrow S$.[1] The other type of contingency is embodied in the conditional probability that if a particular stimulus event has occurred, the subject has previously emitted a behavior within a predetermined period of time. Watson represents this conditional probability with the symbol $P/R \leftarrow S$. If both of these conditional probabilities are equal to one, then the subject should have little difficulty recognizing the contingency between its action and the occurrence

---

[1] Watson (1978) has developed his own representation of traditional Bayesian conditional probabilities, e.g., $P/R \rightarrow S$ for $P(S/R)$ and $P/R \leftarrow S$ for $P(R/S)$, where R and S are the subject's response and the subsequent stimulus change in the environment, respectively. He prefers such representation because it provides information not only about the direction of the contingency (symbolized by the direction of the arrow)—as does the conventional model of representing conditional probabilities—but also about the temporal relationship between R and S (symbolized by the left–right order of R and S), which the conventional representation does not.

of the stimulus event, assuming the predetermined time period is not too long in duration. However, more interesting situations arise when either or both of these probabilities are less than unity.

Consider the case where $O < P/R \rightarrow S < 1$. Here, the stimulus event does *not* occur after every one of the subject's relevant behaviors. In other words, the subject's behavior is not always sufficient to produce the stimulus event. This situation should be familiar with students of instrumental conditioning, for it represents a case of partial reinforcement. A common example for a human infant in a natural setting would be cases in which its mother came to its crib some, but not all, of the times when the infant began to cry (c.f. Gewirtz & Boyd, 1977).

Now consider the case where $O < P/R \leftarrow S < 1$. Here, the behavior of the subject does not always precede the occurrence of the stimulus event in question, i.e., the subject's behavior is not always *necessary* for the stimulus event to occur. This would be the case if the mother came to her infant's crib occasionally when it was not crying. Of course, an extreme case in which the subject is not in control of relevant stimulus events could well lead to perceptions of helplessness by the subject according to Seligman (1975), as was previously discussed. At any rate, Watson (1978) argues that situations in which both types of contingencies are less than perfect (i.e., both types of conditional probabilities are less than 1) are probably far more common—at least for infants in the presence of social stimuli—than are cases where there is a perfect contingency between subject behavior and subsequent social stimulation. Thus, the young subject is frequently faced with a potential problem in detecting such less-than-perfect contingencies, especially when social stimulation is involved.

According to Watson, the extent of this problem is in large part a function of the degree to which the two types of conditional probabilities are different from the base-rate probabilities for the occurrence of the subject's behavior and/or the stimlus event [P(R) and P(S), respectively] within the predetermined time period. If such differences are relatively large, then the subject should have an easy time perceiving a contingency between its behavior and the stimulus event. To use the previous example, the infant should have relatively little difficulty in detecting a contingency between its crying and the appearance of its mother if the mother's base rate of approaching is quite low but her likelihood of approaching when her infant cries is quite high. The infant should also have little difficulty detecting a contingency if it seldom cries, but, nearly every time that it does, the mother suddenly appears. In contrast, the infant should, in theory, have a much more difficult time detecting a contingency if the mother is equally likely to appear when the infant is not crying as when it is crying. Of course, if the mother is far more likely to appear following the infant's cries than she is when the infant is not crying, the contingency again becomes relatively easy to detect. It is the *discrepancy* between conditional and base-rate probabilities that is most important, according to Watson, not the absolute values of such probabilities.[2]

However, Watson (1978) does not believe that absolute levels of these various probabilities are unimportant in consideration of perception of contingency. On the contrary, he presents a convincing model demonstrating that perception of contingency becomes increasingly difficult as the absolute value of either the base rate of the subject's behavior [P(R)] or the base rate of the stimulus event [P(S)] increases in absolute value. In terms of our example, the infant will have an increasingly difficult time detecting a contingency between its crying and its mother's appearance as its base rate of crying increases and/or as the mother's tendency to approach her infant generally increases. All other things being equal, an infant that cries a great deal will have more trouble perceiving a contingency between its crying and its mother's actions than an infant who seldom cries. Likewise, the infant whose mother routinely comes to its crib will have more difficulty perceiving a contingency than one whose mother seldom appears.

Watson (1978) further argues that perception of contingency should be influenced by the *unit of time* between behavior and stimulus event used by the subject to evaluate possible contingency. In general, the greater the discrepancy between the subject's subjective time unit and the actual time from behavior to appearance of the relevant stimulus, the more difficult the perception of contingency between the two. Note that it is not necessarily the case that longer periods between behavior and stimulus automatically result in poorer perception of contingency. For example, if an infant is expecting, on the basis of previous experience, that its mother will appear about 15 seconds after it begins crying, and if in fact she appears in only 2 seconds, then because the infant is not "expecting" her so early it will have more trouble detecting a contingency than if she indeed appeared 15 seconds after crying began.

Finally, the present perception of contingency model suggests one effective strategy a subject can employ to improve its capability to detect a contingency between its activities and subsequent changes in its immediate environment. The strategy involves altering the base rate of the subject's target responses and subsequently monitoring the base rate of the suspected target stimulus event for any corresponding changes. To return to the previous example, if our hypothetical infant suddenly increased its rate of crying and then noted marked increases in its mother's rate of approach, its chance of perceiving a

---

[2]There are (at least) two alternative ways to represent discrepancies between conditional and base-rate probabilities: one based on the absolute difference between the two, $P(S/R) - P(S)$, the other based on the ratio between the two, $P(S/R)/P(S)$. Watson (1978) uses the ratio form, which is the Bayesian representation. At least some authors may use the other form.

contingency between crying and maternal approaches would be much greater than if its crying rate and that of maternal approach continued at the same absolute rate of occurrence. Similarly, voluntary decreases (or even cessation) of crying bouts by the infant should increase its chance of detecting the contingency over that afforded by keeping the response rate constant (cf., Watson, 1978). In contrast, changes in the base-rate occurrence of the relevant environmental event that are independent of the subject's behavior should, according to a model, make the infant's task of detecting a contingency more difficult.

Using an ingenious laboratory paradigm, Watson (1978) has been able to make direct tests of some of the above hypotheses on 8- to 14-week-old human infant subjects. His earlier research (e.g., Watson & Ramey, 1972) had shown that infants in this age range would initiate and maintain kicking behavior by means of special pillows placed under the infants' legs, when such activity resulted in contingent activation of a mobile hanging above the infants' crib. Indeed, not only did such a contingency produce significant increases in leg movements over levels displayed during a noncontingent baseline period (when kicking did not activate the mobile), but also many of the subjects began to direct smiles, coos, and other "social signals" toward the mobile when they activated it. In his more recent work, Watson (1978) has manipulated the strength of the contingency between a subject's leg movements and activation of the mobile in two independent ways. First, the probability that any one kick by a subject will activate the mobile is systematically varied between p = .5 and p = 1.0, i.e, some subjects are placed on partial reinforcement schedules. Second, the mobile can be activated at a predetermined rate independent of any behavior by a subject; this rate of noncontingent activation (e.g., 4 times per minute, 2 times per minute, etc.) is also systematically varied across infant subjects. Thus, in this paradigm, Watson has been able to manipulate both the strength of the contingency and the frequency of noncontingent stimulation, and he can measure the subject's ability to perceive the contingency by calculating the relative rates of increase in leg movement over baseline for subjects exposed to different contingencies and/or different base rates of mobile activation.

In general, data from studies employing this and similar infant paradigms have supported most of the hypotheses concerning perception of contingency that have been outlined. For example, subjects who display high rates of baseline kicking are less likely to increase their rate of kicking than those with lower baselines, independent of either the experimentally manipulated strength of the contingency or the base rate of noncontingent mobile movement. However, one of Watson's (1978) findings was not predicted by any of those hypotheses: In cases where less-than-perfect contingency existed between kicking and mobile activation, optional learning did *not* occur when noncontingent rates of activation were minimized. Instead, subjects showed the greatest responsiveness when the strength of the contingency between their behavior and mobile activation "matched" the rate of noncontingent mobile movement. For example, although subjects with perfect contingency (p = 1.0) between kicking and mobile activation learned best when there was no noncontingent activation, infants with a p = .75 contingency learned best when the rate of noncontingent activation was 8/minute. Subjects in the p = .5 contingency condition learned best when the noncontingent activation rate was 4/minute.

These findings are potentially important because they call into question the assumption that the infant subjects were perceiving the experimentally controlled contingencies according to Bayesian probabilities. Watson's infants did not behave as if they were making perceptual judgments about contingency according to the same standards or "rules" that are embodied in our mathematically based laws of probability. In at least some of Watson's experimental conditions, the performance of subjects whose perception of contingency should have been "optimal," according to Bayesian probabilities, was actually inferior to that of subjects who, according to Bayesian probability analysis, should have been faced with a far more difficult perceptual task. Such findings suggest that 8- to 14-week-old human infants do not make judgments about contingency in the same manner as would a student steeped in probability theory, given the same information about the relative occurrence of the contingency in question.

Other data from a very different line of research indicate that human infants may not be the only individuals who fail to follow the laws of probability theory in making judgments about contingency-based outcomes. For example, Tversky and Kahneman (1974) and Goude (1980), among others, have shown that a wide range of adult human subjects consistently make judgments about the likelihood of certain contingent events occurring that are systematically inaccurate from the standpoint of probability theory, even though such subjects are provided with all the information needed to arrive at the "correct" judgment, according to straightforward calculation of Bayesian probabilities. Thus, there may be some real problems associated with theoretical models of contingency perception that have their basis in classical conditional probability theory.

If perception-of-contingency models based on Bayesian probabilities do *not,* in fact, always provide accurate accounts of the perceptual processes used by subjects in arriving at judgments about contingencies in their respective environments, then the study of effects of contingency upon behavior is clearly made far more difficult. A veritable Pandora's box of problems and questions emerges. If subjects are not following the rules of probability in arriving at judgments about contingencies, what rules *are* they following? Indeed, do all subjects follow the same set of perceptual rules (whatever they may be)? Does a subject change its rules for judging contingencies with increasing age and/or experience? Are contingencies involving different types or classes of stimuli all judged according to the same standards?

These questions become relevant when one abandons the assumption that subjects always perceive contingency in the mathematically "correct" way (i.e., that perceptual systems in advanced animals and humans have been "selected for" making mathematically accurate judgments of probabilistic events). Consideration of these questions enormously complicates the task of studying the effects of contingency on behavior, as is shown in the next sections (see also Brunswik, 1956 and Petrinovich, 1979 for detailed presentations of the perceptual problems involved).

CONTINGENCIES INVOLVING SOCIAL STIMULI

In most previous experimental investigations of contingencies between a subject's behavior and events or stimuli in the test environment, the events and/or stimuli have typically been of a nonsocial nature. Thus, delivery of food or water, onset or termination of electric shock, and a variety of lights, bells, and buzzers have been much more common events and stimuli in these experiments than has been behavior displayed by a conspecific. Often, the decision to use nonsocial stimuli in such experiments has been based in large part on issues of control and convenience: Lights, buzzers, and bells are usually easier to turn on and off in a systematic fashion than are most activities of conspecifics, even if they are paid confederates of the experimenter. Still, the assumption is typically made that the principles discovered using such nonsocial stimuli do generalize to real-life situations involving social stimuli. Recent data from a variety of perspectives have called into serious question the validity of such an assumption. Instead, it appears that the perceptual processes involved with at least some social stimuli are not identical to those involved in the perception of most nonsocial stimuli.

First, it is clear that members of many animal species have perceptual systems that are "tuned" to be especially sensitive to particular social stimuli. Such perceptual biases are thought to be the product of evolution. As such, they may reflect genetically determined, prewired "feature detectors" in the subject (e.g., Sackett, 1963) or represent the product of experience during "critical" or "sensitive" periods (phases) in the subject's development (e.g., Immelmann & Suomi, 1980; Scott, Stewart, & DeGhett, 1974). Most of the stimuli that are the objects of these perceptual biases are social in nature, and most of these social stimili come from conspecifics. Classical ethologists recognized the existence of "innate releasing stimuli" (e.g., Tinbergen, 1951) for many species of animals, while more recent evidence has documented perceptual biases by human infants for certain social signals emitted by their mothers, and vice versa. Thus, some social stimuli may be far more salient for a subject than most other stimuli it might be exposed to, either in its natural environment or in a laboratory setting. Indeed, some authors (e.g., Bischof, 1975; Dawkins, 1976) have proposed that a regular hierarchy of relative salience exists for most social stimuli. The more salient stimuli will clearly be the focus of greater attention by the subject than will "ordinary" stimuli, which, in turn, could very well influence the subject's perception of contingency when prepotent social stimuli are involved. Under these circumstances, principles involved in perception of contingency with "ordinary" stimuli may not always generalize to situations that contain prepotent social stimuli.

A second "unique" characteristic of at least some social contingencies stems from the dynamic qualities of complex social interactions. In an interactive bout that involves several mutual exchanges of activity among the participants, neither participant is usually in total "control" of the other; instead, the coordinated actions of both are required to keep the interaction going. In such a case a subject may well perceive strong contingencies between its activities and those of its partner, but additionally it may be aware that its own actions are themselves dependent, to some degree, on the particular behavior displayed by the partner at any one moment. The epitome of such mutual activities is seen in synchronous behavior, wherein each participant adjusts its own activities to mesh smoothly with those of its partner (see Watson, 1978, for a thorough discussion of the unique characteristics of synchronous interactions vis-a-vis perception of contingency). Synchronous interactions among members of highly social species are hardly uncommon, and they include such diverse activities as "meshing" between mother and infant rhesus monkeys (e.g., Hinde & Simpson, 1975) and sexual intercourse resulting in mutual orgasm among adult human dyads (e.g., Masters & Johnson, 1966). It is worth noting that true synchronous behavior between two (or more) participants usually is not achieved without some degree of practice on the part of at least some of the participants.

A subject's perception of social contingency need not be limited to cases in which the occurrence of some behavior by another individual is dependent upon the subject's own behavior. Indeed, as was mentioned previously, in cases of synchronous interactions a subject must also be able to perceive contingencies between the behavior of its partner and its own response. Perception of contingency between another's actions and one's own responses is certainly not limited to cases of interactive synchrony. Indeed, an individual living in a complex social group who is unable to perceive in what ways or to what degree its behavioral options are limited by the particular activities of fellow group members is unlikely to survive group living very long. Moreover, at least in advanced primate social groups, a socially sophisticated individual can readily perceive contingencies between the actions and responses of other individuals, i.e,. it can observe the interactions of others and perceive social contingencies that need not involve its own behavioral participation.

Such characteristics of contingencies involving social stimuli (and responses) make modeling of a subject's perception of these social contingencies a difficult task, indeed, for any investigator. Even if subjects did perceive social contingencies in accordance with laws of Bayesian probability (which they do not, as was previously discussed), the task would be formidable. One would still have to take into account possible differences in prepotent salience of the various social stimuli perceived by the subject, the degree to which behavioral control of the interactions under analysis was mutually distributed among the participants, and the involvement of the subject itself in the interactions. Moreover, there are developmental considerations that are discussed next.

DEVELOPMENTAL ASPECTS OF
CONTINGENCY PERCEPTION

Earlier in this chapter, Seligman's (1975) hypotheses concerning the possibly profound developmental consequences of restricted opportunities to discover contingencies involving one's own behavior and events in one's environment were outlined. It was then pointed out that direct and conclusive evaluation of these hypotheses regarding helplessness required some means of assessing a subject's perception of such contingencies. The difficulty of such an assessment task has been compounded enormously by the finding that subjects do not (always) perceive contingencies strictly according to the laws of Bayesian probability, and thus calculations of contingency based on Bayesian probability may not accurately represent a given subject's perception of that contingency. The problem of assessing the subject's perception becomes even more complex when the stimuli involved are social in nature.

The difficulties encountered in trying to assess a subject's perception of contingency should not distract us from the potentially important application of learned helplessness theory to our understanding of social and cognitive development. Yet, it is true that a developmental perspective also introduces additional complications to the problem of assessing a subject's perception of social contingencies. The complications arise from the strong possibility that a subject's perceptions of contingency may undergo fundamental change during ontogeny. There are at least four means by which such developmental changes in perception of contingencies might occur.

First, a subject's perceptual sensitivity to particular stimuli may undergo some changes during different stages or phases of development. For example, there is now evidence that visual areas of the brain of precocial birds like Zebra finches exhibit increased growth followed by a sharp increase in the rate of cell death during the period of maximal sensitivity to imprinting stimuli, a period when subjects appear to be far more interested in watching and following conspecifics than before (Immelmann & Suomi, 1980). Rhesus monkey infants display a marked increase in responsiveness to social threat stimuli at 60–80 days of age; the same stimuli presented earlier in life fail to elicit any noticeable reactions in these infants (Sackett, 1966). In human infants, the stimulus threshold for elicitation of the smiling responses changes in qualitative fashion in around 3 months of age (Spitz & Wolf, 1946). Also in humans, changes in sensitivity to secondary sex characteristics of members of the opposite sex appear to occur with the onset of puberty. Thus, during development, an individual's perception of a given contingency in its environment may change simply because its perceptual sensitivity for the stimuli involved in the contingency undergoes change.

Another means by which a subject's perception of social contingencies can change during ontogeny involves changes in the nature of the contingent stimuli themselves. Members of many social species do not behave the same way toward infants as they do toward adolescent and/or adult conspecifics. For example, it is well-documented that adult humans of both sexes simplify their grammatical structures, exaggerate their pronunciations, and repeat their words and phrases when speaking to infants, relative to their speaking habits toward adolescents and adults (e.g., Leiderman, 1980; Studdart-Kennedy, 1980). Suomi (1979a) has demonstrated that socially sophisticated rhesus monkey juveniles, adolescents, and adults of both sexes direct qualitatively different behavior patterns toward infants than they direct toward older conspecifics. Indeed, in many species of birds and mammals, infants have unique physical characteristics (e.g., natal coats) that clearly differentiate them from other conspecifics; when these physical characteristics disappear, the "special treatment" by conspecifics generally ceases (e.g., Grzimek, 1977). Thus, there is good reason to suspect that in many species an individual's perception of social contingencies may change as it grows older, in part because the nature of the social stimulation that it receives changes substantially, i.e., the contingencies themselves to which it is exposed change as it grows older.

A third reason one would expect an individual's peception of social contingencies to change during ontogeny involves maturation of that individual's cognitive capabilities. Cognitively oriented developmental psychologists, from Piaget (1951) to several contributors to the present volume, have argued that during ontogeny an individual undergoes major transformations in the way he or she perceives the world; indeed, several authors have explicitly pointed to ontogenic changes in how one perceives causality as a prominent exemplar of such cognitive transformations. Parallel ontogenic changes in cognitive capabilities, at least early in life, have been reported for advanced nonhuman primates (e.g., Chevalier-Skolnikoff, 1977; Harlow, 1959; Parker, 1977). The most obvious assumption would be that as both human and nonhuman primate infants mature cognitively, they become more capable of detecting contingencies that are increasingly subtle, with greater separation of the contingent events (actions, behaviors) from each other in time and space. On the other hand, increased cognitive capabilities could also lead one to perceive that no real contingency exists in some cases for which less cognitively mature individuals might routinely (and incorrectly) infer that their behavior caused the event in question.

A final means by which one's perception of contingency might change during development is that of simple experience. A given subject exposed over an extended period of time to the same general set of stimuli and contingent relationships among them may well change its perception of the reasons why events occur in the environment when it has additional opportunities to observe (and/or participate in) such events. Such "experiential" changes in perception of contingencies may be quite independent of maturation per se, but they may also be quite important for the individual. For example, a stranger entering an established social group can be at a tremdous disadvantage within the group until he or she can learn about intragroup interactions, relationships, power structures, and lines of communication. This usually requires some observation, if not actual physical interaction, whether the target group is a troop of rhesus monkeys, a class of kindergarten children, a clique of high school students, or the membership of a country club. In such cases, it takes time and experience to be able to perceive and correctly identify relevant contingent relationships amidst all the activity occurring within the group.

Thus, there is ample reason to conclude that an individual may undergo considerable change in both the manner and the precision with which it perceives contingencies, particularly social contingencies, during the course of its development. As was pointed out at the beginning of this section, these developmental considerations do not make the task of assessing a subject's relative perception of a particular contingency any easier for the researcher trying to test empirically the developmental predictions of learned helplessness theory.

CURRENT EMPIRICAL APPROACHES
TO DEVELOPMENTAL STUDY
OF SOCIAL CONTINGENCIES

Despite the extreme difficulties involved in attempting to assess a subject's perception of a particular contingency, there is a diversity of current research designed to investigate the developmental consequences of exposure to various social contingencies, including those which afford little, if any, control of stimulus events by the subject. Many of these studies have focused on comparisons of subjects exposed to various social contingencies with those for whom such exposure was either denied or constrained in some fashion. Virtually all of such studies have been conducted under laboratory conditions rather than in naturalistic settings. Their protypical design is one in which two (or more) randomly selected groups of subjects, following a base-line assessment period, are differently exposed to social stimulation; often, this stimulation is provided by a model or surrogate rather than a real conspecific. A follow-up period, in which all subjects are tested under conditions of identical (or closely matched) stimulation, is usually included in the experimental design. Studies of this sort have been carried out on both human infants and young animal subjects (see Watson & Ramey, 1972).

It should be obvious that studies of this design, which use human infants for subjects, have been quite restricted in terms of the strength of the social contingency manipulation, the period of time during which the manipulation is in force, and the duration of the follow-up period, for quite proper ethical and practical reasons. Thus, virtually all of these studies have used manipulations involving presentation of "safe" stimulation, such as Watson's mobiles, for less than a half-hour period, with follow-up testing of similar duration. The scope of possible effects that would be produced and observed in such studies should be trivial compared to some of the postulated effects of "real-life" social contingencies. This is desirable from an ethical point of view, but not necessarily from a scientific one—it would be nice to know how well laboratory findings generalize to naturalistic settings, and vice versa.

Occasionally, however, investigators can be lucky, as was Watson's research group (1977) a few years ago:

> A study of 8-week-old infants learning to control a mobile with head movement was carried out ... The single-session laboratory experiment involved a 10-minute learning period that was preceded by a 10-minute exposure to the mobile turning noncontingently for half of the 32 subjects. To our dismay, however, neither the group with nor the group without prior noncontingent stimulation showed any general learning. Examination of interview records with the mothers of the infants revealed that more than 60% of these infants were presently being exposed to at least one automatic "wind-up" mobile at home. The usual variety of this wind-up mobile turns while playing a nursery tune for approximately 5 minutes after being wound. Similar interview data available from a study carried out 6 years previously showed that only 12% of our samples (N = 48) were then being exposed to this automatic mobile. Since the old and new samples were at the same age and from the same social class and geographic locale, the contrast implies a very significant shift upward ($X^2 = 21.92$; $p < 0.001$) in at least one form of noncontingent stimulation in the child-rearing practices of the San Francisco Bay Area middle class.
>
> Of equal interest to this sharp rise in exposure to commercially produced automatic mobiles was the result of a post hoc analysis of learning records,

which indicated that those infants who obtained high individual learning scores (as assessed by rate change in the contingent period) either had no automatic mobile or, if they had one, also were described by their mothers as having gained control (by kicking or batting) of some toy hanging over their crib....

It would seem, then, that the recent rise in exposure to noncontingent stimulation has not been without consequence for these infants. Whether our measures of learning are all that have been affected or whether this interference effect has a wider range of transfer for these infants is not yet known.... The case illustrates well the potential invasive possibilities for interference effects from positive noncontingent stimulation [pp. 135-136].

Other studies of similar design, but using nonhuman subjects, have been able to employ more prolonged and powerful manipulations, and in some cases investigators have been able to conduct follow-up testing throughout much of the subject's period of ontogeny. Social stimulation is often simulated or modeled under the direct control of the experimenter in these studies. For example, Latane, Joy, Meltzer, and Lubell (1972) provided rat weanlings with daily stimulation via "interaction" with gloved human hands, while other rats received equivalent exposure to similar-sized inanimate models of the hand. Latane et al. (1972) found that the rats exposed to the interactive hand displayed much greater interest in the stimulus than did those exposed to the stationary counterpart, as indexed by contact and orientation scores; the former subjects also explored more and were more active than those exposed to the stationary, "nonsocial" stimulus. In follow-up tests, these advantages were maintained.

Mason (1978), in an ingenious series of studies, examined the effects of rearing rhesus monkeys with animate surrogates instead of real mothers. These subjects were compared throughout infancy and into adolescence with monkeys reared with inanimate surrogates. In an early study, the animate surrogate was simply a terrycloth-covered wooden dummy mounted at the end of a long horizontal pole attached to a motor which, when activated, turned so as to make the surrogate revolve around it in a circle. Otherwise, the surrogate was an identical model of the stationary surrogate with which control monkeys were reared. Mason found that the infants reared with mobile surrogates showed less fear, greater exploratory tendencies, and virtually none of the stereotypic disturbance behavior that characterized the control monkeys' repertoires. Group differences persisted into adolescence.

In a later study, Mason raised infant rhesus monkeys in outdoor enclosures where they lived alone except for a surrogate "mother," which also occupied the enclosure. Some of these infant monkeys had surrogates that were modified spring-mounted hobbyhorses, each capable of jiggling about when mounted but otherwise inanimate. The remaining monkey infants were given a multiparous adult female dog for a surrogate mother. The dogs were kept tied to short leads so they could not follow the infants around their respective enclosures and, in that respect, they were comparable to the hobbyhorse surrogates. Unlike the hobbyhorses, however, the dogs could and would interact socially with the infants, although they clearly did not possess anywhere near the same behavioral repertoire as a real monkey mother. In all other respects, both groups were exposed to identical rearing environments.

On most measures of exploration, activity, and cognitive skills the dog-reared infants were found to be superior to those reared with hobbyhorse surrogates. Moreover, as juveniles and adolescents, the dog-reared monkeys adjusted to living in conspecific groups far more rapidly and more completely than did the hobbyhorse-reared subjects. Mason (1978) has concluded that these group differences could be attributed to experience with social contingencies gained by subjects who could interact with their canine foster "mother" and denied to subjects whose surrogate could jiggle in response to physical stimulation but otherwise remained inanimate. These differences were strong enough to carry over to behavior patterns years after the surrogates had been removed from the subjects' respective housing units.

During the past few years, Suomi and Perez (1978) have carried out a series of studies at Wisconsin that also involved rearing infant rhesus monkeys with artificial surrogates differing in their capability to produce social stimulation and to provide contingency experience for their respective infants.[3] Unlike previous surrogates used as artificial "mothers," these surrogates were explicitly designed to serve as surrogate "peers" that could reproduce behavior patterns and interaction sequences modeled on that of real conspecific peers, except that they would be under the direct control of the experimenter. An example of a surrogate "peer" is pictured in Fig. 8.1; it is basically a hand puppet with appendages, body, and face made to resemble that of a 4-month-old rhesus monkey with respect to size and features. When operated by a well-trained experimenter, it can be used to mimic specific response sequences exhibited by various classes of social stimuli.

The objective of the first study in the series was to compare the behavior of infants in the presence of like-reared age mates as opposed to behavior in the presence of animate surrogate "puppets" made to mimic age mates in both appearance and behavior. Infant monkeys were separated from their mothers at birth and reared for the first 30 days of life in the neonatal nursery, after which they were moved to individual cages where they could see and hear, but not physically contact, other monkeys. Beginning at 30 days, each subject was removed from its home cage and placed in a 1 × 1.3 × .8 meter wire-mesh test cage for a 20-minute period, 4 days each week. The test cage contained either a like-reared peer or a similar-sized and colored "puppet" surrogate, hand

[3]This surrogate research was supported by U.S.P.H.S. Grant No. MH-11894 from the National Institute of Mental Health and by funds provided by the Graduate School of the University of Wisconsin–Madison.

FIG. 8.1.   A puppet "peer" surrogate. The puppet is approximately the size of a 4-month-old rhesus infant. A skilled operator controls its activity, including arm movements and facial displays.

operated by a tester with 17 years of experience with young monkey subjects. The tester was directed to reproduce, to the best of her ability, the activity of an age mate, within the limits of predetermined rules. Thus, each subject interacted with a peer 40 minutes per week and with a surrogate made to operate like a peer 40 minutes per week. Each subject remained in its individual living cage at all other times. During all interaction sessions, all behaviors displayed by both the subject and its partner/surrogate were recorded in sequence by two trained observers.

The data analyses revealed very few differences in either frequency or duration measures in behavioral levels displayed by subjects when interacting with peers as opposed to interacting with surrogates. Moreover, sex differences between subjects and changes in levels of behavior over successive weeks were highly parallel between sessions with surrogates and sessions with age mates.

More specifically, of the frequency measures, differences between surrogate and peer sessions were found only in a single behavior—proximity (closer than .5 meters but greater than .2 meters to social target)—with slightly but consistently higher scores during surrogate interactions throughout the test period. In contrast, sex differences were disclosed for a total of eight behaviors (females exhibited more proximity, withdrawal, fear, and self-mouthing than males did, whereas males exhibited more close proximity, social exploration, masturbation, and environmental exploration). Moreover, changes in levels over weeks were found, in interactions with surrogates and with peers, for a total of seven behaviors (proximity, close proximity, social exploration, and self-mouthing—decline over weeks; aggression, locomotion, and play—increase over weeks). Similar results were found for duration measures of behaviors during interaction sessions. The only substantial surrogate–peer difference was again found for proximity behavior, with higher durations of proximity displayed toward surrogates than peers. On the other hand, similar sex differences and changes over weeks were apparent in both surrogate and peer sessions, as was the case for frequency measures. Moreover, individual differences between subjects were consistent across both sets of interactions. These data all suggest that the young monkeys were reacting to our puppet surrogates in the same manner that they reacted toward age mates.

In a second study, subjects were reared with age-mate partners but also given exposure to surrogates whose "behaviors" followed specifically predetermined contingency schedules, rather than having the operator "free-lance" as in the previous study. Subjects were initially presented on each test day with one of two surrogates, one who remained stationary throughout the entire test session, the other who reciprocated every social initiation by the subject and mimicked every nonsocial behavior exhibited by the subject as well. For example, if the subject moved closer to this surrogate, the surrogate would move closer to the infant; if the subject groomed the surrogate, the surrogate would groom back; if the subject withdrew to a corner and manipulated the mesh, the surrogate would move to an opposite corner and do likewise. Subjects were exposed to these surrogates for a total of 8 weeks. The results of this study revealed that infants more readily approached the stationary surrogate initially, although they explored and clung to the reciprocating surrogate more often. Levels of environmental exploration and self-directed behavior were similar in the presence of either surrogate type. By the end of the 8-week period, the infants were approaching the reciprocating surrogate more than they approached the stationary puppet, reversing their earlier trend.

A subsequent study compared surrogates that mimicked a subject's behavior entirely, as in the work just discussed, with surrogates that initiated proximity and/or contact behavior whenever a period of more than 20 seconds elapsed during which no social behavior occurred. The same subjects encountered each type of surrogate for four 10-minute sessions per week, for a total of 8 weeks. The results of this study revealed substantial differences between the two surrogate conditions in the relative incidence of several behavior patterns. In the presence of the initiating surrogate, subjects were much more likely to approach and explore, and much less likely to cling to, the surrogate than they were when the surrogate only mimicked their behavior. Levels of exploration were higher, and those of the self-directed activity lower, for the initiating surrogate condition.

These pilot studies demonstrate that socially naïve rhesus monkey infants rapidly develop interest in social stimuli that can produce a variety of contingencies involving the subject's behavior, whereas they tend to habituate to highly predictable stimuli that are either inanimate or capable only of simple, mirror-like reciprocation. Subsequent experiments are being designed to test responses to specific types and degrees of social contingency, as expressed by particular predetermined schedules of surrogate interaction patterns.

CURRENT CONCLUSIONS AND FUTURE PROSPECTS FOR DEVELOPMENTAL STUDY OF SOCIAL CONTINGENCY

The general theme of this chapter has been that discovery of, and experience with, contingencies involving social stimulation are probably crucial for development of behavioral repertoires and interaction patterns that will enable an individual to cope with the complexities of group living. Direct tests of some intriguing predictions of learned helplessness theory, regarding developmental consequences of perceiving noncontingency between one's behavior and salient social stimuli, are exceedingly difficult to carry out, due largely to problems of assessing any subject's *perception* of social contingencies. Nevertheless, there is empirical evidence that infants, both human and animal, who are exposed to settings in which contingencies exist (in the Bayesian sense) between their behavior and actions of social stimuli will be more socially active and proficient than infants exposed to similar though noncontingent stimuli, and those with no exposure. How long such group differences persist or to what degree they generalize to other situations has yet to be determined. Also, additional data have shown that infant monkeys appear to develop preferences for stimuli associated with more elaborate contingencies as they grow older, suggesting that maturation and/or experience can change a subject's ability to deal with different contingent relationships. Still, we presently lack detailed knowledge regarding normative longitudinal changes in social contingencies that may coincide with development, and the extent to which a subject's perception of social contingencies is altered in the process. Finally, we do not know whether differences in exposure to specific contingencies result in social and cognitive differences among the subjects involved.

A useful strategy for pursuing these problems might begin with attempts to describe the normative changes in social contingencies to which a subject is exposed as it grows up. To accomplish this, say, for rhesus monkey infants, one might gather observational data on group-living infants (cf. Miller, 1977), including sequential records of interactive exchanges between each subject and other group members. If the scoring system utilized were exhaustive in nature and hierarchically organized (e.g., as described in Suomi, 1979b), then it would be possible to generate a data set that could be used to search for various contingency patterns in the data.

One procedure that might be employed in such a search has been suggested by Sackett (1977). Sackett asks the question: "What should true interactions look like, in terms of sequences of behavior?" One way to answer the question is to develop various "models" of interactive sequences and then test the goodness-of-fit of an empirical data set with the models' predictions. The simplest model might be: "All behaviors by A and B are equally likely to occur," (i.e., this model implies a totally random distribution of behaviors). Such a model would rarely describe an interaction of interest. A second model might be: "All behaviors of A are autocorrelated, i.e., $P(A_T) = f(A_{T-M})$." Such a model implies that A and B both have cyclicity, but their cycles are independent and thus any "interaction" between them is entirely coincidental. A third model might be that the behaviors of A are autocorrelated, but the behaviors of B are conditionally dependent upon A, i.e., $P(B_T) = f(A_{T-X})$. Other models, of course, could also be constructed. The actual interaction sequences could be quantified by means of the nonparametric-lag sequential analysis program developed by Sackett (1978), and the resulting transformations could be tested against the various models for goodness-of-fit, according to Sackett's (1979) procedure. Such goodness-of-fit tests could show the degree to which changes in patterns of interactions involving the infant subjects changed over successive time periods, e.g., those of 1 month's duration. The resulting protypical interaction models could be used to estimate the actual contingencies involved.

In addition to providing normative data regarding changes in social contingency during development, such models could be reproduced in tightly controlled experimental settings using "surrogate" stimuli, as were employed in the Wisconsin studies previously described. In these settings, specific contingencies could be produced and directly compared. Finally, the generality of the experimental findings could be assessed by returning to the previously obtained "normative" data set, searching for "naturally occurring" equivalents of the experimental manipulations, and testing for the consistency between the experimental findings and the selected subset of normative data.

This strategy represents one possible approach to the study of social contingencies and their impact on the development of social capabilities. This and other approaches may lead to more direct tests of some of the developmental implications of learned helplessness theory. If such tests can be carried out and if at least some of the predictions are supported, then additional research might well focus on the establishment of therapeutic and/or preventive strategies for infants who, for one reason or another, are being exposed to environments whose available social stimulation does not provide adequate experience with the "appropriate" social contingencies. There presently exists considerable data suggesting, albeit indirectly, that knowledge of contingencies can be important for our understanding of social and cognitive development. How important such knowledge is remains to be determined.

REFERENCES

Abramson, L. Y., Seligman, M. E. P., & Teasdale, J. D. Learned helplessness in humans: Critique and reformulation. *Journal of Abnormal Psychology,* 1978, *87,* 49–74.

Alloy, L. B., & Seligman, M. E. P. On the cognitive component of learned helplessness and depression. In G. H. Bower (Ed.), *The psychology of learning and motivation* (Vol. 13). New York: Academic Press, 1979.

Bischof, N. A systems approach to the functional connections of attachment and fear. *Child Development,* 1975, *46,* 801–817.

Brunswik, E. *Perception and the representative design of psychological experiments.* Berkeley: University of California Press, 1956.

Chevalier-Skolnikoff, S. A Piagetion model for describing and comparing socialization in monkey, ape, and human infants. In S. Chevalier-Skolnikoff & F. Poirier (Eds.), *Primate biosocial development.* New York: Garland Press, 1977.

Dawkins, R. Hierarchial organization: A candidate principle for ethology. In P. P. G. Bateson & R. A. Hinde (Eds.), *Growing points in ethology.* New York: Cambridge University Press, 1976.

Ferster, C. B., & Skinner, B. F. *Schedules for reinforcement.* New York: Appleton-Century-Crofts, 1957.

Garcia, J., Ervin, F. R., & Koelling, R. A. Learning with prolonged delay of reinforcement. *Psychonomic Science,* 1966, *5,* 121–122.

Gerwirtz, J. L., & Boyd, E. F. Does maternal responding imply reduced infant crying? *Child Development,* 1977, *48,* 1200–1207.

Gormezano, I. *CS-CR and CS-IR conditioning paradigms.* Paper presented at the 18th meeting of the Pavlovian Society, Madison, Wisconsin, October 1977.

Goude, G. Psychobiological aspects of the function of probability judgments. In G. Barlow, K. Immelmann, M. Main, & Petrinovich (Eds.), *Early development in animals and man.* New York: Cambridge University Press, 1980.

Grzimek, B. *Encyclopedia of ethology.* New York: Nostrand Reinhold, 1977.

Harlow, H. F. The development of learning in the rhesus monkey. *American Scientist,* 1959, *47,* 459–479.

Hinde, R. A., & Simpson, M. J. A. Qualities of mother-infant relationships in monkeys. In the parent-infant relationship. Ciba Foundation Symposium 33 (new series). Amsterdam: Elsevier, 1975.

Immelmann, K., & Suomi, S. J. Sensitive phases in development. In G. Barlow, K. Immelmann, M. Main, & L. Petrinovich (Eds.), *Early development in animals and man.* New York: Cambridge University Press, 1980.

Latane, B., Joy, V., Meltzer, J., & Lubell, B. Stimulus determinants of social attraction in rats. *Journal of Comparative and Physiological Psychology,* 1972, *79,* 13–21.

Leiderman, P. H. The critical period hypothesis revisited: Mother to infant bonding in the neonatal period. In G. Barlow, K. Immelmann, M. Main, & L. Petrinovich (Eds.), *Early development in animals and man.* New York: Cambridge University Press, 1980.

Mason, W. A. Social experience and primate cognitive development. In M. Bekoff & G. Burghardt (Eds.), *Ontogeny of behavior.* New York: Garland, 1978.

Masters, W. H., & Johnson, V. E. *The human sexual response.* Boston: Little, Brown, 1966.

Meyer, D. R., Treichler, F. R., & Meyer, P. M. Discrete-trial training techniques and stimulus variables. In A. M. Schrier, H. F. Harlow, & F. Stollnitz (Eds.), *Behavior of nonhuman primates* (Vol. 1). New York: Academic Press, 1965.

Miller, D. B. Roles of naturalistic observation in comparative psychology. *American Psychologist,* 1977, *32,* 211-219.

Miller, I. W., & Norman, W. H. Learned helplessness in humans: A review and attribution theory model. *Psychological Bulletin,* 1979, *86,* 93-118.

Parker, S. T. Piaget's sensory-motor series in an infant macaque: A model for comparing unstereotyped behavior and intelligence in human and nonhuman primates. In Chevalier-Skolnikoff & Poirier (Eds.), *Primate biosocial development.* New York: Garland Press, 1977.

Pavlov, I. *Conditioned reflexes.* London: Oxford University Press, 1927.

Petrinovich, L. Probabilistic functionalism: A conceptin of research method. *American Psychologist,* 1979, *34,* 373-390.

Piaget, J. *The child's perception of physical causality.* London: Routledge & Kegan Paul, 1951.

Rescorla, R. A., & Wagner, A. R. A theory of Pavlovian conditioning: Variations in the effectiveness of reinforcement and nonreinforcement. In A. H. Black & W. F. Prokasy (Eds.), *Classical conditioning II: Current research and theory.* New York: Appleton-Century-Crofts, 1972.

Sackett, G. P. A neural mechanism underlying unlearned, critical period, and developmental aspects of visually controlled behavior. *Psychological Review,* 1963, *70,* 40-50.

Sackett, G. P. Monkeys reared in isolation with pictures as visual input: Evidence for an innate releasing mechanism. *Science,* 1966, *154,* 1468-1472.

Sackett, G. P. *A paradigm for determining characteristics of interactions using lag sequential analyses.* Paper presented at the Zentrum fur interdisziplinare Forschung, University of Bielefeld (West Germany), December 1977.

Sackett, G. P. The lag sequential analysis of contingency and cyclicity in behavioral interaction research. In J. Osofsky (Ed.), *Handbook of infant development.* New York: Wiley, 1978.

Sackett, G. P. Lag sequential analysis as a data reduction technique in social interaction research. In D. Sawin (Ed.), *Psychosocial risks during pregnancy and early infancy.* Austin, Tex.: University of Texas Press, 1979.

Scott, J. P., Stewart, J. M., & DeGhett, V. J. Critical periods in the organization of systems. *Developmental Psychobiology,* 1974, *7,* 489-513.

Seligman, M. E. P. *Helplessness: On depression, death, and development.* San Francisco: Freeman, 1975.

Seligman, M. E. P., et al. (Contributors), *Journal of Abnormal Psychology,* 1978, *87,* #1 (entire issue).

Skinner, B. F. *The behavior of organisms: An experimental approach.* New York: Appleton-Century-Crofts, 1938.

Spitz, R. A., & Wolf, K. M. The smiling response: A contribution to the ontogenesis of social relations. *Genetic Psychology Monographs,* 1946, *34,* 57-125.

Studdart-Kennedy, M. Learning which languages to speak. In G. Barlow, K. Immelmann, M. Main, & L. Petrinovich (Eds.), *Early development in animals and man.* New York: Cambridge University Press, 1980.

Suomi, S. J. Differential development of various social relationships by rhesus monkey infants. In M. Lewis & L. A. Rosenblum (Eds.), *The social network of the child.* New York: Plenum, 1979a.

Suomi, S. J. Levels of analysis for interactive data collected on monkeys living in complex social groups. In M. E. Lamb, S. J. Suomi, & G. R. Stephenson (Eds.), *Social interaction analysis: Methodological issues.* Madison: University of Wisconsin Press, 1979b.

Suomi, S. J., & Perez, A. M. *Studies with surrogate "peers."* Unpublished data, Department of Psychology, University of Wisconsin-Madison, 1978.

Tinbergen, N. *The study of instinct.* Oxford, England: Oxford University Press, 1951.

Tversky, A., & Kahneman, D. Judgment under uncertainty: Heuristics and biases. *Science,* 1974, *185,* 1124–1131.

Watson, J. S. Depression and the perception of control in early childhood. In J. G. Schulterbrandt & A. Raskin (Eds.), *Depression in childhood: Diagnosis, treatment, and conceptual models.* New York: Raven Press, 1977.

Watson, J. S. Perception of contingency as a determinant of social responsiveness. In E. B. Thoman (Ed.), *The origins of the infant's social responsiveness.* Hillsdale, N.J.: Lawrence Erlbaum Associates, 1978.

Watson, J. S., & Ramey, C. T. Reactions to response-contingent stimulation in early infancy. *Merrill–Palmer Quarterly,* 1972, *18,* 219–227.

Webster's Third New International Dictionary. Springfield, Mass.: Merriam, 1963.

9 The Relation Between Emotion and Cognition in Infant Development

Dante Cicchetti
Petra Pogge-Hesse
Harvard University

> *Emotion both subjectively in its experiential or feeling aspect*
> *and objectively in its expressive or behavioral aspect, involves*
> *the organism at many levels of psychological integration. It is*
> *primarily because of this wide-spread influence and interactions*
> *with other psychological processes (before emotion finds*
> *expression in behavior) that the concept has been so difficult to*
> *deal with... Everyone knows something of what is meant by*
> *emotion but not precisely what.*
>
> —Sheer, 1961, p. 433

During the first 2 years of life, the infant emerges as a socially organized, emotionally expressive human being. In studying the unfolding of joy, distress, fear, and the other emotions, the integrated, organized nature of development very quickly becomes apparent. We encounter such processes as intentionality, relational abilities, the ability to distinguish persons, the formation of expectation, memory, and other major themes in cognitive development. Cognitive development clearly influences affective development, as when an infant's developing memory enables it to laugh in anticipation of the caregiver's return in "peekaboo" (Cicchetti & Sroufe, 1976; Sroufe & Wunsch, 1972). Likewise, affective growth influences social and cognitive development, as when a baby's smiles of recognition encourage the caregiver toward a more cognitively stimulating interaction (Sroufe & Waters, 1976; Stern, 1974). Moreover, through its gaze, motor activity, vocalization, and facial expression, an infant can communicate its emotional state, thereby initiating, maintaining, and terminating social interactions (Brazelton, Koslowski, & Main, 1974; Oster, 1978; Oster & Ekman, 1977;

Stern, 1977). Because the infant's primary experience is made up of sensation, action, and feeling rather than thought, emotion crucially reflects the meaning of its transactions with the world (Sroufe, 1979; Stechler & Carpenter, 1967).

According to this viewpoint, the study of emotional development is central in obtaining a truly comprehensive picture of the infant's development. It involves an understanding of the growing child as an integrated, organized, and dynamic system. Cognitive, social, and affective development proceed in a mutually supportive, interlocking manner. This process is the same for normal and retarded, sighted and blind infants (Cicchetti & Pogge-Hesse, in press b; Cicchetti & Sroufe, 1976, 1978; Fraiberg, 1977).

Stimulated in large part by the publication of Darwin's seminal work, *The Expression of the Emotions in Man and Animals* (1872), and by the appearance of Darwin's diary of observations of his own children in the journal *Mind* (1877), interest in the study of affect was much greater at the beginning of this century than it has been throughout the last 40 years. During the intervening period, the empirical study of the human emotions was largely neglected both within the field of psychology, in general, and within the area of developmental psychology, in particular. However, more recently, considerable work has been done in exploring the area of early emotional development and expression (e.g., Ainsworth, 1973; Bronson, 1972; Charlesworth & Kreutzer, 1973; Emde, 1979; Emde, Gaensbauer, & Harmon, 1976; Izard, 1978; Lewis & Rosenblum, 1974, 1978; Oster & Ekman, 1977; Ricciuti, 1968; Sroufe, 1977a, 1977b, 1979; Sroufe & Waters, 1976, 1977; Stern, 1977).

GOALS OF THIS CHAPTER

The present chapter does not claim to discuss emotional and cognitive development and their interrelationship exhaustively. Rather, it deals schematically with some of the positions that have been advanced in the past and sketches some perspectives for future empirical and theoretical endeavors. More detailed accounts follow in subsequent papers.

Past discussions of emotions have been mainly concerned with emotional development beyond the period of infancy. However, a discussion of development is meaningful only if an attempt is made to relate earlier and later stages of ontogenesis (cf. Kaplan's [1966] and Kosslyn's [1978] arguments in favor of a teleological approach to development). Therefore, our discussion takes all of development into account, rather than dealing exclusively with infancy.

This chapter provides a justification for studying emotional development both as a domain in its own right and in its relation to cognitive development.

It summarizes the problems and challenges developmental theorists have faced thus far and will have to deal with in the future, as they attempt to formulate a comprehensive theory of emotional development. Cognition has already been well established as a viable developmental domain. Moreover, it makes good sense to study the emotions based on the universal interest people have in their own and other's emotions. Boring, Langfeld, Weld, et al. (1935) have noted: "Scientific knowledge concerning emotion is neither comprehensive nor overly exact. Human interest in emotion on the other hand, is universal. This disparity between universal interest and meager psychological knowledge is a continuous challenge to the scientist [p. 397]." Because cognitive and emotional phenomena occur contemporaneously, it is unlikely that these two behavioral systems are completely independent of one another. Acordingly, some ways of conceptualizing the interrelationship of these two systems are delineated. Past and present philosophical as well as psychological theories of emotion are discussed with special consideration paid to their possible bearings on a theory of emotional development. As the standard views on emotion advanced so far have favored different approaches—that is, introspective, physiological, or functional—the consequences of such a variety of points of view are considered both with respect to a comparison between theories and with respect to the meaningfulness of integrating these different levels of discourse within the framework of *one* theory. Lastly, a future perspective for theory and research is formulated with the aim of distinguishing between the more and the less promising candidates for a theory of emotional development.

EMOTION AS A DEVELOPMENTAL DOMAIN

Are there good scientific reasons for studying the emotions? Perhaps one way of answering this question is to examine the major reasons why emotional development in humans has received such scanty attention in the past half century. Two psychological traditions have hindered, or at least failed to encourage, the study of this developmental domain: behaviorism and Piagetian cognitive psychology.

Behaviorism, on the one hand, sought to reduce emotions to propensities or likelihoods to act in certain ways with respect to a range of different stimuli (Berlyne, 1978; Skinner, 1953), and thus tried to overcome the accepted view of emotions as a unique domain of the human mind, distinguishable through introspection (Brentano, 1924; Wundt, 1912).

Piaget, on the other hand, decided to focus on the investigation of cognitive development. Because the experimental paradigms he created proved to be so fruitful and attractive, they brought about a whole wave of replication and modification studies. As such, interest in emotional development was virtually non-existent for a while, except for the literature on attachment. That is, psychology's preoccupation with cognitive over emotional development was artifactual; it did not reflect accurately a real aspect of human development, but was based mostly on the power of Piaget's work and the excitement it engendered. Because this exclusive focus on cognition provided an incomplete picture of development, researchers have been motivated to become concerned once again with human emotions.

Historical support for the increased interest being paid to the emotions can be found in the longstanding tradition of distinguishing among the three faculties of the human mind: cognition, emotion, and will (cf. Bain, 1868; Brentano, 1924; Kant, 1781). An excellent account of this tradition is provided by Baldwin (1890) who gives the following, widely accepted summary of the standard justification for the tripartite classification of mental functions in terms of intellect, feeling, and will: "representative states have as their common characteristic their reference to a thing or object . . . the affective states, as states of feeling, lack of this element of objectivity and carry with them only reference to the self . . . volitional states stand out in consciousness distinguished by a characteristic foreign to the other two, the sense of effort or exertion [pp. 36-37]."

An additional impetus for the resurgent interest in emotions has been generated by the awareness that emotional behaviors have been used as indicators to gauge underlying cognitive competence (Charlesworth, 1966, 1969; Haviland, 1976; Hunt, 1965; LeCompte & Gratch, 1972; Piaget, 1952, 1954a, 1977; Shultz & Zigler, 1970; Sroufe & Wunsch, 1972; Zelazo & Komer, 1971; Zigler, Levine, & Gould, 1966). Some of the most widely used scales for assessing infant cognitive development (e.g., the Bayley and Uzgiris-Hunt scales) rely on the infant's affective responses as indices of cognitive capabilities (Haviland, 1976). Emotional reactions of infants on the "visual cliff" have been shown to be a useful means of assessing perceptual and cognitive competence as well (Campos, Hiatt, Ramsay, Henderson & Svejda, 1978; Cicchetti & Sroufe, 1978). Piaget postulates states of disequilibrium as characteristic of transitional phases between stages of cognitive development, and emotional states are used as symptoms of those disequilibria. Moreover, the whole tradition concerned with the discrepancy hypothesis (Berlyne, 1960, 1978; Hebb, 1949; Kagan, 1971; McCall & McGhee, 1977; Thomas, 1971) rests on the assumption that emotional responses—distress in the case of an event too discrepant to be assimilated, pleasure/joy in the case of a moderately discrepant stimulus, and boredom in the case of a familiar stimulus—can serve as indicators of the degree of discrepancy with respect to stimuli, and thus at the same time as indicators of the complexity of an infant's cognitive representations.

Two viewpoints, one theoretical and the other methodological, have converged to encourage the burgeoning interest in the emotions: 1) ethology and its search for the evolutionary underpinnings of affective expression (e.g., Blurton-Jones, 1971; Charlesworth & Kreutzer, 1973; Chevalier-Skolnikoff, 1973; Eibl-Eibesfeldt, 1970; Ekman & Friesen, 1975; Hinde, 1966; Izard, 1977; Tompkins, 1962, 1963; Van Hooff, 1972; Vine, 1973); and 2) technological advances in the measurement of the psychophysiological correlates and the neurophysiological substrates of emotion (e.g., Black, 1975; Brady, 1975; Campos, Emde, Gaensbauer, & Henderson, 1975; Cicchetti, Mans, & Breitenbuecher, 1977; Cicchetti & Sroufe, 1978; Emde et al., 1976; Gellhorn, 1968; Grossman, 1967; Pribram, 1967; Waters, Matas, & Sroufe, 1975; Weil, 1974).

Implicitly expressed in the previous paragraphs is the need for, and interest in, comprehensive theories of the human mind and its development. Inasmuch as Piaget has provided us with a fairly exhaustive and widely accepted framework for the study of cognitive development, it is not too surprising that attempts are being made to come up with analogous theories for other developmental domains, emotion being one of them. Future research and theorizing will show whether one theory can account for several systems of development, whether different theories will have to be formulated for them, or whether an extended version of one of the traditional theories is sufficient for cognitive, emotional, and possibly even other domains of development. For example, it is not clear whether all developmental domains can be characterized in terms of the same or different formalizations of stage structures, or some combination thereof.

Meta-theoretical discussions of the emotions are often found in the literature and indeed we should consider some of these before proceeding. For example, Duffy (1934, 1941) advanced many objections to considering emotions as a separate domain. She noted that all of the distinctions suggested between emotions and other types of behavior (e.g., physiological mechanisms, degree of arousal, intensity of reactions, disorganization of behavior, descriptions of the content of consciousness, and so on) have not succeeded in qualifying the emotions as different in kind, rather than degree, from other behavioral domains. Because these differences in degree have not been precisely determined, clear distinctions between the different kinds of emotions cannot be made. Although Duffy admits that, intuitively, we cannot deny the existence of emotions, she claims (1941) that the components of emotional experience, "awareness of the stimulus situation and its significance, awareness of the set for response, and awareness of certain physiological changes which are occurring in the individual [p. 289]" are characteristic of all states of consciousness, and not just of emotions. If attempts are made to distinguish emotions from other states of consciousness having the same components, one has to distinguish them both in kind and in degree. The problem that remains to be solved, then, is how we are able to distinguish with reasonable accuracy between cognitive, perceptual, and emotional functions of the mind in everyday contexts. Futhermore, if one accepts Duffy's argument that all of consciousness functions alike, one must disqualify cognition and volition as unique domains also.

More recently, Mandler (1975) has advanced additional arguments against considering emotion as a unique domain. He regards emotions as conglomerations of mechanisms and processes, arousal as setting the nonspecific stage for emotional behavior and experience, and the cognitive or meaning analysis of the arousal state as determining the particular quality of the emotion. In this vein, Mandler postulates that theories of emotions can never be independent of, or different from, a more general analysis of human processing systems.

If it is meaningful to ask what makes emotions different, one must first agree on criteria that justify the study of emotion in its own right—that is, what are the criteria by which emotion can be defined as a unique domain? If emotional development unfolds along a course different from cognitive or language development, would that finding qualify it as a separate domain? Are the underlying structures and organizations of emotional development different from other developmental domains? Does it require its own language (Kendler, 1965; Kessen, 1971)? Do the behavioral expressions elicited by emotional stimuli differ in kind and degree from those elicited by cognitive stimuli? Do emotions effect changes in behavior or are emotions essentially epiphenomenal? All of these questions must be addressed in identifying the criteria for regarding emotion as a developmental domain. In answering these questions, emotions must be related to the other domains of development because of the following systematic problem: emotions can be talked and theorized about only in cognitive or cognitive/linguistic terms. Whereas theorizing about cognitive development is thus "self-reflexive," cross-mapping between components is intrinsic to theory and research on emotional development. Consequently, the problems connected with cross-mapping, changes in meaning, and loss of information cannot be avoided in the study of emotions.

TASKS THAT DEVELOPMENTAL THEORISTS MUST SOLVE

Once such a basis for a theory of emotions is agreed upon, the initial characteristics one wants to assign to the infant must be made explicit (Kessen, 1971). That is, one must distinguish between innate and acquired behaviors, one must determine the role of the infant in the construction of reality (e.g., whether the infant is viewed as an active constructor or passive receptor of the environment), and one must ascertain how the infant represents the information it takes in.

Likewise, one has to specify the role that is attributed to the environment in the developmental process (Kessen, 1971). It must be determined whether environmental input is necessary at all for the infant's development, whether there is an interaction between the infant's organization and the environmental input, or whether the environmental input is directly translated or translated like an image into the infant's representations.

The importance of obtaining a solution to these tasks becomes even more apparent when attempting to account for the *motivation* for development. The necessary and sufficient conditions that bring about developmental change have to be conceptualized and empirically confimed in order to explain the phenomenon of change or transition between stages. Indeed, a decision has to be made as to what is acceptable as an explanation at all. As Deutsch (1960) put it:

> There is no concord among psychologists about what the facts they have accumulated are evidence for. This does not mean that they are merely in disagreement about the edifice they wish to erect; they have not even decided what constitutes a building. . . . As a result, it is not sufficient only to put foward a theory to explain the facts; it is also necessary to put forward a theory to justify the type of theory put forward [p. 1].

In this context, the respective roles of environmental input and the infant's structures have to be specified. Is development brought about only as a function of change in the environment, or, as Piaget has suggested, as a function of contradictions between schemes?

Once change is initiated, the problem of what constitutes a solution arises. At what point do we consider later stages or phases of development as solutions for the conflicts or disequilibria arising at earlier stages (Kessen, 1971)? This question is especially important in view of the possible universality of the stage sequence. That is, out of a range of possible solutions to problems, children tend universally to pick the same one. This phenomenon can be accounted for in terms of maturation or in terms of the necessity with which the stages follow each other.

Flavell (1972) has provided us with a vocabulary for conceptualizing the types of sequences characteristic of cognitive development. He has delineated five major sequential models: addition, substitution, modification, inclusion, and mediation. An account of development in terms of addition would state that there is an accumulation of behaviors in the course of ontogenesis. Early and later emerging behaviors would be posited to coexist throughout development. A substitution model would refer to the possibility that later emerging behaviors might replace earlier ones. Of course, behaviors that occur earlier in ontogenesis may themselves undergo developmental transformations into behaviors that are displayed at a later period in time.

This description captures the modification model of development. Developmental sequences may also be characterized in terms of an inclusion model. Here, earlier and later emerging behaviors become progressively coordinated into larger wholes, with the earlier behaviors becoming elements of the later developing organizations. Mediation models are very similar to modification models in that both assert that early developing behaviors undergo transformations leading to the emergence of new behaviors or levels of organization. However, contrary to modification, mediation sequences assume that these transformations are only necessary but not sufficient for the emergence of new behaviors. This type of sequence postulates that additional factors are necessary to make the transition to new, more articulated, and integrated levels of organization.

Of course, it is by no means obvious that emotional development can be characterized in terms of a stage sequence at all. Even if one agreed on describing emotional development as a sequence of stages, it is not clear that these stages can be characterized in terms of structures, perhaps analogous to Piaget's logical structures of cognitive development. However, once one attempts to formulate the logical structures underlying emotional development, the same objections that Feldman and Toulmin (1975) have advanced with respect to cognitive development apply to emotional development: "What does it tell us about the empirical phenomena represented in cognitive psychology that they are susceptible of being cast in such formal terms at all? Can it be shown that casting them in such terms augments our scientific power to explain the phenomena? In short, what exactly is gained by casting theory in logico-mathematical form, and how do such theories relate to our empirical experience? [p. 410]."

In view of structural approaches, it is not clear what constitutes a test for the existence of structures, especially because it is not clear what sort of "entities" these structures are supposed to be. Further more, the adequacy of formal systems is judged according to nonempirical criteria, e.g., parsimony, consistency, and completeness. Thus, they do not necessarily fit the empirical data. It is also true that for any given logic there exists an unlimited number of other, alternative logics. The use of formal criteria, therefore, can never guarantee that a theoretical model is a good one in terms of its ability to give the most empirically adequate expression to the psychological theory in question.

As indicated by the concept of décalage in Piaget's theory, by Flavell's (1971) discussion of the gradual onset and decline of the stages postulated by Piaget, and by the resulting overlap of different stage structures, the clear-cut definitions of stage sequences and the structures characteristic of them oftentimes are problematic (see Brainerd, 1978). Therefore, Feldman and Toulmin suggest that we conceive of developmental sequences in terms of family resemblances of performances and procedures instead of logical structures. They avoid the problem of determining the defining characteristics or critical features of the respective stages (see also Rosch & Mervis [1975] for a discussion of the advantages connected with conceiving of concepts in terms of family resemblances). Future research and theoretical considerations will determine how fruitful these alternative conceptualizations are.

In summary, in constructing a theory of emotional development, we have to solve several problems. The first of these is to specify the respective roles of the organism and the environment, especially how they impact upon developmental changes and bring about solutions to transitory phases of development. Second, we should make it clear whether developmental sequences ought to be conceived in terms of stages or some alternative organization. Third, we should specify the relationship between earlier and later emerging phases of development. In this context, we should be explicit about the criteria by which we evaluate explanations in developmental psychology. Finally, we should elucidate the ways in which theory and data are related, paying more attention to the testability and refutability of theories (cf. Meehl, 1978; Popper, 1959).

SOME HISTORICAL CONCEPTUALIZATIONS OF THE RELATIONS BETWEEN EMOTION AND COGNITION

In this section, we consider several general psychological conceptions of the emotions and their relation to cognition in light of some philosophical and historical traditions. Traditionally, the relationship between emotion and cognition in infancy has been discussed infrequently. Consequently, the present discussion centers on those related issues that *have* been influential in the past and that shape current conceptions of emotional development. Taking this broader perspective is a fruitful strategy for several reasons. First, the very persistence of some traditions throughout history indicates their power to integrate the emotions into our general conception of the mind. For example, the notion that cognition and emotion function in parallel has been proposed by thinkers as disparate as Piaget and Gerson, who was a medieval thinker (see Gardiner, Metcalf, & Beebe-Center, 1937). Second, some conceptions of emotion and cognition, when examined from a broad perspective, are found to have limited explanatory power. These conceptions persist throughout history, yet with little scientific progress. Third, understanding to what extent current conceptions are shaped by enduring traditions is the first step toward hypothesizing more creative, more explanatory theories.

It should be noted that psychology has always been notoriously vulnerable to the scientific fashions of the age: Freud theorized in terms of hydraulics; Lewin adapted field theory from physics; present-day cognitive psychologists employ metaphors from the computer field. Taking a broader perspective enables us to determine what is of enduring worth in theories that employ differing metaphors. For example, concerning conceptions of emotion and cognition, the Greek idea of emotions, which indicated disequilibria of bodily fluids, has been transformed into the current notion of conflicting tendencies in the nervous system. The metaphors have changed, but the main ideas have stayed the same—with little conceptual advance.

It is worth mentioning that, historically, the developmental approach has usually meant an emphasis on biology, function, and hierarchical integration. Concepts such as intellect, feeling, and will, when considered developmentally, are snatched from the realm of reification and the a priori and are brought back down to earth. An example of this from the history of psychology can be found in the writings of William James. James is a particularly good example, for his philosophical position reflects his psychological stance, and vice versa. James, the pragmatist philosopher, argued that the "cash value"—to use his expression—of terms such as "truth" or "belief" should be found in the actions of people. In a complementary way, James the psychologist (1892) emphasized the biological and functional roots of the mental:

> So long as they (the emotions) are set down as so many eternal and sacred psychic entities, like the old immutable species in natural history, so long all that *can* be done with them is reverently to catalogue their separate characters, points, and effects. But if we regard them as products of more general causes (as 'species' are now regarded as products of heredity and variation), the mere distinguishing and cataloguing becomes of subsidiary importance [p. 375].

Interestingly, in the foregoing quotation, James compares the effect of a developmental approach to the emotions with the impact evolution had on biology. A brief examination of the history of classification of emotions makes this point clear.

Past attempts to classify the emotions have embraced two strategies. The first strategy is to reduce the manifold emotions that can be reliably identified to a circumscribed set of primary emotions or feelings, which are characterized as "fundamental" in some sense. From this small set, all of the emotions are said to be derived. Descartes employed this strategy when he tried to derive all of the emotions from admiration, love, hate, desire, joy, and grief (see Gardiner et al., 1937). Curiously, the behaviorist, Watson (1925) also took such an approach in reducing all of the emotions to an innate set of "primary" emotions: love, fear, and rage. The emergence of all the other emotions could be explained, according to Watson, in terms of stimulus and response generalizations of these primary emotions. Plutchik (1965), Woodworth and Schlosberg (1954), and Wundt (1912) also represent this strategy of reducing the phenomenal complexity of emotions. However, their approaches differ in that they try to conceptualize the emotions in terms of a small set of dimensions within a framework where all emotions are assigned coordinates. The second strategy used to classify emotions is simply to describe and discriminate as many emotions as possible. Some medieval philosophers, Bain, and J. M. Baldwin are representatives of such an approach.

The problem with attempts to classify emotions is not so much in what they do as in what they do not do. As James (1892) wrote: "Many German psychological text-books are nothing but dictionaries of synonyms when it comes to the chapter on Emotion [p. 374]." Distinctions and divisions, although having the appearance of scientific rigor, are unhelpful if no reason or purpose for those distinctions is provided. Comparison can be made with the classification of the affective disorders in psychiatry. Countless schemes enumerating various kinds of depression have been put forward, but nosologies are fruitful only if they are in some way relevant to etiology, treatment, or prognosis. The developmental approach takes this lesson seriously and emphasizes that, when classifying emotions, reference must be made to developmental antecedents, interaction, and developmental sequelae (these correspond analogously to etiology, treatment, and prognosis, respectively, in the field of psychopathology). Thus, classifications of emotion can be fruitful if they take into account the biological function of emotions and if they delineate their differentiation through hierarchic integration.

Explanations of emotion that have traditionally been put forward fall into several groups according to how the functions of the organism are related to the expression and awareness of the emotions. For example, one tradition attempts to account for emotions in terms of *bodily processes*. Thus, as mentioned, the Greeks thought of different mixtures of bodily fluids as responsible for bringing about different emotions. Again, modern counterparts are easy to find: James (1892) and McDougall (1923) assume that emotions are the awareness of bodily changes. Another tradition searches for the origin of emotions as located in certain *organs* or *body parts:* the tongue, the diaphragm, the heart, and others have been implicated. Just as Descartes posited that the pineal gland is the seat of the soul, so this tradition looks for some body part (usually below the head) as being the "seat of the emotions." As physiology has become more and more sophisticated, the seat of the emotions has been pushed back from more external organs, such as the tongue, to more and more internal locations, such as parts of the brain, thus becoming more and more unrelated to felt changes in the body. Flourens, for example, accepted the explanation of emotion in terms of brain function, and recent trends reflect the tradition of identifying the parts of the brain that are involved in the "causation" of emotions (see Gardiner et al., 1937). For instance, Head and Holmes (1911), Cannon (1927, 1931), and Dumas (1932) have defined emotions as awareness of changes in the thalamus. Such an approach can be made conveniently consonant with an *evolutionary perspective.* For example, many behavioral biologists agree in identifying the hypothalamic-limbic system as the origin of the emotions and speculate about its evolutionary significance. Unfortunately, such speculation yields no insight into the *proximate* cause of emotions: That is, how it is that the activity of the hypothalamic-limbic system *does* result in the psychological phenomena of emotions. Finally, another tradition stresses the *teleological character* of the biological foundation of emotions. Spinoza, for example, referred to pleasure as indicating a person's passage from greater to lesser perfection. Some recent theories such as Bowlby's (1969) theory of attachment and Izard's (1977) differential emotions theory emphasize the biological adaptiveness of emotions to the socioemotional development of the organism. "Teleological" explanations of emotions, though highly suggestive, can become especially fruitful if the adaptiveness of an emotion is described in terms of the advantageous function of that emotion.

The *mind-body problem* looms when we discuss the relationship between the organism and the phenomenological experience of emotion (see Table 9.1). Clearly, how one answers the mind-body problem will influence how one explains emotions. Consequently, explanations of emotion can be characterized as roughly isomorphic to solutions of the mind-body problem: *epiphenomenalist, interactionist, parallelist, functionalist,* and *reductionist.*

For example, emotion can be viewed as developing *in parallel* to cognitive growth. In some of his writings on affect, Piaget (1954, 1972) postulates this kind of relationship, holding that cognition and emotion are irreducible to each other and that they do not necessarily undergo developmental changes at the same time. That is, they follow different developmental courses and show different types of organizations with respect to their developmental sequences. Thus, the task for psychologists representing this position is to demonstrate that cognition and emotion *are* different developmental domains.

Emotions can also be viewed as *epiphenomena* of cognitive development or vice versa. All behavioral and introspectively felt "by-products" of development are considered epiphenomena if they do not contribute to any change in the developmental process. Piaget (1936) views needs in such an epiphenomenal sense. Although needs occur wherever there is cognitive disequilibrium, Piaget argues that they only *reflect* cognitive conflicts and do not constitute conflicts in themselves. Rather, cognitive disequilibrium is conceptualized in terms of conflicts between cognitive schemes or between

TABLE 9.1
Parallels Between Positions Held in the Discussion of the Relationship Between Mind and Body and Cognition and Emotion

Mind/Body	Cognition/Emotion
A. *Dualist*	
1. *parallelist:* mind and body act in parallel, no actual causation	1. *parallelist* (e.g., Piaget, 1954); cognitive and emotional development coexist, without influencing each other
2. *interactionist:* mind and body interact causally	2. *interactionist* (e.g., Sroufe, 1979): cognitive development affects the emergence of certain emotions and vice versa
3. *epiphenomenalist:* mind exists, but plays no causal role with respect to the body, and vice versa	3. *epiphenomenalist* (e.g., Piaget, 1936, 1973): emotions are only by-products or cognition *or* vice versa
B. *Monist*	
1. *functionalist:* mind is understood as a function of body action[a]	1. *functionalist* (e.g., Claparède, 1928): emotion and cognition are distinguished on the basis of the functions or purposes they fulfill
2. *reductionist:* mind is understood only in terms of body action	2. *reductionist* (e.g., radical behaviorist, Skinner, 1953): emotions can be reduced to propensities to act in certain ways

[a]We are aware that the philosophical and psychological interpretations of "functionalism" differ (see text).

new information and schemes. Needs do not contribute to the changes in development arising from the cognitive conflicts. The changes are conceptualized as cognitive reorganizations or as new stage structures. According to this interpretation, cognitive factors cause emotional states or are necessary and sufficient conditions for emotional states, but emotional states do not possess the same causal power. They merely reflect the cognitive process and do not contribute to any change in the course of development. Piaget (1954) writes: "If affectivity 'causes' behavior, if it intervenes without interruption in the functioning of intelligence, even if it speeds up or slows down intellectual development, it does not in itself engender cognitive structure, nor does it alter the structure in whose function it intervenes [p. 5]." Such an interpretation does not take into consideration that states of need may bring about reequilibrations or that emotional factors may cause actions and new cognitive developments.

Emotional and cognitive development may proceed *independently* of one another with some necessary links occurring between the two domains. According to this viewpoint, emotional and cognitive development follow their own sequences and laws of development but become necessary for each other at certain points. In other words, it is argued that certain cognitive structures are necessary prerequisites for the development of certain emotions and vice versa. Piaget (1954, 1972), for example, suggests that formal operations are necessary in order for the development of emotions of a moral or political nature.

Emotional development can be depicted as continuously *interactive* with cognitive development. This position is potentially problematic because the mutual impact of emotion and cognition is quite complex: It is necessary to consider both aspects of development with their respective influence on the developmental process, but in so doing, the distinction between cognitive and emotional aspects of behavior becomes more difficult to ascertain.

It should be noted that theorists who adopt an interactionist conception of the relation between cognition and affect can differ in their emphasis of the direction of causality between the two. James (1958), for instance, tends to stress the effect that a particular emotion has on the mind: "Strong feeling about one's self tends to arrest the free association of one's subjective ideas and motor processes. We get the extreme example of this in the mental disease called melancholia [p. 143]." A particularly relevant example of an interactionist theorist emphasizing the effect that cognition has on emotion is Aaron Beck (1967) who stresses the role that cognition plays in perpetuating the mood disorder of the depressive.

In conclusion, we have found that particular notions of classification of the emotions and also of the mind-body relationship have persisted in the philosophical and psychological traditions. These conceptualizations are of interest because they surface when discussing recent theories of emotions. This should come as no surprise. As noted earlier, the lack of interest in human emotions in the past 40 years is coincident with the dominance of the behaviorist movement in American psychology. From its inception, the behaviorist framework had strong ties to a particular antimentalistic philosophy. In fact, a great deal of Watson's work reads more like polemical philosophy than experimental psychology (cf. Watson, 1919). In the past 2 decades, resurgent interest in higher mental processes has entailed challenging the philosophical presuppositions of behaviorism (cf. Herrnstein, 1977; Segal & Lachman, 1972). Therefore, we are concerned with explicitly articulating the conceptualizations underlying recently proposed theories of emotional development. In this section, we argue how concepts that have played a role in the discussion of the emotions have remained basically the same in the course of history, and we warn that what often appears to be conceptual advance is really not that at all. Rather, the content of conceptualizations changes largely because of scientific progress *in fields other than psychology*. Theories of emotion having explicit biological and functional emphasis are notable exceptions, but his special status is contingent upon such theories delineating the functional operation of emotions (cf. Izard, 1977; Sroufe, 1979). In the sections that follow, we examine the developmental theories of the emotions that we believe are most useful in elucidating the relationship between emotion and cognition, paying special attention to the philosophical and general psychological frameworks that shape these theories.

DEVELOPMENTAL THEORIES OF THE EMOTION-COGNITION RELATIONSHIP

Development has been described both as the increasing differentiation of parts into more complex hierarchical organization (Werner, 1948) and as the organism's progression toward self-regulation and balance (Piaget, 1936, 1971). These concepts are not in opposition and can be invoked simultaneously to describe the developmental process. As the organism develops, the principles through which it operates become increasingly differentiated and integrated into more complex structures. Various substructures within the individual are related to each other so that the development of one substructure affects the growth of others. At the same time, under the influence of the processes of assimilation and accommodation, the behaviors of the organism increasingly come under the influence of psychological rather than physiological processes, and tend toward an evermore balanced state (cf. Emde et al., 1976; Spitz, 1965). Central to both of these positions is the assumption that the improved functioning of developmentally advanced states is the result of changes in intrinsic properties of the individual.

One persistent difficulty in developmental analysis is the establishment of constants through the life span. One way of pursuing this difficulty is to establish an adult model of the particular construct in question and then determine how it is that children represent the same construct. However, it is possible that a child's analogous acts may not be an earlier version of the same adult behavior. Additionally, the issues to be studied may not be the same in childhood as they are in adulthood. An alternative method of searching for organizing principles developmentally is to search for behaviors that serve the same *function* in childhood and adulthood. In this way, it is possible to specify accurately the early precursors of later adult behaviors without having to make the assumption that particular behaviors mean the same thing to a child as they do to an adult.

These concepts apply directly to the study of the development of the emotions. The ontogenesis of the emotions should follow a logical process with later emotions unfolding from their precursors and serving identical functions for the organism. Coemergence of different emotions will point to similar underlying structures and will also be related to current major developmental reorganizations in the cognitive and social spheres. Thus, physiological regulation (Sander, 1962), mastery of the object world (Erikson, 1950; Mahler, Pine, & Bergman, 1975), the establishment of attachments (Ainsworth, Blehar, Waters, & Wall, 1978; Bowlby, 1969; Sroufe & Waters, 1977), and the differentiation of self from others (Lewis & Brooks, 1978; Mahler, et al., 1975; Mans, Cicchetti, & Sroufe, 1978), have important implications for the developing emotional life of the infant. Finally, the emotions of an infant, as those of an adult, serve the function of organizing object relations (e.g., DeRivera, 1976; Kanzer, 1979).

There have been four traditions of developmental approaches to the study of the emotions and their relationship to cognition. First, theoreticians of cognitive development have mainly dealt with emotions as they appear in connection with the infant's interaction with the physical environment. Baldwin, Werner, and Piaget are representatives of this tradition. Second, other investigators, within the psychoanalytic framework, have been concerned with emotions as they arise out of social relationships. Freud, Spitz, Hartmann, Klein, and others are the main contributors to this tradition. A third group of researchers have attempted to integrate the first two approaches by relating achievements in the realm of social emotions to those emerging in contact with the physical environment. Bridges' and Sroufe's frameworks exemplify this approach. A fourth theory, advanced by Izard and influenced by the work of Darwin (1872) and Tompkins (1962, 1963), has considered the emotions mainly in the context of their biological foundations and adaptiveness. In the following section, we present the theories proposed in the four traditions.

EMOTIONS ARISING OUT OF THE INFANT'S INTERACTION WITH THE PHYSICAL ENVIRONMENT

Baldwin, Werner, and Piaget are exemplars of cognitive developmental theorists whose theoretical predilections lead them to discuss the emotions only in so far as they arise out of the infant's transactions with the world of physical objects.

A. Baldwin's Perspective on Emotional Development

James Mark Baldwin (1890, 1891, 1894) wrote about emotional development in childhood and provided a detailed classification of human emotions as well. Although Baldwin did not delineate a specific developmental theory of the emotions, his writings on the topic are sufficient to permit us to construct at least a tentative model of emotional development with which he would agree.

In his book *Mental Development in the Child and the Race* (1894), Baldwin defined emotion in the following way:

a phenomenon of instinct purely, the "emotions" which a baby a year old has already got, such as fear, anger, jealousy, sympathy, etc.

a phenomenon of ideas—something that the baby has yet to get, such as the emotions, or sentiments, which involve thought about things, contemplation, the more or less adequate understanding of the *meanings* of things in relation to the person who is affected. A child, for example, starts at a loud noise, and shows all the signs of the emotion of fear; but the adult fears a loud noise only when he has some reason to think that it means danger to him [p. 224].

In *Feeling and Will* (1891), Baldwin developed a general taxonomy of feelings, dividing them essentially into "sensuous feelings" (organic, muscular, cutaneous, kinesthetic feelings, and feelings of innervation) and "ideal feelings" (common ideal feelings: interest, feeling of reality and belief; and special ideal feelings or emotions: presentative emotions and emotions of relation—see Table 9.2). However, Baldwin did not address the issue of how these two types of feelings are ontogenetically related. Thus, for Baldwin, early on in life the infant is an instinctual being and some of its instincts can be called emotional. Later on, when the infant is no longer ruled by these instincts, but by cognition or thought and affect, and probably volition as well, the different types of emotions come to the fore. What remains an open question is whether Baldwin wanted to claim that one of the functions of the mind (affect, intellect, or volition) provides the organization for the infant's

TABLE 9.2
James Mark Baldwin's Classification of Feelings and the Emotions

Sensuous Feeling		Ideal Feeling
1. organic	A. COMMON	B. SPECIAL
2. muscular	1. interest	I. *Presentative Emotions*
3. cutaneous	2. reality feeling	1. of activity
4. kinesthetic	3. belief	2. of content
5. feelings of innervation		3. of self
		4. objective
		5. expressive
		6. sympathetic
		7. representative
		II. *Emotions of Relation*
		1. logical
		2. conceptual
		3. feelings for system
		4. ethical
		5. aesthetic

mind and thus for the other two functions, or whether he assumed certain general characteristics of the mind that are characteristic of all three functions or domains.[1] In either case, Baldwin would have to provide an explanation for the emergence of the structures of later stages and an account of the way in which earlier and later stages are related. The general characteristics of the mind's functioning that Baldwin (1894) postulates as being characteristic of all of ontogenetic and phylogenetic development (e.g., the formation of habits, accommodation or adaptation, and dynamogenesis or "the regular connection between the sensory and motor sides of all living reactions as to amount of process [p. 226])," cannot account for any particular transitions in development, such as from the "instinctual" infant to the "intellectual" adult mind. Nowadays, Baldwin's work may be considered useful because he tried to develop a very detailed taxonomy of feelings and emotions.

As most of the emotions that are listed in Table 9.2 are subdivided into several even more specific feelings or emotions, this classification may be helpful for the future study of the differentiation of emotions in the course of ontogenesis. It seems to guarantee a more exhaustive description of the emotions than those systems that try to reduce the study of emotion to a small set of emotional dimensions (e.g., Plutchik, 1965; Woodworth, 1940; Woodworth & Schlosberg, 1954; Wundt, 1912) or to a small set of prototypical emotions (e.g., Izard, 1977, 1978; Tomkins & McCarter, 1964; Watson, 1919, 1925). In so far as the ideal feelings imply the involvement of cognitive processes, their definition may even contribute to future investigations of the relationship between cognitive and emotional phenomena. However, because the relationship between cognitive and emotional states has not been dealt with by Baldwin, the conceptual analysis of this relationship will have to precede the future use of this taxonomy.

B. Werner's Organismic-Developmental Perspective on the Emotions

Like Baldwin, Heinz Werner's organismic-developmental theory—though not an explicit conceptualization of emotional development—may prove to be a fruitful perspective for understanding the ontogenesis of the emotions and their relationship to other developing systems. The organismic-developmental perspective of development refers to the way in which

---

[1]The question may not pose itself for Baldwin, because he emphasizes the unity of the functions of the mind, intellect, affect, and volition. In his work *Senses and Intellect* (1890), he states that "they have unity of end," "they are one in their collective activity," and that "they find their formal unity in consciousness [pp. 40-41]."

behaviors are hierarchically integrated into more complex patterns within developmental systems. It refers to relationships between systems and the effect that advances and lags in one system have on other systems. From an organismic-developmental point of view, which emphasizes the way in which part functions are integrated into wholes (Werner & Kaplan, 1964), it is assumed that a specific behavioral system or means–ends relationship can be adequately understood only if its goal and its interrelatedness to other behaviors with the same goal are taken into consideration (Serafica, 1978).

Werner's discussion of emotional development can be summarized as follows: Because a syncretic state of behavior characterizes the immediate postnatal period, cognitive, emotional, and perceptual aspects of behavior cannot be distinguished during the early stages of development. But they become specifically cognitive, perceptual, and emotional (that is, differentiated into their respective developmental domains) only at a later time.

As a consequence of this point of view, Werner discusses many examples of affective organization of cognitive categories. However, it is not quite clear which of the following alternatives Werner favors: (1) that at the beginning of ontogenesis, because of the initial state of syncretism, cognitive categories are affectively penetrated as well as affective categories cognitively influenced; (2) that during the initial syncretic stage, there is a preponderance of affect over cognition, and thus only cognitive categories are formed based on affective qualities; or (3) that whatever organization develops out of the early cognitive stage, it is essentially cognitive. That is, whereas the early stage of development is characterized by a state of fusion of affect, cognition, and perception, the three developmental domains become differentiated later on under the guidance of the organization of the cognitive domain. Of course, the aforementioned possibilities are not necessarily mutually exclusive. For example, the latter two alternatives may be regarded as complementary because the syncretic stage could be predominantly affective, whereas the later stages may be preponderantly cognitive. However, because Werner's evidence consists largely of illustrations rather than systematically obtained experimental results, it is impossible to infer a detailed picture of the early affect-dominated organization or the later cognition-dominated organization. Moreover, it is difficult to specify precisely how the transition from affective to cognitive organization is brought about.

Whereas what has been said is mainly concerned with the differentiation *between* developmental domains, Werner also claims that there is a differentiation *within* these respective domains. With respect to the domain of emotional development, Werner (1948) states that there is "the increasing differentiation of emotional content [p. 479]." Werner seems to base his evidence for this differentiation within developmental domains on Bridges'

(1930, 1932) account of the differentiation of the emotions during infancy (see later). However, he does not attempt to present an approach of his own. Such a schematic representation is needed especially to demonstrate that the emotions continue to undergo differentiation beyond infancy and to illustrate how this differentiation comes about. Furthermore, Werner postulates an increase in hierarchic integration of emotional behaviors, but as he does not present a detailed account of their differentiation during the course of development, he cannot show the manner in which earlier and later emerging emotions are related. What is missing in Werner's approach is an account of the organization and thus integration (possibly even a hierarchic one) of the later emerging, increasingly differentiated emotions.

Finally, Werner deals not only with the development of content and form within and between developmental domains, but also with the "development" of the environmental aspects eliciting emotional behavior. Werner distinguishes between immediate and concrete stimuli bringing about emotional behavior at the beginning of development and nonimmediate, imaginative, and anticipatory stimuli causing the emotional behavior at later points in development. Again, he does not provide an explanation for this transition, nor does he describe the possible changes in function the different types of stimuli may undergo in the course of ontogenesis.

In summary, the major problems with Werner's approach to emotional development are that it is rather anecdotal and eclectic. He does not provide a precise account of the relationship between emotion and cognition for the early syncretic stage or for the later stages of development. Additionally, he does not give a detailed account of the differentiation of particular emotional contents, their hierarchic organization, or the evolving importance of more and more distant, imaginative stimuli causing emotional behavior. However, Werner's ideas about emotional development provide a framework within which to study the relationship between emotional and cognitive development. Further experimentation will have to be conducted to enable us to form a better picture of how the relationship among cognition, affect, and perception can be conceptualized at the beginning of development (cf. Stechler & Carpenter, 1967; Wolff, 1960, 1966). It remains to be demonstrated how the later differentiated and hierarchically integrated stages of development can be conceived of in terms of their content and structure. Research should be conducted to determine what a taxonomy of the stimuli-eliciting emotional and cognitive behaviors at different points in development should look like (e.g., Hiatt, Campos, & Emde, 1979; Izard & Buechler, 1979). Werner does not deal explicitly with the nature of the transitional phases between stages—that is, the explanatory aspects of developmental sequence—nor with the type of sequence he considers as characteristic of emotional development and its relation to the cognitive domain. Again, these must be dealt with in future research.

C. The Role of Affect in Piaget's Theory

Jean Piaget has often been accused of having neglected, or even ignored, the domain of affect in his theory of child development. However, there are some places where he has articulated his point of view regarding affect (1936, 1954a, 1972, 1973, 1977). Because Piaget has basically focused on the study of cognitive development, it is not too surprising that he deals with the development of affect only in its relation to cognition. Even though Piaget has never worked out a formal position on the relation between cognitive and affective development, his sketch of possible relationships may serve as a framework. The problem associated with Piaget's perspective can be discussed so as to develop the requirements an adequate theory must fulfill.

Piaget has held two major positions concerning the relationship between cognition and affect. In keeping with his concern with the structures and the content of the various stages of development, Piaget (1973) has argued that these two domains exist in parallel. That is, affect and cognition possess similar or even identical structures along with other underlying mechanisms, although these domains are neither completely nor partially reducible to each other. In connection with his equilibration model, Piaget (1977) has introduced the possibility that affect may be an epiphenomenon of cognition. This implies that the appearance of affects is indicative of cognitive disequilibrium and is important in explaining stage transitions in development.

1. Parallelism of Cognitive and Emotional Devleopment. One of Piaget's approaches (1954a) to the relation between cognitive and affective development tries to spell out what a structure or logic of affect might be, and how one might conceive of a sequence of stages of affective development corresponding to his already established stages of cognition. Furthermore, Piaget discusses the possible roles cognition and affect might play with respect to each other. However, he does not tackle the question of how transformations or transitions between stages take place.

Briefly summarized, Piaget claims that affect (sentiments, in particular— emotions, tendencies, the will) provides the energy, whereas cognition provides the structures for development. Affect and cognition do not entertain causal relationships. As Piaget and Inhelder (1969) put it:

> There is no behavior pattern, however intellectual, which does not involve affective factors as motives. Behavior, therfore, has a unity even if the structure (cognitive) does not explain its energetics (affective) and if vice versa its energetics do not account for its structures. *The two aspects, affective and cognitive, are at the same time inseparable and irreducible.* In other words, intelligence cannot cause affect nor can affect cause intelligence. The relationship is rather one of correspondence. [p. 158, emphasis added].

However, Piaget claims that affect may have either an accelerating or retarding influence upon cognition.

Although he claims that cognition and affect play independent, complementary roles throughout development, Piaget (1954a, 1972) considers affective development in terms of its structuralization. That is, the categories that he has constructed to describe the characteristics of cognitive development emerging at different stages are cast over affective development as well. This conceptualization brings about the problem that although Piaget describes the 'new' affects emerging at every stage as complementary to cognition, he excludes the possibility that their development follows its own regularities. Furthermore, the contribution of affect as an energizing factor for development is not spelled out in sufficient detail.

Piaget's description of the sensorimotor stage of development is most lucidly explained in *The Origins of Intelligence* (1936) and in *The Construction of Reality in the Child* (1945). During this period, the concepts of object permanence, space, time, and causality develop in the cognitive domain. However, Piaget does not have too much to say about the affects that are developing during the sensorimotor stage. He refers to joy, pain, and the distinction made between the pleasant and unpleasant as occurring in connection with perceptions and as having activating or terminating effects on actions. However, he does not describe the exact conditions under which joy, pain, and pleasant/unpleasant distinctions occur, nor precisely how he wants to define them. At approximately 6 months a differentiation between needs and interests arises, together with the infant's general decentration (i.e., differentiation of goals and means in the cognitive domain). Interests involve a qualitative or value aspect in addition to their quantitative or energy aspect. According to Piaget, the intensity of the interest corresponds to the energetic regulation; the content of the interest constitutes the value. In connection with values, a kind of judgement capacity develops enabling the infant to prefer certain objects and experiences to others and to ultimately arrive at a hierarchy of values. Piaget emphasizes the complementarity of cognition and affect to refute the belief that attachments or object relations formed at around 8 months of age are exclusively emotional. For Piaget insofar as other people are objects of the environment, the perception of and knowledge about them undergo changes that are characteristic of the object concept in general. Persons have a special status only because they are the most interesting and pleasure-providing objects that infants encounter.

Piaget does not provide us with an exhaustive classification of affect, in terms of either their behavioral criteria or their environmental and stimulus characteristics. Nonetheless, his notion of affective-cognitive parallelism is worthy of discussion because it provides a potentially fruitful theoretical framework. Several problems with this approach are important because their solution may determine the type of theoretical framwork one chooses for the investigation of affective development.

One such problem is that it is not quite clear what sort of a developmental model Piaget wants to suggest with respect to the development of affect. On the one hand, he claims that earlier feelings are not displaced by newly arising ones (1954a). Using Flavell's (1972) terminology, this would be an addition model. On the other hand, Piaget argues against Flavell's substitution model in favor of a reconstruction or inclusion model (1954). This implies that, although new sentiments may emerge in the course of development, the old ones do not just stay the same throughout development, but undergo a transformation or reconstruction themselves. It would be strange, indeed, if the structural transformations of the various stages—which, according to Piaget, are also manifest in the affective domain—would not influence the sentiments developed at earlier stages as well. If Piaget wants to adhere to an addition model—proposing that later emerging sentiments are simply added to already existing ones—he has to specify the external or internal factors that are necessary and sufficient, or at least sufficient, to explain the occurrence of the later emerging emotions. Furthermore, he has to demonstrate that the earlier emotions remain the same and do not become transformed (e.g., because of interactions with the newly emerged sentiments). If Piaget wants to claim that only an inclusion model represents the developmental sequence adequately, he not only has to account for the emergence of new sentiments, but also for the transformation that earlier sentiments undergo when "integrated" into or related to later developing ones. He would have to specify the identity criteria with respect to which one could, say, consider anger or fear to be the same at different developmental levels. The problem with the inclusion model is that it asks for the specification of more than correlational factors in the explanation of newly emerging emotions because it is tied to the notion of structures characteristic of the respective developmental levels, and the relation between earlier and later stage structures. To relate earlier and later stage structures, a conceptual analysis is requried of the "internal" relations of later structures. To accomplish this task, it first has to be ascertained what "elements," "structures," and "logic" are supposed to represent. Can they all be expressed in terms of behavior (that is, content) or only as formalizations that depict competencies supposedly underlying behavior? Indeed what is acceptable as a formalization at all? Furthermore, it has to be determined whether one wants to conceive of emotional development in terms of a logic of development in Piaget's sense. To obtain a thorough solution to this problem it would not suffice to find a universal developmental sequence. Rather, the manner (mechanism) by which earlier and later stages are related would have to be specified.

The fact that the structures of the suggested developmental states are all ill-defined is problematic, especially when we consider whether or not they are identical in the cognitive and affective domains. On the one hand, Piaget claims that the cognitive domain is structural whereas the affective domain is energetic. On the other hand, when he introduces interests in terms of values, and at later stages the notions of a logic of sentiments and reversibility, it becomes obvious that he wants to attribute a structural component at least to certain emotions.

What does it mean that emotions become structuralized or intellectualized? The following interpretations seem plausible to us:

1. Piaget just wants to claim that there are discernible stages in cognitive development and that certain emotions correspond to the cognitive activities (perception, judgments) at every stage. Assuming a tendency towards greater cognitive complexity (or intellectualization) in the course of development, one could argue that emotions corresponding to later stages of cognitive development are "intellectualized" insofar as they correspond to more complex cognitive processes. However, that does not say anything with respect to the structure of the emotions themselves, and is thus irreconcilable with Piaget's claim that more and more complex structures underlie the emotions.

2. The emotions actually undergo a transformation, becoming cognitive insofar as they develop structures underlying them. Emotions undergoing these changes would not be affective any more, but cognitive. One remaining problem would be that as we become "more structured" in the course of our development, we should have fewer emotions. However, this does not seem to correspond with the developmental literature. This interpretation seems to be consonant with a number of Piaget's remarks, one of them being that one can apply transitivity to emotions in the same sense that one can say that a goal g_1 is more interesting than g_2, g_2 more interesting than g_3, and therefore g_1 more interesting than g_3. However, the problem is that there seems to be a difference between "feeling" emotions and "comparing" them, the latter not being an emotion itself. In other words, the fact that we can make transitive judgments does not imply that we feel "transitively," but rather that we have feelings of different intensities toward objects or persons and rank them by means of judgment, which is cognitive.

3. This suggests a third construal of Piaget's position. Insofar as infants cannot reflect upon their emotions, one may say that they are not intellectualized. One can therefore state that the more children interpret their emotions, or reflect on them propositionally in the course of their cognitive development, the more structured their reflections, judgments, and so on, become, but not the emotions themselves. This interpretation implies a narrower definition of emotions than Piaget has originally posited. It reduces them to different intensities (or energies) and attributes the interpretation of these intensities to cognitions. Thus, we can say that our interpretations of these energies become more structured, but not necessarily the energies themselves.

2. Affects as Epiphenomena of Cognition   Piaget has not only been concerned with the structuralization of affect, but also with its energic aspect

(1936, 1973). In connection with his consideration of the motivations for action, and the indicators of cognitive disequilibrium he first introduced his concept of need in *The Origins of Intelligence* (1936).

To discuss Piaget's concept of need, we have to introduce the different types of equilibration distinguished by Piaget. It is only with regard to these that Piaget (1936) can talk about the cognitive imbalances that he considers as states of need from the infant's point of view—that is, as affective states: "Desirability is the indication of a rupture in equilibrium or of an uncompleted totality to whose formation some element is lacking [pp. 10-11]." This is interesting within the framework of our discussion of the relationship between cognitive and emotional development because, in the case of cognitive disequilibria, emotional and cognitive states seem to be most clearly related. That is, whereas the discussion of Baldwin's and Werner's positions somehow includes both cognitive and affective phenomena without precisely relating them, this position of Piaget's attempts an analysis of their interrelationship. Furthermore, because disequilibria are indicative of developmental changes according to Piaget's theory, the analysis of the respective involvement of cognitive and affective states in disequilibria may reveal something about the mechanisms and thereby the explanatory factors that underlie changes in both cognitive and emotional development.

Piaget (1977) differentiates cognitive states of equilibrium from mechanical (static) and thermodynamic ones (the latter being "a state of rest after the destruction of the structures of a system [p. 11]"). He compares them instead with biological equilibria because cognitive systems, like organisms, are open in one direction (exchange processes with the environment) and closed in another ("cycles" of schemes, which can also function without intervention of the environment). With respect to the first direction, he introduces his concepts of assimilation and accommodation under the aspect of adaptation. With respect to the second, under the aspect of inner organization of the subject, he introduces schemes and developing subschemes (differentiation) that are combinable by means of reciprocal assimilation and ordered hierarchically into a structure (integration).

Accordingly, Piaget discriminates among three different types of equilibration. Because of the interaction between subject and object from the very beginning of a newborn's life, the equilibration of the assimilation of objects to schemes of action and the accommodation of these action schemes to objects can be discerned. This type of equilibrium is external insofar as it refers to the infant's relation to its (physical/social) environment.

The two other types of equilibration refer to the internal organization of the organism. The second type focuses on the relations of subsystems (e.g., parts of independent schemes, like sucking, grasping, and so on) to the extent to which they are combined with one another because of reciprocal assimilation. The third type of equilibration refers to the relationship of differentiation and integration of the hierarchical organization of subsystems into a whole. Differentiation occurs as a result of accommodation; integration occurs as a result of assimilation. Equilibration is achieved as a consequence of the reciprocal assimilation and accommodation *not* only of juxtaposed subsystems as in the second type of equilibrium, but also of parts of the same system.

To achieve the equilibration of certain schemes, A, B, and C, and the corresponding objects A′, B′, and C′, the objects must have certain properties a′, b′, and c′ that the infant can recognize and distinguish from certain other properties, e.g., non-a′, non-b′, non-c′, which are *not* characteristic of these objects. Only if these latter properties can be considered as not belonging to certain assimilated objects A′, B′, and C′, does it make sense to talk about discrepancies or imbalances between schemes and nonassimilated objects, because only then does a malproportion of negative and positive properties become obvious.

Similar processes of differentiation between properties and nonproperties have to be resolved by the infant with respect to the relationship of different juxtaposed subsystems (those related by reciprocal assimilation have to be separated from those that are not) and subsystems belonging to a whole, superordinate scheme or a structure consisting of schemes (the former have to be differentiated from those belonging to other totalities).

Thus, these states of disturbance are due to either the perturbations engendered by unassimilable objects or the differing rates of maturation of the various subschemes. Two major types of disequilibria can occur. The processes of assimilation and accommodation may be inhibited. Additionally, even when the assimilation of objects to schemes and the correspondent accommodation of schemes to objects has been achieved, they may lack the necessary stimulation to be activated fully. The corresponding types of regulations that the infant uses to overcome these interferences are negative and positive feedbacks. With regard to negative feedbacks, one can discern compensations by inversion and reciprocity. With respect to positive feedbacks, one observes a tendency or a state of need for the infant to resolve the imbalance.

Within a developmental framework, one can differentiate between three stages of regulation and compensation: one in which interference can be completely ignored and not integrated into the system; a second in which interference can be partially integrated into the system; and a third in which minimal interference can occur because virtually all possible intrusions are anticipated by the system.

Piaget accounts for the tendency toward more coherence shown during this developmental course by postulating an inherent propensity of the infant to seek more and more consistency in its organization. Several problems remain unsolved by this functional analysis of the concept of equilibration as it relates to emotional development. For example, what is to be understood by the states of need to which Piaget alludes? He refers to them in a very global way as introspective equivalents of states of disequilibrium and implies that they correspond to different states of disproportion between affirmative and negative properties as represented by infants. Although this analysis can account for states of imbalance, it cannot account for the fact that they tend to be resolved. Why, for instance, does an infant repeat a *specific* action and not another one? Why does it even try to resolve these states of disequilibria?

Taking a developmental perspective, it will have to be determined whether the states of need corresponding to cognitive conflicts are the same throughout development. As the content of the cognitive conflict changes depending on the child's developmental stage, it is very likely that the respective states of need are expressed in different ways as well. Contemporary developmentalists, most notably Sroufe in his work on the role of *tension* in promoting development (Sroufe, 1979; Sroufe & Waters, 1976), are conducting research that will shed important light on these issues.

In addition, these two major approaches that Piaget has advanced will have to be related to each other (see Cicchetti & Pogge-Hesse, in press a, for an integration of these two approaches). If our interpretation of the first approach is correct, it is very similar to the second one though seemingly different at first sight. That is, in both cases affective states are conceived of as energies or needs, whereas cognitive states account for the structural aspects of development.

EMOTIONS ARISING IN THE
COURSE OF SOCIAL RELATIONSHIPS:
THE PSYCHOANALYTIC VIEW
OF AFFECTIVE DEVELOPMENT

Psychoanalytic theories of the emotions have made three major contributions. They have discussed emotions as they develop within an interpersonal context rather than in terms of the organism's interaction with the physical environment. In this regard, psychoanalytic approaches complement those of Baldwin, Werner, and Piaget. Second, they have related the discussion of the emotions to issues in the realm of psychopathology, an area rarely touched upon within the framework of the cognitive-developmental theories. Finally, they have studied the relationship between the emotions and language, reaching conclusions that closely resemble those of some nonpsychoanalytic theorists (Luria & Subbotski, 1978). However, we are not going to deal with the latter two contributions because they are beyond the scope of infancy.

The majority of the psychoanalytic theories of emotional and cognitive development in infancy adopt similar fundamental beliefs. At birth, the infant is endowed with a set of *innate reflexes or response tendencies*. One can attribute neither cognition nor emotion to the infant, but only states of arousal or tension and tension reduction, which may be experienced as pleasurable or unpleasurable by the infant. Though analytic authors disagree as to when the beginning of social development occurs, there is general agreement that the newborn infant experiences only states of undifferentiated tension or tension reduction and that these *physiological prototypes* serve as the foundation upon which the psyche will erect its structures (cf. Spitz, 1965). These feelings of pleasure or displeasure are the precursors of later emotions. Blau (1955) referred to this stage of development as follows: "During the first 3 months of life there is as yet no real psychology of emotion, only a physiology of emotion. Psychology of emotions begins when the integrating functions of the central nervous system and the ego mature sufficiently to link the ego with the inner organism and with the outside world [p. 79]."

At approximately 2 or 3 months of age, with the emergence of primitive ego functions such as increases in memory capacity, the first "real" emotions can be recognized. Joy, for example, is reflected in the infant's first social smiles. Though the interpretation of this event differs for ego psychologists and object-relations theorists, the underlying implication is the same. That is, the emotions cannot develop without the *simultaneous development of cognition,* for it is the cognitive changes that qualitatively differentiate the innate quantitative sensations of pleasure and displeasure. Sigmund Freud (1936) expressed this development in the following way: "Anxiety is an affective state which can of course be experienced only by the Ego . . . the Ego is the real seat of anxiety . . . (the) anxiety proper cannot be produced before the Ego is differentiated from the Id [p. 80]." Ego functions make it possible for the infant to attach meaning to its experience, but it is the tension or emotional change that is the force that urges development onward (Emde et al., 1976; Spitz, 1959, 1965).

From 6 to 10 months, further changes in the cognitive domain bring about the first signs of object permanence; the socioemotional manifestation of these cognitive changes is separation anxiety or "eight-month anxiety" (Spitz, 1950, 1959). Still more sophisticated developments in cognition such as the awareness of self-control and the capacity for symbolic and representational functions allow for the emergence of guilt, pride, and shame. This theme of cognitive and socioemotional concomitance continues throughout development and underscores another fundamental belief of psychoanalytic theoreticians. That is, *the infant develops from a primitive, undifferentiated mass of tension to more and more complex forms of behavior and psychic experience* (cf. A. Freud, 1965; Spitz, 1959, 1965).

The Historical Roots of Psychoanalytic Theory on Emotion

Sigmund Freud defined the general rules and assumptions on the theory of emotional development that became the foundation for subsequent psychoanalytic authors. He also posed the questions they attempt to answer and left some aspects of his theory ambiguous or contradictory. It is for this reason that neoanalytic writers have departed from Freudian theory in distinct directions. Though psychoanalytic writers debate the ambiguous points in Freudian theory endlessly, the basic assumptions are retained throughout the literature (e.g., Rapaport, 1953, 1960).

Freud (1900, 1915) conceived of affect as a measurable quantity of energy of which the ego strives to rid itself. These tensions or excitations interfere with psychic functioning, and the ego seeks their discharge. *Affect, then, indicates disorganization* as the ego strives for the state of quiescence. The origin of affect is distinguished from the origin of its ideational representatives; the ontogenesis of affect is viewed as a *quantity* rooted in the biological aspect of the species, whereas ideas originate in the ego as it transforms the emotional *quality* into an acceptable form in consciousness. Green (1977) writes: "One could say that the goal of the psychic apparatus is less to derive the maximum from the wealth of affective experience than to be able to master such an experience by thought and confront it with the known facts of the external and internal worlds [p. 131]."

Freud did not pay as much attention to the experience of affects as he did to the meaning of the event. Affects are viewed as evidence of the failure of the defensive system. Freud (1915) wrote, "to suppress the development of affect is the true aim of repression and . . . its work does not terminate if this aim is not achieved [p. 110]." Similarly, when experienced in transformation, Freud focused his attention on the defensive process by which the affects become disguised or transformed. It is consistent within the tradition of psychoanalysis that Freudian theory tended to subordinate the role of affect to its ideational representations. Psychoanalysis is essentially an intellectual pursuit—a "talking cure"—hence the study of meaning or ego functioning (cognition) took precedence over affective or emotional experience. Though Freud did begin to distinguish qualitative differences in affects (especially anxiety) in his later writings (Freud, 1926, 1933), he never departed from the fundamental view that affects are to be mediated by ego defense mechanisms and that an excess of excitation may have traumatic effects.

What remains, though, is the question of whether the sensation after tension discharge—that pleasurable state of quiescence—is to be considered in itself an affective experience. Freud remained ambiguous on this point throughout his writings, and this ambiguity was responsible for a major division in post-Freudian theory, namely the split between the ego psychologists (e.g., Brenner, 1974; A. Freud, 1954; Hartmann, 1950; Mahler et al., 1975; Spitz, 1950, 1959, 1965) and the object-relations school of thought (e.g., A. Balint, 1949; M. Balint, 1949; Bowlby, 1958; Fairbairn, 1949, 1951; Klein, 1952). How emotional development is conceived for each of these schools can be seen by examining their respective beliefs on the nature of the mother-infant relationship.

The Ego Psychologist's Point of View
on Emotional Development

The ego psychologists have built upon Freud's notion of an "anaclitic" relationship. This notion proposes that love for the mother ultimately derives from ("leans up against") gratification of the primary needs of nourishment. The notion is parallel to the Hullian proposition that the bond between mother and infant is based on the acquisition of a secondary drive formed via mother's association with reduction of primary drives such as hunger or thirst (Dollard & Miller, 1950; Sears, 1963). For the ego psychologists, the newborn is a wholly nondifferentiated organism whose emotional life varies from states of tension to states of quiescence. The infant experiences states of need and states of need gratification only. Affects, whose emergence depends on the existence of a true object relationship, do not develop at this stage. The relationship that exists between the mother and the infant develops solely around the vicissitudes of the infant's needs as is evident in Anna Freud's (1946b) description of the first year:

> When (the infant) is under pressure of urgent bodily needs, as for instance hunger, it periodically establishes connections with the environment which are withdrawn again after the needs have been satisfied and the tension is relieved. These occasions are the child's first introduction to experiences of wish fulfillment and pleasure. They establish centers of interest to which libidinal energy becomes attached. An infant who feeds successfully "loves" the experience of feeding (narcissistic love) [p. 124].

The newborn is shielded largely from the outside world because of an extremely high stimulus barrier in its perceptual apparatus (Benjamin, 1965; Spitz, 1965; Tennes, Emde, Kisley, & Metcalf, 1972). Stimuli from the external world are perceived only when their intensity exceeds that of the barrier threshold. Furthermore, the infant at this time cannot distinguish between sensations that originate from within itself and those that are sensory inputs from the external world. The infant essentially experiences everything as part of itself and is primarily narcissistic—the libido that drives the infant toward need gratification is *objectless*, and the affective bond that develops between the infant and its mother is essentially anaclitic. That is, the "love" that is felt is a blissful feeling of need fulfillment rather than attachment to the object for the object itself. The distinction here lies between a bond formed in response to gratification of physiological needs (a "dependent" bond) and a more emotional, affective "love" bond specific to the object (Ainsworth, 1969). This stage of development is therefore referred to as "primary narcissism" or "objectless" and is governed by the "Nirvana" or "Pain Quiescence" Principle (Spitz, 1965).

Anna Freud did not mark the transformation from narcissistic libido into object libido until the second year of life. However, most psychoanalytic writers have observed object-seeking behaviors much earlier. Spitz and Wolf (1946) observed smiling responses by infants aged 3 to 6 months to elements of the human face and marked the emergence of these smiles as symptoms of the first developmental organizer. Spitz attributes these responses to an increase in memory capacity and infers that a division in the psychic apparatus has taken place. The familiar topography of the psyche as split into conscious, preconscious, and unconscious parts is now applicable to the infant, though in rudimentary form. This structure replaces the threshold protection of the stimulus barrier as the ego is able to mediate intput from the environment (Spitz, Emde, & Metcalf, 1970). Though the infant's emotional reactions become more specific, its object relations are still in response to human faces in general and not to the mother in particular. It is for this reason that Spitz calls this the *preobjectal* stage.

At approximately 8 months, the second developmental organizer of the psyche is observed as the infant displays definite signs of anxiety when confronted with strangers or when it is separated from its caregiver. Spitz maintains that this "eight-month anxiety" marks a distinct development in ego functioning—that is, the capacity for longer-lasting memory traces, the functions of judgment, and the ability to make decisions. The ability to cathect onto "reliably stored memory traces" (Spitz, 1965) reflects the establishment of a true object relation and the emergence of love in an organized, directed sense. A correspondent fusion of the representations of the mother as the good object and the mother as the bad object is assumed to be due to the infant's increasing memory capacity and indicates a synthesizing capacity in ego functioning. This stage is characterized by true object relations, and subtle affective shadings emerge such as jealousy, anger, envy, love, joy, and affection (Spitz, 1965).

Between 18 and 24 months, the emergence of negativity signals the onsetting development of the self-concept and the beginning of the infant's sense of autonomy. According to Spitz, negativity indicates the emergence of the third developmental organizer on an emotional level. An increase in vocabulary and the capacity for more differentiated representations develop in the language and cognitive domains, respectively. According to Spitz, negativity is not possible to the same extent before this stage because it requires the simultaneous representation of the goals the infant wants and does not want to obtain.

Brenner (1974) explicitly distingishes only two phases of emotional development corresponding to Spitz's objectless and preobjectal stages. The first is characterized by sensations of pleasure and unpleasure. These two sensations can be defined at this stage only in terms of intensity. It is with the onset of the second stage, marked by the development of the ego, that emotions emerge as complex phenomena. Brenner (1974) defines these emotions as affects that include the sensations of pleasure and unpleasure as well as their associated ideas:

> Affects, whether pleasurable or unpleasurable, are complex mental phenomena which include (a) sensations of pleasure, unpleasure, or a mixture of the two, and (b) thoughts, memories, wishes, fears—in a word, ideas. Psychologically an affect is a sensation of pleasure, unpleasure, or both, plus the ideas associated with that sensation. *Ideas and sensation together, both conscious and unconscious, constitute an affect* [p. 535, emphasis added].

For Brenner, then, a theory of emotional development will consist of reconstructing the developmental sequence in terms of (cognitive) interpretations of the sensations of pleasure and unpleasure. In his view, not only is the evolution of affect wholly dependent on ego (cognitive) development, but it is seen as an aspect of ego (cognitive) development and often serves as a measure of the level of ego functioning. The question arises as to whether these sensations remain the same throughout the development of changing cognitive interpretations. Brenner (1974) assumes that they do. However, he points to the lack of general knowledge in this area and attempts to fill this informational void by specifying the experience of pleasure/unpleasure and its intensity, and by distinguishing between these on the basis of their content and the origins of their associated ideas.

Schur (1969), in contrast, accounts not only for changes in *cognitive interpretations* of affective states, *but also for changes in the affective states themselves*. He postulates a separate ontogenetic sequence for the emotions:

> It is not only the cognitive sector of all affects which has its history. The sector of an affect which is generally considered the main or the only one deserving of the name affect—if we equate this with feeling, or more precisely conscious feeling—also has its history, which is an integral part of our maturation and development [p. 652].

Although Schur points to the immense complexity of affective experience, it is unclear how changes in sensations of pleasure and unpleasure can be discovered apart from their cognitive interpretations.

The Object-Relations Theory of Emotional Development

The main difference between ego psychology and object-relations theory is that the latter expressly denies the existence of a primary objectless stage of development. A distinction is made between Freud's hedonistic depiction of libido as primarily pleasure-seeking and his subsequent allusions to libido as primarily object-seeking (Fairbairn, 1949, 1951). The fact that the infant generally becomes attached to the primary caregiver is a coincidence of logistics. That is, the caregiver is not merely the source of physiological gratification but also the most salient object in the infant's severely constricted world. The fundamental assumption underlying all object-relations theory is that human beings are *always* in relationship with one another; the neonate is born in relation to its parents just as the orphan's relationship with its parents is conspicuous because it involves loss. Melanie Klein (1952) gives evidence of the existence of an affective bond between the mother and the infant quite early in life:

> Babies as young as three weeks interrupt their sucking for a short time to play with the mother's breast or to look towards her face... young infants—even as early as in the second month—... in wakeful periods after feeding lie on the mother's lap, look up at her, listen to her voice and respond to it by their facial expression; such behavior implies that gratification is as much related to the object which gives the food as to the food itself [p. 239].

"Holding" and "clinging" behaviors are also used as indices of the early object relation (A. Balint, 1949; Winnicott, 1948, 1953, 1960). Fairbairn (1952) cites the ethological literature as demonstrating object-specific behaviors in the newborn. Furthermore, proximity-seeking behaviors, seen in animals and in humans, are viewed as evidence for the existence of primary affection (Bowlby, 1958, 1969).

Object-relations theorists posit a variety of psychodynamic ego structures and mechanisms arising from the *introjection* of representative part or whole objects. That is, in order to facilitate the process of object permanence, the love object is internalized to maintain the attachment bond in the instance of the object's absence. Likewise, the part of the love object that is experienced as frustrating or rejecting is internalized as the infant attempts to master or control it. This process of introjection—a function of the ego—gives rise to the inevitable internal battles between good and bad part-objects (i.e., mother as nurturing and mother as rejecting, respectively) and is responsible for subsequent "splits" that militate against ego integration (see Fairbairn, 1951). Following Freud, the *disorganizing* effect of affect is brought to the fore.

Whether social interaction is viewed as developing secondarily or primarily, the theme of *coemergence* of cognitive (ego) functioning and socioemotional development is consistent throughout the psychoanalytic approach in general. This assumption is made by ego psychologists and object-relations theorists alike, regardless of their respective beliefs on the origins of interpersonal relationships.

Psychoanalytic Taxonomies of the Emotions

The sequence of emotional development suggested by Blau (1955) and Schmale (1964) differ from those of the other psychoanalysts in that they are mainly taxonomical. They do not link cognitive and emotional development so specifically. Rather, they refer to a variety of *learning mechanisms* as the organizers of emotional development.

Blau describes affects as divided into three components: enteroceptive, the basic visceral tensions; proprioceptive, the ideational representations of the impluse for action (i.e., wish or inclination); and verbal, the affect's identification in words. The implication of this view is that only a small portion of the affective experience—namely, the visceral tension—is innate. The large part of affect and its emotional expression is acquired through learning about one's inner and outer worlds.

The infant learns to interpret and place significance upon its inner events as it is better able to perceive these events. Along with developing motor capacities, the infant learns to use these capacities toward goal-directed activity. Furthermore, the child learns conventional ways of acting through the increasing awareness of its culture and with the growing capacity for the language it learns to designate its experiences and communicate it to others (Blau, 1955).

Blau's approach lacks precision in accounting for the factors that facilitate emotional development. He attempts rather a more global description of affect and designates anxiety as the primary innate emotion of displeasure from which all other displeasurable emotions evolve. Anxiety is a basic physiological response to the disturbance of the balance of visceral economy (Blau, 1955). The secondary and tertiary emotions evolving from anxiety are not innate but are learned responses that acquire their significance from the various motor, linguistic, and ideational developments previously described. Fear, rage, and depression are examples of secondary emotions; guilt, shame, and disgust comprise the third set. The distinction between the secondary and tertiary emotions is described by Blau (1955) as a "fuller maturation of the personality [p. 91]." The beginnings of autonomy and ego ideals are cited as evidence of more mature emotional functioning.

By proposing such a hierarchy, Blau offers an ordered system of emotional expression. He describes mature emotions at the upper end of the hierarchy as complicated combinations or blends of the more basic emotions at the lower end. However, he does not describe them more specifically than that, nor does he mention the ages at which the transitions within the hierarchy occur.

Schmale (1964) presents a more detailed taxonomy of the emotions emerging during infancy. He proposes that "affects begin as a psychic awareness of mostly biological material [p. 288]" and differentiate in accordance with the integration and maturation of the psychic system. Like Blau, Schmale points to the experiences in the external world that urge the process of differentiation onward.

In the first few weeks of life, the infant responds rather globally and reflexively to a limited set of stimuli, and the primitive, undifferentiated ego gives rise to affects that are largely somatic. Schmale postulates anxiety as the undifferentiated affect experienced by the infant at this time; anxiety is viewed as the first psychic awareness of discomfort and is the prototype from which all other affects are derived. The psychic process that corresponds to this developmental stage is referred to as *incorporation* and is characterized by its passive mode.

By the third or fourth month, the infant is capable of more active behavior such as reaching and holding (Schmale, 1964). Schmale proposes that these behaviors give rise to the affects of fascination/anger because they refer to object-directed activity. The infant can now associate gratification with activity. According to Schmale (1964) it is much less a passive incorporator and this process of "actively taking in gratification [p. 291]" is referred to as *introjection.*

With further developments in the infant's sensorimotor apparatus, the infant at 6 to 10 months learns to approach and withdraw. Schmale proposes that this capacity gives rise to the affects of bliss (as the infant is able to further regulate its gratifying experiences) and fear (as the infant finds itself unable to avoid ungratifying ones). The gaze-averting behavior observed when the infant is separated from its mother is an example of this newly acquired capacity to withdraw. Schmale marks this stage as the onset of the intrapsychic process *projection,* the active displacement of the source of unpleasure onto an object representation of the external world. Along with Hartmann, Kris, and Lowenstein (1946), Schmale marks the age of 12 to 16 months of life as the time when the infant transforms its psychic relation with regard to objects from primary narcissism to object cathexis. This coincides with the infant's cognitive realization that it is separate from, and dependent on, the laws of the external world. The affect of helplessness reflects this awareness as the infant finds itself unable to gratify its needs alone.

Schmale's (1964) classification scheme, like Blau's, is hierarchical. He maintains that "... in the differentiation of each affect, there are elements of the former affects in the subsequent ones. Take fear, for example; there are elements of anxiety and anger in what is described as feeling tense with a desire to find gratification and to avoid or overcome unpleasure [p. 292]."

However, neither Blau nor Schmale go beyond the claim that emotional development is hierarchical in nature. They do not describe the conceptual and empirical relations between earlier and later emerging emotional behaviors in detail. Furthermore, they do not account for the external and internal factors and mechanisms of change that cause this hierarchy, other than to propose their schemes justified largely for their parsimony.

In summary, most psychoanalytic authors view affect as reflections of a particular stage in development. They are epiphenomenal in this sense. Though they underscore the coemergence of cognition and emotion, the causal relationship most often described is essentially one-way. The role of affect is to manifest tension that the ego is responsible to organize. Freud viewed affect as tension or psychic distress that *signals* conflict and must be controlled (1926) or as a *reaction* to severe trauma that must be discharged or repressed (1900). Spitz's (1959, 1965) particular affect at each stage *indicates* the onset of a new organizer in development. For Brenner (1974), the evolution of affect serves to *measure* the level of ego functioning. Even for the object-relations theorists, the affective bond evident in the neonate is a *manifestation* of the existence of an organized object relationship, and it is the emergence of ego defenses (i.e., introjection, fragmentation, and so on), which is responsible for the evolution of the object relation (see, for example, Fairbairn, 1951; Klein, 1952). Though Schmale and Blau refer to learning mechanisms that organize development, they do not view the infant's experience of its own affect as a stimulus for learning. Rather, for example, the experience of helplessness *reflects* the infant's cognitive awareness of itself as separate from the external world (Schmale, 1964).

What the psychoanalytic theories that have been discussed omit is the organizing, in a sense *effective,* role affect plays in human development. Affect not only *signals* the onset of particular stages, it is oftentimes responsible for the groundbreaking and transition from one stage to the next.

It is possible that the psychoanalytic authors cited do not mean to imply such a one-way causal relationship. However, emotional behaviors can be observed more directly than cognitive structures. Therefore, they are, of necessity, cast into the role of indicating or signaling the emerging stages of development. In addition, because language resides within the cognitive domain, it is impossible to describe changes in affective development other than to attack the problem via cognition. However, given these inherent difficulties, most psychoanalytic authors maintain that affect plays a disorganizing role and that the infant is driven toward affect reduction. It should be kept in mind that these psychoanalytic theories have been encumbered by the energy-distribution and drive-reduction conceptions of affect, integral to Freud's classic closed hydraulic model. Even Spitz assumes that tension increase is unpleasurable, whereas tension relief is pleasurable and that need gratification is central in human emotion (cf. Sroufe, 1979). This is in direct contradiction with much of the developmental data that shows ample evidence of tension-seeking behaviors (see Sroufe, 1979; Sroufe & Waters, 1976, 1977). The object-relations theorists are exceptions among the majority of psychoanlysts in this vein. Their recognition of object-seeking behaviors that serve to facilitate affective bonding takes into account the infant's need for stimulation.

EMOTIONS ARISING OUT OF
THE INFANT'S INTERACTION WITH
THE SOCIAL AND PHYSICAL ENVIRONMENT

A. Bridges' Account of the Ontogenesis
of the Emotions

As noted, Werner's (1948) account of emotional development was profoundly influenced by the work of Bridges (1930, 1932, 1933, 1934, 1936). Indeed, the theorizing of Bridges continues to have an impact on current researchers in infant emotional development (e.g., Sroufe, 1979). Descriptions of the differentiation of emotional behavior are most succinctly stated in her paper, "A Genetic Theory of the Emotions" (Bridges, 1930) and in her article, "Emotional Development in Early Infancy" (Bridges, 1932).

Bridges believes that emotion is more than simply a "visceral pattern reaction," although that may be the core of an emotional behavior. The same visceral reaction can be a component of different emotions. Likewise, a given infant's manifestation of one emotion can involve several visceral reactions on different occasions. Accordingly, it is not a good idea to formulate a one-to-one correspondence between a given visceral reaction and an emotion. Emotions also include reflexes and instinctive reactions, motor habits and combination, and circulatory and glandular patterns. Bridges (1930) prefers to describe emotions as "certain changes in the behavior of the total personality, including particularly visceral and glandular changes and the effects of these upon instinctive, habitual, and other overt behavior [p. 514]."

Then again, although individual differences do exist, by age 2 there are certain general visceral responses characteristic of certain emotions (e.g., joy usually includes relaxation or normal muscle tonus, and partial dilation of the peripheral blood vessels). Bridges borrows from Dashiell (1928) the notions that emotions are more usefully classified in terms of social significance (i.e., the situations that elicit them) than in terms of visceral reactions and that there may be no innate patterns of visceral reactions at all. Rather, Bridges feels that all may be acquired through experience by the process of conditioning.

At birth, visceral responses are relatively undifferentiated and uncoordinated. The primitive, single, undifferentiated emotion, elicited by strong stimuli creating a disturbance, is excitement (akin to Watson's [1925] primary emotions of fear, love, and anger). In the excitement reaction, all parts of the autonomic nervous system are probably activated, and there may be an alternation of sympathetic and parasympathetic activity. Excitement very early on becomes differentiated into distress and delight as a result of experience. Bridges says these two emotions are already apparent in a 3-week-old infant. Delight takes somewhat longer to become differentiated from general excitement than does distress. These two emotions, in turn, are further differentiated into the spectrum of emotions. Although Bridges is somewhat vague on this point, it appears that she believes visceral components of the entire distress/delight reaction to be isolated, associated with certain situations, and integrated with other components to form more sophisticated emotional reactions.

Emotional development takes place in three ways: (1) differentiation from general excitement; (2) change in the form of behavior according to the level of developing motor and social skills; (3) change in situations that arouse different emotions. With increasing age, there is an accompanying increase in specificity of emotional behavior. The stimuli that arouse a given emotion become more circumscribed, and the form of the response becomes more specific.

It is difficult to identify the specificities in the differentiation process Bridges postulates. First of all, Bridges states that the differentiation of excitement to distress and delight occurs very early: Her end points are several hours after birth to 2 or 3 weeks after birth. If the differentiation occurs at least in part through a conditioning process, a problem is presented because it is highly unlikely that a neonate can be conditioned in the way Bridges describes. Second, her theory does not account for the interesting differences between early distress and delight. For example, how would it explain why distress is differentiated from excitement prior to delight, or why the form early distress takes is so much more active than that of early delight, which is more a matter of passive content? Third, if differentiation relies so heavily on conditioning through experience (e.g., associating certain visceral reactions with certain stimuli), how does the infant ever develop any flexibility in its emotional repertoire? That is, how does the infant acquire the capacity to react with, for example, anger—to two overtly different stimuli that still share an underlying frustrating element? Finally, as Sroufe (1979) has noted, Bridges does not call upon general development knowledge to explain why particular emotions appear when they do.

B. Sroufe's Organizational Perspective

As we have seen, developmental theories of the social emotions have been largely psychoanalytic in their orientation. Freud proposed that affect orginated in the internal tension aroused by stimulation, which was invariably experienced as unpleasure. The infant then sought to discharge the tension—the success of which resulted in the experience of pleasure. However, it is now apparent that there are several problems with this "hydraulic" model of affect (see White, 1959). Infants are active seekers of stimulation. Moreover, the build-up of tensions can be a pleasurable experience for the baby. Additionally, with increasing perceptual, cognitive, and neurological maturation, the infant can tolerate and even thrive on increasing amounts of stimulation. Finally, the cessation of pleasurable stimulation can be experienced as unpleasurable.

Bowlby (1969) has refuted the notions of tension release and distribution of a fixed quantity of energy as explanatory concepts for behavior. Instead, information regarding the attainment of set goals (e.g., proximity seeking) reaches the infant and activates its behavior. Such behavior will persist until the baby accomplishes its goal. It is therefore unnecessary to postulate drives or motives in this system. Similarly, Mandler (1975), although not postulating a developmental theory, also describes a control-systems/ information theory to account for the emotions. Here, according to Mandler

(1964), the "interruption of plans" produces arousal and, depending on the evaluation of contextual factors, the various emotions are evoked. Mandler states that these interruptions are, on the whole, disruptive because they usually block the activity that is most appropriate to the situation at hand. However, no drive or energy concepts are proposed.

Sroufe and Waters (1977) have recently criticized theories of attachment that do not postulate tension, motives, or feeling states. They argued that Bowlby's perspective, even though it could account for the activation of attachment behaviors, cannot explain the changing sensitivity of infants to subsequent separation following a prior one or, more generally, why the set goal of the infant changes even though the external situation remains the same. Additionally, the set goal of proximity seeking is not consistent with findings in the developmental literature. For example, Waters (1978) has shown that infants seek less proximity with age, even though they still remain attached to their caregivers. Accordingly, Sroufe and Waters (1977) state that only an affective construct like "felt security" is developmentally robust enough to explain the complex manifestation of attachment behavior (see also Bischof, 1975, in this regard).

Moreover, the need to retain the concept of tension, including tension *cumulation* and *fluctuation,* becomes clear in examining positive affect and the relationships between positive, neutral, and negative affect developmentally (Cicchetti & Sroufe, 1978; Sroufe & Waters, 1976). Frequently, positive affect occurs in the smooth flow of behavior without any conflict or interruption as would be required by purely cognitive theories, of which Mandler's is only one example. Tension seems necessary to account for the range of emotions and their precursors, the positive emotions in particular, the vigor of affective response, and the continuity and discontinuity in the development of emotion (Sroufe, 1979). Also, it captures the quality of dynamic engagement of the infant at play. Freud's extreme position of stating that tension build-up is entirely unpleasurable and the discharge entirely pleasurable underscores the problems of the hydraulic model. The concept of affect being related to building-up and falling-off of stimulation remains, however, and is supported by recent empirical evidence.

Sroufe (1977b, 1979) ties together four diverse instances of rising and falling stimulation based on developmental research to portray the role of tension in emotional experience. The first, from the work of Emde et al. (1976), suggests that during the REM sleep of infants, the more primitive subcortical portions of the brain rhythmically discharge, creating rising and falling cycles of neurological excitation. The endogenous smile of the neonate occurs when the level of excitation rises above and then falls below a postulated threshold. The second instance, based on the work of Berlyne (1969), postulates that an "arousal jag," or sudden increase and then decrease in the ongoing level of excitement, is required to produce laughter. The third instance, based on Kagan's discrepancy hypothesis (1971), proposes that as an infant is processing incongruity, tension mounts until the baby has assimilated or mastered the conflict. As the tension dissipates, positive affect results. Finally, Sroufe's own work on positive affective expression in infants demonstrates that the stimuli most effective in producing strong positive affect are steep gradients of tension with rapid recovery. Thus, it is tension *cumulation* and *fluctuation,* produced by the infant's engagement of the world, that leads to the arousal associated with affective expression (see, for example, Cicchetti & Sroufe, 1976; Sroufe & Waters, 1976). As Sroufe and Waters (1976) state: "The function of the tension-release mechanism . . . goes beyond the modulation of prevailing levels of arousal. It serves . . . to help the infant maintain commerce with novel or provocative stimulus situations *and thereby promotes both cognitive and emotional growth* [pp. 183–184, emphasis added.]"

Sroufe's theory, however, remains a heavily cognitive one—in fact, tension is the "arousal" produced by *cognitive processes.* The amount of tension that is tolerable varies widely due to cognitive, social, situational, and individual factors. Except at very high levels, no amount of tension automatically leads to negative emotional reactions. In agreement with Arnold (1960), Mandler (1975), and others, it is the evaluation of the situation that determines the hedonic tone of the affective response. Strong arousal, such as that elicited by vigorous jiggling, may result in positive affect when produced by the caregiver but negative affect when elicited by a stranger (Sroufe, Waters, & Matas, 1974). Thus, a subjective relationship between the infant and the object world is implied. Tension, produced through the infant's engagement of the world, leads to affective experience. The elicitation of the particular emotions depends on the evaluation of circumstances surrounding the tension increase.

Thus, it is clear that cognitive and control-systems models must be integrated with motivational, feeling, and tension constructs to account adequately for the ontogenesis of the emotions. Sroufe's "organizational perspective" attempts such an integration. Sroufe's work is also unique among nonpsychoanalytic developmental theories in its interpersonal focus—that is, the nature of emotional development is intimately related to the infant's relations with persons.

Sroufe's (1977b, 1979; Cicchetti & Sroufe, 1976, 1978; Sroufe & Waters, 1976, 1977) view of the relation of affect and cognition in infancy is basically interactionist. He relates the ontogenesis of the emotional systems to parallel changes occurring in Piaget's sensorimotor stages of cognitive development. However, his account of the process of development is largely Wernerian.

Similar to Werner's (1948, 1957) organismic-developmental position, Sroufe states that there are general developmental tendencies toward greater specification, precision, coordination, hierarchization, and reorganization of behavioral systems. Following Spitz (1959) and his colleagues (Emde et al.,

1976), Sroufe states that there are three developmental reorganizations during the first 2 years of life. These reorganizations are qualitative changes in behavior marked by affective growth and followed by different transactions with the environment. As the infant's brain and neuromuscular systems develop and as it experiences the world, its physical responses to stimulation become more specific, more highly organized, and more effective. In other words, changes in object relations occurring developmentally are concomitant with marked changes in emotional expression and cognitive organization.

To Sroufe, cognitive development and affective development *interact*. The interaction occurs both for affect as it relates to the development of attachment and for the ontogenesis and differentiation of the specific emotions. Sroufe's theory views the affective and cognitive systems as mutually influencing and interlocking. For Sroufe (Sroufe & Waters, 1976) "... it is a distortion to discuss the cognitive underpinnings of affect without also noting the interdependence of cognitive activity with affect [p. 184]." Furthermore, *"Neither the cognitive nor the affective system can be considered dominant or more basic than the other ... It is as valid to say that cognition is in the service of affect as to say that affect reflects cognitive processes* [p. 187, emphasis added]."

Sroufe notes a series of changes in the sense in which the baby is receptive to stimuli. Its capacity to tolerate tension and to produce tension cognitively are also factors in the infant's receptivity. Sroufe's account of the interaction between socioemotional and cognitive development may be characterized as follows.

In the first month of life, an object will elicit visual following, but the infant is much less attentive than it will be in another month or two, when the tension tolerance also increases markedly. At that time, the infant can be said to "subject itself" to stimulation, with engagement becoming more continuous. The infant at this time has schemes for familiar objects, though they are not yet well-articulated. These schemes first appear between the fifth and twelfth weeks of life, the age at which the infant will smile in response to any smiling, immobile face.

As the infant develops during the first year, it will become able to produce cognitive tension more quickly and in response to events that are cognitively, but not physically, stimulating. Evidence for this is provided from studies on the ontogenesis of positive and negative affect in normal and Down's syndrome babies (Cicchetti & Mans, 1976; Cicchetti & Sroufe, 1976, 1978; Sroufe & Wunsch, 1972). As the infant progresses through the first year, it also becomes better able to produce schemes and process relationships between them more quickly, resulting in the ability to laugh at more cognitively sophisticated, less physically stimulating items. In an example of the interlocking nature of development, as schemes become better articulated the infant becomes able to distinguish familiar persons from strangers. In the fourth month of life, coordination of schemes advances as the baby becomes able to watch the act of touching and use the sense of touch to explore objects.

Intentionality first appears in about the fifth month of life, when the infant has gained mastery of the schemes for some actions (e.g., seeing and grasping). Once the schemes are initiated, the infant is motivated to exercise the complete action and will cry if it cannot. Of course, as memory and object permanence develop, the possible foci of the infant's intentionality broaden. Sroufe sees intentionality as an important component in defining the specific emotions. For instance, he thinks that true joy (as opposed to pleasure) is dependent on intentionality, as are true anger (an interpersonal affect to Sroufe), true fear (as opposed to wariness), and so on (see, for example, Bronson & Pankey, 1977; Cicchetti, Mans, & Breitenbuecher, 1977; Sroufe, 1977a).

The development of memory and object permanence are closely linked, as indeed are all the themes of development. Recall memory is obviously necessary for remembering that an object not currently in sight continues to exist. According to Sroufe, both are usually fairly well-developed by about the eighth month of life. Object permanence is necessary for the development of a stable attachment to a being other than the self. Another prerequisite for attachment is the differentiation of other persons and of the self. The newborn does not differentiate between sensations emanating from "in here" and "out there"; by the second or third month, when the infant is more awake and alert, its greater attentiveness to its surroundings helps the baby begin to differentiate the internal and external worlds. The beginning of imitation, in the fifth month, probably reflects a further sense of differentiation of self from others. The experience of specific emotions helps the infant's sense of self to differentiate further.

During the second year, the infant, by now well aware of the "out there" and of its own feelings, also becomes aware of the self as experiencing and the self as actor. Evidence for self-recognition, self-assertion, and feelings about the self emerge. Shame, affection (spontaneous love pats), and defiance emerge during the second year. They could not have emerged before this level of self-cognition and self-differentiation; they automatically emerge now.

Attachment also develops over the first 2 years of life. Of course, this is dependent on the development of object permanence, differentiation of self and others, development of receptivity to stimulation, and the development of coordination of schemes. Definite attachment first appears with the beginnings of object permanence in about the seventh month of life. As the infant becomes attached, it eventually becomes capable of affection and of using the caregiver as a secure base for exploration (Ainsworth et al., 1978). Thus, Sroufe believes that the relationship between the development of attachment and the development of cognition is one in which the two systems are mutually influencing and interdependent.

Sroufe divides the human emotions into three basic systems: pleasure/joy, wariness/fear, and rage/anger. He states that the first true emotions within each system emerges at about the same time, 3 to 4 months, when the infant becomes capable of reacting as a result of a *specific* event. Likewise, joy, fear, and anger emerge in the third quarter-year of life, when *the meaning of the event to the infant* (for example, fear of an adult who is not the caregiver) becomes central and the infant becomes a truly emotional being. Elation, anxiety, and angry mood emerge by the end of the first year. At about 18 months, shame, affection, and defiance emerge together; pride, love, and guilt appear at approximately three years. Each of these three sets of emotions requires a new higher level of self-awareness and self–other differentiation.

Sroufe comments on the relation of affect and cognition at a given point in time. He believes that cognition can cause *expressed* affects. For instance, an infant of 3 months can, upon observing an object several times, form a scheme of that object and on further presentations *effortfully* assimilate the object to that scheme. The effortful assimilation results in the production of tension, which then falls after assimilation is accomplished, finally resulting in a smile (see, for example, Shultz & Zigler, 1970). A similar process explains laughter that, with development, can result from an "arousal jag" (Berlyne, 1969) caused by *cognitively produced* tension. Sroufe also notes that, in later infancy, *context* cues play an important role in producing affect as discrete emotion at a given point in time (Sroufe et al., 1974). An infant in a state of disequilibrium in a secure context may resolve the disequilibrium by experiencing either distress/fear or pleasure. Context cues are cognitive; they are an infant's evaluation of safety and of what is likely to happen (see also Bischof, 1975).

Sroufe implies that he sees the relation of affect and cognition at a given point in time much as Piaget does. That is, if it is the infant's evaluation of security that causes it to be able to play or fearfully cling to its mother, then cognition—a cognitive evaluation ("appraisal," cf. Arnold, 1960)—has produced affect. Similarly, for the mind to focus on a particular event and cognitively evaluate it, the affect of interest must be present. There is another sense in which Sroufe seems to believe that cognition can directly produce affect; at about 9 months of age, novel stimulation (novelty being a cognitive judgment) arouses two strong motives, curiosity and mastery, as well as avoidance/wariness motives. This fact is related to Sroufe's comments on the *relation of affect and cognition to each other as forces in the press for development,* for depending on whether curiosity/mastery or avoidance/ wariness motives prove stronger, the infant will or will not engage its environment and thereby develop its cognitive structures. Therefore, according to Sroufe, affect-as-object relations (i.e., a secure attachment in which the infant can use the caregiver as a base for exploration) and affect-as-interest become important forces in the press for cognitive development.

Sroufe sees the infant's joy in mastery, an affect likely to yield cognitive development, as the psychological foundation for development (cf. Bühler's [1930] "function pleasure"). The infant's belief in its own effectance is likely to come first from caregiver-infant play, which according to Sroufe helps teach the infant to tolerate increasing amounts of tension without breaking contact *and without its behavior becoming disorganized.* Tension tolerance and sustained attention in the face of challenging complexity are foundations for important learning. The responsivity, mutuality, reciprocity, and cooperativeness of the caregiver are important, and also themselves feed into the creation of a secure attachment. The infant's smile, its expressed affect, is a signal of pleasure to the caregiver. This encourages the caregiver to repeat the event or provide new stimulation, which then becomes another force in the press for cognitive development. Object relations and interest are forces in the press for cognitive development in another sense, for the caregiver is likely to be the first object that is more than the sum of separate impressions (see Bell, 1970). In turn, the fact that the infant develops this capacity to respond to the caregiver as an integrated entity after repeatedly exercising its separate capacities to see, hear, and touch him or her, underscores the importance of cognition as a force in the development of object relations.

To his credit,, Sroufe (Sroufe & Waters, 1976) is one of the very few nonpsychoanalytic theorists who discusses the reciprocal influence that affect has on cognition: "In a reciprocal manner, cognitive changes promote exploration, social development, and the differentiation of affect; and affective-social growth leads cognitive development [p. 187]." Moreover, he has generated an impressive body of research to support many of his theoretical conceptualizations. However, Sroufe's position, although based on a synthesis of several existing perspectives (e.g., Piaget, Werner, Bridges, and psychoanalysis), contains several problems that need to be explicated more precisely in future work.

Because Sroufe postulates a *dynamic interactionist* model of socioemotional development, it is hard to discern *how* cognitive states become translated into affect and vice versa. Sroufe describes cognition and emotion as mutually reciprocal processes, but as currently stated it is hard to differentiate his position from other competing alternatives (e.g., epiphenomenal accounts).

Sroufe states that affective development may be viewed as proceeding through stages analogous to Piaget's stages of cognitive development. However, he himself admits that our present empirical evidence is still too weak to allow for a conceptual analysis of the organization or structures of emotions in terms of stages. Thus, Sroufe's proposal to conceive of emotional development as a sequence of stages should be considered as tentative at this point and awaits additional research.

Because Sroufe cannot yet account for the sequences and structural organizations of emotional development, he is unable to delineate the specific mechanisms underlying developmental change and reorganization. For example, Sroufe (1979) describes the role that the caregiver provides in the organization of the infant's development: "The sensitive caregiver provides the proper affective climate, helps the infant achieve and maintain an optimal level of tension, and actually helps it to organize the behavior to which she then contingently responds [p. 499]." However, Sroufe does not state precisely how the caretaker's actions could explain the possible universality of the sequences and organization of the emotions in the course of development. In this regard, Sroufe (Sroufe & Waters, 1976) recognizes the limitations of his perspective as currently articulated: "In a manner yet to be specified, both cognitive and social factors promote evolution from the pleasant physiological state reflected in the neonatal smile and the pleasure of early recognitory smiles, to the joy of mastery and engagement [p. 187]." Future research should be conducted to uncover what these underlying explanatory processes might be and how they might operate.

INFANT EMOTIONS IN THE CONTEXT OF THEIR BIOLOGICAL FOUNDATIONS

In many ways, it may seem strange to include Izard's differential emotions theory (1977, 1978) in a chapter focusing on the interrelationship between cognition and emotion in infant development. Izard has only begun to detail the applications of his theory to development in infancy. As such, he has not dealt with emotional development in its relationship with cognition in an explanatory fashion. Rather, much of Izard's work on the ontogenesis of emotion-cognition interrelationships is descriptive and awaits the results of future experimentation. However, Izard's differential emotions theory is one of the few current efforts to integrate the vast array of information on human emotions. Although the differential emotions theory is not primarily developmental, Izard (1978; Izard & Buechler, 1979) has recently proposed an interpretation of the ontogenesis of emotion in infancy.

Metatheoretical Assumptions

Several major ideas delimit and provide the superstructure for the particulars of Izard's theory. Among these is the concept that emotions are adaptive and purposive. Our facial expressions are not the vestigial remains of our primate communications system, but rather the essential mode of social expression and the crucial mediator for subjective emotional feeling. In the infant, emotions are seen as emerging as they become adaptive. These views are examples of the highly teleological bent of Izard's theory.

A second assumption is that emotions are discrete. Izard does not posit an undifferentiated state of arousal at any stage. Even in infancy, the discrete emotions of distress, interest, and enjoyment are thought to be present in rudimentary form. The discrete emotions are fundamental because their properties cannot be attributed to any smaller unit of emotional organization.

A third assumption is a corollary to the second. It states that the discrete emotions have the capacity to combine and create dyadic, triadic, and even more complex configurations of either harmonious or conflicting emotions. Izard does not state it explicitly, but the implication is that the emotions other than the fundamental ones are formed by this process.

A final assumption, and one that especially distinguishes Izard's theory, is his contention that "emotion" is not defined by a subjective feeling but may occur without its unique subjective experience. Most theorists, among them Freud and Arnold (1960), see emotion as first and foremost a felt experience. In fact, Freud saw stored informational bits of affectively charged experiences as the ideational counterpart of the emotion proper (see, for example, White & Pillemer, 1979). Within Izard's framework, it is possible to either feel an emotion and show no physical sign, or, to show signs but not subjectively experience the emotion.

Izard's Differential Emotions Theory

Izard defines an emotion as a neural pattern that is in the somatic nervous system, the system responsible for control over voluntary actions. The observable components of emotions are behavioral patterns—such as facial expression, postural change, and visceral-glandular responses—and the conscious experience of the emotion. The crux of Izard's theory is that feedback from bodily and facial expressions of an emotion is directed to the cortex, which registers the "felt" emotion. In other words, we make facial expressions for the fundamental emotion before actually feeling the emotion itself. Izard maintains that "emotions" have neurophysiological, subjective (phenomenological), and expressive components. However, he (Izard & Buechler, 1979) advocates that infant researchers focus on the expressive component of emotion for two reasons. First, Izard states that we will probably never be able to study the subjective component of infant emotional experience. Second, he notes that there are inherent difficulties in inferring emotional experience from physiological responses recorded in isolation. That is, unless these responses are studied in relation to other behavioral domains, it is seldom possible to conclude that they are reliable indicators of the presence or absence of an emotion.

Izard posits 10 fundamental discrete emotions: interest-excitement, enjoyment-joy, surprise-startle, distress-anguish, anger-rage, disgust-repulsion, contempt-scorn, fear-terror, shame/shyness-humiliation, and guilt-remorse. The hyphenated pairs indicate the continuum of intensity along which a given emotion may vary. Not only does a discrete emotion have many different strengths, but the emotions are also organized into a hierarchy, such that, depending on the stimulus intensity, attention might become surprise or surprise might become fear.

Emotion comprises the major motivation in human psychology and is always granted a functional role in all activities of the organism. However, the personality is conceived of as having six different subsystems, labeled the homeostatic, drive, emotion, perceptual, cognitive, and motor systems. The differentiation seems at first to be a semantic one because Izard repeatedly states that the six systems are in constant interaction. Their separability becomes of theoretical interest when Izard states that it is possible for each of these systems to act separately, and that although they can amplify, inhibit, and attenuate one another, it is possible to have a "pure emotion," completely independent of these subsystems. In Izard's system, the young infant is primarily an affective being because the primary systems in early infant development are the homeostatic, drive, and emotion subsystems.

The six subsystems of personality in combination bring about, according to Izard, four distinct kinds of motivation: drives, emotions, cognitive-affective interactions, and cognitive-affective structures. Drives result from purely physiological needs; emotions and drives are what Izard calls "affect." Cognitive-affective interactions are "one-shot" relationships formed between a cognitive awareness and an emotional reaction to events in which the cognition and affects serve to intensify, block, mitigate, or otherwise transform one another. Although Izard is somewhat vague in this definition, it might be best to think of these interactions as our basic mode of interpreting events both within and around us. Cognitive-affective structures are organizations of specific cognitive and affective interactions that are fairly stable across time, due to repetition. We may think of them as trait-like in nature.

Because all of the six systems have motivational properties, the emotion system is viewed as the primary motivational system throughout the life span. The emotions are the principal organizing factors in consciousness. Indeed, Izard states that they provide the motivation for the integration of the other personality subsystems over the life span.

According to Izard, the neural mechanisms for emotional expression and emotional experience are innate. The facial expression serves a two-fold function. First, it provides sensory data to the brain, which in turn activates hormonal and other systems and produces an emotional experience. Second, it provides social signals that are important to the caregiver (see also in this regard the work of Brazelton et al., 1974; Cicchetti & Sroufe, 1978; Emde, Katz, & Thorpe, 1978; Stern, 1977, which illustrates how deviations and asynchronies in affect-signaling systems can have a deleterious effect upon caregiver-infant interaction). In Izard's system, the ontogenesis of a particular fundamental emotion is primarily a function of maturational processes and secondarily a function of learning and experience.

Izard states that although the ontogenesis of emotion consists mainly of processes that are a function of age-related biological changes and to a lesser extent of developmental processes influenced by experience, *affective-cognitive structures* develop primarily as a function of ecological variables and learning and secondarily as a function of age-related biological processes. Affective-cognitive structures result from the infant's pairing certain affects with certain cognitions. Izard does not believe that these form until the second half-year of life because they depend on the ability to store and retrieve information. (At that age, it seems that these structures are exactly comparable to what Sroufe [Cicchetti & Sroufe, 1978; Sroufe, 1979] calls "affectively-toned schemes," which he believes emerge at about 9 months.) Affective-cognitive structures are, to Izard, the predominant motivational features in consciousness after language and symbolization appear. Prior to the emergence of language and symbol systems, Izard notes the significance of three processes:

1. *Sensory-affective processes,* which have their highest significance during the first 2 postnatal months. During this period, changes in stimulation or information processing and the differential selective and organizing functions of receptors produce different affects.

2. *Affective-perceptual processes,* which are most salient between the second and ninth months of life. During this time, different objects are said to elicit different affects that differentially focus interest and attention. Attachment begins during this period.

3. *Affective-cognitive processes,* which begin about the ninth month. The prerequisites for the emergence of these latter structures are the ability to form and store memories, the increased differentiation of self and other, and the sharpening of self-awareness and the self-concept.

As the different emotions emerge, these three kinds of processes become integrated and interrelated.

As noted, Izard believes that each discrete emotion emerges as it becomes adaptive in the life of the infant. Each emotion, as a unique quality of consciousness, tends to instigate a broad class of responses that are generally adaptive in relation to the eliciting event. Each emotion adds to the complexity of consciousness, increasing the capacity for processing and responding to different types of information. Izard believes that the relation of affect and cognition as forces in the press for development is such that each specific emotion appears, mostly as a result of biological maturation, at a time when it becomes adaptive in the life of the infant. He maintains that the infant is born with the ability to experience and to express the emotions of distress, interest, and enjoyment in rudimentary form and to react differentially—both affectively and perceptually—to changes in stimulus and information input. As each emotion emerges, it establishes the beginning of a critical period for certain types of experience and for the learning of specific types of responses that are important to the salient developmental issues at that particular stage. However, Izard does not say what it is that causes each emotion to emerge, nor does he state how a primarily biological unfolding could be reacting to so subtle a stimulus as (within broad limits) the infant's relation with its caregiver.[2]

For example, it seeems as if an infant from an abusive family might best adapt to the immediate environment by not expressing certain affects. However, according to Izard, this would have an adverse impact on cognitive development, not from damage due to lack of stimulation or to energy being bound up in dealing with survival rather than learning, but rather in a more direct way as the critical experiences do not occur. It is difficult to see how the emergence of a facial expression (to those who do not agree with Izard that neural feedback from the face causes phenomenological emotions) could affect anything other than the infant's relation to its caregivers.

It seems somewhat inconsistent for Izard to state that sensory-affective processes, which are predominant in the first 2 months of life, produce different affects via the differential organizing functions of receptors when most of the specific affects do not emerge until later. Also, his belief that the rudiments of distress, interest, and pleasure are all present at birth seems to place Izard closer to Sroufe—in his belief that various affect systems evolve in parallel—than Izard realizes.

According to Izard, there are two main kinds of affective development: affect as emotions and affect as experiences. The first is the above mentioned way in which the basic discrete emotions emerge separately over the first 2 years of life, with each emotion continuing in consciousness after its first emergence. The second is that each emotion becomes more organized and centered after it emerges. Izard believes that these developmental changes in emotional experiences do not reflect a change in the quality of the phenomenon in consciousness. Rather, he asserts that a more organized, specific emotional experience allows for concomitant cognitive processes that increase the infant's ability to act appropriately to cope with the situation.

---

[2]In a more recent paper (Izard & Buechler, 1979), he suggests that more research is needed on the relative influence of maturational versus environmental variables in directing the ontogenesis of expressions.

Izard believes that the phenomenological component of emotions may become less diffuse and have different effects partly as a result of the maturation of the underlying neural substrates of the emotion and the corresponding developmental changes in other systems, especially self-recognition. This belief that the experience of a given emotion becomes less diffuse with age seems to be similar to Werner's and Sroufe's belief that development yields to organization, specification, and hierarchic integration. Izard and Buechler (1979) state that a given emotion should be studied for the way it emerges, peaks, and declines to each given salient stimulus situation, so that one is not justified in saying, for instance, that fear emerges at a particular age on the basis of responses to a single stimulus situation. Again, this is fairly consistent with Sroufe's (1979) developmental viewpoint.

According to Izard, the increased differentiation of self and other, the sharpening of self-awareness and the self-concept, and the ability to store memories are what enable the infant to begin the development of affective-cognitive structures—the linking of affect with images and symbols, including words and ideas. Izard states that emotions play a part in the development of self-recognition and the self-concept, and self-related cognition in turn influences emotional responses and emotion-behavior sequences. He states that there are important relationships between self-recognition and the self-concept and contempt, fear, shame, and guilt. Izard believes that shame/shyness emerges very early, occurring after the infant has the capacity to discriminate self from other and familiar person from strange person. He believes that the heightened consciousness of self that occurs with shame has motivational value for developing self-identity and self-esteem, and that eventually the anticipation of shame will motivate the development of competences that increase self-worth and decrease the likelihood of experiencing shame.

Although shame/shyness and anger/disgust play a special role in the differentiation of self and others in the first half-year of life, in the second half-year new emotions emerge to play a role in facilitating the development of self-cognition and self-control. Izard states that there are no self-perceptions or self-cognitions until some time after the infant has begun differentiating itself from others, except for sensations that compose a "bodily sense of me." Izard contends that virtually all of the emotions play some role in the self-related perceptions and cognitions that lead to self-concept or to self-identity and self-control. In particular, fear, emerging during the second half-year of life, is the experience of self endangered and generates cognitions about the self in this mode. Guilt, which according to Izard emerges in the second year of life, plays an important role in the development of self-responsibility. Izard does not state why he thinks so, but he claims that around 8 to 9 months of age—and increasing rapidly in the second year—a sharper demarcation of the boundaries of the self emerges. Clearly, empirical research is sorely needed to further clarify these assertions.

Izard and Sroufe disagree on the ways in which emerging emotions contribute to the development of the self. Sroufe (1977b, 1979) puts more emphasis than does Izard upon the role of the caregiver in producing differentiation of self and others, as well as emphasizing the role of differentiation in producing attachment. Sroufe agrees that emotions such as shame promote self-awareness and, in some way, *are* self-awareness. He also stresses the importance of the infant's use of motor and representational skills in promoting the discovery of the self. Sroufe implies that *any* affect, *any* strong feeling, will help the infant differentiate itself and come to know itself as an affective being. This belief that the cognitive evaluation is in some way a part of the phenomenal emotion leads him to differ from Izard on the role of affects in promoting self–other differentiation, as does his different conception of the cognitive prerequisites and consequences of individual emotions. Sroufe does not believe that affect generates cognition in the very young infant. Rather, he believes that in very early infancy affects terminate interaction with the surroundings. By the beginning of the fourth quarter, when the infant has become a truly emotional being, Sroufe states that affect comes as a result of an anticipated event. The infant at this age has an awareness of the affect itself, and affects now forecast further behavior. Early in the second year of life, affect provides a frame for behavior. That is, the infant now has *moods,* such as elation, sadness, and petulance, and its prevailing affective state provides a context for behavior. Izard attributes much more cognitive sophistication to the infant than does Sroufe (e.g., he has several of the emotions emerging much earlier). Moreover, Izard attributes much more separateness to the affective and cognitive systems than does Sroufe.

Izard makes several comments on the relation of affect and cognition at a given point in time. He believes that affect is caused by the brain's reception of sensory feedback from the face. However, due to our imprecise knowledge of neurophysiology, he does not explain the exact mechanisms by which the facial expression arrives on the face in the first place. Izard states that context has effects on both perception (what is actually perceived) and the cognitive-interpretive process (the imagery and symbolization associated with the emotion in consciousness). These effects, in turn, trigger neural activity that activates a specific emotion or pattern of emotions.

As just implied, Izard believes that drives and emotions interact with the perceptual and cognitive processes, with the affect determining the selectivity and direction of these processes. He states that the emotions facilitate infant-environment transactions and positive affective interchange.

In summary, Izard's differential emotions theory is one of the few truly integrative theories of the emotions in the field of psychology. The accomplishment of this difficult and much needed task is commendable. However, some underlying theoretical assumptions need to be addressed more explicitly in future research. For example, Izard has little to say about the relation between the development of affect and the development of cognition because his theory deals very little with cognitive development per se. Izard fails to define cognition and sufficiently explore its relation to emotion, hence leaving us with an unclear picture of what interaction between these two systems really entails. The absence of a definition would not present many problems if the interaction of separated systems were not the underlying principle of Izard's theory. Izard states that emotion can operate "relatively independent" of any cognitive process. However, the question we must ask is how it is that emotion acts independently of cognition. For an answer, it is perhaps most fruitful to examine Izard's process model. The events that trigger the emotion process are one of two kinds: internal events such as memory, imaging, anticipatory thinking, proprioceptive and endocrine activity, and external events that are channeled into the organism via perception. Cognition clearly plays a part in all these causes of emotion. Motor and hormonal activity do not spontaneously generate emotion even in Izard's model, bur rather serve to amplify and sustain it. This effect is largely a product of cognitive processing of the meaning of activities. Perception of outside stimuli do not bring about emotional experience until meaning is attached to them.

Cognition also plays a role in various other processes. Memory traces of the "feeling" and a facial pattern can preempt the actual visible patterning and cause the subjective emotion directly. In one of the last steps of Izard's process model, the cortex integrates feedback from the sensory cortex as well as information from the other systems. Although Izard does not say this information is necessarily processed, its presubjective nature makes it hard to discern whether it is or not. Finally, it is possible to store the integrated message as a unit in the memory, which is a cognitive operation. All of these processes support the idea that cognition plays an essential role in the feeling and facial patterning of emotion.

Many of the problems with elucidating the role of cognition also hold true for the role of memory. Izard's theory never explicitly links cognition with memory or emotion with memory except in a linear cause-and-effect fashion. Thus, it is difficult to determine whether Izard sees memory as a conscious awareness of past experiences or rather as a *mechanism* by which events and emotional meanings are stored.

The divorce of memory from the discussion of emotional properties is characteristic of the treatment of memory throughout. This is partly due to the learning-theorist slant of Izard's "affective-cognitive structures," which largely subsume the role of memory. The trait-like structures are formed by repetition of specific affective-cognitive interactions. The emphasis on repetition subordinates the role of memory both by neglecting to assign differential weight to certain experiences and by neglecting to specify what factors participate in choosing which affects and which cognitions form affective-cognitive interactions.

Relevant questions about the role of memory can be asked if we integrate memory into the existing structures posited by Izard. For instance, can an affective-cognitive interaction be a "past–present" interaction, and is it possible for one to override the other? What is the relative power of present and past factors in determining a mood or ongoing affective state? How is an emotion retrieved from the memory store? Are emotions stored as fundamental emotions, undifferentiated affect, cognitive-ideational counterparts of subjective feeling, neural patterns of facial expressions, or possibly some combination of these? These kinds of questions should be addressed in future research.

As is also true of the other developmental theorists discussed in this chapter, Izard should elucidate the *processes* whereby complex emotions emerge and develop from simpler ones. Izard sees each emotion as an *addition* to the capacities of an already emotional infant. Unlike the majority of the developmental theories, emotions do not differentiate from undifferentiated emotional prototypes but are relatively complex when they first appear. This is inevitable if Izard believes that complex emotions such as guilt and contempt are present in the repertoire of the young infant. Emotions emerge when they serve a specific adaptive function, rather than serving the general function of increasing the overall flexibility and adaptiveness of the organism. The addition of guilt, for instance, takes place when awareness of the social community and a regard for ethical norms is "adaptive" for the child. A crucial difference between structural-developmental theories (e.g., Sroufe, Werner) and differential emotions theory is that the latter conceives of phenotypic behaviors as having stable meanings across time. Facial expressions always have the same meaning but are limited in infancy by the undeveloped cortex, which is unable to fully process subjective emotions. However, the contention that emotions such as guilt, shame, and fear have the adaptive value of promoting self-cognition and self-recognition can severely limit our view of the uses for these behaviors. It assumes that what we observe—namely, self-cognition and self-recognition—are necessarily purposive goals of certain emotions, rather than one of many goals, or possibly even by-products. Moreover, the theory places too much emphasis on innate neural programming and too little on the adaptive value of having flexibility of cortical functioning.

Although we have pointed to a number of issues that we feel merit attention, this does not gainsay the usefulness of Izard's theoretical perspective. In fact, as Izard's theory is perhaps the most well-articulated account of the ontogenesis of the emotions, the strengths as well as the problematic areas are more visible. The clarity of Izard's theory, although lending itself to criticism on one hand, serves to generate future research questions on the other, and this facilitates the momentum of scientific advancement.

SOME COMMON FEATURES AND PROBLEMS
OF THE THEORIES OF COGNITIVE
AND EMOTIONAL DEVELOPMENT

Despite the theoretical heterogeneity that characterizes existing viewpoints on emotional development in infancy, there are underlying similarities common to the majority of these perspectives. For example, most theories assume a fairly diffuse or global stage at the beginning of the infant's development. Depending on the theoretical framework on which this initial stage is conceptualized, it is conceived of as excitement, tension and tension reduction, arousal, instinct, or general lack of differentiation. Along with the assumption of an initial state of emotional diffuseness, all theorists postulate an increasing degree of complexity or differentiation and integration of emotions in the course of ontogenesis.

Two major conceptualizations of these developmental trends have been advanced. On the one hand, the later emerging, more complex emotions are hypothesized to occur as a result of the more sophisticated cognitive structures that accompany energetic or feeling states of different intensities. On the other hand, these later unfolding emotions are thought to occur as a result of increasing differentiations of the energetic (i.e. emotional) system itself. Adherents of this latter viewpoint normally implicitly recognize the simultaneous development of increasing degrees of complexity in both the cognitive and the affective domains. However, none of the theorists has dealt explicitly with the question of the organization or structuralization of the emotions. That is, if there are separate stages or phases of emotional development, what is the manner in which these are to be conceived?

In this context, the different possible descriptions of the sequential organization of emotional development suggest differing conceptualizations of the way in which emotional structures might be conceived. An addition sequence implies emotional differentiation by summation—that is, emotions are accumulated over time and coexist without necessarily entertaining relationships among themselves. Conversely, a substitution sequence suggests that earlier emotions disappear as later, more complex ones take their place. This process again occurs with no interchange implied among the earlier and later emotions. Thus, addition and substitution sequences do not reveal anything with respect to the structure or organization of emotional development because they do not specify the relationships different emotions entertain. This is in contrast with the sequences of mediation, modification, and inclusion where a connection between earlier- and later-developed emotions is necessary. That is, a later, more complex emotion is the result of some process of transformation between earlier, less differentiated emotions. The process of mediation suggests an interaction between earlier emotions from which a new emotion is derived. Modification is the process by which an earlier emotion is transformed into a later one. The inclusion model implies organizational patterns of earlier and later emotions that are hierarchical in structure. Thus, insofar as the latter three types of sequences account for the relationships emotions entertain in the course of development, they deal with their organization or structure. What remains to be done in future empirical and conceptual investigations is a closer analysis of the processes involved in inclusion, modification, and mediation sequences. Unless we know *how* earlier-developed emotions become transformed (modification), *how* they interact to develop into later emerging ones (mediation), or *how* they coexist in a hierarchical organization (inclusion), we cannot decide whether there are structures of emotional development or how exactly they might be conceived.

In their various efforts to account for contemporaneous developments in both the affective and cognitive domains, all of the theorists adopt a position (implied or stated explicitly) on the nature of the relationship between emotion and cognition. However, the exact process by which cognition effects a change in emotion or vice versa is not clarified, nor is the process that effects changes *within* each of the two domains. If an interactional or epiphenomenal view is posited, it remains unclear exactly how a change in one domain effects a change in the other. Similarly, the parallelists fail to describe the process of transformation within each domain itself. Indeed, such an analysis is needed to demonstrate that cognition and emotion can be conceived of as independent and therefore parallel. This obscurity is in part a result of the fact that causality is always inferred rather than directly observed. In analyzing the empirical evidence, a theoretical position must eventually be adopted even though it can be "proven" only on the basis of temporal sequences of development. In any event, the different changes within each domain need to be closely monitored in order to enable us to formulate their necessary and sufficient conditions in greater detail on a conceptual or theoretical level.

In summary, there are a variety of problems that require explication regarding the tasks that developmental theorists of the emotions confront. Thus far, theoreticians have not classified the emotions throughout development with sufficient detail. Furthermore, the nature of the developmental sequence and organization must be described explicitly, and an explanation for why emotional changes occur at all is needed. Lastly, the problem of how cognition and emotion are related must be explored.

IMPLICATIONS FOR FUTURE RESEARCH

Among the most fundamental questions raised in this chapter is whether or not emotion should be viewed as a separate developmental domain. How this question is answered will affect the way the relationship between emotion and cognition is viewed in subsequent empirical and theoretical conceptualizations. Although the criteria that characterize a domain as unique have yet to be delineated, there are specific areas of investigation that will help to answer this question. Findings about the nature and course of emotional development—about its stages, sequences, and the processes by which a new emotion becomes integrated with other emotions and other developmental systems—will bear directly on this issue. Individual differences and variations in emotional expression will be factors that must be accounted for. This is of particular concern, for example, when diagnosing the presence or absence of an emotion in a given context. Here, differences in arousal thresholds, temperament, speed of information-processing capacity, and so on, will all influence the behavioral expression of the emotion. Careful naturalistic and experimental observations that catalogue and classify the emotions as they emerge must be undertaken in a variety of contexts. Furthermore, analyses must be sensitive to the differentiations that develop with special attention paid to the process of these transformations.

Baldwin (1891), Bridges (1930), Izard (1977, 1978), and Sroufe (1979) have provided us with four *classificatory schemes* that, though lacking in precision, can be fruitful in guiding research. In order to cast more light on the question of the definition and classification of the emotions, we have developed a diary of children's language of the emotions, and several linguistic and nonlinguistic classification tasks. We think that an ontogenetic reconstruction of "common-sense" definitions and classifications of the emotions will be helpful in overcoming the confusions and conflicts that have been caused by the traditional armchair definitions and taxonomies.

In the emotional language diary, we ask parents to describe the antecedents and consequences of their own and their children's use of emotion-words. Thus, we want to answer the following two questions: 1) which behavioral and other clues do children use when they learn to talk about their so-called "internal states"; and, 2) how do parents teach them these words? By answering these questions, children's implicit definitions of the emotions will emerge and we will be able to study them through the course of their development.

In addition, experimentally based information will be obtained by asking children to identify emotions as displayed by people in pictures under two conditions: 1) when given the emotional label by the experimenter, they are asked to point at the right picture out of an array of pictures presented to them; and, 2) when given the picture displaying different emotions, they are asked to label the emotions themselves. Furthermore, as soon as the children are more linguistically competent, we will ask them what their definitions of the emotions are.

With regard to the classification of the emotions, we have developed tasks in which we ask children to sort pictures that portray emotions. We expect that children use different sorting categories depending on their level of development. We are also working on categorization tasks similar to the ones used by Rosch and her colleagues with respect to natural objects and perceptual categories (e.g. Rosch & Mervis, 1975). We expect that children—in the course of their ontogenesis—learn to conceive of emotions in terms of different levels of abstraction (e.g. laughter, joy, happiness; crying, sadness, depression; and so on). We suggest that these levels of abstraction be considered "natural taxonomies" of the emotions.

Regarding the specification of the infant's *emotional maturity at birth,* Izard (1977) has given the most detailed account of the infant's emotional sophistication. He has managed to distinguish more than just states of tension and tension reduction in newborns. Thus, Izard's theory suggests that more emotions are innate than has been suspected and that the young infant may be more emotionally complex than previous accounts have led us to believe.

In order to increase our knowledge about the emotions present at birth and/or developing throughout infancy, we have developed a diary for parents in which they describe the situations where their infants display emotions. By asking the parents to describe the situational context, the infant's and their own behaviors, and the emotion they infer from their infant's behavior, we want to ascertain whether only the situations that tend to elicit emotions change or whether the emotions displayed in different situations change as well.

To supplement the information provided by parents, we film the infants in various naturalistic and laboratory contexts. Babies are observed during feedings and during free-play and structured situations (alone, with their caregivers, and with peers). The emotions characteristically displayed in each of these different situations are coded and related to a variety of other cognitive measures we have collected on the same infants (e.g., Bayley and Uzgiris-Hunt scales). The results of these investigations will provide us with invaluable information about which emotions are innate and which undergo development, and about the situations that elicit these emotions at different phases of development.

Regarding the *processes* by which emotions are integrated into the behavioral repertoire of the infant, Bridges (1930) asnd Sroufe (1979) provide tentative proposals for an Inclusion sequence of emotional development, which seem to confirm the psychoanalystic position that affective states have their own structure. Izard (1978) also provides suggestions about the sequencing of emotional development. His position implies a Mediation sequence in that he appears to believe that several earlier-emerging emotional states must be linked in certain ways for a new emotional state to emerge. We have found evidence for an Inclusion sequence when analyzing for their emotional content the behavioral observations of Piaget's children as presented in his trilogy on infant development—*The Origins of Intelligence in Children* (1936), *The Construction of Reality in the Child* (1937), and *Play, Dreams and Imitation in Childhood* (1945) (Cicchetti & Pogge-Hesse, in press-a). The results of our diary on the development of emotional expressions, and the corresponding naturalistic and experimental situations discussed earlier, will yield a more comprehensive account of the type of sequence characteristic of infant and child emotional development.

Another fundamental question that we addressed in this chapter is the issue of *explaining* emotional and cognitive development. What are the motivating factors that account for the need for such transformations? Environmental input and contextual variables must always be accounted for, but internal states may be causal factors as well. Piaget's (1936) discussion of states of need as motivating factors for development is useful in that it provides us with a preliminary framework for accounts on transitions in emotional and cognitive development.

Experiments in which we observe both the types of emotions children display in various cognitive tasks and the degree of their emotional reaction in its relation to their problem-solving activity will generate hypotheses about the role of emotions in motivating cognitive development. We are looking in particular at the phases of transition between Piaget's stages, because they should yield more emotional reactions if Piaget is right in his conception of emotions as symptoms of cognitive disequilibria. In addition, we are developing cognitive conflict tasks on the basis of Inhelder, Sinclair and Bovet's work (1974). These tasks should be more likely to produce emotions and should provide us with a better understanding of the types and degrees of emotions manifested in situations of cognitive conflict. An inspection of the emotions will enable us to learn which of these facilitate and/or decrease problem-solving activity.

The *relationship between cognition and emotion* is crucial in understanding development in general. Furthermore, the way this relationship is viewed will directly influence how emotional development itself is conceptualized. We believe that emotion and cognition should be studied *concurrently* with special attention paid to their interdependence in encouraging growth. For example, the distinction between self and other is a necessary prerequisite for the infant's capacity to invest emotionally in the outside world (Lewis & Brooks, 1978). On the other hand, the infant learns much about itself and the world as it interprets its emotional states. How each system does or does not affect changes in the other is the underlying question.

In terms of the theories presented herein, Sroufe (1979) and Schmale (1964) have attempted to relate emotional development in infancy to Piaget's sensorimotor stages, Sroufe claiming interaction as characteristic of the relationship between cognition and emotion. Piaget himself has provided us with at least two different ways of conceptualizing this relationship (parallelism and epiphenomenalism). Future research will show which of the three positions with respect to the relation between cognition and affect proves to be the most meaningful.

Studies of atypical and handicapped infants may be helpful in discriminating among the possible ways that affect and cognition relate to each other. For example, in the rapidly developing normal infant, the simultaneous emergence of various behaviors or behavioral systems may be viewed as coincidental or as epiphenomena of chronological age. In the case of the atypical infant, the pace of development is generally slowed down. If it can be demonstrated, despite heterogeneity in etiology and rate of development, that affective stages correspond exactly to the development of cognitive stages, then true convergences and discontinuities in development may be specified.

We are conducting studies with three types of atypical or "at-risk" infants: 1) infants with Down's syndrome (Cicchetti & Pogge-Hesse, in press b; Cicchetti & Sroufe, 1976, 1978); 2) infants who have been maltreated by their caregivers (Cicchetti & Aber, in press; Cicchetti, Taraldson, & Egeland, 1978); and 3) infants who are the offspring of affectively ill parents (Cicchetti & Rizley, 1980). We are attempting to learn about the *process* of development in these groups of infants and are focusing on their intersystemic organization. If we uncover commonalities in the developmental processes of these diverse groups of infants, we will be able to show that certain processes are common to all atypical infants, regardless of differences in etiology or risk factors. Likewise, differences that are obtained among these groups will elucidate our understanding of how these divergent outcomes arose.

We believe that the psychology of atypical developmental processes can make many other significant contributions to our theory of how emotional and cognitive development relate in the normal course of development. We may be able to find convergent developments with other domains as well (e.g. language, perception, neurophysiology). By observing how lags in one domain either affect or do not affect development in other domains, we will be able to make inferences as to the nature of their respective relationships.

Researchers must move from the microscopic level of analysis to a more integrative level and attempt to formulate a comprehensive theory of the relation between emotional and cognitive development. Though we believe that no such comprehensive theory exists as yet, the theories that have been formulated are complementary in various respects that may be fruitful in guiding research.

Izard's (1978) and Sroufe's (1979) theories are important because of their focus on the development of systems. Although they differ on whether the systems are reflective of the same underlying process (Cicchetti & Sroufe,

1978; Sroufe, 1979) or independent separate processes (Izard, 1978), they provide a crucial first attempt at integrating not only cognitive and emotional development, but also the development of the other systems of the human mind. Our current research on the relationship between emotional, language, and cognitive development aims to provide an in-depth integration of the different systems of development and the respective roles they play in the developmental process.

Sroufe's position may be considered the most advanced, because it is an integration of many of the existing perspectives. First, he relates emotional systems emerging during infancy to Piaget's cognitive stages. Second, he generates a rich classification scheme. Third, he incorporates and extends Spitz's (1965) theory and hence most of the psychoanalytic theories, by developing eight stages—instead of Spitz's three (re)organizers—of emotional development in the course of the first 2 years. Finally, he integrates Werner's orthogenetic principle as a potential explanatory principle within his own framework. What remains to be accomplished is a more careful integration of these three theoretical traditions—Piaget, Werner, and psychoanalysis—in particular combining their different theoretical terminologies within one framework.

Concerning the *teleological aspects of development,* Piaget has been the most explicit about later stages of emotional ontogenesis, postulating social emotions and emotions with respect to ideal states as characteristic of later development. Although these more complex stages are beyond the scope of this chapter, Piaget has provided us with some excellent ideas about what the endstate of the child's emotional development might look like. These should guide researchers in future investigations of the child's later-developing emotions.

Sroufe and his colleagues have initiated programmatic research looking at the relationship between early socio-emotional competence and later adaptation (see Sroufe, 1979). Within this organizational framework, continuity refers to the prediction that competence in dealing with one developmental issue (e.g., the formation of a secure attachment relationship) will be related to competence with respect to subsequent ones (e.g., successful integration into and mastery of the peer world). The salient methodological issues are to utilize broad-band, age-appropriate measures of competence and to select age-appropriate situations, each of which elicit a variety of behavioral patterns that are more or less adaptive for that developmental period. From the organizational framework, continuity in the organization of attachment behavior and even relationships to later individual differences in adaptation have been clearly demonstrated (Arend, Gove, & Sroufe, 1979; Matas, Arend, & Sroufe, 1978; Waters, 1978; Waters, Wippman, & Sroufe, 1979). Other investigators must follow the lead of Sroufe and carry out longitudinal studies that examine the relation between emotion and cognition throughout the life span.

Finally, affect may also prove to be a better *prognostic index for later adaptation* than cognitive measures. For example, in their longitudinal work with Down's syndrome infants, Cicchetti and Sroufe (1978) found that cognitive development in the second year was predicted by laughter and other indices of affective expression in the first year of life. We feel that early laughter to the complex events studied in the Cicchetti and Sroufe research was such an excellent predictor because it tapped the motivational, attentional, affective, and cognitive capabilities—in short, the competence— of the infant. Though various indices of affect (e.g., crying, laughter, smiling, and so on) are closely interrelated and are closely tied with measures of cognitive development that suggesting one system as causal seems inappropriate, we underscore the predictive power of affect because of the difficulty of obtaining accurate, meaningful cognitive assessments early in life (see also Haviland, 1976, in this regard).

Knight, Roff, Barrnett, and Moss (1979) have shown that ratings of affectivity and interpersonal competence were better predictors of later outcome in schizophrenics than ratings of thought disorder—the core cognitive symptom of dysfunction in schizophrenia. At the very least, we believe researchers in psychopathology should pay increased attention to the emotional domain as well.

It is clear that the widespread influence that the emotions have on other developmental domains cannot be ignored. Indeed, we believe that continued research and theorizing about the relation between emotional development and other ontogenetic domains will prove to be a rich source of knowledge about the mechanisms of the human mind.

ACKNOWLEDGMENTS

The authors would like to extend their gracious appreciation to Andrea Celenza, whose critical thinking and emotional support during this project was invaluable, and to Michael Pakaluk, whose thoughtful suggestions led us to examine the theories at a deeper level. We have also profited greatly from our discussions with Linda Mans, Hazel Rovno, and Aviva Wasserman. We offer our sincerest thanks to Dr. Michael Lamb, both for the feedback he has provided on two earlier drafts of this chapter and for the understanding and patience that he displayed throughout our work on this manuscript.

REFERENCES

Ainsworth, M. D. S. Object relations, dependency and attachment: A theoretical review of the infant-mother relationship. *Child Development,* 1969, *40,* 969–1025.

Ainsworth, M. D. S. The development of infant-mother attachment. In B. Caldwell & H. Ricciuti (Eds.), *Review of child development research* (Vol. 3). Chicago: University of Chicago Press, 1973.

Ainsworth, M. D. S., Blehar, M., Waters, E., & Wall, S. *Patterns of attachment.* Hillsdale, N.J.: Lawrence Erlbaum Associates, 1978.

Arend, R., Gove, F., & Sroufe, L. A. Continuity of individual adaptation from infancy to kindergarten: A predictive study of ego-resiliency and curiosity in preschoolers. *Child Development,* 1979, *50,* 950–959.

Arnold, M. *Emotion and personality* (2 Vols.). New York: Columbia University Press, 1960.

Bain, A. *Mental science.* New York: Appleton, 1868.

Baldwin, J. M. *Senses and intellect.* New York: Holt, 1890.

Baldwin, J. M. *Feeling and will.* New York: Holt, 1891.

Baldwin, J. M. *Mental development in the child and the race.* London: Macmillan, 1894.

Balint, A. Love for the mother and mother-love. *International Journal of Psycho-Analysis,* 1949, *30,* 251–259.

Balint, M. Early developmental states of the ego. Primary object love. *International Journal of Psycho-Analysis,* 1949, *30,* 265–273.

Beck, A. T. *Depression: Causes and treatment.* Philadelphia: University of Pennsylvania Press, 1967.

Bell, S. The development of the concept of object as related to infant-mother attachment. *Child Development,* 1970, *41,* 291–311.

Benjamin, J. Developmental biology and psychoanalysis. In N. Greenfield & W. Lewis (Eds.), *Psychoanalysis and current biological thought.* Madison: University of Wisconsin Press, 1965.

Berlyne, D. *Conflict, arousal, and curiosity.* New York: McGraw-Hill, 1960.

Berlyne, D. E. Laughter, humor, and play. In G. Lindzey & E. Aronson (Eds.), *Handbook of social psychology* (Vol. 3). Boston: Addison-Wesley, 1969.

Berlyne, D. E. Struktur und motivation. In G. Steiner (Ed.), *Die Psychologie des 20. Jahrhunderts* (Vol. 7). Piaget und die Folgen, Kindler Verlag AG, Zurich, 1978.

Bischof, N. A systems approach towards the functional connections of fear and attachment. *Child Development,* 1975, *46,* 801–817.

Black, P. (Ed.) *Physiological correlates of emotion.* New York: Academic Press, 1975.

Blau, A. A unitary hypothesis of emotion: I. Anxiety, emotions of displeasure, and affective disorders. *Psychoanalytic Quarterly,* 1955, *24,* 75–103.

Blurton-Jones, N. G. Criteria for use in describing facial expressions of children. *Human Biology,* 1971, *43,* 365–413.

Boring, E. G., Langfeld, H. S., Weld, H. P. et al. *Psychology, A factual textbook.* New York: Wiley, 1935.

Bowlby, J. The nature of the child's tie to his mother. *International Journal of Psycho-Analysis,* 1958, *39,* 350–373.

Bowlby, J. *Attachment and loss* (Vol. 1). New York: Basic Books, 1969.

Brady, J. V. Towards a behavioral biology of emotion. In L. Levi (Ed.) *Emotions: Their parameters and measurement.* New York: Raven Press, 1975.

Brainerd, C. The state question in cognitive-developmental theory. *The Behavioral and Brain Sciences,* 1978, *1,* 173–182.

Brazelton, T. B., Koslowski, B., & Main, M. The origins of reciprocity: The early mother-infant interaction. In M. Lewis & L. Rosenblum (Eds.), *The effect of the infant on its caregiver.* New York: Wiley, 1974.

Brenner, C. On the nature and development of affects: A unified theory. *Psychoanalytic Quarterly,* 1974, *43,* 532–556.

Brentano, F. *Psychologie vom empirischen Standpunkt.* Leipzig: Felix Meiner, 1924.

Bridges, K. M. A genetic theory of the emotions. *Journal of Genetic Psychology,* 1930, *37,* 514–527.

Bridges, K. M. Emotional development in early infancy. *Child Development,* 1932, *3,* 324–341.

Bridges, K. M. A study of social development in early infancy. *Child Development,* 1933, *4,* 36–49.

Bridges, K. M. Measuring emotionality in infants. *Child Development,* 1934, *5,* 36–40.

Bridges, K. M. The development of the primary drives in infancy. *Child Development,* 1936, *7,* 40–56.

Bronson, G. Infants' reactions to unfamiliar persons and novel objects. *Monographs of the Society for Research in Child Development,* 1972.

Bronson, G., & Pankey, W. On the distinction between fear and wariness. *Child Development,* 1977, *48,* 1167–1183.

Bühler, C. *The first year of life.* New York: Day, 1930.

Campos, J., Emde, R., Gaensbauer, T. & Henderson, C. Cardiac and behavioral interrelationships in the reactions of infants to strangers. *Developmental Psychology,* 1975, *11,* 589–601.

Campos, J., Hiatt, S., Ramsay, D., Henderson, C., & Svedja, M. The emergence of fear on the visual cliff. In M. Lewis & L. Rosenblum (Eds.), *The development of affect.* New York: Plenum, 1978.

Cannon, W. The James-Lange theory of emotions: A critical examination and an alternative theory. *American Journal of Psychology,* 1927, *39,* 106–124.

Cannon, W. Again the James-Lange and the thalamic theories of emotion. *Psychological Review,* 1931, *38,* 281–295.

Charlesworth, W. R. *Development of the object concept: A methodological study.* Paper presented at the meeting of the American Psychological Association, New York, September 1966.

Charlesworth, W. R. The role of surprise in cognitive development. In D. Elkind & J. Flavell (Eds.), *Studies in cognitive development.* London: Oxford University Press, 1969.

Charlesworth, W. R., & Kreutzer, M. Facial expressions of infants and children. In P. Ekman (Ed.), *Darwin and facial expression.* New York: Academic Press, September 1973.

Chevalier-Skolnikoff, S. Facial expression of emotion in nonhuman primates. In P. Ekman (Ed.) *Darwin and facial expression.* New York: Academic Press, 1973.

Cicchetti, D., & Aber, J. L. Abused children—abusive parents: An overstated case? *Harvard Educational Review,* in press.

Cicchetti, D., & Mans, L. *Down's syndrome and normal infants' responses to impending collision.* Paper presented at the annual meeting of the American Psychological Association, Washington, D. C., September 1976.

Cicchetti, D., & Pogge-Hesse, P. Affect and intellect: Piagetian and neo-Piagetian contributions to the study of emotional development. In G. Butterworth (Ed.), *Infancy and epistemology.* England: Harvester, in press. (a)

Cicchetti, D., & Pogge-Hesse, P. Possible contributions of the study of organic retardates to developmental theory. In E. Zigler & D. Balla (Eds.), *Developmental and difference theories of mental retardation.* Hillsdale, N.J.: Lawrence Erlbaum Associates, in press. (b)

Cicchetti, D., & Rizley, R. *Maternal and child depression: Research and theoretical perspectives.* Presented at the Harvard University Department of Psychiatry, March 1980.

Cicchetti, D., & Sroufe, L. A. The relationship between affective and cognitive development in Down's syndrome infants. *Child Development,* 1976, *47,* 920–929.

Cicchetti, D., & Sroufe, L. A. An organizational view of affect: Illustration from the study of Down's syndrome infants. In M. Lewis & L. Rosenblum (Eds.), *The development of affect.* New York: Plenum, 1978.

Cicchetti, D., Taraldson, B., & Egeland, B. Perspectives in the treatment and understanding of child abuse. In A. Goldstein (Ed.), *Prescriptions for child mental health and education.* New York: Pergamon Press, 1978.

Cicchetti, D., Mans, L., & Breitenbuecher, M. *The ontogenesis of fear in Down's syndrome infants: Implications for the study of brain development.* Paper presented at the biennial meeting of the Society for Research in Child Development, New Orleans, La., March 1977.

Claparède, E. Feelings and emotions. In M. L. Reymert (Ed.), *Feelings and emotions: The Wittenberg symposium.* Worcester, Mass.: Clark University Press, 1928.

Darwin, C. *The expression of the emotions in man and animals.* London: Murray, 1872.

Darwin, C. A biographical sketch of an infant. *Mind,* 1877, *2,* 285-294.

Dashiell, J. Are there any native emotions? *Psychological Review,* 1928, *35,* 319-327.

DeRivera, J. A structural theory of emotions. *Psychological Issues Monographs,* 1976.

Deutsch, J. A. *The structural basis of behavior.* Chicago: University of Chicago Press, 1960.

Dollard, J. & Miller, N. E. *Personality and psychotherapy.* New York: McGraw-Hill, 1950.

Duffy, E. Emotion: An example of the need for reorientation in psychology. *Psychological Review,* 1934, *41,* 184-198.

Duffy, E. An explanation of "emotional" phenomena without the use of the concept "emotion." *Journal of General Psychology,* 1941, *25,* 283-293.

Dumas, G. *Nouveau traité de psychologie.* Paris: Alcan, 1932.

Eibl-Eibesfeldt, I. *The biology of behavior.* New York: Holt, Rinehart, & Winston, 1970.

Ekman, P. & Friesen, W. *Unmasking the human face.* Englewood Cliffs, N.J.: Prentice-Hall, 1975.

Emde, R. Levels of meaning for infant emotions: A biosocial view. In W. A. Collins (Ed.), *Minnesota Symposia on Child Psychology* (Vol. 13). Hillsdale, N.J.: Lawrence Erlbaum Associates, 1979.

Emde, R., Gaensbauer, T., & Harmon, R. *Emotional expression in infancy: A biobehavioral study.* New York: International Universities Press, 1976.

Emde, R. N., Katz, E., & Thorpe, J. Emotional expression in infancy: II. Early deviations in Down's syndrome. In M. Lewis & L. Rosenblum (Eds.), *The development of affect.* New York: Plenum, 1978.

Erikson, E. *Childhood and society.* New York: Norton, 1950.

Fairbairn, W. R. D. Steps in the development of an object-relations theory of the personality. *The British Journal of Medical Psychology,* 1949, *22,* 152-161.

Fairbairn, W. R. D. A synopsis of the development of the author's views regarding the structure of the personality. *The British Journal of Medical Psychology,* 1951, *24,* 162-179.

Fairbairn, W. R. D. *Psycho-analytic studies of the personality.* London: Tavistock, 1952.

Feldman, C., & Toulmin, S. Logic and the theory of mind. In D. Levine (Ed.), *Nebraska Symposium on Motivation.* Lincoln: University of Nebraska Press, 1975.

Flavell, J. H. Stage-related properties of cognitive development. *Cognitive Psychology,* 1971, *2,* 421-453.

Flavell, J. H. An analysis of cognitive-developmental sequences. *Genetic Psychology Monographs,* 1972, *86,* 279-350.

Fraiberg, S. *Insights from the blind.* New York: Basic Books, 1977.

Freud, A. *The ego and the mechanisms of defense.* New York: International Universities Press, 1946. (a)

Freud, A. The psychoanalytic study of the infantile feeding disturbances. *Psychoanalytic Study of the Child,* 1946, *2,* 119-132. (b)

Freud, A. Psychoanalysis and education. *Psychoanalytic Study of the Child,* 1954, *9,* 9-15.

Freud, A. *Normality and pathology in childhood: Assessments of development.* New York: International Universities Press, 1965.

Freud, S. *The interpretation of dreams* (The Basic Writings). New York: Modern Library, 1938. (Originally published, 1900.)

Freud, S. Instincts and their vicissitudes (Vol. 14 of the *Standard Edition*). London: Hogarth, 1968. (Originally published, 1915.)

Freud, S. *Inhibitions, symptoms and anxiety* (Vol. 20 of the *Standard Edition*). London: Hogarth, 1968. (Originally published, 1926.)

Freud, S. *New introductory lectures on psychoanalysis* (Vol. 22 of the *Standard Edition*). London: Hogarth, 1968. (Originally published, 1933.)

Freud, S. *The problem of anxiety.* New York: Norton, 1936.

Gardiner, H. M., Metcalf, R. C., & Beebe-Center, J. G. *Feeling and emotion: A history of theories.* New York: American Book Company, 1937.

Gelhorn, E. *Biological foundations of emotion.* Glenview, Illinois: Scott-Foresman Press, 1968.

Green, A. Conceptions of affect. *International Journal of Psycho-Analysis,* 1977, *58,* 129–156.

Grossman, S. P. *Physiological psychology.* New York: Wiley, 1967.

Hartmann, H. Psychoanalysis and developmental psychology. *The Psychoanalytic Study of the Child,* 1950, *5,* 7–18.

Hartmann, H., Kris, E., & Loewenstein, R. M. Comments on the formation of psychic structure. *Psychoanalytic Study of the Child,* 1946, *2,* 11–38.

Haviland, J. Looking smart: The relationship between affect and intelligence in infancy. In M. Lewis (Ed.), *Origins of infant intelligence.* New York: Plenum, 1976.

Head, H., & Holmes, G. Sensory disturbances from cerebral lesions. *Brain,* 1911, *34,* 102–254.

Hebb, D. O. *The organization of behavior.* New York: Wiley, 1949.

Herrnstein, R. J. The evolution of behaviorism. *American Psychologist,* 1977, *32,* 593–603.

Hiatt, S. W., Campos, J., & Emde, R. Facial patterning and infant emotional expression: Happiness, surprise, and fear. *Child Development,* 1979, *50,* 1020–1035.

Hinde, R. A. *Animal behavior: A synthesis of ethology and comparative psychology.* New York: McGraw-Hill, 1966.

Hunt, J. McV. Intrinsic motivation and its role in psychological development. In D. Levine (Ed.), *Nebraska Symposium on Motivation.* Lincoln: University of Nebraska Press, 1965.

Inhelder, B., Sinclair, H., & Bovet, M. *Learning and the development of cognition.* Cambridge: Harvard University Press, 1974.

Izard, C. *Human emotions.* New York: Plenum, 1977.

Izard, C. On the development of emotions and emotion-cognition relationships in infancy. In M. Lewis & L. Rosenblum (Eds.), *The development of affect.* New York: Plenum, 1978.

Izard, C., & Buechler, S. Emotion expressions and personality integration in infancy. In C. Izard (Ed.), *Emotions in personality and psychopathology.* New York: Plenum, 1979.

James, W. *Psychology: The briefer course.* New York: Holt, 1892.

James, W. *Talks to teachers.* New York: Norton, 1958.

Kagan, J. *Change and continuity in infancy.* New York: Wiley, 1971.

Kant, I. *Kritik der reiner Vernunft.* Leipzig: Felix Meiner, 1781.

Kanzer, M. Object relations theory: An introduction. *Journal of the American Psychoanalytic Association,* 1979, *27,* 313–325.

Kaplan, B. Meditations on genesis. *Human Development,* 1966, *10,* 65–87.

Kendler, H. H. Motivation and behavior. In D. Levine (Ed.), *Nebraska symposium on motivation.* Lincoln: University of Nebraska Press, 1965.

Kessen, W. Early cognitive development: Hot or cold? In T. Mischel (Ed.), *Cognitive development and epistemology.* New York: Academic Press, 1971.

Klein, M. Some theoretical conclusions regarding the emotional life of the infant. In M. Klein, P. Heimann, S. Isaacs, & J. Riviere (Eds.), *Developments in psychoanalysis.* London: Hogarth, 1952.

Knight, R., Roff, J., Barrnett, J., & Moss, J. Concurrent and predictive validity of thought disorder and affectivity: A 22-year follow-up. *Journal of Abnormal Psychology,* 1979 *88,* 1–12.

Kosslyn, S. M. Imagery and cognitive development: A teleological approach. In R. S. Siegler (Ed.), *Children's thinking: What develops?* Hillsdale, N.J.: Lawrence Erlbaum Associates, 1978.

Le Compte, G. K., & Gratch, G. Violation of a rule as a method of diagnosing infants' levels of object concept. *Child Development,* 1972, *43,* 385–396.

Lewis, M., & Brooks, J. Self-knowledge and emotional development. In M. Lewis & L. Rosenblum (Eds.), *The development of affect.* New York: Plenum, 1978.

Lewis, M., & Rosenblum, L., (Eds.), *The effect of the infant on its caregiver.* New York: Wiley, 1974.

Lewis, M., & Rosenblum, L. *The development of affect.* New York: Plenum, 1978.

Luria, A. R., & Subbotski, E. W. Zur frühen Ontogenese der steurenden Funktion der Sprache. In G. Steiner (Ed.), *Die Psychologie des Jahrhunderts* (Vol. 7). Piaget und die Folgen, Kindler Verlag AG, Zurich, 1978.

Mahler, M., Pine, G., & Bergman, N. *The psychological birth of the infant.* New York: Basic Books, 1975.

Mandler, G. The interruption of behavior. In D. Levine (Ed.), *Nebraska symposium on motivation.* Lincoln: University of Nebraska Press, 1964.

Mandler, G. *Mind and emotion.* New York: Wiley, 1975.

Mans, L., Cicchetti, D., & Sroufe, L. A. Mirror reactions of Down's syndrome infants and toddlers: Cognitive underpinnings of self-recognition. *Child Development,* 1978, *49,* 1247–1250.

Matas, L., Arend, R., & Sroufe, L. A. Continuity of adaptation in the second year: The relationship between quality of attachment and later competence. *Child Development,* 1978, *49,* 547–556.

McCall, R., & McGhee, P. The discrepancy hypothesis of attention and affect. In F. Weizmann & I. Uzgiris (Eds.), *The structuring of experience.* New York: Plenum, 1977.

McDougall, W. *Outline of psychology.* New York: Scribner, 1923.

Meehl, P. E. Theoretical risks and tabular asterisks: Sir Karl, Sir Ronald, and the slow progress of soft psychology. *Journal of Consulting and Clinical Psychology,* 1978, *46,* 806–834.

Oster, H. Facial expression and affect development. In M. Lewis & L. Rosenblum (Eds.), *The development of affect.* New York: Plenum, 1978.

Oster, H., & Ekman, P. Facial behavior in child development. In W. A. Collins (Ed.), *Minnesota symposia on child psychology* (Vol. 11). Hillsdale, N.J.: Lawrence Erlbaum Associates, 1977.

Piaget, J. *Play, dreams and imitation in childhood,* 2nd ed. (1945). New York: Norton, 1951.

Piaget, J. *The origins of intelligence in children,* 2nd ed. (1936). New York: International Universities Press, 1952.

Piaget, J. *The construction of reality in the child.* New York: Basic Books, 1954. (Originally published 1937.) (a)

Piaget, J. *Les relations entre l'affectivité et l'intelligence dans le developpement mental de l'enfant.* Paris: Centre de Documentation Universitaire, 1954. (b)

Piaget, J. *Biology and knowledge.* Chicago: University of Chicago Press, 1971.

Piaget, J. The relation of affectivity to intelligence in the mental development of the child. In S. Harrison & J. McDermott (Eds.), *Childhood psychopathology.* New York: International Universities Press, 1972.

Piaget, J. The affective unconscious and the cognitive unconscious. *Journal of the American Psychoanalytic Association,* 1973, *21,* 249–261.

Piaget, J. *The development of thought: Equilibration of cognitive structures.* New York: Viking Press, 1977.

Piaget, J., & Inhelder, B. *The psychology of the child.* New York: Basic Books, 1969.

Plutchik, R. What is an emotion? *Journal of Psychology,* 1965, *61,* 295–303.

Popper, K. *The logic of scientific discovery.* New York: Harper & Row, 1959.

Pribram, K. H. Emotion: Steps toward a neuropsychological theory. In D. C. Glass (Ed.), *Neurophysiology and emotion.* New York: Rockefeller University Press and Russell Sage Foundation, 1967.

Rapaport, D. On the psychoanalytic theory of affects. *International Journal of Psycho-Analysis,* 1953, *34,* 177–198.

Rapaport, D. Psychoanalysis as a developmental psychology. In B. Kaplan & S. Wapner (Eds.), *Perspectives in psychological theory.* New York: International Universities Press, 1960.

Ricciuti, H. Social and emotional behavior in infancy: Some developmental issues and problems. *Merrill-Palmer Quarterly,* 1968, *14,* 82–100.

Rosch, E., & Mervis, C. B. Family resemblances: Studies in the internal structure of categories. *Cognitive Psychology,* 1975, *7,* 573–605.

Sander, L. Issues in early mother-child interaction. *Journal of the American Academy of Child Psychiatry,* 1962, *1,* 141–166.

Schmale, A. A genetic view of affects. *Psychoanalytic Study of the Child,* 1964, *19,* 287–310.

Schur, M. Affects and cognition. *International Journal of Psycho-Analysis,* 1969, *50,* 647–653.

Sears, R. R. Dependency motivation. In M. R. Jones (Ed.), *The Nebraska Symposium on Motivation.* Lincoln: University of Nebraska Press, 1963.

Segal, E., & Lachman, R. Complex behavior and higher mental process. *American Psychologist,* 1972, *27,* 46–55.

Serafica, F. C. The development of attachment behaviors: An organismic-developmental perspective. *Human Development,* 1978, *21,* 119–140.

Sheer, D. E. Emotional facilitation in learning situations with subcortical stimulation. In D. E. Sheer (Ed.), *Electrical stimulation of the brain: An interdisciplinary survey of neurobehavioral integrative systems.* Austin: University of Texas Press, 1961.

Shultz, R., & Zigler, E. Emotional concomitants of visual mastery in infants: The effects of stimulus movement on smiling and vocalizing. *Journal of Experimental Child Psychology,* 1970, *10,* 390–402.

Skinner, B. F. *Science and human behavior.* New York: MacMillan, 1953.

Spitz, R. Anxiety in infancy: A study of its manifestations in the first year of life. *International Journal of Psycho-Analysis,* 1950, *31,* 138–143.

Spitz, R. *A genetic field theory of ego formation.* New York: International Universities Press, 1959.

Spitz, R. *The first year of life: A psychoanalytic study of normal and deviant development of object relations.* New York: International Universities Press, 1965.

Spitz, R., Emde, R., & Metcalf, D. Further prototypes of ego formation: A working paper from a research project on early development. *The Psychoanalytic Study of the Child,* 1970, *25,* 417–441.

Spitz, R. A., & Wolf, K. M. The smiling response: A contribution to the ontogenesis of social relations. *Genetic Psychology Monographs,* 1946, *34,* 57–125.

Sroufe, L. A. The developmental significance of the construct of wariness. *Child Development,* 1977 (b), *48,* 731–746.

Sroufe, A. *Knowing and enjoying your baby.* Englewood Cliffs, N.J.: Prentice-Hall, 1977 (b).

Sroufe, L. A. Socioemotional development. In J. Osofsky (Ed.), *Handbook of infant development.* New York: Wiley, 1979.

Sroufe, L. A., & Waters, E. The ontogenesis of smiling and laughter: A perspective on the organization of development in infancy. *Psychological Review,* 1976, *83,* 173–189.

Sroufe, L. A., & Waters, E. Attachment as an organizational construct. *Child Development,* 1977, *48,* 1184–1199.

Sroufe, L. A., Waters, E., & Matas, L. Contextual determinants of infant affective response. In M. Lewis & L. Rosenblum (Eds.), *The origins of fear.* New York: Wiley, 1974.

Sroufe, L. A., & Wunsch, J. P. The development of laughter in the first year of life. *Child Development,* 1972, *43,* 1326–1344.

Stechler, G., & Carpenter, G. A viewpoint on early affective development. In J. Hellmuth (Ed.), *Exceptional infant* (Vol. 1). New York: Brunner/Mazel, 1967.

Stern, D. The goal and structure of mother-infant play. *Journal of the American Academy of Child Psychiatry,* 1974, *13,* 402–421.

Stern, D. *The first relationship.* Cambridge, Mass.: Harvard University Press, 1977.

Tennes, K., Emde, R., Kisley, A., & Metcalf, D. The stimulus barrier in early infancy: An exploration of some formulations of John Benjamin. In R. Holt & E. Peterfreund (Eds.), *Psychoanalysis and contemporary science.* New York: Macmillan, 1972.

Thomas, H. Discrepancy hypotheses: Methodological and theoretical considerations. *Psychological Review,* 1971, *78,* 249–259.

Tomkins, S. *Affect, imagery, consciousness* (Vol. 1). New York: Springer, 1962.

Tomkins, S. *Affect, imagery, consciousness* (Vol. 2). New York: Springer, 1963.

Tomkins, S., & McCarter, R. What and where are the primary affects? *Perceptual and Motor Skills,* 1964, *18,* 119–158.

Van Hooff, J. A comparative approach to the phylogeny of laughter and smiling. In R. Hinde (Ed.), *Non-verbal communication.* Cambridge, England: Cambridge University Press, 1972.

Vine, I. The role of facial signalling in early social development. In M. von Cranach and I. Vine (Eds.), *Social communication and movement: Studies of men and chimpanzees.* London: Academic Press, 1973.

Waters, E. The reliability and stability of individual differences in infant-mother attachment. *Child Development,* 1978, *49,* 483–494.

Waters, E., Matas, L., & Sroufe, L. A. Infants' reactions to an approaching stranger: Description, validation and functional significance of wariness. *Child Development,* 1975, *46,* 348–356.

Waters, E., Wippman, J., & Sroufe, L. A. Attachment, positive affect, and competence in the peer group: Two studies in construct validation. *Child Development,* 1979, *50,* 821–829.

Watson, J. B. *Psychology from the standpoint of a behaviorist.* Philadelphia: Lippincott, 1919.

Watson, J. B. Experimental studies on the growth of the emotions. *Pedagogical Seminary,* 1925, *32,* 328–348.

Weil, J. L. *A neurophysiological model of emotional and intentional behavior.* Springfield, Illinois: Thomas, 1974.

Werner, H. *Comparative psychology of mental development.* New York: International Universities Press, 1948.

Werner, H. The concept of development from a comparative and organismic point of view. In D. Harris (Ed.), *The concept of development.* Minneapolis: University of Minnesota Press, 1957.

Werner, H., & Kaplan, B. *Symbol formation: An organismic-developmental approach to language and the expression of thought.* New York: Wiley, 1964.

White, R. Motivation reconsidered: The concept of competence. *Psychological Review,* 1959, *66,* 297–333.

White, S. H., & Pillemer, D. B. Childhood amnesia and the development of a socially accessible memory system. In J. F. Kihlstrom & F. J. Evans (Eds.), *Functional disorders of memory.* Hillsdale, N.J.: Lawrence Erlbaum Associates, 1979.

Winnicott, D. W. Pediatrics and psychiatry. *British Journal of Medical Psychology,* 1948, *21,* 229–240.

Winnicott, D. W. Transitional objects and transitional phenomena. *International Journal of Psycho-Analysis,* 1953, *34,* 1–9.

Winnicott, D. W. The theory of the parent-infant relationship. *International Journal of Psycho-Analysis,* 1960, *41,* 585–595.

Wolff, P. *The developmental psychologies of Jean Piaget and psychoanalysis.* New York: International Universities Press, 1960.

Wolff, P. The causes, controls, and organization of behavior in the neonate. *Psychological Issues Monographs,* 1966.

Woodworth, R. S. *Psychology,* New York: Holt, 1940 4th ed.

Woodworth, R. S., & Schlosberg, H. S. *Experimental psychology.* New York: Holt, 1954.

Wundt, W. M. *An introduction to psychology.* London: G. Allen, 1912.

Zelazo, P., & Komer, M. Infant smiling to non-social stimuli and the recognition hypothesis. *Child Development,* 1971, *42,* 1327–1339.

Zigler, E., Levine, J., & Gould, L. The humor response of normal, institutionalized retarded, and noninstitutionalized retarded children. *American Journal of Mental Deficiency,* 1966, *71,* 472–480.

10 Perception, Appraisal and Emotion: The Onset of Social Referencing

Joseph J. Campos
Craig R. Stenberg
University of Denver

The recent history of the study of emotion has been dominated by approaches stressing cognitive factors. In theories of adult emotional response, cognitive appraisal now functions as the central construct. In infancy research, cognitive theories have also been predominant. However, the operation of appraisal as a mediator of the elicitation, regulation, expression, and recognition of emotion has been largely neglected. Instead, theoretical emphasis has been placed on the development of memory, in particular evocative (recall) memory and object permanence, as a necessary precondition for the ontogeny of several discrete emotions. Despite the persistence of this notion in recent theorizing, there is now good reason to suspect that the role of memory may have been overstated and that of appraisal understated. In this paper, we present an alternative conceptualization of the role played by cognitive factors in emotional development and regulation. It emphasizes sensitivity to the affective perceptual information provided by others as a significant factor in the acquisition of the capacity to appraise and react emotionally. We review evidence for the possible emergence of this perceptual sensitivity between 5 and 9 months of age, identify empirical predictions stemming from these notions, and discuss their implications for normal and abnormal personality development.

THE ROLE OF COGNITION IN AFFECT—
THEORIES ABOUT AFFECT IN ADULTS

Any complete theory of emotion must address at least five distinct processes: (1) the *elicitation* of emotion; (2) the central nervous system *mechanisms* of emotion; (3) the peripheral, autonomic, facial, and skeletal *expressions* of emotion; (4) the *perception* of emotion in others, resulting in regulation of the perceiver's behavior; and (5) the *interaction* among these variables, such as how peripheral feedback influences both the central processes and the sensitivity to affect elicitors.

Historically, investigations of affect have concentrated on the second and third processes. For instance, the early theoretical controversies dealt with how the conscious awareness of emotional states was generated: Was it through the perception of visceral and skeletal feedback, as postulated by the James (1890) and Lange (1885) theories of emotion, or was it solely a central phenomenon, controlled either by the thalamus and hypothalamus as Cannon (1927) and Bard (1950) proposed, or by the limbic system as Papez (1937) and MacLean (1949) hypothesized? Simultaneously, there was considerable empirical research and theorizing concerning specificity of emotional expression in the autonomic and facial actions of individuals— particularly whether emotional expression was comprised only of general activation and undifferentiated peripheral reaction (Duffy, 1941). With a few exceptions, such as Freud's treatment of signal anxiety (1926), there was little effort to relate eliciting factors to emotions in early theories. Thus, neither James nor Cannon speculated much about what produced the physiological feedback or thalamic activation in the first place. The major elicitors that they considered were typically limited to a narrow set of unconditional stimuli, such as loud sounds or electric shocks, and to stimuli associated with them. Indeed, Freud's theory of signal anxiety, which today would be categorized as a classic appraisal theory for its emphasis on evaluation of both danger and the means of coping with it, was reduced to conditioning terminology by Mowrer (1939) and many others (e.g., Miller, 1944; Skinner, 1953).

By 1960, however, theoreticians began to place increasing emphasis on the three remaining factors, particularly the cognitive factors involved in the elicitation of emotion. Cognitive theorists regarded conditional stimuli as an unacceptably restrictive set of events producing emotional reactions (Lazarus, 1968). Indeed, they argued that no particular class of stimuli was the crucial cause of emotional reactions. In their view, it is not the physical stimulus that matters, but how that stimulus is made sense of by the organism. Through attentive processes, some stimuli are highlighted and their impact enhanced, whereas others are ignored and their effects circumvented. Through attitudes and sets, the subject can selectively misinterpret some events and realistically interpet others. Hence, cognitive theories of emotion emphasized perception (or more technically, apperception) and the cognitive loops intervening between stimulation and emotional reaction. Even in behaviorist theories, images and thoughts began to be given roles formerly occupied only by environmental stimuli (Wolpe, 1958). Expectations were also given crucial theoretical roles, especially the anticipation of future consequences even if these had never before been experienced directly. In addition, the perceiver was not restricted to previously learned emotional expressions. The evaluation of the situation permitted novel reactions and emotional expressions or coping reactions different from those the subject had previously learned. Therefore, previous conditioning could be transcended. Variables such as these were subsumed under the term *cognitive appraisal*, leading to a more elaborate conception of the elicitors of emotional states and of the range of responses available to the subject.

Many theorists exemplify this major change in the *zeitgeist* of emotion theory. We cite four of the more influential in order to illustrate the shift from associationistic and physiological approaches to cognitive ones:

1. Arnold (1960) defines emotion as the felt tendency toward anything intuitively appraised as good (i.e., beneficial), or away from anything intuitively appraised as bad (i.e., harmful). She (1960) proposes that: "There must be a psychological capacity of appraising how a given thing will affect us, whether it will hurt or please us, before we can want to approach it or avoid it. To call upon mere 'learning,' 'past experience,' or the 'conditioned reflex' for an explanation is futile. Without such an appraisal, learning would be impossible, and past experience, fruitless [p. 173]." Thus, for her, a situation (whether in the past, present, or future, and whether real or imagined) elicits an evaluation. The direct, immediate outcome of this evaluation is an emotional state, unless the appraisal is that the event is of no consequence. Although Arnold states that emotions can be categorized along a pleasantness–unpleasantness dimension, she describes as many as 12 discrete emotions (and numerous possible blends of the 12) resulting from the process of evaluation. She also describes a process of *secondary appraisal*, such as noticing the physiological consequences of emotional arousal, which can augment or reduce the perceived intensity of the emotion elicited by the *primary evaluation.* An important corollary of the appraisal process—and one that is crucial for the argument to be made later in this chapter—is that the recognition of emotion in others is similarly the result of an intuitive appraisal of facial patterning and other sources of information. Implicit in her position, then, is the possibility of two related but distinct types of appraisal: The intrinsic appraisal by the individual of the good or harm of an event, and the social appraisal of how another individual is reacting emotionally to that event.

2. Lazarus (1968) takes a position that is similar in substance, though somewhat different in emphasis, from that of Arnold. Every emotion is said to flow from appraisal processes by which the person or infrahuman animal

evaluates the adaptive significance of the stimulus. There are two general types of appraisal outcomes. Benign appraisal results from the anticipation that an event is not likely to be harmful because: (1) the person possesses well-rehearsed and successful coping strategies; (2) there is reappraisal of threat on the basis of new evidence; or (3) positive outcomes are expected. In the last case, love, elation, and similar emotions will result. Threat appraisals produce negatively toned emotional states like fear and anger and direct action such as attack and avoidance. The major difference between Lazarus and Arnold resides in the immediacy of the appraisal, given the perception of the situation. Arnold believes that for emotion to occur, appraisal must be immediate and intuitive. Lazarus gives much more emphasis to conscious reflection, deliberation, and even verbal instruction as major factors in affect elicitation and regulation.

3. Schachter and Singer's (1962) theory of emotion further demonstrates the importance of evaluation. Like Arnold and Lazarus, they emphasize the importance of cognitive variables for determining discrete affect states and argue that the detection of physiological arousal generates an evaluative need—a search for possible causes of a stirred-up physiological state. In their words (1962): "The cognition, in a sense, exerts a steering function. Cognitions arising from the immediate situation as interpreted by past experience provide the framework within which one understands and labels his feelings. It is the cognition which determines whether the state of physiological arousal will be labeled as anger, joy, fear, or whatever [p. 380]."

In contrast to most other theories of appraisal, Schachter and Singer do not see cognitions and appraisals as causes of physiological arousal in the first place, but rather as providing an interpretation for the arousal. In a sense, then, what Schachter and Singer are proposing seems to be very similar to what Arnold calls secondary appraisal, except for one important point: Discrete emotions or their absence are not accompanied by perceptible differences in physiological states (a proposition central to Arnold's theory) but are produced solely by the subject's attribution of the cause of his or her stirred-up state.

4. The use of cognitive variables in accounting for emotional states extends to the domain of psychopathology. Numerous theorists have posited that cognitive distortions produce affective disorders of one type or another (Ellis, 1962; Seligman, 1975). Beck (1974), for example, has advanced an influential theory of depression arguing that the affective, motivational, and physical manifestations of depression result from persistent negative evaluations and misinterpretations. These mistaken interpretations are categorized within a triad of cognitive sets: the negative interpretation of experience, the negative evaluation of the self, and the negative expectation of the future. In short, the entire array of depressive clinical phenomena is seen to result from cognitive misappraisals, and depression results from a malfunction in the individual's evaluative capabilities.

COGNITION AND AFFECT—
THEORIES OF EMOTION IN INFANCY

There has been very little correspondence between theories of emotion in adulthood and infancy. The former generally fail to speculate about the ontogenesis of emotions and the potential role of emerging cognitive capacities as mediators of emotional epigenesis, whereas the latter have neglected many of the parameters that are regarded as crucial in theories about adults, most notably appraisal. In more recent theorizing, this neglect has been acknowledged (see Kagan, 1974; Lewis & Brooks, 1974), and a few theories now incorporate the concept (e.g., Sroufe, Waters, & Matas, 1974). But theorists otherwise sympathetic to the appraisal notion have argued that the appraisal of events (conceptualized in terms of anticipation of beneficial or undesirable consequences) may not emerge until the second year of life (Kagan, 1974).

This neglect of the appraisal concept in theories regarding emotion in infancy does not extend to cognitive determinants in general. In fact, three of the major theoretical traditions in the field—the psychoanalytic, Hebbian, and neo-Piagetian—have used cognitive variables, especially memory and object permanence, to account for discrete emotional states such as joy, fear, and affection. In theories about adults, by comparison, the importance of cognitive factors has only recently been recognized.

The emphasis infancy researchers have placed on the acquisition of memory capacities derives from the role given to memory by psychoanalytic theories. Best exemplified by the work of Spitz (e.g., 1965), these theories postulate that four apparently universal affective developments—the social smile, separation anxiety, its derivative stranger anxiety, and the capacity to experience sadness and depression—result from changes in memory abilities.

According to Spitz's formulation, the rise of the social smile at approximately 2 months of age comes about because the infant has acquired a rudimentary memory that permits the child to respond differentially to certain stimuli in the environment. Initially, the infant enters the world in an affectively undifferentiated state devoid of any true emotions or memories, except for excitement tinged with a hint of unpleasure (Spitz, 1965). This excitement generates needs states from which the infant desires immediate release. The release, in turn, takes place in large part as a consequence of maternal ministrations. Delays in drive reduction cause certain stimuli in the environment to be more readily cathected—i.e., more easily differentiated from the perceptual background and invested with importance—than others. Initially, the infant's rudimentary memory stores only selective and exceedingly limited information, which encompasses certain features of the human face—the so-called *sign gestalt* consisting of the eyes, nose, hairline, and forehead, in motion. At this stage, the infant is responsive both to human faces that display these features and inanimate representations as well.

Discrimination of mother from nonmother is not possible. Memories are quite unstable and are retrievable only while the sign gestalt is physically present. The infant can only recognize the sign gestalt, and as a consequence of this recognition, a genetically preprogrammed affective response—a smile—immediately results, so long as the gestalt is a sign of drive reduction. If it has become a sign of forthcoming unpleasure, as in the case of Evamar (Spitz & Wolf, 1946), immediate distress, rather than smiling, results.

These new perceptual, cognitive, and affective capacities—called the first organizer by Spitz—usher in a stage where specific associations can be formed between certain events in the environment and certain pleasant or unpleasant consequences. For example, contrary to some recent theoretical positions (e.g., Bronson, 1978), Spitz (1950) believes that by 3 months of age, the infant can learn specific fears based on the recognition that certain stimuli now present in the perceptual field have led to negative consequences before. The most significant memory traces laid down in this period, in Spitz's view, are associations between perceptual features of the mother and frustration or satisfaction of a drive-based need. These traces become organized in memory under the rubric of "good" and "bad" mother. As Spitz (1966) put it: "(The mother) became a bad object when she refused to gratify the desire of the baby, for this refusal triggered his aggressive drive; when shortly thereafter she gratified his wish or rather his need, she became the good mother, toward whom libidinal drives were directed [p. 137]."

At first, the memory-based good and bad mothers are distinct. The eventual interweaving of the two part-objects into a coherent whole depends on the emergence of a new skill, evocative memory. Once this type of memory exists (around 6 to 8 months of age) in the form of a stable representation of the mother, a number of new emotional phenomena arise, including stranger and separation anxiety. Stranger anxiety is particularly noteworthy because distress is shown to a person even in the absence of any negative experiences with that person. According to Spitz, this rules out the operation of recognition memory in this phenomenon. Spitz (1957) describes the emergence of separation and stranger anxiety as follows:

> The child produces first a scanning behavior, namely seeking for the lost loved object, the mother. A decision is now made by the function of judgment "whether something which is present in ego as an image can also be rediscovered in perception" (Freud, 1926). The realization that it cannot be rediscovered in the given instance provokes a response of unpleasure. In terms of the eight-months anxiety, what we observe can be understood as follows: The stranger's face is compared to the memory trace of the mother's face and found wanting. This is not mother, she is still lost. Unpleasure is experienced and manifested [p. 54].

Spitz thus argues unequivocally for a necessary role of recall memory in stranger and separation anxiety (see also Fraiberg, 1969).

In Spitz's view, the ability to maintain a stable, mental image of the mother also has profound clinical implications, and major differences are expected in the reactions of infants when they are separated from their mothers before 6 months of age and after. In his famous "hospitalism" study (Spitz, 1945), infants whose mothers were taken from them before 6 months of age showed severe developmental lags, contracted marasmus, and many died. By contrast, infants who were separated from their mothers somewhat later (at 6 to 8 months of age) displayed a much greater capacity to survive. Unlike the younger sample, they reacted with weepiness, sadness, terror at the approach of strangers, insomnia, weight loss, and other symptoms of what Spitz labeled "anaclitic depression" (Spitz, 1946).

The explanation for this startling shift from dire somatic consequences to milder ones, and from marked psychological disorganization to affective distress upon maternal separation hinged on the presence or absence of the stable mental image of the mother. Before representation, when the infants were deprived of an object in the external world, the aggressive drives normally directed at the mother were turned toward their own bodies. The effect of the aggression turned against the self became evident in the marasmus and eventual death. However, the existence of a stable memory image of the mother allowed the intervention of delay of gratification, the neutralization of libidinal and aggressive energies, and thus the capacity to deflect some of the drives from their more direct aim. Consequently, when the mother is removed from the infant at this more advanced stage of ego functioning, the infant can partially defend him or herself from the aggressive drives by channeling the destructive energy away from the body or the whole self. Through the process of grief and mourning and through the experience of sadness and depression, the infant is able, at least in part, to transform drive energies and use them for aims consistent with survival.

Spitz, then, used recognition memory to explain the social smile, acquisition of specific fears, and hospitalism. He used recall or evocative memory to account for separation anxiety, stranger anxiety, and anaclitic depression.

Although there are some differences between Spitz's views and those of other major psychoanalytic writers, this theoretical tradition has largely upheld the importance of recognition and recall memory in accounting for early emotional development. Recently, McDevitt (1975), in reviewing his and Mahler's (Mahler, Pine, & Bergman, 1975) research, emphasized anew the significance of these concepts and argued for a timetable of their emergence quite similar to Spitz's. Even where tradition has departed from Spitz's views on the importance of recall memory, the spirit of his argument has been maintained. Many analysts today argue that maternal separation may result in a number of consequences besides marasmus, death, or anaclitic depression. Speculations abound concerning the impact of separation both on the individual's appreciation of others as separate human beings and on the person's conceptualization of him- or herself. Moreover, the presence or absence of a mental representation of a primary libidinal object is generally thought to demarcate certain forms of later pathology from others. For example, psychoses as well as narcissistic personality disorders are thought by many to originate prior to the formation of the ability to evoke a stable, mental image of the loved object (Ornstein, 1974). Neurotic difficulties, on the other hand, are thought to presuppose this capacity (Blanck & Blanck, 1974).

Ironically, the second major source of the preoccupation with memory factors as causes of emotion originated within a theoretical tradition that rejects or ignores many tenets of psychoanalysis: Hebbian theory. In his classic paper, "On the Nature of Fear" (1946), Hebb advanced the claim that animals and humans display fear reactions that cannot be accounted for simply by associationistic learning principles. Included are fears by apes of dismembered, motionless, or mutilated bodies. These reactions were described by Hebb as *spontaneous fears* because they occur in response to novel stimuli and can not be built up by association, yet at the same time are not "innate" because there are definite factors of past experience involved. Hebb regarded fear of strangers as a paradigmatic example of spontaneous fears in humans.

In characterizing this position, now frequently referred to as "incongruity theory," many authors (e.g., Kenney, Mason, & Hill, 1979) describe Hebb's arguments as follows: The source of fear is the divergence between a perceived object and a central representation of a familiar set of objects. Fear does not exist when the child first sees a stranger. Rather, according to Hebb (1946): "It is dependent on the fact that certain perceptions have become habitual, a limited number of central neural reactions to the sight of human beings have been established with great specificity by repeated experience [p. 268]." Once the central memory representation has been acquired, fear occurs because a strange human is enough like familiar humans to set into motion neurophysiological memory circuits (in Hebb's terms, phase sequences), yet sufficiently different not to be able to maintain the smooth central nervous system network of neural activity. The resulting central nervous system disruption produces fear.

There is a major problem with this frequently repeated account, however. It assumes a connection between incongruity and fear which is ambiguous in Hebb's 1946 account and which is clearly rejected in a chapter of his 1949 book, *The Organization of Behavior.* Contrary to the proposition that discrepancy is a sufficient condition for fear, Hebb suggests that the disruption of temporally and spatially organized cerebral activities is observed not only in fear, but also in rage (Hebb, 1946). Moreover, the state of disruption of coordinated cerebral activity may result in at least three outcomes—flight, aggression, or fawning. Consequently the outcome of incongruity need not necessarily be fear. In the 1946 account, then, discrepancy was regarded as perhaps a necessary, but not a sufficient, condition for fearful reactions to unfamiliar stimuli.

In the 1949 account, Hebb went even further. He argued that *incongruity is neither necessary nor sufficient to account for negative reactions to the strange.* To begin with, Hebb (1949) abandoned the concept of spontaneous fears and instead reinterpreted anthropoid responses to dismemberment, motionlessness, and mutilation as "a source of profound excitation, rather than specifically fear producing [p. 243]." He described how the same event could produce fear, aggression, surprise, friendliness, or "a confusing mixture of all these reactions," depending on the animal. Finally, he posited that specific learning mechanisms and maturationally based sensitivities are required to account for the transformation of undifferentiated emotional disturbance into discrete emotions like anger or fear.

Despite Hebb's disclaimers, numerous researchers have continued to advocate incongruity theory (e.g., Bateson, 1971; Bronson, 1968; Dimond, 1970; Scott, 1962), and it is still the most widely discussed explanation of the elicitation of wariness in infants in the second half-year of life (Haith & Campos, 1977). However, some researchers, although maintaining the conviction that cognitive factors underlie the affective developments between 5 and 9 months of age, have speculated that a more complex capability may be involved. The development of Piagetian object permanence is the most frequently proposed cognitive alternative to incongruity.

Two reports by Schaffer have been particularly influential in advancing this view. In an early study of the effects of hospitalization, Schaffer (1967) noted two types of reactions exhibited by hospitalized infants upon their return home. One reaction, called the "global syndrome," was characterized by extreme preoccupation with the environment. As Schaffer (1967) states: "For hours on end sometimes the infant would crane his neck, scanning his surroundings without apparently focusing on any particular feature, and letting his eyes sweep over all objects without attending to any particular one [p. 628]." The other reaction was called the "overdependent syndrome" and featured excessive crying when the infant was left alone by the mother, much fear of strangers, continual clinging, and the desire to be nursed. There was a clear age break between infants showing these two reactions, the differentiating age being approximately 7 months. Schaffer (1967) explained these results as follows:

> The most useful way of approaching this problem appears to be through a consideration of the type of *cognitive structure* to be found in infancy, i.e., the

way in which perceptions are organized and related to each other and to their external sources by the individual...In the early months, according to Piaget,...objects...do not exist in their own right but only as functional elements serving the infant's own activities, and are assimilated in terms of the present need of the individual. Moreover, once the object is out of the perceptual field the infant behaves as though it has ceased to exist...There is consequently no conservation of the object, and the world is centered on the child's own activity. There is, furthermore, no appreciation of the own body as one element amongst others, and it is thus not recognized as being part of a world of distinct, stable objects.

It is only in the second half of the first year that Piaget finds a new type of cognitive structure developing. It is only then that objects become detached from action and the first fundamental step taken in attributing to them a separate, independent existence [p. 631].

In another report, Schaffer (1966) described an explanation for what was to him a puzzling time gap between the infant's ability to discriminate his mother from strangers, which studies of the social smile had placed at 3–4 months of age, and the onset of fear of strangers, which Schaffer had noted to take place at around 8 months of age. In fact, fear of strangers took place 1 month or so after the formation of specific attachments. Once again, Schaffer postulated that the infant needed to develop a cognitive capacity concerning the mother as a complete individual before fear of strangers was possible and that object permanence provided the cognitive capacity. Others taking similar viewpoints include Bowlby (1969) and Ainsworth (1973; Ainsworth, Blehar, Waters, & Wall, 1978). Indeed, so persuasive was the theorizing underlying the postulation of object permanence as accounting for emotional development (in this case, of attachment to mother) that object permanence became a logically necessary prerequisite for the formation of attachment, and no longer an empirical hypothesis. For instance, Stayton, Ainswroth, and Main (1973) completely dismissed differential crying to the mother's departure as positive evidence of the infant's attachment to the mother at 5 months of age because at that age infants cannot be expected to possess object permanence. Stayton et al. (1973)wrote: "It has been generally agreed that mere discrimination and preference do not constitute attachment, and that a baby must first have acquired at least a rudimentary concept of object permanence, an acquisition that Piaget (1954) placed about about 8 months of age [p. 222]."

Very serious difficulties beset all of these approaches, as well as other recent ones, which in one way or another revise some of the ideas just mentioned (e.g., Décarie, 1974; Kagan, 1974; Kagan, Kearsley, & Zelazo, 1978; Schaffer, 1974; Stern, 1977). Perhaps the most fundamental difficulty with all of these positions is that they fail to take an evolutionary perspective of the affective phenomena they are attempting to explain. Lower animals, including inframammalian species, possess rudimentary memory processes, and except for the great apes, show no evidence for representation or recall memory. Yet, separation and stranger distress are universal in these species, signs of depression upon prolonged maternal departure can be seen in animals ranging from goats to monkeys and apes, and positive behaviors corresponding to the attachment to caregivers are observable from early life in these species. Because these phenomena are readily seen along the phylogenetic scale, advanced cognitive competencies like object permanence or recall memory appear unnecessary to account for their emergence in either animals or humans.

Furthermore, each of the three types of theory—Spitzian, Hebbian, asnd neo-Piagetian—has serious intrinsic logical difficulties, as well as a lack of empirical support. For instance, Spitz failed to draw a convincing case for the necessity of recall memory in stranger and separation anxiety. As Fraiberg (1969) argued, failure of recognition is the most advanced cognitive skill possibly needed for these affective reactions. She also pointed out the discrepancy between Spitz and Piaget on the age of onset of representation in infancy. Rather than being present at 6–8 months as Spitz had postulated, recall memory is a capacity that Piaget had shown to develop between 12 and 18 months, a conclusion in agreement with some recent research (cf. Haith & Campos, 1977; Ramsay & Campos, 1978). The frequent argument in favor of a "décalage" producing earlier representation of the mother than of an inanimate object is now known not to be of sufficient magnitude to account for representation at such an early age as Spitz's theory requires (Jackson, Campos, & Fischer, 1978).

Hebb's theory received probably its best—and certainly its earliest— critique from Hebb himself, as we have already noted. However, psychologists persuaded by his earlier views have provided a body of evidence to indicate that Hebb was indeed justifed in his rejection of "incongruity theory." For instance, it now seems clear that incongruous events produce arousal and not necessarily fear (Sroufe et al., 1974), and that novel toys and nonhuman objects produce interest but little aversion (Bronson, 1972).

The approaches stressing object permanence are difficult to criticize because they were never very clearly formulated in the first place. It has never been made clear why the development of stage 4 of object permanence should suddenly result in the capacity to experience fear of strangers, or form an attachment relationship, except that there is an apparent coincidence in age of onset. No argument or empirical evidence had ever been presented to differentiate coincidence from prerequisite. By now, however, a considerable body of evidence has accumulated on the relationship of Piagetian sensorimotor stage assessments and stranger and separation distress. There is widespread agreement that assessments such as those of object permanence are not related to any emotional development (Haith & Campos, 1977; Kagan et al., 1978). As Décarie (1974) states:

Postulating that the appearance of the negative reaction to strangers was related to a new capacity of interpretation of reality, we predicted that in an operational context there would be a close correspondence between the type of reaction to strangers and the Piagetian stages of object concept and causality.

Now, however, in view of the findings of Goulet and Brossard, we can no longer hold to the original hypothesis, and by the same token, must contradict the assertions of the few authors who assumed that a certain stage of object concept or causality concept has been reached when the fear of strangers appears [pp. 188-189].

Décarie, then, in anticipation of the position that we take in this paper, goes on to say: "Nevertheless, we believe that it would be hasty to reject out of hand the hypothesis that the evolution of certain cognitive processes is what precipitates the negative reaction to strangers by making possible a new reading of the immediate environment [p. 189]."

In the remainder of this chapter, we speculate about the cognitive processes that may be involved in affective reactions—not just to strangers but to a much broader class of events. We put these cognitive factors into a phylogenetic perspective that leads us to emphasize both the growing sensitivity of the human infant to perceptual factors closely linked to the elicitation of affect and the development of a readiness to form certain associations. We eventually subsume these phenomena under the rubric of *social referencing*. Furthermore, without denying the importance of memory in accounting for perceptual development, learning, and emotion, we present evidence to indicate that there are more immediate cognitive phenomena than memory or object permanence, which may account for emotional developments.

SENSORIMOTOR FACTORS
IN EMOTIONAL DEVELOPMENT:
THE VISUAL CLIFF AND SOCIAL REACTIONS

Developmental Shift on the Visual Cliff

Research with the visual cliff has yielded data that can be explained parsimoniously by reference to perceptual development, especially that which results from the intercoordination of sensorimotor schemes. It has also demonstrated a close connection between the development of cognitive processes and the type of coping strategy used by the infant when faced with danger. In addition, it suggests that an unsuspected type of learning may be occurring in infancy.

Traditionally, theorists and researchers have construed avoidance of heights as present at birth, or as merely awaiting the maturation of the *locomotor* or *expressive* capacity. Indeed, the typical argument holds that fear of heights is a "natural clue to danger" that has enormous survival value for the species because, by preventing possible lethal injury to the young, it facilitates survival and reproduction. In addition, an impressive body of evidence has been amassed in animals of various species, generally supporting the conception that avoidance of the deep side of the cliff is present from the earliest testing opportunity (Walk, 1978). Hence, many theorists have inferred that human infants are also innately fearful of depth. Yet there is now ample evidence that this inference is in error.

Three sources of evidence support the conclusion of a developmental shift in the fear of heights. The first is maternal report. We have interviewed well over a hundred mothers and, with very few exceptions, they typically report that there is a period during which their infants are not afraid of heights. The mothers describe their infants as readily going over the edge of a bed, off a changing table, down a set of stairs, or off a countertop. Infant clumsiness no doubt accounts for some of these behaviors, as does failure to attend to the drop-off point. However, many mothers deny that clumsiness and lack of attention explain their infants' behaviors and insist that the babies appear to be unconcerned about the consequences of falling. These mothers also report that eventually, generally around 9 months of age, the infants stop such acrobatics and hastily retreat from any height. It should be noted that these observations have been reported before (Freedman, 1974), but they were dismissed as an artifact of insufficient height.

A second line of evidence confirmed the maternal reports, and has argued against the artifact explanation. In a recently reported study (Campos, Hiatt, Ramsay, Henderson, & Svejda, 1978), infants were brought to the laboratory shortly after the onset of locomotion, as assessed by maternal report. These infants were then tested longitudinally every 10 to 14 days on the visual cliff, using a slight variation of the Walk and Gibson (1961) visual-cliff locomotor-crossing paradigm. That is, infants were placed on a center board atop the cliff table and called by their mothers from either the deep or the shallow side, respectively. Two trials were given at each test point on each side of the cliff table. Figure 10.1 presents the data on latency to cross to the mother on each side on the first test day—when infants had minimal locomotor experience— as well as on the second, and final test day. (Infants had varying numbers of test sessions, but all babies had at least three.)

These results indicated a statistically nonsignificant difference in crossing to the mother over the two sides of the cliff on the first test day. More specifically, 10 of the 15 infants tested readily crossed the deep side to their mothers and the other five also did so on the subsequent session. (Why the other five infants did not cross the deep side is the source of speculation in a later section of this chapter.) Thus, consistent with maternal report, the data from the first test session showed that most infants did not avoid heights.

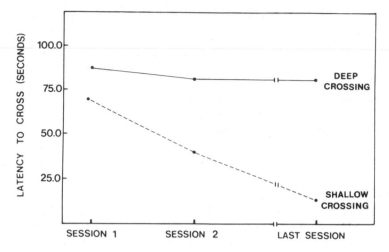

FIG. 10.1.   Mean latencies to cross to the mother over the deep and the shallow sides of the visual cliff. The final test session point for deep-side crossing is an average of a bimodal trend: Six infants failed to cross the deep side altogether and received latency scores of 120 seconds, whereas nine infants crossed to the mother very rapidly over the deep side, but via a "detour."

Furthermore, despite repeated trials confirming that the table was covered by a transparent but solid surface, despite the increasing likelihood of attachment to their mothers and obedience to their commands, and despite (in some cases) the absence of any falling experiences in the interim, the remarkable finding of this study was that six of the infants eventually stopped crossing to the mother altogether on the deep-side trials on the final two test sessions. The other nine infants (including the five who on day 1 refused to cross at all) crossed to the mother on these later sessions using a very curious behavior, which we called "detour" crossing. These infants, who previously had come to their mothers over the deep side on a "beeline," now approached the mother as closely as possible over the shallow side before they ventured onto the glass over the deep side, thus minimizing the distance to cross over the cliff. As this detour behavior was not necessitated by any physical obstacle, we have inferred that the infants were reacting to a psychological obstacle—the emerging fear of heights. Detour crossing seemed to be a compromise in the conflict between obeying the mother and avoiding the deep side.

The third line of evidence demonstrated the importance of intercoordination of the schemes of vision and self-produced lcomotion for the onset of wariness of heights and favored a perceptual and learning explanation, rather than one based on object permanence, memory development, or falling experiences. One study in this series is particularly instructive. This study, also reported in Campos et al. (1978), was designed as a 2 x 2 factorial that crossed self-produced locomotion and its absence with assessments of stage 3 versus stage 4 of object-permanence development as determined by the Uzgiris-Hunt procedure (Uzgiris & Hunt, 1975). We had previously observed that infants frequently appeared to tense up as they were being lowered to the deep of the cliff, but not the shallow side. Because of the well-known relationship between motoric tensing and heart-rate change (Obrist, 1976), and because of our prior work relating heart-rate acceleratory changes to distress in infants (Campos, 1976), we decided to assess the infant's heart rate as he or she was lowered toward the visual-cliff table, that is, prior to contact with the glass. Because infants in this procedure are almost without exception looking downward at the deep or shallow surface they are approaching, heart-rate changes should clearly reflect the infant's visual perception of each side of the cliff.

This study produced dramatic evidence for a cardiac developmental shift as a function of *locomotion,* rather than of sensorimotor stage assessment. As can be seen in Figure 10.2, when approaching the shallow side, infants in all groups showed a mean heart-rate change of +2.0 beats per minute, which is not significantly different from zero. When approaching the deep side, prelocomotor infants showed a slight, nonsignificant deceleration. Locomotor infants, whether assessed in stage 3 of object permanence or beyond, showed a highly significant acceleration of nearly 8 beats per minute as they were lowered to the deep side.

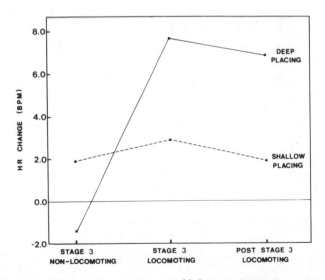

FIG. 10.2.   Mean heart-rate responses of infants as they are lowered to the deep and shallow sides of the visual cliff. Heart rate is assesed prior to contact with the glass surface. Prelocomotor stage 4 infants were very difficult to obtain and hence their data are not presented in the figure.

These findings have recently been replicated in our laboratory by Schmid (1978). Her prelocomotor and locomotor infants were matched for age (7.1 months), but the locomotor infants had 7 days to 10 weeks of locomotor experience. As in the Campos et al. study, Schmid found a (nonsignificant) modest acceleration of heart rate as infants—locomotor or prelocomotor—were being lowered to the shallow side of the cliff. Locomotor infants, on the other hand, showed a marked (over 7 beats per minute) maximum acceleration as they approached the deep side, with the acceleration increasing linearly with each succeeding second of descent. Schmid further reported that infants with a minimal amount of locomotor experience (7–14 days locomoting) showed a median heart rate difference of +2.4 beats per minute between the deep and the shallow sides, whereas those infants with a maximal amount of locomotor experience (8–12 weeks) showed a median difference of +5.6 beats per minute. Furthermore, as in the earlier study, assessment of the infants with the Uzgiris-Hunt scales of object permanence produced no relationship between object-permanence level and visual-cliff reaction. Experiences with falls also failed to differentiate cardiac reactions to the deep side of the cliff.

The Role of Perception, Cognition, and Emotion on the Onset of Fear of Heights

This line of research implies that the wrong aspects of Piagetian theory may have been emphasized in previous attempts to relate sensorimotor developments to the ontogeny of emotion and that appraisal may play a more significant role in emotions in the first year of life than previously suspected. More specifically, object permanence does not seem to account for the developmental shift on the visual cliff. However, there are several other sensorimotor accomplishments that may be related to the onset of wariness of heights and that may prove to have more general explanatory value. Three such sensorimotor developments are suggested by the work just reviewed: (1) the perceptual developments resulting from the intercoordination of sensorimotor schemes; (2) the possibility that the infant acquires an avoidance of heights through vicarious learning—that is, through having noticed in the past the *emotional reactions* of another to situations like the one the infant is currently facing; (3) the development of detour behavior as a coping strategy based on sensorimotor cognitive skills.

The intercoordination of vision with self-produced motoric activity must result in important perceptual consequences, specifically, the calibration of the absolute distance of an object or surface from the perceiver. As several reviewers have noted (Bower, 1974; Gogel, 1977; Kaufman, 1974), the traditional primary sources of visual information about depth, such as binocular disparity and monocular parallax, provide only relative depth information. For instance, binocular disparity can specify whether an object is closer or farther than the point of fixation, but it cannot specify—without additional, nonvisual information—how far away the point of fixation is, or how far from the fixation point other objects are. A similar consideration applies to monocular parallax. Although convergence can, in principle, provide an absolute scale of depth, it requires information about interocular distance. Inasmuch as that distance changes with growth, even an innate knowledge of that parameter would require updating and recalibration as the infant's head grows larger. Hence, the prelocomotor infant may have depth information available, such as stereopsis (as Aslin, Shea, Dumais, & Fox, 1979 demonstrated with 4- to 6-month-olds), yet lack knowledge of the absolute distance of a surface in space. It seems plausible that the intercoordination of vision with self-produced locomotion may provide such a calibration of visual information, resulting in more precise appraisal of the distance of an object from the observer. Indeed, this seems to be at the heart of Piaget's theory of spatial cognition in the sensorimotor period. It also accounts for his otherwise puzzling postulation of a distinction between near and far space. Near space is the space calibrated by reach; far space is that calibrated by self-produced crawling (see Piaget, 1954). These considerations further imply that negative reactions to looming stimuli (e.g., Cicchetti & Sroufe, 1978; Yonas, Bechtold, Frankel, Gordon, McRoberts, Norcia, & Sternfels, 1977) would occur earlier than those to the visual cliff because looming stimuli necessarily intrude into "near space."

What relates these theoretical conceptions about levels of processing of depth information to the previous studies on the developmental shift on the visual cliff is that the typical infant is showing the shift only after the intercoordination of two complex schemes—vision and self-produced crawling. To the extent that intercoordination facilitates the calibration of distances, it may be that the immediate outcome of the calibration is a realization that the surface at the bottom of a drop-off point is very far away. Such a perceptual appraisal might then result in the spontaneous elicitation of fear. This is a somewhat different conception of the role of releaser stimuli in the triggering of affective reactions than ethological theories usually propose. Ethological speculations generally postulate *innate* sensitivity and not sensitivity resulting from perceptual development. However, the process of perceptual differentiation followed by the apparently immediate triggering of affect is not unknown in the field of infant emotion and may be what is taking place in the development of the social smile to the "face gestalt." Indeed, Spitz comes close at times to adopting just such a theory (see Spitz, 1965).

However, there may be an alternative mechanism for the emergence of wariness of heights that involves vicarious learning. Walk (1966), Schmid (1978), and Campos et al. (1978) have presented data suggesting that discrete learning experiences such as falls may not be necessary to produce fear of heights. However, Piaget (1952) specifies a new cognitive acquisition—prevision—at stage 4 of sensorimotor development. It involves the emergence of the capacity to use one environmental event to serve as a signal for the occurrence of another environmental event. In brief, the child becomes capable of higher-order conditioning. With respect to heights, such higher-order conditioning may come about when infants begin to note the contingency between their approach to an edge and their mothers' facial, vocal, and gestural reactions cautioning the infants that there is danger ahead. To the extent that such observational or vicarious learning is possible *before* the intercoordination of vision with locomotion, one should expect to find some infants showing evidence of wariness of heights either prior to or simultaneous with the onset of self-produced locomotion, as we have found in some of our studies. Specifically, a drop-off point in near space can come to signal an expectation of a negative maternal reaction, and avoidance may then ensue even when falls do not occur. This analysis suggests the emergence of heretofore undiscussed appraisal capabilities in the human infant and puts the role of specific learning in affective reactions into a rather different light: Vicarious learning, which has never been seriously considered as a factor in the ontogeny of emotion, may provide the infant with a capacity to use the appraisals of socially significant others to guide his or her emotional reactions to environmental events.

The emergence of the capacity for detour behavior on the visual cliff highlights the importance of still another appraisal capacity that has not been systematically considered in theories of cognition-emotion relationships in infancy. One aspect of the appraisal process, perhaps most clearly articulated by Lazarus (1968), concerns the role of coping processes in appraisal. For Lazarus, appraisal may include the choice of alternative responses to a danger. The visual-cliff study demonstrated that infants can react in multiple ways to the danger of height. The cognitive prerequisite for one such alternative—detour behavior—is generally not available to the human infant before stage 5 of sensorimotor development, when one of the criteria of the group concept, which Piaget calls associativity (see Piaget, 1960, 1970), is first demonstrated. Associativity is evident when the infant can use multiple means to the same end; detour behavior is a clear instance. A striking aspect of the stage 4 infant's behavior, such as the 8-month olds in Bruner's (1970) task that required detour reaching around a transparent barrier preventing the grasp of a desired toy, is the persistence of direct approaches to the goal, followed by giving up. At a later age, the infant fortuitously discovers the tactic of circumventing the transparent barrier. On the visual cliff, similarly, we see the emergence of detour behavior—to a psychological obstacle—after a period of direct, beeline approach to the mother. The development of detour crossing over the deep side of the cliff to the mother, in some cases including the use of the sides of the cliff to hold onto and to "hitch" along to get to mother, clearly demonstrates the close connection between the emergence of cognitive competencies (the associativity criterion in this case) and coping strategies.

Perceptual Factors in Stranger Distress

We previously noted that the wrong aspects of cognitive development—object permanence and recall memory—had been emphasized in attempts to explain another major affective phenomenon: the onset and intensity of negative reactions to strangers. There is little doubt that stranger distress is a multidetermined phenomenon (Sroufe, 1977). However, recent research suggests that the consideration of the perceptual processes involved in reactions to strangers may organize parsimoniously what appear to be disparate experimental results.

A major source of evidence for the importance of perceptual factors in the elicitation of stranger distress is the study by Brooks and Lewis (1976). They contrasted the reactions of infants between 7 and 24 months of age to an adult female, a female midget of the same age as the adult, and a male and female child of approximately the same height as the midget. Brooks and Lewis reasoned that, in terms of predictions from discrepancy theory, all four strangers—adults or child, tall or short—were equally unfamiliar and hence should elicit similar patterns of negative responding. However, if something about physical size and height were important, then negative reactions should be directed predominantly to the adult female, and little to the midget and two children. Finally, they argued that if facial configuration was a significant variable, then the reactions of the infants to the midget and the two children should differ, with more negative reactions to the midget and more positive reactions to the children.

The results did not support any of the major theories that have been reviewed—Hebbian, Spitzian, or neo-Piagetian—and were especially damaging to incongruity theory. Height and facial configuration were found to be independent contributors to the quality and intensity of affect. Much more gaze aversion was observed during the approach of the adult female than during the approach of any of the other three strangers. The female child, in fact, elicited no gaze aversion whatsoever. Although visual attention was very high to the approach of all strangers, every infant was observed to look continuously at the midget during the closest approach phase of the study. Because children and the midget seemed to elicit similarly low rates of gaze aversion, the role of size seemed to be of particular importance in stranger reactions (Brooks & Lewis, 1976).

The importance of facial configuration was suggested by the finding that the infants smiled much more to the two child strangers than to the two adults, who elicited similarly low rates of smiling. Brooks and Lewis speculated on the possible influence of the elicitation of positive affect by something analogous to the "babyness gestalt." Lorenz in 1943 (cited in Eibl-Eibesfeldt, 1970) proposed the existence of an innate releaser of affiliative and affectionate reactions consisting of a pattern of: (1) large head in relation to body size; (2) large, protruding forehead in relation to the rest of the face; (3) large eyes below the midline of the head; (4) round, protruding cheeks. Although 5-year-old children do not possess all of these features, enough may be evident to trigger positive reactions in the infant subjects.

One more perceptual feature—the proximity of the stranger to the infant—proved important in this study. There was a dramatic increase in both gaze aversion and frowning at close distances—when the stranger was 3 feet from the infant or touching the infant's hand. A similar pattern has been observed in other studies (see Sroufe, 1977). For instance, Campos, Emde, Gaensbauer, and Henderson (1975) studied cardiac and behavioral responses of infants at 5 and 9 months of age to the approach of a stranger. When the stranger was 4 meters from the infant and the mother was present in the room, only 2 infants were rated as distressed, and cardiac reactions were predominantly deceleratory. However, when the stranger was within .1 meter of the infant, 9 of the 20 infants were rated as distressed, and cardiac reactions were frequently acceleratory. Behavioral reactions of 5-month olds showed no such trend: Global distress reactions were equally unlikely to be observed when the stranger was either at a distance or near. A very similar pattern of findings has been reported by Skarin (1977).

The similarity of these findings on stranger proximity takes on theoretical significance because of their relationship to adult research on personal space. One principle emerging from such research (Harper, Wiens, & Matarazzo, 1978) is that the intrusion of a nonintimate individual into one's zone of surrounding proximity is likely to lead to feelings of discomfort and upset even in adults. This suggests that the infant's growing structuring of space— not only between objects, but also between him- or herself and others— combines with the establishment of an attachment relationship in contributing to negative reactions to strangers.

Vertical space is also an important perceptual parameter of negative reactions to strangers. In previous reports, Greenberg, Hillman, and Grice (1973) and Brooks and Lewis (1976) noted that male strangers sometimes elicited more negative reactions than female strangers did. They speculated on the possibility that it was not the stranger's gender, but the greater height of the male that would make them more aversive. Recently, Weinraub and Putney (1978) investigated the separate influences of absolute and relative height on stranger distress in 11-month-old infants. Absolute height was manipulated by having tall (6 feet, 2 inches) or short (5 feet, 6 inches) male strangers serve as experimenters. Relative height was manipulated by having the infants placed on platforms that created three viewing heights: low (infants' eyes 35 inches from the floor), medium (50 inches from the floor), and high (eyes 72 inches from the floor).

The absolute height of the strangers did not play a significant role in negative reactions. Both short and tall strangers elicited similar reactions within each viewing height. However, relative height was found to be very important: Infants in the high viewing condition were reported to be less likely to avert gaze or move away from the stranger, and more likely to concentrate on the stranger. They also tended to fuss less in the high viewing condition than in the low. Weinraub and Putney (1978) concluded:

> What accounts for infants' greater negative responding in the low and medium conditions than in the high condition? We believe that one factor which may contribute to whether unfamiliar persons are responded to positively or negatively is whether or not the strangers "tower" over the infant. The results of this study suggest that this effect may be dichotomous rather than continuous. The absence of differences between infants' responses in the medium and low viewing conditions and the absence of differential responding to tall and short stimulus persons suggest that, at least within the conditions tested, greater towering may not lead to stronger negative responsiveness [p. 601].

The Possibility of Maturationally Determined Perceptual Sensitivity

Perceptual factors are significant not only in processing the physical distance of strangers, but in the detection of biologically and socially significant information in the environment. Evidence for this proposition comes from studies of socially isolated infrahuman primates.

For instance, Sackett (1966) showed an emerging affective sensitivity to both positive and negative stimuli in the absence of social stimulation. Sackett reared eight rhesus monkeys from birth to 9 months of age in individual cages. Five sides of the cages were covered by opaque panels, and the sixth side was covered by a ground-glass rear projection screen. Except for a brief period of hand feeding, which ended at 5 to 9 days of age, these monkeys were exposed to no social stimulation from either monkeys or humans. Each week, the experimenter presented every infant with slides that in some cases were contingent with lever pressing and in other cases were noncontingent. The content of the slides varied. Some showed monkeys in various postures such as threat, play, fear, withdrawal, exploration, or sexual activity. Other slides showed infant monkeys, mother and infants, or adult monkeys who were "doing nothing." A set of control slides contained pictures of objects other than monkeys.

The results of this study supported the hypothesis of a maturationally determined sensitivity to visual configurations. The content of some of the slides was found to elicit negative affect, and the content of other slides was found to elicit positive affect. Specifically, Sackett found that beginning at 2½ months of age, noncontingent pictures of monkeys in threat posture elicited considerable fear in the infants, as evident in withdrawal, rocking, and huddling behavior. Vocalizations also increased sharply at this age. A sharp drop in the operant rate of lever pressing when the threat slide was the reinforcer further suggested that threat slides were aversive. The only observation contrary to the conclusion that the sight of threat-display slides elicited negative affect was a sharp simultaneous increase in frequency of play—a finding for which Sackett had no interpretation, but which could have reflected a confusion by raters of fearful activity and playful activity. Fearful behavior to this slide declined with age and with repeated presentations.

On the other hand, slides of infant monkeys elicited positive affect in the isolate-reared monkeys. Not only was lever-touching behavior highest when infant slides were the reinforcers, but play activity, exploration, and climbing were also high when infant slides were presented. As Sackett (1966) noted:

> These data lead to several important conclusions. First, at least two kinds of socially meaningful visual stimuli, pictures of monkeys threatening, and pictures of infants, appear to have unlearned, prepotent, activating properties for socially naive infant monkeys. From the second month of life these stimuli produced generally higher levels of all behaviors in all subjects. Second, the visual stimulation involved in threat behavior appears to function as an "innate releasing stimulus" for fearful behavior. This innate mechanism appears maturational in nature. Thus, at 60 to 90 days, threat pictures release disturbance behavior, although they fail to do so before this age. These fear responses waned about 110 days after birth. This could be due to habituation, occurring because no consequences follow the fear behavior released by threat pictures—consequences that would certainly appear in a situation with a real threatening monkey.
>
> One important implication of these results concerns the ontogeny of responses to complex social communication in primates. These data suggest that at least certain aspects of such communication may lie in innate recognition mechanisms, rather than in acquisition through social learning processes during interactions with other animals [p. 1473].

A recent study by Kenney, Mason, and Hill (1979) provides further support for the hypothesis of a close linkage between age and visually elicited emotionality in isolate-reared monkeys. It also supports the notion that experience can facilitate the process of affective sensitivity to which Sackett alluded. In the Kenney et al. study there were three groups of monkeys. An enclosed group (N = 6) was housed in individual cages with four opaque walls. A visual group (N = 10) had cages with clear plastic front panels, which allowed the animals to see human caretakers and other monkeys similarly housed. A neighbor group (N = 10) had cages adjoining that of another monkey, the two cages being separated by a transparent plastic wall, which allowed a monkey to see its age mate and the interior of the adjacent cage.

The study showed that even in the enclosed group, infant monkeys reacted with affiliative behavior (lip smacking) to their reflections in a mirror, but with fear or distress responses (grimacing) and almost no lip smacking to a human face maintaining eye-to-eye contact with the monkey. As in Sackett's study, age was a factor. The negative reactions were first evident at 35 days of age in the enclosed group and increased in frequency until the end of the study. Visual experience also played a role, with negative reactions to the human occurring earlier, and more frequently, in the visual group than in the enclosed. Kenney et al. (1979) concluded that there are "inherent differences in the potency of visual configurations as sources of affective responses in primates [p. 182]."

PERCEPTION, COGNITION
AND APPRAISAL IN INFANCY:
THE CONCEPT OF SOCIAL REFERENCING

Recent studies thus highlight three processes that appear to be important in the development of emotion in the first year of life: perceptual development, socially significant releasers of positive or negative affect in the infant, and cognitive prerequisites for learning and coping. We now argue that these processes play a very important and a very general role in emotional development in the first year of life by making possible an appraisal process that has not been adequately considered in the field of infant emotion. We call this process *social referencing,* and postulate that there are six aspects to its development:

1. There are major changes taking place in the perception of patterned visual information between 5 and 9 months of age. These perceptual changes foster the detection of affective information previously unavailable to the human infant.
2. There are patterns of facial, vocal, and gestural behaviors that directly elicit discrete emotions in the infant.
3. The detection of this patterned information follows a developmental sequence between 5 and 9 months of age.
4. The mother becomes the target of social referencing. Through facial, vocal, and gestural patterning, she expresses her affective appraisal of events, some of which may otherwise exceed the infant's cognitive capacity to appraise.
5. Social referencing makes possible the vicarious learning of either approach or avoidance of environmental situations.

6. After the mother has become a crucial evaluation resource, her inaccessibility may be perceived by the infant as a frustration and becomes manifest in negative reactions.

We would like to evaluate each of these postulates in turn.

Postulate 1.   There Are Developmental Changes in Form-Perception Capacities in the Human Infant that Eventually Enable the Infant to Detect Affectively Significant Information.   There is little doubt that a major change in the form-perception capabilities of the human infant takes place between the ages of 4 and 9 months. This developmental change is characterized by a dramatic improvement in whole-form perception and in the extraction of invariances from sensory displays. This conclusion contrasts markedly with the view that emerged in the mid-1960s, when two separate lines of evidence suggested rather emphatically that the neonate or very young infant possessed quite sophisticated form perception abilities. It now appears that these abilities emerge much later. For instance, the early studies by Fantz (1961) with neonates concluded that the newborn's discrimination of a patterned visual display from an unpatterned one, or of a face stimulus from something else, indicated that infants were capable of perceiving whole forms or visual gestalts shortly after birth. A few years later, Bower (1964, 1965, 1966) presented striking evidence that 2-month olds could perceive size and shape constancy. Unfortunately, further studies showed both lines of evidence to be seriously flawed. Some recent studies, for instance, have failed to confirm the conclusion that 2-month olds have size constancy (McKenzie & Day, 1972) or shape constancy (Caron, Caron, & Carlson, 1978), although some positive evidence on the latter has recently been reported (Caron, Caron, & Carlson, 1979; Caron, Caron, Carlson, & Cobb, 1979). Fantz's conclusions were challenged on different grounds. Critics argued that the neonate's apparent discrimination was mediated not by whole-form perception, but by some simpler capability. For instance, Cohen, DeLoache, and Strauss (1979) presented compelling evidence that the basis for neonatal discrimination of faces from nonfaces, or of patterned from unpatterned stimulation, lay in the complexity of the stimulus, as reflected in contour density (see Bond, 1972).

Studies of infant scanning, such as those of Haith (in press) or Salapatek (1975), further documented that neonates are attracted to simple features of a stimulus display—such as edges, slits, or bars—and not to whole forms. When infants were presented with faces to scan, neonates and infants up to 8 weeks of age scanned the exterior of the face and generally ignored any interior detail. Given the limited peripheral vision of the infant, it was not likely that infants before 2 months of age were perceiving the whole face. But by 2 months, infants began to scan the internal features of the face, such as the eyes. However, whole-form perception continued to be dubious because of the tendency to ignore the mouth region.

In fact, it is not until about 5 months of age that infants may begin to note and detect the region of the mouth in face stimuli and to respond to the face "as a whole." This conclusion is best supported in a study by Caron, Caron, Caldwell, and Weiss (1973), a heroic investigation involving hundreds of infants studied with a habituation–dishabituation paradigm in order to determine what features of the face were discriminated at 4 and 5 months of age. Although seriously limited in generalizability because of its use of schematized, two-dimensional face stimuli, the study nevertheless provided evidence for the following conclusions:

1. At 4 months of age, the nose-mouth region of the face was not very salient. Whether the nose-mouth region was totally absent, horizontally displaced, scrambled, or inverted, infants failed to differentiate this condition from a standard, control face. By contrast, any change in the eye region caused significant discrimination from the normal, control face. Hence, Caron et al. concluded that at four months the eyes were more salient than the nose-mouth region.

2. The property of "faceness"—the invariant configuration of eyes, nose, and mouth—is not yet perceptually organized at 4 months of age, because major distortions of the nose-mouth region or inversion of the features of the interior of the face were not yet discriminable.

3. By 5 months of age, three major perceptual developments had taken place: The distortions of the mouth region were now clearly discriminated, infants became sensitive to inversions of the interior features of the face, and the emergence of the "face configuration" was inferred from the infants' ability to detect changes in features that heretofore had not been discriminated.

This study, then, provides one important source of evidence for the conclusion that facial communication patterns, especially those involving the mouth region, become increasingly available to the infant following 5 months of age, and that the use of patterned visual information involving the whole face is not likely to occur before 5 months.

Further perceptual changes are taking place after 5 months of age. Ten years ago, Gibson speculated that between 6 and 7 months of age the infant would be able to perceive unique faces for the first time, and by 7 months would isolate invariant expressions of the face (Gibson, 1969). A recent study by Cohen and Strauss (1979) further demonstrated the development of perceptual capabilities in 5- to 7-month-old infants. In this study, 18-, 24-, and 30-week-old infants were assigned to several conditions, one of which involved the repeated presentation fo the same female face having a different orientation and facial expression on each trial. After habituation had taken place, the infants were then presented with a novel face in a novel orientation, or the familiar face in the novel orientation. Only the 7-month-olds could extract invariant aspects of the face from different orientations; they generalized their habituated responses more to the previously seen face in the novel orientation than to the new face. By contrast, younger infants responded similarly to the familiar face and to the novel one. A similar result with 7-month-olds had been reported previously by Fagan (1976).

Two other research projects suggest a major improvement in the capability of infants to extract configurational information from their environments after 6 months of age. Ruff (1978) investigated the detection of form invariance in displays that differed in three irrelevant dimensions. Infants were shown the same configuration for six trials, but on each trial it differed in its size, colors, and orientation. On two subsequent test trials, the infants' task was to discriminate a totally novel form from the previously familiarized one. Both forms were presented in sizes, color, and orientations not shown previously. Ruff reported that 9-month-olds consistently responded to the novel form. Six-month olds, on the other hand, failed the task, responding equally to novel forms and novel instances of a familiar form.

The other line of research explored developmental changes in sensitivity to the subjective contour illusion, an example of which is given in Figure 10.3. Subjective contour stimuli have long been used to study adult visual organization and form perception because a phenomenally vivid shape is evident that has no physical basis for most of its perimeter, and hence must reflect the cerebral organization of stimulus input. In the study of infant form perception, subjective contour stimuli are useful because they allow the researcher to disentangle the effects of discrimination based on whole-form perception from a discrimination based on simpler features. Thus, the same four elements of figure 10.3 can be organized either to produce an illusion, or

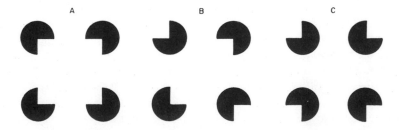

FIG. 10.3. Examples of stimuli that result in the perception of subjective contours (a), or which do not (b and c). Dishabituation of infants from (b) to (c) does not produce response recovery in 5- or 7-month-olds. Dishabituation involving the subjective contour stimulus (a) produces highly significant response recovery.

not to do so. If one finds that a change from nonillusion to illusion (or the reverse) is discriminated more than a change from one nonillusion to another, one can infer that the basis for the extra discrimination is produced by the detection of the illusion, and hence that whole-form perception is present in the infant. Using this rationale, Bertenthal, Campos, and Haith (in press) reported that 7-month-olds consistently discriminated arrays producing the illusion from arrays that did not. Five-month-olds, on the other hand, did not make the discrimination consistently. Seven-month-olds thus provided clear evidence for whole-form perceptual organization in this study.

Thus, between 5 and 9 months of age, the infant's ability to organize visual information changes dramatically. In particular, major advances in face perception—characterized by the ability to respond for the first time to the face as a whole, and to the face in varying orientations and contexts—are evident. Other studies suggest dramatic improvement in the ability of infants to extract perceptual invariance from their visual fields.

Postulate 2.   Facial, Vocal, and Gestural Information Specify Affect.   Recent theories and research suggest that there may be a process of *psychophysical correspondence* whereby higher-order invariants of visual stimulation, as well as of auditory stimulation, directly specify discrete affect to a perceiver, whether an adult or an infant. By psychophysical correspondence we mean that there is a one-to-one relationship between the pattern of stimulation in the environment and the perception of emotion by an observer, in a manner very similar to what Gibson (1950) described as the psychophysical correspondence between invariants such as texture gradients and the perception of surfaces oriented in depth. These psychophysical correspondences need not be innate. Maturation and perceptual learning facilitate their detection, but once detection occurs, the experience results directly. Certain facial expressions constitute one example of a fairly well-described visual-affect specifier, whereas some types of paralinguistic (vocalic) phenomena constitute another.

During the past 10 years, there has been an upsurge of interest in the relationship between the experience of emotion by a subject and the expression of emotion information in the face. For decades prior to the 1960s, psychologists had believed that, at best, facial expressions reflected either the general level of arousal or the hedonic tone of the individual. However, the theorizing by Tomkins (1962) and the empirical work of Ekman (1971) and Izard (1971) suggested that the human face expressed more than general dimensions of emotion. Rather it expressed discrete emotions. For example, when a subject experiences sadness, a particular pattern of facial components is observable, and the pattern is different from that when surprise, fear, or happiness is being experienced. Furthermore, it appeared that such response patterns may be universal, and thus probably innate, because they were observed in both Eastern and Western cultures (Izard, 1971) as well as in nonliterate cultures (Ekman, Sorenson, & Friesen, 1969).

Ekman's and Izard's work has received some criticism for its heavy reliance on the use of actor-posed peak facial expression, which may have no relationship to the real expressions of individuals experiencing real emotions. Furthermore, the emphasis on maximal expressions left open the question about the similarity of patterning of less intense emotions of the same kind. However, recent studies with human infants have utilized eliciting circumstances designed to produce moderate degrees of several discrete emotions in infants too young to be likely to have learned cultural display rules for emotional reactions. These studies have provided strong evidence for the predicted patterning of facial-response information for the emotions of happiness, surprise, and anger, and to a much lesser extent, fear (Hiatt, Campos, & Emde, 1979; Stenberg, Campos, & Emde, in preparation). At least for these discrete emotions, then, as well as for emotions related to the pain experience recently studied in infants by Izard (Izard, Huebner, Rissner, McGinnes, & Dougherty, 1980), the facial-response patterns specified by Ekman and Izard appear to be correct in broad outline.

However, facial expressions are more than responses. Many theoreticians have conceptualized these expressions as patterned visual *stimuli* with innate communicative value to conspecifics (e.g., Darwin, 1872; Ekman, Friesen, & Ellsworth, 1972). When detected by others, facial expressions elicit affect (e.g., happiness upon seeing a smile; distress upon seeing an anger face), and they specify the action consequences to be expected (Camras, 1978).

These ideas have not gone unchallenged: For decades, critics have maintained that information about emotion is specified by the observer's knowledge of the eliciting circumstances, and not by the facial expressions. But, this challenge seems unfounded in light of recent evidence that stimulus-context-free facial response components do, in fact, communicate affect. In the study by Hiatt, Campos, and Emde (1979), six eliciting circumstances were used to obtain naturalistic facial responses of infant subjects in emotional settings. Two circumstances were designed to elicit happiness, two to elicit surprise, and two to elicit fear. A set of judges then scored 28 facial-response components, which had been identified on the basis of the descriptions and photographs supplied by Ekman and Friesen in *Unmasking the Face* (1975). Examples of response components included "raised, curved, high eyebrows," "brows are lowered and drawn together," "corners of the lips are down or the lip is trembling." Each of the 28 components was theoretically linked to one, or at most two, discrete emotions. For example, the first component just described is linked to surprise, the second to anger, and so on.

Three judges rated the *presence* or *absence* of each component in a videotaped segment lasting 5 or 10 seconds (depending on condition) that contained no information about eliciting circumstances. A different set of judges looked at the same videotaped segment but with a different task: They judged on nine-point scales their confidence that each of six fundamental emotions (sadness, surprise, anger, disgust, fear, happiness) plus a neutral state was being expressed. Then, two separate sets of analyses were performed to determine whether components of facial behavior are related to observer's judgments of emotion, in the absence of contextual information. The first analysis correlated the number of observed facial-expression components that should be involved in that emotion and the confidence rating that such an emotion had in fact occurred. The results showed that, with one exception (in which a restricted range kept down the magnitude of the correlation coefficient), the more components of an emotion expression that were detected by one set of judges, the greater was another set of judges' confidence that that emotion was being expressed (range of r's = +.40 to +.54).

The second analysis tested whether the presence of a given facial component determined which of six emotions was being perceived by a judge. For example, lowering and drawing the brows together is a component of anger, according to Ekman's theory. When observed in a subject's face, it should tend to produce judgments of "anger" by raters. The results suggested that discrete affective information was, in fact, conveyed by single response components. Forty-one percent of the components that were observed a sufficient number of times to allow statistical analyses were significantly related to judgments that the infant was showing the emotion linked theoretically to that component. Only seven components were significantly related to other, unpredicted, emotions. These analyses thus confirm that information in the face specifies affect to a perceiver.

There is also growing evidence that patterned information in the *voice* can similarly specify affective information. Although the stimulus dimensions that enter into the specification of emotion information have not been as carefully delineated for the voice as they have for the face, Scherer (1974) has made an attempt to describe how various acoustical dimensions may differ in different emotional situations. These dimensions are described in Table 10.1. From the information in the table, it can be seen that anger, for instance, can be differentiated from other negative emotions on the basis of ascending pitch contour, moderate pitch variation, high pitch level, extreme lack of overtones, and minor tonality of vocal expressions. Although fear expressions share many of the same dimensions as anger expressions, fear expressions show amplitude variations and rhythmicity in the voice not evident in anger.

A number of recent studies have attempted to verify that the voice alone, independent of semantic content, may convey emotional information (Davitz, 1964). For example, Davitz and Davitz (1959) asked subjects to read letters of the alphabet imagining that they were in one of 10 emotional states, ranging from simple emotions such as anger and fear to complex emotions

TABLE 10.1
Concomitants of Acoustical Dimensions

AMPLITUDE	Moderate	Pleasantness, Activity, Happiness
VARIATION	Extreme	Fear
PITCH VARIATION	Moderate	Anger, Boredom, Disgust, Fear
	Extreme	Pleasantness, Activity, Happiness, Surprise
PITCH CONTOUR	Down	Pleasantness, Boredom, Sadness
	Up	Potency, Anger, Fear, Surprise,
PITCH LEVEL	Low	Pleasantness, Boredom, Sadness
	High	Activity, Potency, Anger, Fear, Surprise
TEMPO	Slow	Boredom, Disgust, Sadness
	Fast	Pleasantness, Activity, Potency, Anger, Fear, Happiness, Surprise
DURATION (SHAPE)	Round	Potency, Boredom, Disgust, Fear, Sadness
	Sharp	Pleasantness, Activity, Happiness, Surprise
FILTRATION (LACK OF OVERTONES)	Low	Sadness Pleasantness, Boredom, Happiness
	Moderate	Potency, Activity
	Extreme	Anger, Disgust, Fear, Surprise
	Atonal	Disgust
TONALITY	Tonal-Minor	Anger
	Tonal-Major	Pleasantness, Happiness
RHYTHM	Not Rhythmic	Boredom
	Rhythmic	Activity, Fear, Surprise

Table reproduced from Scherer (1974).

such as pride and sympathy. All emotions were judged accurately by a group of 30 raters listening to tapes of the emotional reading of the letters of the alphabet. The results were quite impressive: Every one of the 10 emotions being acted was judged with accuracy far greater accuracy than chance. Happiness, sadness, "nervousness," and anger were particularly likely to be detected correctly.

Using a totally different procedure, Scherer (1974) also found agreement among judges in the attribution of emotion to abstract acoustical patterns generated by a Moog synthesizer. The synthesizer was used to manipulate five acoustic parameters independently: pitch variation, amplitude variation, pitch level, amplitude level, and tempo. Each level of these dimensions was crossed with every level of other dimensions to create acoustical patterns that were then presented to raters, whose task was to code whether each of the 64 resulting stimulus samples expressed interest, sadness, fear, happiness, disgust, anger, surprise, elation, or boredom. In addition, judges rated 10-point scales of pleasantness, evaluation, activity, and potency. Results showed a significant degree of agreement among raters in their emotion judgments, especially for the dimensions of tempo and pitch variations. Extreme pitch variations led to ratings of highly pleasant, active, and potent emotions such as happiness, interest, and surprise. Fast tempo led to attributions of high activity and potency, as in the emotions of interest, fear, happiness, anger, and surprise.

Thus, both the face and voice provide patterned stimulus information for the elicitation and/or communication of affect in adults. There may be other sources of patterned stimulus information that also directly specify affect. Gestures, tempo of movement, and patterns of eye contact are among the social signals that deserve further research. In the next section, we review the evidence that infants are sensitive to these sources of affective information.

Postulate 3. There Are Developmental Trends Toward Increasing Sensitivity to Affective Information, and Increasing Use in the Regulation of Behavior.   In a recent review of the literature on this issue, Klinnert (1978) has documented three levels in the reactions of human infants to facial-affective information. At the most basic stage (birth to 3 months), there is consistent failure to find evidence of differential reaction to facial expressions. For instance, Spitz and Wolf (1946) reported that infants were just as likely to smile to a friendly face as to an angry one at these ages.

At the second stage, infants begin to show sensitivity to some aspects of facial expressions and can *discriminate* some expressions from others. However, the research on facial discrimination does not make clear that the facial *affect* is being identified, because discriminations between one facial expression and another can be made on the basis of numerous nonaffective features (e.g., greater contour density of some expressions than others). However, between 3 and 7 months, several studies have provided evidence of discrimination of surprise from sadness and happiness (Young-Browne, Rosenfeld, & Horowitz, 1977), of joy from anger and neutral expressions (LaBarbera, Izard, Vietze, & Parisi, 1976), and of fear from happiness (Nelson, Morse, & Leavitt, 1979). (Interestingly, Young-Browne et al., 1977 did not find that 3-month olds could discriminate joy from sadness. These two emotions are usually quite easily discriminated by adults. However, if 3-month-olds are indeed generally inattentive to the region of the mouth, as mentioned earlier, such a finding might be explainable as a result of failure to notice the difference between the smile of joy and the downturned lips of sadness.)

At the third stage, there is evidence that infants not only discriminate facial expressions, but react in different emotional ways to different facial expressions. For example, Kreutzer and Charlsworth (1973) tested infants between 4 and 10 months of age by exposing them to a model acting out angry, happy, sad, or neutral facial and vocal displays. Four-month olds reacted indiscriminately to the four posed expressions. However, 6-month and older infants responded with more negative emotion to the angry and sad conditions than to the happy and neutral ones. Earlier, Bühler and Hetzer (1928; cited in Kreutzer & Charlesworth, 1973) compared infants' reactions to a positive face, a negative face, to positive and negative voices, and to threatening and affectionate arm gestures. By the fifth month, infants were reportedly capable of acting "appropriately" to angry facial expressions, and by 7 months, 100% of the infants' responses to the angry face were said to be negative. Bühler (1930) subsequently designed a developmental scale with norms demonstrating that at 5 months infants responded with the appropriate affect to combinations of facial and vocal affective cues; at 6 months they responded to vocal affective cues without accompanying facial expressions; at 7 months they respond to facial expressions without vocalizations; and at 9 months they responded to threatening versus friendly gestural information. In the development of this scale, care was taken to rule out imitative responses by the infant. The child had to demonstrate the affective impact of the modeled expressions through a different response than the modeled ones.

This developmental sequence then points to the age period of 5 to 9 months as the time when affective information in social settings is first recognized by the human infant. It is not clear whether humans learn the process of affect communication by way of social interactions, or whether it emerges in the course of maturation. The previously cited studies of isolate-reared monkeys and the adaptive value of these expressions would seem to argue, at the very least, for biologically-prepared learning of these communication patterns. For the present, however, we merely take as a given the psychophysical correspondence between stimulus pattern and elicited affect to which we alluded earlier, and a development of the capacity to *notice* these arrays in the environment.

Postulate 4.   The Mother Becomes the Target for Social Referencing. There are two sources of evidence suggesting that in the course of development the infant begins to seek facial, vocal, and gestural affect-specifying messages from the mother and other socially significant individuals. One source is an intriguing study by Carr, Dabbs, and Carr (1975), which challenged the widespread belief that it is the physical presence of the mother in an unfamiliar setting that helps to provide the child with a "secure base for exploration." This study showed that 2-year-old infants needed to be within "eyeshot" of the mother, even at the risk of abandoning the exploration of interesting environmental objects.

The study compared the behavior of infants when the mother was in one of three positions: visible in the room and facing the child, visible in the room but turned away from the child, or present in the room but not visible behind a partition. The children were free to move about the room, but an attractive set of toys was located in a corner diagonally opposite the mother's chair. For our purposes, the most significant finding was that infants tended to orient themselves so that they would be in the mother's visual field. When the mother was out of sight, the infants went behind the partition and positioned themselves within mother's view over 45% of the time. When the mother was present but facing away, they did likewise, spending 50% of the time in her visual field. Finally, in the facing-toward condition, the infants stayed in the mother's visual field almost 100% of the time, presumably because of the joint influence of the mother's facial orientation and the attractiveness of the toys.

Why should the mother, present but turned away, be no more satisfying than her visual absence? And why should infants find it so important to stay within their mothers' visual field? Our answer is that infants placed in an unfamiliar setting have heightened needs to evaluate the situation, and staying within their mothers' visual field is one means of maintaining access to facial and gestural information provided by the mother. The mother thus becomes a source of affective evaluation of uncertain situations—a source that must be within visual access, even if glancing at the mother occurs only briefly and intermittently.

The second line of evidence comes from a frequently cited observation in the stranger-distress literature. many researchers have noted that upon the entrance of a stranger, the infant first stares at the unfamiliar person and then glances at the mother, in a repetititve alternation suggesting to some researchers (e.g., Schaffer, 1971, 1974) that a process of comparison was taking place between two faces, the outcome of which was a Hebb-like incongruity reaction.

This comparison process emerges at 5 months (Emde, Gaensbauer, & Harmon, 1976), but does not stop even at ages when the infant must have a well-articulated central representation of the mother. Feinman (personal communication), for instance, reports the presence of the back-and-forth facial comparison well into the second year of life. What seems much more plausible to us is that the entry of an unfamiliar person creates uncertainty in the infant, who looks to the mother not to make a facial comparison, but to search for affective information, which may disambiguate the event for the infant.

There are a number of testable consequences of this notion. For instance, we would predict that the nature of the facial, gestural, and vocal expression noted by the infant upon referencing will change his or her reaction to the uncertain event in the direction of the mother's affective communication. Pleasant expressions from her will shift the infant's reaction in a positive direction; unpleasant expressions, in a negative direction. Furthermore, the effects of social referencing should be evident even when the stimulus event that leads to the referencing intrinsically elicits a discrete emotion. Thus, the unpleasant reaction of the infant to a noxious stimulus can be attenuated, and in some cases even reversed, by the appropriate maternal expressions. By the same reasoning, the infant's emotional reaction can be exaggerated by maternal signals in the same direction as the reaction elicited intrinsically by a stimulus. For example, the infant's fear on an amusement park ride may be shifted to laughter by maternal glee, or the infant's distress can be turned to terror by maternal fearfulness. Similarly, infants frequently look to the mother after falls or other painful events, and crying can be prevented or augmented depending on the mother's reaction to the event.

In addition, the effects of maternal referencing will be evident in behaviors that are not merely imitations of the mother's affective expression. Rather, maternal referencing will lead to regulation of the infant's behavior: His or her *actions* will differ as a function of the maternal communication, and will be morphologically different from those of the mother. We also believe that the infant will increasingly rely on vocal cues when the mother is out of sight. Finally, when the infant is held or touched by the mother, the need for social referencing may decline substantially, or be eliminated altogether. In these cases, the infant does not need to regulate his or her own behavior but instead expects the mother to do so by picking up, cuddling, or any of a number of actions.

Postulate 5. Social Referencing Makes Possible Some Types of Vicarious Learning. Classic behavioristic conceptions of early emotional learning involve the association of a response or an event with a primary positive or negative consequence. This viewpoint has never been influential in the study of human infants because the primary positive or negative reinforcers have frequently been difficult to identify. Strangers, for instance, have typically not been associated with pain or noxious consequences, yet at some point in their lives, infants nearly universally react negatively to unfamiliar adults. A similar consideration applies to discrete-learning explanations of the developmental shift on the visual cliff.

Furthermore, it would be very maladaptive biologically for the infant to acquire emotional responses by virtue of learning mediated by primary reinforcers. The need for such emotional learning in the first year of life is extremely great. As infants become more mobile, they encounter potentially dangerous objects such as electrical outlets, poisonous plants, household cleansing chemicals, and so forth. A more adaptive basis for learning is one that bases positive or negative emotional learning on the association of environmental events with maternal communication to the infant. Especially because semantic comprehension is so limited in the first year of life, communication is most likely to take place through the facial, vocal, gestural, and instrumental behaviors of the mother, as delineated in Postulate 2. We have already speculated on the potential importance of this type of learning in accounting for visual-cliff avoidance, especially in those infants who had not experienced falls. Traditionally, this type of learning is called *vicarious learning* to convey the notion that the learning is not based on the direct firsthand experience of the subject, but rather depends upon detection and response to the affective expressions of others (see Bandura, 1969).[1]

The relevance of vicarious learning to the appraisal concept is fairly direct. Vicarious learning provides the infant with the capacity to capitalize "symbiotically" on the appraisal of an environmental event by a significant other. With increasing age, and with the advent of language, children come to develop their own internalized strategies of evaluation, and therefore come to depend less on social referencing. However, it does not seem likely that social referencing is ever completely dispensed with. Rather, it is a basic strategy likely to be invoked whenever circumstances are affectively ambiguous and evaluative needs run high in the individual. The target of the social referencing may shift with age, of course, and become centered on peers, teachers, and other socially significant individuals. Nevertheless, for its developmental onset, social referencing requires only the sensorimotor skills available to infants by 9 months, as described in Postulate 3.[2]

Postulate 6.   Maternal Inaccessibility and Its Consequences to the Infant.   As infants repeatedly encounter ambiguous circumstances in which they experience an evaluative need and successfully use affective information from the caretaker to cope with the circumstance, they learn that the caretaker is a worthwhile resource. One consequence of this recognition is that emotional accessibility of the mother (as in cases of physical absence or inattention), is a condition with a high probability of eliciting distress in the infant. This distress results from the frustration of the infant's need for evaluative support whenever the caretaker actually leaves the child's presence or becomes involved in something besides attending to the infant's needs.

---

[1]There are many sorts of vicarious learning. For instance, there is *observational learning:* The child observes that event X leads to a particular reaction from person A. (The mother yells "ouch" as she touches a hot radiator.) There is also *vicarious learning through referencing directed at the subject:* The child observes that his or her involvement in an event is contingent with an affective reaction from person A. (The child approaches a hot radiator, leading the mother to yell out urgently, "Johnny, be careful!," followed by a rush to remove the child from the situation.) Finally, there is a combination of the two previous types of learning: The child observes that person B's approach to situation X leads person A to react emotionally. (The child notices that the mother yells out, "Helen, be careful!," then rushes to prevent Helen from touching the hot radiator.)

[2]The ideas in this section were suggested to us by Charlotte Henderson.

Furthermore, environmental events that come to signal the impending emotional inaccessibility of the social-referencing resource may eventually lead to anticipatory distress. Such a process may account, in part, for the infant's negative reactions to strangers. That is, the stranger may not signal pain or discomfort to the infant, but may signal that the mother will focus her attention on the stranger or will physically depart from the infant. If this is so, then a significant number of instances of "fear of strangers" may not involve fear at all, but rather anger and generalized negative responding to a frustration.

This conceptual framework has implications for understanding aspects of sibling rivalry and jealousy. Although Brooks and Lewis (1976) reported that unfamiliar children typically did not elicit distress in infants, we feel that there may be a number of instances in which either a younger or older child may be perceived by the infant as making the mother less accessible. If so, there will be some occasions when children will elicit distress in infants, and, for that matter, infants will elicit distress in toddlers and older siblings. In addition, we would predict that this type of negative reaction would decrease in older children in conjunction with the decline in their need for social referencing. We know of no literature bearing on this important and socially significant point.

CONCLUSION

We began this chapter by contrasting the importance of the concept of appraisal in adult theories of emotion with the neglect of the concept in theories of infancy. We have presented a case for the importance of one type of appraisal in infancy—social referencing—and for the consideration of different cognitive and perceptual variables than those usually discussed in connection with emotional development in the human infant. We have also suggested that both learning and memory have been too narrowly conceptualized to be useful in explaining emotional development. In particular, we believe that perceptual learning and vicarious learning need to be studied more carefully, not only because of their intrinsic importance, but because evidence now exists that they are important for understanding emotional changes in infancy.

We also believe that research with infants modeled after the work on nonverbal communication (Harper et al., 1978) promises to be extremely fruitful for understanding both how emotions can be elicited and how they can be learned. We believe that there are clear consequences of this conceptual framework for understanding normal and abnormal personality development. For instance, great significance has been given to so-called "double-bind" messages in the formation of adult and child psychopathology, but such a theoretical notion has not had much influence on research with infants. The double bind, of course, usually refers to a contradiction in the affective tone of messages conveyed verbally and nonverbally, and hence is irrelevant for understanding the preverbal infant. But it is now apparent that infants can be faced with inconsistent messages presented in two nonverbal channels. What are the consequences for subsequent personality development of being faced with such inconsistent messages, with minimal nonverbal affective messages, or with heightened intensity of such communications? With few exceptions, such as the postdictive study by Milmoe, Novey, Kagan, and Rosenthal (1974), there has been little attention to these issues. It is our hope that this chapter helps to focus research in this neglected but important area of social and emotional development.

ACKNOWLEDGMENTS

This chapter was prepared with the support of NIMH grant MH-23556 to the first author. It draws heavily from a history of collaborative research with Robert Emde, James Sorce, Mary Klinnert, Hill Goldsmith, Marilyn Svejda, and Charlotte Henderson. The notion of social referencing first emerged in discussions with Dr. Saul Feinman.

REFERENCES

Ainsworth, M. The development of infant-mother attachment. In B. Caldwell & H. Ricciuti (Eds.), *Review of child development research* (Vol. 3). Chicago: University of Chicago Press, 1973.

Ainsworth, M., Blehar, M, Waters, E., & Wall, S. *Patterns of attachment.* Hillsdale, N.J.: Lawrence Erlbaum Associates, 1978.

Arnold, M. *Emotion and personality* (Vols. 1 & 2). New York: Columbia University Press, 1960.

Aslin, R., Shea, S., Dumais, S., & Fox, R. *Stereoscopic depth perception in young infants.* Paper presented at the meetings of the Society for Research in Child Development, San Francisco, March 1979.

Bandura, A. *Principles of behavior modification.* New York: Holt, Rinehart & Winston, 1969.

Bard, P. Central nervous system mechanisms for the expression of anger in animals. In M. Reymert (Ed.), *Second international symposium on feelings and emotions.* New York: McGraw-Hill, 1950.

Bateson, P. Imprinting. In H. Moltz (Ed.), *The ontogeny of vertebrate behavior.* New York: Academic Press, 1971.

Beck, A. The development of depression: A cognitive model. In R. Friedman & M. Katz (Eds.), *The psychology of depression: Contemporary theory and research.* Washington, D.C.: Winston & Sons, 1974.

Bertenthal, B., Campos, J., & Haith, M. Development of visual organization: The perception of subjective contours. *Child Development,* in press.

Blanck, G., & Blanck, R. *Ego psychology: Theory and practice.* New York: Columbia University Press, 1974.

Bond, E. Perception of form by the human infant. *Psychological Bulletin*, 1972, *77*, 225–245.

Bower, T. Depth perception in the premotor human infant. *Psychonomic Science*, 1964, *1*, 365.

Bower, T. Stimulus variables determining space perception in infants. *Science*, 1965, *149*, 88–89.

Bower, T. Slant perception and shape constancy in infants. *Science*, 1966, *151*, 832–834.

Bower, T. *Development in infancy*. San Francisco: Freeman, 1974.

Bowlby, J. *Attachment and loss* (Vol. 1). New York: Basic Books, 1969.

Bronson, G. The fear of novelty. *Psychological Bulletin*, 1968, *69*, 350–358.

Bronson, G. Infants' reactions to unfamiliar persons and novel objects. *Monographs of the Society for Research in Child Development*, 1972, 32, (4, Serial No. 112).

Bronson, G. Aversive reactions to strangers: A dual process interpretation. *Child Development*, 1978, *49*, 495–499.

Brooks, J., & Lewis, M. Infants' responses to strangers: Midget, adult, and child. *Child Development*, 1976, *47*, 323–332.

Bruner, J. The growth and structure of skill. In K. Connolly (Ed.), *Mechanisms of motor skill development*. New York: Academic Press, 1970.

Bühler, C. *The first year of life*. New York: Day, 1930.

Campos, J. Heart rate: A sensitive tool for the study of emotional development in the infant. In L. Lipsitt (Ed.), *Developmental psychobiology: The significance of infancy*. Hillsdale, N.J.: Lawrence Erlbaum Associates, 1976.

Campos, J., Emde, R., Gaensbauer, T., & Henderson, C. Cardiac and behavioral interrelationships in the reactions of infants to strangers. *Developmental Psychology*, 1975, *11*, 589–601.

Campos, J., Hiatt, S., Ramsay, D., Henderson, C., & Svejda, M. The emergence of fear on the visual cliff. In M. Lewis & L. Rosenblum (Eds.), *The development of affect*. New York: Plenum, 1978.

Camras, L. Facial expressions used by children in a conflict situation. *Child Development*, 1978, *48*, 1431–1435.

Cannon, W. B. The James-Lange theory of emotions: A critical examination and an alternative theory. *American Journal of Psychology*, 1927, *39*, 106–124.

Caron, A., Caron, R., Caldwell, R., & Weiss, S. Infant perception of the structural properties of the face. *Developmental Psychology*, 1973, *9*, 385–399.

Caron, A., Caron, R., & Carlson, V. Do infants see objects or retinal images? Shape constancy revisited. *Infant Behavior and Development*. 1978, *1*, 229–243.

Caron, A., Caron, R., & Carlson, V. Infant perception of the invariant shape of objects varying in slant. *Child Development*, 1979, *50*, 716–721.

Caron, R. F., Caron, A. J., Carlson, V. R., & Cobb, L. S. Perception of shape-at-a-slant in the young infant. *Bulletin of the Psychonomic Society*, 1979, *13*, 105–107.

Carr, S., Dabbs, J., & Carr, T. Mother-infant attachment: The importance of the mother's visual field. *Child Development*, 1975, *46*, 331–338.

Cicchetti, D., & Sroufe, L. An organizational view of affect: Illustration from the study of Down's syndrome infants. In M. Lewis & L. Rosenblum (Eds.), *The development of affect*. New York: Plenum, 1978.

Cohen, L., DeLoache, J., & Strauss, M. Infant visual perception. In J. Osofsky (Ed.), *Handbook of infant development*. New York: Wiley, 1979.

Cohen, L., & Strauss, M. Concept acquisition in the human infant. *Child Development*, 1979, *50*, 419–424.

Darwin, C. *The expression of emotion in man and animals*. London: John Murray, 1872.

Davitz, J. *The communication of emotional meaning*. New York: McGraw-Hill, 1964.

Davitz, J., & Davitz, L. The communication of feelings by content-free speech. *Journal of Communication*, 1959, *9*, 6–13.

Décarie, T. *The infant's reaction to strangers*. New York: International Universities Press, 1974.

Dimond, S. Visual experience and early social behavior in chicks. In J. Crook (Ed.), *Social behaviour in birds and mammals*. New York: Academic Press, 1970.

Duffy, E. An explanation of "emotional" phenomena without the use of the concept "emotion." *Journal of General psychology*, 1941, *25*, 283–293.

Eibl-Eibesfeldt, I. *Ethology: The biology of behavior*. New York: Holt, Rinehart & Winston, 1970.

Ekman, P. Universals and cultural differences in facial expressions of emotion. In J. Cole (Ed.), *Nebraska symposium on motivation*. Lincoln: University of Nebraska Press, 1971.

Ekman, P., & Friesen, W., & Ellsworth, P. *Emotion in the human face: Guidelines for research and an integration of findings*. New York: Pergamon, 1972.

Ekman, P., Sorenson, E., & Freisen, W. Pancultural elements in the facial expression of emotion. *Science*, 1969, *164*, 86–88.

Ellis, A. *Reason and emotion in psychotherapy*. New York: Lyle Stuart, 1962.

Emde, R., Gaensbauer, T., & Harmon, R. Emotional expression in infancy: A biobehavioral study. *Psychological Issues* (Vol. 10, No. 37). New York: International Universities Press, 1976.

Fagan, J. Infants' recognition of the invariant features of faces. *Child Development*, 1976, *47*, 627–638.

Fantz, R. The origin of form perception. *Scientific American*, 1961, *204*, 66–72.

Fraiberg, S. Libidinal object constancy and mental representation. *Psychoanalytic Study of the Child*, 1969, *24*, 9–47.

Freedman, D. *Human infancy: An evolutionary perspective*. Hillsdale, N.J.: Lawrence Erlbaum Associates, 1974.

Freud, S. *Inhibitions, symptoms, and anxiety*. (Std. ed. 20: 87–172). London: Hogarth, 1926.

Gibson, E. *Principles of perceptual learning and development*. New York: Appleton-Century-Crofts, 1969.

Gibson, J. *The perception of the visual world*. Boston: Houghton Mifflin, 1950.

Gogel, W. The metric of visual space. In W. Epstein (Ed.), *Stability and constancy in visual perception: Mechanisms and processes*. New York: Wiley, 1977.

Greenberg, D., Hillman, D., & Grice, D. Infant and stranger variables related to stranger anxiety in the first year of life. *Developmental Psychology*, 1973, *9*, 207–212.

Haith, M. *Rules that newborns look by*. Hillsdale, N.J.: Lawrence Erlbaum Associates, in press.

Haith, M., & Campos, J. Human infancy. *Annual Review of Psychology*, 1977, *28*, 251–293.

Harper, R., Weins, A., & Matarazzo, J. *Nonverbal communication: The state of the art*. New York: Wiley, 1978.

Hebb, D. On the nature of fear. *Psychological Review*, 1946, *53*, 259–276.

Hebb, D. *The organization of behavior*. New York: Wiley, 1949.

Hiatt, S., Campos, J., & Emde, R. Facial patterning and infant emotional expression: Happiness, surprise, and fear. *Child Development*, 1979, *50*, 1020–1035.

Izard, D. *The face of emotion*. New York: Appleton-Century-Crofts, 1971.

Izard, C., Huebner, R., Risser, D., McGinnes, G., & Dougherty, L. The young infant's ability to produce discrete emotion expressions. *Developmental Psychology*, 1980, *16*, 132–140.

Jackson, E., Campos, J., & Fischer, K. The question of decalage between object permanence and person permanence. *Developmental Psychology*, 1978, *14*, 1–10.

James, W. *Principles of psychology*. New York: Henry Holt, 1890.

Kagan, J. Discrepancy, temperament and infant distress. In M. Lewis and L. Rosenblum (Eds.), *The origins of fear*. New York: Wiley, 1974.

Kagan, J., Kearsley, R., & Zelazo, P. *Infancy: Its place in human development*. Cambridge, Mass.: Harvard University Press, 1978.

Kaufman, L. *Sight and mind: An introduction to visual perception*. New York: Oxford University Press, 1974.

Kenney, M., Mason, W., & Hill, S. Effects of age, objects, and visual experience on affective responses of rhesus monkeys to strangers. *Developmental Psychology,* 1979, *15,* 176–184.

Klinnert, M. *Facial expressions and social referencing.* Unpublished doctoral dissertation prospectus, Psychology Department, University of Denver, Denver, Colo., 1978.

Kreutzer, M., & Charlesworth, W. *Infants' reactions to different expressions of emotions.* Paper presented at the meetings of the Society for Research in Child Development, Philadelphia, March, 1973.

LaBarbera, J., Izard, C., Vietze, P., & Parisi, S. Four- and six-month-old infants' visual responses to joy, anger, and neutral expressions. *Child Development,* 1976, *47,* 535–538.

Lange, C. 1885. Cited in Grossman, S. *A textbook of physiological psychology.* New York: Wiley, 1967.

Lazarus, R. Emotions and adaptation: Conceptual and empirical relations. In W. Arnold (Ed.), *Nebraska Symposium on Motivation.* Lincoln: Unversity of Nebraska Press, 1968.

Lewis, M., & Brooks, J. Self, other and fear: Infants' reactions to people. In M. Lewis & L. Rosenblum (Eds.), *The origins of fear.* New York: Wiley, 1974.

MacLean, P. Psychosomatic disease and the "visceral brain": Recent developments bearing on the Papez theory of emotion. *Psychosomatic Medicine,* 1949, *11,* 338–353.

Mahler, M., Pine, F., Bergman, A. *The psychological birth of the human infant,* New York: Basic Books, 1975.

McDevitt, J. Separation, individuation, and object constancy. *Journal of the American Psychoanalytic Association,* 1975, *23,* 713–742.

McKenzie, B., & Day, R. Object distance as a determinant of visual fixation in young infants. *Science,* 1972, *178,* 1108–1110.

Miller, N. Experimental studies of conflict. In J. McV. Hunt (Ed.), *Personality and the behavior disorders* (Vol. 1). New York: Ronald Press, 1944.

Milmoe, S., Novery, M., Kagan, J., & Rosenthal, R. The mother's voice: Postdictor of aspects of her baby's behavior. In S. Weitz (Ed.), *Nonverbal communication: Readings with commentary.* New York: Oxford University Press, 1974.

Mowrer, O. H. A stimulus–response theory of anxiety and its role as a role reinforcing agent. *Psychological Review,* 1939, *46,* 553–565.

Nelson, C., Morse, P., & Leavitt, L. Recognition of facial expressions by seven-month-old infants. *Child Development,* 1979, *50,* 1239–1242.

Obrist, R. The cardiovascular-behavioral interaction—as it appears today. *Psychophysiology,* 1976, *13,* 95–107.

Ornstein, P. On narcissim: Beyond the introduction, highlights of Heinz Kohut's contributions to the psychoanalytic treatment of narcissistic personality disorders. *Annual of Psychoanalysis,* 1974, *2,* 127–149.

Papez, J. A proposed mechanism of emotion. *Archives of Neurology and Psychiatry,* 1937, *38,* 725–744.

Piaget, J. *The origins of intelligence in children.* New York: International University Press, Inc., 1952.

Piaget, J. *The construction of reality in the child.* New York: Basic Books, 1954.

Piaget, J. *The psychology of intelligence.* Paterson, N. J.: Littlefield, Adams & Co., 1960.

Piaget, J. Piaget's theory. In P. Mussen (Ed.), *Carmichael's manual of child psychology* (3rd ed.). New York: Wiley, 1970.

Ramsay, D., & Campos, J. The onset of representation and entry into stage 6 of object permanence development. *Developmental Psychology,* 1978, *14,* 79–86.

Ruff, H. Infant recognition of the invariant forms of objects. *Child Development,* 1978, *49,* 293–306.

Sackett, G. Monkeys reared in isolation with pictures as visual input: Evidence for an innate releasing mechanism. *Science,* 1966, *154,* 1468–1473.

Salapatek, P. Pattern perception in early infancy. In L. B. Cohen & P. Salapatek (Eds.), *Infant perception: From sensation to cognition* (Vol. 1). New York: Academic Press, 1975.

Schachter, S., & Singer, J. Cognitive, social, and physiological determinants of emotional state. *Psychological Reivew,* 1962, *69,* 379–399.

Schaffer, H. R. The onset of fear of strangers and the incongruity hypothesis. *Journal of Child Psychology and Psychiatry,* 1966, *7,* 95–106.

Schaffer, H. R. Objective observations of personality development in early infancy. In Y. Brackbill & G. Thompson (Eds.), *Behavior in infancy and early childhood: A book of readings.* New York: Free Press, 1967.

Schaffer, H. R. Cognitive structure and early social behaviour. In H. Schaffer (Ed.), *The origins of human social relations.* New York: Academic Press, 1971.

Schaffer, H. R. Cognitive components of the infant's response to strangeness. In M. Lewis & L. Rosenblum (Eds.), *The origins of fear.* New York: Wiley, 1974.

Scherer, K. Acoustic concomitants of emotional dimensions: Judging affect from synthesized tone sequences. In S. Weitz (Ed.), *Nonverbal communication: Readings with commentary.* New York: Oxford University Press, 1974.

Schmid, D. *The role of self-produced locomotion on the development of fear of heights.* Unpublished undergraduate honors thesis, Psychology Department, University of Denver, Denver, Colo., 1978.

Scott, J. Critical periods in behavioral development. *Science,* 1962, *138,* 949–958.

Seligman, M. *Helplessness: On depression, development and death.* San Francisco: Freeman, 1975.

Skarin, K. Cognitive and contextual determinants of stranger fear in six- and eleven-month-old infants. *Child Development,* 1977, *48,* 537–544.

Skinner, B. *Science and human behavior.* New York: Macmillan, 1953.

Spitz, R. Hospitalism. *Psychoanalytic Study of the Child,* 1945, *1,* 53–74.

Spitz, R. Anaclitic depression. *Psychoanalytic Study of the Child,* 1946, *2,* 313–342.

Spitz, R. Anxiety in infancy: A study of its manifestations in the first year of life. *International Journal of Psychoanalysis,* 1950, *31,* 138–143.

Spitz, R. *No and yes: On the genesis of human communication.* New York: International Universities Press, 1957.

Spitz, R. *The first year of life.* New York: International Universities Press, 1965.

Spitz, R. Metapsychology and infant observation. In R. Loewenstein, L. Newman, M. Schur, & A. Solnit (Eds.), *Psychoanalysis—A general psychology.* New York: International Universities Press, 1966.

Spitz, R., & Wolf, K. The smiling response: A contribution to the ontogenesis of social relations. *Genetic Psychology Monographs,* 1946, *34,* 57–125.

Sroufe, L. A. Wariness of strangers and the study of infant development. *Child Development,* 1977, *48,* 731–746.

Sroufe, L. A., Waters, E., & Matas, L. Contextual determinants of infant affective response. In M. Lewis & L. Rosenblum (Eds.), *The origins of fear.* New York: Wiley, 1974.

Stayton, D., Ainsworth, M., & Main, M. Development of separation behavior in the first year of life: Protest, following and greeting. *Developmental Psychology,* 1973, *9,* 213–225.

Stenberg, C., Campos, J., & Emde, R. *The expression of anger in seven-month-old infants.* Manuscript in preparation, 1979.

Stern, D. *The first relationship: Infant and mother.* Cambridge, Mass.: Harvard University Press, 1977.

Tomkins, S. *Affect, imagery, consciousness* (Vol. 1). New York: Springer, 1962.

Uzgiris, I., & Hunt, J. *Assessment in infancy: Ordinal scales of psychological development.* Urbana,: University of Illinois Press, 1975.

Walk, R. The development of depth perception in animals and human infants. *Monographs of the Society for Research in Child Development,* 1966, *31* (Whole No. 5).

Walk, R. Depth perception and experience. In R. Walk & H. Pick (Eds.), *Perception and experience.* New York: Plenum, 1978.

Walk, R., & Gibson, E. A comparative and analytical study of visual depth perception. *Psychological Monographs,* 1961, *75* (15, Whole No. 519).

Weinraub, M., & Putney, E. The effects of height on infants' social responses to unfamiliar persons. *Child Development,* 1978, *49,* 598–605.

Wolpe, J. *Psychotherapy by reciprocal inhibition.* Stanford, Calif.: Stanford University Press, 1958.

Yonas, A., Bechtold, A., Frankel, D., Gordon, F., McRoberts, G., Norcia, A., & Sternfels, S. Development of sensitivity to information for impending collision. *Perception and Psychophysics,* 1977, *21,* 97–104.

Young-Browne, G., Rosenfeld, H., & Horowitz, F. Infant discrimination of facial expressions. *Child Development,* 1977, *48,* 555–562.

11 Developmental Changes in Strategies of Social Interaction

Douglas Frye[1]
Yale University

Defining social interaction in infancy is difficult. It is not possible to say for the infant, as it might be for the adult, that social interactions are those which occur with people as opposed to objects. Despite more than a decade of study (see Lewis & Brooks, 1975 for a review), there is no consistent evidence that the infant differentiates people and objects at the beginning of life. Even at 2 or 3 months, when it can be demonstrated that people and objects, or faces and objects, are differentially recognized, the child's interactions with the two may not be sufficiently unalike to justify calling one social and the other nonsocial. To make such a distinction, it is necessary to specify what in itself makes social interaction special.

The infant's interactions with people hold the prospect of being special because people, to state the obvious, are capable of doing more than objects are. People are more likely to respond contingently to the infant's behavior than objects are (Lewis & Brooks, 1975; Lewis & Brooks-Gunn, 1979). Even when objects do react to something the infant does (move after being pushed for instance), they do so in set and specified ways (Glick, 1978). People's reactions can be more varied. A simple example, from Glick, is that people can move themselves; they need not be pushed. People, unlike objects, can not only react, but they can act too. In general, social interactions will not be possible with entitites that can only react in set and unchangeable ways.

Damon (1979, in press) has given this argument clear and precise form by designating the importance of intention for social interaction. In social

---

[1]Now at the Department of Experimental Psychology, University of Cambridge, Downing Street, Cambridge, England, CB2 3EB.

interactions, the thoughts, perspectives, actions, and reactions of one person are coordinated with those of another person. It is this coordination that is at the center of paradigmatic social phenomena like reciprocal exchanges and communication. It is altogether likely that these phenomena would not exist if people could not intentionally coordinate their actions; if they could not respond, but at the same time add something new; if they could not react, but at the same time act. Social interactions are "mutually intentional relations" (Damon, in press). It is this feature which makes them special and unique.

If social interaction depends on mutual intentionality, the status of objects is, of course, no longer a problem. The infant's interactions with objects will not be social. The problem now, however, becomes the infant. Doubtless, adults meet the intentionality requirement. So long as they choose to, they can be full participants in a social exchange. But what of the infant? With the new criterion, interactions between infants and others will not become social until the infant becomes able to behave intentionally. Social interaction in infancy should depend, then, on intention, and changes in the strategies infants use in social interaction should follow the development of intention.

To explore the role of intention in infant social development, it is first necessary to discuss intention and its development in infancy. In the following pages, a theory of the development of intention is taken up. The theory is Piaget's, for his is the most extensive available. What is known about intention is then applied to some familiar infant social developments including smiling, attachment, early communication, and coordinated play. The importance of intention for infant-infant and infant-adult social interactions is considered in light of these developments.

INTENTION

Intention has made its most recent entry into infancy research through speech-act analyses of early communication (Bates, 1976; Dore, 1975). Largely because of this work, psychologists in the past several years have been more willing to talk of intention, although they have not always stated exactly what they were talking about. Fortunately, the topic has been extensively explored in contemporary philosophy. A comprehensive explication of intention can be found in Anscombe's (1957) early book on the subject. Following Anscombe (1957) and Von Wright (1971), we may say in short and rough form that intention is doing something in order to bring about something else, where the "something else" is typically some future state of affairs and what is being done is directed toward attaining that state of affairs.

Piaget's (1952) writings seem to be in accord with this characterization, although his theory uses the more familiar terms of means and ends. Infants begin to be intentional when they do one thing (use a means) to accomplish something else (an end or a goal). We have evidence that a goal is being pursued when infants, if their efforts are blocked by some sort of obstacle, are able to try a new means to the goal (see also Schaffer, 1979). Being able to change means is evidence of the independence of means from ends and makes intention apparent.

As an aside, it is worth noting that the link between means–ends use and awareness of self has already been sketched (Lewis & Brooks-Gunn, 1979; Piaget, 1954). To the extent that infants fail to match means and ends, and thus fail to reach a goal, they themselves learn to distinguish their actions from their effects or, in other words, themselves from the world. Anscombe's (1957) work may be used to draw the connection between intention and awareness of self in another way. In doing something intentionally, we cannot become aware of what we are doing only during or after it is done. If we did, we could have acted without plan or reason, that is, by accident or under some external cause. Intentional actions belong to that class of things we know without observation, know without having to look. The nonobservational knowledge that we have of what we do intentionally may in part constitute our awareness of self.

Returning to intention, it is clear that under the proposed definition, the development of intention will involve the development of the infant's ability to act in order to bring other things about. Or, in Piaget's language, the development of intention concerns the differentiation of means from ends and the changes in the way means and ends are combined. If in infancy work little has been written about what intention is, there have also been only a few studies on how intention develops during this period.

The Development of Intention

Bower, Broughton, and Moore (1970) claim to have shown that neonatal reaching is intentional because neonates were found to reach accurately for objects and to become upset if they encountered a virtual or projected image of an object instead of the object itself. Later work has tended not to support these observations. It is doubtful whether neonates can accurately reach for objects (Ruff & Halton, 1978; White, 1971), and a study (Field, 1977) testing 3-, 5-, and 7-month olds in the virtual-object situation found that it was only at 7 months that the infants expected an object they were reaching for to be solid.

Piaget's (1952) is the only major study of the development of intention in infancy and of course it is based on only three subjects. Unlike Bower et al., Piaget does not claim that intention is present neonatally. He argues that intention first appears at 8 or 9 months, near the middle of infancy, although he acknowledges that it has precursors before that time and that it undergoes considerable development afterwards. Piaget's study of intention has not generated as much subsequent research as other parts of his theory, but it has been shown (see, for example, Uzgiris & Hunt, 1975) that the behavioral changes described by the study do occur and in the order Piaget suggests.

Piaget's Work on Intention

Piaget divides the development of intention into six familiar stages. The stages are fully described in *The Origins of Intelligence in Children* (1952). The chapter headings in this book give a succinct summary of each stage and are adapted here. Because the developments of each of the stages are well-known, there is no need to detail them. It is interesting to note, however, why Piaget believes the particular behavior patterns of some of the stages are intentional whereas those of others are not. In his view, the first three stages encompass the preintentional, the last three reflect the development of intention per se.

Stages I and II: Reflexes and the Primary Circular Reactions.   The reflexes of the first month of life, exemplified by rooting and sucking, appear to be the least likely candidates for intentionality. These behavior patterns are apparently controlled by prior physical stimulation. In the case of rooting, for example, touching the infants' cheeks is sufficient to make them turn their heads. The range of effective elicitors narrows with development, but it is always possible to trigger the reflex in situations that have nothing to do with nursing. Consequently, it seems unlikely that at this point children root to take the nipple or suck to ingest milk, although these may be typical results of their movements.

Smiling at familiar sights, grasping objects, and carrying objects to the mouth—some of the primary circular reactions of the next stage—must also be deemed unintentional. These reactions are not present at birth. They are acquired, but all are heavily dependent on chance for their acquisition. Even in learning something as simple as thumb sucking, the infant goes through an observable process of hit and miss. And, once a reaction is acquired, bringing objects to the mouth for instance, it becomes virtually automatic and is used indiscriminately on almost every graspable object.

Stage III: Procedures to Make Interesting Sights Last—The Secondary Circular Reactions.   The secondary circular reactions of the period from 4 to 8 or 9 months are very nearly intentional. When infants kick in their cribs, they appear to anticipate the effect, the movement of the suspended rattle. These reactions cannot quite be counted as intentional, however, because again they are formed in part by chance. Typically, the infants' normal movements make something happen and this is then noticed. Infants will then reproduce their movements so that the "interesting spectacle" will reoccur. Anticipation comes only after the reaction is acquired. Even so, the anticipation does not seem to lead to a modification of the reaction. Infants do not seek to discover new movements, nor do they experiment to see which movements have an effect and which do not. At best, they will simply generalize the movements to other situations where they may or may not be appropriate.

Stage IV: Application of Familiar Means to New Situations—The Coordination of Secondary Circular Reactions. In Stage III, infants are active in making interesting events reoccur. In the several months that follow, they can become agents in bringing about events they have not stumbled upon by chance. These comprise the first signs of intentionality. They are most readily detected in situations involving obstacles. When infants find a completely covered toy, they act first on the cover in order to then reach the toy. One is a means to the other. The infants' appreciation of means and ends can also be seen in their reactions when adults swing a mobile. To make the sight continue, they may push the adult's hand toward the mobile, rather than trying to act on the mobile itself. The means and ends in Stage IV are secondary circular reactions that have been set together. These coordinations do not seem to be formed fortuitously and they do not arise as a by-product of the infant's ongoing behavior. The ability to coordinate allows the infant to act intentionally in Stage IV. Intentionality is limited in this stage because only secondary circular reactions can be coordinated. In other words, the behaviors the infant displays in Stage IV are not novel, but joining them into means and ends is new.

Stage V: Discovery of New Means Through Experimentation. The infant's ability to behave intentionally does not change radically at the outset of the second year. Means and ends are coordinated in the same fashion as before, but now new means may be formed. When infants are not confronted with a problem, but are merely doing something well-practiced, they will often spontaneously vary their actions. In the course of this experimenting, they may discover, although they have no need to, how to do something new. In the course of throwing objects to the floor, for example, infants may discover they only have to let the objects go to achieve the same result. New means may also be found when they are needed. If presented with a stick and an out-of-reach toy, infants are able to discover, again through experimentation or "directed groping," how the stick may be used as a tool. These improvements do not mark a decisive change in the infants' intentionality, but they do expand greatly the things they can do intentionally.

Stage VI: The Invention of New Means. In the last stage of infancy, from 18 to 24 months approximately, infants gain a great advantage. Means and ends begin to be combined mentally. Infants follow the same process of discovering new means as in Stage V, except that now each step in the process does not have to be acted out. The infants can test various means—ends combinations mentally and forestall acting until they have found a means that seems appropriate for the goal they are pursuing. The child who wants to slip a long chain into a box may not try one end of the chain and then the other, but may pause and then roll the entire chain into a ball that can easily be placed inside. Intention in these circumstances seems clear and well-defined. Confronted with a new problem, the infant makes a deliberate choice of means. In more than a few cases, the infants' choices will be wrong, but their actions at this age show not only a good appreciation of what they are capable of, but also a fundamental understanding of the workings of the world and, perhaps, of people in the world.

Piaget's observations speak in behalf of a complex course for the development of intention, one which covers the entire period of infancy. Following the argument presented in this chapter—that social interaction requires intention—the infant's strategies of social interaction should follow a similarly rich and extended development. Of course, applying Piaget's theory to infant social development has strong precedents in work on attachment (Bell, 1970; Bowlby, 1969) and early language development (Bloom, 1973; Corrigan, 1976). Most of this work, however, has focused almost exclusively on Piaget's description of the development of object permanence. Nelson (1979) has reviewed some of the difficulties involved in using object permanence to explicate early language development. Object permanence would also seem to be a very opaque lens through which to view social development, especially if differential reactions to objects and people are being assessed, since object permanence is exactly the feature that objects and people should share. Intention, on the other hand, is exactly what should hold objects and people apart. The development of intention may reveal how the infant's interactions with objects and people change, such that one becomes social. Moreover, examining the infant's interactions with people drawn from different points in the development of intention, the infant's age mates compared to her or his caregivers, may help explain the different kinds of infant social interaction.

SOCIAL INTERACTION

Preintention

Gazing, vocalizing, and smiling are the behaviors that have traditionally been identified as holding social significance during the first 6 months of life, the period corresponding to Piaget's Stages I, II, and III. In this period the infant is not—according to Piaget—intentional, so it is worth considering whether in these months the behaviors can be said to be truly social. Of the three, smiling has been the most extensively researched (see Sroufe & Waters, 1976 and Zelazo, 1972 for reviews) and so may be the most profitable to discuss.

The developmental course of early smiling is well-charted. The first smiles are reflexive. In the weeks immediately following birth, smiles occur either spontaneously, that is with no apparent cause, or they may be elicited, for example by light tactile stimulation (Wolfe, 1963). The first "social" smiles, smiles to a passive face, start at about 2 months, peak at 14 weeks, and decline thereafter (Ambrose, 1961). These smiles have been characterized as recognitory (Zelazo, 1972) or as the consequence of the assimilation of faces to an emergent schema (Kagan, 1967). The smiling that occurs following the recognitory smile has been linked to mastery (Schultz & Zigler, 1970; Sroufe & Waters, 1976) because it seems to accompany the infant's contingent responding.

Although the 2-month smile has been called social, smiling to nonsocial stimuli has been documented (Salzen, 1963; Schultz & Zigler, 1970; Watson, 1972; Zelazo & Komer, 1971) throughout the period preceding intentionality. The types of stimulation found to have been effective follow the same developmental progression as for "social" stimuli: from the purely visual to static displays to moving displays and displays that move contingent on the infant's behavior. These similarities place early smiling to faces in a group of phenomena, one that is not necessarily social. Of course, infants' smiles have the effect of attracting and engaging people, especially caregivers, but it is uncertain that smiling at this age is directed toward that result. The effects of nonsocial stimuli suggest that it is not. Adults may interpret infant smiles to be social, perhaps because they cause the smile (Richards, 1974), but there are no strong grounds for presuming that smiling in the first 6 months has a social meaning *for the infant.*

Finding that the infant smiles at both "social" and nonsocial stimuli might seem to challenge the conclusion, drawn mainly from studies on gazing, that faces and objects are discriminated very early in life (Lewis & Brooks, 1975). This conflict is more apparent than real however. The gaze studies may show that the infant discriminates faces from other displays, but they do not show that the infant treats the two differently. Faces may be looked at more (although see Carpenter, 1974 and Koopman & Ames, 1968 for exceptions), but the infant still looks at both, just as it smiles at both. Without a difference in the type of reaction shown, it is difficult to tell what meaning, if any, the discrimination has for the infant. One of the few studies that offers evidence of differential infant reactions to people and objects in the first 3 months is Brazelton, Koslowski, and Main's (1974), but it compared a responsive caregiver with an object that merely moved into reach. A similar study by Rheingold (1961) compared the infant's reactions to people and to a toy rattle. Rheingold found very little difference in the nature of the reactions shown and concluded that at this age it was the degree of responsive stimulation, and not whether the stimulation was social or nonsocial, that determined the infant's reaction.

Detailed studies of infant-caregiver interactions at 3 and 4 months have confirmed the importance of stimulation. Stern's (1974) work on patterns of gazing has shown that it is the adult who initiates the majority of exchanges and works to reestablish mutual gazing if it is interrupted. Blehar, Lieberman, and Ainsworth (1977) observing a full range of maternal and infant behaviors, again found that it was the mother who initiated the majority of face-to-face interchanges. What is more, they discovered that maternal playfulness and contingent responding engendered the infant responses of smiling, vocalizing, and bouncing. Except for bouncing less, the infants did not behave differently with an interactive stranger than they did with their own mothers.

The results of the studies on interaction, like those on smiling, tend to show that at this point in development infants are not social, just as Piaget says they are not intentional. Contingent stimulation would seem to account for the infant's part in infant-caregiver interactions at 3 and 4 months. This sort of outcome is what would be expected if the infant were beginning to form the secondary circular reactions of Stage III. As secondary circular reactions appear to represent both an elicitation and reinforcement of behavior (Cavanagh & Davidson, 1977), they may be perfectly suited to explain how adult responsiveness can both prompt and prolong the infant's responding in infant-caregiver interactions. Of course, some events in the environment will have the power to do the same thing. All in all, in the first 6 months, if there is a difference in the infant's responses to social and nonsocial stimuli, or people and objects, it will only be a difference in degree and it will result from what the two types of stimuli do, rather than from what the infant does.

The Beginnings of Intention with Stage IV

Attachment, heeded as one of the fundamental developments of the first year, marks an unmistakable change in the infant's behavior. Becoming attached is surely social. Just as surely, attachment shows that infants come to treat people and objects in qualitatively different ways. As has been mentioned, object permanence in Piaget's sense and attachment have been frequently linked (for example, Bowlby, 1969). It has been thought that infants must have some rudimentary conception of people as permanent entities before they can become attached to them and, indeed, there is some evidence that object permanence and attachment are interrelated (Bell, 1970). Although contrary to Bell's results and Piaget's (1954) speculations, a recent study (Jackson, Campos, & Fisher, 1978) failed to find that permanence for people developmentally precedes object permanence. In addition, Bates, Benigni,

Bretherton, Camaioni, and Volterra (1977a) found that quality of attachment was correlated with means–ends development and not with the development of object permanence. Permanence, or the start of it, may very well be necessary for attachment, but intention, for several reasons, may prove to be more apposite.

An important, but almost implicit, argument for permanence is that, because it starts with Stage IV, it can explain why attachment does not appear before the seventh or eighth month of life. Intention, because it too begins in Stage IV, enjoys this same advantage, yet it accounts for the "why" of attachment while permanence does not. The first time infants can place a value on something, independently of their own activity, is when means and ends are separated (Piaget, 1952). A goal has an estimated *worth* for children, and a means may or may not have a *use* in attaining the goal. Before intention, the infants' estimations of things in the world are tied strictly to their own activity. When infants smile at someone, the smiles tell as much about the infants' own state as they do about the worth of the person. With intention, indications of the infants' state and their estimations of things becomes separated. Infants may place a positive value on their caregiver and at the same time express that value by crying, if by crying they bring the caregiver closer.

Seeing attachment as an intentional activity has several merits. It retains the spirit of the original characterization that the infant's goal is to come into comforting proximity to a caregiver (Bowlby, 1969; Schaffer & Emerson, 1964). It makes sense of the findings that stress enhances the show of attachment (Sroufe & Waters, 1977), since stress would give the infant a reason for seeking proximity. When infants are not stressed, they are able to pursue other goals intentionally, e.g., explore the surroundings. An intention account would accept that infants could become attached to caregivers besides their mothers (Fox, 1977; Lamb, 1977, 1978), so long as they were important to them and responded to their pleas, although it would acknowledge that they might represent different ideals or different sorts of goals for babies (see Lamb, Chapter 7). Intention would also accept that there might not be impressive correlations among "attachment behaviors" (Masters & Wellman, 1974; Weinraub, Brooks & Lewis, 1977). For intention, it is not important that particular behaviors are shown, rather that the infant's behavior functions in particular ways, that is, as a means to influence the caregiver.

Piaget's work on intention would predict that the first attachment behaviors will not be new. They should, if they occur in stage IV, merely be old behaviors pressed into new service. Given the list of behaviors that have been thought to index attachment—crying, approaching, touching, greeting, smiling, etc.—this generalization would seem to hold. More to the point, Bell and Ainsworth (1972) found that an old behavior, crying, comes to have a new signaling function during the last quarter of the first year. Since the behaviors are not new, it will be necessary to demonstrate, as Bell and Ainsworth begin to, that infants use them to gain comfort from their caregivers. Hay (1977), for example, in a clever series of experiments, found that following mother does not necessarily give evidence of attachment, although it may count as exploration because infants did not follow their mothers preferentially, and following did lead to exploration. Hay acknowledges that under different circumstances following may be a sign of attachment. If infants are acting intentionally, it will be necessary to determine what goal they are actually pursuing, something which cannot always be divined straight away. In these terms, confirming the validity of attachment as a theory will require sound evidence that infants in the appropriate circumstances do seek the goal of gaining comfort from their caregivers.

In social interactions like those described by attachment, the infant is a participant of standing. His or her role is not subsumed by the adult's, but obviously the more fully intentional adult does much to support the interaction. The "intentional relations" at this point cannot be completely mutual. Just how much the adult structures the interchange can be seen by contrasting infant-caregiver and infant-infant interactions. Differences between the two will indicate how much more the adult contributes over a partner at the infant's own developmental level. Of course, this comparison is confounded with others. Peers and caregivers differ in their familiarity to the infant, affective value, relative size, and so on. General differences in the infant's social interactions, however, may be likely to reflect the effects of level of intention rather than these other more specific factors.

As the intention hypothesis would predict, there appears to be very little interaction between infants before 8 months (Maudry & Nekula, 1939; Mueller & Lucas, 1975). After 8 months, there is social interaction of a kind. In the presence of a peer, infants of this age or slightly older issue simple, socially directed behaviors like waving or offering a toy (Becker, 1977; Bronson, 1975; Eckerman & Whatley, 1977; Eckerman, Whatley, & Kutz, 1975). Peer reaction to the overture is not a high probability event however (Becker, 1977; Bronson, 1975). A major difference between infant-infant and infant-caregiver interactions at this age has to be that the infant is not yet consistently responsive to social overtures. When a peer does respond, the response is not likely to maintain the exchange. A peer may simply duplicate the infant's actions on a toy (Eckerman, 1978) or, if offered a toy, may accept but not offer the toy back again, as an adult might. Infants at this age would seem to be able to initiate interactions, although *they* do not have, as adults do, the wherewithal to keep them going.

The New Means of Stage V

The first considerations of the importance of intention for infant social cognition came in work on early communication and language development. The use of intention in this work rests on Piaget and speech-act analysis (Austin, 1962). As with attachment, Piaget's discussions of object permanence have also been applied to the development of communication and language in infancy (Bloom, 1973; Corrigan, 1976), although the research evidence now shows means–ends relations, rather than object permanence, to be more closely related to developments in these realms (Bates et al., 1977a; Corrigan, 1976). At present, Piaget's work on intention has had its most useful application to early communication and language.

Efforts to explain the infant's development of communicative skills have centered around Piaget's Stage V. It has been hypothesized that the first communicative gestures arise as new means to accomplish an end (Bates et al., 1977a; Bretherton & Bates, 1979). In the prototypical situation, the infant must enlist an adult's aid to reach a toy. Before Stage V, the infant acts on the toy or the adult, probably with intention, but has no way of effectively joining the two (Sugarman, 1978). With Stage V, a gesture like pointing, along with looking back and forth between the adult and the toy, can be used to direct the adult's attention to the toy. The infant will persist in these actions until the adult has been induced to move the toy into reach. In form, these episodes exactly resemble the tool use characteristic of Stage V, except now the infant's tools are gestures. Clearly, the infant's use of these developing tools is intentional.

The infant's vocalizations at this point have also been found to be intentional. Harding and Golinkoff (1979) judged whether infants were in Stage IV or V on the basis of two Piagetian causality tasks. They then subjected the infants to a situation where adult aid was necessary and counted as intentional any vocalizations the infants made which were accompanied by eye contact with the adult. Vocalizations of this sort were only made by the infants who were judged to be in Stage V. These results can be interpreted as showing that vocalization while making eye contact with the "listener" develops as a means during Stage V.

The infants who scored as Stage IV in Harding and Golinkoff's study did not look at the adult and vocalize, but they did look back and forth between the adult's hand and the object that they needed help with. This behavior pattern is reminiscent of pushing the adult's hand toward a goal, the phenomenon Piaget observed in Stage IV. In Stage IV, the infant was found to treat objects and people in qualitatively different ways, so much so that it has been said that at this age the infant's world is divided into the social and nonsocial (Nelson, 1979). Part of what must reinforce the division and help the infant further realize that objects and people behave differently is the development of new means in Stage V. These means necessarily reflect the difference between objects and people. For example, it is difficult to imagine how an object could be affected by being gestured to, or looked and vocalized at.

In Stage V, infants gain in what they can do intentionally, but probably not enough to allow them to take an equal role in most social interactions. The infants' communicative gestures, although they are much clearer in intent than what came earlier, still demand active interpretation to make them comprehensible. As before, the preponderant role of the adult can be seen from the negative examples of like-intentioned or infant-infant interaction. Mueller and Lucas (1975) found that peer social interchanges did occur during the second year. These included occasions when one infant would run while the other chased, or when one infant would look and vocalize at his partner and his partner would laugh in response (all the subjects were male). The first behavior in these interchanges was socially directed, complex, often new, and did draw a contingent response from the peer, but the interchanges themselves were usually limited to the same exchange repeated over and over.

The contrast in infant-adult interaction can be seen in Bruner's studies of peekaboo (Bruner & Sherwood, 1976; Ratner & Bruner, 1978). Peekaboo may be played from the sixth month through the end of infancy. The game, like the peer interchanges previously discussed, has a set structure, which in the first year consists mainly of the adult taking the agent's moves. Several months into the second year, at the time of the repetitive peer interactions, the infant can be either agent or recipient when playing peekaboo and will typically switch back and forth between the two. Some of the skills that the infant acquires are merely the new means necessary to do what the agent does, and the infant still depends on the adult to rescue the interchange if it goes wrong. Nevertheless, in the second year, the infant in the context of a well-practiced game may approach mutuality in a social interchange.

The Mental Combination of Means and Ends in Stage VI

Language development during Stage VI has been related almost exclusively to the final steps in object-permanence development (Bates et al., 1977a; Bloom, 1973; Corrigan, 1976). It has been thought, for instance, that the referential use of single words requires the symbolic and representative capacity implied by object permanence. This hypothesis may very well be true, but it does not preclude an interpretation of first-word use based on intention. In Stage VI, infants may understand that words are the paradigmatic means for expressing intent. They may realize that when they hear a word they must seek the speaker's intent and when they wish to express their intent they should seek a word. Infants ought to be able to handle this task in Stage VI because for the first time they can mentally form and test combinations of means and ends. Their new mental ability does not exempt them from making linguistic mistakes, of course, but these mistakes should be attributable to the misdiagnosis or misexpression of intent, rather than to a misunderstanding of what language is about.

Regardless of the role the development of intention plays in language acquisition, it is obvious from the fact they hold conversations with adults, that infants can participate fully in social interactions at the end of the second year. A conversation must certainly be a mutually intentional relation. The intentional status of infants is underscored, moreover, by their peer relations, which now also become truly social, as is shown by the appearance of coordinated play (Eckerman, 1978; Mueller & Lucas, 1975). Toward the end of the second year, infants may play together by putting a piece of paper on a wall or building a tower of blocks. In these activities, both infants pursue a common goal. Both are working to build the tower. Their roles are complementary, they take the other into account, and they are reversible. Blocks are stacked in turn, and either infant may start or end the game. All the elements of social interaction are present. The relation between peers in coordinated play is intentional and mutually so.

PERCEIVED INTENTIONALITY

Given the intentionality account of infant social relations, it is worth making a final note on the problem of differentiating people and objects. As we have seen, if social interaction requires mutual intentionality, infants will not necessarily become social as soon as they distinguish people from objects. When the development of intention allows infants to be social, however, they will need to be able to differentiate people and objects, and presumably they will need to do so using the criterion that people alone are intentional. Infants should be aware that objects are not candidates for sharing mutually intentional relations.

Golinkoff and Kerr (1978) have done one of the very few studies bearing on the question of the infant's perception of the intentionality of others. They investigated whether infants between 15 and 18 months expected people, and people alone, to be agents by determining whether the sight of a chair pushing a man across a room was treated as an anomaly. Using an habituation paradigm with films of various events as stimuli and cardiac deceleration as a response, they did not observe a reaction to this discrepant event. Of course, it is difficult to interpret a finding of no effect, especially without a body of related research, but this result is so important that it needs to be studied in other ways. For example, if infants saw a real chair push a man across a room, would they look, smile, or gesture to it as they might to a person?

Piaget claims that intention and the understanding that other people are intentional develop contemporaneously. In Stage IV, when the infant gently pushes the adult's hand, urging it to do some particular thing, the child is acting and also showing a beginning recognition of the adult as an independent center of activity. This claim is consistent with the development of social relations as they have been reviewed in this chapter. The infant begins to behave intentionally in Stage IV, and at the same time there occurs, with attachment, the first clear differentiation between people and objects in the infant's behavior. Attachment, to the extent it is intentional, represents the infant's ability to act and also a beginning awareness that people and not objects are the ones who are likely to reply to these acts.

At present, Golinkoff and Kerr's results and Piaget's observations are at variance on the question of the infant's perception of the intentionality of others. Without further research it is impossible to settle the issue, but certainly for the intentionality account of infant social development it is important that the issue be further investigated.

SUMMARY

The problem of the infant's entry into social relations is unsolvable without some specification of what social relations are. It is not reasonable to merely assume, as is often done, that once people and objects are discriminated on some dimension the infant immediately begins to treat people socially. Mutual intentionality defines the central feature of social relations and provides a chart for when the infant will begin to be social. By the criterion of mutual intentionality, the infant's interactions with objects will never be social. Interactions with people will not be social at first, but they will come to be social as the infant comes to be intentional. The first social relation, attachment, accompanies the beginnings of intention in Stage IV. Rudimentary social relations with peers are apparent at the same time, but a comparison of the infant-infant and infant-adult situations shows that early social exchanges suffer greatly if there is not an adult to play the preponderant role. The development of infants' intentional abilities expands what they can do socially as is evidenced by changes in early communication and language skills. These developments also narrow the gap between infant-infant and infant-adult social interactions since they allow the infant to take a more flexible role. By the end of infancy the child can assume a full role and, as the example of coordinated play shows, distinctly social peer, along with infant-adult, relations become possible.

REFERENCES

Ambrose, A. The development of the smiling response in early infancy. In B. Foss (Ed.), *Determinants of infant behavior I*. New York: Wiley, 1961.

Anscombe, G. E. M. *Intention*. London: Blackwell, 1957.

Austin, J. L. *How to do things with words*. London: Oxford University Press, 1962.

Bates, E. *Language and context: The acquisition of pragmatics*. New York: Academic Press, 1976.

Bates, E., Benigni, L., Bretherton, I., Camaioni, L., & Volterra, V. From gesture to first word: On cognitive and social prerequisites. In M. Lewis & L. Rosenblum (Eds.), *Origins of behavior: Communication and language*. New York: Wiley, 1977.(a)

Bates, E., Benigni, L., Bretherton, I., Camaioni, L., & Volterra, V. Personal communication, 1977.(b)

Becker, J. A learning analysis of the development of peer oriented behaviors in nine-month-old infants. *Developmental Psychology*, 1977, *13*, 481-491.

Bell, S. The development of the concept of the object as related to infant-mother attachment. *Child Development*, 1970, *41*, 291-311.

Bell, S., & Ainsworth, M. D. Infant crying and maternal responsiveness. *Child Development*, 1972, *43*, 1171-1190.

Blehar, M., Lieberman, A., & Ainsworth, M. D. Early face-to-face interaction in the first year of life. *Child Development*, 1977, *48*, 182-194.

Bloom, L. *One word at a time*. The Hague: Mouton, 1973.

Bower, T., Broughton, J., & Moore, M. Demonstration of intention in the reaching behavior of neonate humans. *Nature*, 1970, *228*, 679-680.

Bowlby, J. *Attachment and loss* (Vol. 1). New York: Basic Books, 1969.

Brazelton, T. B., Koslowski, B., & Main, M. The origins of reciprocity: The early mother-infant interaction. In M. Lewis & L. Rosenblum (Eds.), *The effect of the infant on its caregiver*. New York: Wiley, 1974.

Bretherton, I., & Bates, E. The emergence of intentional communication. In I. Uzgiris (Ed.), *Social interaction and communication during infancy*. San Francisco: Jossey-Bass, 1979.

Bronson, W. Developments in behavior with age mates during the second year of life. In M. Lewis & L. Rosenblum (Eds.), *Friendship and peer relations*. New York: Wiley, 1975.

Bruner, J., & Sherwood, V. Peekaboo and the learning of rule structures. In J. Bruner, A. Jolly, & K. Sylva (Eds.), *Play: Its role in development and evolution*. New York: Basic Books, 1976.

Carpenter, G. Visual regard of moving and stationary faces in early infancy. *Merrill-Palmer Quarterly*, 1974, *20*, 181-194.

Cavanagh, P., & Davidson, M. The secondary circular reaction and response elicitation in the operant learning of six-month-old infants. *Developmental Psychology*, 1977, *13*, 371-376.

Corrigan, R. *Patterns of individual communication and cognitive development*. Unpublished doctoral dissertation, University of Denver, 1976.

Damon, W. Why study social-cognitive development? *Human Development*, 1979, *22*, 206-212.

Damon, W. The developmental study of children's social cognition. In J. Flavell & L. Ross (Eds.), *New directions in the study of social-cognitive development*, in press.

Dore, J. Holophrases, speech acts, and language universals. *Journal of Child Language*, 1975, *2*, 21-40.

Eckerman, C. *The attainment of interactive skills: A major task of infancy*. Colloquium address delivered at the University of Virginia, Charlottesville, October 1978.

Eckerman, C., & Whatley, J. Toys and social interaction between infant peers. *Child Development*, 1977, *48*, 1645-1656.

Eckerman, C., Whatley, J., & Kutz, S. Growth of social play with peers during the second year of life. *Developmental Psychology*, 1975, *11*, 42-49.

Field, J. Coordination of vision and prehension in young infants. *Child Development,* 1977, *48,* 97–103.

Fox, N. Attachment of kibbutz infants to mother and metapelet. *Child Development,* 1977, *48,* 1228–1239.

Glick, J. Cognition and social cognition: An introduction. In J. Glick & A. Clarke-Stewart (Eds.), *The development of social understanding.* New York: Gardner, 1978.

Golinkoff, R., & Kerr, J. Infants' perception of semantically defined action role changes in filmed events. *Merrill–Palmer Quarterly,* 1978, *24,* 53–61.

Harding, C., & Golinkoff, R. The origins of intentional vocalizations in prelinguistic infants. *Child Development,* 1979, *50,* 33–40.

Hay, D. Following their companions as a form of exploration for human infants. *Child Development,* 1977, *48,* 1626–1632.

Jackson, E., Campos, J., & Fischer, K. The question of decalage between object permanence and person permanence. *Developmental Psychology,* 1978, *14,* 1–10.

Kagan, J. On the need for relativism. *American Psychologist,* 1967, *22,* 131–142.

Koopman, P., & Ames, E. Infants' preferences for facial arrangements: A failure to replicate. *Child Development,* 1968, *39,* 481–487.

Lamb, M. Father-infant and mother-infant interaction in the first year of life. *Child Development,* 1977, *48,* 167–181.

Lamb, M. Qualitative aspects of mother- and father-infant attachments. *Infant Behavior and Development,* 1978, *1,* 265–275.

Lewis, M., & Brooks, J. Infants' social perception: A constructivist view. In L. Cohen & P. Salapatek (Eds.), *Infant perception: From sensation to cognition* (Vol. 2). New York: Academic Press, 1975.

Lewis, M., & Brooks-Gunn, J. Toward a theory of social cognition: The development of self. In I. Uzgiris (Ed.), *Social interaction and communication during infancy.* San Francisco: Jossey-Bass, 1979.

Masters, J. & Wellman, H. The study of human infant attachment: A procedural critique. *Psychological Bulletin,* 1974, *81,* 218–237.

Maudry, M., & Nekula, M. Social relations between children of the same age during the first two years of life. *Journal of Genetic Psychology,* 1939, *54,* 193–215.

Mueller, E., & Lucas, T. A developmental analysis of peer interaction among toddlers. In M. Lewis & L. Rosenblum (Eds.), *Friendship and peer relations.* New York: Wiley, 1975.

Nelson, K. The role of language in infant development. In M. Bornstein & W. Kessen (Eds.), *Psychological development from infancy: Image to intention.* Hillsdale, N.J.: Lawrence Erlbaum Associates, 1979.

Piaget, J. *The origins of intelligence in children.* New York: Norton, 1952.

Piaget, J. *The construction of reality in the child.* New York: Basic Books, 1954.

Ratner, N., & Bruner, J. Games, social exchange, and the acquisition of language. *Journal of Child Language,* 1978, *5,* 391–401.

Rheingold, H. The effect of environmental stimulation upon social and exploratory behavior in the human infant. In B. Foss (Ed.), *Determinants of infant behavior I.* New York: Wiley, 1961.

Richards, M. *The integration of a child into a social world.* London: Cambridge University Press, 1974.

Ruff, H., & Halton, A. Is there directed reaching in the human neonate? *Developmental Psychology,* 1978, *14,* 425–426.

Salzen, E. Visual stimuli eliciting the smiling response in the human infant. *Journal of Genetic Psychology,* 1963, *102,* 51–54.

Schaffer, H. R. Acquiring the concept of the dialogue. In M. Bornstein & W. Kessen (Eds.), *Psychological development from infancy: Image to intention.* Hillsdale, N.J.: Lawrence Erlbaum Associates, 1979.

Schaffer, H. R., & Emerson, P. The development of social attachments in infancy. *Monographs of the Society for Research in Child Development,* 1964, *29* (3, Serial No. 94).

Schultz, T., & Zigler, E. Emotional concomitants of visual mastery in infants: The effects on stimulus movement on smiling and vocalizing. *Journal of Experimental Child Psychology,* 1970, *10,* 390–402.

Sroufe, L. A., & Waters, E. The ontogenesis of smiling and laughter: A perspective on the organization of development in infancy. *Psychological Review,* 1976, *83,* 173–189.

Sroufe, L. A., & Waters, E. Attachment as an organizational construct. *Child Development,* 1977, *48,* 1184–1199.

Stern, D. Mother and infant at play: The dyadic interaction involving facial, vocal and gaze behaviors. In M. Lewis & L. Rosenblum (Eds.), *The effect of the infant on its caregiver.* New York: Wiley, 1974.

Sugarman, S. Description of communicative development in the prelanguage child. In I. Markova (Ed.), *The social context of language.* New York: Wiley, 1978.

Uzgiris, I., & Hunt, J. McV. *Assessment in infancy: Ordinal scales of psychological development.* Urbana: University of Illinois Press, 1975.

Von Wright, G. H. *Explanation and understanding.* London: Routledge & Kegan Paul, 1971.

Watson, J. Smiling, cooing, and "the game." *Merrill–Palmer Quarterly,* 1972, *18,* 323–340.

Weinraub, M., Brooks, J., & Lewis, M. The social network: A reconsideration of the concept of attachment. *Human Development,* 1977, *20,* 31–47.

White, B. *Human infants: Experience and psychological development.* Englewood Cliffs, N.J.: Prentice-Hall, 1971.

Wolff, P. Observations on the early development of smiling. In B. Foss (Ed.), *Determinants of infant behavior II.* London: Methuen, 1963.

Zelazo, P. Smiling and vocalizing: A cognitive emphasis. *Merrill–Palmer Quarterly,* 1972, *18,* 349–365.

Zelazo, P., & Komer, M. Infant smiling to nonsocial stimuli and the recognition hypothesis. *Child Development,* 1971, *42,* 1327–1339.

12

Early Person Knowledge as Expressed in Gestural and Verbal Communication: When Do Infants Acquire A "Theory of Mind"?

Inge Bretherton
Sandra McNew
Marjorie Beeghly-Smith
University of Colorado

> *"The child's image of the world is mirrored twice, once directly and again as a representation of the representation of others. His image of himself is also mirrored twice, once with direct knowledge of his internal states and again by his representation of his behavior in the eyes of others. Each image extends and modifies the other.*
>
> —Shields, 1978

INTRODUCTION

During the first year of life, infants come to know about objects by manipulating, shaking, banging, finding, hiding, pushing, pulling, throwing, stacking, and nesting them. By acting on objects, infants discover—paradoxically—that objects have properties that are independent of the infant's action, that objects continue to exist in space and time whether the baby perceives them or not, and that objects can sometimes act without being acted upon (a toy car can roll down an incline without being pushed). Infants also discover that one object can act indirectly on another, making it possible to obtain one object (for example, a necklace) by means of another (the cloth on which it rests). During the first year of life, infants also come to know about people by interacting with them in everyday routines and games, discovering that people can act without being acted upon, that they are agents who continue to exist in time and space independent of the infant's perception. Further, babies discover that a person can also be used as a means to an end—as a social tool through whom the infant can obtain a desired action by using a communicative gesture such as pointing. Person permanence and object permanence (Bell, 1970; Jackson, Campos, & Fischer, 1978) and social and nonsocial tool use (Bates, Camaioni, & Volterra, 1975; Bates, Benigni, Bretherton, Camaioni, & Volterra, 1979) seem to develop more or less in step with one another, suggesting that the same underlying processes may come into play in the acquisition of object and person knowledge. Or do they?

We believe, in common with a number of other researchers (Shields, 1978; Shotter, 1978; Trevarthen & Hubley, 1978; Bruner, 1977; Newson, 1977) and philosophers (Habermas, 1972; Hamlyn, 1974), that there are fundamental differences between person knowledge and object knowledge even though both types of knowledge are constructed by a child through feedback from his or her own actions. The differences are evident both in the way in which person knowledge and object knowledge are acquired (through dialogue with a person, compared to acting upon an object) as well as in what is acquired (knowledge of physical laws, as compared to knowledge of others and of oneself as a psychological agent wth intentions, beliefs, emotions, and the ability to communicate). For example, a baby playing with a rattle obtains *interesting effects* (noises, visual and tactile stimulation) depending only on the skill with which he or she manipulates the toy. From people, on the other hand, a baby receives a *reply* to his or her action by a more experienced partner who treats the baby's action as socially meaningful behavior. For example, when a mother responds to her baby's cry as if it were a communicative signal, she allows the baby to discover eventually that crying (and other behaviors) can be used as communicative signals. Mothers thus provide a scaffold (Wood, Bruner, and Ross, 1976) within which babies can begin to make sense of their own and their mothers' actions. As Hamlyn (1974) phrases it: "The child could come to have the idea of what a person is only *via* and in the context of *being* a person; and for this to have any real sense the child must be treated as a person [p. 34]."

In dialogue, infants very early discover the rudiments of turn taking (Stern, 1977), how to achieve affective synchrony in interaction with others (Brazelton, Koslowski, & Main, 1974), the capacity to predict the behavior of others (see Lamb, this volume, for a review), and the capacity to *influence* another's behavior intentionally. Even 3-month-old infants can recognize their ability to make a partner repeat his or her behavior by repeating their own behavior (Rheingold, Gewirtz & Ross, 1959). Later, around 7 months of age, babies tend to repeat the antics that lead an adult to laugh, seeming to anticipate further laughter (Bates, et al., 1975). Both examples qualify as *intentional behavior designed to influence other persons,* but not yet as *intentional communication* as the term is used in this paper.

Intentional communication as well as a host of other new achievements become possible as the result of a far-reaching discovery on the part of the infant, which dramatically alters the nature of his or her relationship to other human beings. Infants come to recognize not only that others possess agency (can activate themselves) and resemble them physically, but that others are like them *psychologically* and yet distinct from them (see also Lewis & Brooks-Gunn, 1979, for a discussion of this point). It is this discovery that makes experiential sharing or intersubjectivity possible (Trevarthen & Hubley, 1978). Whereas the capacity for intersubjective sharing is prefigured in the neonate's ability to imitate facial expressions (Meltzoff & Moore, 1977), to show empathetic distress (Hoffman, 1975), and to adapt to the micro- and macrorhythms of the caregiver (Sander, 1977), it truly blossoms around 9 months, as demonstrated by the following list of capacities that emerge between then and 12 months, inspired by a similar list by Trevarthen and Hubley (1978). All of the examples except those specifically acknowledged were collected in a study jointly undertaken by Bates, Benigni, Bretherton, Camaioni, and Volterra (1979):

1. Obeys simple gestural or verbal requests such as "Give me the cup" said with an outstretched open palm extended to the baby. Begins to make gestural requests.
2. Points to objects (first without [later with] checking whether the addressee is attending) and follows the pointing gesture of an adult (Murphy & Messer, 1977).
3. Reliably turns his or her regard in the same direction as that of an adult (Scaife & Bruner, 1975).
4. Requests adult help to obtain an object or to "fix" it.
5. Shakes head or says "no-no" in refusal, also occasionally in self-reproof.
6. Shows manners by appropriate waving or saying "hi" and "bye-bye" and by saying "thank you" when handing over, or being handed, an object.
7. Begins to use conventional labels for objects such as balls, bottles, and teddy bears. Also requests labels with "Whassa?" Begins to name persons and pets.
8. Demonstrates affection in the learned form of hugging and kissing. Kisses, hugs, and pats favorite dolls and teddy bears.
9. Initiates, with appropriate gestures, games such as peekaboo and patty-cake.

10. Plays at carrying out adult activities such as mopping the floor, driving the car (turning the steering wheel), telephoning, reading books, putting on clothes, brushing and combing hair, dancing and singing.
11. Imitates conventional actions with objects (driving a car), but resists imitating counterconventional use (drinking from a car) (Killen & Uzgiris, 1978).

The emergence of these behaviors is difficult to explain unless one assumes that the child has come to recognize the psychological similarity as well as the separateness of self and others (a rudimentary form of identification) and is operating within a shared meaning system that he or she has developed through interaction with another person.

In later childhood, the knowledge that others are more than self-activating agents, but persons who perceive, feel, and intend in much the same way as the children themselves can be applied in complex social situations where the other persons' feelings, viewpoints, thoughts, and intentions may *differ* from one's own (i.e., role taking, see Flavell, Botkin, & Fry, 1968, for a review). But before children can conceive of others as having *different* viewpoints, they must first recognize that *others can have viewpoints and other mental processes at all* (Flavell, 1974).

Thus, the young child's psychological model of persons may at first not be very much concerned with possible differences of viewpoint, but rather with the similarity of self and others. Shields (1978), in discussing the minimum psychological model required for intentional communication and preceding the role-taking skills of preschool children, proposed the following dimensions:

1. Persons have identity over time despite changes in location, behavior and appearance.
2. Persons are self moving or animate, and influence over the course of their behaviour has to be negotiated by invoking interest or a shared frame of constraint.
3. Persons identify each other and can react to each other.
4. Persons can see, feel, hear, touch and smell, i.e., they have a perceptual field.
5. Persons intend their actions.
6. Persons conceptualize and construct their world in roughly similar ways.
7. Persons have moods and states such as anger and fear, and also wants, likes and dislikes.
8. Persons can send and receive messages based on gestures and words which are related to context in stable ways.
9. Persons have an action potential, i.e., things they can and can't do.

10. Persons can retain previous experience and structure their present behavior by it.
11. Persons can replicate previous behaviors in new contexts.
12. Persons share sets of rules about what is appropriate within particular frames of action [pp. 553–554].

Is Shield's model a realistic one? There are many windows into a child's person knowledge, and therefore many different ways in which Shield's model could be tested: through the observation of dyadic interaction, the study of symbolic play, and the study of intentional communication through gesture and word. In this paper, we focus on the last topic, but we do so in full awareness that verbal and gestural communicative skills do not represent the sum total of a young child's person knowledge. Knowledge that can be mapped onto a communicative medium does, however, have special status by being more shareable than the private knowledge of imagery and more explicit than the observable knowledge expressed in action. In his early work, Piaget was criticized (see Flavell, 1963) for investigating young children's understanding through interviews instead of asking children to act out solutions to problem situations. Although it is interesting that children *can* understand and solve a problem at the level of doing (without being able to give a coherent verbal account of their actions), communicable knowledge—especially communicable knowledge of others and the self as perceiving, intending, feeling, cognizing, and moralizing beings—is, we believe, an extremely important aspect of person knowledge in its own right. It is both an indicator of present knowledge available for linguistic symbolization and communication, and it probably also facilitates the further acquisition of such knowledge. This remains true even if verbally expressible person knowledge is not the first and only form of such knowledge that a child possesses.

The data with which we are buttressing our arguments come from many published sources, but also include data that were collected by us as part of a larger joint project with Elizabeth Bates on the prerequisites to language and the emergence of symbols. In this study 32, middle-class Boulder, Colorado infants were observed in the presence of their mothers at 10½ and 13 months. Twenty-seven of these infants were seen again at 20 months (with an additional three infants to bring the sample size up to N = 30) in a number of structured and unstructured situations at home and in the laboratory. An extensive interview of the mother was also conducted at each age. We have in the past found interviews to be reliable (i.e., to correlate strongly with comparable observational data), provided we confined our questions to the present and provided we asked the mother to supply concrete examples of behavior. The latter procedure is very effective at eliminating potential misunderstandings (see also Bates et al., 1979). The data presented here are taken from the maternal interview and from a comprehension test of emotion labels. The sample is referred to as the Boulder Sample.

PERSON KNOWLEDGE VIEWED THROUGH THE WINDOW OF GESTURAL AND VERBAL COMMUNICATION

Babies appear to communicate intentionally from about 9 months of age (Bates et al., 1979; Bates et al., 1975); that is, they begin at this age to use conventional gestures (and sometimes sounds) such as giving, showing, pointing, requesting, shaking the head "no" or saying "no-no-no," waving bye-bye, saying "hi," clapping the hands in applause, and so forth. Table 12.1 shows how many such communicative conventions had already been mastered by the Boulder Sample at 10½ and 13 months.

What makes such gestural and vocal conventions communicative? Instead of straining to reach an unattainable object, a baby who is attempting to communicate a request will reach toward the object without straining, open and close the hand while intermittently glancing up at mother's face, perhaps with an imperative 'eheheh." Functional reaching and grasping behavior gradually becomes abbreviated and ritualized as it turns into a communicative gesture. Similarly, the arms-up gesture emerges out of cooperation with the mother: As the mother extends her arms toward the baby in order to pick him or her up, the baby responds by lifting its arms. Later, the baby may start to raise the arms as soon as mother enters the room in the morning in the *expectation* of being picked up. Eventually, an infant comes to use the arms-up gesture communicatively, that is, the child spontaneously approaches his or her mother in order to *request* a pick-up (Edwards, 1978). Other gestures, like waving "bye-bye," are not ritualizations of actions in context, but have to be acquired through imitation.

Before the advent of conventional communication, the baby is already engaging in behavior designed to influence adults (see p. 335), but intentional communication requires more than this. Bates (1979) writes:

> Intentional communication is signaling behavior in which the sender is aware, *a priori,* of the effect that the signal will have on his listener, and he persists in that behavior until the effect is obtained or failure is clearly indicated. The behavioral evidence that permits us to infer the presence of communicative intentions include (a) alternations in eye contact between the goal and the intended listeners, (b) augmentations, additions, and substitution of signals until the goal has been obtained, and (c) changes in the form of the signal toward abbreviated and/or exaggerated patterns that are appropriate only for achieving a communicative goal [p. 36].

TABLE 12.1
Percentage of Children in the Boulder Sample Using
Conventional Gestures in Communication at 10½ and 13 Months
(According to Maternal Report)

Convention	Used at 10½	Used at 13 Months
Communicative Gestures and Sounds		
Shows an object	66%	94%
Gives an object	75%	100%
Requests an object by pointing	9%	50%
Requests an object with out-stretched arm, accompanied by grasping motions and/or ritual sound	9%	66%
Requests object by banging on or shaking container	0%	25%
Requests pick up with arms-up gesture	100%	97%
Refuses with head shake	33%	44%
Refuses by saying "no," "nanana," etc.	25%	28%
Affirms with head nod	0%	9%
Requests attention by pointing and visual check to adult	34%	69%
Greetings		
Waves bye or hi (mostly bye)	59%	69%
Says bye-bye or bye	6%	34%
Says hi	19%	65%
Affective Expression		
Kisses	9%	84%
Hugs	50%	75%
Applauds self	not known	53%
Joins in applause with others	not known	78%

Implicit in Bates' definition is the fact that the infant recognizes a partner's capacity to *understand* a message. In other words, the infant attributes an internal state of *knowing* and *comprehending* to the mother as he or she communicates, and thus must have what Premack and Woodruff (1978) have called a "theory of mind." According to these authors, an organism is said to have a theory of mind if:

he imputes mental states to himself and others (either to conspecifics or to other species) as well. A system of inferences of this kind is properly viewed as a theory, first, because such states are not directly observable and second, because the system can be used to make predictions specifically about the behavior of others.... Purpose or intention is the state we impute most widely; several other states are not far behind, however. They include all those designated by the italicized term in each of the following statements: John *believes* in ghosts; He *thinks* he has a fair chance of *winning;* Paul *knows* that I don't *like* roses; She is *guessing* when she says that; I *doubt* that Mary will come; Bill is only *pretending.* This list is in no way exhaustive. [p. 515].

Even the ability to impute internal states to self and others is, in and of itself, not enough. In order to communicate intentionally, a baby must have recognized that his or her mind can be *interfaced* with that of a partner (Bretherton & Bates, 1979). This interfacing is possible only because both partners: (1) share a *framework of meaning;* (2) share an *interfacible medium* (language or conventional gestures) into which underlying intentions can be encoded by the speaker and from which they can be decoded into something corresponding to the speaker's underlying intentions by the addressee. The notion of interface has, surprisingly, been taken for granted by philosophers concerned with the transmission of meaning. For example, according to Grice (1958) as rephrased in our terms, a baby who means something by his or her gesture or utterance would like his or her mother: (1) to understand the meaning or content of his or her communication; (2) to either act upon it or at least acknowledge its receipt. That the production of mutually comprehensible messages is possible is simply taken for granted by Grice.

When suggesting that infants as young as 9 months of age have something as outlandish as a theory of interfacible minds, we do not mean to suggest that they are *aware* of using such a theory, nor that they can impute *any* mental state, nor that their inferences are likely to be as sophisticated as those ascribed to naive adult psychologists by Heider (1958). Let us make this clear by way of an analogy: When at around age 2, babies begin to use syntax in the construction of utterances, their knowledge of syntactic rules is only implicit. Late in the third year of life, however, some young children start correcting the speech of younger siblings and even come up with simple etymological explanations (Clark, 1978). They have become aware of some of the rules underlying language. Similarly, a baby's use of a theory of interfacible minds remains at first implicit and fairly rudimentary. It becomes somewhat more explicit as children gain experience with repairing misfired nonverbal messages, a phenomenon that has been noted but not systematically studied in infants. A particularly striking example is reported by Rubin and Wolf (1980) in a longitudinal study of J., who was 12 months at the time of the following observation:

J. has been playing in his room. There he found his jack-in-the-box sitting on the table with a block resting on its lid. He cranked the handle, the jack popped up, sending the lock flying off behind a shelf. J. wants to make this grand event happen again, but he has lost his block. He runs to the kitchen, calling out his father's name. He pulls his father back into the room and points behind the shelf, saying "there, there." His father has a hard time understanding and tries several guesses, pulling out first one favorite book, then another. J., somewhat exasperated, at last takes his father's hand in his own, places them both on top of the jack-in-the-box, makes a kind of explosive noise, and moves his and his father's hand in an arc toward the bookcase. J. then reaches his own hand down behind the bookcase, making somehwhat conventionalized effort sounds to signal reaching. Still looking at his father, he says something like "block" [p. 18].

Such heroic efforts at communicating are hard to explain unless one assumes that the child knows that one's intentions can be transmitted to another via messages which implies that the child has a theory of interfacible minds. It is especially noteworthy that J. did not assume that because he himself knew that he wanted the block, his father must automatically know it too (the egocentric position). He seemed to assume, however, that by making his father see and experience the situation from *his* (J.'s) viewpoint, he could somehow convey his meaning.

That at least some very young children can demonstrate simple role-taking skills in their communications is illustrated also by the example of Jacqueline Piaget (Piaget, 1954) at 16½ months:

Jacqueline has just been wrested from a game she wants to continue and placed in her playpen from which she wants to get out. She calls, but in vain. Then she clearly expresses a certain need, although the events of the last ten minutes prove that she no longer experiences it. No sooner has she left the playpen then she indicates the game she wishes to resume!

Thus we see how Jacqueline, *knowing* that a mere appeal would not free her from her confinement, has *imagined* a more efficacious means, *foreseeing* more or less clearly the sequence of actions that would result from it [p. 297, italics added].

Not only did Jacqueline know that she could communicate her wish to get out of the playpen, she could also envisage which type of presumed need on her part would be most effective in getting her parents to act as she wished, an attempt at deception with all the hallmarks of role-taking skill.

The recognition that self and others are objectively and subjectively similar but distinct is *implicit* in intentional communication when it first emerges. It becomes *explicit* in three aspects of language development during the subsequent 2 years. The three aspects to be discussed in turn are: (1) the establishment of one-to-one correspondence between the physical self and the physical other as shown in language through comprehension and then production of labels for corresponding body parts; (2) reference to self and other by personal names as well as the mastery of pronouns, which because of their deictic properties require simple role-taking skills; (3) the verbal expression of mental states imputed to self and other (perception, physiological states, affects, cognitions, and moral judgments).

Self and Other: the Labeling of Body Parts

In his book *Play, Dreams and Imitation in Childhood* (1962), Piaget gives very detailed descriptions of his children's struggles with imitation, especially when they could not see themselves perform the actions that they were trying to replicate. Thus Lucienne, at 11 months, first opened and closed her fist, and then later her mouth in response to Piaget's demonstration of opening and closing the eyes. Only 3 months later did she finally master the correct movement. Laurent also started by confusing mouth with eyes, although he required only 1 month to achieve correct imitation after his first erroneous attempt at imitating eye opening and closing. Jacqueline struggled from 11½ to 12½ months before she was able to touch her index finger to her forehead like the model and not her eye instead.

Piaget (1962) theorizes that the idea of one-to-one correspondence of invisible bodily (facial and head) features is acquired through the use of indices:

> Although the child cannot picture his own mouth (and does not need to do so) he understands through the sound he hears that the movements he sees made by the mouths of others are concomitant with a certain tactilo-kinesthetic impression in his own mouth. In other words, thanks to the index, the child assimilates the visual and auditory model to the auditory motor schema with which he is familiar in himself, and imitation becomes possible through accomodation to this schema. The sound then becomes unnecessary, whereas if it were a signal it would have to persist as a stimulus, or, in case of transfer, itself be produced as a result of visual perception. When a silent, visual suggestion does in fact produce a vocal motor response (obs. 30) it is only transitory, and the sound very soon disappears.[p. 42–43].

The index can be established also via direct tactile comparison, as when babies explore their own and the model's mouth with their fingers.

Thus, there is evidence that the recognition of which *invisible* body parts on oneself correspond to which *visible* body parts on another human being is no easy achievement. We believe, however, that Piaget may have underestimated the contribution of language in the establishment of this one-to-one correspondence. Although we did not ask the mothers of the Boulder Sample how often they played body-part-labeling games with their infants, we did ask which labels the infants comprehended at 10½ and 13 months as well as how the mother inferred comprehension. Very frequently the answer turned out to be that the baby indicated comprehension by pointing to the correct part on self or other in response to the question: "Where's your nose, ears, eyes? Where's Mommy's nose, ears, eyes?" Interestingly, the body parts best known in comprehension at 10½ and 13 months and most frequently labeled at 20 months are precisely the head and facial features for which one-to-one correspondence is most difficult to discover (see Table 12.2).

TABLE 12.2
**List of Body-Part Labels Understood by the Boulder Sample
At 10½ and 13 Months and Produced at 20 Months
(Percentage of Sample)**

Body Part	Comprehended at 10½ Months (N = 32)	Comprehended[a] at 13 Months (N = 32)	Labeled at 20 Months (N = 30)
Head Area			
Nose	10%	22%	67%
Eye(s)	3%	25%	60%
Hair	3%	6%	60%
Ear(s)	3%	3%	57%
Mouth	3%	19%	47%
Teeth	–	–	43%
Face	–	–	23%
Cheek(s)	–	–	20%
Tongue	3%	–	13%
Beard	–	–	3%
Chin	–	–	3%
Eyebrow(s)	–	–	3%
Head	–	3%	3%
Neck	–	3%	3%
Shoulder-Arm Area			
Hand(s)	3%	–	37%
Finger(s)	–	3%	30%
Arm(s)	–	–	20%
Elbow	–	–	7%
Shoulder	–	–	3%
Thumb	–	–	3%
Wrist	–	–	3%
Trunk Area			
Tummy (Belly)	3%	12%	37%
Bellybutton	–	3%	33%
Penis	–	12% (of males)	47% (of males)
Bottom (Butt)	–	–	13%
Back	–	–	7%
Chest	–	–	3%
Leg Area			
Feet (foot)	3%	25%	40%
Toes	3%	9%	37%
Knee(s)	–	–	30%
Leg(s)	–	–	23%

[a]Only two infants produced body-part labels at 13 months.

When do children also find out that one sees with the eyes, hears with the ears, tastes with the mouth and tongue, and smells with the nose? When do they discover that sight can be excluded by covering the eyes, sounds by covering the ears, and smell by holding the nose? There is no systematic information except for vision, although Yarrow and Waxler (1977) mention a child who held her hand over her ears during a parental quarrel, and Piaget (1962) describes Jacqueline, who at the age of 28 months, pulled her doll's hair away from the ears in order to make her listen to music.

In a study of two-year olds, Masangkay, McCluskey, McIntyre, Sims-Knight, Vaughn, and Flavell (1974) found that quite young children could accurately specify the object in an array of four at which an adult was gazing. Lempers, Flavell, and Flavell (1977) corroborated these results and also showed that 18- to 24-month olds when required to *prevent* an adult from seeing an object hit upon the idea of turning the adult away from the object. It was more difficult for children of this age to "fix it" so that an adult or doll with closed eyes could see an object (the child had to open the adult's eyes or turn the doll from a prone to a supine position).

Learning to label body parts on self and others and learning to label the associated sensory activities (seeing, smelling, hearing, tasting) are presumably instrumental in drawing young children's attention to the correspondence of their own to other people's sensory organs and associated perceptions, even though nonverbal cues may also be of help in establishing the correspondence.

Self and Other: Names and Pronouns

Using first-, second-, and third-person pronouns requires more than the discovery of a one-to-one correspondence between self and other selves, as observed in the acquisition of body-part labels. *I* and *you, my* and *your* are deictic words; that is, they point from a speaker to an addressee. Their correct usage therefore requires simple role-taking skills, because the reference shifts depending on who is speaker and who addressee. Personal pronouns are mastered earlier than other deictic word pairs, such as *come,* and *go, here* and *there, this* and *that,* which have a directional or distance component as well as a deictic component pointing to a speaker or addressee (Clark & Sengul, 1978).

Most of the Boulder Sample had begun to produce the labels Mommy or Daddy at 13 months (69% produced Mommy, 69% produced Daddy, and 81% produced Daddy or Mommy). On the other hand, only 10% of the children could say a version of their own name at this age on request or in response to seeing their image in a mirror. They did not use it to refer to themselves in communication. By 20 months, the situation had changed dramatically in some respects. Mother and father were still addressed as

Mommy and Daddy, but 60% of the children could now say their names, although only 23% used their own names to refer to themselves in communication (i.e., Betty night-night). On the other hand, 75% had mastered at least one first-person pronoun, and all of these were used in communication. Table 12.3 lists the pronouns acquired, as well as how many children produced one, two, three, and four first-person pronouns. It also provides examples of how the pronouns were used in multiword utterances. The pronoun "I" only appeared in two-word or multiword utterances in this sample (we did not count formulaic uses such as a slurred "Iyuvyou" at bedtime). In spite of the fact that first-person-pronoun-use was so frequent, only two children had started to address others as "you."

We know from other sources that children are often confused about the use of first- and second-person pronouns (Bloom & Lahey, 1978; Clark & Sengul, 1978; Stern & Stern, 1928). There are even examples in the literature of children who consistently refer to themselves as "you" (Halliday, 1975), but we do not know how long such errors usually last and whether they appear more frequently in complex rather than simple utterances. The children in the Boulder Sample seemed to have chosen the strategy of acquiring the first-person pronouns for self-reference while still addressing others by name, using the principle of mastering one thing at a time. There are occasional anecdotes illustrating the reasoning process that some children go through in the process of acquiring correct pronouns. For example, Cathy (25 months) systematically inquired about ownership of the potty: "Is this my potty?"..."Is it Tara's potty?"..."Is it Mommy's potty?"..."Is it Daddy's potty?" before finally concluding "It is OUR potty." The strategy of personal pronoun use deserves much more systematic study. Everytime a child acquires the use of these pronouns, he or she rediscovers the person

TABLE 12.3
First-Person Pronouns Used by the Boulder Sample (According to Maternal Interview)

No. of Pronouns	No. of Children Using Pronouns at 20 Months	Type of Pronouns	Examples of Pronoun Use in Multiword Utterances
0	6	—	—
1	6	5 mine or my	mine toy
		1 me	me out
2	6	4 me/my	my baby
		2 my/mine	
3	10	4 I/my/mine	I'm hungry
		3 I/me/mine	
		2 me/my/mine	
		1 I/me/mine	
4	6	6 I/me/my/mine	

knowledge already built into the language, thus mastering the naïve psychology of roles, i.e., who is relating to whom and in what way as speaker, addressee, and bystander.

Self and Other: Imputing Mental States

The mere fact that infants engage in intentional communication requires, as we suggested earlier, that they impute mental states to themselves and to others. But can one be more specific about *which* states are imputed? By using the technique of "rich interpretation" (interpreting communicative behavior within its total context; see Bloom, 1970; Brown, 1973), one can infer that a child who habitually uses vocalizations to request objects or actions probably imputes auditory perception to others and that a child who systematically uses manual gestures such as pointing probably imputes vision to others. Furthermore, a child who habitually bangs on a container while looking back and forth from the container to mother (requesting what is inside) probably imputes shared *knowledge* and *memory* to the mother. A young child who takes a security blanket to a crying playmate probably imputes *distress* and knows that this state is changeable (Hoffman, 1975). It is from the consistency with which children engage in such behaviors, as well as from associated cues such as tone of voice and facial expression, that an observer may infer that the children are imputing specific mental states to themselves and to others. With the child's acquisition of first words, the observer's inferential task becomes thankfully somewhat easier. A child who says "no" as her mother reaches for a toy probably imputes *wanting* to her mother; a child who says "there ball" to his brother is probably imputing *shared perception;* a child who says "man cry" (see Main, Weston, & Wakeling, 1979) to a crying clown in a sad tone of voice seems to be imputing *distress;* a child who takes a toy to her mother saying "fix" imputes *ability and knowledge* to the mother that the child does not have herself. A child who says "horsie allgone" when driving past a field that used to contain horses or a child who asks "where Daddy?" when his father is not present is fairly obviously imputing *memory* to his partner. Piaget (1954) reports a particularly striking example of the latter:

> OBS. 173a. At 1;6(15) Jacqueline weeps while calling her mother. I imitate her, repeating, "Mama, Mama," in a tearful tone, and she laughs. Two days later, at 1;6(17); we play at reproducing the sounds of animals and Jacqueline inserts this memory into the game: "How does the goat go?" "Meh." "And the cow?" "Moo." "And the dog?" "Voovoo." "And Jacqueline?" "Mama." This final answer is given by imitating exactly the tone of the other day and with a *meaningful smile,* which demonstrates clearly that Jacqueline is *alluding* to a past behavior pattern and is not making up a new game [p. 347, italics added].

The onset of language makes it easier for researchers and mothers to infer what the child is implicitly imputing because the messages become more precise. But, when do children begin to label states or processes of perception, physiological deprivation, affect, cognition, and moral judgment explicitly? In an attempt to probe the first emergence of a variety of internal-state labels, we interviewed the mothers of the Boulder Sample (see Table 12.4). The mother was first asked whether the child produced the particular label at all, and then whether she or he used it to refer to her/himself, to others, or to pictures and representations of others. For each use, the mother was requested to supply a concrete example. Labels that describe affect expression (kiss, cry) as well as psychological labels (love, happy, sad, mad, scared) were included on the assumption that reference to emotional behavior would precede labels for emotional states. However, labels of emotional expression *were* assumed to have strong connotations of emotional state and, conversely, the psychological labels to have strong connotations of emotional expression (at 13 months many mothers used the expression "give Mommy love" to request a hug). Some of the perceptual labels included in the questionnaire could be projected inward to refer to a mental state of self or other, or, they could be projected outward to describe the state of an object. When an object is described as "cold" for example, the child refers to perceived property, but the coldness is presumed to reside in the object (outward projection). If a child refers to feeling cold herself, she is labeling a perceptual state (the feeling of coldness resides in herself). The frequencies given in the table for hot, cold, wet, dry, dirty, good, and bad always refer to labels applied to person rather than to a thing being hot (such as a stove) or bad (such as food). There are other potential uses such as "the ice feels cold" or "the milk tastes bad" in which the perceptual quality is emphasized, but we did not ask about perceptual verbs in this preliminary study.

As expected, the concrete expressive labels (cry, kiss) were indeed mastered by a large number of infants at 20 months, but note that not one child produced the label "smile" even though a number of children could apply the corresponding psychological label "happy" appropriately. Perhaps the smile is not so distinct behaviorally as tears, a puckered face, and the sound effects that one labels "crying." Sadness may be more tied to one of its behavioral referents, namely "crying," than happiness is to "smiling."

In addition to "happy," a small but not negligible number of children referred to themselves and/or others as hungry thirsty, tired, sad, mad, and scared (all psychological rather than behavioral labels). The word "hot" was produced by almost all children in the sample to refer to stoves or liquids, but much more rarely to refer to a perceptual state. A larger number of children spoke of themselves as "cold," particularly in the form "brr-cold," a fact that might relate to the season during which the data were collected. The perception of pain (or inference of pain in others) is labeled very frequently, but as yet more often by the conventionalized pain-cry "ouch" than the adult term "hurt," although one child said "hurt" when her mother called out "ouch" in pain. Despite the fact that many children already used the adult

TABLE 12.4
Number of Children in the Boulder Sample Who Used the Following Internal-State Words
at 20 Months (According to the Maternal Report)

State Word	Applied to Self	Applied to Other Persons	Applied to Doll or Picture
Perceptual			
Cold and Brr-cold	8	2	0
Brr	3	1	0
Hot	5	0	0
Wet	14	4	0
Dry	5	1	0
Hurt	9	4	0
Ouch, Owie	21	9	1
Physiological			
Hungry	4	0	0
Thirsty	3	0	0
Sleep	7	7	5
Sleepy	4	4	0
Tired	2	0	0
Night-night, Bye-bye			
(to mean sleepy or sleeping)	11	6	4
Emotional			
Positive			
Happy	5	1	0
Smile	0	0	0
Funny	1	2	0
Kiss	14	13	4
Love	11	6	2
Emotional			
Negative			
Sad	0	2	1
Cry	4	13	8
Mad (Angry)	0	1	1
Scared	2	0	0
Dirty (Disgust)	12	8	1
Yuck (Ick, etc.)	12	6	0
Gross	1	0	0
Messy	0	0	0
Phtew	1	0	0
Ability			
Hard (difficult)	2	1	0
Moral			
Good	12	4	0
Nice	7	10	2
Gentle	3	2	0
Bad	6	7	1
Naughty	0	0	1
No-no (meaning bad)	2	0	1

labels "tired," "sleepy," an equal number extended the meaning of the bedtime greeting "night-night" to refer to the state of sleeping as well as to the feeling of sleepiness.

The meaning of mental state and its correlated external expression are intertwined in the early use of these labels. Do they therefore only refer to external behavior? We do not think so. There is indirect evidence that words such as "sleepy" carry state meaning. For example, a child who says "tired" when her eyes are not closed and she is not lying down is *informing* her mother of an internal state that the mother may already have inferred from the child's sluggishness or whining. Verbatim examples of the way in which 20-month-old infants of the Boulder Sample referred to mental states and affective expression in self and others are presented in the Appendix to this chapter.

In addition to interviewing the mothers of the Boulder Sample about their infants' production of internal-state labels, we conducted a comprehension test for emotion labels. The infants were shown a book containing nine pairs of test pictures that had been pretested during another study of preschool children (Blackmon, personal communication) with filler items to retain the baby's interest. Pictures of children and infants, each showing a distinct emotion, were presented in pairs as follows: sad–happy, happy–mad, sad–happy, crying–smiling, happy–serious, sad–mad, happy–sad, and sad–happy. For each emotion pair, the tester would point and say: "Here's a baby (boy, girl) and here's another baby (boy, girl). Can you show me the happy (sad, mad, crying, smiling) baby (boy, girl)?" The book was shown twice, asking first for one, then for the other expression. Because this test was part of a large correlational study, the pictures were presented in the same order to all children, but randomized with respect to which emotion (positive or negative) was requested first and where the first target picture was located (right or left page). Had responses been entirely random—and most children recognized that they were required to point to a picture—about 50% correct responses could have been expected overall. Because the pictures were presented in pairs, random responding would have resulted in 25% correct identifications of both members of a pair, 25% incorrect identifications of both members of a pair, and 50% correct identifications of one picture in a pair. For the whole sample, we found significantly more instances of correct pointing to *both* members of a pair than incorrect pointing to *both* members $(X^2 (1) = 6.9, p < .01)$, but this result was largely due to one sad–happy pair that was identified correctly by 40% of the children. Only four children correctly identified four picture pairs out of nine. Thus, it appears that comprehension is not far ahead of the production of emotion labels in 20-month-old infants.

Spontaneous production of labels (not counting echoing) also concurred during this comprehension test. Most instances of labeling involved the word "cry," a result that corroborates the mothers' report about the frequent use of that word (see Table 12.4). Twelve of the children (six boys and six girls) spontaneously labeled pictures of sad children as "he cry," "crying," "baby cry," "uh-oh, cry," sometimes with wiping of tears, imitation of crying noises, and kissing the baby picture. Only in two cases did this happen as an echoing response when the child was asked to point to the crying baby (see pair 5); *in no case was a mad or happy face labeled as crying.* Saying "uh-oh" and kissing and wiping the tears of the child in the picture could be interpreted as evidence for concern (and therefore as evidence that the word had affective as well as behavioral connotations).

The findings on internal-state labeling by 20-month olds led us to conduct a literature search for examples of internal-stage language in young children up to 36 months of age. Only utterances for which the context was also supplied were included, and our major sources were: (1) Stern and Stern (1928) who describe the language development of their three children as well as quoting from other contemporary diaries; (2) a series of studies by Bloom and her colleagues (Bloom, 1970; Bloom, 1973; Bloom & Lahey, 1978; Bloom, Lightbown, & Hood, 1975; Hood & Bloom, 1979). In addition, we collaborated with Lynn Tracy who for 8 weeks collected utterances made by her 25–26-month-old daughter, Cathy (Cathy's mother had, incidentally, *not* noticed that Cathy had begun to use words labeling internal states and processes until she began to write down Cathy's utterances systematically). The results of our compilation are listed verbatim (with context and source) in the Appendix and are summarized in Table 12.5 according to six categories (perception, physiology, emotion, volition and ability, cognition, and moral judgment).

A large number of the utterances containing emotion labels came from data collected or reported by parents (Stern & Stern, 1928; the Boulder Sample; Cathy's mother) rather than from direct observations made by researchers. This bias in the collection of utterances makes it difficult to draw quantitative conclusions about the data. Nevertheless, we would like to note that some internal-state labels were encountered so often during our literature search that only a sample could be included in the Appendix. These were statements about seeing, wanting, hunger, fatigue, and feeling pain. For the remainder of the labels, almost every example we found is included in the Appendix.

In tabulating the utterances listed in the Appendix, we were not only interested in the variety of labels used (although we think it impressive), but in whether the children applied the label to others as well as to themselves. Table 12.5 shows that many of the labels were indeed applied to others, although we discovered more instances of self-labeling than other-labeling. Only a developmental study could show whether self-labeling generally precedes other labeling. Note that Table 12.4 lists a few examples to the contrary in 20-month-old infants (the verb *cry* was used by more children to label others, and *mad* was used by two children about their mother, but not to label their own

TABLE 12.5
Summary of Internal-State Words Used by Children up to 36 Months

Type of Internal-State Word	Age First Reported (in Months)	Applied to Self	Applied to Other	Applied to Doll or Picture	Negated, Used in Past or Future Tense or Question	Used in Causal Sentence
Perceptual						
See, look	11	X	X	X	X	X
Watch	24	X	X			X
Hear	14½	X	X		X	
Listen	22		X			
Taste	26	X	X		X	X
Feel (to touch)	24½	X				
Cold	20	X	X	X	X	X
Freezing	25	X			X	X
Hot	20	X				X
Warm	25			X		
Hurt	20	X	X	X		X
Ouch, boo-boo	18½	X	X			X
Physiological						
Hungry	20	X		X	X	
Starving	25	X				
Thirsty	20	X			X	
Sleep	20	X	X	X	X	X
Sleepy	20	X				
Tired	17		X		X	
Awake, wake up	28		X	X	X	X

(continued)

TABLE 12.5 (continued)

Type of Internal-State Word	Age First Reported (in Months)	Applied to Self	Applied to Other	Applied to Doll or Picture	Negated, Used in Past or Future Tense or Question	Used in Causal Sentence
Emotional						
Positive						
Happy, pleased	20	X	X	X	X	
Fun	25	X			X	
Funny	20	X	X		X	
Feel (emotional)	25	X	X		X	
All right	25		X			
Nice	20	X	X			
Like	22½	X	X		X	
Love	20	X				
Hug	20	X		X		
Kiss	20	X	X	X	X	
Negative						
Sad	20	X	X	X	X	
Mad	20	X	X	X	X	X
Scared	20	X				
Scary	20	X	X	X		
Dirty	20	X	X	X		X
Messy	20	X	X			
Bad (feeling)	20	X	X			
Cry	17	X	X	X	X	X

	Age					
Volition and Ability						
Want	20	X	X		X	X
Need	22	X	X	X		X
Have to	25	X			X	
Can	20	X	X		X	X
Hard	20	X	X			
Cognition						
Know	15	X			X	
Think	23½	X	X		X	
Remember	26	X			X	
Believe	26	X			X	
Maybe	33	X			X	
May	33	X			X	
Seem	29	X	X			
Understand	28		X			
Pretend	29	X	X	X		
Moral Judgment						
Good	20	X	X	X		
Bad, naughty	20	X	X	X		
May	25	X	X			
Let	25		X		X	X
Supposed to	25	X	X		X	X
Must	34	X				X

Note: The table indicates the age at which each word was first used, whether it was applied to self and/or others, and the types of utterance. The data were obtained from the Boulder Sample, a pilot study, and various published sources as identified in the Appendix.

353

state). Whether a label is first applied to the self or to another may depend on the individual label, but *when* a label is appropriately applied both to self and others by the same child, we have evidence that psychological one-to-one correspondence has been achieved for that label, and that the state can be symbolically represented.

In addition to noting the person to whom the label is applied, we were also interested in the extent to which a child could use a label *outside* the situation in which the particular emotion or state was felt or experienced. If a child says "me hungry," he or she is talking about a state presently being experienced. But if a child says "I was hungry," he or she is talking about past experience. The first statement could be replaced by pointing at food and making a peremptory sound; the second statement could not. The second type of statement indicates that the child cannot only label the state when it occurs, but can use it for the symbolic manipulation of knowledge and for the symbolic sharing of such knowledge outside the narrow context of the experience itself. The same is true of statements in which a state is denied ("Me no hungry") or couched in the future tense ("I will be hungry"). (See Table 12.5 for how frequently such statements were found in the literature.)

Another extremely important aspect of knowledge and communication about the internal states of self and others is the attribution of cause and effect (including as cause or effect a person's internal state and behavior). Table 12.6 illustrates that causal utterances about the internal states of self and others appear almost as early as internal-state labeling itself. Note that almost half of the statements that we collected were made by children under 26 months of age.

TABLE 12.6

Child Utterances About the Possible Cause or Resolution (Termination) of Internal States Experienced by Self and Others[a]

State	Utterance	Age	State of Self	State of Other
Perceptual States				
SEE	"Want out/see wow-wow."	22½	X	
	"Seen enough today/Go night-night again. (also under WANT)	27		X
WATCH:	"I left it open, because I wanna watch it (TV)."	31	X	
COLD:	"Brr-cold. Get jacket."	20	X	
	"Cold. Cold feet. Put heater up."	21	X	
	"Baby blanket—cold." (about doll)	23		X
	"Close (window)—so Bubi doesn't freeze."	26½	X	
HOT:	"If I get too hot, I sweat."	33	X	
HURT:	"Head-ouch-cut."	17	X	
	"Doctur hurt Mommy/stone-stick." (threat)	20		X
	"Christy fell down/hurt self."	24½	X	
	"I'm putting medicine on the lamb's leg cause he had a boo-boo." (pretend play)	31½		X

TABLE 12.6 *(continued)*

State	Utterance	Age	State of Self	State of Other
Physiological States				
SLEEP:	"Daddy sleep. Mustn't shout. Daddy finish sleeping—me can shout again.	31		X
TIRED:	"Tired, tired? Chair-yes? Sit."	21½	X	
WAKE UP:	"Don't ring the bell either. Jenny will wake up."	35		X
Emotional States				
SAD:	"Her eyes are crying—her sad."	26		X
	"I'm sad I popped it." (balloon)	25	X	
	"Goes train. We sad." (about father's trip)	30	X	X
	"Today (we will) both go on trip. Else (should) not be sad. . . . .(because we will) come back."	33		X
HAPPY:	"Günther made Mommy happy."	31		X
PLEASED:	"He pleased of (about) Hilde."	33		X
MAD:	"If I cry I'm mad. If you cry I'll be mad."	26	X	X
SCARE:	"That doesn't scare me." (scare is causative)	20	X	
	"Those ladies scare me."	25	X	
DIRTY:	"Baby/splash/dirty."	20½		X
BAD:	"Daisy gone. No more in garden. (I feel) bad."	25½	X	
CRY:	"Baby cry/hurt/breast." (Baby needs to be fed)	17		X
	"Don't say shhh to me. I wanna cry." (also under MAD and WANT)	26	X	
States of Volition and Ability				
WANT:	"(Child is) crying/want Mommy."	24½		X
	"I want to go door see my Mommy." (also under SEE and CRY)	25½	X	
NEED:	"You need a stool to climb up."	25½		X
CAN:	"Can't. Too hard."	20	X	
	"The door is open so I can get in."	33	X	
	"When I was a little girl I could go 'geek-geek' like that, but now I can go 'this is a chair.'"	34	X	
	"Now you can try one/cause I teached you." (also under KNOW)	35		X
Cognitive States				
KNOW:	"Could you read this to me, cause I don't know how."	35½	X	
States of Moral Obligation				
MUST:	"Doll is going to sleep. Must be quiet." (also under SLEEP)	34	X	

[a]See the Appendix for the sources of these utterances, as well as the context in which they occurred.

Hood and Bloom (1979) also analyzed causal utterances produced by children in their second and third years. They found that the majority of causal statements made by the children in their sample were concerned with the activities and internal states of people ("I want to go door see my Mommy"), rather than with the behavior of physical objects ("Cup fall so it broke"). Physical objects obey the laws of what Aristotle has called efficient causality (direct push, gravity, etc.) whereas persons usually influence each other via what Aristotle has called final causality (will, motivation). As scientists, we know much more about efficient causality in the domain of physical reality than about final causality as it is exercised in personal interaction. Yet it appears, on the basis of Hood and Bloom's findings, that psychological causality is much more salient for young children than physical causality. Moreover, our own inventory of causal statements would suggest that children are as interested in explaining others' internal states as they are in explaining their own.

Lastly, the fact that young children sometimes *question* others about their internal states ("Are you alright?"), or question one person about the internal state of a third ("Is Tara mad at me?") indicates awareness that the states of others are not always easy to infer. The same is true of statements indicating uncertainty such as "I think that man is going camping" or "He may want to play with the truck." It appears that at a very young age children are *beginning* to realize that the interfacing of minds has to be achieved through communication, that intersubjectivity is not automatic. Thus, young children are neither radical egocentrists, nor radical behaviorists.

CONCLUSIONS

From a theory of interfacible minds (see page 000), which is *implicit* in infants' first attempts at intentional communication at the end of the first year, young children progress to an *explicit, verbally expressible* theory of mind that begins to emerge at the end of the second year. At this stage in their development, children become capable of exchanging verbal information about internal states as experienced by themselves and by others and the fact that they do so allows us to make a number of inferences about the state of their person knowledge.

Let us now return to the 12-point person model proposed by Shields (1978) as a minimum prerequisite for the occurrence fo communication and for the later development of role-taking skills. The data on the development of language and communication that we have presented lend support to each of Shields' 12 points and to two additional points of our own. In their language, children between 12 and 36 months of age *explicitly* (as well as implicitly) express the knowledge:

1. that persons have identity over time despite changes in location: by talking about "daddy at work"; persons have identity despite changes in behavior, state, and appearance by commenting on "daddy sleeping," "mommy mad.";

2. that persons are self-moving or animate: by making requests for actions or objects; influence over the course of their behavior has to be negotiated by "look," "watch," "listen.";

3. that persons identify each other: and can react to each other by naming and correctly using personal pronouns;

4. that persons see, hear, smell, feel (touch), feel temperature, and feel pain: by using the appropriate labels for these experiences; persons have a perceptual field by asking "did you see?", or commenting "I can't see," "want to see," "daddy didn't hear";

5. that persons intend their actions: by "I want," "you want," "baby wants," "I'm going to.";

6. that persons conceptualize and construct their world in roughly similar ways: through language itself, but also by asking questions or stating "I know," "you know.";

7. that persons have moods and states such as joy, anger, sadness, and fear as well as likes and dislikes: (mad) by words denoting these feelings and states: "mom " "K. likes me," "I love K..";

8. that persons can send and receive messages based on gestures and words: that are related to context in stable ways by using the medium of language for communication; the messages are sometimes successfully, sometimes unsuccessfully, received by "understand," "daddy didn't hear";

9. that persons have an action potential: by commenting "I can," "I know how," "I don't think I can"; some persons have a higher action protential than others by "only daddy can," "now you can try cause I teached you";

10. that persons can retain previous experience and structure their present behavior by it: through requests for repetition and words like remember; that people can sometimes forget previous experience or knowledge by "I don't remember";

11. that persons can replicate previous behavior in new contexts: by "pretend that...," "I know how...," "You can...";

12. that persons share a set of rules about what is appropriate behavior within particular frames of action: by "you supposed to," "good boy," "bad girl," and polite language like "hi," "bye," "please," "thank you";

13. that interpersonal behavior is regulated by reciprocal consent: using words such as "let," "may," "may not";

14. that the internal states of others are not always unambiguously expressed and have to be inferred: by "Is T. mad at me?," "Moo. Dyahear?"

There can be no question that very young children have a fairly sophisticated model of others and of themselves as psychological beings, even though they still make many errors of attribution and find it difficult to manipulate many aspects of their person knowledge simultaneously, as required in the traditional egocentrism tests (see Flavell et al., 1968).

But is the capacity to talk about internal states related to interpersonal functioning? It would seem reasonable to suppose that being able to give verbal expression to one's states should facilitate interaction and lead to the acquisition of further knowledge through feedback (having one's misconceptions corrected). Until the research results are in, however, we cannot be sure that this is so.

Furthermore, it is likely that were we to look, we would discover individual differences in the extent to which children talk about the perceptions, intentions, feelings, thoughts, and activities of persons and the degree to which they talk about the properties of physical objects. In play, analogous differences have been noted by Shotwell, Wolf and Gardner (1979), who observed that some children prefer to reenact person-related events in symbolic play (dramatists), and others explore the structure of the physical world in combinatorial play (patterners). Clarke-Stewart (1973) found boys at 20 months to be more object-oriented and girls to be more person-oriented. Are these differences also reflected in the vocabulary of the children? What we have in mind is slightly different from the expressive-referential dichotomy described by Nelson (1973) when she studied the acquisiton of the first 50 words. Some of her subjects used language as a tool for *regulating* interaction (expressive) and some to talk *about* the object world (referential). We are instead interested in whether there are children who specialize in *analyzing* the social rather than the object world—in infant psychologists versus infant physicists. Does preference for combinatorial play go with a more sophisticated object vocabulary and preference for symbolic play go with a more articulated internal-state vocabulary?

If individual differences such as these are found to exist, where do they originate? Are they associated with the child's temperament (and related cognitive style) or with the harmoniousness of mother-child interaction? Or are they perhaps more specifically related to how often internal-state words are mentioned by adults in the child's environment and *when* a state is labeled (while the child is experiencing it or attending to someone else experiencing it)? These and many other research questions remain to be answered.

APPENDIX TO CHAPTER 12
Utterances Made by Children up to 36 Months About Internal (Mental) States Experienced by Self and Others

Child	Utterance and Context	Age (in months)	Source
	Perceptual Terms		
LOOK/SEE/WATCH			
Ty:	"See." (while pointing and turning to listener for eye-contact)	11	Volterra et al., 1979
Ky:	"I see a car." (looking out of window)	20	Present study[a]
Eric:	"Let me see."	20½	Bloom et al., 1975
Christy:	"Want out/see wow-wow."	22–22½	Bowerman, 1974
Tr:	"Watch, Mommy." (trying to get M to look at her play)	24	Present study
Hilde:	"Look, Momma, come, a pretty one, see?" (wants mother to look at her scribble)	24	Stern & Stern, 1928
Eric:	"I saw it." (looks for object, sees it, and goes after it)	25	Bloom et al., 1975
Jacqueline:	"You see the lake and the trees." "You see a carriage, a horse, etc. (to doll, holding it through balcony railings facing street)	25	Piaget, 1962
Hilde:	"Seen enough today. Go night-night again." (after mother put little brother back into baby carriage)	27	Stern & Stern, 1928
Hilde:	"Pappa look—Hilde has done." (meaning: "Look at what Hilde has done.")	30	Stern & Stern, 1928
Paul:	"I left it open, because I wanna watch it." (regarding TV, which is on)	31	Hood & Bloom, 1979
HEAR			
Günther:	"Moo? Dyahear?" (at cow mooing outside)	14½	Stern & Stern, 1928
Hilde:	"Listen. Daddy roll." (She had asked her father to get her a roll. This was said when she heard his returning steps.)	22	Stern & Stern, 1928
Kathryn:	"I hear childrens." (on hearing voice of children playing outside)	24	Bloom et al., 1975
Jacqueline:	"Daddy didn't hear." (after father did not respond to her call)	28½	Piaget, 1962
Hilde:	"Listen. Thunder." (during storm)	30	Stern & Stern, 1928

(continued)

Child	Utterance and Context	Age (in months)	Source
TASTE			
Hilde:	"Taste good?" (to parents at mealtime)	26	Stern & Stern, 1928
Hilde:	"No, doesn't taste good." (after father tries to get her to eat her soup by suggesting it tastes so good)	30	Stern & Stern, 1928
FEEL (to touch)			
Christy:	"Want feel slide cool now."	24½	Bowermann, 1974
COLD			
Ni:	"Brr-cold. Get jacket."	20	Present study
Kathryn:	"Cold. Cold feet. Put heater up." (touching window)	21	Bloom et al., 1975
Hilde:	"Baby cold." (on looking at naked cherub in Rafael painting)	23	Stern & Stern, 1928
Jacqueline:	"Baby blanket—cold." (to doll before covering it up)	23	Piaget, 1962
Cathy:	"I am freezing."	25	Present study
Bubi:	"Close, so Bubi doesn't freeze." (asks to have window closed)	26½	Stern & Stern, 1928
Hilde:	"Momma cold?" (feels mother's cheek, which is warm) "No." (meaning not cold)	30	Stern & Stern, 1928
HOT			
Js:	"Hot." (when hot, moving sweater away from body)	20	Present study
Cathy:	"They are nice and warm." (on looking at picture of children wearing snowsuits)	25	Present study
Kathryn:	"I got too hot, oh. If I get too hot, I sweat."	33	Bloom & Lahey, 1978
HURT, OUCH			
P:	"Head-ouch-cut."	18½	Guillaume, 1978
	"Doctor hurt Mommy/stone/stick." (threatens doctor whom he blames for mother's illness)	20	Guillaume, 1978
Dr.:	"Hurt." (after mother said ouch on hurting herself) "Hurt finger." (said about hurting her own finger)	20	Guillaume, 1978
Ni:	"Poor J. Owie." (when brother hurt himself)	20	Guillaume, 1978

J:	"Ouch. It hurts. Be better soon. Poor baby." (said to doll wearing bandaid. J had hurt himself several hours before, and parents had put bandaid on doll to comfort him. Mother had said to J what J now, several hours later, said to doll.)	20	Rubin & Wolf, 1979
Allison:	"Hurt knee." (after putting a toy pig against sharp corner of truck on which she herself had hurt herself some moments before)	22	Bloom, 1973
Christy:	"Christy fell down/hurt self."	24½	Bowermann, 1974
Eric:	"I'm putting medicine on the lamb's leg cause he had a boo-boo." (pretending)	31½	Hood & Bloom, 1979

Physiological States

HUNGRY

Nt:	"I hungry." (said appropriately)	20	Present study
Kathryn:	"Hungry, mm. Girl hungry. Daddy. No Daddy hungry. Daddy up. Mommy hungry, boy hungry." (on looking at picture of mother and two children sitting at table, father carrying in food)	22½	Bloom & Lahey, 1978
Cathy:	"I was hungry."	25	Present study
Gia:	"I am starving." (said appropriately)	25½	Bloom et al, 1975
	"Lamb hungry." (while holding toy lamb)		

THIRSTY

Tr:	"I thirsty." (when wants drink)	20	Present study
Ky:	"I was thirsty." (after having taken a drink)	20	Present study
Scupin's son:	"No, a little thirst." (when mother is trying to get him to drink by saying he has a big thirst [literal translation])	20	Stern & Stern, 1928

SLEEPY, SLEEP

Ls:	"Seepy." (when tired)	20	Present study
	"Seep." (to doll in play, putting hand over doll's eyes)	20	Present study
Gi:	"Sleep." (closes eyes in pretend sleep)	20	Present study
	"He's sleeping." (of person in TV program)		
Ky:	"I go to sleep." (in bed)	20	Present study
Eric:	"Mommy sleeping." (putting Mommy form flat on board)	23½	Bloom et al, 1975
Hilde:	"Slept well?" (questions parents)	26	Stern & Stern, 1928
Günther:	"Daddy sleep. Mustn't shout. Daddy finish sleeping—me can shout again." (while father is napping)	31	Stern & Stern, 1928

(continued)

Child	Utterance and Context	Age (in months)	Source
TIRED			
Allison:	"Tire." (for self when pretend sleeping and for others lying down with eyes closed)	17	Bloom, 1973
Nt:	"I tired." (used appropriately)	20	Present study
Ky:	"I'm tired." (used appropriately)	20	Present study
Kythryn:	"Baby tired." (to picture of sleeping baby)	21	Bloom, 1970
Hilde:	"Tired, tired? Chair—yes? Sit." (when tired wants to be put in chair. Unclear whether addressed to parents or self)	21½	Stern & Stern, 1928
Kathryn:	"I not tired." (context not given)	24	Bloom, 1970
Eva:	"Are you tired?" (on seeing someone yawn)	26	Bloom, 1970
AWAKE			
Günther:	"Hilde awake, Daddy awake, all awake."	28	Stern & Stern, 1928
Hilde:	"Look. It woke up." (about doll, a little while after she had put the doll to bed)	29	Stern & Stern, 1928
Peter:	"Don't ring the bell either. Jenny will wake up." (commanding)	35	Hood & Bloom, 1979

Emotional Terms
POSITIVE EMOTIONS

Child	Utterance and Context	Age (in months)	Source
HAPPY			
Dw:	"Happy." (when he sees people smile)	20	Present study
Js:	"Happy." (of self when seems to feel happy)	20	Present study
Ky:	"I'm happy." (when he seems to feel happy)	20	Present study
Et:	"Et is happy now." (habitually said on calming down after having been upset)	21	Present study
Gia:	"I'm not unhappy."	27	Bloom, 1970
Günther:	"Günther made Mommy happy." (when mother laughs while she praises his drawing)	31	Stern & Stern, 1928
Hilde:	"He pleased of (meaning about) Hilde." (said when little brother laughs at Hilde's dancing)	33	Stern & Stern, 1928

Hilde:	"How pleased doll is."		
	"Doll making a pleased face." (to mother during pretend play with doll)	36	Stern & Stern, 1928
FUN			
Peter:	"That fun." (rolling small objects down slide and making them crash)	25	Bloom et al., 1975
Cathy:	"That was fun."	25	Present study
FUNNY			
Tr:	"Funny." (about self when she is the star attractin, also about dog's antics)	20	Present study
Allison:	"Funny." (while crushing a cup)	20½	Bloom, 1973
Günther:	"Have cut—looks funny." (what he has cut looks funny)	31	Stern & Stern, 1928
FEEL (emotion)			
Cathy:	"You feel better now, Tara?" (to sister, after she had been sent to her room)		
	"Are you all right?" (to mother after she had been angry)		
	"I feel bad." (meaning sad, also under BAD)	25	Present study
An:	"Nice girl." (of self)	20	Present study
Ni:	"Nice baby." (patting doll in play)	20	Present study
Ky:	"R is a nice boy." (about his friend)	20	Present study
Ec:	Comes over and slaps mother who says: "You can't do that."		
	Ec replies by stroking mother and saying: "Make nice."	20	Present study
KISS			
Hn:	"Kiss." (when making two dolls kiss each other)	20	Present study
Ni:	"Give kiss." (when going over to kiss somebody)	20	Present study
	"Kiss baby." (when going over to kiss a baby)		
Ky:	"I'll give the dog a kiss." (about kissing dog)	20	Present study
	"Kiss the doll." (command to mother)		
Eric:	"I want kiss it/I want kiss." (trying to reach baby sister in crib)	25	Bloom et al., 1975
Hilde:	"Momma come. Give kiss." (asking mother for a kiss)	30	Stern & Stern, 1928
LIKE			

(continued)

Child	Utterance and Context	Age (in months)	Source
Kathryn:	"I no like celery." (not taking celery when offered by mother)	22½	Bloom, 1970
	"Daddy like coffee, Lois no coffee." (prompted by talk about a coffee store)	22½	Bloom, 1970
	"Kathryn, me like crackers." (during pretend play with Lois, on being asked if she likes nuts)	24	Bloom, et al., 1975
Scupin's soon:	"Like cake better."	24	Stern & Stern, 1928
Eric:	"I no like to." (on being asked if he wanted to go on a roller coaster again)	24	Bloom, 1970
Cathy:	"K likes me." (said when friend's dog nuzzles her)	26	Bloom, 1970
Hilde:	"Like to eat carrot better." (on being fed soup)	30	Stern, 1927
LOVE, HUG			
Nc:	"I love you." (bedtime formula)	20	Present study
Ct:	"Ov." (when she hugs someone)	20	Present study
Cl:	"Hug." (when asking to be hugged)	20	Present study
Cr:	"Hug." (looking at picture of people hugging)	20	Present study
	"Love." (when embracing her mother)	21	Stern & Stern, 1928
Hilde:	"I love K" (said when playing with friend's dog after overcoming initial apprehension)	26	Present study
	NEGATIVE EMOTIONS		
SAD			
Ky:	"Boy sad." (about boy crying in picture)	20	Present study
Ar:	"Mommy sad. Mommy cry." (about mother crying)	20	Present study
Cathy:	"I'm sad I popped it." (about balloon)	25	Present study
Cathy:	"Her eyes are crying. .(pause). . her sad." (Looking at a picture of herself taken at her birthday party. In the picture she was not crying, but her eyes were partly shut)	26	Present study
Günther:	"Goes train. We sad." (about father leaving for a trip)	30	Stern & Stern, 1928
Günther:	Telling a story about self and sister: "Today both go on trip. Else not be sad." (Parents reply Else, the nursemaid, will cry.) "Oh, no, come back."	33	Stern & Stern, 1928

MAD, ANGRY

Speaker	Quote	Age	Reference
N:	"Mom, mad."	20	Present study
Cathy:	"Mommy, is Tara mad at me?" (question to mother when sister was indeed angry at Cathy)	25	Present study
	"I'm mad at you, Mommy." (when mother says dinner isn't ready yet)	26	Present study
Cathy:	"If I cry, I am mad." (trying to explain something to mother, also under CRY)	26	Present study
Hilde:	"Doll is making a mad (bös) face." (to mother during pretend play with doll)	34	Stern & Stern, 1928

SCARED, AFRAID

Speaker	Quote	Age	Reference
P:	"Afraid." (when strange woman picks him up, and in many other contexts)	15	Guillaume, 1927
Dr:	"Scared." (when father makes scary faces)	20	Present study
Ky:	"I'm not scared."		
	"That doesn't scare me." (habitually said in situations when he is really scared)		
Hilde:	"A scare." (on seeing cold washcloth)	20	Present study
Cathy:	"Those ladies scare me." (after swimming teachers tried to put her in the pool)	23	Stern & Stern, 1928
Cathy:	"I'm scary. You're scary." (playing ghost game with sister	25	Present study
J:	"Dat scary lion." (on seeing a small lion previously used in elicited pretend play. Takes lion and hides it away across room)	26	Present study
		28	Rubin & Wolf, 1979

DIRTY

Speaker	Quote	Age	Reference
Bt:	"Dirty." (when brother is dirty)	20	Present study
Ky:	"I have dirty hands"		
	"Doll has dirty hands."		
Ni:	"Messy." (when self is dirty)	20	Present study
	"J is messy." (of brother)	20	Present study
Allison:	"Baby/splash/dirty." (when mother gives baby doll a bath in a cup)	20½	Bloom, 1973

BAD (feeling)

Speaker	Quote	Age	Reference
Dr:	"Bad." (on hearing a baby cry)	20	Present study

(continued)

Child	Utterance and Context	Age (in months)	Source
Tr:	"Doo-doo my head." (on bumping head. Doo-doo is her word for bad.)	20	Present study
Cathy:	"I feel bad." (when she feels sad)	25	Present study
Luise:	"Daisy gone. No more in garden. Bad."	25½	Stern & Stern, 1928
CRY			
Pi:	"Baby cry/hurt/breast." (on hearing baby cry, asks for baby to be nursed)	17	Guillaume, 1927
Jacqueline:	"Cry, cry." (to her toy dog. She then imitated the sound of crying.)	19	Piaget, 1962
Nt:	"I cry."		
	"Mom cry." (both said appropriately)	20	Present study
Ky:	"I'm crying." (when pretending to cry)		
	"Baby is crying." (looking at picture of crying baby)	20	Present study
Js:	"I cried." (after he genuinely cried)	20	Present study
Tr:	"Cry." (command to grandmother in game where he hits her and she pretends to cry)	20	Present study
Cathy:	"Baby cry, Mommy." (telling M that a baby is crying)	20	
	"If you cry, you get mad." (Said when no one had been crying or been mad that day. Mother asked her to explain and she continued.) "If I cry, I am mad. If you (meaning mother) cry, I'll be mad."		
	"Don't say shhh to me! I wanna cry." (when Cathy fell off air mattress during camping and parents tried to shush her)	26	Present study

Expressions of Volition and Ability

Child	Utterance and Context	Age (in months)	Source
WANT			
Ln:	"Want juice." (request)	20	Present study
Ky:	"I wanta take a nap now."	20	Present study ·
Eric:	"I don't want baby." (on dropping baby doll)	20½	Bloom et al., 1975
Christy:	"Want out see wow-wow." (wants to go outside to see dog)	22½	Bowerman, 1974
Christy:	"Crying. Want mommy." (about crying child)	24½	Bowerman, 1974
Cathy:	"I want to do it myself." (assertion)	25	Present study

(continued)

Speaker	Utterance	Age	Reference
Gia:	"I want go door see my mommy."	25½	Bloom et al., 1975
Eric:	"Baby Nancy want bottle." (about baby sister who is crying)	25	Bloom et al., 1975
Hilde:	"Doll wants to look at pictures."	34	Stern & Stern, 1928
Allison:	"You want it on/you have it on." (said when mother takes microphone back from Allison)	28	Bloom & Lahey, 1978
NEED, HAVE TO			
Eric:	"ə need book." (when Lois teases him that she's going to take his book)	22	Bloom et al., 1975
Cathy:	"I don't have to go." (meaning to bathroom)	25	Present study
Gia:	"I need it/I want need it." (Gia draws on counter; Lois trying to take pencil from Gia)	25½	Bloom et al., 1975
Eric:	"You need a wrench to get up/you need a stool to climb up and you need a wrench." (Baby sitter comments that she can't reach the frying pan. Eric proposes stool to get up and wrench to unlock the cabinet, although it doesn't have a lock.)	33	Bloom & Lahey, 1978
CAN			
Ky:	"I can do it." "I can't get it."	20	Present study
Ni:	"Can't. Too hard."	20	Present study
Gia:	"Can't do it. You do it." (has trouble putting lamb in hollow block)	25½	Hood & Bloom, 1979
Cathy:	"I can do it myself."	25	Present study
Smith's son:	"Only Daddy can say 'jup.'" (after father tried to get him to say "jump" properly)	30	Smith, 1973
Kathryn:	"The door is open, so I can get in." (while going to her bedroom)	33	Bloom & Lahey, 1978
Unspecified:	"When I was a little girl I could go 'geek-geek' like that but now I can go 'This is a chair.'"	34	Limber, 1973
Kathryn:	"Now you can try one/cause I teached you how." (K is trying to get Lois to turn a somersault after giving her a demonstration.)	35	Bloom & Lahey, 1978
HARD			
Ar:	"Hard. Hard." (on trying to obtain an object by means of a stick)	20	Present study
Ni:	"Can't. Too hard." (when unable to do something)	20	Present study

Child	Utterance and Context	Age (in months)	Source
Ky:	"That's hard work." (when unable to do something)	20	Present study
Cathy:	"That's too hard for me." (when unable to do something)	25	Present study
	Cognitive Terms		
KNOW			
J:	"I don't know." (said while gesturing with hands turned up when asked, "Where's X?")	15	Present study
Tr:	"I don't know." (when asked for something and she cannot find it)	20	Present study
Cathy:	"I know how to turn it on." (said about faucet)	26	Present study
Mariana:	"Could you read this to me, cause I don't know how." (bringing book to L)	35½	Hood & Bloom, 1979
THINK			
Eric:	"No ə think so."	23½	Bloom, 1970
Cathy:	"I think I can't." (Mother asked her to get blanket, but the bedroom door, which she can't open yet, was shut.)	26	Present study
H. Neugebauer's son:	"The cow is thinking something." (about a cow that is looking at him steadily)	26	Stern & Stern, 1928
Ky:	"I think it's a propeller airplane." (when asked what kind of airplane it is. Father is teaching him the difference between different kinds of airplanes.)	26½	Present study
Tögel's son:	"I thought it would be dark." (context not given)	29	Stern & Stern, 1928
Günther:	"I think, rice soup." (on seeing soup being served at table. When it was carried in, he misidentified it as 'snow-soup.')	33	Stern & Stern, 1928
Günther:	"Miss Schmidt thought two." (Günther had been given three cookies. Miss Schmidt teased him by saying he had two.)	33	Stern & Stern, 1928
Allison:	"I think he'll play with the truck." (about baby to whom she had given a truck to play with)	33	Bloom & Lahey, 1978

REMEMBER		
Cathy:	"I don't remember/ man's name." (visiting another family and being asked to name family members)	26	Present study
BELIEVE		
Cathy:	"I don't believe it/that Brian went to A..." (tries to say Arizona). (A 6-year-old neighbor boy had left for Arizona the previous night. This was uttered the next morning before anyone had mentioned Brian.)	26	Present study
MAYBE, MAY, SEEM		
Günther:	"Is that cake, maybe?" (on seeing an unfamiliar dish)	33	Stern & Stern, 1928
Allison:	"He may want to play with the truck."	33	Bloom & Lahey, 1978
	"Maybe he'll play with the truck." (putting down a truck for the baby to play with)		
Meringer's daughter:	"What Mommy got! Seems she brought plums."	29	Stern & Stern, 1928
UNDERSTAND		
Günther:	"Emma understood." (He couldn't think of the name of a stirrer, so he successfully used a stirring gesture to request it instead.)	28	Stern & Stern, 1928
PRETEND		
Unspecified:	"I going out Mommy. Mommy you (pre)tend to cry." (giving order to mother)	29	Gardner & Wolf, 1979
Günther:	"Pretend Christine is here."	29½	Stern & Stern, 1928
Eric:	"He pretending himself is a beetle." (had set down a wire man in very awkward position, with legs twisted around the body. Answer to Lois' question, "Am, does that man stand?")	33	Bloom & Lahey, 1978

Moral Terms

GOOD (usually meaning well-behaved)		
Js:	"Good Daddy." (when father does something Js wanted him to do)	20	Present study
Ky:	"I'm a good boy." (in praise of self)	20	Present study
Hilde:	"Good children." (she used a German term, "artig," meaning well-behaved)	23	Stern & Stern, 1928
Cathy:	"I'm a good girl." (in praise of self)	25	Present study

(continued)

369

Child	Utterance and Context	Age (in months)	Source
BAD (moral sense)			
Dr:	"Bad boy." (at picture of old lady spanking boy)	20	Stern & Stern, 1928
Ky:	"K was bad." (after being naughty)	20	Stern & Stern, 1928
	"Naughty dog." (at picture of dog chewing up a book)	20	Stern & Stern, 1928
Rb:	"Rb bad, no-no." (looking at electric socket)	25	Bloom et al. 1975
Eric:	"Də bad boy/a naughty boy." (after Mother says, "I sometimes hit you when you're a bad boy.")	25½	Bloom et al. 1975
Gia:	"Bad, bad boy baby." (looking at picture of bad baby)	28	Rubin & Wolf, 1979
J:	"Go back bad lion." (talking for doll who is being chased by a lion in elicited pretend play)	31	Stern & Stern, 1928
Günther:	"I is bad." (after tearing up a paper sun and being asked why)		
LET, MAY (permission)			
Cathy:	"May I please have cookie?" (asking for cookie)	25	Present study
	"Tara won't let me have it." (about sister)	25	Present study
Allison:	"May I/I wanna sit on here." (after having climbed onto big chair)	28	Bloom & Lahey, 1978
Eva:	"Why may I not eat downstairs?"	28½	Stern & Stern, 1928
SUPPOSED TO, MUST (obligation)			
Cathy:	"I'm not supposed to pee-pee on the floor."	25	Present study
	"Mommy, you supposed to talk to me?" (after mother had spent time talking to sister)	25	Present study
Hilde:	"Doll is going to sleep. Must be quiet." (during doll play)	34	Stern & Stern, 1928

[a] All utterances labeled present study were obtained from the Boulder Sample, from a pilot study by the senior author, and from Cathy's mother (Lynn Tracy).

ACKNOWLEDGMENTS

During the writing of this paper, the authors were supported by a grant from the Spencer Foundation. The research reported in this paper was funded by a grant from the National Science Foundation (BNS76-17624) and a grant from the Spencer Foundation to E. Bates and I. Bretherton. We would like to express our appreciation to the mothers and infants of the Boulder Sample and to Vicki Carlson, Karlana Carpen, Andy Garrison, Cecilia Shore, and Carol Williamson who helped with the data collection and analysis. We also thank Lynn Tracy for recording her daughter's internal-state utterances.

REFERENCES

Bates, E. Intentions, conventions, and symbols. In E. Bates et al., *The emergence of symbols: Cognition and communication in infancy.* New York: Academic Press, 1979.

Bates, E., Benigni, L., Bretherton, I., Camaioni, L., & Volterra, V. Cognition and communication from 9–13 months: Correlational findings. In E. Bates, *The emergence of symbols: Cognition and communication in infancy.* New York: Academic Press, 1979.

Bates, E., Camaioni, L., & Volterra, V. The acquisition of performatives prior to speech. *Merrill-Palmer Quarterly,* 1975, *21*(3), 205–226.

Bell, S. M. The development of the concept of object as related to infant-mother attachment. *Child Development,* 1970, *41*, 291–313.

Bloom, L. *Language development; Form and function in emerging grammars.* Cambridge, Mass.: MIT Press, 1970.

Bloom, L. *One word at a time.* The Hague: Mouton, 1973.

Bloom, L., & Lahey, M. *Language development and language disorders.* New York: Wiley, 1978.

Bloom, L., Lightbown, P., & Hood, L. Structure and variation in child language. *Monograph of the Society for Research in Child Development,* 1975, No. 2.

Bowerman, M. Learning the structure of causative verbs: A study in the relationships of cognitive, semantic and syntactic development. *Papers and reports on child language,* Linguistics Department, Stanford University, 1974.

Brazelton, T. B., Kozlowski, B., & Main, M. *The origins of reciprocity: The early mother-infant interaction.* In M. Lewis & L. A. Rosenblum (Eds.), *The effect of the infant on its caregiver.* New York: Wiley, 1974.

Bretherton, I., & Bates, E. The emergence of intentional communication. In I. Uzgiris (Ed.), *New directions for child development* (Vol. 4). San Francisco: Jossey-Bass, 1979.

Brown, R. *A first language: The early stages.* Cambridge, Mass.: Harvard University Press, 1973.

Bruner, J. S. Early social interaction and language acquisition. In H. R. Schafer (Ed.), *Studies in mother-infant interaction.* New York: Academic Press, 1977.

Clark, E. Awareness of language: Some evidence from what children say and do. In A. Sinclair, R. T. Jarvella, & W. T. M. Levelt (Eds.), *The child's conception of language.* New York: Springer-Verlag, 1978.

Clark, E. V., & Sengul, C. J. Strategies in the acquisition of deixis. *Journal of Child Language.* 1978, *5,* 457–475.

Clarke-Stewart, K. A. Interactions between mothers and their young children: Characteristics and consequences. *Monographs of the Society for Research in Child Development,* 1973, *37,* No. 153.

Edwards, D. Social relations and early language. In A. Lock (Ed.), *Action, gesture and symbol.* New York: Academic Press, 1978.

Flavell, T. H. *The developmental psychology of Jean Piaget.* New York: Van Nostrand, 1963.

Flavell, T. H. The development of inferences about others. In T. Mischel (Ed.), *Understanding other persons.* Totowa, N.J.: Rowan & Littlefield, 1974.

Flavell, T. H., Botkin, P. T., & Fry, C. L. *The development of role-taking and communication skills in young children.* New York: Wiley, 1968.

Gardner, H., & Wolf, D. *The development of symbolic capacities.* Grant proposal submitted to the Carnegie Corporation, 1979.

Grice, H. P. Utterer's meaning, sentence-meaning, and word-meaning. *Foundation of Language,* 1968, *4,* 1–18.

Guillaume, P. First stages of sentence formation in children's speech (1927). In L. Bloom (Ed.), *Readings in child development research.* New York: Wiley, 1978.

Habermas, T. *Knowledge and human interests.* London: Heinemann, 1972.

Hamlyn, D. W. Person-perception and our understanding of others. In T. Mischel (Ed.), *Understanding other persons.* Oxford: Blackwell, 1974.

Halliday, M. A. *Learning how to mean: Explorations in the development of language.* London: Edward Arnold, 1975.

Heider, F. *The psychology of interpersonal relations.* New York: Wiley, 1958.

Hoffman, M. L. Developmental synthesis of affect and cognition and its implications for altruistic motivation. *Developmental Psychology,* 1975, *11,* 607–622.

Hood, L., & Bloom, L. What, when and how about why: A longitudinal study of early expressions of causality. *Monograph of the Society for Research in Child Development,* 1979, *44,* Serial No. 181.

Jackson, E., Campos, J. J., & Fischer, K. W. The question of decalage between object permanence and person permanence. *Developmental Psychology,* 1978, *14,* 1–10.

Killen, M., & Uzgiris, I. *Imitation of actions with objects: The role of social meaning.* Paper presented at the International Conference on Infant Studies, Providence, R. I., March 1978.

Lempers, T., Flavell, E., & Flavell, T. H. The development in very young children of tacit knowledge concerning visual perception. *Genetic Psychology Monographs,* 1977, *95,* 3–53.

Lewis, M., & Brooks-Gunn, J. Toward a theory of social cognition: The development of self. In I. Uzgiris (Ed.), *New directions for child development* (Vol. 4). San Francisco, Jossey-Bass, 1979.

Limber, J. The genesis of complex sentences. In T. E. Moore (Ed.), *Cognitive development and the acquisition of language.* New York: Academic Press, 1973.

Main, M., Weston, D., & Wakeling, S. *"Concerned attention" to the crying of an adult actor.* Paper presented at the Biennial Meeting of the Society for Research in Child Development, San Francisco, March 1979.

Masangkay, Z., McCluskey, K., McIntyre, C., Sims-Knight, J., Vaughn, B., & Flavell, J. The early development of inferences about the visual percepts of others. *Child Development,* 1974, *45,* 357–366.

Meltzoff, A., & Moore, M. K. Imitations of facial and manual gestures by human neonates. *Science,* 1977, *198,* 75–78.

Murphy, C. M., & Messer, J. D. Mothers, infants and pointing: A study of a gesture. In H. R. Schaffer (Ed.), *Studies in mother-infant interaction.* New York: Academic Press, 1977.

Nelson, K. Structure and strategy in learning to talk. *Monographs of the Society for Research in Child Development,* 1973, *48,* Serial No. 149.

Newson, T. An intersubjective approach to the systematic description of mother-infant interaction. In H. R. Schaffer (Ed.), *Studies in mother-infant interaction.* New York: Academic Press, 1977.

Piaget, J. *The construction of reality in the child.* New York: Basic Books, 1954.

Piaget, J. *Play, dreams and imitation in childhood.* New York: Norton, 1962.

Piaget, J. *The origins of intelligence in children.* New York: 1963.

Premack, D., & Woodruff, G. Does the chimpanzee have a theory of mind? *The Behavioral and Brain Sciences,* 1978, *1,* 516–526.

Rheingold, H. L., Gewirtz, J. L., & Ross, H. W. Social conditioning of vocalization in the infant. *Journal of Comparative and Physiological Psychology,* 1959, *52,* 68–73.

Rubin, S., & Wolf, D. The development of maybe: The evolution of roles into narrative. In E. Winner (Ed.), *New directions for child development* (Vol. 6). San Francisco: Jossey-Bass, 1980.

Sander, L. W. The regulation of exchange in the infant-caregiver system and some aspects of the context-content relationship. In M. Lewis & L. A. Rosemblum (Eds.), *Interaction, conversation and the development of language.* New York: Academic Press, 1977.

Scaife, M., & Bruner, J. S. The capacity for joint visual attention in the infant. *Nature,* 1975, *253,* 265–266.

Shields, M. M. The child as psychologist: Construing the social world. In A. Lock (Ed.), *Action, gesture and symbol.* New York: Academic Press, 1978.

Shotter, T. The cultural context of communication studies: Theoretical and methodological issues. In A. Lock (Ed.), *Action, gesture and symbol.* New York: Academic Press, 1978.

Shotwell, J., Wolf, D., & Gardner, H. Exploring early symbolization: Styles of achievement. In B. Sutton-Smith (Ed.), *Play and learning.* New York: Gardner Press, 1979.

Smith, N. V. The acquisition of phonology: A case study. Cambridge, England: Cambridge University Press, 1973.

Stern, C., & Stern, W. *Die Kindersprache: Eine psychologische und sprachtheoretische Untersuchung,* (4th ed.). Leipzig: Barth, 1928.

Stern, D. *The first relationship: Infant and mother.* Cambridge, Mass.: Harvard University Press, 1977.

Trevarthen, C., & Hubley, P. Secondary intersubjectivity: Confidence, confiding and acts of meaning in the first year. In A. Lock (Ed.), *Action, gesture and symbol.* New York: Academic Press, 1978.

Volterra, V., Bates, E., Benigni, L., Bretherton, I., & Camaioni, L. First words in language and action: A qualitative look. In E. Bates, *The emergence of symbols: Cognition and communication in infancy.* New York: Academic Press, 1979.

Wood, D., Bruner, J. S., & Ross, G. The role of tutoring in problem solving. *Journal of Child Psychology and Psychiatry,* 1976, *17,* 89–100.

Yarrow, M. R., & Waxler, C. Z. The emergence and functions of prosocial behaviors in young children. In B. Sutton-Smith (Ed.), *Play and learning.* New York: Gardner Press, 1979.

13

The Effects of Social Experience and Social Style on Cognitive Competence and Performance

Marguerite B. Stevenson
University of Wisconsin-Madison

Michael E. Lamb
University of Utah

The orientation of this chapter differs substantially from that of most others in this book. Our focus is upon the manner in which social experience affects cognitive development, whereas the other chapters deal for the most part with the implications of cognitive development for social and emotional development. It is likely, of course, that both types of relationships exist, and it is important not to overlook the complexity of the interface between cognitive and socioemotional development (Sroufe, 1979). Indeed, it is well to remember that the distinctions between cognitive, social, and emotional development are arbitrarily drawn by theorists for analytic purposes rather than because clear, substantive differences exist (Lamb & Campos, in press).

We begin this chapter with a brief review of the evidence suggesting that social or socially mediated experiences can facilitate or retard cognitive development. Thereafter, we describe and evaluate the mechanisms proposed to explain how social experiences affect cognitive development, noting that the putative mechanisms are largely complementary rather than mutually exclusive. Finally, we illustrate the complexity of the relationship between social experience and cognitive development by showing how the infant's personality and social style partially determine its social experiences and thereby affect its cognitive development.

DOES SOCIAL EXPERIENCE AFFECT
COGNITIVE DEVELOPMENT?

It is commonly believed that individual differences in the cognitive capacities of children are jointly determined by congenital differences and by the varied experiences the children have had. Experiences may involve interactions with social or nonsocial objects, and we are primarily interested here in experiences that are socially mediated. Four types of evidence suggest that rearing environments indeed influence cognitive development in infancy. First, institutionalized infants often develop more poorly than home-reared infants. Because infants raised in institutions are not provided with many of the experiences commonly available to home-reared infants, the deficient environment is often viewed as the source of their intellectual deficiencies. Second, the caretaking practices of lower- and middle-class parents differ substantially, and children from lower-class homes seem to develop more slowly. Again, differences in rearing environments are deemed responsible. Third, some of the experimental intervention programs designed to facilitate the development of lower-class infants by "enriching" their experiences have indeed accelerated infant development. Finally, measures of the caretaking environment are significantly correlated with measures of infant cognitive competence. Researchers assume that the direction of effects is from experience to competence, though the alternative possibility has never been entertained seriously. The following paragraphs summarize the evidence concerning the relationship between infant social experience and cognitive development.

Institutionalization

In 1945, Spitz published the results of his research comparing institutionalized infants with those reared at home. He reported that by the end of the first year, infants in one of the institutions appeared to be grossly retarded. Although this early study had many methodological weaknesses (see critique by Pinneau, 1955), subsequent research confirmed that, from the first year onward, the development of infants in many institutions lags behind that of infants reared in natural, foster, or adoptive homes (Ainsworth, 1966; Bowlby, 1951; Dennis & Najarian, 1957; Kohan-Raz, 1968; Provence & Lipton, 1961; Rutter, 1972).

There are many differences between institutional and home environments, and there has been considerable controversy about which differences are crucial. Some writers have followed Spitz and Bowlby in stressing the affective deprivation of the institutional environment, whereas others have emphasized the lack of social and physical stimulation available to infants in institutions. Both factors were probably debilitating, although improvements in institutional practices since 1951 have made the deprivation less extreme. It remains true that infants in institutions are often not provided with many of the experiences commonly available to home-reared infants (Casler, 1961; Rheingold, 1960; Rutter, 1972) and their cognitive development is retarded. Nevertheless, it is possible to improve the quality of institutional care sufficiently to insure normal development (Tizard, Cooperman, Joseph, &

Tizard, 1972). This suggests that differences in rearing environments are responsible for differences in infant development.

Social-Class Differences

Several studies have shown that infants are treated differently by middle- and lower-class mothers (Baylay & Schaefer, 1960; Lewis & Wilson, 1972; Tulkin & Cohler, 1973; Tulkin & Kagan, 1972). As a result, researchers have attempted to determine whether there are social-class differences in infant performance. The data are mixed. Standardized measures of infant cognitive performance do not reliably show social-class differences in infant performance (Bayley, 1935, 1965; Furfey, 1928; Golden & Birns, 1968; Hindley, 1960; Knobloch & Pasamanick, 1960; Lewis & Wilson, 1972), although social-class differences are clearly evident among slightly older children (Golden, Birns, Bridger, & Moss, 1971; Yando, Seitz, & Zigler, 1979). Social-class differences do, however, become apparent when low-birth-weight infants from lower- and middle-class families are compared (Drillien, 1964; Werner, Simonian, Bierman, & French, 1967). In addition, class differences are evident in several more specific areas of functioning than are assessed by the standardized measures of developmental quotient. By one year of age, lower-class infants perform more poorly on Piagetian object-permanence tasks (Wachs, Uzgiris, & Hunt, 1971), and may be more difficult to test than middle-class infants (Golden & Birns, 1968). One-year olds from lower-class backgrounds vocalize to their mothers less frequently than middle-class infants do (Messer & Lewis, 1972). In addition, middle-class 1-year-olds appear better able to differentiate between their mothers' voices and those of strangers (Tulkin, 1973). These social-class differences may result from differences in the rearing environments, although there are social-class differences in nutrition, medical care, and genetic endowment that may also account for the observed differences in infant competence.

Intervention Programs.

Additional evidence of environmental influences on cognitive development has been gathered in intervention studies designed to facilitate the development of lower-class infants. Although some of these programs have been successful in improving infant performance relative to control groups (e.g., Andrews, Blumenthal, Bach, & Weiner, 1975; Badger, Elsas, & Sutherland, 1974), others have shown effects on none (Caldwell, Elardo, & Elardo, 1972), or only some (Lally, 1969), of their assessment measures. Lambie, Bond, and Weikart (1974) found that early differences between experimental and control groups largely disappeared as the infants grew older, and this appears to be quite common (Bronfenbrenner, 1974). Gutelius and her colleagues (Gutelius, Kirsch, MacDonald, Brooks, McErlean, & Newcomb, 1972) reported another type of fadeout: Their program became progressively less effective with successively entering groups of infants.

For our present purposes, the existence of fadeout effects is irrelevant, because if infant cognitive development could be accelerated—even temporarily—by an intervention program, it would demonstrate the susceptibility of cognitive development to environmental influences. Unfortunately, the results of the intervention studies are inconsistent, and it is not clear whether the interventions produce general effects on competence (as some would claim) or improvements that are limited to specific areas or items on which training was focused. Consequently, the results of intervention programs provide only weak evidence for the formative effects of environmental influences on early cognitive development.

Correlational Studies

The final type of evidence suggesting a relationship between environmental variables and the development of infant competence is correlational. Most commonly, measures of mother-infant interaction have been correlated with contemporaneous or subsequent measures of cognitive competence, and significant relationships between infant functioning and aspects of the social environment have been found (Beckwith, Cohen, Kopp, Parmelee, & Marcy, 1976; Clarke-Stewart, 1973; Elardo, Bradley, & Caldwell, 1975; Wachs, 1976; Yarrow, Rubenstein, & Pedersen, 1975). Because the evidence is correlational, it is not possible to asert that variations in parental behavior are indeed responsible for variations in cognitive performance, but the correlations at least suggest that such a relationship exists.

HOW DOES EXPERIENCE AFFECT COGNITIVE DEVELOPMENT?

As the preceding paragraphs suggest, there are several lines of evidence *suggesting* that early experiences affect cognitive development. The experiences involved are invariably multimodal, but they always involve the participation of a social agent. Consequently, we can consider them as examples of social experiences even though (as indicated later) the emphasis placed on the social element of the experiences varies from one explanatory model to the next. In this section, we wish to focus on the mechanisms whereby experience is said to affect cognitive development. Several such mechanisms have been proposed, and our goal is to explain and evaluate the putative mechanisms. Understanding how experience affects cognitive development is crucial to the formulation of intervention efforts that are likely to be successful.

A survey of the pertinent literature reveals five perspectives from which the effects of social experiences on cognitive development have been considered and explained. Casler (1961) has emphasized the importance of the total *amount* of stimulation received by infants. Caldwell and her colleagues (Elardo, Bradley, & Caldwell, 1975) have described *variety* of stimulation as the key determinant of individual differences in cognitive development. According to another view (Dennis & Najarian, 1957), caretakers facilitate cognitive development by structuring the environment to insure *experiences,* which are *appropriate* to the infant's current level of attainment. Researchers like Lewis (Lewis & Coates, 1980; Lewis & Goldberg, 1969) and Watson (1966, 1979) emphasize the need for stimulation that is *contingent* upon the infant's own behavior. Finally, Bruner (1977) and Schaffer (1977) suggest that the turn taking and *patterning* of social interaction teach infants the structural roles implicit in communication and language. Clearly, no one of these proposed mechanisms can explain all the variation in cognitive functioning. Each has some explanatory power, and they should not be viewed as mutually exclusive explanations. After reviewing each perspective, we suggest that they may be viewed as complementary rather than alternative perspectives on the effects of social experience on the development of cognitive competence in infancy.

Quantity of Stimulation

After reviewing research on the effects of institutionalization on infant development, Casler (1961) proposed that the amount of stimulation received was the most important variable. Infants in institutions received far less sensory stimulation and human contact than did home-reared infants, and Casler saw this as the cause of developmental retardation among institutionalized infants. If amount of stimulation accounted for the difference between home-reared and institutionalized infants, perhaps variations in the performance of home-reared infants can likewise be attributed to variations in the quantity of stimulation they received. To investigate this hypothesis, researchers have gone into homes to tally the frequency of various types of maternal stimulation. Yarrow and his colleagues (Yarrow et al., 1975), for example, made home observations to determine what types of stimulation mothers provided for their infants during the first 6 months of life. They found significant correlations between measures of the social and inanimate stimulation and the infants' scores on the Bayley Scale of Mental Development, underscoring the formative significance of the quantity of stimulation infants received.

This emphasis on the amount of stimulation is shared by Beckwith and her colleagues (Beckwith et al., 1976). During home observations that took place when the infant subjects were 1-, 3-, and 8-months-old, observers recorded the frequency of several maternal behaviors. A significant proportion of the variation in scores on cognitive tests at 9 months was predicted by measures of the amount of maternal stimulation observed during the earlier observations. In a previous study, Beckwith (1971) was able to predict variation in Cattell scores from behavioral observations made 6 weeks earlier.

Clarke-Stewart (1973) used an approach somewhat similar to Beckwith's in her longitudinal study of 9- to 18-month-old lower-class infants. During seven home observations, the occurrence of 23 infant and 26 maternal behaviors was recorded; observations were made at 10-second intervals. The frequencies with which mothers engaged in each behavior were subsequently calculated. The data were further summarized by use of a factor analysis yielding an "optimal-care" factor. Included on this factor were measures of the amount of verbal, social, and object-mediated stimulation, as well as measures of responsiveness to both distress and social elicitations. This factor was significantly related to several cognitive measures.

On the assumption that amount of stimulation was a crucial determinant of cognitive development, Casler designed three intervention programs for institutionalized infants (Casler, 1965a, 1965b; Casler, 1975). By providing extra stimulation, he hoped to facilitate or accelerate the cognitive development of institutionalized infants. When supplementary tactile stimulation was provided, Casler's program was successful (Casler, 1965a), but neither verbal nor vestibular stimulation had any measurable impact on cognitive development (Casler, 1965b, 1975).

The importance of sensory stimulation for early development has long been recognized (Bronfenbrenner, 1968; Casler, 1961, 1965a; Hebb, 1958; Schaffer, 1958). Animals reared with additional sensory stimulation from regular handling develop better physically, socially, and cognitively. Several aspects of development are likewise accelerated or facilitated when animals are raised in enriched environments. Unfortunately, one can only speculate about the processes by which supplementary stimulation affects the rate of development. As changes in brain chemistry and the density of neural connections and pathways are known to occur following exposure to enriched environments in rats (Casler, 1965a; Rosensweig, Krech, Bennett, & Diamond, 1968), it is quite likely that sensory stimulation can also affect neural development in human infants. On the other hand, it is unlikely that repeated exposure to the same stimuli will be beneficial. Because of this, several theorists have argued that the variety, rather than the amount, of stimulation is important.

Stimulus Variety

Caldwell and her colleagues (Elardo et al., 1975) stress the importance of variety in the types of experiences to which infants are exposed, and these researchers have developed an instrument to quantify the stimulus potential of rearing environments. Infants who are exposed to a more varied environment in the home and who are frequently exposed to experiences outside the home receive high scores on the "Home Observation for Measurement of the Environment" (HOME) instrument (Caldwell, 1974). Scores on this instrument at 12 months correlate significantly with scores on the Bayley Mental Development Scale at 12 months and with Stanford-Binet IQ scores at 36 months (Elardo et al., 1975). Using this measure of the caretaking environment, Bradley and Caldwell (1976) have also been able to predict changes in infant cognitive performance between 6 and 36 months. Unfortunately, however, this instrument is not sufficiently sensitive to quantify differences among middle-class families; most of these families receive scores in a relatively narrow range at the top of the index (Stevenson & Lamb, 1979).

Research with an instrument similar to Caldwell's has suggested to Wachs (1976; Wachs et al., 1971) that the "optimal" home environment is one that provides an intermediate level of stimulation. He argues that both over- and understimulation are undesirable. The items that showed significant positive correlations with Wachs' cognitive-outcome measure were those related to the orderliness of the home and neighborhood and to the opportunity for varied experiences. Overstimulation—in the form of noise and activity from which the infant could not escape—was negatively correlated with cognitive performance. In reaching his conclusions, however, Wachs was relying on a small number of significant correlations out of many correlations. Thus, his findings have to be viewed cautiously until replicated.

In addition to these correlational studies, at least one intervention program explicitly attempted to facilitate cognitive development by increasing the variety of experiences to which infants were exposed (Caldwell et al., 1972). Tutors brought toys to the homes of disadvantaged infants and made suggestions to their mothers about ways in which they could enrich their infants' experiences. As expected, the program increased the variety of infant experiences, but it did not have a measurable impact on cognitive development.

Although empirical support remains equivocal, it seems reasonable that exposure to a wide variety of experiences should be beneficial. Infants exposed to a variety of experiences are constantly challenged by novel demands and opportunities to act upon the environment. By having to adapt to various circumstances and challenges, these infants should be forced to develop a diverse array of cognitive strategies and thus should appear more competent than infants who have less complex and variable experiences.

Appropriate Experiences

Rather than focusing on quantity or variety of stimulation, other theorists have argued that the environment needs to be structured so as to provide the infant with appropriate opportunities. By this they mean that infants benefit most when asked to practice newly developed skills or to perform tasks demanding slight, but attainable, improvements in their abilities. In an investigation founded on this belief, Dennis and Najarian (1957) first identified institutionalized infants whose ability to sit was retarded. They then gave these infants the opportunity to practice sitting. As expected, their sitting skills developed quickly. In addition, once they were able to sit, the infants' hands were free to explore and to manipulate toys, and this was also beneficial. Although this is an extreme example, it does illustrate the importance of specific and appropriate experiences.

The value of individually appropriate experiences was also demonstrated in a study of infants raised in an Iranian institution (Hunt, Mohandessi, Ghodssi, & Akiyama, 1976). These infants were so retarded that they even seemed incapable of pseudoimitation of vocal sounds, yet after only a few days of verbal interaction the researchers were able to elicit vocal play in these infants. Hunt and his colleagues also discussed a group of disadvantaged infants in the United States who developed mastery of object-concept tasks sooner than did an upper-middle-class sample. The success of the disadvantaged group was informally attributed to the extensive opportunity they had to play with a toy in which things could be hidden and then found. In other words, the infants who were able to practice certain skills made progress in these areas.

Badger, Elsas, and Sutherland (1974) developed an intervention program designed to provide specific and developmentally appropriate experiences for disadvantaged infants. The developing skills of the babies were discussed with their lower-class mothers so that the mothers could provide activities that were appropriate for, or "matched," their infants' level of development. A post-test showed that the cognitive performance of these infants was superior to that of a control group. In other words, when infants were provided with opportunities appropriate to their developmental level, their cognitive devleopment was facilitated.

Reviewing evidence of this nature, Hunt (1961, 1979) has argued that infants clearly need a sufficient amount of varying stimulation that is appropriate for their existing level of competence. He thus accepts the claims that amount of stimulation is important and that stimulus variability is important, but adds an important qualification in the form of stimulus appropriateness. Hunt notes that each developmental achievement builds on previous achievements. Infants who are given the opportunity to practice skills at their own level are able to develop at an optimal rate. Each time new skills are mastered, infants have the prerequisites to move on to new challenges. It is the caretakers' task to provide new challenges that demand of the infant slightly more than it is currently capable of: Hunt labels this "the problem of the match." Development is cumulative, and successes at one level allow (but do not guarantee) progress to the next level.

Contingent Stimulation

Watson (1971, 1979) has suggested that the crucial variable is not the amount or variety of stimulation provided for infants, but the contingency between the stimulation and the infants' behavior. Watson (1979) has described contingency as the "focal structure of experience." He believes that infants have an innate need to detect contingencies between their own behavior and environmental consequences and that the detection of such contingencies is positively reinforcing. In support of this claim, Watson has shown that infants provided with mobiles, which only moved when the infants moved their heads, enjoyed controlling the movements of the mobile, increased their rate of head turning, and later learned to control the movements of a new mobile more rapidly than control infants who did not have the contingency experience (Watson, 1966, 1971; Watson & Ramey, 1972). A later investigation by Finkelstein and Ramey (1977) confirmed that experience with contingently responsive stimulation facilitated learning in a different situation. A correlational study by Yarrow and his colleagues (Yarrow et al., 1975), meanwhile, found that those 6-month-old infants who had more toys that were responsive were more advanced cognitively than those infants who had fewer such toys. Findings like these led Hunt and his colleagues (1976) to fashion an intervention program in which one group of infants was provided with "highly responsive" play materials in addition to audio-visual stimulation. Infants in this group developed better than those not provided with such experiences.

Although these researchers have looked at inanimate sources of contingent stimulation, it seems likely that contingently responsive adults facilitate infant development in the same way. Several studies show this to be the case. Most recently, Lewis and Coates (1980) found no relationships between the frequency of several maternal behaviors and the cognitive performance of 3-month-old infants although the probability of contingent maternal response was significantly related to cognitive performance, as was the relative frequency with which the mothers responded to infant smiles. Earlier, Lewis and Goldberg (1969) found that infants with mothers who responded contingently to cries and vocalizations learned better in a habituation task than infants with less responsive mothers. Furthermore, all three of Clarke-Stewart's (1973) measures of maternal responsiveness were good predictors of infant competence. These measures included an overall measure of responsiveness, a measure of maternal responsiveness to social signals, and a measure of maternal responsiveness to signals of distress. In Yarrow's research (Yarrow et al., 1975), responsive mothers also had the most cognitively advanced infants.

As Lamb and Easterbrooks point out in Chapter 6, parents who respond contingently are sensitive and responsive to the small cues emitted by their infants. According to Ainsworth and Bell (1969), sensitivity to infant signals determines the security of the attachment bond between infant and parent. When secure attachments have developed, infants are able to use the adults as secure bases from which to explore the environment and thereby develop mastery and cognitive competence. Ainsworth and Bell (1974) thus propose that sensitive parental responsiveness results in the development of secure attachment relationships, and that this in turn enhances cognitive development through the facilitation of exploration. Consistent with this hypothesis, Bell (1970) found advanced cognitive development in infants who had secure attachments to their mothers. Several years earlier, Rheingold (1956) reported the findings of an experimental study with implications for this hypothesis. In this study, Rheingold herself provided individualized care for eight institutionalized infants in hopes that the extra attention and the opportunity to become attached to a single caretaker would enhance cognitive development. The intervention was only partially successful. The infants in the experimental group became more socially responsive, but they did not obtain higher scores on measures of cognitive development. As noted earlier, however, Clarke-Stewart (1973) found that infants who had more sensitive mothers (and thus, presumably, were securely attached) were more cognitively competent.

Communicative Competence

Schaffer (1977) and Bruner (1977) provide yet another perspective on the relationship between social experience and cognitive development in infancy. According to these theorists and their students, social interaction teaches infants the basic structural rules that underlie language communication. They point out that the preverbal interactions between mothers and infants involve synchronized and reciprocal exchanges. Kaye's (1977) research is exemplary, for his description of mother-infant interaction during feeding evokes the image of a dialogue. When neonates paused between bursts of sucking, for example, he found that mothers jiggled the nipples or the infants. When this stimulation ceased there was an increased probability that sucking would resume. Thus, turn taking occurs between mothers and infants from early in the infants' lives.

Turn taking may also be evident in the vocal exchange between mothers and their infants. As early as 3 months of age, infants spend some time alternating vocalizations with their mothers, although at this age babies and mothers are more likely to talk simultaneously than in alternating turns (Stern, Jaffe, Beebe, & Bennett, 1975; Strain & Vietze, 1975). Indeed, mothers talk most of the time when conversing with 2½-month-olds, but as the infants grow older, mothers talk less and allow the infants a greater role in the conversation (Vietze, Strain, & Falsey, 1975). Interestingly, even when no infant vocalizations follow the mothers' utterances, mothers pause after vocalizing as if anticipating a response (Stern, 1977). Long before infants comprehend the content of conversation, therefore, they are being exposed to, and entering into, interactions that have the form of conversations.

Turn taking is also an important element in the "give-and-take" games or routines that characterize a great deal of mother-infant interaction during the first year (Bruner, 1977). For example, Bruner describes a game in which mother and infant alternatively offer a toy to, and accept it back from, one another. According to Bruner, the infant learns the sequence of actions comprising the game, the regularized pattern of which becomes an exemplary model for the give and take of verbal communication. Bruner (1977) refers to this as an "action dialogue" preceding the development of true verbal dialogue.

In a recently reported intervention study (Crittenden & Snell, 1979), mothers of infants at risk for developmental delay were taught to hold their infants in a face-to-face position. In this position, mothers interacted more with their infants and had more opportunity for turn taking.

According to this viewpoint, infants have the capacity to enter into active interchanges with their caretakers from early in their lives. Through feeding, vocalizing, and playing, it is believed that infants practice the form of conversation. However, although many researchers have described turn taking in early interactions, no one has yet shown that infants who have more early turn taking experiences have a cognitive advantage over infants who have fewer turn taking experiences.

Summary

The theorists discussed emphasize somewhat different elements of the formative environment in their description of influences on cognitive development, yet, for the most part, their views do not contradict one another. Few would contest the claim that infants need at least a certain amount of stimulation (too much might be detrimental), preferably of a varying rather than of a repetitive type. And it is intuitively obvious that stimulation will be most effective when it is appropriate to the recipient's current capacities and needs.

However, these three perspectives have a common deficiency: the portrayal of infants as passive recipients of stimulation. The last two approaches recognize that infants interact with the people and objects around them. Proponents of these two views stress that the crucial "information" is contained in the relationship between the infants' behavior and the responses of others. Unlike the three earlier approaches, these two perspectives explicitly account for motivational consequences of social stimulation, thereby explaining more satisfactorily how long-term effects may result from social stimulation. Environmental events set in motion endogenous processes that insure continued cognitive acceleration. The mechanisms whereby enduring effects are mediated have not been adequately addressed by proponents of the first three approaches.

The two last perspectives are not inconsistent with those reviewed earlier, for they emphasize different components of social experiences. The first three views emphasize the content of the stimulation, whereas the other two are concerned primarily with the structure or patterning of the stimulus input. Most transactions with the environment probably accord infants both structural and substantive information, and it would be premature, in our current state of ignorance, to limit focus to only one type of information. Both types are surely of formative significance.

EFFECTS OF INFANT SOCIAL STYLE

Even though the contingency and communication perspectives emphasize the lessons infants learn from dyadic social interactions, they still tend to ignore the extent to which individual differences among infants affect the types of social experiences to which they are exposed. We think it important to recognize that the personality and social style of each infant (whether these are inborn or the products of earlier experiences) may influence both its cognitive development and its performance on cognitive tests. Both McCall and his colleagues (McCall, Hogarty, & Hurlburt, 1972) and the present authors (1979) have argued that the relationship between characteristics of the caretaking environment and the infant's cognitive performance cannot be examined meaningfully without considering the sociability of the infant. The infant's mode of responding to unfamiliar people surely influences its interactions with an examiner during a testing session. It may be easier, for example, for the examiner to elicit responses from the friendly, responsive infant than from the reserved, uncooperative infant. In addition, sociable and affable infants may elicit more frequent and more sensitive affectionate attention from caretakers and others, and the evidence reviewed suggests that the cognitive development of these infants could be accelerated. By assessing infant sociability, social interaction, and cognitive performance, it should be possible to obtain a clearer picture of the relationship between social experience and cognitive performance than when only assessing the social environment and the infants' cognitive competence.

As early as 1933, Bayley recognized the importance of the infant's interactions with the examiner and thus developed the 24-item Infant Behavior Record (IBR). This instrument enables examiners to quantify their impressions of the infants' behavior during testing sessions. Three of the items on the IBR directly assess the infants' sociability: They involve ratings of cooperativeness, social responsiveness, and general emotional tone. When

Bayley and Schaefer (1964) used the IBR to predict cognitive performance, they found that males who were rated as happy and positively responsive to the examiner received higher test scores than less sociable infants did. (When older, however, these sociable infants were the ones who performed more poorly.) Crano's (1977) later reanalysis of data from the Berkeley Growth Study found significant correlations between scores on the Mental Development Index of the Bayley Scales and ratings of social responsiveness made a few months later.

Seegmiller and King (1975) tested 14- and 22-month-old infants and found that their scores on the Mental Development Index were significantly correlated with ratings made by the examiners on the IBR. There were significant correlations between MDI scores and responsiveness to the examiner at 22 months; between MDI scores and cooperation with the examiner at 14 months; and between MDI scores and general emotional tone at both 14 and 22 months. Matheny, Dolan, and Wilson (1974) summed the scores on these three sociability items to yield an extraversion score that was significantly correlated with Bayley MDI scores for females from 6- to 24-months-old and for males at 24 months only. Using a similar set of rating scales, Birns and Golden (1972) found significant correlations between cognitive performance and the infant's cooperativeness during testing. However, their rating of shyness did not correlate with cognitive scores.

In all of these studies, infant sociability was rated by the examiner at the end of the testing session. The relationship between sociability and performance would be even more impressive psychologically if infant sociability was measured outside the testing situation and was still significantly related to performance on tests of cognitive competence. Infant sociability could then be considered a relatively enduring characteristic of the infant rather than a situational measure of the infant's behavior in a specific test session. Several researchers have thus attempted to assess sociability outside the test situation, usually by recording the infant's initial reactions to an unfamiliar adult.

In an early study, Rheingold (1956) recorded the reactions of institutionalized infants to the approach and social bids of familiar and unfamiliar adults. Although Rheingold did not relate sociability to cognitive performance, Clarke-Stewart (1973) used Rheingold's work as the basis for developing an "approach sequence" for the assessment of infant social responsiveness. During this sequence the infant was looked at, smiled at, talked to, approached, touched, picked up, and left alone. The sequence was repeated four times—by a familiar and unfamiliar adult, with and without the mother present. Performance on this sociability index did not, however, correlate with any measures of infant cognitive competence.

By contrast, Beckwith and her colleagues (1976) showed that a measure of sociability outside the test situation indeed predicted cognitive-test performance. Observers tallied the number of 15-second time units of a home observation during which the infant smiled at or vocalized to the observer. In regression analyses, these scores were significant predictors of some of the cognitive-outcome measures. In our own work (Stevenson & Lamb, 1979), sociability measured independently both before and during cognitive testing predicted cognitive performance in 1-year olds extremely well. When many of the same children were tested again as 2-year olds, furthermore, the same relationship was found (Stevenson, in preparation). On the other hand, Ramey and Campbell (1979) reported that IBR ratings of fearfulness were not related to test performance at 6, 12, or 18 months of age.

The research documenting the relationship between sociability and level of cognitive development raises an interesting question: Is infant sociability related to cognitive *competence,* or does it only influence *performance* during cognitive assessments? One possibility is that sociable, friendly babies invite more social stimulation from adults, which in turn facilitates the infants' cognitive development. Alternately, sociable, friendly babies may be no more competent than less sociable peers; they may simply give of their best in test situations, whereas less sociable babies do not perform as well as they are capable of performing. Additionally, of course, both processes may account for the relationship between sociability and cognitive performance. Unfortunately, none of the data currently available speaks to this issue.

Whichever way the performance/competence question is resolved, infant sociability will remain an important variable for us to consider. Infants' reactions to testers clearly influence how testing sessions proceed. Sociable, friendly infants and somber, withdrawn infants have very different test sessions, and so it is of crucial importance to supplement information about cognitive-test performance with information about sociability. The methodological implications of this are enormous. Researchers tend to assume that developmental tests measure cognitive capacity whereas test performance may be as much (or more) a function of sociability as of cognitive capacity: In Stevenson and Lamb's (1979) research, the correlations between the various measures of sociability and test performance were between .43 and .60 (N = 40 1-year-olds). When one uses cognitive-test scores to assess the effectiveness of intervention programs, therefore, it is most important to recall that test scores reflect sociability as well as cognitive abilities. Similarly, any assessment of the cognitive competence of an individual infant must be viewed as a reflection of both sociability and cognitive ability.

This makes it important to ask about the origins of sociability as well as about the origins of cognitive competence. Little information of relevance is available. When Stevenson and Lamb (1979) assessed infant sociability, they also rated the caretaking environment with Caldwell's HOME inventory. The only scale that was significantly correlated with infant sociability was the scale measuring the emotional and verbal responsivity of the mother: The sociable infants had sociable mothers. Earlier, Main (1973) reported that sociable and cooperative infants had secure attachment relationships with their mothers. She proposed that maternal sensitivity promoted secure attachment (cf. Ainsworth, Bell, & Stayton, 1974) and that this in turn promoted cooperativeness with others.

It is also possible that infant sociability depends on the diversity of prior experiences with nonfamily members: It seems plausible that infants who spend more time with nonfamily members would respond more positively to unfamiliar adults in a testing session. Unfortunately, preliminary data indicate that this is not the case (Stevenson, in preparation). Perhaps, sociability is influenced only by major variations in social experiences—for example, the difference between home rearing and institutionalization. Tizard and Joseph (1970) found that 2-year-old children raised in an institution were much less friendly with a stranger than were those reared at home. Similarly, Ramey and Campbell (1979) factor analyzed scores on the IBR ratings and found that scores on a responsiveness/fearfulness-to-examiner factor differed depending on the child's enrollment in a full-day intervention program. At 6, 12, and 18 months, children enrolled in the center were significantly more socially competent (and less fearful) than children in a matched control group.

Finally, it is also possible that sociability is an innate and persistent characteristic of the infant; this has been suggested by the results of the New York Longitudinal Study (e.g., Thomas & Chess, 1977). As Carey (1973) and Rothbart and Derryberry (in press) have developed measures of infant temperament based on parental reports, future researchers will be able to search for relationships between early temperament, sociability, and cognitive competence.

CONCLUSION

The attempt to understand how social experience affects cognitive development has been complicated considerably by evidence concerning infant sociability. We do not yet know whether sociability only affects performance, or whether it should also be viewed as a mediating variable with implications for the development of cognitive competence. If it is a mediating variable—as seems likely—then each of the putative mechanisms described earlier becomes more complicated. Any attempts to explain the rate of cognitive development would have to include measures of infant sociability in their predictive equations.

Individual differences in sociability affect the type of social stimulation infants receive. There are also individual differences in the capacity of infants to process and benefit from stimulation. The "appropriate-experience" perspective reviewed earlier emphasized developmental differences among infants, but there are also substantial individual differences within groups of infants at the same developmental level. Some of the dimensions tapped by temperament scales—distractibility and persistence, for example—are relevant here, but a great deal more work needs to be done in this area before we will be able to measure individual differences reliably and comprehensively.

It is not surprising that the importance of individual differences has been ignored until recently. First, American developmental psychologists have long portrayed infants as passive and homogeneous recipients of formative stimulation—both social and nonsocial. Second, and more importantly, theorists have been attempting to demonstrate *that* the mechanisms of influence we reviewed are operative, whereas individual differences are of greatest significance when one asks the next question: *How much* influence does this or that stimulation have? Clearly, we now need research acknowledging that multiple modes of influence mediate the effects of social stimulation on cognitive development, and seeking to determine the relative importance of these different modes. Such research will have to take individual differences more seriously.

REFERENCES

Ainsworth, M. The effects of maternal deprivation on cognitive and intellectual development. In O. J. Harvey (Ed.), *Experience, structure and adaptability*. New York: Springer, 1966.

Ainsworth, M. D. S., & Bell, S. M. Some contemporary patterns of mother-infant interaction in the feeding situation. In A. Ambrose (Ed.), *Stimulation in early infancy*. New York: Academic Press, 1969.

Ainsworth, M. D. S., & Bell, S. M. Mother-infant interaction and the development of competence. In K. J. Connolly & J. S. Bruner (Eds.), *The growth of competence*. New York: Academic Press, 1974.

Ainsworth, M. D. S., Bell, S. M., & Stayton, D. J. Infant-mother attachment and social development: Socialisation as a product of reciprocal responsiveness to signals. In M. P. M. Richards (Ed.), *The integration of a child into a social world*. Cambridge, England: Cambridge University Press, 1974.

Andrews, S. R., Blumenthal, J. M., Bache, W. L., & Weiner, G. *The New Orleans model: Parents as early childhood educators*. Paper presented at the meeting of the Society for Research in Child Development, Denver, April 1975.

Badger, E., Elsas, S., & Sutherland, J. *Mother training as a means of accelerating childhood development in a high risk population*. Paper presented at the Society for Pediatric Research, Washington, May 1974.

Bayley, N. *The California first-year mental scale*. Berkeley: University of California Press, Syllabus Series No. 243, 1933.

Bayley, N. The development of motor abilities during the first three years. *Monographs of the Society for Research in Child Development*, 1935, *1*(1).

Bayley, N. Comparisons of mental and motor test scores for ages 1–15 months by sex, birth order, race, geographical location, and education of parents. *Child Development,*1965, *36*, 379–411.

Bayley, N., & Schaefer, E. Relationships between socio-economic variables and the behavior of mothers toward young children. *Journal of Genetic Psychology,* 1960, *96,* 61–77.

Bayley, N., & Schaefer, E. Correlations of maternal and child behaviors with the development of mental abilities: Data from the Berkeley Growth Study. *Monographs of the Society for Research in Child Development,* 1964, *29*(6,Whole No. 97).

Beckwith, L. Relationships between attributes of mothers and their infants' I.Q. scores. *Child Development,* 1971, *42,* 1083–1097.

Beckwith, L. Cohen, S. E., Kopp, C. B., Parmelee, A. H., & Marcy, T. G. Caregiver-infant interaction and early cognitive development in preterm infants. *Child Development,* 1976, *47,* 579–587.

Bell, S. M. The development of the concept of the object as related to infant-mother attachment. *Child Development,* 1970, *41,* 291–311.

Birns, B., & Golden, M. Prediction of intellectual performance at three years from infant tests and personality measures. *Merrill-Palmer Quarterly,* 1972, *18,* 53–58.

Bowlby, J. Maternal care and mental health. *Bulletin of the World Health Organization,* 1951, *3,* 355–534.

Bradley, R. H., & Caldwell, B. M. Early home environment and changes in mental test performance in children from 6 to 36 months. *Developmental Psychology,* 1976, *12,* 93–97.

Bronfenbrenner, U. Early deprivation: A cross-species analysis. In G. Newton (Ed.), *Early experience and behavior.* Springfield, Ill.: Charles C. Thomas, 1968.

Bronfenbrenner, U. *Is early intervention effective?* Washington, D.C.: Department of Health, Education, and Welfare, 1974.

Bruner, J. S. Early social interaction and language aquisition. In H. R. Schaffer (Ed.), *Studies in mother-infant interaction.* New York: Academic Press, 1977.

Caldewll, B. M. *Instruction manual: Inventory for infants.* Unpublished manuscript, University of Arkansas at Little Rock, 1974.

Caldwell, B. J., Elardo, P., & Elardo, R. *The longitudinal observation and intervention study: A preliminary report.* Paper presented at the meeting of the Southeastern Conference on Research in Child Development, Williamsburg, Va., April 1972.

Carey, W. B. Measurement of infant temperament in pediatric practice. In J. C. Westman (Ed.), *Individual differences in children.* New York: Wiley, 1973.

Casler, L. Maternal deprivation: A critical review of the literature. *Monographs of the Society for Research in Child Development,* 1961, *26*(2, Serial No. 80).

Casler, L. The effects of extra tactile stimulation on a group of institutionalized infants. *Genetic Psychology Monographs,* 1965, *71,* 137–175. (a)

Casler, L. The effects of supplementary verbal stimulation on a group of institutionalized infants. *Journal of Child Psychology and Psychiatry,* 1965, *6,* 19–27. (b)

Casler, L. Supplementary auditory and vestibular stimulation: Effects on institutionalized infants. *Journal of Experimental Child Psychology,* 1975, *19,* 456–463.

Clarke-Stewart, K. A. Interactions between mothers and their young children: Characteristics and consequences. *Monographs of the Society for Research in Child Development.* 1973, *38*(6–7, Whole No. 153).

Crano, W. D. What do infant mental tests test? A cross-lagged panel analysis of selected data from the Berkeley Growth Study. *Child Development,* 1977, *48,* 144–151.

Crittenden, P. M., & Snell, M. E. *Intervention to improve mother-infant interaction and development.* Paper presented at the Society for Research in Child Development, San Francisco, March 1979.

Dennis, W., & Najarian, P. Infant development under environmental handicap. *Psychological Monographs,* 1957, *17*(7, Whole No. 436).

Drillien, C. M. *The growth and development of the prematurely born infant.* London: E. & S. Livingstone, 1964.

Elardo, R., Bradley, R., & Caldwell, B. M. The relation of infant's home environments to mental test performance from six- to thirty-six months: A longitudinal analysis. *Child Development,* 1975, *46,* 71–76.

Finkelstein, N. W., & Ramey, C. T. Learning to control the environment in infancy. *Child Development,* 1977, *48,* 806–819.

Furfey, P. H. The relation between socio-economic status and intelligence of young infants as measured by the Linfert-Hierholzer scale. *The Pedagological Seminar and Journal of Genetic Psychology,* 1928, *35,* 478–480.

Golden, M., & Birns, B. Social class and cognitive development in infancy. *Merrill–Palmer Quarterly,* 1968, *14,* 139–149.

Golden, M., Birns, B., Bridger, W., & Moss, A. Social class differences in cognitive development among black preschool children. *Child Development,* 1971, *42,* 37–45.

Gutelius, M. F., Kirsch, A. D., MacDonald, S., Brooks, M. R., McErlean, T., & Newcomb, C. Promising results from a cognitive stimulation program in infancy: A preliminary report. *Clinical Pediatrics,* 1972, *11,* 585–593.

Hebb, D. O. The motivating effects of exteroceptive stimulation. *American Psychologist,* 1958, *13,* 109–113.

Hindley, C. B. The Griffiths scale of infant development: Scores and predictions from 3 to 18 months. *Journal of Child Psychology and Psychiatry,* 1960, *1,* 99–112.

Hunt, J. McV. *Intelligence and experience.* New York: Ronald Press, 1961.

Hunt, J. McV. Early experience. *Annual Review of Psychology,* 1979, *30,* 103–143.

Hunt, J. McV., Mohandessi, K., Ghodssi, M., & Akiyama, M. The psychological development of orphanage-reared infants: Interventions with outcomes (Tehran). *Genetic Psychology Monographs,* 1976, *94,* 177–226.

Kaye, K. Toward the origin of dialogue. In H. R. Schaffer (Ed.), *Studies in mother-infant interaction.* New York: Academic Press, 1977.

Knoblock, H., & Pasamanick, B. Environmental factors affecting human development, before and after birth. *Pediatrics,* 1960, *26,* 210–218.

Kohan-Raz, R. Mental and motor development of kibbutz, institutionalized, and home-reared infants in Israel. *Child Development,* 1968, *39,* 489–504.

Lally, J. R. A study of the relationship between trained and untrained twelve-month-old environmentally deprived infants on the "Griffiths Mental Development Scale." In I. J. Gordon (Ed.), *Relationships between selected family variables and maternal and infant behavior in a disadvantaged population.* ERIC report ED 47784, 1969.

Lamb, M. E., & Campos, J. J. *Human infancy: A personal perspective.* New York: Random House, in press.

Lambie, D. S., Bond, J. T., & Weikart, D. P. *Home teaching with mothers and infants.* Ypsilanti, Mich.: High/Scope Educational Research Foundation, 1974.

Lewis, M., & Coates, D. Mother-infant interaction and infant cognitive performance. *Infant Behavior and Development,* 1980, *3,* 95–105.

Lewis, M., & Goldberg, S. Perceptual-cognitive development in infancy: A generalized expectancy model as a function of the mother-infant interaction. *Merrill–Palmer Quarterly,* 1969, *15,* 81–100.

Lewis, M., & Wilson, C. D. Infant development in lower-class American families. *Human Development,* 1972, *15,* 112–127.

Main, M. *Exploration, play, and cognitive functioning as related to child-mother attachment.* Unpublished doctoral dissertation, Johns Hopkins University, 1973.

Matheny, A. P., Jr., Dolan, A. B., & Wilson, R. S. Bayley's infant behavior record: Relations between behaviors and mental test scores. *Developmental Psychology,* 1974, *10,* 696–702.

McCall, R. B., Hogarty, P. S., & Hurlburt, N. Transitions in infant sensorimotor development and the prediction of childhood IQ. *American Psychologist,* 1972, *27,* 728–746.

Messer, S., & Lewis, M. Social class and sex differences in the attachment and play behavior of the year-old infant. *Merrill–Palmer Quarterly,* 1972, *18,* 295–306.

Pinneau, S. The infantile disorders of hospitalism and anaclitic depression. *Psychological Bulletin,* 1955, *52,* 429–452.

Provence, S., & Lipton, R. *Infants in institutions.* New York: International Universities Press, 1961.

Ramey, C. T., & Campbell, F. A. Compensatory education for disadvantaged children. *School Review,* 1979, *87,* 171–189.

Rheingold, H. L. The modification of social responsiveness in institutionalized babies. *Monographs of the Society for Research in Child Development,* 1956, *21* (Whole No. 63).

Rheingold, H. L. The measurement of maternal care. *Child Development,* 1960, *31,* 565–575.

Rosensweig, M. R., Krech, D., Bennett, E. L., & Diamond, M. C. Modifying brain chemistry and anatomy by enrichment or impoverishment of experience. In G. Newton & S. Levine (Eds.), *Early experience and behavior.* Springfield, Ill.: Charles C. Thomas, 1968.

Rothbart, M. & Derryberry, D. Development of individual differences in temperament. In M. E. Lamb & A. L. Brown (Eds.), *Advances in developmental psychology (Vol. 1).* Hillsdale, N. J.: Lawrence Erlbaum Associates, in press.

Rutter, M. *Maternal deprivation reassessed.* Harmondsworth, England: Penguin, 1972.

Schaffer, H. R. Objective observations of personality development in early infancy. *British Journal of Medical Psychology,* 1958, *31,* 174–183.

Schaffer, H. R. Early interactive development. In H. R. Schaffer (Ed.), *Studies in mother-infant interaction.* New York: Academic Press, 1977.

Seegmiller, B. R., & King, W. L. Relations between behavioral characteristics of infants, their mother's behaviors, and performance on the Bayley Mental and Motor Scales. *The Journal of Psychology,* 1975, *90,* 99–111.

Spitz, R. A. Hospitalism: An inquiry into the genesis of psychiatric conditions in early childhood. *Psychoanalytic Study of the Child,* 1945, *1,* 53–74.

Sroufe, L. A. Socioemotional development. In J. D. Osofsky (Ed.), *Handbook of infant development.* New York: Wiley, 1979.

Stern, D. *The first relationship: Infant and mother.* Cambridge, Mass.: Harvard University Press, 1977.

Stern, D. N., Jaffe, J., Beebe, B., & Bennett, S. L. Vocalizing in unison and in alternation: Two modes of communication within the mother-infant dyad. *Annals of the New York Academy of Science,* 1975, *263,* 89–100.

Stevenson, M. B. *Changes in sociability, cognitive performance, and the caretaking environment from 12 to 24 months and causal interrelations among these.* In preparation.

Stevenson, M. B., & Lamb, M. E. Effects of infant sociability and the caretaking environment on infant cognitive performance. *Child Development,* 1979, *50,* 340–349.

Strain, B. A., & Vietze, P. M. *Early dialogues: The structure of reciprocal infant-mother vocalization.* Paper presented at the biennial meeting of the Society for Research in Child Development, Denver, April 1975.

Thomas, A., & Chess, S. *Temperament and development.* New York: Brunner/Mazel, 1977.

Tizard, B., Cooperman, O., Joseph, A., & Tizard, J. Environmental effects on language development: A study of young children in long-stay residential nurseries. *Child Development,* 1972, *43,* 337–358.

Tizard, B., & Joseph, A. Cognitive development of young children in residential care: A study of children aged 24 months. *Journal of Child Psychology and Psychiatry,* 1970, *11,* 177–186.

Tulkin, S. R. Social class differences in infants' reaction to mother's and stranger's voices. *Developmental Psychology,* 1973, *8,* 137.

Tulkin, S. R., & Cohler, B. J. Childrearing attitudes and mother–child interaction in the first year of life. *Merrill–Palmer Quarterly,* 1973, *19,* 95–106.

Tulkin, S. R., & Kagan, J. Mother–child interaction in the first year of life. *Child Development,* 1972, *43,* 31–41.

Vietze, P. M., Strain, B., & Falsey, C. *Contingent responsiveness between mother and infant: Who's reinforcing whom?* Paper presented at the Southeastern Psychological Association, Atlanta, March 1975.

Wachs, T. D. Utilization of a Piagetian approach in the investigation of early experience effects: A research strategy and some illustrative data. *Merrill–Palmer Quarterly,* 1976, *22,* 11–30.

Wachs, T., Uzgiris, I., & Hunt, J. McV. Cognitive development in infants of different age levels and from different environmental backgrounds: An exploratory investigation. *Merrill–Palmer Quarterly,* 1971, *17,* 283–317.

Watson, J. S. The development and generalization of contingency awareness in early infancy: Some hypotheses. *Merrill–Palmer Quarterly,* 1966, *12,* 123–135.

Watson, J. S. Cognitive-perceptual development in infancy: Setting for the seventies. *Merrill–Palmer Quarterly,* 1971, *17,* 139–152.

Watson, J. S. Perception of contingency as a determinate of social responsiveness. In E. B. Thoman (Ed.), *Origins of infant social responsiveness.* Hillsdale, N.J.: Lawrence Erlbaum Associates, 1979.

Watson, J. S., & Ramey, C. T. Reactions to response contingent stimulation early in infancy. *Merrill–Palmer Quarterly,* 1972, *18,* 219–227.

Werner, E., Simonian, K., Bierman, J. M., & French, F. E. Cumulative effect of perinatal complications and deprived environment on physical, intellectual, and social development of preschool children. *Pediatrics,* 1967, *39,* 490–505.

Yando, R., Seitz, V., & Zigler, E. *Intellectual and personality characteristics of children.* Hillsdale, N.J.: Lawrence Erlbaum Associates, 1979.

Yarrow, L. J., Rubenstein, J. L., & Pedersen, F. A. *Infant and environment: Early cognitive and motivational development.* New York: Wiley, 1975.

14 Self-Knowledge: A Social Cognitive Perspective on Gender Identity and Sex-Role Development

Michael Lewis
Educational Testing Service

Two views of human nature dominate our theories of development. According to the first view, humans are acted on by forces around and within them. According to the second, humans act on these forces. The passive view generates two major theoretical positions: the biological (or maturational) and the social-control paradigms. The active view, on the other hand, has generated the constructivist or cognitive-developmental theoretical paradigm. It is to the latter paradigm that we wish to turn our attention (see Lewis & Weinraub [1979] for a fuller treatment of the other paradigms).

In both the biological/maturational and social-control paradigms, the causes of developmental change are forces that act on the organism. These causes may be the internal biological features of the species, the external social controls of the conspecifics (i.e., the reinforcement patterns), or the differential construction of the social world. In all cases, the organism is acted on, and its behavior is shaped or formed independently of its action, will, thought, or plans.

In contrast to this passive view is the constructivist paradigm, which holds that the organism acts on its environment by participating in, by being influenced by, and by influencing those forces that determine development. This view does not necessitate the discarding of either the biological control or the social control of behavior because humans are both biological and social creatures. Hence, both biological and social control must to some degree and in some combination affect development. We prefer to think of the biological and social forces as nothing more than the material for the construction of cognitive and affective structures. Thus, although biological and social forces act on the organism and are used by the organism to construct its world, they do not correspond in any simple one-to-one relationship with the structures so created. An example may clarify this distinction: A loud noise has the biological capacity to force us to turn toward the sound source and to startle, but fright is the consequence of our interpreting the noise and our changing physiological state. The study of psychology must study both the action (loud noise and physiological changes) and the attribution that we give to those actions. In the study of emotional behavior, this distinction has been emphasized because it is both the action and interpretation that characterize emotional experience (James, 1890). We would argue, therefore, that the study of development is not merely the study of action. It is also the study of the child's interpretation of the event, including the interpretation of its own behavior. The developmental task for the young organism is to make sense of a variety of events, some of which are external and some of which are internal to it. If the developmental task is learning that internal and external events are different, then it follows that the task of perceiving, ordering, and interpreting events involves the self–other differentiation.

We believe that the study of self as a developmental process has been seriously neglected and that this issue is central to the area of infant social cognition and the understanding of children's development (Lewis & Brooks-Gunn, 1979a). For us, the construction of knowledge requires the interaction of the self and others. These others can be either objects in the child's world or people. Our theories of interaction have stressed the acquisition of knowledge through interaction of the child with its object world. Through these interactions the child learns about its world, develops structures, and undergoes change as a consequence of the interaction of these structures with experience. The focus has been on the development of structures related to knowledge of the object. Although clearly relevant, little attention has been paid to the knowledge and structures that the child acquires about itself. It is hard to imagine, for example, how infants can know about the permanence of objects (independent of their perception of them) without at the same time having a notion about self and self-permanence! We believe in the duality of knowledge in which interaction creates both knowledge of the others (either object or person) and, at the same time and in the same way, knowledge of the self (Lewis & Brooks-Gunn, 1979b). That is, in our interactions with objects and people, we learn both about them and about ourselves. For example, reaching for a block tells us something about objects in space and also about the length of our arms. Indeed, I cannot reach for something unless I know about both myself and the object. Spatial knowledge, by necessity, involves the relationship of self to other in space. By the same token, what we learn about people we also know about ourselves. One of the things we learn about people is that they have thoughts and feelings about us. Moreover, how we interpret and behave toward others—either objects or people—is a function of the relationship of the structures of self and of the others' actions.

Thus, self-knowledge is both a consequence of interaction and also an aid in determining that interaction. We employ the acquisition of gender identity, a self-category which is acquired early, to articulate this interactive perspective, arguing that gender identity—a specific attribute of self-identity—is the important determinant of subsequent sex-role behavior. That is, the young child utilizes the information about itself and others to affect its behavior; in this case, to be more like same-sex people than like opposite-sex people. Moreover, sex-role differentiation contributes to the acquisition of gender identity. The knowledge of gender identity and the nature of like-gender people are themselves developmentally linked. Nonetheless, the early acquisition of gender identity facilitates the process of sex-role acquisition.

Although all theorists and researchers recognize the interactional influence of biological, environmental, and cognitive factors, differences in emphasis exist. Those who focus on the role of biological factors argue that sex role is directly tied to gender; individuals' sex roles, in large part, are determined by their hormonal level.

Those who focus on the role of environmental factors argue that sex roles are learned primarily as a consequence of differentially administered rewards and punishments. Such a view holds that the individual's sex-role behavior is, to a large degree, learned as a result of cultural reinforcement patterns. Though there is a paucity of supporting data demonstrating a direct relationship between differential reinforcement and the child's sex-role behavior (Lewis & Weinraub, 1979), this view has a considerable number of adherents. However, given that the rejection of this view often implies the acceptance of the biological view, it is no wonder that the importance of environmental factors is often accepted without sufficient evidence.

There is, of course, an alternative to both the biological and social reinforcement views of sex-role development. We have called it the cognitive-motivational approach (Lewis & Brooks-Gunn, 1979a). Although each of these three factors—biological, environmental, and cognitive—makes a contribution to development, it is the child's active construction of sex role through cognition that we consider most important for the development of early sex-role behavior. Sex role is influenced by both biological and environmental factors. However, the coalescence of these factors around the child's growing cognitive abilities is the critical factor in the development of sex-role behavior, and it is to this development that we now turn.

COGNITIVE MOTIVATIONAL STRUCTURES

Cognitive influences in the development of appropriate sex-role behavior have received far less attention than they deserve. The emphasis on a cognitive-motivational theory of gender identity does not deprecate the role of environment or biology. These forces, however, are not seen as the prime determinants of sex-role behavior. Rather, they are seen as factors that supply young organisms with information they need in order to acquire appropriate sex-role behavior. This information contains data on both how to act and what others think is appropriate action. Sex-role development is related to the construction of knowledge and, in particular, knowledge about the self. Young children as well as adults construct beliefs, values, and knowledge from their interaction with the environment. The actions of others, either in the patterns of reinforcement, the construction of reality, or the action of the self in one's own biologically mediated behavior, may have their most significant effects upon the constructions formed by the child. Self-knowledge or identity is one of the first and most central social constructions that the child creates. Its centrality is due to its effect on all other social cognitions and on the social activity of the organism who utilizes its knowledge of itself in forming and maintaining social relationships (Lewis & Brooks-Gunn, 1979a). One attribute of self-identity is gender identity which, for the most part, controls the acquisition and development of sex-role behavior. We first turn our attention to self-identity and its acquisition in order to demonstrate how self-identity, gender identity, and gender knowledge coalesce into the social cognitions necessary to sustain and develop appropriate sex-role behavior.

Self-Identity

Although gender identity has received some consideration, especially in the last few years, hardly any attempt has been made to relate this particular aspect of identity to a larger theory about the self; this is especially true for the infancy period. This lack is particularly critical if, as we have argued elsewhere (Lewis & Brooks-Gunn, 1979b), self-knowledge as well as knowledge of others is a result of the infant's interaction with its world (both social and nonsocial). The duality of knowledge—that is, knowledge about both self and others—is the natural consequence of any interaction. In all likelihood, such knowledge acquisition is bidirectional, with the discovery of self informing us about others and the discovery of others telling us about self. In a recent chapter on the child's construction of self, Bannister and Agnew (1977) presented a similar analysis: "The ways in which we elaborate our construing of self must be essentially those ways in which we elaborate our construing of others, for we have not a concept of self but a bipolar construct of self—not self or self–other [p. 99]." Thus, self-knowledge about gender (gender identity) and knowledge of others (gender differentiation) develop concurrently. It is to the problem of self-identity that we should like to turn, because gender identity is just one aspect of the acquisition of self and the development of social cognition.

The study of social cognition involves, at least, knowledge of self, knowledge of others, and knowledge of our relationship to others, as well as knowledge of the relationship between others. Toward such a view, we have articulated the position that the child's knowledge of others is developed through interaction with them. More importantly, through interaction with others the infant gains self-knowledge at the same time that he or she acquires knowledge of others. Such a view is shared by Merleau-Ponty (1964) and Hamlyn (1974) as well as Mead (1934). The parallel development of self and other knowledge is acquired through interaction of the self and others. Thus, interaction (Lewis & Feiring, 1979; Lewis & Weinraub, 1976) becomes the major content of social cognition, because both self and other knowledge is derived through interaction. For example, whenever I engage in a social exchange with another person, I learn about that person. At the same time as I learn about the other person, I learn about what the other person learns about me. This may even have an analogy to spatial knowledge. When I interact with another person, I look at and see that person. In the same way, that person looks at me. But where is this me? Notice that when the other person looks at me, he or she looks at the one locus in space that I can not see because I occupy that space. This spatial fact can hardly escape notice and is related to the child's development of self as having a specific and defined locus in space.

In regard to social cognition concerning gender and sex role, we hold that knowledge of the self and others is vital, and the desire to act consistently with others similar to the self determines the young child's behavior. These views can be stated briefly:

1. The infant acquires knowledge about itself and, at the same time, acquires knowledge about others in a reciprocal process.
2. Gender identity and sex-role knowledge are acquired early and constitute an important aspect of social knowledge.
3. The infant is attracted to, and acts in a manner consistent with, "like-self" objects.

The Acquisition of Self

A distinction between the self as subject and object has been made in order to reflect the dual nature of the self. Self as subject—or as Lewis and Brooks (1975) called it, the existential self—is the self as distinct from others. This subjective self, like other cognitive structures, is created from the material of interaction, yet it holds no relationship to those interactions. That is, the subjective self is simply a structure representing self as distinct from others; it does not represent any particular kind of self. The second aspect of self, self as object, or the categorical self, includes the categories by which one is defined—the attitudes, attributes, abilities, and values of one's self. In the present discussion, gender is such a category. The self as object involves different types of categories: some remain invariant across the life span, some undergo transformation, and finally, others disappear.

In trying to study self-knowledge, one is confronted with any number of difficulties. Without language, the study of self-knowledge is limited. However, if we assume that self-recognition reflects some form of self-knowledge, our work becomes easier. In a series of studies, Lewis and Brooks-Gunn (1979a) have shown that the infant's knowledge of self, as measured through self-recognition, begins within the first year of life. By 2 years, the infant demonstrates a clear self-knowledge. For example, self-recognition was studied through the use of mirrors, still pictures, and videotape representations. In one set of studies, infants 9 to 24 months of age were led to a mirror behind which a TV camera recorded their behavior. After recording their behavior in front of the mirror, rouge was applied to the infants' noses, and they were led back to the mirrors. Figure 14.1 represents the different scores for mark-directed (nose) behavior. Mark- or nose-directed behavior consists of the child touching its nose after the rouge was applied and while the child was looking in the mirror. The difference score consists of the difference between the number of nose-touches after rouge application minus the number of nose-touches before application. In a variety of studies, nose-directed behavior increased over the 2 years and ranged from 25% at 18 months in one study to over 40% in another. Similar results have been reported by Amsterdam (1968). Figure 14.2 shows body-directed behavior. Body-directed behavior consists of all body touching, not including the nose. Most often, it consisted of facial touching. the difference score was obtained also by subtacting any body touching before rouge application from body touching after application. In this case, self-recognition is apparent even by 9

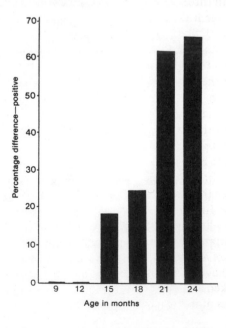

FIG. 14.1. Nose-directed behavior: percentage difference between the no rouge and rouge 1 conditions by age.

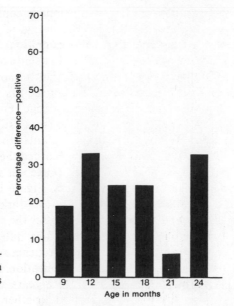

FIG. 14.2. Body-directed behavior: percentage difference between the no rouge and rouge 1 conditions by age.

months. The difference in measurement may reflect the increased ability to point to a particular location, which is a function of neuromuscular development.

In another set of studies, TV representations were used. Infants 9- to 24-months-old were presented with three conditions: (1) a TV that was just like a mirror—we called this a contingent self-condition; (2) a TV tape of the child made 1 week earlier—it looked like the subject but the image was not contingent; (3) a TV tape of another child made 1 week earlier, which was the same age and sex as the subject—this was a nonself, noncontingent condition. We were interested in whether the infant was more likely to imitate the self, noncontingent condition than the nonself, noncontingent condition. Imitation was defined as the subject's attempt to repeat the behavior seen on the screen. Figure 14.3 presents the data and indicates that from 12 months infants are more likely to imitate self than nonself representations.

Considerably more data have been collected and can be found in *Social Cognition and the Acquisition of Self* (Lewis & Brooks-Gunn, 1979a). We need, therefore, only summarize the results of our efforts on self-recognition. Within the last quarter of the first year of life, infants already appear to possess some demonstrable ability to recognize themselves. The 9- to 12-month-old is able to differentiate between contingent and noncontingent representation of self. Papoušek and Papoušek (1974) have shown that even 5-month-old children already have this skill. We have found that infants are able to differentiate the unmarked and marked mirror conditions and are able to differentiate between pictures of self and others. Between 15 and 18 months

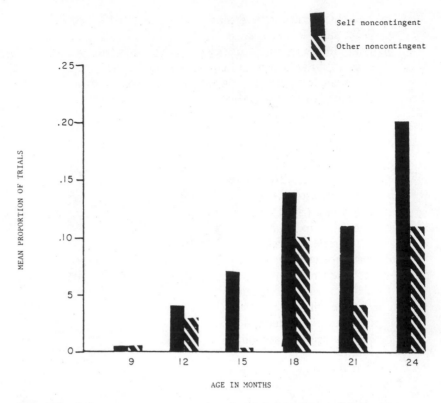

FIG. 14.3. Imitates tape: mean proportion of trials by stimulus condition and by age.

of age, self-recognition becomes more organized and less dependent on the contingency of the reflected surface. In noncontingent representations, infants exhibit differential attention, imitation, and affect between representations of self and others. They are also able to label and point to pictures themselves. A more detailed breakdown by age suggests a shift at 14–15 months a toward greater self-recognition. Between 18–19 and 24 months, there is a general increase in the number of infants demonstrating self-recognition abilities across a wide range of representational modes. At the same time, personal pronouns begin to be used. In brief, there is an increase in the child's ability to recognize itself during the first two years of life. Self-recognition is highly dependent on both contingency (it does what I do) and feature recognition (what I look like). At around 15 months, feature recognition becomes the more critical dimension in self-recognition.

These data have bearing on a theory of self-development and its relationship to affective and cognitive growth. Our work suggests that there are four organizing features of self-knowledge: (1) infants are attracted to babies as a class of stimuli, including the self; (2) infants learn cause and effect relations and, in particular, one cause and effect: self as both action *and* outcome in the same locus in space; (3) infants acquire the ability to hold an enduring belief in the existence of objects over time, which must include a locus in space; (4) infants begin to acquire self-categories. Thus to be oneself and to be different from others requires that this distinction be defined. This definition is related to what we have called the categorical self, which is seen in the child's ability to recognize itself on the basis of features.

This process of self-identity, derived from both our data and from the general theory of development we espouse, has the following time frame and characteristics. Table 13.1 represents this progression in which the development of self, cognitive ability, and affective growth are represented. In the table, we have attempted to relate general cognitive development with development of self. (See Lewis and Brooks-Gunn [1979a] for more details.)

Period one (birth to 3 months) is characterized by biological determinism and is primarily reflective in nature. Infants have interest in and positive affect toward social objects, particularly other babies. Differentiation of other social objects and single action-outcome pairings (primary circular reactions) occur. Concurrent with contingent events is the beginnings of self as different from others. The self–other differentiation has only begun inasmuch as this process involves the intended actions with objects. Means-and-ends development, as seen in secondary circular reactions, has not begun to emerge.

In period two (3 months to 8 months), social activity and social control of behavior is established. Elaborate action-outcome pairings occur along with means-and-ends relationships both in the social and nonsocial domain. Mirror contingency (that is, effecting response contingencies in reflecting surfaces) becomes of interest as part of the action-outcome behavior. Moreover, through this action, self-recognition, dependent on these mirror contingencies, now can be demonstrated. The distinction between self and others is consolidated, but self-identity remains situationally determined and fleeting until the onset of self and object permanence.

The most critical feature of period three (8 to 12 months) is the establishment of self-permanence, which solidifies the self–other distinction and signifies that the conservation of self or identity is independent of any particular situation, event, or person. In addition, the self now has a location in space that is unique. More complex means-and-ends relationships are established, and intentionality is present. Contingent play is of particular interest because the self–other distinction is consolidated due to self-permanence. Self-recognition is established and can be demonstrated in reflected-surface or in other conditions involving contingency relationships. The establishment of self-permanence represents the beginning of self-identity. With self-identity, we can see the emergence of a truly social organism, one which knows some things about self as well as others. During

TABLE 14.1

Development of Self-Knowledge, Emotional Experience, and Cognitive Growth[a]

Age	Self-Knowledge	Emotional Experience	Cognitive Growth
0–3 mos	Interest in social objects: Emergence of self–other distinction.	Unconditioned responses to stimulus events (loud noise, hunger, etc.).	Reflexive period, primary circular reactions.
3–8 mos	Consolidation of self–other distinction, recognition of self through contingency.	Conditioned responses (strangers, incongruity).	Primary and secondary circular reactions.
8–12 mos	Emergence of self-permanence and self categories; Recognition of self through contingency and onset of feature recognition.	Specific emotional experiences (fear, happiness, love, attachment).	Object permanence, means-ends, imitation.
12–24 mos	Consolidation of basic self categories (age, gender, emergence of efficacy); feature recognition without contingency.	Development of empathy, guilt, embarrassment.	Language growth; more complex means-ends; symbolic representations.

[a]Table 14.1 appeared in Lewis and Brooks-Gunn (1978).

this period, early features of a categorical self begin to emerge, and self-recognition independent of contingnecy appears in its first form.

Period four (12 and 24 months) is best characterized as the beginning of representational behavior, including social representation and the representation of self. During the middle of this period, self-recognition becomes less dependent on contingency. Categories of self begin to emerge and include gender. The impact of these events on affect development is considerable. Prior to self-identity, it would be difficult to talk about the ability to experience an emotion because such experiences as "I am fearful" require the acquisition of self. We have attempted to deal with this problem by making a distinction between emotional states characterized by facial expression, physiological change, etc., and emotional experiences that requires self-development (Lewis & Rosenblum, 1978). Some emotional experiences emerge in the third period, especially those emotions requiring little social comparison. Emotional experiences that involve learning or a comparison of a child's behavior to a standard—either an internalized or external standard—must await the further elaboration of the categorical self. As such, they emerge only in the fourth period.

That children can be shown to demonstrate knowledge of themselves comes as no surprise given the number of other social and cognitive competencies the child shows in other areas. The child's knowledge of others is considerable (Lewis & Feiring, 1979; Weinraub, Brooks, & Lewis, 1977), and it is difficult to imagine that the child's knowledge of the complex social space does not include knowledge of self. Thus, the data indicate that the development of identity begins early in the child's life.

Gender and Sex-Role Knowledge

Our theory of the acquisition of self necessitates that the infant first differentiates itself from others (the self as subject) and then develops categories of self (the self as object). One of the earliest categories that the child acquires is gender, others being age, efficacy, and familiarity (Lewis & Feiring, 1978, 1979). We focus on gender identity because there has been less attempt to relate this category to self-knowledge than other categories. It is our belief that gender knowledge, both about self (gender identity) and others, occurs somewhere between 1 and 2 years. This age estimate differs significantly from Kohlberg's (1966), which is around 5 to 6 years. According to Kohlberg, gender identity does not appear until age 3, consistent gender labeling does not appear until age 4, and gender constancy does not appear until age 6. These estimates no longer appear to be accurate and may be questioned on several grounds. For one, Kohlberg's estimates were based on studies in which children were asked verbally to identify themselves and others as "boy" or "girl" (Gesell, Halverson, Ilg, Thompson, Castner, Ames,

& Amatruda, 1940; Rabban, 1950). The technique used by Rabban and Gesell et al. may have confounded gender knowledge and gender identity with language sophistication. Another difficulty was in the estimate of the age of gender constancy. For Kohlberg, gender constancy is the child's ability to maintain its gender in the face of transformations. Not unlike other types of knowledge, gender constancy or conservation was thought to exist around 6 years, and it was only after constancy was established that its effect on sex role was thought to take place. Both notions have been challenged.

Except for Kohlberg's original formulations about gender identity and constancy, there has been relatively little work on the stages of gender constancy. Emmerich, Goldman, Kirsh, and Sharabany (1977) and Emmerich (1979) have made such an attempt and have questioned the view that constancy represents the last stage in gender knowledge. Rather, constancy may be a characteristic associated with each stage of gender-identity development. Furthermore, there is no reason to believe that a mature gender identity (or gender constancy) is necessary for all aspects of sex-role or sex-typed behavior. Gender information in the form of gender identity, a knowledge of the existence of the categories male or female (or some variation thereof), and the ability to perceptually discriminate between the sexes may be sufficient to produce some forms of sex-role and sex-type appropriate behavior. Indeed, the evidence points to just that conclusion. In this regard, then, early forms of gender identity may supply sufficient cognitive information to allow for the generation of early sex-role (typed) behavior. The development of gender identity (constancy) and, at the same time, the onset of the more sophisticated cognitive processes may allow the child to generate even more complex notions of what is appropriate sex-role behavior. Nonetheless, there is reason to believe that this process is started early and is mediated by some form of gender identity.

Beside the work we present, there are several studies indicating that the concept of gender identity and appropriate sex-role behavior begin at earlier ages than was previously thought. Slaby and Frey (1975) found evidence for gender identity and constancy in children 2- to 5-years-old. Kuhn, Nash, and Brucken (1978) looked at gender identity and sex-role stereotypes in 2- and 3-year olds. Children as young as 2 years possess substantial knowledge of the sex-role stereotypes that exist in this culture. Moreover, gender identity and constancy, assessed in a manner similar to Slaby and Frey (1975) and DeVries (1969), was found to be advanced vis-à-vis the scales used to assess it. Finally, and most important to theory, gender identity was significantly related to sex-role behavior (Kuhn, Nash, & Brucken, 1978; Slaby & Frey, 1975).

By 2 years of age, children have clear notions of which toys and games are stereotyped male and female and show corresponding sex-typed toy preferences. Mere labeling of neutral activities as appropriately or inappropriately sex-typed can influence the preferences for, and performances in, these activities (Liebert, McCall, & Hanratty, 1971; Montemayor, 1974; Stein, Pohly, Pohly, & Mueller, 1971) even in children as young as 2 years of age (Thompson, 1975). Moreover, most impressive are the clinical observations of Money, Hampson, and Hampson (1957) who noted that, regardless of genetic or hormonal background, children's gender could be reassigned through surgery and other techniques to either sex between the ages of 18 to 36 months. After this age, gender reassignment led to significant emotional and behavioral adjustment problems. Personal observation of the mislabeling of the gender of children 2 to 3 years and older has shown that children become quite upset over mislabeling. The degree of affective involvement, as measured by their protests, appears to be an indication of children's cognitive-affective commitment to their gender.

Part of the difficulty in studying very young children's knowledge of gender and sex roles is the inability to use language, either to instruct them in what we wish to discover (for example, asking them to categorize male and female activities), or to elicit verbal responses that tell us about their level of knowledge. It is important, therefore, that we do not confuse methodological difficulties with a lack of results. The Blakeman, LaRue, and Olejnik (1979) study is a good case in point. When they asked 2-year olds to sort toys in "boy" and "girl" piles, the children were unable to do so. However, these same children were able to choose in a sex-role stereotype fashion. The demonstration of knowledge of gender and sex roles, especially with very young children, is dependent on the nature of the task presented. With this in mind, it is necessary to look at a series of studies that use techniques appropriate for young age levels. These include perceptual-cognitive abilities, naturalistic studies of social interaction that take into account the sex of subject and of object, modeling studies, and finally, the early use of verbal labels.

Perceptual-Cognitive Abilities. Lewis and Brooks (1975) have already reported that infants tend to look more at pictures of same-sex infants than at pictures of opposite-sex infants. These results recently have been partially replicated (Lewis & Brooks-Gunn, 1979a). Moreover, in a recent study on children's perceptual-cognitive responses to pictures of their parents, infants between the ages of 9 to 24 months smiled more to the same-sex parent than at the oppsite-sex parent (Brooks-Gunn & Lewis, 1979).

Naturalistic Studies. Most naturalistic studies that contribute to our understanding of sex knowledge involve the observation of parent–child differences as a function of the sex of both parent and child. There are several studies that show differences in children's behavior as a function of their sex and that of their parents. If boy children act in a different way to their fathers than mothers and if girl children act in a different way to their mothers than fathers, we may be able to conclude that the children both know of their own sex (gender identity) as well as knowledge of their parents' gender. There are unfortunately relatively few data on same-sex/opposite-sex in parent-child interaction. This lack of data emphasizes one of the shortcomings of the study of sex-role differences (Block, 1976). Especially in infancy, the lack of data on the father's role in socialization and the reliance on the mother in most studies of parent-child relations does not provide us with enough information to analyze these interactions. The studies that do exist provide some support for gender knowledge. Lewis and Weinraub (1976) studied sex-of-child/sex-of-parent interactions in 1- and 2-year olds in a free-play situation. Significant sex-of-parent/sex-of-infant interactions were noted. For example, at both 1 and 2 years of age, children looked more at the same-sex parent than at the opposite-sex parent. This result was also reported by Lamb (1975).

In terms of peer relations, children of preschool age (and younger) sort themselves into same-sex play groups. Recently, Jacklin and Maccoby (1978) have demonstrated this effect in 33-month-old children, and a study of peer interaction with 1- and 1½-year olds—16 sets of 4 children, 2 males and 2 females in each—revealed that the boy infants look more at male infants than at female infants, whereas the reverse is true for girls (Brooks-Gunn & Lewis, 1979).

Some caution should be given to the interpretation of these data in that the parents are also acting differentially to their children. Because of this, it is unclear whether children act in a particular manner because they have knowledge of their own gender and the gender of their parents or because of the past differential reinforcement history.

Modeling Studies.   Modeling is another way of observing gender knowledge of both the self and others. Unfortunately, there are almost no data on this subject for infants. However, data for older children do exist and may prove to be helpful. There is a lack of clarity in the literature on the modeling of same-sex behaviors. Maccoby and Jacklin's review (1974) notes that children do not consistently imitate same-sex adult models, yet the data suggest that children between the ages of 3 and 5 years imitate same-sex parents. The four studies of children under 5 years of age imitating parental behavior reviewed by Maccoby and Jacklin (1974) show that children are more likely to imitate the behavior of the same sex-parents (DuHamel & Biller, 1969; Hartup, 1962; Hetherington, 1965; Hetherington & Frankie, 1967). Several factors may contribute to the lack of clarity that exists. The task to be modeled seems to be a quite important factor. Indeed, it is sometimes more important than the sex of the model. Barkley, Ullman, Otts, and Brecht (1977) report that the child's free-play and modeling behavior, after seeing a videotape of a man and woman playing with a masculine- or feminine-type toys, revealed an interaction between model and activity. Children imitate same-sex behavior regardless of sex of model. White (1978) also found that males were more interested in the model's activity independent of the sex of the model whereas females preferred to model a female engaged in female behavior. The interaction of sex of task and sex of model on modeling behavior of boys and girls also holds for children as young as 34 months (Lynch & Cassel, 1979). Given these data, the issue of same-sex modeling among peers and parents at early ages needs to be reconsidered. Nonetheless even these data point to knowledge of sex-role appropriateness of some tasks. Although sufficient data are not available to answer this question, there is indication of a preference for same-sex models even before 3 years of age.

Verbal Labeling. Perhaps the most convincing data on gender knowledge comes from verbal labeling and comprehension. In a series of tasks, infants were shown pictures of faces and asked to label or point to various ones. The faces varied by gender, age, and familiarity (Brooks-Gunn, & Lewis, 1979; Lewis & Brooks-Gunn, 1979a). By 18 months of age, when most infants had some labeling ability, 90% of the time infants labeled adults correctly on the basis of gender. Approximately 80% of the infants who had labels for boy and girl applied these labels correctly. Moreover, some of the infants, when asked to label pictures of themselves, applied gender labels of boy or girl. In no cases were these labels used incorrectly. Of particular interest in infants' labeling behavior is their overgeneralization of labels. The label "daddy" or some derivative, for example, first appeared (and appeared correctly) by 15 months. By 18 months, this label was overgeneralized to include other faces. The nature of the errors is instructive because 90% of the errors were applied to *adult male* faces. We know that children of this age can discriminate pictures of their father from other males. What seems to be at work is that these children, when asked to label a picture for which they have no label, apply the label that is most like the picture. Thus, not until 30 months—when they have the label for "man"—are infants able to produce the semantically correct label. The discriminable features of males and females would seem to be known at least by the second year of life. It does appear that infants acquire information about themselves and others quite early and that this knowledge emerges at about the same time as sex-differentiated behavior. We make no claim about the form of this knowledge because, without verbal ability, this issue is difficult to explore. Nor do we believe that the knowledge is fixed. But, certainly, the concepts of gender and sex role are emerging. Nevertheless, some form of knowledge both of self and of others is present before 2 years of age.

Attraction for Like Self

Although infants may have gender knowledge both about themselves and others, it is not clear why they should behave in a sex-appropriate fashion. We need to address the motivational aspects of sex-role behavior. One motivational view is that of Mischel (1970) who believes that the reinforcement contingencies of the social environment motivate the child's behavior. We believe the motivational system of the child rests on the assumption that if I am an "A" and I can differentiate other "A's" and "not A's," I will, under most conditions, act like the other "A's." This motivational principle of "attraction of like" exists across a wide range of psychological phenomena, some of which has been summarized by Byrne (1971). Evidence for this phenomenon in young children can be found in the modeling and in the peer-play literature that we have presented. In principle, this motivational component is both derived from the information of self and the differentiation of the social world. It is also derived from cognition, but it may operate independently in such a manner as to encourage further cognitive growth. Thus, wanting to be like other males (or females) motivates the child to seek out differences, which in turn become more perceptually differentiated; these produce further differences and generate new hypotheses. Thus, cognitive growth and motivational factors work in tandem to produce a more committed and differentiated child vis-à-vis sex-role behavior. The infant's development of categories of self include age, familiarity, and efficacy in addition to gender. This motivational principle of attraction to "like-self" would operate on any of the categories the child is capable of conceptualizing and would change as new categories are added and old ones dropped. For example, we have evidence for age as one category. Infants and young children appear to be attracted to same-aged children (Edwards & Lewis, 1979) in much the same fashion as they are attracted to same-sex social objects.

SUMMARY: SOME GENERAL PRINCIPLES UNDERLYING THE ACQUISITION OF SEX-ROLE BEHAVIOR

A cognitive theory of sex-role development has been offered that holds as its central points:

1. Self-identity emerges within the first year of life, certainly by 8–9 months of age.
2. Gender knowledge of self and others is acquired at the same time through the interaction of infants with their social world.
3. Gender identity, an aspect of self-identity, although not fixed, exists in some form before 2 years of age.
4. Some forms of sex-role and sex-type behavior are displayed by the infant within the first year of life.
5. Sex-role appropriate behavior is initiated by children in their desire to be like same-sex people.

6. Sex-role behavior is constructed by infants and young children from the biological and cultural differences that exist around them. These constructions are developmentally organized and have correspondences to other levels of knowledge in that the processes necessary for their construction remain the same.

In general, the theories of cognitive influences on sex-role development share several factors. The first is that gender knowledge of self, or gender identity, is believed to play an important role in sex-role behavior. The second is gender knowledge of another's gender, including the behaviors classified as appropriate by the culture (Kohlberg, 1966; Mischel, 1966, 1970). Although recognizing the development of both sets of knowledge, the present theory of sex-role development argues for the acquisition of self-identity and other gender knowledge as a dual process. Moreover, the acquisition process occurs rather early, within the first 2 years of life. The third factor, necessary in addition to the cognitive component, is a motivational component that seeks to explain why children choose to behave in a sex-role appropriate fashion. Lewis and Kohlberg have argued that the desire to do and be like same-sex objects is the underlying motive. Although this difference has not been resolved, the child's knowledge about gender (its own and others) constitutes the material used to construct sex-role behavior.

The infant is evoking knowledge about self and others within the first years of life; this knowledge involves gender, sex roles, and sex-typed behavior. We have focused on gender because it has been underexamined from the viewpoint of infant social cognition. Moreover, as an active organism—one that acts on its environment and constructs the schema that govern its actions—the infant chooses to be like those who have similar characteristics and labels. This choice, based on the level of development at any specific time, provides the material for the next phase of construction. In this way, additional information continually leads to increased conformity. Thus, for example, the earliest forms of gender knowledge may be based on the smallest difference (for example, hair length, type of clothes, or labels such as proper names). These cues provide the first information necessary for differentiation of self and others. On the basis of this differentiation, gender identity, and the principle of attraction, the infant moves towards conformity in sex-role behavior.

ACKNOWLEDGMENTS

This chapter is based in part on a paper presented as a Masters' Lecture at the American Psychological Association meetings, New York, September 4, 1979. Portions of it appear in a paper by the author and Marsha Weinraub (1979). I should like to express my debt to her effort while retaining for myself the responsibility for any shortcomings. The paper was supported by NICHD grant #N01-HD082849.

REFERENCES

Amsterdam, B, K. *Mirror behavior in children under two years of age.* Unpublished doctoral dissertation. Chapel Hill: University of North Carolina, 1968.

Bannister, D., & Agnew, J. The child's construing of self. In J. Cole (Ed.), *Nebraska symposium on motivation, 1976.* Lincoln: University of Nebraska Press, 1977.

Barkley, R., Ullman, D., Otts, L., & Brecht, J. The effects of sex typing and sex appropriateness of modeled behavior on children's imitation. *Child Development,* 1977, *48,* 721–725.

Blakeman, J., LaRue, A., & Olejnik, A. Sex-appropriate toy preference and the ability to conceptualize toys as sex-role related. *Developmental Psychology,* 1979, *15*(3), 339–340.

Block, J. H. Issues, problems, and pitfalls in assessing sex differences: A critical review of *The psychology of sex differences. Merrill-Palmer Quarterly,* 1976, *22,* 283–308.

Brooks-Gunn, J., & Lewis, M. Why "Mama and Papa"? The development of social labels. *Child Development,* 1979, *50,* 1203–1206.

Byrne, D. E. *The attraction paradigm.* New York: Academic Press, 1971.

DeVries, R. Constancy of generic identity in the years of three to six. *Monographs of the Society for Research in Child Development,* 1969, *34* (Serial No. 127).

DuHamel, T. R., & Biller, H. B. Parental imitation and nonimitation in young children. *Developmental Psychology,* 1969, *1,* 772.

Edwards, C. P., & Lewis, M. Young children's concepts of social relations: Social functions and social objects. In M. Lewis & L. A. Rosenblum (Eds.), *The child and its family.* New York: Plenum, 1979.

Emmerich, W. *Developmental trends in sex-stereotyped values.* Paper presented at the biennial meeting of the Society for Research in Child Development, San Francisco, March, 1979.

Emmerich, W., Goldman, K. S., Kirsh, B., & Sharabany, R. Evidence for a transitional phase in the development of gender constancy. *Child Development,* 1977, *48,* 930–936.

Gesell, A., Halverson, H. M., Ilg, F. L., Thompson, H., Castner, B. M., Ames, L. B., & Amatruda, C. S. *The first five years of life: A guide to the study of the preschool child.* New York: Harper, 1940.

Hamlyn, D. W. Person-perception and our understanding of others. In T. Mischel (Ed.), *Understanding other persons.* Totowa, N.J.: Rowman & Littlefield, 1974.

Hartup, W. W. Some correlates of parental imitation in young children. *Child Development,* 1962, *33,* 85–96.

Hetherington, E. M. A developmental study of the effects of sex of the dominant parent on sex-role preference, identification, and imitation in children. *Journal of Personality and Social Psychology,* 1965, *2,* 188–194.

Hetherington, E. M., & Frankie, G. Effects of parental dominance, warmth, and conflict on imitation on children. *Journal of Personality and Social Psychology,* 1967, *6,* 119–125.

Jacklin, C. N., & Maccoby, E. E. Social behavior at 33 months in same-sex and mixed-sex dyads. *Child Development,* 1978, *49,* 557–569.

James, W. *The principles of psychology.* New York: Holt, 1950. (Originally published, 1890.)

Kohlberg, L. A. Cognitive-developmental analysis of children's sex-role concepts and attitudes. In E. E. Maccoby (Ed.), *The development of sex differences.* Stanford, Calif.: Stanford University Press, 1966.

Kuhn, D., Nash, S. C., & Burcken, L. Sex role concepts of two- and three-year-olds. *Child Development,* 1978, *49,* 445–451.

Lamb, M. E. Fathers: Forgotten contributors to child development. *Human Development,* 1975, *18,* 245–266.

Lewis, M., & Brooks, J. Infants' social perception: A constructivist view. In L. Cohen & P. Salapatek (Eds.), *Infant perception: From sensation to cognition* (Vol. 2). New York: Academic Press, 1975.

Lewis, M., & Brooks, J. Self knowledge and emotional development. In M. Lewis & L. Rosenblum (Eds.), *The development of affect: The genesis of behavior* (Vol. 1). New York: Plenum, 1978.

Lewis, M., & Brooks-Gunn, J. *Social cognition and the acquisition of self.* New York: Plenum, 1979. (a)

Lewis, M., & Brooks-Gunn, J. Toward a theory of social cognition: The development of self. In I. Uzgiris (Ed.), *New directions in child development: Social interaction and communication in infancy.* San Francisco: Jossey-Bass, 1979. (b)

Lewis, M., & Feiring, C. The child's social world. In R. M. Lerner & G. D. Spanier (Eds.), *Contributions of the child to marital quality and family interaction through the life-span.* New York: Academic Press, 1978.

Lewis, M., & Feiring, C. The child's social network: Social object, social functions and their relationship. In M. Lewis & L. Rosenblum (Eds.), *The child and its family: The genesis of behavior* (Vol. 2). New York: Plenum, 1979.

Lewis, M., & Rosenblum, L. (Eds.). *The development of affect: The genesis of behavior* (Vol. 1). New York: Plenum, 1978.

Lewis, M., & Weinraub, M. The father's role in the child's social network, In M. E. Lamb (Ed.), *The role of the father in child development.* New York: Wiley, 1976.

Lewis, M., & Weinraub, M. Origins of early sex-role development. *Sex Roles,* 1979, *5*(2), 135–153.

Liebert, R., McCall, R., & Hanratty, M. Effects of sex-typed information on children's toy preferences. *Journal of Genetic Psychology,* 1971, *119,* 133–136.

Lynch, K., & Cassel, T. Z. *Children's modeling of sex role behaviors: Sex of child and model, and family communication styles.* Paper presented at the biennial meeting of The Society for Research in Child Development, San Francisco, March 1979.

Maccoby, E. E., & Jacklin, C. N. *The psychology of sex differences.* Stanford, Cal.: Stanford University Press, 1974.

Mead, G. H. *Mind, self, and society.* Chicago: University Press, 1972. (Originally published, 1934.)

Merleau-Ponty, M. *Primacy of perception.* J. Eddie (Ed.) & W. Cobb (Trans.). Evanston, Ill.: Northwestern University Press, 1964.

Mischel, W. A social-learning view of sex differences in behavior. In E. E. Maccoby (Ed.), *The development of sex differences.* Stanford, Cal.: Stanford University Press, 1966.

Mischel, W. Sex-typing and socialization. In P. H. Mussen (Ed.), *Carmichael's manual of child psychology* (Vol. 2). New York: Wiley, 1970.

Money, J., Hampson, J., & Hampson, J. Imprinting and the establishment of gender role. *Archives of Neurology and Psychiatry,* 1957, *72,* 333–336.

Montemayor, R. Children's performance in a game and their attention to it as a function of sex-typed labels. *Child Development,* 1974, *45,* 156–166.

Papousek, H., & Papousek, M. Mirror-image and self-recognition in young human infants: I. A new method of experimental analysis. *Developmental Psychology,*1974, *7,* 149–157.

Rabban, M. Sex-role identification in young children in two diverse social groups. *Genetic Psychological Monographs,* 1950, *42,* 81–158.

Slaby, R. C., & Frey, K. S. Development of gender constancy and selective attention to same-sex models. *Child Development,* 1975, *56,* 849–856.

Stein, A. H., Pohly, S., Pohly, R., & Mueller, E. The influence of masculine, feminine, and neutral tasks on children's achievement behavior, expectancies of success, and attainment values. *Child Development,* 1971, *42,* 195–207.

Thompson, S. K. Gender labels and early sex role development. *Child Development,* 1975, *46,* 339–347.

Weinraub, M., Brooks, J., & Lewis, M. The social network: A reconsideration of the concept of attachment. *Human Development,* 1977, *20,* 31–47.

White, D. Effects of sex-typed labels and their source on the imitative performance of young children. *Child Development,* 1978, *49,* 1266–1269.

Author Index

Numbers in *italics* refer to pages on which complete references are listed.

415

Subject Index